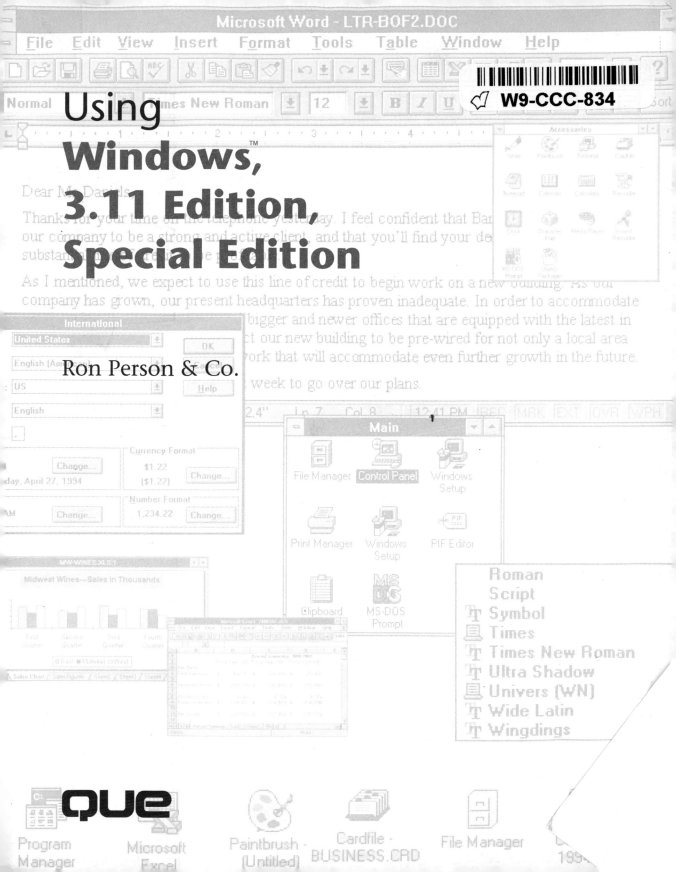

Using
Windows,™
3.11 Edition,
Special Edition

Ron Person & Co.

W9-CCC-834

que

Using Windows, 3.11 Edition, Special Edition

Library of Congress Catalog No.: 94-66720

ISBN: 1-56529-807-1

97   96   95   4

Interpretation of the printing code: the rightmost double-digit number is the year of the book's printing; the rightmost single-digit number, the number of the book's printing. For example, a printing code of 94-1 shows that the first printing of the book occurred in 1994.

Publisher: David P. Ewing

Associate Publisher: Michael Miller

Publishing Director: Joseph B. Wikert

Managing Editor: Michael Cunningham

Product Marketing Manager: Greg Wiegand

Credits

Publishing Manager
Brad R. Koch

Acquisitions Editor
Angela J. Lee

Product Directors
Robin Drake
Bryan Gambrel
C. Kazim Haidri
Lisa D. Wagner

Production Editor
Nancy Sixsmith

Copy Editors
Lori Cates
Patrick Kanouse
Jeanne Lemen
Lori Lyons
Lynn Northrup
Andy Saff
Maureen Schneeberger
Linda Seifert
Kathy Simpson

Technical Editors
J. David Shinn, CNE
Robert Zigon

Book Designer
Amy Peppler-Adams

Composed in *Stone Serif* and *MCPdigital*
by Que Corporation

Cover Designer
Karen Ruggles

Production Team
Steve Adams
Stephen Carlin
Karen Dodson
Teresa Forrester
Joelynn Gifford
Aren Howell
Bob LaRoche
Stephanie Mineart
Tim Montogomery
G. Alan Palmore
Caroline Roop
Dennis Sheehan
Johnna VanHoose
Sue VandeWalle
Mary Beth Wakefield
Donna Winter
Lillian Yates

Indexer
Charlotte Clapp

Acquisitions Coordinator
Patricia J. Brooks

Editorial Assistant
Michelle Williams

About the Author

Ron Person has written more than 12 books for Que Corporation, including *Using Excel 5 for Windows*, Special Edition and *Using Word 6 for Windows*, Special Edition. Ron is the principal consultant for Ron Person & Co. He has an M.S. in physics from The Ohio State University and an M.B.A. from Hardin-Simmons University.

Ron Person & Co., based in San Francisco, has attained Microsoft's highest rating for Microsoft Excel and Word for Windows consultants—Microsoft Solutions Partner. Ron was one of Microsoft's 12 original Consulting Partners. The firm trains Excel and Visual Basic for Applications developers and support staff for corporations nationally and internationally. If your company plans to develop applications using Microsoft Excel or integrating multiple Microsoft applications, you will gain significantly from the courses taught by Ron Person & Co. For information on course content, on-site corporate classes, or consulting, contact Ron Person & Co. at the following address:

Ron Person & Co.
P.O. Box 5647
Santa Rosa, CA 95402

Acknowledgments

Using Windows, 3.11 Edition, Special Edition, was created through the work and contributions of many professionals. We want to thank the people who contributed to this effort.

Thanks to everyone at Microsoft. Their energy and vision have opened new frontiers in software—software that is more powerful, yet easier to use. Windows has changed the face of computing.

Thanks to the following software consultants and trainers who helped us write *Using Windows*, 3.11 Edition, Special Edition:

Karen Rose has written five books for Que Corporation, including *Using Microsoft Windows 3*, Second Edition; *Using Word 6 for Windows*, Special Edition; and *Using WordPerfect 5.0/5.1*. Karen has taught for the University of California, Berkeley Extension, and Sonoma State University. Karen is currently the owner and publisher of *Little Red Book Press*, publishers of handbound books.

Robert Voss, Ph.D., has been an important contributor to many Que books. Robert applied his knowledge of many Windows applications to the chapters on Windows accessories, Windows Graph, Mail, and Schedule+. Again, Robert has done a conscientious and in-depth job. Robert is a senior trainer in Microsoft Excel and Word for Windows for Ron Person & Co.

Don Roche is the DOS and Windows expert who contributed to the chapters on working with DOS applications under Windows. Don has extensive software and publishing experience. Don is Publishing Director for Que Corporation.

Roger Jennings wrote Chapter 20, "Using Windows with CD-ROM and Video." Roger is a multi-path with an impressive knowledge of many fields, including databases and multimedia. Roger is the author of the best-selling books, *Using Access 2* from Que, and *Database Developers Guide with Visual Basic 3* from Sams. Roger is the president of OakLeaf Systems in Oakland, California.

Doug Bierer contributed Chapter 26, "Networking Windows 3.1x." Doug has written *Connecting Windows for Workgroups 3.1*, *Tuning Windows 3.1*, and was a contributing author for *Using MS-DOS 6*, Special Edition for Que. Doug is a Certified Netware Instructor and Engineer (CNI/CNE), and has worked with

Netware, Banyan, and LANtastic for nine years. Doug currently works for Futronics in San Jose, CA.

Micheal Hader wrote Chapter 25, "Installing Windows for Workgroups 3.11." He has written *Networking Windows 3.1* and has been a contributing author for *Killer DOS Utilities*, *Killer Windows Utilities*, and *Killer WordPerfect 6 Utilities* for Que. He is founder and president of Hader & Associates and its subsidiary, Atrium Learning Center, in Hendersonville, Tennessee.

Ralph Soucie contributed to Chapter 3, "Controlling Applications with Program Manager," and to Chapter 4, "Managing Files with File Manager." A longtime contributing editor to *PC World* and author of a popular book on Microsoft Excel, he is also a Microsoft Excel consultant. Ralph works out of Jonesport, Maine.

Allen Wyatt updated the File Manager and network tools topics for DOS 6. Allen is president of Discovery Computing Inc., in Sundance, Wyoming. Allen's company has years of experience in all facets of computer book writing, editing, and publishing.

Matt Fogarty is the talented artist who drew the pictures of the guitarist and pelicans using PaintBrush, and of the horse race and the old man's character study using Microsoft Draw.

The skillful pens of our editors and the gallons of late night oil they burn for Que ensure that our books are consistent and easy to read. That they succeed in their jobs is evident by the comments of our corporate clients on the quality and value of Que books. Thanks also to:

Brad Koch, Publishing Manager, brought his years of technical experience to ensure that *Using Windows*, 3.11 Edition, Special Edition was updated and restructured to aid the book's more knowledgeable and technical audience.

Angela Lee, Acquisitions Editor, for gracefully keeping us on track and on schedule.

Trademarks

Contents at a Glance

Running and Customizing

Troubleshooting Windows

Installing Windows

Appendixes

Contents

5 Simple Data Sharing   189

6 Advanced Data Sharing   199

7 Customizing with Control Panel   231

III Using Windows Accessories   333

10 Using Windows Write   335

11 Using Windows Paintbrush   363

22 Running, Installing, and Configuring DOS Applications — 731

23 Introducing Visual Basic for Applications   795

VI Installing Windows   809

24 Installing and Optimizing Windows 3.1   811

VII Troubleshooting Windows   977

27 Troubleshooting Windows   979

Introduction

The phenomenal success of Windows, which came of age with the release of Version 3.0, surprised many people. The success didn't surprise the engineers and evangelists at Microsoft, who have praised Windows since the beginning, and it didn't surprise users who have appreciated the benefits of a graphical interface, multitasking, and connectivity between applications for years. Windows' success, however, surprised people accustomed to the command-line interface of DOS and who never really thought computers should be easy to use. Computers, after all, are serious business tools.

The following reasons demonstrate why a PC running Windows is a very serious business tool:

- Windows is easier to use than DOS. Windows commands are listed in menus that you can pick from easily, not hidden in some technical tome. Because commands are easier to find and understand, you will use more of them.

- If you need further assistance, most Windows applications provide a Help command that displays on-screen documentation.

- Windows applications are consistent: the *select, then do* method of operating Windows extend to all Windows applications.

- Because learning one application moves you well along the way toward using any other Windows application, you will be comfortable using more applications, and you will learn the applications faster.

- Windows offers multitasking. Each Windows application runs in its own *window*, and you can have many windows on-screen at the same time. To move from one application to another, point to the window containing the application you want to use and click (or press a key combination if you don't use a mouse). Running two applications side-by-side is easy.

■ With Windows, you can share data between applications. copying and moving data within and between Windows applications is simple. You can forge links between applications so that updating one file updates all those files linked to it. You can even create compound documents that enable you to start one application from within another.

Not only are Windows and Windows applications easier to use than DOS and DOS applications, they also are very powerful. The word processing program Word for Windows includes advanced capabilities for formatting documents, creating and editing tables, adding tables of contents and indexes, using reference tools like bookmarks and annotations, proofing documents with a spell checker and a thesaurus, automatically creating bulleted and numbered lists, quickly printing envelopes, and much more. The worksheet program Microsoft Excel includes formatting and charting capabilities that rival annual report quality. Excel has more math, scientific, and finance functions than any other worksheet and includes a robust programming language. With its toolbars, drag-and-drop techniques, and help system, however, Excel is easy to use. Powerful applications also exist for database management, presentation development, illustration, photo editing, desktop publishing, multimedia production, accounting, and more. Many of these Windows applications outperform their DOS counterparts.

Besides being easier to use and very powerful, many Windows applications are highly customizable as well. They are packed with features right out of the box but also can be enhanced to meet your specific needs. Word for Windows and Microsoft Excel, for example, include built-in programming languages that far surpass the capabilities of simple macros. Both applications also include customizable toolbars displaying icons that you can click for instant access to commands you use frequently.

Windows 3.1 and Windows 3.11

Windows 3.1, released in the spring of 1992, adds many features to the already powerful Windows 3.0. Windows 3.11, with additional software drivers and network features, was released in the Spring of 1994. To make the upgrade easy, all Windows 3.0 applications are completely compatible with Windows 3.1+. You have to upgrade only Windows—not your applications.

The most important new features of Windows 3.1 include TrueType font technology, object linking and embedding (OLE), a new File Manager, drag-and-drop moving and copying, and built-in multimedia extensions.

TrueType is a revolutionary new technology that brings the magic of fonts to anyone who owns a computer and a printer. In brief, TrueType provides outline fonts that can be scaled to any size and used on both your screen and your printer—at any resolution. With TrueType, you do not need expensive PostScript, and you do not need downloadable fonts that take up a great deal of space on your hard disk and are slow. TrueType is discussed in Chapter 8, "Managing Fonts."

Object linking and embedding (OLE) augments (and greatly expands) what Windows 3.0 knew as *dynamic data exchange*, or DDE. To understand OLE, you need to understand that an *object* is anything—data, picture, or chart—that becomes associated with an application other than the application used to create it; *linking* is including an object within a different application but leaving the object linked to the application used to create it so that the linked object is updated when the original changes; *embedding* puts data from a server application within the document of a client application. This leaves all the data in the final document—data is not linked back to its original application. Through OLE, you can create compound documents made up of objects created by diverse applications. In the most recent applications using OLE 2.0, when you edit an embedded OLE object, the menu bar and toolbars change to the menu bar and toolbars of the application that originally created the OLE object. For example if you are in Word 6 for Windows and edit an embedded Excel 5 chart, Word's menus and toolbars change to the menus and toolbars used in Excel for charting.

If the new File Manager included with Version 3.1 had added only much greater speed, it would have been a hit with veteran Windows users. Besides being considerably faster, however, the new File Manager also offers a whole new look and new features. Its split window shows the contents of a disk on one side and the contents of a selected directory on the other. You can open multiple File Manager windows and display a different drive or directory in each. Using Windows' drag-and-drop feature to move or copy files between drives or directories is easy in Version 3.1. If you use Windows for Workgroups 3.11, you gain a toolbar that is helpful for file and disk management. The toolbar contains tools for frequent file and disk management tasks such as copying and deleting files, sharing drives on the network, and so on.

The new drag-and-drop feature is useful in File Manager and in many Windows applications. In the new File Manager, you can drag a data file onto its application icon to start the application and load the file; you can drag a data file or application file onto Program Manager to create a program item icon; you can drag a data file onto the running Print Manager to print the file; and as before, you can drag files of any type onto a disk or directory icon to copy or move the files. The drag-and-drop feature also is evident in many Windows applications. You read about the drag-and-drop feature throughout this book.

New multimedia extensions enable you to turn your PC into a musical composition workstation, into a video production studio, or into a reference library. Multimedia means the integration of many media; therefore, a multimedia presentation may consist of text, animation, music, and voice. You can create your own multimedia productions, or you can purchase them premade. You need special equipment to turn your PC into a multimedia workstation: a CD-ROM drive, a sound board, and speakers.

Many other aspects of Windows also have been improved with the release of Version 3.1 and Version 3.11; you read about these changes throughout the book.

Windows for Workgroups

By the fall of 1992, more than one million new people were using Windows each month. But many faced problems with communicating and sharing data between people working on the same projects or working in the same organization.

Although Windows 3.1 and its applications gave individuals more productivity, it did nothing to aid the productivity of people working together in groups. People were forced to walk a floppy disk of files across a building, send internal messages that the company mail room routes through Siberia, and deal with a general lack of coordination. One solution to these problems was to put Windows 3.1 on a network. But most networks require money, a lot of time, and technical expertise.

Microsoft's solution to increasing the productivity of groups of Windows users who work together is Windows for Workgroups. Windows for Workgroups is Windows 3.1 with enhancements that give it networking capability and features to help people work together.

Windows for Workgroups is based on the idea that most work gets done in small groups of people. These groups are usually organized around performing a common task, reaching a common goal, or having a common flow of work and communication. Windows for Workgroups helps these groups by giving them a low-cost, easy-to-install network and application that help people share and communicate.

Windows for Workgroups makes connecting a network of computers almost as easy as installing Windows 3.1 by itself. Most networks require one computer to act as a dedicated *server* that controls the network, but Windows for Workgroups shares the networking overhead between all the computers on the network. This reduces the cost of the network. Most networks also require a system administrator who has had technical training. In the peer-to-peer network used by Windows for Workgroups, each user is responsible for his own password, and each user controls who can and can't access her files and printer.

In addition to creating an easy-to-install network, Windows for Workgroups adds features to Windows 3.1 that are designed to help groups of people work together. If you are familiar with Windows 3.1, you will recognize File Manager and Print Manager in Windows for Workgroups, but these features have been enhanced. With the Windows for Workgroups File Manager and Print Manager, you can share your directories and printers with others in your workgroup. These *shared resources* can even have two levels of sharing so that you can give different people different levels of use.

Windows for Workgroups also includes five powerful applications to help you and your workgroup work together:

- **Mail** is a message-passing system. People in your workgroup can send messages, memos, and files to others in the workgroup. A network *post office* stores and forwards mail so that you can pick up your mail when it is convenient to you.

- **Remote Access** gives you the ability to log on to a Windows NT server over the telephone. This enables you to connect your laptop-based Windows computer to the network in your office while you are traveling. Its as though you are a normal part of the network within the office.

- **PC Fax** gives people on the Windows for Workgroups network the ability to share a common Fax. When compatible Fax hardware is used it makes sending a Fax from a computer on the network almost as easy as sending an mail message.

- **Schedule+** is a personal or group scheduling application. It helps you manage your time and appointments and monitor when groups of people are available for a meeting. It ties into Mail so that you can notify people of a meeting and confirm when the meeting time is added to their schedule.

- **Clipbook** enables everyone in your workgroup to share data. It acts like a central scrapbook for everyone in the workgroup. Workgroup users can paste or link data from the Clipbook into their documents. When the chart, table, or data in the Clipbook changes, everyone in the workgroup gets the updated version.

Windows for Workgroups also recognizes when one of its workgroup members is attached to other networks, such as LAN Manager and Novell, and gives you access to the other network. If you need to expand the horizons of Windows for Workgroups, you can buy Microsoft Mail and Schedule+ Extensions, a product from Microsoft, which enables you to link Windows for Workgroups to large networks, mainframes, or off-site (remote) Windows users.

How This Book Is Organized

Using Windows, 3.11 Edition, Special Edition is divided into seven parts, beginning with the most basic information and progressing to the most advanced. At the end of the book are appendixes that describe how to use Windows from a keyboard, the files that are loaded by Windows, and the contents of the INI files as they are initially created when Windows is installed.

Part I

Part I, "Getting Started," includes two chapters for those who are new to Windows. If you have never used Windows, these two chapters are a must because they contain basic information on operating Windows, menus, and dialog boxes. This information is not repeated in individual chapters. Even if you have been using Windows for a while, you may want to scan Chapters 1 and 2 for tips.

Chapter 1, "Operating Windows," teaches you how to perform basic Windows functions. You learn how to start Windows, start an application and how to use menus and dialog boxes. You learn how to run multiple applications simultaneously and how you can cut and paste information between documents in different applications. You also learn that many things you do in one Windows application are the same in all Windows applications, making it easier to become familiar with more Windows applications.

Chapter 2, "Getting Help," begins with an overview of Windows Help features and commands. Many Windows applications, including the Windows accessories, include easy-to-use on-line documentation in the form of Help files. You can access Help through a menu, and the Help files in each application work similarly. Windows Help also enables you to search for information by choosing from an index of key topics.

Part II

Part II, "Managing Your Windows Work Session," includes chapters that detail the essential elements of Windows, how to use File Manager, how to move data between applications, and how to use Control Panel. In these chapters, you learn how to customize Windows and how to use features shared by all Windows applications. You also learn how to manage the TrueType fonts available with Windows and how to most effectively control your printer.

Chapter 3, "Controlling Applications with Program Manager," presents Program Manager, which is the heart of Windows. When you start Windows, Program Manager is what you see on-screen. This highly customizable manager of your Windows session includes several group windows, each containing a group of program item icons that you use to start applications. You can create your own program item icons, and you can organize them inside your own custom windows.

Chapter 4, "Managing Files with File Manager," shows how you can use File Manager to copy or move files or groups of files. You also learn to delete or rename files, create or remove directories, format disks, view files in almost any order, and search for files that meet specified criteria. This new, faster File Manager makes extensive use of Windows' drag-and-drop feature to manage files. If you use DOS 6, you'll want to learn about its Undelete, Anti-Virus, and Backup features that are available through Windows.

If you are using Windows for Workgroups, you learn to share your directories with other members of the workgroup. You also see how to get information from the shared directories of other members of the workgroup.

Chapter 5, "Simple Data Sharing," introduces you to simple copying or cutting of data from one location and pasting it into another location. The two locations may even be in different applications. You learn how to move data between Windows applications as well as between DOS and Windows applications or between two DOS applications.

Chapter 6, "Advanced Data Sharing." illustrates how to copy and paste line data between applications so that when the original data changes, the copy automatically reflects the change. You also learn about object linking and embedding, or OLE, which is another exciting Windows innovation. OLE objects are created by one application and then embedded into another application. For example, a chart may be created in Excel and then embedded as a chart into Word for Windows. The Word document contains not only the graphic display of the OLE object, the chart, but it also contains the original data used to create the OLE object. This means that the recipient of a document containing an OLE object can edit or modify the object.

If you are using OLE 2-compatible applications such as Excel 5 and Word 6 when you edit an embedded object, the menus and toolbars of the application change to reflect the type of menus and toolbars used to originally create the object.

If you are part of a workgroup using Windows for Workgroups, you learn to reduce work among the group's members by using the Clipbook. The Clipbook is like a scrapbook in which you can store your personal clippings. But the workgroup Clipbook can share text, tables, and charts with anyone in your workgroup. If workgroup members link to data in the Clipbook, their document updates whenever the data in the Clipbook updates. The Clipbook makes it easy to keep a group document up-to-date.

Chapter 7, "Customizing with Control Panel," shows how to take control of Control Panel, which includes a suite of applications you can use to customize your Windows environment. A Colors application enables you to choose screen colors; a Desktop application enables you to choose background patterns and a screen saver; and a Sounds application enables you to assign sounds to events. You can customize your keyboard, your mouse, and your numeric formats.

Chapter 8, "Managing Fonts," introduces one of Windows' most exciting features—TrueType, a font technology that provides you with high-quality fonts on any printer. TrueType scalable font outlines adapt to screen and any printer that Windows supports (at any resolution) and are instantly available to Windows and Windows applications. To preserve your investment in other types of fonts, TrueType works seamlessly with existing font technologies, such as downloadable and PostScript fonts.

Chapter 9, "Printing with Windows," shows you how to use Print Manager to *spool* print jobs. When you print a file from a Windows application, you don't have to wait impatiently until your printer is finished printing before you can start using your computer again. Instead, Print Manager spools print jobs to the printer, taking over management of printing functions while you continue working. You also can use Print Manager to install new printers.

If you need better print management, print scaling, and so forth, you should examine the features available with the Windows Printing System described in this chapter.

When you are printing in Windows for Workgroups, you can use Print Manager to monitor your print job even if it is printing on a printer located at someone else's computer.

Part III

Part III, "Using Windows Accessories," teaches you how to use the accessory applications that come with Windows. Windows accessory applications include a word processor, a painting application, a communications application, a macro recorder, and others.

Chapter 10, "Using Windows Write," discusses Windows Write, a simple but powerful word processing application that comes with Windows. In Write, you can enter, edit, and format text just as in any word processor, and you can add tabs, headers, and footers. Write lacks advanced features like spell checking and automatic tables of contents but is upward-compatible with more powerful word processors like Word for Windows, making Write a perfect springboard for moving up to an advanced word processor. Write is an OLE client, into which you can embed objects.

Chapter 11, "Using Windows Paintbrush," discusses Windows Paintbrush, a fun and colorful painting program you can use to create illustrations in a rainbow of colors and shades. Use Paintbrush's many painting tools to create fanciful works of art or serious illustrations for business use. Paintbrush is an OLE server that you can use to create objects embedded in client documents.

Chapter 12, "Using Windows Terminal," shows how you can use Windows Terminal (if your computer is equipped with a modem) to manage your communications. For easy access to modems or on-line services that you use frequently, such as CompuServe, you can create files containing all the information you need to make a connection. Use Terminal to connect to another computer and to upload and download files.

Chapter 13, "Using Windows Recorder," shows how many of the tasks you perform over and over can be automated using a macro. The Recorder records as a macro a series of steps that you perform in one or more Windows applications. With the Recorder application running, you can play back your macro to instantly duplicate the keystrokes and mouse movements you recorded.

Chapter 14, "Using Desktop Accessories," describes each of the smaller accessory programs that come with Windows. Using the Cardfile, you can keep track of names and addresses in a file that looks like a stack of indexed cards. You can even automatically dial a phone number on a cardfile card, if your computer has a modem. Calendar provides you with a visual calendar into which you can schedule your appointments for years to come. You can mark important appointments with a beep to remind you when it is time for your appointment. Start up Calculator to do quick or complex scientific calculations and copy the results into your primary application. Use Clock when you need to watch the time, minimizing Clock to an icon at the bottom of your screen.

Chapter 15, "Using Windows for Workgroups Mail and PC Fax," discusses Mail, which is a full-featured electronic mail system that comes as part of Windows for Workgroups. By using Mail, you can send, receive, and store messages over the network. You can even attach files to messages so that you can send a message that includes the backup document, spreadsheet, or charts. If you have a FAX on your network, you can use the shared FAX capability of Windows for Workgroups 3.11.

Chapter 16, "Using Windows for Workgroups Schedule+," discusses how to help you and everyone in your workgroup schedule your time, meetings, and common resources, such as meeting rooms. Schedule can be used as a personal scheduler to help you keep appointments. Schedule+ even prints schedules in standard time management notebook sizes. Schedule is also designed to work with Mail to make it easy to review when a group of people have a common block of time available for a meeting. Mail incorporates a note for scheduling and confirming group meetings.

Chapter 17, "Using Clipbook Viewer, Chat, and WinPop-Up," describes how to share data between users on your network by copying information to Clipbook Viewer where it can be shared. Chat is a simple two-way typing screen on which you and anyone else in your workgroup can type simultaneously. You can *chat* back and forth in Chat and get more immediate results than sending a message by Mail. When you want to get a quick message to someone who is currently working on the network use Pop-up. It allows you to pop-up a note on their computer screen while they are working.

Chapter 18, "Using Windows for Workgroups Management Tools," discusses Windows accessories that are used to help you manage your computer on the Windows for Workgroups network. The WinMeter accessory shows how your computer's time is being spent between your applications and its network housekeeping duties. The Net Watcher accessory lets you see who is using the files, directories, and printers that you are sharing with others in your workgroup. When you work away from your network you can still be part of it. Through the use of Remote Access, available with Windows for Workgroups 3.11, you can connect your computer to a Windows NT network server over the telephone line.

Part IV

Part IV, "Windows Multimedia," guides you into the world of multimedia. By adding sound cards, CD-ROMs, and even video cards you can turn your computer into a multimedia computer. You have the ability to compose and play music, edit video tapes, and run CD-ROMs that contain over 600 megabytes of data or programs.

Chapter 19, "Using Windows Multimedia," introduces the two accessory programs that you can use with your multimedia equipment. Sound Recorder enables you to create your own music, blend and mix tunes, and record your own voice. Media Player enables you to play existing music files, and Windows comes equipped with two 2-minute tunes that sound pretty amazing, coming out of your computer. To take advantage of multimedia, you need to equip your PC with a sound board, a CD-ROM drive, and speakers. Optionally, you can add a MIDI-based keyboard, a microphone, a VCR, and other equipment. With a multimedia-equipped PC (or MPC), you can create your own multimedia productions or take advantage of animated, speaking stories and reference libraries available for purchase.

Chapter 20, "Using Windows with CD-ROM and Video," helps you choose the right type of CD-ROM drive to meet your needs. If you want to edit videos, you definitely want to read this chapter to learn about using full-motion video in Windows and the type of video adapter cards you need.

Part V

Part V, "Running and Customizing Applications," teaches you how to install and configure Windows and DOS applications. It also describes the new Visual Basic for Applications that enables power-users and programmers to write programs that use the features and components found in programs such as Excel, Word for Windows, Access, and Project.

Chapter 21, "Installing and Configuring Windows Applications," describes the process of installing a new Windows application on your computer so that it performs well and takes up the least amount of disk space. You also learn how to uninstall applications from your computer. The chapter also teaches you how to use the RegEdit application to repair problems that arise with incorrect installations or applications that have been moved to new directories.

Chapter 22, "Running, Installing, and Configuring DOS Applications," illustrates how to configure Windows to get the best performance from your DOS applications. You also learn how to optimize the performance of DOS applications by customizing PIFs. A PIF is a program information file that contains technical specifications. Although a PIF already exists for many DOS applications, you can improve performance by optimizing the PIF for your own computer configuration. In this chapter, you also learn how to create a PIF for DOS applications that don't have one.

Chapter 23, "Introducing Visual Basic for Applications," gives a quick overview of Microsoft's new language that is used as the *glue* to bind together Windows applications. Visual Basic for Applications is first available as the macro language in Excel 5 and Project 4. It provides a common language used by all of Microsoft's applications that run under Windows.

Part VI

Part VI, "Installing Windows," gives you the information to fine-tune Windows for optimal performance and teaches you how to set up Windows and Windows for Workgroups to run on a network.

Chapter 24, "Installing and Optimizing Windows 3.1," shows you how to install Windows and improve performance or modify its operating characteristics by making changes to its configuration and INI files. Turn to this chapter to get the most out of your computer and Windows.

Chapter 25, "Installing Windows for Workgroups 3.11," begins with a short description and definitions to help you understand how networks work. It then shows you how to get on and off the network and how to share such resources as disk drives and printers with other members of your workgroup. Because groups of people and networks are dynamic, you also learn how to change workgroup, user names, and your password. This chapter also gives tips on improving performance when using Windows for Workgroups.

Chapter 26, "Networking Windows 3.1x," teaches you how Windows works with common networks, such as Novell. If you are setting up Windows to run on a network, turn to this chapter.

Part VII

Part VII, "Troubleshooting Windows," brings together some of the most common problems users face with Windows and how to solve those problems.

Chapter 27, "Troubleshooting Windows," provides solutions to the problems that everyone runs into with their computer now and then. Many times, you will find that the fix is simpler than you expect. This chapter also includes a list of who to call to get answers to pressing questions and where to turn for on-going support. Despite all your best efforts at finding the answer yourself, sometimes you need help.

Appendixes

The appendixes contain a listing of the files installed for Windows that lets you know which files you can delete if you need to gain more disk space. The INI files listed in the appendix are used by Windows for startup settings and to store the characteristics of hardware or software working under Windows.

The appendixes also describe how to control Windows using the keyboard. Although most work in Windows involves a mouse, as you become more familiar with Windows and Windows applications, you will find that you can gain speed with a few keyboard techniques. Knowing how to use the keyboard is almost mandatory if you spend much time with a laptop computer or working with a laptop while traveling.

How To Use This Book

To use this book, start with Part I, especially if you are a beginner. To get right to work, go to the specific chapters that interest you. To become more familiar with Windows, focus on Part II, where you can learn the details of working with Windows.

Two important reference tools begin and end the book: a table of contents and an index. When you are not sure exactly what you want to learn, browse through the table of contents at the beginning of the book to get an overview of Windows features and applications. Then turn to the chapter that seems most relevant. If you know exactly what you want to find, look it up in the index at the end of the book. After you become familiar with Windows, take some time to browse through the table of contents to look for features you may have passed over when you were a beginner.

Conventions Used in This Book

As with all Windows applications, you can use the mouse, the keyboard, or shortcut keys for most operations. In some cases, you may need to use key combinations. In this book, a key combination is joined by a comma or a plus sign (+). For example, Alt+letter means hold down the Alt key, press the letter key, and then release both keys.

This book uses the following special typefaces:

Typeface	Meaning
Italic	This font is used for optional items in functions and for terms used for the first time.
Boldface	This font is used for things you type, such as commands and functions. It also indicates "hot keys" which you can use to access commands from the keyboard.
`Special font`	This font is used to represent system and screen messages, and on-screen results of functions.

Tip
This paragraph format suggests easier or alternative methods of executing a procedure.

Note

This paragraph format indicates additional information that may help you avoid problems or offer advice to aid you in using Windows.

Caution

This paragraph format warns you of hazardous procedures that can lead to an unexpected or unpredictable result, including loss of data.

Troubleshooting

This paragraph format provides guidance on ways to find solutions to common problems.

▶ "Section title," p. xx

For Related Information cross-references help you access related information in other parts of the book. Right-facing triangles point you to later chapters; left-facing triangles point you to information in previous chapters.

Part I

Getting Started

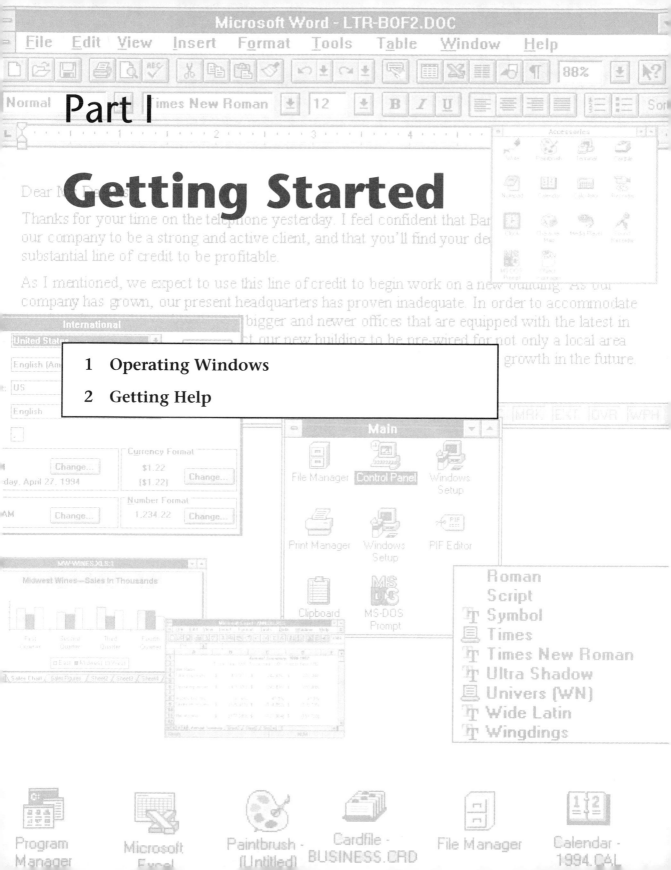

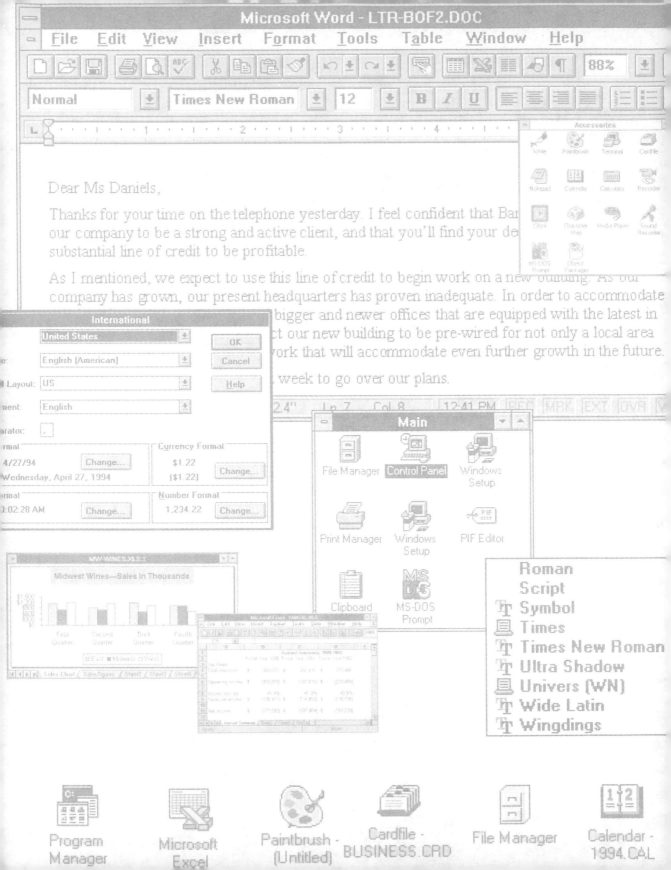

Chapter 1

Operating Windows

Windows is a graphical working *environment* that makes it easier to use your computer. Under Windows, each *application* (program) runs in a *window* (rectangular box) on-screen that you can open or close. You can run multiple applications at the same time, each in its own window, and you can easily switch between applications. Your knowledge of one application transfers to each new application you use because all Windows applications operate in a similar way.

What you learn in this chapter helps you operate any Windows application. You learn that Windows is easy to operate and that operating one Windows application is similar to operating another. This "learning carry-over" is important—when you start a new Windows application, you already understand most of the concepts necessary to operate it. You know how to choose, find, and use most commands and how to manipulate application windows. After completing this chapter, you should learn how to use the Windows Help system, as described in Chapter 2, how to start and manage applications with Program Manager, as described in Chapter 3, and how to manage your disk and files with File Manager, as described in Chapter 4. From there, you can jump to any other chapter in this book.

This chapter shows you how to control the location, size, and status of windows that contain applications. The focus in this chapter is on using the mouse to control windows, although some shortcut key combinations that are particularly useful are presented when appropriate. See Appendix C, "Using the Keyboard To Control Windows," for complete coverage of Windows keyboard commands and shortcuts.

In this chapter, you learn how to:

- Start and exit Windows

- Work in the Windows environment

- Control windows and icons

- Work with applications

Starting and Exiting Windows

Tip
If you have not yet installed Windows, turn to Part VI, "Installing Windows," to learn how.

You can run Windows in one of two modes (Standard or 386 Enhanced), depending on the processor in your computer and how much memory your computer has. Unless you specify otherwise, Windows selects the mode automatically. Sometimes you can force Windows to run in a different mode. See the section "Choosing an Operating Mode," later in this chapter, for more information on operating modes.

This section provides instructions on starting and exiting the Windows program. If you are unfamiliar with using menus, commands, or the mouse in Windows, follow the instructions for starting Windows and skip to later sections to learn more Windows basics. When you are ready to exit the Windows program, return to this section to learn how to exit safely and properly.

Starting Windows

Depending on your system setup, Windows may start automatically when you turn on your PC, you may need to select a Windows option from a menu, or your system may require a special command to start the Windows program. If you need help in using a custom setup like this, talk to your system administrator before attempting to start Windows.

If you set up Windows (or it was set up for you) with the default Microsoft Windows setup procedure, starting Windows is very simple. Follow these steps:

1. If necessary, change to the drive containing Windows. (If your PC defaults to drive C, for example, and Windows is on drive D, type **D:** at the DOS prompt and press Enter.)

2. Type **CD C:\WINDOWS** and press Enter to change to the directory that contains Windows. (Substitute a different drive letter or directory, if necessary.)

3. Type **WIN** and press Enter to start Windows.

When you start Windows, Program Manager appears on-screen as a window that contains other windows and icons (see fig. 1.1). If you don't see the Program Manager window, Windows may have been customized to start with Program Manager minimized as an icon. To open the Program Manager window, double-click the Program Manager icon at the bottom of the screen.

Tip
If you let Windows modify the AUTOEXEC.BAT file during installation, you can start Windows from any prompt.

Getting Started

──Program group window

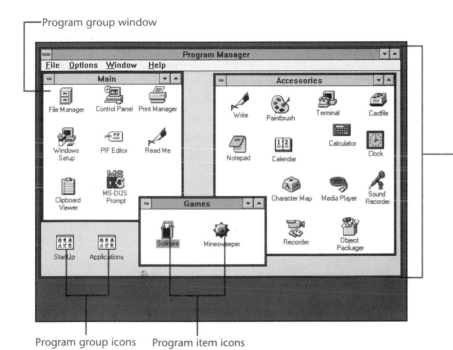

Fig. 1.1
Program Manager with the Main, Accessories, and Games group windows open.

Program Manager window

Program group icons   Program item icons

Program Manager acts as the coordinator of frequently used applications and documents. In the Program Manager window are *group windows* that contain groups of applications and associated documents. The Main group is one of these windows. Some group windows may be reduced to *group icons* at the bottom of the Program Manager window.

The *icons*, or small pictures, inside each group window are known as *program item icons*. Each program item icon starts one application and optionally one document. Grouping program item icons together in a group window makes it easy for you to work with applications and data used for a specific task.

When you first install Windows, you see that Program Manager contains the Main window, which includes utilities to help you manage files, work with DOS, customize Windows, and install new printer drivers. Program Manager also includes the Accessories window, which contains several small applications—including a simple word processor, a drawing application, and a communications program—that allow you to become productive in Windows right away without purchasing additional applications. Program Manager also includes the Games window, which contains two games you can play to learn how to use Windows; and, if Windows detects existing Windows applications, an Applications window, which contains your Windows and DOS applications.

As you'll learn in this chapter and in Chapter 3, you can customize your Windows start-up screen in many ways. You can create new windows and new icons to go in the windows. Each icon can represent an application, or an application and a file (so that when you start the application the file opens automatically). The applications and files can be located in different directories on your disk, and different icons can represent the same application in different windows. If you customize Program Manager, windows and icons different from those shown in figure 1.1 may appear when you start Windows.

> ### Note
>
> You can start Windows and an application from the DOS prompt by typing **WIN**, pressing the space bar, entering the application name, and then pressing Enter. To start Windows and Word for Windows, for example, type **WIN WINWORD** at the DOS prompt and then press Enter. The path for the application must be included in the PATH statement in your AUTOEXEC.BAT file. (Most applications automatically update the AUTOEXEC.BAT file when installed.)

Exiting Windows

To exit Windows and return to DOS, close the Program Manager window by opening the File menu and choosing Exit, or by pressing Alt+F4. Windows gives you the chance to cancel this command and remain in Windows.

If Windows applications are running, Windows closes them. If you changed documents in the applications since they were last saved, you are prompted to save them.

In the following explanation of how to quit Windows, the convention Alt+*key* indicates that you hold down the Alt key as you press the indicated letter or key. When you are asked to click an object, move the pointer so that the tip is on the object, and then quickly press the left mouse button.

To exit Windows when applications are running, follow these steps:

1. Activate Program Manager if its window is not open and on top of the other windows. Click the Program Manager window if it is visible, or press Alt+Tab until the Program Manager title appears in the center of your screen, and then release both keys. You can also press Ctrl+Esc, select Program Manager in the Task List, and choose OK.

2. Open the **F**ile menu and choose E**x**it Windows to close Program Manager and exit Windows (or press Alt+F4).

3. Choose OK when the message box advising you that This will end your Windows session appears.

   If you don't want to exit Windows, choose Cancel instead of OK.

4. If a Windows application is still running with a document containing unsaved changes, you are prompted to save your changes. Choose **Y**es to save changes, **N**o to discard changes, or Cancel to return to Windows. If you choose **Y**es to save changes to an unnamed file, the application's Save As dialog box appears, and you must name and save the file. If a DOS application is still running, Windows tells you to return to the application and quit it in the usual way before you can exit Windows.

You also can quit Windows from Program Manager's Control menu. The Control menu box is the square icon in the upper left corner of the Program Manager window. Normally, you use the Control menu to close an application's window; however, when you close the Program Manager window, you also close the Windows program. To close Windows from the Program Manager's Control menu, follow these steps:

1. Save any documents and quit all applications.

2. Click the Control menu box to open Program Manager's Control menu.

3. Click the **C**lose command or press **C**.

4. Choose OK from the alert box that says `This will end your Windows session`, or choose Cancel to return to Windows.

5. If an application is still running that contains a file with unsaved changes, you are prompted to save changes.

Note

Double-clicking the Control menu box that appears at the top left corner of each document or application window closes that window. If you made changes in the document or application since the last save, you are asked whether you want to save the changes. Double-clicking the Control menu box at the left corner of the Program Manager's title bar closes the Program Manager window *and* closes Windows.

Hands On: Exiting

To learn how to exit a Windows application, practice by exiting the Calendar. First, open the Calendar application by double-clicking its icon in the Accessories group. Click anywhere in the Calendar window and type a few characters. Then follow these steps to exit the program:

1. Open the **F**ile menu and choose E**x**it from the Calendar. The dialog box shown in figure 1.2 appears, asking whether you want to save changes to the document.

Fig. 1.2
A dialog box asks whether you want to save documents that have changed before you exit an application.

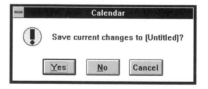

2. Choose **Y**es or press Enter. Because this document has not been saved before, the File Save As dialog box appears. (If you previously saved the file, choosing **Y**es or pressing Enter saves the document to its previous file name.)

3. Type a file name of one to eight characters. Use letters and numbers, but don't use spaces. For this example, enter **practice**.

4. Choose OK or press Enter.

   The Calendar window disappears.

To close all applications at once, activate and then close Program Manager. Follow these steps to practice this task:

1. Activate Program Manager in the following manner:

   Click the Program Manager window if you can see it; or press Alt+Tab until the Program Manager box appears, and then release both buttons. You can also use the Task List dialog box by pressing Ctrl+Esc to open the Task List dialog box, and then selecting Program Manager from the list and pressing Enter.

2. Exit Program Manager to exit Windows and all applications: double-click Program Manager's Control menu box (in the top left corner of the Program Manager window), or use the shortcut key Alt+F4.

3. The Exit Windows dialog box appears. Choose OK or press Enter to exit Windows and all Windows applications.

▶ "Operating Program Manager," p. 92

You return to the DOS prompt.

Working in the Windows Environment

Windows uses concepts that, for many people, make computers easier to use. The basic organizational concept is that all applications run on a *desktop*, and each application runs in its own window. Windows can run multiple applications just as you can have stacks of papers on your desk from more than one project. You can move the windows and change their size just as you can move and rearrange the stacks of papers on your desk.

Within Windows are two types of windows: application windows and document windows (see fig. 1.3). An *application window* contains the application itself. In figure 1.3, the application window has the title Microsoft Excel. The menu bar that controls the application is always at the top of the application window, underneath the application's title. Depending on the type of processor and amount of memory you have, you can run multiple applications at one time in Windows. Each application appears in its own application window.

A *document window* is located in an application window. In figure 1.3, the two document windows have the titles MW-WINES.XLS and MW-WINES.XLC. Document windows contain the data or document on which the application works. Some applications, such as Windows Write, can have only one document window open at a time. With other applications, such as Microsoft Excel and Word for Windows, you can have multiple document windows open at a time.

Fig. 1.3

Multiple document windows open within the Excel application window.

Application window

Document window

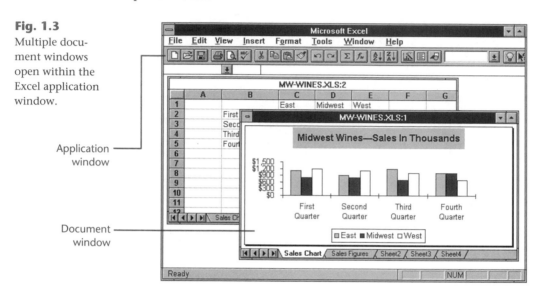

Just as you can cut, copy, and paste parts between papers on your desk, Windows enables you to cut or copy information from one application and paste the information into another. With some applications, you can even share information through linking. You can, for example, insert and link a table of data from a Microsoft Excel worksheet into a Microsoft Word for Windows document. If you make changes to the original data in Excel, the linked data is automatically updated in the Word document.

Making entries, edits, and changes to information is similar in all Windows applications. The basic procedure is as follows:

1. Activate the window containing the desired application.

2. Select the text or graphics object you want to change.

3. Choose a command from the menu at the top of the application.

4. Select options from a dialog box, if one appears, and complete the command by choosing OK or pressing Enter.

Parts of the Windows Screen

Figure 1.4 shows a Windows desktop containing multiple applications, each in its own window. The parts of a typical Windows screen are labeled in the figure.

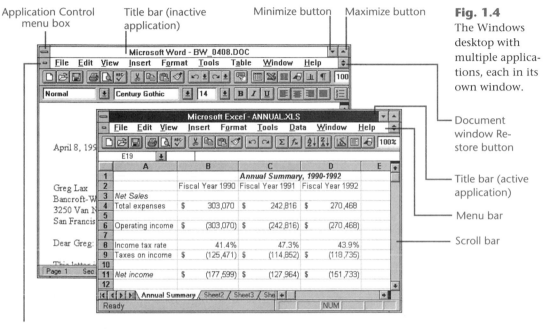

Application Control menu box

Title bar (inactive application)

Minimize button   Maximize button

Document Control menu box

Fig. 1.4
The Windows desktop with multiple applications, each in its own window.

Document window Restore button

Title bar (active application)

Menu bar

Scroll bar

With the mouse, you can control Windows applications quickly and intuitively. It enables you to choose commands, select options, and move on-screen items. When you move the mouse, the *mouse pointer* moves accordingly. The mouse pointer changes shape at different locations on-screen to indicate that it has different capabilities at that point. You select items on-screen by positioning the pointer on the item to be selected, and then pressing or holding down the mouse button. You use three actions to control the pointer in Windows: *clicking*, *double-clicking*, and *dragging* (see table 1.1 later in this chapter for definitions).

The *Control menu box* opens a menu that contains commands to control window location, size, and status (open or closed). See "Controlling Windows and Icons," later in this chapter, for information on how to use the Control menus.

The *title bar* at the top of each window contains the name of the application. After you save a file, the title bar also shows the file name. The title bar is one color when the window is active and another color when the window is inactive. (The *active window* is the window in front; it contains the currently running application.)

Menu names are located in the *menu bar* directly under the title bar. Windows applications use the same menu headings for common functions (such as **F**ile, **E**dit, **W**indow, and **H**elp) to make it easy for you to learn new applications. Select a menu by clicking it with the left mouse button or pressing Alt and then the underlined letter in the menu name. (This book shows the letter you press in **bold** type: for example, **F**ile.)

Icons are small pictorial representations. Some icons in Windows represent applications in memory that do not currently occupy a window. The Program Manager and Solitaire icons at the bottom of the desktop in figure 1.4 are *application icons*. In Program Manager, program groups can be reduced to *group* icons that appear inside the Program Manager window. To reduce the clutter of a filled desktop, you can minimize windows to icons. When you want to work with the application, restore icons to windows by using mouse techniques or the Control menu, as described in the section titled "Controlling Windows and Icons," later in this chapter.

Application windows are the windows containing applications. *Document windows* appear inside application windows and contain documents. In many (but not all) applications, you can have several document windows open at a time; you switch between them by pressing Ctrl+F6 or by selecting the document you want from the **W**indow menu.

In applications, you use *scroll bars* to move up and down in a document or from left to right in documents wider than the screen. You learn techniques for working with windows and icons in the section titled "Controlling Windows and Icons," later in this chapter.

Understanding Windows Terminology

Table 1.1 introduces terms that describe certain actions. The first part of the table contains general terms describing Windows actions. The next part defines mouse actions that produce consistent results in most Windows applications. See Appendix C, "Using the Keyboard To Control Windows," for a table of keyboard actions that can be used in Windows.

Getting Started

Table 1.1 Windows Terms and Conventions	
Term	**Definition**
Choose	Execute a command or close a dialog box, executing the selection mode.
Select	Select an item to activate it so that you can change it. Selecting a command or option turns it on but does not complete it. Selected text or menu names/items appear in reverse type or a different color. Selected options show a black dot or an x. Selected graphics appear enclosed by a dashed line or fenced in by boxes known as *handles*.
Unselect or Deselect	Remove the selection.
Point	Move the mouse so that the arrow pointer is on the desired menu name, command name, or graphic object; or so that the I-beam pointer (used in text) is where you want the insertion point (cursor) to be.
Pointer	The on-screen symbol controlled by the mouse. As you move the mouse on the desk, the pointer moves on-screen. The pointer changes shape to indicate the current status and the type of functions and selections available. An arrow means that you can select menus, commands, or objects. An I-beam means that the pointer is over text that you can edit. A two-headed or four-headed arrow means that you can move the edge or item. An hourglass means that you must wait while the application works. A crosshair means that you can draw.
I-beam	When the mouse pointer is in an area of text that you can edit, the pointer appears as a vertical I-beam. Reposition the flashing insertion point (cursor) by positioning the I-beam and clicking.
Mouse button	The mouse usually has two buttons. (Some mice have three.) Normally, clicking the left button completes an action; clicking the center or right button does nothing in Windows. (Clicking the right mouse button performs a specific function in some Windows applications.) You can switch the action of the left and right buttons through Control Panel.
Click	Quickly press and release the mouse button as you point to the item indicated. Clicking is used to reposition the insertion point in text, select a menu, choose a command from a menu, or select an option from a dialog box.
Drag	Select multiple text characters, or move objects by pointing to them and holding down the left mouse button as you move the mouse.

(continues)

Table 1.1 Continued	
Term	**Definition**
Double-click	Rapidly press and release the left mouse button twice as you point to the indicated item. Double-clicking an icon or file name opens an application or window related to that icon or file name.
Shift+click	Press and hold down the Shift key as you click. Use Shift+click to select multiple consecutive file names, or to select text between the current insertion point and where you press Shift+click.
Ctrl+click	Press and hold down the Ctrl (Control) key as you click. Use Ctrl+click to select multiple nonconsecutive file names or item choices.

Note

A comma in a key combination indicates that you release the first key before pressing the second key. A plus (+) indicates that you press and hold down the first key and then press the second key. Then release both keys.

Using the Mouse

The *mouse* is a hand-held pointing device that controls the position of a pointer on-screen. As you move the mouse across your desk or mouse pad, the pointer moves across the screen in the same direction. The mouse acts as an extension of your hand, enabling you to point to objects on-screen. The mouse works particularly well for people unfamiliar with a keyboard, new users, or people using graphics and desktop publishing applications.

To use a mouse, hold it so that the cable extends forward from your fingers and the mouse's body nestles under the palm of your hand. Place your index finger and second finger on the buttons. Move the mouse on your desk to move the pointer on-screen; click the left mouse button to make a selection. (Windows and Windows applications use the left button to indicate most selections, but you can use Control Panel to make the right button the primary button if you find that button more convenient.) The most common use of the mouse is to select menus, commands, tools, text, graphic objects, or windows so that you can change them with a command. In graphics applications and desktop publishing applications, you usually use the mouse to select menus, options, and icons; and to select and move objects on-screen.

The mouse senses movement through the rotating ball on its undercarriage. To use a mouse, your desktop surface must be smooth and clean. If possible, do not run the mouse on paper or cardboard surfaces; the lint from paper or cardboard can clog the ball and cause the pointer to skip. The ideal surface is a specially designed mouse pad. If you have an optical or laser mouse, you may have a special surface on which you must move your mouse.

To use a mouse, you need a clear area on your desk next to the keyboard. You don't have to clean your whole desktop—you only need a six- or eight-inch square of space for the mouse. Using Control Panel, you can increase or decrease the sensitivity of the mouse so that you need a smaller or larger area to move the mouse.

To select an object or menu item using the mouse, follow these steps:

1. Move the mouse so that the tip of the mouse pointer, usually an arrow, is on the name, graphic object, or text you want to select.

2. Quickly press and release the left mouse button.

Throughout this book, this two-step process is called *clicking*. Clicking the mouse button twice in rapid succession while pointing is called *double-clicking*. Double-clicking produces an action different from clicking. In a word processing application, for example, you click to position the insertion point, but you double-click to select a word.

You can also use the mouse for *dragging*. Dragging *selects* multiple text characters or moves graphic objects such as windows. In figure 1.5, a sentence in the Write word processor is selected.

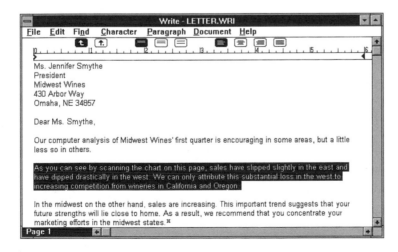

Fig. 1.5
Selected text appears in a reversed color scheme that contrasts with the rest of the document in the window.

To drag with the mouse, follow these steps:

1. Move the mouse so that the tip of the pointer is on the object or at the beginning of the text you want to select. (When over text, the pointer appears as an I-beam.)

2. Press and hold down the mouse button.

3. While holding down the mouse button, move the mouse. If you are dragging a graphical object, the object moves when you move the mouse. If you are selecting text, the highlighted text area expands when you move the mouse.

4. Release the mouse button.

Table 1.2 Mouse Pointers	
Pointer	**Appears When...**
⌨	Pointing to menus, options, or buttons
I	Inserting text
↔	Stretching the side or corner of a graphics frame
⊹	Adjusting column width in a spreadsheet program
╪	Adjusting row height in a spreadsheet program
⇔	Dragging the side or bottom of a window to resize it
⬈	Dragging the corner of a window to resize it
⇧	Selecting cells in a spreadsheet program
╪	Splitting a window horizontally
╫	Splitting a window vertically
⌕	Zooming in on a section of a document
☝	Selecting an item in the Help window
+	Dragging a spreadsheet cell to copy it
⌨?	Clicking an object or command to get related Help information
+⊾	Placing a chart or graph

Pointer	Appears When...
+	Stretching a chart or graph; placing objects when creating dialog boxes
↖↕	Moving rulers and other tools on-screen
+⁺	Dragging a spreadsheet cell to copy and increment it in contiguous cells
⧗	Indicating that the system is busy starting a program, getting data, calculating, and so on
↓	Pointing to a column in a word processing table

Many applications include specialized pointers for particular functions. Consult your program's documentation for specific information.

The mouse and the keyboard work as a team for controlling Windows applications. You can perform some tasks more easily with the mouse and other tasks more easily with the keyboard. Most Windows applications can perform all functions with either. This chapter emphasizes using the mouse to control Windows. See Appendix C to learn how to use the keyboard in Windows and Windows applications. Experiment with the mouse and the keyboard and use each where it works best for you.

Using Menus and Dialog Boxes

Every Windows application operates in a similar way. Commands are listed in menus whose names appear at the top of the window. You can choose commands from a menu by using the mouse or the keyboard (many timesaving shortcuts exist for choosing commands, too). If a program needs information from you to execute a command, a dialog box appears after you choose the command. You can use the mouse or the keyboard to choose options or enter values in dialog boxes.

Choosing Menus and Commands

When a menu is selected as shown in figures 1.6 and 1.7, its commands appear in a list. If you're not sure where to find a command, try browsing through the menus until you find the command you need. Many applications use similar commands for similar actions—a practice that makes learning multiple Windows applications easier.

► "Using the Mouse with Program Manager," p. 107

► "Using the Keyboard To Control Windows," p. 1,037

Getting Started

Fig. 1.6
Microsoft Word's
Edit menu.

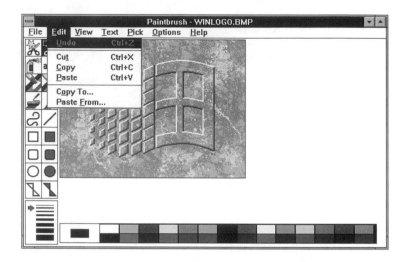

Fig. 1.7
Excel 5.0's **F**ormat
menu with a
submenu
displayed.

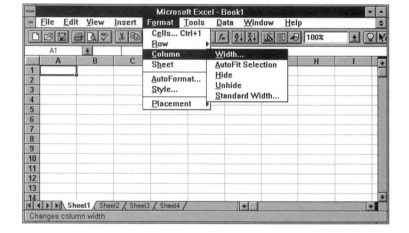

To choose a command with the mouse, follow these steps:

1. Position the tip of the mouse pointer on the menu name in the menu bar and click the left mouse button.

2. Click the command name in the menu.

Commands with an arrowhead next to them, such as the **R**ow command in figure 1.7, have *cascading menus* (also called *submenus*) that list additional commands.

You cannot choose commands that appear in gray in a menu (these options are called *grayed* or *dimmed*). You can see the gray command, but you cannot choose it. If a command you want to choose appears in gray, you probably forgot a step that is required before you can choose it. For the **E**dit **C**opy command to appear in bold type, for example, you must select what you want to copy.

Command names followed by an *ellipsis* (...) display an additional dialog box or window from which you can choose options or enter data. If you choose **E**dit **F**ind... from a Windows application, for example, a dialog box appears in which you type the word you want to find.

Commands with a check mark to the left are commands that *toggle* on and off. A check mark indicates the command is on; no check mark indicates the command is off. In Windows Write, for example, a check mark next to the **B**old command in the **C**haracter menu indicates that bold is on for the currently selected text.

Commands with key combinations listed to the right have shortcuts. In Word for Windows, for example, the **E**dit **C**opy command lists a shortcut of Ctrl+C. To copy text, you can open the **E**dit menu and choose **C**opy, or press Ctrl+C.

Note

When instructing you to use a command, this book sometimes uses the following phrase:

> Choose the *menuname commandname* command.

In this phrase, *menuname* refers to the name on the menu bar, and *commandname* refers to the name of the command in the pull-down menu. The phrase *choose the Find Find command*, for example, means that you should open the **F**ind menu and then choose the **F**ind command from that menu.

Note

Many Windows applications have menus that can be modified. If you share your computer with someone else, or if someone else set up your system for you, the menus in your programs may not appear exactly as indicated in the program documentation in this book. You may have different or additional shortcut keys available or additional menu commands, for example.

If you don't want to make a choice after displaying a menu, click the menu name a second time or click anywhere outside the menu. If you are using the keyboard, press Esc to close the open menu but leave the menu bar active; press Esc a second time to leave the menu bar.

If you are in a dialog box, you can click the Cancel button or press Esc to close the dialog box without making any changes to your document.

Many Windows applications have an Undo command. If you complete a command and then decide you want to undo it, check the **E**dit menu for an Undo command. You must choose the Undo command immediately after issuing the command to undo it.

Selecting Options from Dialog Boxes

Some commands need additional information before you can complete them. To use the F**o**rmat C**e**lls Number command in Excel, for example, you must specify which formats you want to use. The command displays a dialog box containing a list from which you can choose formats and a text box in which you can type new formats.

Commands that require more information display a *dialog box*—similar to those shown in figures 1.8 and 1.9. Dialog boxes like the one in figure 1.8 have areas for you to enter text (the File **N**ame *text box*) or to select from a scrolling list of choices (the **D**irectories list).

Fig. 1.8
The Save As dialog box with a text box, a list box, drop-down lists, and command buttons.

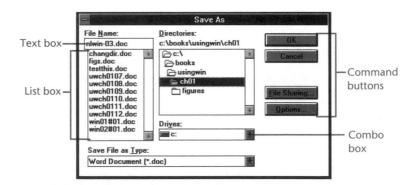

Many dialog boxes include *drop-down list boxes* (also called *combo boxes*) with lists that appear when you click the arrow button on the right side of the box. Figure 1.9 shows *option buttons* (also called *radio buttons*) and *check boxes*. The round option buttons are clustered in groups, and you can select only one of the options. The square check boxes, like the Parity Chec**k** box in figure 1.9, are toggles; you can turn each one on or off.

Option button ——

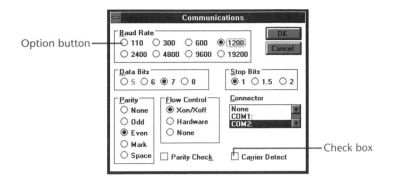

I

Getting Started

— Check box

Fig. 1.9
The Communica-
tions dialog box
in the Terminal
application, with
option buttons
and check boxes.
Groups of options
or check boxes are
often surrounded
by thin or dotted
lines.

Tip
If a dialog box
hides some-
thing that you
want to see on-
screen, you can
move the dia-
log box with
the mouse by
dragging the
dialog box by
its title bar to a
new position.

After you select options or make text entries, you accept the contents of the
dialog box by choosing the OK button (also called a *command button*) or
pressing Enter. Notice that the OK button has a dark shadow around the
button. This shadow indicates that the OK button is *active*. When a button is
active, pressing Enter activates that active button. In most dialog boxes, the
OK button is active most of the time. You can cancel most dialog boxes by
choosing the Cancel or Close button or pressing Esc. The selections you have
made will not be accepted if you choose Cancel or Close.

In this section, you learn how to make selections in a dialog box using the
mouse. You can also use the keyboard to make selections in a dialog box. See
Appendix C, "Using the Keyboard To Control Windows," to learn how to use
the keyboard in a dialog box.

To select an option button or check box, click it. Clicking a check box the
first time puts an x in it, signifying that the check box is selected. Clicking a
check box a second time turns off the x. To turn off an option button, click
one of the other buttons in the group.

To select command buttons such as OK, Cancel, Yes, or No, click them.

Select the *optionname* Option

This book uses the phrase *select the optionname option* to instruct you to turn on an
option or move the insertion point into an option. In this phrase, *optionname* refers
to the name of the option button, check box, text box, or scrolling list. For example,
the phrase *select the Inch option in the Page Layout dialog box* means that you should
turn on that option so that a dot appears in the circle to the option's left.

To deselect a round option button so that the black dot does not appear in it, click a
different option from the group that button is in. To deselect a square check box so
that the X disappears, click the check box a second time.

To select a text box so that you can type in it, click in the box. Reposition the cursor by moving the I-beam to a new location and clicking. The flashing insertion point is where your typed characters or edits appear. Select multiple characters by holding down the mouse button and dragging the I-beam across the text you want selected. (Text entry and editing is described in "Editing Text in Text Boxes," later in this chapter.)

To select from a list box, select the list box by clicking in it. Scroll through the list by clicking the up- or down-arrow button at the right side of the box. Make large jumps through the list by clicking in the shaded area of the scroll bar. Drag the scroll box to new locations for long moves. When the desired selection appears in the list box, click that selection once.

Some Windows applications use drop-down list boxes. These list boxes appear like figure 1.10 when closed, and like figure 1.11 when opened. To select from a drop-down list, click the down arrow button. When the list appears, select from it in the same way you select from any scrolling-list box—click the item you want.

Fig. 1.10
A closed drop-down list box.

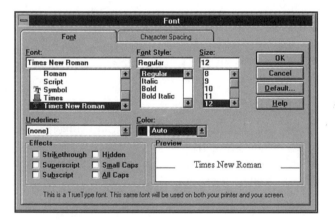

In some dialog boxes, double-clicking an option button or an item in a list selects that option and simultaneously chooses the OK command button. In the Open dialog box, for example, you can double-click a file name to select and open the file. Experiment with the dialog boxes in your applications to determine whether double-clicking is a viable shortcut.

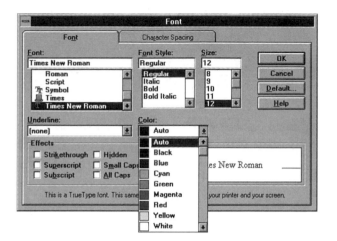

Fig. 1.11
An opened drop-down list box.

Using the Keyboard with a Drop-Down List Box

To use the keyboard to select from a drop-down list box, first select the list by pressing Alt+*letter*. In some dialog boxes, this automatically drops down the list. In others, you must press Alt+down-arrow key to drop down the list so that you can see its contents. In the Color dialog box, as in some others, you can select from a list without dropping it down—press Alt+*letter* to select the list and then press the down- and up-arrow keys to cycle through the items on the list. Each item appears in turn in the list's text box.

Changing Directories in a List Box

In many Windows applications, the Save As and Open dialog boxes contain hierarchical **D**irectories and Dri**v**es list boxes with icons—other dialog boxes used for locating files may have similar lists (see fig. 1.12). To change the directory, you must navigate through this hierarchical list.

The topmost entry in the **D**irectories list box represents the current drive. To its left is an icon that represents an open folder, indicating that the contents of the drive are displayed. The entries below it represent directories. They have closed folder icons, indicating that the directory contents are not listed, or they have open folder icons, indicating that the directory contents are listed. To see what's in a directory, you must open this folder.

When you open a folder, any subdirectories contained within the directory are listed below the directory in the **D**irectories list box, and any files contained in the directory are listed in the File **N**ame list box. Figure 1.12 shows the Windows Write Save As dialog box; other dialog boxes may have lists that look slightly different or have different list names.

Fig. 1.12

A hierarchical **D**irectories list box.

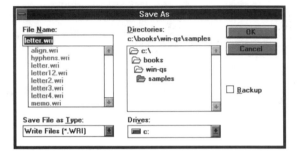

To open a directory or subdirectory in a **D**irectories list box, follow these steps:

1. Select the **D**irectories list box.

2. Scroll the **D**irectories list box to display the directory you want to open. Click the down arrow in the scroll bar to scroll the list. Hold down the mouse button to scroll continuously.

3. Double-click the directory name to open the directory.

4. Open the subdirectory in a directory by using the same technique as for opening a directory.

You can close a subdirectory by using the reverse procedure: select an open directory higher in the hierarchy than the subdirectory you want to close and press Enter (or double-click the higher directory).

Editing Text in Text Boxes

You can use the text-editing techniques you learn in this section in all Windows applications. These editing techniques are described for text boxes inside dialog boxes, but they also work when editing text in other locations in Windows applications.

To edit text in the text box with the mouse, position the I-beam pointer over the text where you want the insertion point to be and click. To delete multiple characters, drag across the characters so that they are selected and then press Del.

To deselect text in the text box, click somewhere else in the text or press End, Home, or the right or left arrow. When you select text, the characters you type are inserted at the insertion point. (The insertion point is the vertical flashing bar.)

To delete a character to the right of the flashing insertion point, press Del. Press Backspace to delete a character to the left of the insertion point.

Replace existing text with new text by selecting the text you want to replace and then typing. Select with the mouse by dragging the I-beam across the text as you hold down the mouse button.

When you are editing text in an application, you can use **E**dit commands such as **U**ndo, **C**opy, and **P**aste, but these commands do not work in dialog boxes. However, the keystroke equivalents—Ctrl+C, Ctrl+X, and Ctrl+V for copying, cutting, and inserting text, respectively—do work.

Scrolling Windows

Most applications include scroll bars at the right and bottom edges of the screen. You can use the vertical scroll bar at the right to scroll up and down in your document. You can use the horizontal scroll bar to scroll left and right. To scroll a small distance, click the scroll arrow at either end of either scroll bar; you scroll in the direction the arrow points. To scroll a larger distance, click in the gray area next to the arrow or drag the scroll box to a new location. In many applications, the scroll bars are optional: if you want more working space, you can turn them off.

You can scroll using the keyboard by pressing the arrow keys to move a character or line at a time or the PgUp or PgDn keys to move a screen at a time. The Home key scrolls you to the left margin, and the End key takes you to the end of the line or the right side. Holding down the Ctrl key when you press any other scrolling key changes the scroll: Ctrl+Home, for example, takes you to the beginning of your file; Ctrl+End takes you to the end of the file; Ctrl+the left- or right-arrow key moves you a word at a time instead of a character at a time. Most applications have many shortcuts for scrolling. To learn more about using the keyboard in Windows, see Appendix C.

In most applications, if you scroll using the scroll bars, the insertion point does not move; it remains where it was before you scrolled. If you scroll by using the keyboard, the insertion point moves as you scroll. Scroll bars are shown in figure 1.13.

Fig. 1.13
Scroll bars enable you to scroll up and down or left and right in your document.

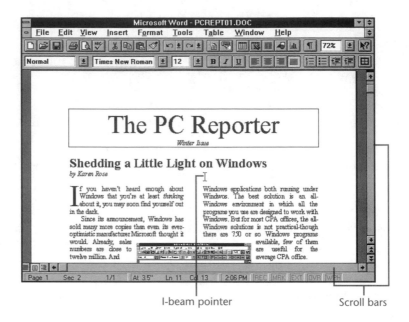

I-beam pointer

Scroll bars

Controlling Windows and Icons

Just as you move papers on your desktop, you can move and reorder windows on-screen. In fact, you can resize windows, expand them to full size, shrink them to a small icon to save space, and restore them to their original size.

All these activities take place by choosing options on a Control menu or with a mouse action. Every application and document window has a Control menu box located at the left edge of the window's title bar. Figure 1.14 shows an open application Control menu.

In an application window, the Control menu box looks like a space bar in a box. To activate it with the keyboard, press Alt, space bar. In a document window in an application, the Control menu box looks like a hyphen in a box. To activate it with the keyboard, press Alt, hyphen (-). To activate either Control menu with the mouse, click the Control menu box.

Many of the commands in a document Control menu are the same as those in an application Control menu. The application Control menu, however, controls the application window; the document Control menu controls the document window within the application. The commands in a Control menu are given in the following table.

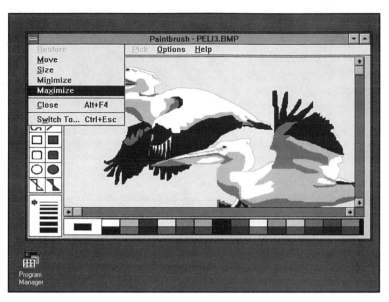

Fig. 1.14
The Paintbrush
Control menu.

Table 1.3   Control Menu Commands

Command	Action
Restore	Restores an icon or maximized window to its *previous* window size. The shortcut-key combination is Ctrl+F5 (for a document window).
Move	Moves the currently selected icon or window to a new location when you press the arrow keys. The shortcut-key combination is Ctrl+F7 (for a document window).
Size	Resizes a window by moving its edge. The shortcut-key combination is Ctrl+F8 (for a document window).
Mi**n**imize	Minimizes a window into an icon. In most cases, this command applies only to application windows.
Ma**x**imize	Increases an application window or icon to its full size. The shortcut-key combination is Ctrl+F10 (for a document window).
Close	Exits an application or closes a document window. If changes were made to the current file since the last save, the application asks whether you want to save the file. The shortcut-key combinations are Alt+F4 (for an application window) and Ctrl+F4 (for a document window).

(continues)

Table 1.3 Continued	
Command	**Action**
Switch To	Displays the Task List so that you can switch to a different application. The shortcut-key combination is Ctrl+Esc.
Next Window	Activates the next document window in applications that enable multiple documents to run simultaneously; works only when multiple document windows are open. The shortcut-key combination is Ctrl+F6.

Moving a Window or an Icon

With Windows, you can move a window to any location on-screen. You can arrange applications on your Windows desktop to be as neat or messy as your real desktop.

To move a window with the mouse, activate the window by clicking it; then place the pointer on the window's title bar, press and hold down the mouse button, drag the outline of the window to the new location, and release the button. Move icons in the same way.

You cannot move a maximized window (if you open the Control menu in a maximized window, the Move command is dimmed—unavailable). To move a maximized window, you must restore it to a smaller size (see the following section).

Changing the Size of a Window

To change the size of a window with the mouse, activate the window by clicking it. Move the pointer to one edge or corner of the window until the pointer changes into a two-headed arrow (see the preceding chart). Press and hold down the mouse button and drag the double-headed arrow to move the edge or corner of the window and resize the window. When the window is the size you want, release the mouse button.

You cannot size a maximized window (if you open the Control menu in a maximized window, the Size command is dimmed—unavailable). To size a maximized window, you must restore it to a smaller size (see the following sections on maximizing, minimizing, and restoring).

Moving Two Edges at the Same Time

To move two edges at once with the mouse, move the pointer to the corner of a window so that the pointer becomes a two-headed arrow tilted at a 45-degree angle. Drag the corner to its new location and release the mouse button.

Maximizing a Window to Full Size

When you are working in an application, you may find it convenient to maximize the application window so that it fills the screen. If the application includes document windows, you can maximize the document windows so that they fill the entire inside of the application window. When you maximize a window, you hide other windows and icons, but they are still active.

To maximize a window with the mouse pointer, click the Maximize button at the top right of the window (the up arrow) or double-click in the title bar. Restore the window to its previous size by clicking the Restore icon that appears at the top right of the window (the double arrow that appears only in a maximized window) or by double-clicking in the maximized window's title bar.

You cannot move or size a maximized window.

Minimizing and Restoring Windows and Icons

When you have too many windows on-screen, you can clean up the screen by changing windows into icons. As you know, *icons* are small pictorial representations of an application (or, in Program Manager, of a closed group window). Usually, application icons are stored at the bottom of the screen (see fig. 1.15). Icons usually show a name, symbol, or shape that indicates the application they represent. They also can show their active file or document. The icons at the bottom of figure 1.15 are for Excel, Paintbrush, Cardfile, Program Manager, File Manager, Clock, and Calendar. In the figure, Word for Windows and its document are sized and positioned at less than the maximum so that you have immediate access to the applications shown as icons at the bottom of the screen.

Application icons represent applications that are in memory but not in a window. Windows applications can continue running even when minimized into an icon. The Clock application, for example, continues to tell time.

With a mouse, you can reduce a window to an icon by clicking the Minimize button (the down-arrow located at the right edge of the application's title bar). Restore an icon into a window by double-clicking the icon (if you cannot see the icon, move the window covering it). You also can restore an icon to a window by activating the Task List and selecting the application from the list (to activate the Task List, double-click the desktop background or press Ctrl+Esc).

You can close an application by choosing the Control **C**lose command. If you made changes to the file since the last save, you are asked whether you want to save the changes. Some DOS applications require special closing procedures. For full details on DOS applications, refer to Chapter 22, "Running, Installing, and Configuring DOS Applications."

Fig. 1.15
Icons representing applications available in memory that are not in a window.

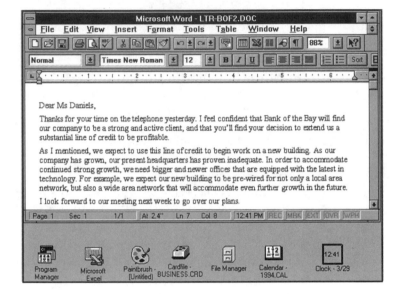

Hands On: Changing Windows and Icons

Now it's time to practice the methods for controlling windows and icons. Use the Program Manager window to learn how to move, resize, maximize, minimize, and restore windows and icons by following these steps:

1. Move the Program Manager window by positioning the tip of the mouse pointer on Program Manager's title bar, holding down the left mouse button, and dragging the window to a new location. Release the mouse button when the window is in position.

   Figure 1.16 shows the Program Manager window as it is being moved.

2. Move the Main group window elsewhere inside the Program Manager window, using the mouse.

3. Practice resizing the document window that contains the Main group so that it is smaller.

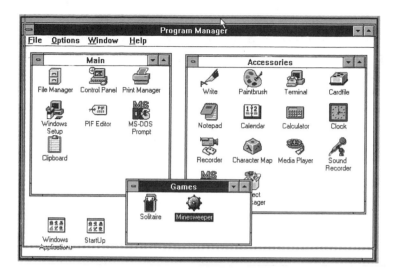

Getting Started

Fig. 1.16
Notice the dotted
outline as the
title bar is being
dragged up and to
the right.

To drag the right edge of the document window inward, move the
mouse pointer over the right edge of the Main group window. When
the pointer changes to a double-headed arrow (see fig. 1.17), press and
hold down the left mouse button and move the mouse to the left. Release the mouse button so that the edge hides one or more of the program item icons. You can resize most window edges or corners in this
manner.

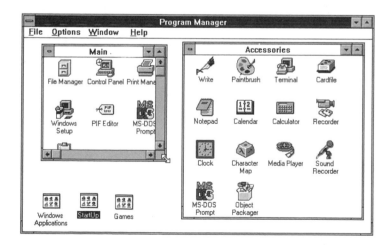

Fig. 1.17
Resizing a window
so that not all of
its contents are
visible.

Notice that when the window becomes too small to show all the icons, *scroll bars* appear at the right and bottom sides of the window (depending on how small you make the window, only one scroll bar may appear). The horizontal scroll bar enables you to scroll left and right through the window contents. You use vertical scroll bars to scroll vertically through data. To use the horizontal scroll bar in the resized Main group window, click the right-pointing arrowhead located at the right side of the horizontal scroll bar. The window scrolls to the right. Click the left-pointing arrowhead to scroll back to the left.

4. Minimize the Main group window to a group icon.

   Click the Document Minimize button (the down arrowhead to the right of the Main group title bar). Make sure that you click the Minimize button for the Main group window and not for the Program Manager. (If you accidentally minimize the Program Manager, it shrinks to an icon at the bottom of your screen. Double-click the icon to restore it to a window.)

   Figure 1.18 shows how the Main group window becomes an icon within the Program Manager window. Minimizing unused windows into icons leaves them accessible but reduces the amount of screen space they use.

Fig. 1.18
Reducing document windows to icons at the bottom of the Program Manager window.

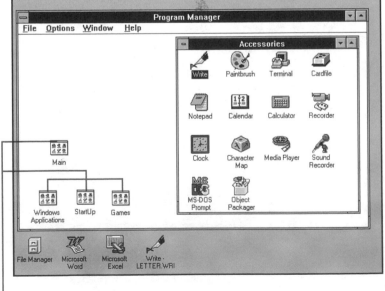

Program group icons

5. Restore the Main program group to a window by double-clicking the Main group icon.

6. Maximize the Main group document window so that it fills the Program Manager window. Click the Maximize button at the far right of the Main group window title bar.

Figure 1.19 shows the Main group window maximized within the Program Manager window. Notice that the Maximize button becomes a Restore button and that the Program Manager title bar is now shared with the Main group window title bar.

Notice that when you maximize a document window, all the other document windows and group icons are hidden.

7. Maximize Program Manager so that it fills the screen. Click the Maximize button at the far right of Program Manager's title bar.

8. Restore the Main group window so that the other groups show within the Program Manager.

Click the double-headed restore icon at the top right corner of the Program Manager window (see fig. 1.19). The double-headed restore icon belongs to the group window and is underneath the Minimize and Maximize buttons that belong to the Program Manager window.

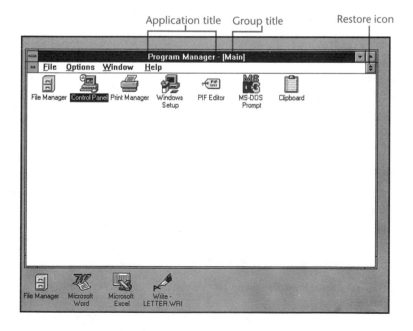

Fig. 1.19
A maximized document window filling the application window.

▶ "Controlling
    Program
    Manager,"
    p. 105

▶ "Customizing
    Groups,"
    p. 95

What you have learned about moving, sizing, maximizing, and minimizing windows and icons applies to application windows and the document windows within them, as well as to group windows.

Working with Applications

Many operations are similar from application to application in Windows. Nearly all Windows applications, for example, start with the File and Edit menus. The File menu includes commands for opening, closing, saving, and printing files. The Edit menu includes commands for cutting, copying, pasting, and other editing commands specific to the application. Operating menus and dialog boxes are the same in all applications. Selecting text and objects also is similar in most Windows applications.

Starting Applications

When you start Windows, Program Manager appears. With Program Manager, which is always running in Windows, you can easily start applications which you work with frequently.

Program Manager usually contains one or more open windows, called *group windows* (refer to fig. 1.1). Program Manager also usually contains one or more *group icons,* which are closed group windows (refer to the earlier section, "Controlling Windows and Icons," to learn how to open and close group windows). Inside each group window are one or more *program item icons.* A program item icon represents an application (and sometimes an associated data file).

The easiest way to start an application is from its program item icon. You can start your application by using the mouse or the keyboard. You also can start an application with File Manager, whether or not the application has a program item icon (described in Chapter 4).

When you are finished using an application, exit it before you exit Windows (especially with DOS-based applications). The procedure for exiting is similar in most Windows applications. Exit DOS applications by using the appropriate technique for that application—even though the DOS application is running under Windows.

> **Note**
>
> If Program Manager does not appear when you start Windows, someone may have
> customized Windows so that Program Manager displays as an icon at the bottom of
> the screen. Double-click the Program Manager icon or press Alt+Tab enough times to
> display the Program Manager window or a box showing its name. When you release
> the Alt and Tab keys, the Program Manager window opens.

When you installed Windows, you had the choice of assigning Windows and
DOS applications to groups. *Group windows* store all applications related to a
specific task together. With group windows, you can find and start applications and get data for a job you do frequently.

If you requested it during the installation, Windows made program item
icons for each application and put them in an Applications group window.
This group appears within Program Manager as a group window or a group
icon at the bottom of the window. If you open the group icon into a window,
the program item icons are displayed. You can start the applications from the
icons. Figure 1.20 shows Program Manager with group windows, group icons,
and program item icons. Application icons appear at the bottom of the screen
to represent running applications.

Tip

If you cannot
see Program
Manager, press
Alt+Tab until
the Program
Manager title
box appears,
and then re-
lease both keys
to display the
Program Man-
ager window.

Program group window

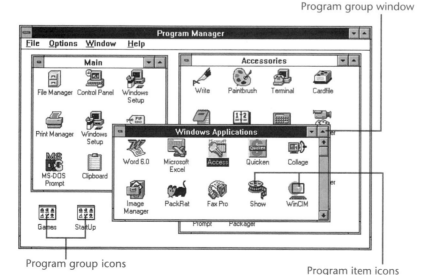

Fig. 1.20
Applications
grouped together
in a program
group window.

Program group icons

Program item icons

If you did not install the applications into a group (or if you added a new application to your system or want to regroup your applications), read Chapter 3 and create your own customized program item icons to hold applications.

Starting Applications from Icons

To start an application from a program item icon, follow these steps:

1. Activate the Program Manager window.

   If the Program Manager window is not open, double-click its icon if you can see it on the desktop or press Alt+Tab until the Program Manager box appears and then release both keys. You can also press Ctrl+Esc to display the Task List and then use the arrow keys to select Program Manager from the list and press Enter (or double-click Program Manager).

2. Open the group icon or activate the group window that contains the application you want to start.

   Double-click the group icon to open and activate the group window. If the group window is already open, click in the window to activate it.

3. Double-click the program item for the application or the application and document you want to start.

Starting Applications with Commands

You may not want applications you use infrequently to clutter the Program Manager. Instead of starting applications from icons, you can start applications and their related data documents by using the **File Run** command in the Program Manager. To start an application by using **File Run**, follow these steps:

1. Open the **File** menu and choose **Run**. The Run dialog box appears (see fig. 1.21).

Fig. 1.21
The Run dialog box.

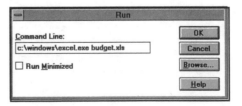

2. Type the full path name and application name in the **C**ommand Line text box.

3. To open a document with the application, type a space after the application name and type the name of the document. If the document is in a different directory from the application, also specify the path name of the document. For example, type the first of the following lines to start Excel, which is located in the EXCEL directory, and open the file BUDGET.XLS, also in the EXCEL directory. Type the second of the following lines if the file BUDGET.XLS is in the FINANCE directory:

    C:\EXCEL\EXCEL.EXE BUDGET.XLS

    C:\EXCEL\EXCEL.EXE C:\FINANCE\BUDGET.XLS

4. If you want the application to shrink to an icon when it starts, select the Run **M**inimized check box.

5. Choose OK or press Enter.

If you are not sure of the path or name of the application you want to start from the Run dialog box, choose the **B**rowse button and select the program from the Browse dialog box. When you choose OK or press Enter, the application's path and name appear in the **C**ommand Line text box. You can return to the DOS prompt while you run Windows. To start the DOS prompt from Program Manager, open the Main group window. Select the DOS Prompt icon with arrow keys and press Enter, or double-click it. When you are finished working from the DOS prompt, type **EXIT** at the prompt and press Enter to return to Windows and Program Manager.

Do Not Run CHKDSK with the /F Argument

You must not run some DOS commands and utilities from Windows. These commands and utilities change the DOS file-allocation table (FAT) or close files that Windows expects to remain open. If you run these commands, Windows can freeze, or you can lose data. A DOS command that causes this problem is CHKDSK /F (used to unfragment disks). You can use CHKDSK by itself to check disk and memory, but you must not use the /F argument. Other utilities that can cause problems are file-compression utilities, disk-optimizer utilities, and undelete-file utilities. To use these types of utilities, exit Windows and run them directly from the DOS prompt. When using Windows and DOS 5, you get the message CHKDSK/F cannot be done in a Windows /DOS Shell Command Prompt.

Getting Started

Hands On: Starting an Application

In this section, you learn how to start an application from Program Manager. Before starting an application, the group window containing the application must be open. In the following steps, you activate or open the Accessories group window containing the desktop applications that come with Windows. From that group, you open Microsoft Write, a simple word processor.

1. Activate the open Accessories group window inside Program Manager by clicking the Accessories window.

   If the Accessories group window is not open, double-click the Accessories group icon to open it.

   The Accessories group window appears (see fig. 1.22). If several windows are open on your desktop, the active window is the one on top (usually the one with a solid or colored title bar).

Fig. 1.22
The Accessories group window.

The Accessories group window displays all the applications it contains. Descriptions and in-depth instructions for these desktop applications can be found in Chapters 10 through 14.

▶ "Starting Applications from a Group Window," p. 93

▶ "Using File Manager's Drag-and-Drop Feature," p. 173

2. Start the Write application by double-clicking the Write program item icon. The Write application window appears, as in fig. 1.23.

You will use the Write application to practice the skills you learn in the next section.

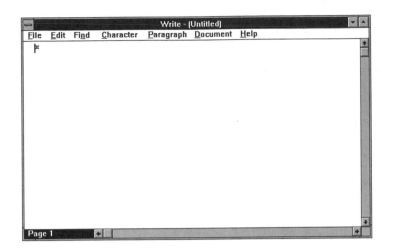

Fig. 1.23
The Write
application
window.

Getting Started

Opening, Saving, Printing, and Closing Files

When first started, many applications present you with a new, empty document—a blank page if the application is a word processing or graphics or desktop publishing application; an empty worksheet if the application is a spreadsheet application. If you finish working on one file, you can start a new file by choosing the **F**ile **N**ew command. Your application may ask you for information about the type of new file to start.

To open an existing file, choose the **F**ile **O**pen command. An Open dialog box similar to the one shown in figure 1.24 appears. In the Dri**v**es drop-down list box, select the drive that contains your file. In the **D**irectories list box, select the directory containing your file and choose OK to display the list of files in that directory. From the list of files presented in the File **N**ame list box, select the file you want to open and choose OK or press Enter. (The File **N**ame list box lists only files with the application's extension; to list other types of files, type a different extension in the File **N**ame list box.)

Tip
To see all files
in the selected
directory, type
. in the File
Name text box.

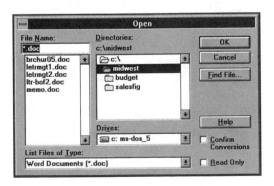

Fig. 1.24
The Open dialog
box in a Windows
application.

The File menu contains two commands for saving files: Save **A**s and **S**ave. Use the **F**ile **S**ave or **F**ile Save **A**s command the first time you save a file so that you can tell Windows where to save it and what name to give your file. You also can choose Save **A**s to create a new version of an existing file by giving the file a new name. The Save As dialog box is often similar to the Open dialog box shown in the preceding figure; in it, you must specify the drive and directory to which you want to save your file and name the file. File names are limited to eight characters with a three-character extension, usually supplied by the application. After you type the file name, choose OK or press Enter to save the file. After you name your file, you can choose the **F**ile **S**ave command to save the file without changing its name or location. This command replaces the original file.

Printing your file may take two steps. Often you first must make some choice about the printer by using a command in the **F**ile menu named something like P**r**int Setup or **T**arget Printer. Use this command to identify the printer you want to use or to change the paper orientation. (After you make these selections, you need not access this menu again until you want to change the setting.) After you identify the printer you will use, you can choose the **F**ile **P**rint command to print your document. You are presented with a Print dialog box (see fig. 1.25) that asks for details about the print job: how many copies to print; what range of pages to print; and other options depending on the application. Make your selections and then choose OK or press Enter. In some applications, like Windows Write and Aldus PageMaker, you can change the printer setup by choosing a special Setup command in the Print dialog box.

Fig. 1.25
The Print dialog box is used to control printing.

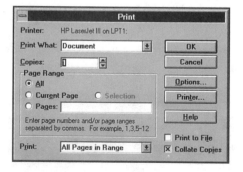

To close a file, you often can choose the **F**ile **C**lose command. Applications that don't allow more than one document to be open at once, however, usually don't include a **F**ile **C**lose command; instead, to close the current file, you open a new file or exit the application. If you choose **F**ile E**x**it, you exit the application. When you close or exit, most Windows applications prompt you to save any changes you made since you last saved your document.

Simple Editing Techniques

Editing text and objects is similar in all Windows applications. When you're working with text in your document or in a dialog box, the mouse pointer turns into an I-beam when you move it onto editable text. You can use the I-beam to move the insertion point and to select text. The flashing vertical insertion point is where text appears when you type.

You can use the mouse or the keyboard to move the insertion point. To use the mouse, position the I-beam where you want the insertion point to move and click the left mouse button. (If you cannot see the insertion point, it may be under the I-beam; move the mouse a little to move the I-beam.) To use the keyboard to move the insertion point, press the arrow keys. For a complete description of how the arrow keys work, refer to Appendix C, "Using the Keyboard To Control Windows." Many keyboard shortcuts also are listed in the table.

To insert text at the insertion point, just begin typing. Most applications push existing text to the right to make room for the new text (though some applications allow you to select an *overtype* mode). To delete text to the left of the insertion point, press the Backspace key. To delete text to the right of the insertion point, press the Delete key.

Selecting Text and Objects

You can sum up one of the most important editing rules in all Windows applications in three simple words: select and do. You must select text or an object before you can do anything to it (if you don't select first, the application doesn't know where to apply your command).

Selecting text with the mouse is fast and easy. To select text with the mouse, position the I-beam at the beginning of the text you want to select, click and hold down the left mouse button, drag to the end of the text you want to select, and release the mouse button. Many Windows applications—for example, word processors—have shortcuts you can use with the mouse to select particular blocks of text. You can select a word, for example, by double-clicking it. To select a length of text with the mouse, you can drag until you

Tip

Most applications contain an "oops" function: the **E**dit **U**ndo command. This command undoes your most recent edit—use it when you make an edit you instantly regret.

touch the end of the screen, which causes the screen to scroll. Refer to Appendix C, "Using the Keyboard To Control Windows," to learn how to select text with the keyboard. Selected text appears reversed (refer to fig. 1.5).

After you select a word, you can turn it bold or change its font. In most applications, typing replaces the selection, so you can replace text by selecting it and typing the new text. If a graphic is selected, you can resize it.

To select an object, such as a picture, with the mouse, click the object. (To select multiple objects, hold down Shift while you click each one in turn.) To select with the keyboard, position the insertion point beside it, hold down Shift, and press an arrow key to move over the object. Selected objects, such as graphics, usually appear with *selection handles* on each side and corner.

Copying and Moving

After you select text or an object, you can use the Edit menu to copy or move it. The commands all Windows applications use to copy and move are **Edit Cut**, **Edit Copy**, and **Edit Paste**. The **Edit Cut** command removes the selection from your document; **Edit Copy** duplicates it. Both commands transfer the selection to the Clipboard, a temporary holding area. The **Edit Paste** command copies the selection out of the Clipboard into your document at the insertion point's location. Your selection remains in the Clipboard until you replace it with another selection.

To copy a selection, open the **Edit** menu and choose **Copy**, move the insertion point where you want the selection duplicated, then open the **Edit** menu again and choose **Paste**. To move a selection, open the **Edit** menu and choose **Cut**, move the insertion point to where you want the selection inserted, and then open the **Edit** menu again and choose **Paste**. Many shortcuts exist for copying and moving. Ctrl+X cuts a selection, Ctrl+C copies a selection, and Ctrl+V usually pastes the Clipboard's contents. Many Windows applications also take advantage of Windows' *drag and drop* feature: you can use the mouse to drag a selection to its new location and drop it into place.

Some Windows applications can link data to other Windows applications. You usually create these links by using **Edit Copy** to copy from the server application and **Edit Paste Link** to paste the shared data into the client application. When data in the server application changes, the linked data in the client application changes. To link data in this way, you use Windows' object linking and embedding (OLE) capability, which is described more fully in Chapter 6 "Advanced Data Sharing." With OLE, you also can embed an object created in one application inside a file created in another application.

You can edit the embedded object in the file where you embedded it, but you use the same application you used to create the embedded object.

Switching between Document Windows

In many—but not all—Windows applications, you can open more than one file and switch between the files easily. Use these techniques when you want to copy or move information from one document to another. To open multiple files, choose the **F**ile **O**pen command multiple times. If your application doesn't support multiple documents, it closes the current file, asking you whether you want to save any changes you made since you last saved.

If your application supports multiple documents, each document opens in its own document window, as shown in figure 1.26. You can use the document Control menu, at the left of the menu bar, to control the size and position of the document window. You also can control the document window using the Restore, Minimize, and Maximize buttons that appear at the right end of the menu bar.

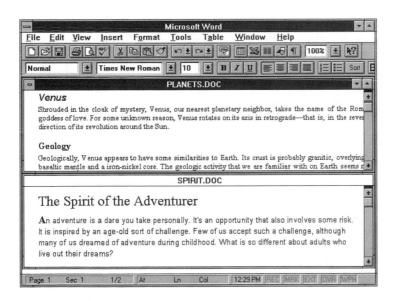

Fig. 1.26
Multiple document windows.

The file you opened most recently is the active file; usually it appears in the top window, and it may hide the other document windows. In some applications, such as Word for Windows, you can use the **W**indow **A**rrange All command to arrange your document windows so that they all are visible. (If you have many files open, the windows may be very small.)

To switch between document windows with the mouse, click the window you want to activate. If the window you want to activate is not visible, you may need to move or size the active window on top (move a window by dragging its title bar; size it by dragging its border). To switch between document windows with the keyboard, choose the **W**indow menu and select the document you want from the list of open windows. In most applications, you can hold down Ctrl while you press the F6 key to switch between open document windows within an application.

Quitting Windows Applications

Most Windows applications abide by the same design rules. Fundamental commands such as saving and quitting are common across different applications. To quit a Windows application, follow these steps:

1. Activate the application by clicking the application window if you can see it, or pressing Alt+Tab until the box for the application appears and then releasing both keys.

2. Open the application's **F**ile menu and choose E**x**it.

Tip
To quickly close an application, double-click its Control menu box.

If you alter documents without saving them, you are prompted to save your changes before the application quits.

To run a non-Windows (DOS) application from Windows, follow the normal procedure to quit or exit that application. Make sure that you save before quitting because you may or may not be prompted to save your work before the application quits. Depending on your Windows settings and on how the DOS application was started, you may return immediately to Windows, or you may return to an empty (inactive) window. If you return to an inactive window, close the window by using the Control menu.

Hands On: Executing Commands and Editing

In this tutorial, you practice many of the skills you learned in this section. You learn how to edit text, choose menus and commands, select options from dialog boxes, and how to save a file.

Typing and editing text is the same in nearly every Windows application. After you practice the techniques described in this section, you can type and edit text in other applications.

In the following steps, you type a list in the Write application, and make a simple editing correction to it. Follow the steps and remember to include the misspelled word *Raketball*.

1. Open the Write application from Program Manager. (See "Hands On: Starting an Application," earlier in this chapter.)

2. Type the following lines (press Enter at the end of each line):

> **Things to do today:**
>
> **Complete cash flow analysis**
>
> **Plan next quarter's goals**
>
> **Raketball at 7:00**

3. Change Raketball to **Racquetball** by using the mouse.

Move the I-beam pointer between the k and the e in Raketball and click once. The flashing insertion point should now be between the k and e. Press the Backspace key to delete the letter k, and type **cqu**.

The result of your typing is shown in figure 1.27.

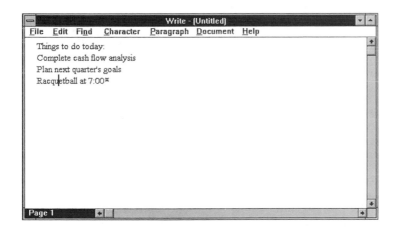

Fig. 1.27
The Write word processor with the corrected list.

What you have learned about editing text in Write applies to editing text in all Windows applications and text-entry boxes. You can learn much more, however, that will save you time. Windows applications have many shortcuts for editing, cutting, and pasting text. These shortcuts are briefly described in the section titled, "Working with Applications," and are described in more detail in Chapter 10, "Using Windows Write."

Every Windows application lists its commands in menus. The menus are listed at the top of the application Window, just below the title bar. You can choose commands by using the keyboard, the mouse, or sometimes by using shortcut keys.

Figure 1.28 shows the Find menu selected so that its commands show. Click the Find menu name to select the menu.

Fig. 1.28

A Windows menu with available commands in bold and commands that lead to dialog boxes with ellipses.

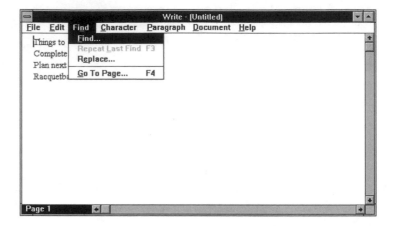

Commands that appear in solid type in a pull-down menu are available for selection; all the requirements necessary for you to select the command have been fulfilled. In the Find menu, Repeat Last Find F3 is shaded gray (see fig. 1.28). A shaded command in a Windows menu is momentarily unavailable. The command may be unavailable because a required preceding step has not been completed or because the command is not appropriate for the type of document active in the application. The F3 to the right of the Repeat Last Find command is the shortcut key for that command. Some shortcut keys are combinations such as Ctrl+C. (Ctrl+C is the shortcut key for the Edit Copy command. This shortcut is executed by holding down the Ctrl key as you press the C key.)

To exit from a menu without executing a command, click anywhere outside the menu or click the menu name a second time.

To change something in a Windows application, you select the text, graphical object, or data cell, and then do something to the selection by choosing a command. In most applications, if you do not select specific text or objects before you choose the command, the command applies only to the location of the insertion point.

In the following steps, you complete a menu command that boldfaces the heading of the list you typed (see fig. 1.29):

1. Select the Things to do today heading.

2. Open the **C**haracter menu and choose **B**old to boldface the selected text.

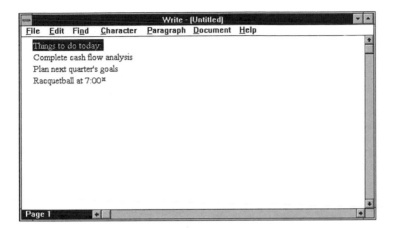

Fig. 1.29
Selected text to be changed by the next edit or character-formatting command.

Windows applications include an **U**ndo command that undoes the last editing action you took. If you look at the command in the **E**dit menu now, it reads **U**ndo Formatting because the last action you took was to format some text in bold. The **U**ndo command changes names, such as **U**ndo Typing and **U**ndo Formatting, depending on the last action you took.

Explore Unfamiliar Menus

You can find out what commands are available in a Windows application by selecting the menus in the application, one by one. After you open a menu, close it by pressing Esc, clicking outside the menu, or using the arrow keys or mouse to open another menu.

In the following steps, you change the document format for the Things to do list that you typed earlier in this section. A set of option buttons and text boxes will appear. (Chapters 10 and 11 go into more detail about the uses of scrolling lists and check boxes.)

To change the document layout of the document you typed earlier, follow these steps:

1. Open the **D**ocument menu and choose **P**age Layout to display the Page Layout dialog box.

When the Page Layout dialog box first appears, the number in the **S**tart Page Numbers At text box is selected (see fig. 1.30). The contents of the text box are highlighted, or the flashing insertion point is in the text box. To replace the selected number 1, type text or a number.

Fig. 1.30
The Page Layout
dialog box.

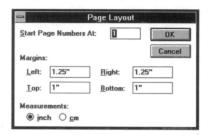

2. Select the **C**m measurement option.

   Notice that the selected option button has a black dot. A dashed line encloses the button name when you first select it.

3. Select the **I**nch measurement option.

4. Select the **T**op margin text box, and type **2** for a 2-inch top margin. (Because inches are the default unit of measurement, you don't have to type the " symbol.)

   Click between the 1 and " characters in the **T**op margin text box, and press Backspace to remove the 1. Type **2**. You also can drag the mouse pointer across the contents of the text box and type **2**, or you can double-click in the text box and type **2**.

5. Execute the command by clicking the OK button or pressing the Enter key.

You can save the document containing your list so that you can add to it later. Follow these steps to save the list:

1. Open the **F**ile menu and choose Save **A**s.

   The File Save As dialog box appears with the flashing insertion point at the beginning of the File **N**ame text box.

2. Type the file name **todo** (see fig. 1.31).

3. Choose OK or press Enter.

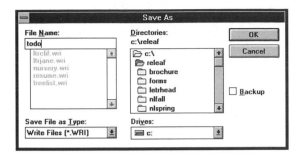

Fig. 1.31
The Save As dialog
box.

You do not have to type a file name extension because Write automatically adds the extension WRI. Notice that after you save the file, the file name, TODO.WRI, displays in the title bar of the Write window.

▶ "Starting
Applications
from a Group
Window," p. 93

▶ "Advanced
Data Sharing,"
p. 199

▶ "Loading and
Running DOS
Applications,"
p. 738

Using Multiple Applications

With Windows, you can run multiple Windows or DOS applications and switch between them. You even can copy and paste data between applications. You can copy tables or charts from a spreadsheet application, for example, and paste them into a word processing report or copy drawings from a design application and paste them into a desktop publishing application.

Switching between Applications

When you run several applications, you need an easy way to switch between the windows.

If you are using a mouse, *activate* another window (or bring it to the top of the stack of windows) by clicking it. If you cannot see the window of the application you want, use a keyboard technique or move the top windows as described in the earlier section, "Controlling Windows and Icons." If the application you want is in an icon, double-click the icon to open it into an active window.

Often you work with your application windows maximized full-screen, so it is more convenient to use the keyboard to switch between applications. There are two methods for using the keyboard to switch to another application. One method uses the Alt and Tab keys, the other method uses the Task List.

To use the Alt and Tab keys to switch between applications, follow these steps:

1. Hold down the Alt key and press Tab.

   Each time you press the Tab key, a box appears on-screen showing the name and icon of the next application (see fig. 1.32). While you hold down the Alt key and each time you press Tab, the next icon and application name appear in a box.

Fig. 1.32
Pressing Alt+Tab cycles you through all open applications.

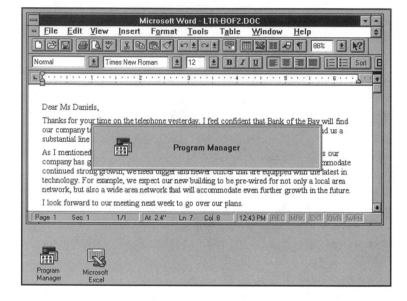

2. When the box for the application you want to switch to appears, release both the Alt and Tab keys.

You also can press Alt+Esc to cycle through application windows, but this method is slower because each window must be completely redrawn before the next window appears.

Whether you use the mouse or the keyboard, you can use the Task List to switch among many applications (see fig. 1.33). The Task List shows which applications are currently running. You can switch between applications by choosing the one you want from the list.

To switch among applications using the Task List, follow these steps:

1. Activate the Task List, either by double-clicking the desktop background or pressing Ctrl+Esc. You can also press Alt, space bar to open the Control menu and then choose the **S**witch To command.

Fig. 1.33
The Task List
dialog box.

2. Double-click the application you want to activate or use the down arrow to select the application and press Enter. Choose the application you want active.

The following table lists the command buttons in the Task List dialog box.

Table 1.4   Task List Command Buttons

Command Button	Action
Switch To	Activates the selected application in the Task List
End Task	Exits the selected application in the Task List
Cancel	Exits the Task List without making a choice
Cascade	Arranges all open application windows in an overlapping cascade from top left to bottom right
Tile	Arranges all open application windows to fill the screen with equal-sized windows
Arrange Icons	Arranges all application icons along the bottom of the desktop

Hands On: Working with Multiple Applications

In this section, you get a chance to work with multiple applications. You learn how to switch between an open application to another and how to transfer data from one application to another.

If you completed the exercise in the previous section, Write should be opened. Now open the Calendar application that comes with Windows. To open Calendar, follow these steps:

1. Switch to Program Manager. Click the Program Manager window if you can see it or press Alt+Tab until the Program Manager box appears and then release both buttons.

2. Activate the Accessories window by clicking in it or by double-clicking the Accessories group icon if the window is closed.

3. Double-click the Calendar program item icon to open Calendar.

Now the Write application is open but in an inactive window. To switch back to Write, click the Write window if you can see it or press Alt+Tab until the Write title box appears, and then release both keys.

You can also use the Task List to switch back to Write:

1. Double-click the desktop if you can see it or press Ctrl+Esc to display the Task List.

2. Double-click the name Write in the list box or press the down arrow to select the name and press Enter.

The To-Do list in Write should now be active. To copy the 7:00 racquetball appointment to the Calendar, follow these steps:

1. Select the statement Racquetball at 7:00, using the mouse. Click to the left of the R in Racquetball, hold down the mouse button, and drag the I-beam pointer across the phrase.

2. Open the **E**dit menu and choose **C**opy.

3. *Activate* (switch to) the Calendar application. Click the Calendar if it is visible or press Alt+Tab until the Calendar box appears and then release both keys.

4. Select the 7:00 time period on the Calendar. Click the down arrow in the vertical scroll bar until 7:00 PM is displayed; click to the right of 7:00 PM.

5. Open the **E**dit menu and choose **P**aste.

The phrase you copied from Write is pasted into the Calendar (see fig. 1.34).

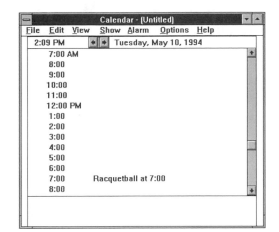

Fig. 1.34
Copying information from one Windows application and pasting it into another.

Choosing an Operating Mode

Windows runs in one of two modes—standard or 386 Enhanced. Your ability to use 386 Enhanced mode depends on your equipment. When you start Windows, the application examines your PC and then runs in the mode best suited for your equipment. (You can force your PC to start in standard mode, however, by typing **WIN/S** at the DOS prompt, and you can force it to start in 386 Enhanced mode by typing **WIN/3** at the DOS prompt.) Each mode has different operating capabilities and uses memory differently. Standard mode operates in extended memory; 386 Enhanced mode operates in extended memory and accesses the virtual memory functions built into the 386 processor so that your PC seems to have more memory than is actually installed.

Windows starts in 386 Enhanced mode if you have a 386 or 486 PC with more than 2M of memory. This default setting is meant for people who are running some DOS applications under Windows. If you aren't running any DOS applications, you are better off running Windows in standard mode. In 386 Enhanced mode, Windows creates *virtual machines* of memory for the DOS applications to use. These virtual machines are about 640K (but are determined by settings in the PIF) because many DOS applications cannot use more than 640K. This setting restricts Windows applications that don't have the 640K memory restriction and can use any amount of memory available to them.

To start Windows in standard mode, type **WIN/S** (or **WIN/2**) at the DOS prompt. You can set up your PC so that you start Windows in standard mode by creating a batch file called WIN.BAT that includes only one command: WIN/S. (If you need to start a Windows session in which you use DOS applications, you can override the batch file and start in 386 Enhanced mode by typing **WIN/3** at the DOS prompt.)

From Here...

In this chapter, you learned the basic skills you need to work in the Windows environment. To gain a more in-depth understanding of ways to use Windows, refer to the following chapters:

- Chapter 2, "Getting Help," shows you how to get on-line help in Windows.

- Chapter 3, "Controlling Applications with Program Manager," teaches you how to manage your applications.

- Chapter 4, "Managing Files with File Manager," explains ways to manage the files on your computer.

- Chapter 7, "Customizing with Control Panel," shows you how to customize the Windows environment.

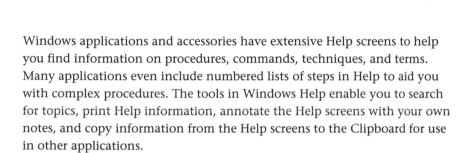

Chapter 2

Getting Help

Windows applications and accessories have extensive Help screens to help you find information on procedures, commands, techniques, and terms. Many applications even include numbered lists of steps in Help to aid you with complex procedures. The tools in Windows Help enable you to search for topics, print Help information, annotate the Help screens with your own notes, and copy information from the Help screens to the Clipboard for use in other applications.

Some Windows applications even include help to aid you in changing from one application to another. Microsoft Excel, for example, contains a keystroke Help feature that accepts Lotus 1-2-3 keystrokes, and then uses those keystrokes to demonstrate how to do the equivalent feature in a Microsoft Excel worksheet. You can learn as you work. Word for Windows has a similar feature that enables you to learn Word for Windows, even as you use WordPerfect keystrokes and commands.

Although Windows applications come from various software manufacturers, most manufacturers use the Help application supplied by Microsoft, the manufacturer of Windows. The Help applications in many different programs, therefore, work similarly. You can learn the basics of using Help in one application and translate what you know to all your other Windows applications.

Help is part of your Windows application, but Help also is a separate application. As such, Help runs in a separate window that overlays your application window. If you expect to use it frequently, you can leave Help open and switch between your application and the Help window. You also can minimize Help to an easily accessible icon at the bottom of your screen.

Tip
Windows comes with a helpful on-line tutorial. To run it, open the **H**elp menu and choose **W**indows Tutorial. Follow the on-screen instructions.

This chapter uses the Help screens in Notepad as examples. Many Windows accessories and applications use the same kinds of commands and procedures as Notepad Help. Because each application's Help screens are different, however, you can learn how to use the application's Help system by starting Help, opening the **H**elp menu (from the Help menu bar), and choosing **H**ow to use Help.

In this chapter, you learn how to:

- Jump between Help screens

- Search for a Help topic

- Customize Help

Understanding Windows Help

You start Help by choosing a command from the **H**elp menu or by pressing the F1 key. Figure 2.1 shows the Help pull-down menu for the Notepad accessory. Other Windows applications may have more or fewer Help menus or buttons.

Fig. 2.1
The Help pull-down menu for the Notepad application.

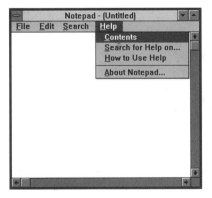

The following list describes the commands found in the **H**elp menu:

- **C**ontents. A table of contents of all Help topics.

- **H**ow to use Help. Basic instructions for using Help.

- **S**earch for Help on. Enables you to search the Help information for specific topics.

■ **About.** Information about the current application, which may include copyright, licensed-user information, the current Windows mode, and memory- and system-resources information.

To start Help, follow these steps:

1. Open the **H**elp menu.

2. Choose the **C**ontents command to display Help contents (see fig. 2.2).

    or

    Choose the **S**earch Hp on command to display the Search dialog box (see "Searching for Topics by Keyword," later in this chapter).

In most applications, you also can start Help by pressing the F1 key.

When you start Help by choosing the **H**elp **C**ontents command, the Help window usually has three sections: the menu bar, the button bar, and the Help text area. Figure 2.2 shows Notepad's Help window.

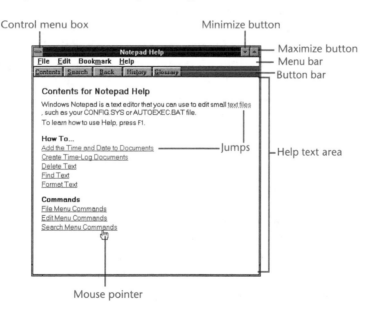

Fig. 2.2
The Notepad Help window, showing the Notepad Help Contents topic.

The Help window uses the standard Windows controls: scroll bars as needed (vertical and/or horizontal), Minimize/Maximize buttons, and the application Control menu box in the upper left corner. The Help window can be resized as needed.

Jumping between Topics

The underlined topics listed in the Help Contents window are known as *jumps,* and are used to display additional information about the topic. Some Help screens may contain graphic jumps, which appear in a second color. When you move the mouse cursor over a jump on a Help screen, the mouse pointer changes to a pointing hand (refer to fig. 2.2). Selecting a jump shows additional information about the item in a text window or displays a Help screen about the topic.

To select a jump, move the mouse pointer over the jump. When the mouse pointer changes to a hand shape, click once to select the item.

Displaying a Definition

Some Help topics contain words that are underlined with a dashed line. The dashed line indicates that a *definition* is linked to this word. To display the word's definition, click the word. Click a second time to remove the definition box.

Getting Help from a Dialog or Alert Box

Many Windows applications are designed to give you help as you work. When a dialog box or alert box appears, try pressing the F1 key. This action may display *context-sensitive help*—information related to what you are doing at the moment. Many applications include a Help button in dialog boxes, which you can click to get context-sensitive help.

◀ "Using Menus and Dialog Boxes," p. 31

In many applications, if you press F1 when a dialog box appears, you see the definitions of what each item in the dialog box does.

If you press F1 when an alert or error box appears, you see an explanation of the cause of—and possibly a solution for—the error.

Viewing Help's Table of Contents

Selecting the **C**ontents command from the **H**elp pull-down menu, or pressing F1 in a Windows application, opens the Help Contents window. The Contents window typically shows a short list of Help's major topics. Each major topic is divided into subtopics, which are shown as underlined text in a different color. You jump to the underlined topic by clicking the topic's name. Continue jumping from topic to topic until you get to the specific information you want.

Using the Help Button Bar

Help screens may have buttons on a button bar. (Some applications may use Help buttons different from those in the standard Windows accessories.)

These buttons enable you to jump to a specific Help window or perform other functions. Some buttons you may see include **C**ontents, **S**earch, **B**ack, His**t**ory, **<<**, **>>**, and **G**lossary.

You use a button by clicking it with the mouse or by pressing the underlined key in the button's label.

Searching for Topics by Keyword

You can use Help's **S**earch button to quickly find information on a particular topic. By using *keywords*—words associated with specific Help topics—you can display on-screen a list of topics that contains information about the keyword.

To search for a Help topic, follow these steps:

1. In the Help button bar, click the **S**earch button.

2. From the Search dialog box that appears (see fig. 2.3), start typing in the text box a phrase or word for which you are searching. The list scrolls to the first entry that most closely matches the characters you type.

Alternatively, scroll through the list of topics and select the one that seems closest to what you want.

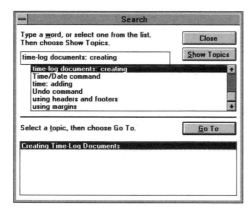

Fig. 2.3
The Search dialog box.

3. Click **S**how Topics or double-click the desired topic in the list.

The bottom box displays a list of subtopics for the selected topic.

4. Select a topic in the bottom box; then click **G**o To to display the Help screen for that topic.

Alternatively, you can double-click the topic to go immediately to that Help screen.

To cancel the search, select Cancel or press the Esc key.

Retracing Your Path through Help

If you move through different Help topics or search on different keywords, you may occasionally want to retrace this path to see where you have been and review previous topics. You can perform this step by clicking the **B**ack button to see the Help topic you viewed most recently. Help tracks the topics that you previously viewed; using the **B**ack button shows these topics in reverse order until the Help Contents screen appears.

Use the << and >> (Previous and Next) buttons in many applications (such as Word for Windows and Excel) to move to the previous or next topic in the Help file. These topics usually are related until you reach the end of a series of Help topics; then the topic may become unrelated. The Previous and Next buttons are useful when you want to go through a series of Help screens about a particular topic.

Reviewing Previous Help Screens

To see a list of all the topics you covered, and even jump back to a previous topic, click the History button. The History button presents a list of up to 40 previously viewed Help screens. You can jump quickly to a Help topic from this list. To use the History button, follow these steps:

1. Choose the History button. The History window displays up to the last 40 topics viewed (see fig. 2.4).

2. Double-click the topic you want.

Fig. 2.4
The History
window.

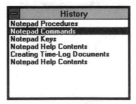

Because the history list appears in a window and not a dialog box, the list remains visible until you close the window. Windows handles the history list in this way, so that you can keep the list visible until you no longer need to select previously used Help screens. To close the history list, double-click the Control menu box at the top left corner of the window, or press Alt+F4.

Viewing Definitions with the Glossary

Some Help button bars include a **G**lossary button that shows a list of defined Windows terms. When you select an item in the glossary, a pop-up window presents the definition of the word or phrase. The **G**lossary button may be unavailable in some Help files.

Shortcut Keys in Help

Several shortcut keys are available in Windows Help, which also are common to many Windows applications. The following table describes the shortcut keys.

Table 2.1   Shortcut Keys

Key	Action
F1	In an application, starts Help and displays the Help contents for that application.
Shift+F1	In many applications, including Word for Windows and Excel, turns the mouse pointer into a question mark. To get information, you click a command, screen region, or press a key combination.
Tab	Moves to the next jump (underlined topic) in the Help window.
Shift+Tab	Moves to the previous jump in the Help window.
Ctrl+Tab	Highlights all jumps in a topic.
Ctrl+Ins	Copies the current Help topic to the Clipboard.
Ctrl+V	Pastes the Clipboard contents in the Annotate dialog box.
Alt+F4	Closes the Help window.

Printing Help Information

Often, having a printed copy of the Help topic in which you are interested can help you more clearly understand the topic or keep you from having to look it up repeatedly. When the topic for which you want information is in the Help window, open Help's **F**ile menu and choose **P**rint Topic to print the topic on the current printer. The entire text for the current Help topic prints. To select a printer or to change printer options, open the Help **F**ile menu and choose **P**rint Setup.

▶ "Printing with Windows," p. 283

> **Note**
>
> Some of the handiest information you can print or copy from Help is an application's shortcut keys. If you didn't get a shortcut keystroke template for the keyboard attached to your computer, look under the Help contents for a topic called Keyboard Shortcuts or similar name. Copy these topics to a word processing program and reorganize them, or print the topics directly from Help. You then can use a photocopier to reduce the printouts for pasting onto 3x5 cards for easy reference.

Exiting Help

While using the Help screens, you can minimize the Help window to an icon, or you can exit Help. To minimize Help to an icon, click the Minimize button.

◀ "Quitting Windows Applications," p. 58

To exit Help, double-click the Help Control menu box, open the **F**ile menu and choose E**x**it, or press Alt+F4.

Customizing Help

◀ "Controlling Windows and Icons," p. 40

◀ "Working with Applications," p. 48

Help is more than just a list of procedures or word definitions. You can print Help screens, copy screens into word processing programs, and even annotate Help with notes so that Help becomes customized for the kind of work you do.

Adding Custom Notes to Help Topics

You can customize Help information in a Windows application to make Help information more useful to you or to coworkers. You may want to include your company's default settings, for example, in a Help window on document formatting, or you may want to attach a note that names the templates for mailing labels to a built-in Help window that describes creating mailing labels. You can use *annotations* to add these notes.

A Help window is marked as having annotated text by showing a paper clip icon next to the topic (see fig. 2.5).

To create an annotation, follow these steps:

1. Display the topic that you want to annotate.

2. Open Help's **E**dit menu and choose **A**nnotate. The Annotate dialog box appears (see fig. 2.6).

I

Getting Started

Fig. 2.5
The paper clip icon indicates that the information includes a custom annotation.

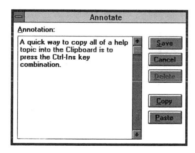

Fig. 2.6
The Annotate dialog box.

3. If you copied text for the annotation to the Windows Clipboard, click the **P**aste button. If not, type the annotation. (By default, text wraps as you type; press the Enter key to start a new line.)

4. Click the **S**ave button.

   A paper clip icon appears to the left of the topic title in the Help window.

To copy text you have typed or pasted in the Annotation text box, select the text and then click the **C**opy button to copy the text to the Clipboard. This feature is useful, for example, if you want to place the same annotation in more than one location in the Help system.

Tip
If the annotation you want to add is lengthy or may need editing, type it in a Windows word processing program or text editor, and use the **E**dit **C**opy and **E**dit **P**aste commands to copy it into the Help screen of your choice.

To view or edit an annotation, follow these steps:

1. Select the topic with the annotation.

2. Click the paper clip icon.

3. Make any desired changes to the annotation; then click the **S**ave button. To return to the topic without making changes, click Cancel.

To remove an annotation, follow these steps:

1. Select the topic with the annotation.

2. Click the paper clip icon.

3. Click the **D**elete button in the Annotate window.

The Annotate window closes and the paper clip icon disappears from the Help topic.

Marking Special Help Topics with Bookmarks

Bookmarks enable you to mark Help topics that you frequently reference. A bookmark is a named location. By assigning a bookmark to a location in Help, you can choose this bookmark's name from a list at any time to quickly go to the location.

To create a bookmark, follow these steps:

1. Display the Help topic that you want to add to the bookmark list.

2. Open Help's Book**m**ark menu and choose **D**efine.

   The Bookmark Define dialog box shows a list of existing bookmarks (see fig. 2.7).

Fig. 2.7
The Bookmark
Define dialog box.

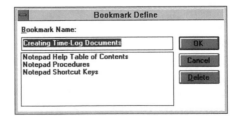

3. In the **B**ookmark Name text box, type a bookmark description (unless you want to use the default topic that Help displays).

4. Click OK or press Enter.

To quickly go to a location you previously marked with a bookmark, follow these steps:

1. Open the Bookmark menu.

2. From the lower part of the menu, select the bookmark name you entered. With the mouse, click the desired bookmark; with the keyboard, press the number associated with the bookmark. If more than nine bookmarks are available, select **M**ore to see the next group of nine bookmarks.

To delete a bookmark, follow these steps:

1. Open the Bookmark menu and choose **D**efine.

   Help displays the Bookmark Define dialog box.

2. Select the name of the bookmark to delete.

3. Click the **D**elete button.

Running Help for Other Applications

In some Help windows (especially those for newer applications), you can read Help information for more than just the application in which you are currently working. From within a Help window, you can open other applications' Help files or use File Manager to open Help for an application.

After you start Help, you can open another application's Help window by following these steps:

1. With the Help window active, open the Help **F**ile menu and choose **O**pen. The Open dialog box appears (see fig. 2.8).

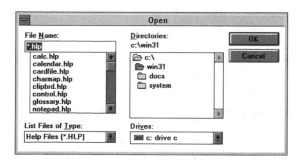

Fig. 2.8
The Open dialog box.

2. In the File **N**ame list box, select the name of the Help file you want to view. (Change drives or directories as needed.)

Alternatively, type the file name (with an HLP extension) in the File **N**ame list box.

3. Click OK or press Enter.

To return to the original Help file, click the **B**ack button enough times to return to the file. You can also select a topic from the original Help file in the Windows Help History window.

Copying Help Information to Another Application

You can create a collection of Help topics by copying Help information and pasting this data into a word processing document file. You can copy and paste into another Windows application any information you see in a Help window. The information transfers as editable text.

Depending on the Windows application you are using, you can copy information from a Help window in two ways. In some applications, you are limited to copying all the text information in a Help window. To perform this operation, display the Help topic in which you are interested, open the Help **E**dit menu, and choose **C**opy. The full text of the window is copied to the Clipboard so that you can paste the text into another application.

In other Help applications, you can selectively copy Help information. To perform this action, take the following steps:

1. Display the Help topic you want to copy, open the Help **E**dit menu, and choose **C**opy. The Copy dialog box appears (see fig. 2.9).

Fig. 2.9
The Copy dialog
box.

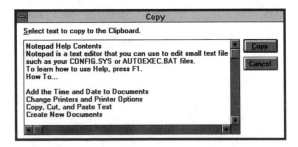

To copy the entire Help topic, press Ctrl+Ins rather than choosing the **E**dit **C**opy command. Then skip to step 4. The entire topic is copied to the Clipboard.

2. Select the portion of the text that you want to copy. With the mouse, drag across desired text; with the keyboard, move the insertion point to the beginning of the selection and then use Shift+arrow key to select.

3. Click the **C**opy button to copy the selected text to the Clipboard.

4. Switch to the application in which you want to paste the information, position the insertion point, open the **E**dit menu, and choose **P**aste.

Creating Your Own Help Files

If you develop your own applications in Windows, using the built-in Visual Basic for Applications language that comes with Microsoft Excel, for example, you can write your own Help files to be used with the application. These Help files can be accessed using WINHELP.EXE, which comes with Windows 3.1 and Windows for Workgroups. This is the same help engine used by commercial applications to access help files.

▶ "Transferring Data with Copy and Paste," p. 190

To create a help file, you need to write the text in Rich Text Format (RTF). Word for Windows can produce RTF files, but it is still a difficult task to insert the required RTF formatting codes required by the Help compiler to create the Help file. Fortunately, there are two tools available that make it much easier to produce the text files needed by the Help compiler.

The first tool is called Doc-To-Help and is distributed by WexTech Systems. Contact WexTech at the following address for more information:

WexTech Systems
60 E. 42nd St.
Suite 1733
New York, NY 10165
212-949-9595
212-949-4007 fax

The second tool is called RoboHELP and is distributed by Blue Sky Software Corporation. Contact Blue Sky at the following address for more information:

Blue Sky Software Corporation
7486 La Jolla Blvd.
Suite No. 3
La Jolla, CA 92037
619-459-6365
800-677-4946

Getting Started

Help, Support, and Resources

Windows is one of the most popular software applications ever written. Therefore, a great deal of support is available for Windows. The resources described in the following sections can help you get the most from Windows.

Telephone Support

Use the following telephone numbers to get technical support or product sales information about Windows or Windows applications.

For questions specific to Windows installation, Program Manager, File Manager, or Windows accessories, call Microsoft Corporation's Windows support line at 206-637-7098.

For technical or sales information regarding a major product, call one of the support lines in table 2.2.

Table 2.2	Technical Support	
Manufacturer	**Software**	**Support Line**
Microsoft Corp.	Corporate	206-882-8080
	Technical (all software, Publisher, Money, and Project)	206-454-2030
	Windows	206-637-7098
	DOS	206-646-5104
	Access	206-635-7050
	Microsoft Excel	206-635-7070
	Word for Windows	206-462-9673
	FoxPro for Windows	206-635-7191
Adobe Systems	Corporate	415-961-4400
	Technical (Adobe Type Manager, Adobe Fonts)	408-986-6530
Aldus Corp.	Corporate	206-628-2320
	Technical (PageMaker, Persuasion, Freehand)	206-628-2040
Asymetrix	Corporate	206-462-0501
	Technical (ToolBook)	206-637-1600
Borland	Corporate	408-431-1000
	Technical (ObjectVision)	408-461-9000

Manufacturer	Software	Support Line
Corel	Corporate	613-728-8200
	Technical (CorelDRAW!)	613-728-1990
Intuit	Corporate	800-624-8742
	Technical (Quicken)	415-858-6003
Lotus	Corporate	617-577-8500
	Technical (recordings) (1-2-3 for Windows, Ami Pro, Freelance)	617-253-9150
Lotus	Technical (pay per call)	900-555-6887
Polaris (PackRat)	Corporate, Technical	619-592-7400
Symantec	Customer Service	800-441-7234
	Technical (Norton Desktop for Windows)	503-465-8420
WordPerfect	Corporate	801-225-5000
	Technical (WordPerfect 6.0 for Windows)	800-228-1029

Getting Started

Support Organizations

Most major cities in the United States have a computer club. Within each club, you usually can find a Windows Special Interest Group (SIG). Clubs usually have meetings monthly, demonstrate new software, maintain a list of consultants, and have free or low-cost training. To contact your local computer club, check newspaper listings under *computer* or call local computer stores.

The Windows User Group Network (WUGNET) is a national organization devoted to supporting its members with information about Windows and Windows applications. WUGNET publishes a substantial bimonthly journal containing tips and articles written by members and consultants. The staff is highly knowledgeable about Windows and Windows applications. Contact WUGNET at the following address:

WUGNet Publications, Inc.
1295 N. Providence Rd.
Media, PA 19063
215-565-1861 voice
215-565-7106 fax

Computer Bulletin Board Forums

Computer bulletin boards are databases from which you can retrieve information over the telephone line (using Terminal, the communication application that comes with Windows, or other communications programs). Some bulletin boards contain a wealth of information about Windows and Windows applications. One of the largest public bulletin boards is CompuServe.

CompuServe contains *forums* where Windows and Windows applications can be discussed. You can submit questions electronically to Microsoft operators who will return an answer, generally within a day. CompuServe also contains libraries of sample files and new printer and device drivers. The Knowledgebase available in Microsoft's region of CompuServe has much of the same troubleshooting information used by Microsoft's telephone support representatives. You can search through the Knowledgebase by using keywords. The Microsoft region of CompuServe is divided into many different areas—for example, Windows users, advanced Windows users, Microsoft Excel, Microsoft languages, and sections of each of the major Microsoft and non-Microsoft applications that run under Windows.

After you become a CompuServe member, you can access the Microsoft user forums, library files, and Knowledgebase. (You must join CompuServe and get a passcode before you can use the bulletin board.) To gain access to one of these areas, type one of the following GO commands at the CompuServe prompt (!) and then press Enter.

Type	To access
GO MSOFT	Overall Microsoft area
GO MSUSER	Overall applications and Windows areas
GO MSAPP	Microsoft applications areas
GO MSEXCEL	Microsoft Excel areas
GO MSACCESS	Microsoft Access areas
GO MSWIN	Microsoft Windows areas
GO WINVEN	Overall non-Microsoft Windows applications areas
GO WINAPA	Non-Microsoft Windows applications area
GO WINAPB	Non-Microsoft Windows applications area

Type	To access
GO WINAPC	Non-Microsoft Windows applications area
GO WINAPD	Non-Microsoft Windows applications area
GO WINAPE	Non-Microsoft Windows applications area
GO WINAPF	Non-Microsoft Windows applications area

To find out which applications are supported in a non-Microsoft Windows applications area, go to the area. You see a listing of the applications supported.

An example of how to log onto CompuServe and enter the Microsoft Windows and applications regions is shown in Chapter 12, "Using Windows Terminal."

For more information, contact CompuServe at the following address:

CompuServe
5000 Arlington Centre Blvd.
P.O. Box 20212
Columbus, OH 43220
800-848-8990

► "Customizing Terminal," p. 418

Consultants and Corporate Training

Microsoft Solution Providers develop and support applications written using Microsoft products for the Windows environment. Microsoft Solution Providers are independent consultants who have met strict qualifying requirements imposed by Microsoft.

Ron Person & Co, based in San Francisco, has attained Microsoft's highest rating for Microsoft Excel and Word for Windows consultants—Microsoft Solution Provider. The firm helps corporations nationwide in consulting and developing in-house programming and support skills with the embedded macro languages in Microsoft Excel, Word for Windows, and Microsoft Access. The firm's macro and Visual Basic for Applications developer's courses have enabled many corporations to develop their own powerful financial, marketing, and business analysis systems in a minimum amount of time. If your company plans to develop applications using Microsoft's macro or Visual Basic for Applications languages, you can gain significantly from the

Getting Started

courses taught by Ron Person & Co. For information on course content, on-site corporate classes, or consulting, contact the firm at the following address:

Ron Person & Co.
P.O. Box 5647
Santa Rosa, CA 95402
415-989-7508 voice
707-539-1525 voice
707-538-1485 fax

From Here...

Now that you know how to get help in Windows, you can learn how to manage your applications and files. Refer to the following chapters:

- Chapter 3, "Controlling Applications with Program Manager," shows you how to manage your applications.

- Chapter 4, "Managing Files with File Manager," explains ways to manage the files on your computer.

Part II

Managing Your Windows Work Session

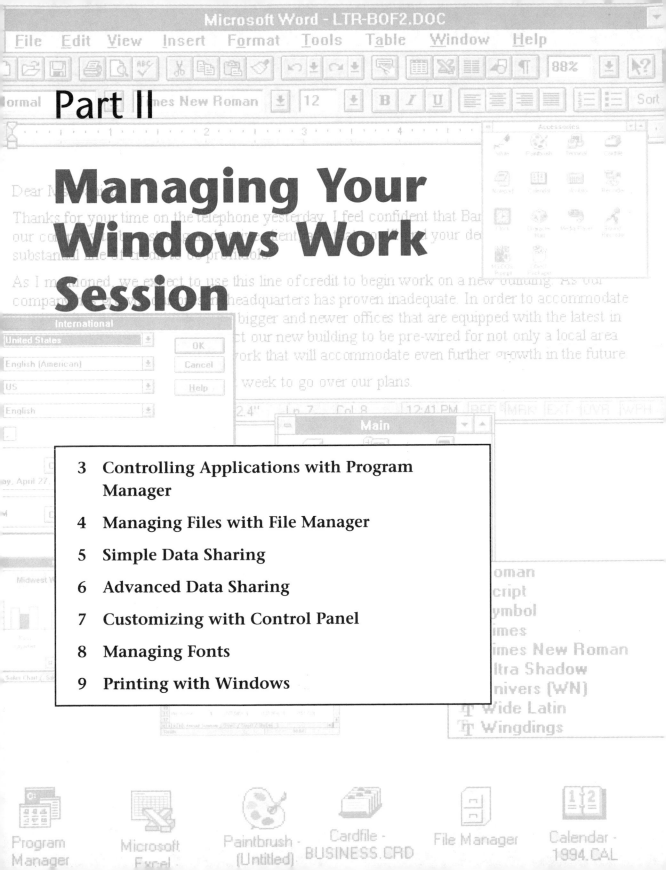

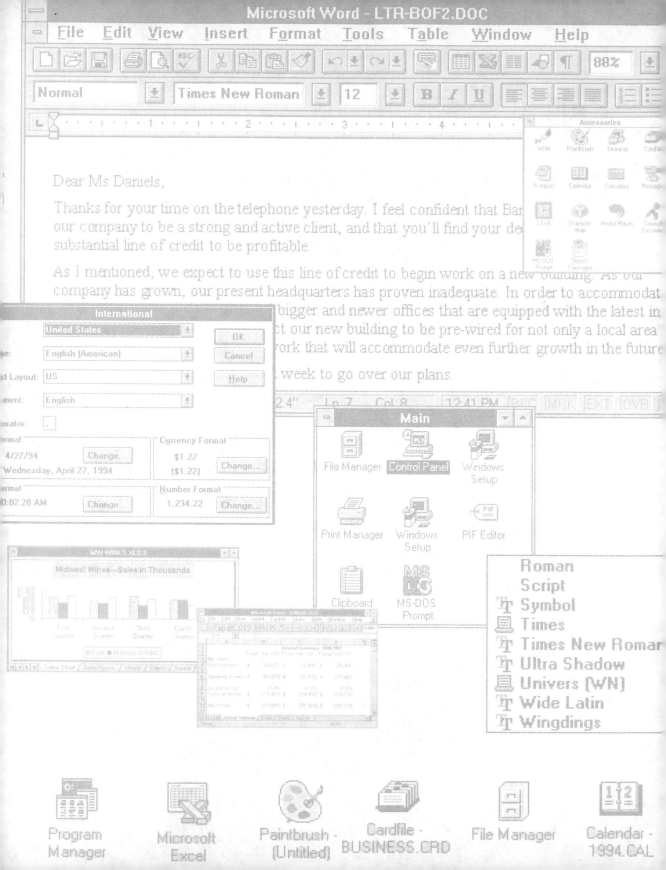

Chapter 3

Controlling Applications with Program Manager

Program Manager is the application and document coordinator for Windows. Program Manager helps you keep together software applications and their associated data by organizing related applications and data into groups.

With Program Manager, you can group applications and files together according to the way you work, and you also can start an application and (optionally) an associated data file.

In this chapter, you learn how to:

- Start applications using the icons in the Program Manager

- Activate and arrange groups and icons

- Create and manage custom groups containing icons for your frequently used applications or documents

- Restrict users from specific applications

- Restrict users from changing the Program Manager

Program Manager contains windows and icons that help you quickly find and run applications and documents you use frequently. Program Manager contains the following parts:

Part	Definition
Program item icon	An icon that represents an application, or a document or data file that is associated with an application. Opening such an icon starts the application and opens the

(continues)

Part	Definition
	document (if one is associated with the icon). You can have a program item icon for each task you perform with an application—in other words, you can have multiple program item icons for the same application. (You *associate* documents or data files to an application with File Manager, an action that is described in Chapter 4, "Managing Files with File Manager.") Program item icons can be copied and moved to different group windows. Create your own program item icons by following the steps in "Adding Applications and Documents to a Group," later in this chapter.
Group icon	An icon that represents a collection of program item icons. Opening such an icon displays the group window, in which you can see the program item icons belonging to that group.
Group window	A window in Program Manager containing a collection of program item icons. Usually a group window contains program item icons that relate to a specific type of work. A group window can contain multiple program item icons that start the same application. Group windows save you time by grouping together similar program item icons, making it easy to start applications and documents related to that group. Create your own group window by following the steps in "Creating Groups of Applications and Documents," later in this chapter.

Program Manager opens as soon as you start Windows and remains as a running application while Windows runs. Closing or quitting Program Manager closes Windows. Program Manager remains ready for you to choose the group of applications and documents you want to work with. The Main group window, shown in figure 3.1, appears inside Program Manager when Windows starts for the first time. After you begin using Windows, you probably will customize your Program Manager to fit your own work habits. If you do, Program Manager will look different from this figure when you start Windows.

Troubleshooting

I arranged the windows and icons in Program Manager just the way I need them when I start Windows, but the next time I restart Windows the windows and icons have moved back to their old positions.

If you want the Program Manager to remember the locations and sizes of group windows and icons, make sure the **S**ave Settings on Exit command is enabled. To do this, open the **O**ptions menu and choose the **S**ave Settings on Exit command. When this command is enabled, the menu shows a checkmark next to the **S**ave Settings on Exit command.

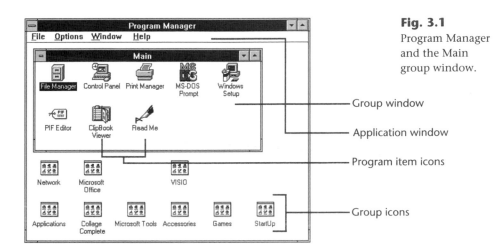

Fig. 3.1
Program Manager and the Main group window.

Group window

Application window

Program item icons

Group icons

At the bottom of the window in figure 3.1, you can see group icons. You can create groups like these that contain the applications and documents you use. When you installed Windows, you had the option of letting Windows create the Applications group for you from applications that Windows found on your hard disk. Regardless of whether you had this group created, Windows automatically installs the Main group, the Startup group, the Accessories group, and a Games group. When you install new Windows applications, the application's setup program may ask you to enter the name of an existing or new group window, in which the new application's group item icons will be placed. Following is a list of the contents of these groups.

Group	Contents
Main group	Includes system applications that help you control files, control printing, set up peripherals, customize the desktop, manage files, and manage your network.
Startup group	Includes applications that Windows activates immediately on startup.

(continues)

Group	Contents
Accessories group	Includes desktop accessories that come with Windows, such as a simple word processor, calendar, calculator, and so on.
Network group	Included with Windows for Workgroups only, this group contains network utilities and programs such as Mail and Schedule+.
Games group	Includes two games, Solitaire and Minesweeper, to help relieve the stress of working long hours at your computer. If you are using Windows for Workgroups, this group also includes the network game of Hearts.

Operating Program Manager

Learning how to operate Program Manager gives you the power to group applications and documents together in the same way you work with them. You also can start applications and documents quickly.

Figure 3.1 shows the four major parts of Program Manager. Because Program Manager is a Windows application, it resides in its own application window. The Program Manager window can contain many group windows or group icons. A *group window* and a *group icon* are two different views of a group of applications and data. A group window reveals all the program item icons. Group windows can be minimized to group icons; group icons can be changed back (restored) to group windows.

In figure 3.1, the Main group window is inside the Program Manager window. The Main group window contains program item icons that represent applications.

Fig. 3.2

You can create your own custom groups containing application and document icons.

Figure 3.2 shows another group window, called Daily Business, opened on top of the Main group window. The Daily Business group contains program item icons referencing applications such as Excel and Word for Windows;

a single document that is used on a daily basis is associated with each application. Each of these applications and its associated document is represented by a program item icon. Each program item icon can contain one application and one associated document. That's why you see several Excel and Word for Windows icons—each contains a different associated document.

Each program item icon represents an application and an associated document. Program item icons in the Daily Business group have been given names such as Letter Template, FAXTemplate, Proposal Template, Sales Report, Sales Trends, and Expense Template. When you create your own groups and program item icons, you can name them to fit the task they perform.

> **Note**
>
> You can drag icons of running applications on top of the Program Manager window or one of the group windows. These icons may appear to be in Program Manager, but they really are not; they merely overlap Program Manager in the same way that windows overlap. If you reselect the Program Manager window by clicking it, you see the Program Manager window without the overlapping icon.

You can start applications from the program item icons in a group window or from File Manager (discussed in Chapter 4, "Managing Files with File Manager.") When an application is running, it occupies its own window. Applications also can be shown as icons on the desktop, but you should not confuse these icons with program item icons. The easiest way to tell them apart is that program item icons appear *inside* the Program Manager window, whereas icons that represent running applications appear *outside* and usually *below* the Program Manager window (unless you drag the icon on top of the Program Manager window). You can switch between applications that are running in a couple of ways, as described in Chapter 1, "Operating Windows."

Starting Applications from a Group Window

When you open a group window in Program Manager, you see program item icons. Each icon refers to an application and, optionally, an associated *document,* or file of data. Sometimes the associated document is simply a new, empty document.

◄ "Using Multiple Applications," pg. 63

To open a group window, follow these steps:

1. Open the Program Manager window (if it isn't open) by double-clicking the Program Manager icon or by pressing Ctrl+Esc and choosing Program Manager from the Task List.

2. Activate the group window or open the group icon containing the program item you want to start. Click a group window to activate it; double-click a group icon to open it; or repeatedly press Ctrl+Tab until the icon or window is selected (then press Enter if you need to open a group icon).

Moving an application to the Startup group causes Windows to start the application automatically when you start Windows. You can add any application you like to the Startup group (for details, see the section "Adding Applications and Documents to a Group," later in this chapter).

Note

Bypass the loading of applications in the Startup group by holding down the Shift key when you start Windows. When you see the Windows logo as Windows starts, hold down the Shift key until Windows is finished loading. This enables you to start Windows quickly when you don't need all the startup applications.

Create your own custom Startup window with its own name by adding the following line to the [Settings] section of the PROGMAN.INI file; The *groupname* is the name of an existing or new group other than the Startup group. You can edit the PROGMAN.INI file using a text editor such as Notepad. The change does not take place until you restart Windows.

    Startup=*groupname*

Troubleshooting

After double-clicking on the program item, the application doesn't start. In some cases, a message says the application or document cannot be found.

The name or directory path to the application or document files may be incorrect. Files may have been moved, renamed, or erased.

To check the path and file name, activate Program Manager and the appropriate group window. Select the program item icon and then choose the **F**ile **P**roperties command. Change the path, application file name, or document file name in the Command Line text box. You can use Browse to find the correct path and file name for the application. The **F**ile **P**roperties command is described in more detail in "Creating Groups of Applications and Documents," later in this chapter.

Customizing Groups

You don't have to limit yourself to the Windows Applications group that may have been created automatically for you. You can create your own customized groups to match the way you work, putting together applications and associated documents that you use to do specific jobs.

Creating and Deleting Groups

You can create your own groups to fit the way you work. Your groups can contain collections of applications and documents you use together for a task. The applications and documents can be located in different locations on your disk, yet they appear together in the group window. Items in a group can contain just an application, or contain an application and one associated document.

◄ "Working with Applications," p. 48

► "Starting Applications and Documents," p. 170, and "Using File Manager's Drag-and-Drop Feature," p. 173

Program Items Contain One Application and Document

Each program item contains either one application and no associated document, or it contains one application and one associated document. Groups can contain many program items that start the same application, but with different documents.

If you want an application to start with multiple documents, create an auto-opening macro that runs when the document is opened. In most applications, such a macro is stored within the document that the program item icon starts. When the application and that document start, the auto-opening macro loads the other documents that are also needed. Auto-opening macros and worksheets for Microsoft Excel are described in *Using Excel Version 5 for Windows,* Special Edition; auto-opening macros and worksheets for Lotus 1-2-3 are described in *Using Lotus 1-2-3 Release 4 for Windows,* Special Edition; auto-opening macros for Word for Windows are described in *Using Word Version 6 for Windows,* Special Edition; auto-opening macros for WordPerfect for Windows are discussed in *Using WordPerfect Version 6 for Windows,* Special Edition. All four books are published by Que Corporation.

Creating Groups of Applications and Documents

Before creating groups, imagine the tasks you perform each day. Divide those tasks into related groups, such as writing proposals, managing a project timeline and budget, or contacting clients and sending follow-up letters. Each of these groups of tasks can become a group window. Within each group window, you add program item icons representing the applications and documents needed to get that work done.

II

Managing Your Work

> **Note**
>
> You can specify the arrangement and order in which group windows and icons appear on startup. To do this, uncheck the **O**ptions **S**ave Settings on Exit command. (This command is a toggle. Each time you choose it, a checkmark appears or disappears next to the command.) Next, arrange windows and icons as you want them on startup. Finally, hold down the Shift key and double-click the System icon at the top left corner of the Program Manager window. With the keyboard, press Shift+Alt+F4. This records the current Program Manager settings in the PROGMAN.INI file. You can do this at any time while you are in Windows. The next time you start Windows, the settings you recorded are used.

To create your own group, start with the Program Manager window active, and follow these steps:

1. Open the **F**ile menu and choose **N**ew.

2. Select the Program **G**roup option.

3. Click OK. The Program Group Properties dialog box appears (see fig. 3.3).

Fig. 3.3
Label the group icon with the Program Group Properties dialog box.

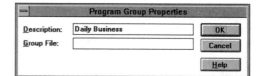

4. In the **D**escription text box, enter the title you want under the group icon or as the title of the group window. Do not make an entry in the **G**roup File text box; Program Manager automatically creates a GRP file for the group you are creating.

5. Choose OK.

The new group window you have created remains open on-screen. If you want to add applications and data to the window, leave it open. If you want to minimize the group window so that it appears as an icon, double-click the Control menu icon of the new group window. As a shortcut, press Ctrl+F4 to change the group window to an icon.

Protecting a Program Group

If you want to prevent changes to a group, designate it as a "read-only" group. Start File Manager, select the group file (usually this is a file located in your Windows directory with a GRP extension), and open the **F**ile menu and choose the **P**roperties command. In the Properties dialog box, select the **R**ead Only option from the Attributes group.

When you make a program group read-only, you can make no further changes to the Group window unless you remove the read-only attribute. For example, you cannot add new program items to, or delete program items from, the protected group. You also cannot move or rearrange the program item icons in the protected group.

Restricting and Protecting Groups and Icons in Program Manager

If you administer computers that are used by others, you may want to restrict or protect features in Program Manager. By putting restrictions on Program Manager, you can prevent users from deleting groups or items, from adding new groups or items, and from running unauthorized programs. This can reduce your support load and make Program Manager less frustrating for inexperienced users.

To make these modifications, open the PROGMAN.INI file using a text editor such as Notepad. PROGMAN.INI is found in the WINDOWS directory. This file contains Program Manager's options and settings in a text file.

Add to the PROGMAN.INI file a section titled [Restrictions]. The word *restrictions* must be enclosed in square brackets. Arguments you can add to the [Restrictions] section are listed in table 3.1.

Table 3.1	Arguments to Restrict Program Manager	
Argument	**Value**	**Result**
NoRun=	1	Prevents users from using the **F**ile **R**un command to run an application. Applications can be started only from the program item icons.
NoClose=	1	Prevents users from closing Windows through any method.

(continues)

Table 3.1	Continued	
Argument	**Value**	**Result**
NoSaveSettings=	1	Dims the **O**ptions **S**ave Settings on Exit command, and prevents the user from saving changes to the window arrangement and icon positions.
NoFileMenu=	1	Removes the **F**ile menu from Program Manager so that users cannot delete or copy groups or icons, or run applications.
EditLevel=		Restricts the changes the user can make, depending on the value specified.
	0	User can make any change.
	1	Prevents creating, deleting, or renaming groups. **N**ew, **M**ove, **C**opy, and **D**elete commands are dimmed.
	2	Creates level-1 restrictions and prevents creating or deleting groups. **N**ew, **M**ove, **C**opy, and **D**elete commands are removed.
	3	Creates level-2 restrictions and prevents users from changing command lines in program items. This prevents them from using an icon to start other applications.
	4	Creates level-3 restrictions and prevents changes to any program item information.

Tip

Quickly load PROGMAN.INI into the Notepad editor by choosing **F**ile **R**un from Program Manager, typing **PROGMAN.INI**, and choosing OK.

When you are finished adding items to the [Restrictions] section, save the PROGMAN.INI file back to its original directory and restart Windows. A finished [Restrictions] section might look like the following:

```
[Restrictions]
NoRun=1
NoSaveSettings=1
EditLevel=4
```

Adding Applications and Documents to a Group

After you create and title a new group window, include in the window the applications and documents you use in this group. The applications and documents you put in a group are called *program items*; they appear as item icons in the group window.

To add items, applications, and documents associated with an application to a new or existing group, follow these steps:

1. Select the group window that will contain the program item.

2. Open the **F**ile menu and choose **N**ew.

3. Select Program **I**tem from the New Program Object dialog box.

4. Choose OK. The Program Item Properties dialog box appears (see fig. 3.4).

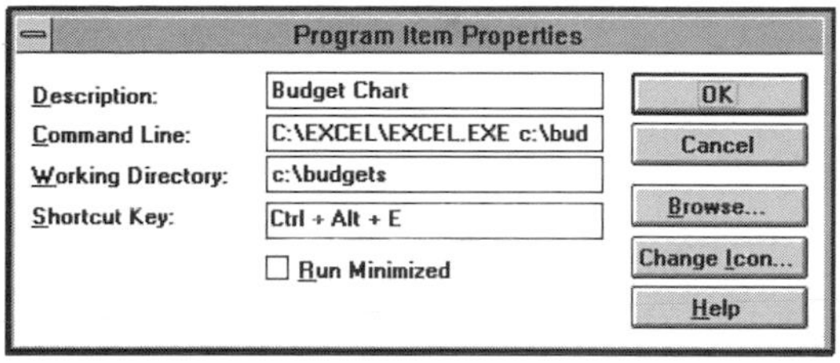

Tip
Microsoft recommends that you do not include more than 40 program items in a single group.

```
┌──────────────────────────────────────────────────────┐
│ ▭              Program Item Properties                │
├──────────────────────────────────────────────────────┤
│  Description:       │Budget Chart          │   ┌──OK──┐│
│  Command Line:      │C:\EXCEL\EXCEL.EXE c:\bud│ ┌─Cancel─┐│
│  Working Directory: │c:\budgets            │   ┌─Browse...─┐│
│  Shortcut Key:      │Ctrl + Alt + E        │   ┌Change Icon...┐│
│                     ☐ Run Minimized            ┌──Help──┐│
└──────────────────────────────────────────────────────┘
```

Fig. 3.4
Specify an icon's label, icon graphic, and shortcut key with the Program Item Properties dialog box.

5. Select the **D**escription text box and type the title you want to appear under the program item icon.

6. Select the **C**ommand Line text box and type the path name, file name, and extension of the program for this item. If you are unsure of the path and program file name, choose **B**rowse to display a list of files and directories (see fig. 3.5). Select the directory containing the application from the **D**irectories list, choose the application from the File **N**ame list, and click OK. (To open a higher, or *parent*, directory, select the parent directory in the **D**irectories list—the one indicated by an "open folder" icon—and select OK.) When you choose OK, the Program Item Properties dialog box reappears with the path and application name copied into the **C**ommand Line text box.

▶ "Using Drag and Drop to Create a Program Item Icon," p. 175

7. If you want a document such as a spreadsheet, letter, or data file to open with the application, type a space after the file name in the **C**ommand Line text box, and then type the path and file name of the document. A completed command line specifying an application and document that are in separate directories might look like this:

```
C:\EXCEL\EXCEL.EXE C:\BUDGETS\JUNE.XLS
```

II

Managing Your Work

Fig. 3.5

Use the Browse dialog box to find the application or document you want to start.

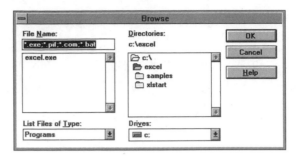

8. In the **W**orking Directory text box, enter the directory you want to be active when you start this application (your program defaults to this directory when opening or saving files).

Tip

Create a shortcut key to start applications you use frequently.

9. Select the **S**hortcut Key text box and press Shift, Shift+Ctrl, or Ctrl while you type a character or function key. You see a shortcut key combination such as Ctrl+Alt, plus your character; press this key combination to switch to the application if it is running.

10. Normally, Windows chooses an icon to represent the program item you are creating. If more than one icon is available to represent the item, the Change **I**con button turns bold. Choose the Change **I**con button, and select the icon you want to represent the application and document. Move through the icons using the scroll bar below the icon window. Choose OK or Cancel to return to the Program Item Properties dialog box.

11. Select the **R**un Minimized icon if you want the application to be minimized to an icon at start-up.

12. Choose OK.

To use icons other than those shown, choose Change **I**con to display the Change Icon dialog box. Some applications contain more than one icon. You can choose the icon you want from the Current Icon list. Additional icons are available in two files that come with Windows. In the **F**ile Name text box, enter **PROGMAN.EXE** or **MORICONS.DLL**, including the full path where those files are located (usually in your Windows directory). To access icons in the MORICONS.DLL file, for example, enter **C:\WINDOWS\MORICONS.DLL**. You also can choose the **B**rowse button to locate these files. Figure 3.6 shows some of the icons located inside MORICONS.DLL.

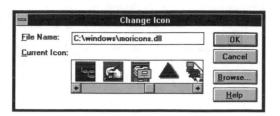

Fig. 3.6
Additional icons
are available in
PROGMAN.EXE
and
MORICONS.DLL.

Troubleshooting

After doing some work with the File Manager, I noticed that some of my custom program item icons have been replaced with simple document icons. The documents and applications still work, but the Program Manager doesn't look cool.

You may have accidentally moved, renamed, or deleted the file(s) containing the icons used by your program items. To return an icon to its previous shape, select the icon and choose the **F**ile **P**roperties command. In the Program Item Properties dialog box choose the Change **I**cons button. If the file containing the icons has been renamed, moved, or deleted, a warning will appear saying that the path to the original icon file is invalid. Note the directory and file name in the warning. Cancel out of all the dialog boxes and go to the File Manager. Use the **F**ile Searc**h** command to look for the missing file. If you find the icon file, move it to its original location or rename it with its original name. If you cannot find the icon file, you may need to access the Program Item Properties dialog box to select an icon from a different file.

Tip
Additional sets
of icons are
available
through database services
such as
CompuServe,
or through
shareware disks
at your local PC
users group.
These sets of
icon files have
extensions of
ICO, DLL, or
EXE.

Figure 3.7 shows a Program Item Properties dialog box that has been filled out to start Excel and one worksheet. A program item can have only one document associated with an application.

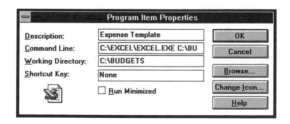

Fig. 3.7
These properties
specify the icon's
title, the application and document file names,
the directory to
start in, a shortcut
key, and the icon.

By default, the Browse window initially shows only application files (files with the extensions EXE, COM, BAT, or PIF). To see all the files in the directory, select the All Files option from the List Files of **T**ype box in the Browse dialog box.

II

Managing Your Work

Creating a Program Item Icon

Another way you can create a program item icon is to run File Manager and Program Manager side by side, locate in File Manager the application for which you want to create an icon, and drag the file name from File Manager into Program Manager. A program item icon appears in the group window where you drop the file name. You can use the File Properties command (described in the next section, "Redefining Groups and Program Items") to associate a document to the application.

Redefining Groups and Program Items

When you gain experience with groups and program items, you may want to change the names you have assigned to them or change the document associated with a specific program item. You can make these changes easily.

To change the title of a group, follow these steps:

1. Select the group icon whose name you want changed (you cannot change the name of an open group window).

2. Open the **F**ile menu and choose **P**roperties.

3. Select the **D**escription text box and type a new description. This text becomes the new title.

4. Click OK.

When you want to change the title of a program item icon, or when you want to change the application associated with a document or data file, follow these steps:

1. Select the program item icon you want to change.

2. Open the **F**ile menu and choose **P**roperties.

3. Change the icon title in the **D**escription text box, or change the application or document name in the **C**ommand Line text box.

4. Click OK.

If you have used version 3.0 of Windows, you may notice that some of the group and application names look different. Version 3.1 limits the width of names on the screen by "wrapping" the text to additional lines. This word-wrap feature is helpful because it can create names up to four lines long.

You may have to shorten some of the group and item names to avoid over-lapping icon and group names, however.

Deleting Groups

If you no longer use any of the program items in a group, or if you find a group unnecessary, you can delete the entire group so that it no longer appears in the Program Manager window. Deleting the group removes the group window and its program items from the Program Manager window; it does not, however, delete the application files or data files from disk. To delete a group, follow these steps:

1. If the group window is open, minimize it to an icon by clicking its Minimize button or double-clicking its control icon.

2. Select the group icon you want to delete by clicking it or by pressing Ctrl+Tab until the group icon is selected.

3. Press the Del key.

4. Choose **Y**es to delete the group.

Troubleshooting

I accidentally pressed the Del key while in the Program Manager. I wasn't paying atten-tion when the alert box appeared, so I pressed Enter. Now the entire group is deleted.

There is no way to undelete the group or program item you accidentally deleted. To re-create the group or program items, use one of the methods described in this chapter.

Note

Deleting a group does not delete the applications or files that were in that group. It only deletes the group window and the program item icons inside the window.

Deleting Program Items

As your job changes, or as you become more familiar with Windows and groups, you frequently will want to keep a group, but move or delete a pro-gram item in that group. Deleting the program item only removes the icon from the group window; it does not delete the application or data file from disk. To delete program items, follow these steps:

Tip

To prevent users from deleting windows or icons, use the [Restrict] section of PROGMAN.INI, as described in this chapter's section titled "Restricting and Protecting Groups and Icons in Program Manager."

II

Managing Your Work

1. Open the group window containing the program item.

2. Select the program item by clicking it or by pressing an arrow key to select it.

3. Press the Del key.

4. Choose **Y**es when asked to verify deletion.

Moving and Copying Program Items

As you become more familiar with your work habits in Windows, you may want to change the contents of your groups, which may mean copying or moving program items between groups. You also may find that one program item can be useful in more than one group window (you can use it repeatedly for different jobs). If that happens, don't re-create the program item in the multiple groups; instead, move or copy the existing program item to other groups where it is needed.

To move a program item to another group, open the group window containing the program item and drag the program item onto the destination group window. You also can drag a program item from one group onto a group icon, but you have no control over where the program item is positioned in the destination window.

To copy a program item to another group, follow these steps:

1. Open the group window containing the program item. Open the destination group window if you want to position the icon in a specific place or position the destination group icon where you can see it.

2. Press and hold down the Ctrl key and drag the program item icon where you want it in the destination group window or over the destination group icon. Figure 3.8 shows a program item icon being dragged to another group window.

3. Release the mouse button.

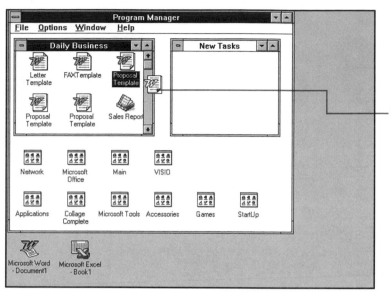

Fig. 3.8
Drag or press
Ctrl+drag to move
or copy icons to
other group
windows.

— Icon being dragged

II

Managing Your Work

Duplicating a Program Item

To duplicate a program item in a group window, hold down the Ctrl key and use the
mouse to drag the program item to a new position in the same group window.
Release the mouse button to copy the program item in the original group window.

Controlling Program Manager

Program Manager is always available in Windows. It may appear on-screen in
its own window or as the Program Manager icon. Activate the window or the
icon to use Program Manager.

If you can see Program Manager or its icon, you can activate it by clicking
anywhere on the Program Manager window, by double-clicking the Program
Manager icon, or by pressing Alt+Tab until the Program Manager icon or
window is selected and then releasing both keys.

If you cannot see the Program Manager window or icon, you can activate it
by pressing Ctrl+Esc or double-clicking the desktop to activate the Task List
(see fig. 3.9).

Fig. 3.9
Task List.

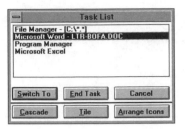

From the Task List, select Program Manager by clicking its name or by pressing the up- or down-arrow key. Choose the **S**witch To button to activate Program Manager.

Using Menu Commands with Program Manager

You can operate Program Manager by using menus, mouse actions, or shortcut keys. The menu commands for Program Manager are listed in table 3.2.

Table 3.2	Program Manager Menu Commands
Command	**Action**
File **N**ew	Adds a new group item to a group or creates a new group
File **O**pen	Starts the selected program item and its associated document
File **M**ove	Moves a program item to another group
File **C**opy	Copies a program item to another group
File **D**elete	Deletes a group or program item
File **P**roperties	Changes the description, program name, document name, or icon for a program item
File **R**un	Starts the application whose name you enter, with or without a document (the application does not have to be a program item)
File **E**xit Windows	Quits Windows
Options **A**uto Arrange	Rearranges icons automatically in the selected group window when you change the window
Options **M**inimize	Shrinks the Program Manager window to an icon when another application starts

Command	Action
Options **S**ave	When a check mark appears next to this Settings on Exit item, Windows saves all changes to window sizes and positions to preserve the current environment for your next Windows session
Window **C**ascade	Arranges windows in an overlapping cascade so that titles remain visible
Window **T**ile	Arranges windows side by side so that each window is visible
Window **A**rrange Icons	Arranges all group icons in a row at the bottom of the screen or all program item icons into neat rows in a selected group window
Window #	Selects a group and opens or activates its window
Help	Defines Program Manager terms and explains its operation

Using the Mouse with Program Manager

By using the mouse, you can open different groups, activate windows, and start items quickly. If you are familiar with the way the mouse works in Windows, you can guess how most of Program Manager operates. Following are some of the basic mouse actions:

Mouse Action	Result
Click an item in the active window	Selects the item
Click a window	Activates the window
Double-click a program item icon	Starts the program item (the application and its associated document)
Double-click a Group icon	Opens the Group icon to a Group window
Drag an item or window title	Moves the item within its group window or moves the group window within the Program Manager window

II

Managing Your Work

Using Shortcut Keys with Program Manager

Although the mouse is the most intuitive method of operating Program Manager, you can touch-type your way through almost any Windows application—including Program Manager. Following are the shortcut keys you can use to operate Program Manager:

Key	Result
Arrow keys	Moves the selection between items in the active group window
Ctrl+F6 or Ctrl+Tab	Moves selection to the next group window or icon
Enter	Starts the selected program item (the application and its associated document) or opens the selected group icon
Shift+F4	Arranges group windows in tiles
Shift+F5	Arranges group windows in a cascade
Ctrl+F4	Closes the active group window
Alt+F4	Exits Windows (you are given a chance to cancel the action)

Minimizing Program Manager to an Icon for Easy Access

Figure 3.10 shows the Windows desktop with Program Manager minimized to an icon in the bottom left corner. Whenever you need room on the desktop or want to remove visual clutter, minimize Program Manager to an icon. When Program Manager shrinks to an icon, all the group windows remain "inside" Program Manager's icon. To minimize Program Manager, click the Minimize button (the down triangle) at the right edge of Program Manager's title bar.

If you use the keyboard, follow these steps to minimize Program Manager:

1. Open Program Manager's Control menu (press Alt+space bar).

2. Select the Minimize command.

To restore Program Manager from an icon to a window, double-click the icon or press Ctrl+Esc and select Program Manager from the Task Manager dialog box.

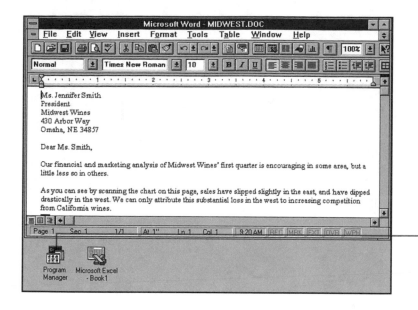

Fig. 3.10
Minimize Program
Manager to an
icon to reduce
clutter on your
Windows desktop.

Program Manager icon

II

Managing Your Work

You can specify that Program Manager minimize to an icon automatically
whenever you start an application. To make this specification, open Program
Manager's **O**ptions menu and select the **M**inimize on Use command. A check
mark appears next to the **M**inimize on Use option when it is selected. To turn
off this command, choose it again.

Opening Group Windows

Before you can open program items (applications and their associated
documents), you must open the group window that contains the items.
Group windows usually are stored as icons at the bottom of the Program
Manager window (see fig. 3.11). The name of the icon appears below each
icon.

If you are using a mouse, double-click the group icon to open it into a
window.

Sizing Group Windows

When you have multiple windows, you may want to change their sizes to see
multiple groups or to maximize one group window so that it fills the inside
of Program Manager. You can resize a group window using the same window-
sizing principles you learned in Chapter 1. (If you are unfamiliar with window sizing, minimizing, and maximizing, review Chapter 1.)

Fig. 3.11
Group icons
arrange them-
selves at the
bottom of the
Program Manager
window.

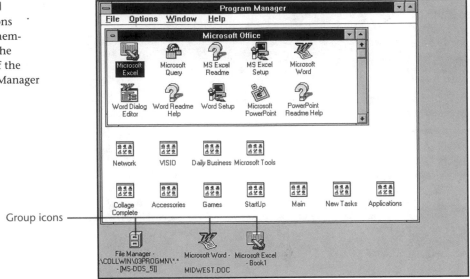

Group icons ————

To resize a group window, move the pointer to a window edge until the
pointer changes to a two-headed arrow. Drag the window edge to a new location and release the mouse button.

Maximizing a Group Window

Double-click the title bar of a group window to maximize the window. You can
restore a maximized window to its previous window size by clicking the Restore icon
(a double-headed arrow in the top right corner of the window).

You can maximize, minimize, and restore group windows in Program Manager just as you can do with application windows (described in Chapter 1).
To maximize, minimize, and restore, click the arrowhead icons located at the
right edge of each group window's title bar. The up arrowhead maximizes a
window; the down arrowhead minimizes the window to an icon; the double
arrowhead restores a maximized window to its previous size.

If you have many group windows, you may find it easier to move between
groups if you minimize group windows you are not using. Another method
of minimizing a group window with the mouse is to double-click the document Control menu icon. This icon is located at the left edge of the title
bar of each group window. If you double-click this icon in an application

window, you close the application window; but because group windows cannot be closed, they become icons when you double-click the document Control menu icon.

Arranging Group Windows and Icons

You can arrange group windows and icons manually, or you can use commands in Program Manager to arrange them. If you want to manually move a group window, drag its title bar with the mouse pointer.

> **Note**
>
> While working in Program Manager, you can arrange the windows and icons in an order that would be a good startup configuration the next time you start Windows. You can save the current Program Manager configuration by holding the Shift key as you double-click the System icon at the top left corner of the Program Manager window. This saves the current configuration to the PROGMAN.INI file. Make sure the **O**ptions **S**ave Settings on Exit command is turned off, or the PROGMAN.INI file will be overwritten when you quit Windows.

If you want a cascading arrangement of overlapping group windows, like that shown in figure 3.12, open the **W**indow menu and choose **C**ascade.

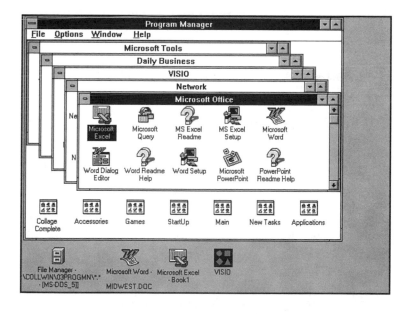

Fig. 3.12
Use cascading windows to organize a large number of open windows.

Cascading group windows are useful when you are working with primarily one group, when you have a large number of program items in each window, or when you have so many group windows that tiling produces small windows. When you have too many group windows to fit in a single cascade, Windows overlaps cascades. (The window that was active before you issued the command is the window on the top of the cascade.)

You can arrange group windows in tiles so that you can see a portion of all open group windows (see fig. 3.13). To achieve this arrangement, open the **W**indow menu and choose **T**ile. Tiling group windows is useful if you need access to the program items from multiple groups. To tile multiple group windows, open the **W**indows menu and choose **T**ile.

You can arrange group icons in the Program Manager window. If you want to move a group icon to a new location, drag the icon with the mouse to its new location. To arrange all the group icons at the bottom of the Program Manager window, first select any group icon and then open the **W**indow menu and choose **A**rrange Icons.

To arrange the program item icons in a group window, select the group window and then open the **W**indows menu and choose **A**rrange Icons. If you want Windows to automatically arrange program item icons whenever you open or resize a window, choose the **O**ptions **A**uto Arrange command. A check mark appears next to the **A**uto Arrange command when it is on. Choose the command again to turn it off.

Fig. 3.13
Use tiled windows for quick access to program item icons in multiple windows.

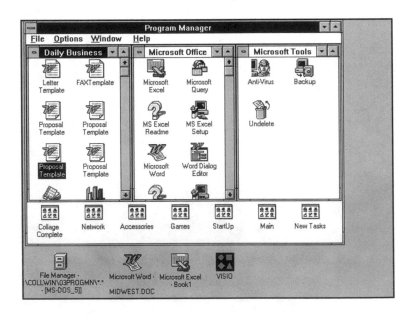

Changing Groups with File Manager

You can perform many of the operations you just learned from File Manager. You also can use File Manager to prevent accidental or unauthorized changes, such as deletions of program items. You learn how to do this in Chapter 4, "Managing Files with the File Manager."

Restoring Program Manager to a Window

If you have been running an application, Program Manager may have been minimized to an icon. If you want to restore Program Manager's icon to a window, double-click Program Manager's icon if you can see it.

If you cannot see the icon, press Ctrl+Esc to display the Task List (see fig. 3.9). The Task List enables you to activate applications that are running in Windows but that are not visible (Program Manager is always running when Windows is running). From the Task List, double-click Program Manager to start Program Manager.

Quitting Program Manager and Windows

Be careful when you quit Program Manager. Program Manager is always running and available because it is the central coordinator for any applications running in Windows. When you close or quit Program Manager, you also quit Windows.

When you are ready to quit Windows, follow these steps:

1. Save the data in your application and then quit the application.

2. Activate Program Manager, opening the icon into a window if necessary.

3. Open the **F**ile menu and choose E**x**it.

4. Click OK.

A quick way to quit any application—including Program Manager—is to press Alt+F4.

From Here...

To learn more, refer to these chapters:

- Chapter 1, "Controlling Windows and Icons," teaches you about window sizing, minimizing, and maximizing.

II

Managing Your Work

■ Chapter 6, "Linking Data Between Applications," explains ways to learn how to integrate applications so that you can pass data between them and use multiple applications for new business solutions.

■ Chapter 21, "Installing and Configuring Windows Applications," shows you how you can make your DOS applications run efficiently under Windows.

Chapter 4

Managing Files with File Manager

File Manager in Windows is a well-designed tool that acts like an office manager to help you organize files; to manage disks; to copy, move, and erase files; and to start applications. When you first start File Manager, you see a window divided into left and right sides. The directory tree area on the left shows the tree-like structure in which directories and subdirectories are organized on a hard disk. The right side of the window shows the files and subdirectories found within the directory selected on the left side. You can have multiple directory windows open—each showing the contents of a different directory in the contents list segment.

In this chapter, you learn how to:

- Use storage, memory, files, and directories

- Understand File Manager's display

- Operate File Manager

- Select and open files and directories

- Control File Manager windows and displays

- Manage files and disks

- Protect your data

- Start applications and documents

- Use File Manager's drag-and-drop feature

- Work with networks in Windows for Workgroups

■ Work with non-Windows for Workgroups networks

■ Work with network drives

With File Manager, you can view and maintain files and directories more easily than with DOS commands. If you have a mouse, for example, you can copy all the files in a directory to a disk by dragging the directory's icon on top of the disk drive icon and releasing the mouse button. Figure 4.1 shows the different parts of File Manager.

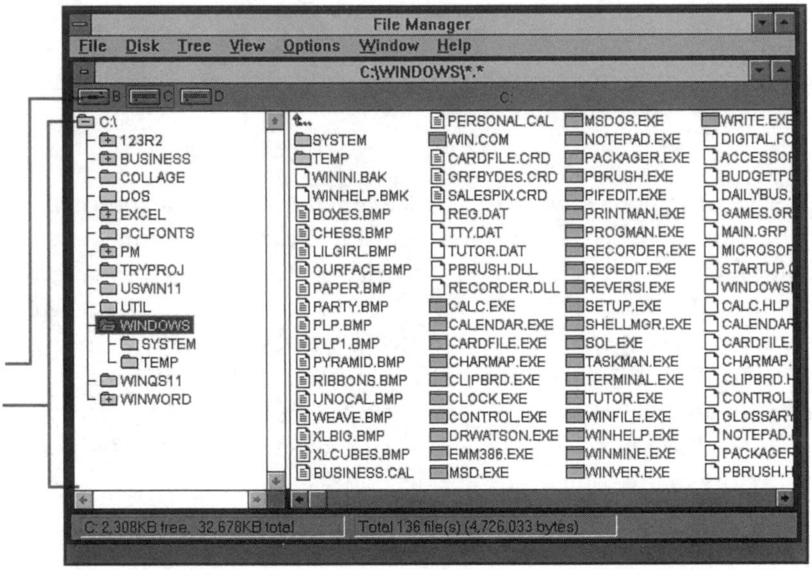

Fig. 4.1

The left side of File Manager shows directories and subdirectories; the right side shows the contents of the selected directory or subdirectory.

Drive icons

Directory tree area

If you are working with Windows for Workgroups, you can connect to shared directories on other computers on your network. Likewise, you can designate directories on your hard disk as shared so that other users can access the files in those directories. You use File Manager to connect to shared directories and to share directories on your computer.

Besides the commands associated with working with shared directories, File Manager in Windows for Workgroups is different from File Manager in Windows 3.1 in a few other ways. The most noticeable difference is the toolbar in the Windows for Workgroups File Manager (see fig. 4.2). The toolbar gives you ready access to frequently used commands. There are a few other minor differences, which are indicated in the appropriate sections throughout this chapter. Features unique to File Manager in Windows for Workgroups are designated with the Windows for Workgroups icon.

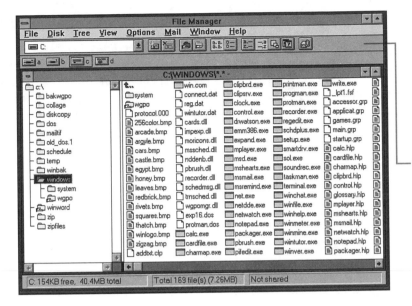

Toolbar

Note

With DOS, you may have used or created batch files that executed multiple commands to copy directories, erase disks, and so on. You can automate File Manager to reproduce many of these procedures by using Windows Recorder. Recorder records the keystrokes you press so that the process can be repeated on request.

When you make a recording to delete, copy, or move files, do not use the mouse. Instead, use keystroke commands, File Manager menus, and explicit file names or DOS wild cards in file names. Doing so enables Recorder to reproduce actions exactly. If you record mouse movements, Recorder may not duplicate the action if files or windows are positioned differently on-screen. (Refer to Chapter 13, "Using Windows Recorder," for more information.)

Understanding Storage, Memory, Files, and Directories

A computer does all calculations and work in electronic memory. (Electronic memory is known as *RAM, random-access memory*.) RAM is where Windows and your applications work. The data you use also resides in RAM. If the computer loses electrical power, the data, application, and Windows are lost from memory. Because electronic memory is limited in size and disappears when electrical power is removed, the computer needs a way to store large amounts of data and applications for long periods of time.

You use magnetic storage to store applications and data for long periods of time or when the computer is turned off. Magnetic-storage media are floppy disks (which are removable and don't contain much space) or hard disks (which are internal to the computer and have vast amounts of space). When you start an application or open a data file, the computer places a copy of the information stored in magnetic storage (on floppy disks or a hard disk) into electronic memory (RAM). If power is lost, the magnetic copy still is available.

You save the work in magnetic files, which store the data on a floppy disk or hard disk. Over time, you may have hundreds or even thousands of files. Searching for a specific file among the thousands of file names that File Manager displays can be very time-consuming.

To make the job of finding files easier, hard disks usually are organized into directories. If you think of the hard disk as a filing cabinet, *directories* are like the drawers in the filing cabinet. In a filing cabinet, each drawer can hold a different category of document. In a hard disk, each directory can hold a different category of file. The files in a directory can be applications (also known as *programs*) or documents.

Within a filing-cabinet drawer, you can further segment the drawer with file folders. Within a hard disk, you can segment a directory by putting *subdirectories* under it. Subdirectories also hold files.

The process of organizing a hard disk is similar to organizing a filing cabinet. With File Manager commands, you can create, name, and delete directories and subdirectories. (Some networks, however, may prevent you from altering or creating directory structures.) For example, you may want a WINWORD directory for word processing jobs. Within the WINWORD directory, you may want subdirectories with names such as BUDGETS, SCHEDULE, LETTERS, and REPORTS.

Large computers and networks have multiple hard disks, and each disk has its own drive letter. In figure 4.1, there are three disks, as shown by the icons for drives B, C, and D. Each disk acts like a separate filing cabinet and can have its own unique directories and subdirectories.

Understanding File Manager's Display

Before you use File Manager, you will find it helpful to understand the different characteristics of File Manager's display. Recognizing the display features enables you to perform file-management tasks more quickly, such as listing the contents of a directory or finding the total space used by a group of files.

If you use Windows for Workgroups, you will find File Manager very similar to the Windows 3.1 File Manager. However, for some of the added features that you get with Windows for Workgroups File Manager, see the section titled "Windows for Workgroups File Manager Display."

Windows 3.1 File Manager Display

When you first start File Manager, the directory window is divided into two parts. In figure 4.3, the directory tree, with the expanded structure of directories and subdirectories on drive C, occupies the left portion of the window. The contents list on the right shows the files in the C:\EXCEL\LIBRARY directory.

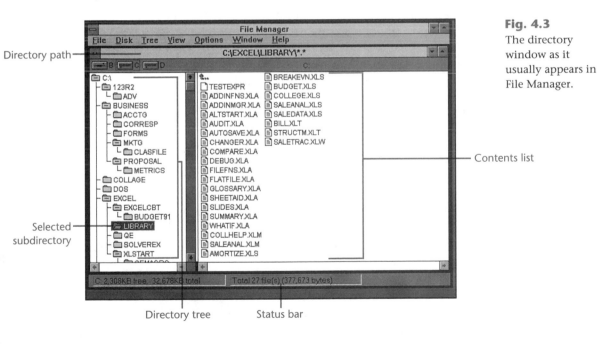

Directory path

Selected subdirectory

Directory tree   Status bar

Fig. 4.3
The directory window as it usually appears in File Manager.

Contents list

II

Managing Your Work

Notice the status bar at the bottom of File Manager. On the right, the bar always displays the number and total size of the files on the selected subdirectory. When the directory tree portion of the window is active, the left portion of the bar shows the available storage on the active disk. When the contents list is active, this area shows the total size in bytes of the selected files. Scroll bars appear on the right and bottom of the directory tree and at the bottom of the contents list. If either segment contains more information than it can show at once, the scroll bar is shaded.

The directory tree contains miniature folder icons, which represent directories and subdirectories. The contents list shows files as miniature icons that represent documents. The first time you start File Manager, a plus sign (+) in a directory or subdirectory icon indicates that additional subdirectories are inside the icon. A minus sign (–) in a subdirectory icon indicates that the directory can be collapsed inside its parent directory. A folder icon without a plus or minus sign indicates that it is the lowest level of subdirectory. (If you cannot see pluses and minuses, open the **T**ree menu and select the **I**ndicate Expandable Branches command to display them.)

When a directory or subdirectory icon is expanded, as shown in figure 4.3, you can see the underlying subdirectories. Notice the vertical lines and indentations that show how directories and subdirectories are dependent. When a directory or subdirectory is open, its icon changes to look like an open folder, and its contents are displayed in the contents list.

At any given time, File Manager's focus is on only one area of the window: the drive bar, the directory tree, or the contents list. The area that has a selection with a highlighted background has the focus. In the area with the focus, you can use the arrow keys on the keyboard to change the selection. Press Tab to move the focus between areas.

File Manager can display multiple directory windows at one time to show the file contents of any directory or subdirectory you select. To make comparing disk contents, or copying or deleting files easy, open multiple directory windows onto different disks and directories.

Windows for Workgroups' File Manager Display

Windows for Workgroups' File Manager is slightly different in appearance from Windows 3.1's File Manager (see fig. 4.4). Just below the menu bar is the toolbar. The buttons on the toolbar enable you to quickly access several frequently used File Manager commands. Each button represents one of the menu commands. You can customize the toolbar so that it includes buttons for whatever commands you want.

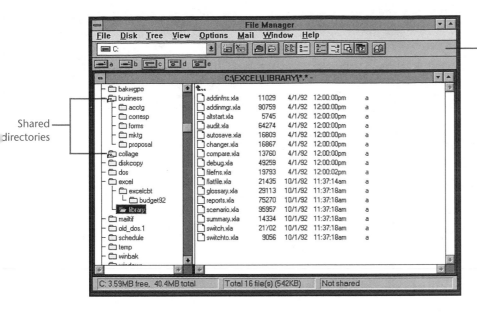

Fig. 4.4
Windows for
Workgroups' File
Manager includes
a toolbar.

Shared
directories

Toolbar

Also located on the toolbar (at the left end) is a drop-down list of all the
drives available for you to use, including *network drives*, which are directories
being shared by other users. The share name and a computer name may
appear next to the names of network drives in this list (see "Working with
Networks in Windows for Workgroups").

When a directory is shared, it is represented in the directory tree as a folder
with a hand underneath it (see fig. 4.4). The BUSINESS and COLLAGE
directories in the figure show that they are shared.

Operating File Manager

As with most Windows applications, you can operate File Manager with the
mouse, by touch typing, or with shortcut keys. Use the method that is most
convenient for you. A combination of mouse actions and typing is fast and
flexible.

Using Commands with File Manager

Table 4.1 lists the commands available in File Manager. You can select these
commands with either the keyboard or mouse.

II

Managing Your Work

Table 4.1 File Management Commands

Command	Description
Disk Connect Network Drive	Connects the computer to a network drive (only displayed if you are on a network).
Disk **C**opy Disk	Copies the contents of one disk to another disk of the same capacity.
Disk **D**isconnect Network Drive	Disconnects the computer from a drive (only displayed if you are on a network).
Disk **F**ormat Disk	Formats a disk.
Disk **L**abel Disk	Creates or changes the volume label on disks.
Disk **M**ake System Disk	Formats a disk and includes the system files for disk start-up.
Disk **S**elect Drive	Selects a different disk drive.
File **A**ssociate	Associates a selected document file with an application so that you can open a document in an application by opening only the document file.
File **C**opy	Copies selected files or directories to a new location.
File Cr**e**ate Directory	Creates a directory or subdirectory within the currently selected directory or subdirectory.
File **D**elete	Deletes selected files or directories.
File E**x**it	Exits and closes File Manager.
File **M**ove	Moves selected files or directories from one location to another.
File **O**pen	Starts the selected application, opens a directory window of the selected directory, or opens the selected document and starts the application associated with the document.
File **P**rint	Prints the selected text file to the current printer.
File Proper**t**ies	Displays some information about a selected file and allows changes to a file's Read Only, Hidden, Archive, and System attributes.
File Re**n**ame	Renames selected file or directory.
File **R**un	Starts a selected application with a data file (if one is associated) or with a start-up argument (if one is associated).

Command	Description
File Sear**ch**	Searches for file or directory names that meet naming patterns you set. You can search the entire disk with this command.
File **S**elect Files	Selects files and directories in the active directory window.
File **U**ndelete	Runs the Microsoft Undelete program. Use this option to recover a file or files you accidentally deleted. This command is only available with DOS 6 or greater.
Mail **S**end Mail	Sends a mail message with selected files attached to the message. This command is only available when you are using Microsoft Mail (see Chapter 15, "Using Mail with Windows for Workgroups").
Options **C**onfirmation	Allows you to specify which file actions File Manager asks for confirmation about before executing.
Options Customize Tool**b**ar	Adds, removes, and rearranges the buttons on the toolbar.
Options **D**rivebar	Displays a bar with drive buttons for each drive connected to your computer. Selecting a drive button displays the contents of that drive in File Manager window.
Options **F**ont	Changes the font, font style, and font size used to display directory and file information.
Options **M**inimize on Use	Minimizes File Manager to an icon when you start an application.
Options **O**pen New Window on Connect	Opens a new directory window whenever you connect to a shared network drive.
Options Save Settings on **E**xit	Enables the automatic saving of current settings of all options in the Options menu.
Options **S**tatus Bar	Displays the status bar at the bottom of File Manager for information about the selected files or directories.
Options **T**oolbar	Displays the toolbar at the top of File Manager with buttons for quickly carrying out several File Manager commands.
Tools **A**ntivirus	Runs the Microsoft Antivirus program. Allows you to check files or a disk drives for the presence of viruses. This command is only available with DOS 6 or greater.

II

Managing Your Work

(continues)

Table 4.1 Continued	
Command	**Description**
Tools **B**ackup	Runs the Microsoft Backup program. Allows you to back up your disk files. This command is only available with DOS 6 or greater.
Tools **D**oubleSpace Info	Provides information about disk volumes formatted with DoubleSpace. This command is only available with DOS 6 or greater.
Tree **C**ollapse Branch	Collapses the lower level subdirectories into the selected directory.
Tree Expand **A**ll	Expands all directories and subdirectories; files are not shown.
Tree Expand **B**ranch	Expands the selected directory to show all lower subdirectories.
Tree E**x**pand One Level	Expands the selected directory to show the next level.
Tree **I**ndicate Expandable Branches	Uses plus (+) and minus (–) symbols to indicate whether a directory contains subdirectories.
View **A**ll File Details	Shows all information about the files and file attributes (name, size, date and time most recently edited, and attributes).
View by File **T**ype	Limits the files displayed to the specified types and/or to files whose names match specified parameters.
View Directory **O**nly	Displays the contents list only.
View **N**ame	Shows the file and directory name in the current directory window.
View **P**artial Details	Shows selected information about the files. (You select what you want to show.)
View Sort by **D**ate	Sorts file names by last modification date (oldest dates first).
View **S**ort by Name	Sorts file names by name (alphabetical order).
View Sort by Si**z**e	Sorts file names by size (from largest to smallest).
View Sort **b**y Type	Sorts file names by type (alphabetically by extension name).
View Sp**l**it	Moves the dividing line between the directory tree and the contents list.

Command	Description
View **Tr**ee and Directory	Displays the directory tree on the left and the contents list on the right
View **Tr**ee Only	Displays the directory tree only.
Window #	Activates the indicated window. All open windows' names are assigned a number in the list.
Window **A**rrange Icons	Arranges minimized directory windows icons in a row at the bottom of the screen.
Window **C**ascade	Arranges windows so that they cascade in overlapping fashion from top left to lower right.
Window **N**ew Window	Opens a new directory window.
Window **R**efresh	Rereads the disk and updates the active window to match the disk contents.
Window **T**ile	Arranges windows to fill File Manager so that the contents of all windows are visible. This command is only available in Windows.
Window Tile **H**orizontally	Arranges open windows horizontally so that the contents of all windows are visible. This command is only available in Windows for Workgroups.
Window **T**ile Vertically	Arranges open windows vertically so that the contents of all windows are visible. This command is only available in Windows for Workgroups.

Using the Keyboard with File Manager

To operate File Manager by using keystrokes, use this section as a quick reference. This section lists the keyboard shortcuts.

When you are in the drive icon area, use the keystrokes in the following list:

Keystroke	Action
Tab	Moves the active area between the disk-drive icons, the directory tree, and the contents list.
Ctrl+*letter*	Selects and opens the drive specified by *letter*. For example, Ctrl+C selects drive C and displays the directories on this drive in the directory tree area.

(continues)

II

Managing Your Work

Keystroke	Action
← or →	Moves the selection among the drive icons if you have tabbed into the drive area of the window.
Enter	Opens the selected drive and displays the contents of the drive in the directory-tree area of the window.

When you are in the directory tree area, use the following keystrokes:

Keystroke	Action
↑ or ↓	Moves the selection to a directory or subdirectory above or below the currently selected directory in the directory-tree section of the window.
→	Selects the first subdirectory (the daughter) within the currently selected and open directory when you are in the directory-tree section of the window.
←	Selects the directory that contains the current subdirectory (the parent) when you are in the directory-tree section of the window.
Ctrl+↑ or Ctrl+↓	Restricts selections to a subdirectory level within the current directory.
PgUp	Selects the directory one window up.
PgDn	Selects the directory one window down.
Home	Selects the root directory for the disk.
End	Selects the last directory in the window.
letter	Selects the next directory or subdirectory, beginning with *letter*.
- (hyphen)	Collapses the selected directory. (The minus sign key also works.)
+ (plus)	Expands the selected directory one level.
* (asterisk)	Expands all branches in the selected directory.
Ctrl+*	Expands all branches on the disk.

When you are in the contents list area, use the keystrokes in the following list:

Keystroke	Action
PgUp	Selects the file or directory one window up.
PgDn	Selects the file or directory one window down.
Home	Selects the first file or directory in the window.
End	Selects the last file or directory in the window.
letter	Selects the first file or directory beginning with *letter*.
Shift+arrow	Selects all files or directories over which you move the selection highlight.
space bar	Selects or deselects the current file or directory when moving the selection with Shift+F8.
Enter	Opens a directory if the directory is selected or starts an application if an application or the associated data file is selected.

Using the Mouse with File Manager

File Manager can be much easier to use with your mouse. It makes selecting and copying nonadjacent files very easy. The following chart lists some activities and the mouse actions you do to achieve them.

Activity	Mouse Action
Select a directory	Click on a directory in the directory tree area.
Select a file	Click on a file in the contents list.
Select multiple adjacent files	Click on the first file; press and Shift+click on the last file.
Select multiple nonadjacent files	Ctrl+click on each file.
Start an application or open a document file	Double-click on the application file or an associated document file.
Expand a directory one level	Double-click on the icon with the plus sign (+) to the left of the directory you want to expand.
Collapse a directory one level	Double-click on the icon with the minus sign (–) on the open folder icon above the directory you want to collapse.
Copy a file	Drag the file name onto another disk drive.
Move a file	Drag a file name into a different directory on the same disk drive.

Using the Toolbar with File Manager

If you are working with File Manager in Windows for Workgroups, you can quickly execute many File Manager commands with the toolbar, which is located below the menu bar. To execute a command, click the button on the toolbar for that command. File Manager has a default set of buttons in the toolbar, which are described in the following table. The table lists the icons (in left-to-right order) as they appear. You can also customize the toolbar so that it includes the commands you use frequently.

Note

When you install some software (for instance, when you update to DOS 6.2 or when you enable Microsoft Mail), the installation program may automatically modify the toolbar for you. This is done so you can access some Microsoft tools quickly and easily.

Icon	Button Name	Description
	Connect Network Drive	For connecting to a network drive
	Disconnect Network Drive	For disconnecting from a network drive
	Share As	For sharing a directory with other users on a network (this button is only available when you are running in 386 Enhanced mode)
	Stop Sharing	Stops the sharing of a directory with other users (this button is only available when you are running in 386 Enhanced mode)
	View Name	Changes display to show file names only
	View All File Details	Changes display to show all file details
	Sort By Name	Sorts files alphabetically by file name
	Sort By Type	Sorts files alphabetically by file name extension
	Sort By Size	Sorts files by size, from largest to smallest

Icon	Button Name	Description
	Sort By Date	Sorts files by date, startingwith most recent files
	Send Mail	Sends a mail message with selected files attached to the message

Selecting and Opening Files and Directories

File Manager follows the primary rule of all Windows applications: Select, then Do. When you want to work on a file or directory in File Manager, you first must find and select the file or directory. After you select a file, you can display information about the file, and start, copy, move, or delete the file. After you select a directory, you can find information about the directory contents, copy or move the directory, or open the directory to see the subdirectories or files it contains.

Selecting a New Disk Drive

Before you can work with files and directories, you must be in the correct disk drive. The disk drives available in the computer appear as icons under the directory window title bar. The currently selected drive appears outlined. If the focus is on the drive icon bar, the currently selected drive also displays with a dark background. To change to a new drive with the mouse, click on the drive icon you want to activate.

When using the keyboard to change to a new drive, first notice whether the focus is in the drive icon area of the window. Press the Tab key to move the focus among the three screen areas.

If the focus is in the drive icon bar, change to a new drive by pressing the left- or right-arrow key to move the focus to a different drive, then press Enter. The highlight moves behind the drive you selected.

If the focus is in the directory tree or contents list area of the window, press Ctrl+*letter* to change to a different drive, in which *letter* is the drive's letter. (If you change to a disk drive containing an unformatted disk, File Manager prompts you to format the disk.)

In Windows for Workgroups' File Manager, you can also select the drive you want to work with by using the drop-down list at the left end of the toolbar (see fig. 4.5). The advantage to using the drop-down list is that you can easily see the shared directory associated with the drive letter.

Fig. 4.5
Selecting a drive
using the drive list
on the toolbar.

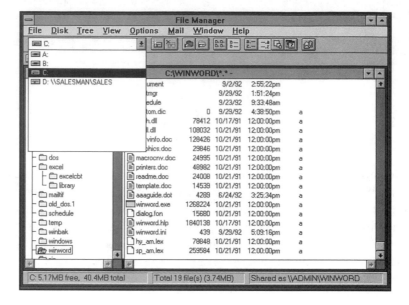

To open this list, click the down arrow to the right of the list or press F2. Click the drive you want to activate or use the up- or down-arrow keys to select the drive you want to activate, and press Enter.

Selecting, Expanding, and Collapsing Directories

The directory window, shown in figure 4.6, always displays in File Manager window. It may be either in its own window or in an icon at the bottom of File Manager window. The directory tree area in the left half of File Manager shows the hierarchical structure of the area of the disk you are currently examining.

Select One Directory at a Time

You can select only one directory at a time in a given directory window. You can, however, open multiple directory windows, each displaying a different directory. Open more than one directory when you want to see the contents of multiple directories at one time. Copying files between directories is easier when you open a source-directory window and a destination-directory window. To learn how to open a second File Manager window, refer to the section, "Opening and Selecting Directory Windows," later in this chapter.

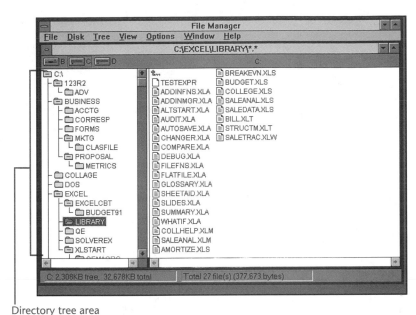

Fig. 4.6
The directory tree
area.

Directory tree area

To select a directory, click on the directory or subdirectory you want. If you cannot see the directory, use the vertical scroll bar on the directory tree area to scroll it into sight before clicking. If you need files in a subdirectory, open the directory above the desired subdirectory first, as described later in this section.

After you select a specific directory, you may want to see the subdirectories beneath it. Or you may want to collapse the fully expanded directory structure so that you can see the directories at a higher level. Figure 4.6 shows a directory structure with directories expanded. The BUSINESS directory is a parent directory that has been expanded to show the ACCTG, CORRESP, FORMS, MKTG, and PROPOSAL subdirectories beneath it. Collapsed directories do not show the subdirectories they contain.

Directory icons appear as file folders. If a directory icon contains a + (plus) sign, the directory contains subdirectories. If a directory icon contains a – (minus) sign, the directory can be collapsed so it does not display its subdirectories. If the directory icon does not contain a + (plus) sign, no subdirectories are contained within this directory (or the plus and minus signs are hidden—to display them, open the **T**ree menu and select the **I**ndicate Expandable Branches command).

To expand or collapse a directory or subdirectory, use one of the following mouse actions:

- Double-click on the + (plus) sign in a directory icon if you want to expand the directory one level.

- Double-click on the–(minus) sign in a directory icon if you want to collapse the directory.

You can also expand or collapse directories with the menu commands, following these steps:

1. Select the directory or subdirectory.

2. Choose one of the following commands:

Command	Action
Tree E**x**pand One Level	Expands the selected directory to show all subdirectories at the next lower level.
Tree Expand **B**ranch	Expands the selected directory to show all lower subdirectories.
Tree Expand **A**ll	Expands all subdirectories on the disk.
Tree **C**ollapse Branch	Collapses the lower level subdirectories into the selected directory.

Opening and Selecting Directory Windows

Tip

To cycle through all the open directory windows, press Ctrl+F6. To arrange all the directory windows on-screen, choose the **W**indow **C**ascade command or the **W**indow **T**ile command.

You can have many directory windows that show the contents of individual directories. Figure 4.7 shows File Manager with numerous directory windows. Notice that each directory window displays a different directory—and even different disks. For any directory window, you have the option of displaying just the directory tree, just the list of files in the directory, or both. Use the **V**iew command to select one of these three options. As you see later in this chapter, having multiple windows open onto different directories and disks is a convenient way to copy or move files with a mouse.

To open a new directory window, open the **W**indow menu and Choose **N**ew Window. The new window will display the path name of the previously active window in the title bar, followed by a colon and 2, which indicates that the window is the second one associated with this particular directory. When you choose another directory, however, the path name in the new window changes.

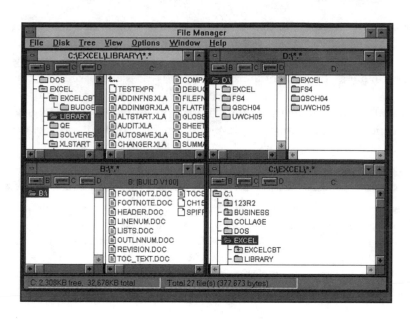

Fig. 4.7
Directory windows, each displaying the contents of different directories.

Each file within a directory window displays an icon that helps identify its type of file. These file shapes are shown in the following list.

Icon	Type of File
Directory Tree Icons	
	Open directory or subdirectory.
	Closed directory or subdirectory.
Contents List icons	
	Application or batch file having the extension EXE, COM, PIF, or BAT (choosing one of these files may start an application).
	Document file associated with an application (choosing one of these files starts the application that created the file).
	Other files.
Shared directory icon	
	Directory that is shared with other users.

Tip
Press Ctrl+F6 to
activate the
next window.

Suppose that you have multiple directory windows open and want a specific window to be active. If you are using a mouse and can see the window you want, click on a portion of this window to make it active. If you are using a keyboard, press Ctrl+F6 until the window you want is active, or select the Window menu and choose the name of the window you want from the menu. (If you have more than nine windows open, the More Windows command appears at the bottom of the Window menu. Choose it to select from a scrolling list of open windows.)

> **Note**
>
> A quick way to open a new window in File Manager is to double-click a disk drive icon. Double-click the icon for disk drive A, for example, to open a new window displaying the contents of a disk in drive A. Double-click the current drive icon to duplicate the window currently displayed. Follow this step by tiling your windows so that you can see the contents of all open windows. A shortcut to tiling your windows vertically is to press Shift+F4.

If you are using Windows for Workgroups, you can select **O**ptions, **O**pen New Window on Connect. This causes File Manager to open a new directory window every time you connect to a remote network drive.

Changing or Closing Directory Windows

Each directory window usually contains both a directory tree and a contents list. However, you can change this to another View option for any given window. You might be doing some intensive disk management, for example, and need to display multiple directory windows for easier moving and copying. To save screen space, you can display one directory tree together with multiple contents lists. To do this, follow these steps:

1. With a single directory window open, choose the **V**iew Tr**ee** Only command.

2. For each directory whose contents you want to see on the screens, open a new window.

3. Select each window in turn and choose the **V**iew Directory **O**nly command. Leave one window in tree-only format and use it for quick perusals of the directory structure.

4. Open the **W**indow menu and choose **T**ile if you want to see all the open directory windows always. If you have more than a few windows open, you might need to maximize the File Manager window to work effectively.

Directory windows are document windows, so you can use the mouse or document Control menu to resize, move, or close each window. Activate the window you want to change by clicking on it or by pressing Ctrl+F6 until it is on top of the other windows.

Tip
Close the active directory window by pressing Ctrl+F4.

Selecting More than One File or Directory

Before you can act on a file, you must select it. In some cases—when copying or deleting files, for example—you may want to select multiple files before choosing any command.

To select a single file, click on the file name. To select multiple adjacent files, click on the first file, press and hold down the Shift key, and click on the last file. All files between the two files you clicked on are selected. To select non-adjacent files, click on the first file and hold down the Ctrl key as you click on other files. If you want to retain current selections but deselect a file, just Ctrl+click on the file you no longer want selected.

You can also select files with the keyboard. Start by pressing the arrow keys to move the selection to the file name you want. To select multiple adjacent files, move the selection to the first file, press and hold down the Shift key, and press an arrow key. To select nonadjacent files, select the first file, press Shift+F8, press an arrow key to move to the next file to be selected, and press the space bar. Move to the additional files you want to select and press the space bar. To deselect a file and retain other selections, move to the selected file and press the space bar. Press Shift+F8 to return to normal mode (selecting a single file at a time).

If you want to select all files in a directory window with a given extension, select a contents list window and choose the File, Select Files command. The dialog box shown in figure 4.8 appears.

In the Files text box, type the name for the file you want to select. You can use a pattern of DOS wild cards in the file name.

Use wild cards, such as * and ?, to search for a group of files or directory names or to search when you don't know the exact name of the file or directory. In the example shown in figure 4.9, the pattern E*.XLS searches for all file names beginning with E and having the extension XLS (an Excel worksheet). Although the file name must begin with E, the rest of the file name can be any group of letters (as specified by *).

II

Managing Your Work

Fig. 4.8
The Select Files
dialog box with
. specified.

Fig. 4.9
The Select Files
dialog box with
E*.XLS specified.

Tip
A quick way to
select all the
files in a se-
lected contents
list is to press
Ctrl+/. To
deselect all files
but one, press
Ctrl+\.

To select all files in the window, choose the Select button while the **F**iles text box displays *.*. If you want to deselect certain files, change the Files param-eter and choose **D**eselect. Choose Close when you finish making the selection(s).

Canceling Selections

If you select the wrong file or directory, you can cancel any selection you do not want. To cancel a single selection with the mouse, click on another file or directory. If you select multiple files, and want to cancel one but retain the others, press and hold down the Ctrl key as you click on the file you want to deselect.

To cancel a single selection with the keyboard, press an arrow key to select another file or directory. If you select multiple files or directories, and want to cancel one but retain the others, press Shift+F8, press the arrow keys to en-close the incorrect selection with the dashed focus line, and press the space bar. Deselect any other incorrect selections and press Shift+F8 to return to normal selection mode.

To cancel a selection while the Select Files dialog box is on-screen, change the Files parameter to *.* and choose the **D**eselect button.

Searching for Files or Directories

Losing a file is frustrating and wastes time. With Windows, you can search disks or directories for file names similar to the file you have misplaced. To search for a file by its name or part of its name, follow these steps:

1. Select the disk drive you want to search.

2. Select the directory (if you want to search a single directory).

    If you do not know the specific directory that contains a file, select the parent directory of all subdirectories that might contain the file.

3. Open the **F**ile menu and choose Searc**h**. The Search dialog box appears (see fig. 4.10).

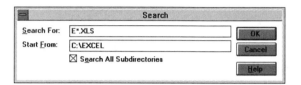

Fig. 4.10
The Search dialog box.

4. In the **S**earch For text box, type the name of the file for which you are searching. You can use a pattern of DOS wild cards in the file name.

5. To search all directories on the current disk, specify the root directory in the Start **F**rom text box. By default, Windows searches all subdirectories beneath the directory you select. To search the specified directory only, turn off the Search All Subdirectories option.

6. Choose OK or press Enter.

A Search Results window, such as the one shown in figure 4.11, displays the paths and file names of all files that match the pattern you were seeking. When you see the file or application you want in the Search Results window, start the document or application by double-clicking it with the mouse, or by selecting it and pressing Enter. You can start documents and applications together if the document has been associated with an application, as explained in "Associating Documents with an Application," later in this chapter.

When you use wild cards in a name pattern, remember that the * wild-card character finds any group of characters in the file name in the same or following positions. The ? wild-card character matches any single character within the file name that is in the same position as ?.

Suppose that you know the directory in which a file is located, and the date or time at which the file was last saved, but you don't know the file name. You can display the time and date of all the files in the directory window to

II

Managing Your Work

help you locate that specific file. Choose the **View A**ll File Details command to show the time and date on which files were last saved. This command also indicates file attribute(s) at the right.

Fig. 4.11
The Search Results window.

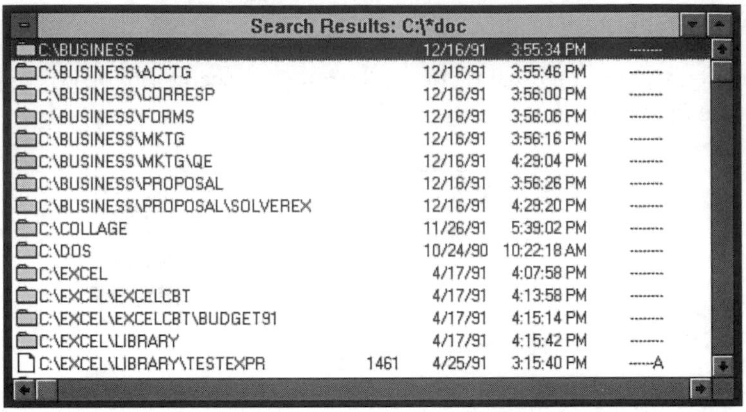

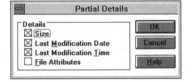

If you want to save screen space, you can choose the **View P**artial Details command and specify which particular file details to display in the Partial Details dialog box (see fig. 4.12).

Fig. 4.12
The Partial Details dialog box.

To sort the files in the directory window by name, type, size, or date, choose the corresponding Sort By command under the **V**iew menu. Figure 4.13 shows a directory window after choosing the **V**iew Sort By **D**ate command.

> **Note**
>
> Some Windows applications, such as Word for Windows, can search through their document files and return a list of all files that contain specific words or phrases. An application's search facility can be more effective and precise than File Manager's search command.

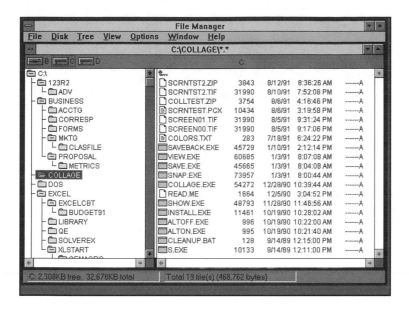

Controlling File Manager Windows and Displays

You can arrange the windows and files in a way that makes it easy to get work done, whether copying files between directories, making backup copies to disk, or deleting files. The following sections explain how to manipulate the appearance of the Windows display screen.

Arranging Directory Windows and Icons

You can arrange directory windows and icons in three ways. You can arrange them by manually sizing and positioning them, by cascading them to show all the window titles, or by placing them in tiles to show each window's contents. You also can minimize windows so that they appear as icons.

To arrange directory windows in a cascade like that shown in figure 4.14, open the **W**indow menu and choose **C**ascade. The active window becomes the top window in the cascade.

To arrange directory windows in tiles so that the screen is evenly divided among the windows (see fig. 4.15), open the **W**indow menu and choose **T**ile. The active window becomes the window at the top left of the screen.

Tip
Press Shift+F5
to cascade
open windows.

Tip
Press Shift+F4
to vertically tile
open windows.

II

Managing Your Work

Fig. 4.14
Windows in a cascade arrangement.

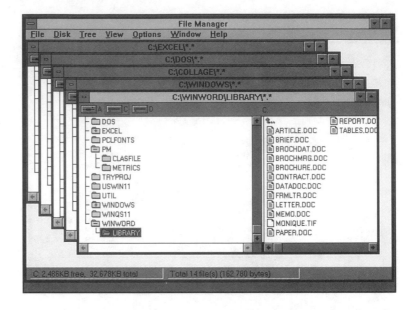

Fig. 4.15
Windows in a tile arrangement.

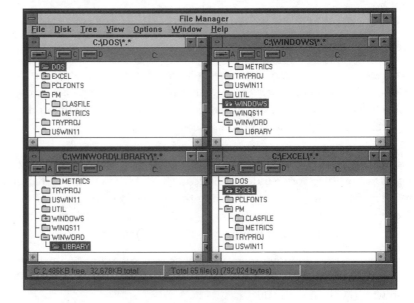

In Windows for Workgroups, File Manager provides two ways to arrange directory windows in tiles. open the **W**indow menu and choose Tile **H**orizontally to distribute directory windows in tiles that are arranged one on top of the other. Open the **W**indow menu and choose **T**ile Vertically to distribute directory windows in tiles that are arranged side by side.

When windows are arranged by cascading or by tiling, you still can use each directory window's Control menu to move a window. Chapter 1 describes how to use the Control menu to move a window.

Note

You can save time if you minimize directory windows that you use frequently to icons (see fig. 4.16). When you want to work with the directory contained within the icon, maximize the icon. To minimize a directory window into an icon, click on the mini-mize button (the down arrow at the top right of the window). Alternatively, press Alt+hyphen (-), N (for Minimize). To maximize a directory icon into a window, double-click on the icon; alternatively, select the icon by pressing Ctrl+F6 and then press Alt+hyphen (-), X (for Maximize). Remember that you move among icons with the keyboard by pressing Ctrl+F6 or Ctrl+Tab. Chapter 1, "Controlling Windows," describes how to minimize windows, maximize icons, and move both windows and icons.

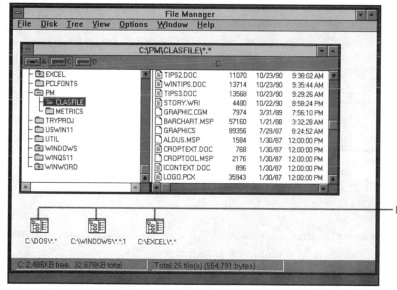

Fig. 4.16
Directory icons keep frequently used directory windows available.

Specifying File-Display Details

You can specify what file information appears in the directory window. **V**iew **N**ame shows only the file names and extensions. **V**iew **A**ll File Details shows all file information. The **V**iew **P**artial Details command enables you to select the information you want displayed. To display file information, follow these steps:

1. Activate the directory window you want to change. If you want to change the display of all subsequent windows you open, activate the directory tree area.

2. Choose the appropriate command. The following chart lists the commands that affect the window display.

Command	Description
View **N**ame	Displays only names and directories.
View **A**ll File Details	Displays the name, size, date and time last saved; and file attributes.
View **P**artial Details	Selects a custom display showing one or more of the following file characteristics:
	Size: displays the file size in bytes.
	Last **M**odification Date: displays the last date the file was modified and saved
	Last Modification **T**ime: displays the last time the file was modified and saved
	File Attributes: displays one of the following letters for different attributes:

A	Archive
S	System
H	Hidden
R	Read Only

3. If you chose **V**iew **P**artial Details, choose OK or press Enter after you select one or more of the options.

You can sort the directory window by any of the characteristics displayed. Use the **V**iew Sort By commands, as explained later in this section. If you want to change a file's attributes, use the **F**ile Properties command, described later in this chapter.

Figure 4.17 shows the Partial Details dialog box, from which you can select the different file characteristics you want to display. Figure 4.18 shows two directory windows, each displaying a different set of file characteristics.

Fig. 4.17
The Partial Details
dialog box.

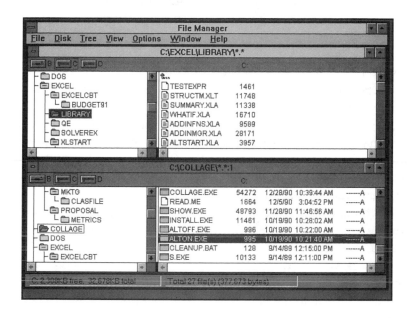

Fig. 4.18
Two directory
windows, each
showing different
file characteristics.

Hiding the Status Bar

You can change some characteristics of the File Manager window. For example, you can hide the status bar at the bottom of File Manager window.

Leave the status bar turned on to see available storage and the number of files. The status bar displays important information about the active window. If the directory tree is selected, the status bar shows the available storage on the disk and the number of files in the current directory. If the contents list is selected, the disk storage information is replaced by the number of selected files and the total size of the selected files.

If you want to find out how much room you have on a disk, change to that disk and look at the status bar.

You may want to remove the status bar from the bottom of File Manager so that you can display more files. In general, however, you should display the status bar so that you can monitor the available disk storage. To turn on the status bar, open the **O**ptions menu and select the **S**tatus Bar command. A check mark appears next to the command when the option is on. Choose the command again to turn off the status bar. (This action also removes the check mark.) All directory windows you open subsequently also omit the status bar.

Hiding the Toolbar and Drivebar

You can choose to display or not display the toolbar and drivebar. If you need more room to display files, or do not use the toolbar, you may want to turn off one or both of these options. To turn off the toolbar, open the **O**ptions menu and select the **T**oolbar command. Choose the **T**oolbar command again to turn the toolbar on. To turn off the drivebar, open the **O**ptions menu and select the **D**rivebar command. Choose the **D**rivebar command again to turn the drivebar on. A check mark appears next to these commands when the options are on. When you turn off the option, the check mark is removed.

Changing the Font

By default, File Manager displays directory and file names in 8-point MS Sans Serif font. This small font is generally optimal for displaying as many entries as possible while still remaining readable. You can change the font, however, with the **O**ptions **F**ont command.

Open the **O**ptions menu and choose the **F**ont command; then select the desired font (typeface), font style, and size from the appropriate list boxes. As you make selections, the Sample box changes to reflect the current state of File Manager's display font. When you are satisfied, choose OK or press Enter.

By default, characters in File Manager appear in upper- and lowercase letters—exactly as you enter them. If you want text in File Manager's window to display in uppercase letters, open the **O**ptions menu and select the **F**ont command. The dialog box shown in figure 4.19 appears. Turn off the **L**owercase option to display file and directory names in uppercase letters.

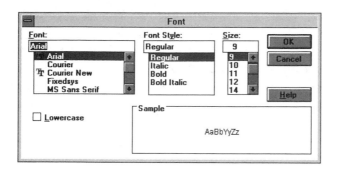

Fig. 4.19
The Font dialog
box.

Updating File Manager's Window

You may need to update a directory window. For example, you may have switched disks. As a result, you may activate File Manager and not see a file you have just saved—a scenario that is more than a little disconcerting. Don't panic; the file is there. All you have to do is to choose the **W**indow **R**efresh command (as a shortcut, press F5). If you still cannot find the file in the directory in which you thought you saved the file, you may have saved it to a different directory or disk. You should search for the file. Open the **F**ile menu and select the Searc**h** command; type the file's name.

Sorting the Display of Files and Directories

Finding files or directories is much easier if you rearrange the contents of a directory window. You can order the window contents alphabetically by file name, alphabetically by file extension, by file size, or by the last date the file was saved. To reorder a window's contents, choose one of the commands in the following chart to sort the window.

Command	Description
View **S**ort by Name	Sorts alphabetically by file name
View Sort **b**y Type	Sorts alphabetically by file extension
View Sort by Si**z**e	Sorts by file size, from largest to smallest
View Sort by **D**ate	Sorts by last date modified, most recent first

You don't have to display the file date or size in the directory window to sort by those attributes. If you want to see the file's date and size in the directory window, open the **V**iew menu and choose **A**ll File Details or **V**iew **P**artial Details.

Filtering Out Unwanted Files from the Display

Another way to easily find a specific type of file in a directory window is to limit the number of files displayed. You can set criteria to filter files so that only files of the type you want are displayed. Specify the type of file to be displayed when you want to see only application files or only document files that end with a specific extension.

To include in the directory window only the files you want, follow these steps:

1. Activate the directory window in which you want to specify the type of file you want to display.

2. Open the **V**iew menu and choose By File **T**ype. The dialog box shown in figure 4.20 appears.

Fig. 4.20
The By File Type
dialog box.

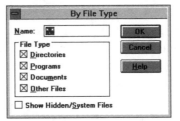

3. Select the **N**ame text box and type a file pattern to display only the files matching the pattern you specify (you can use the wild cards * and ?). Alternatively, select one of the following options:

Option	Description
Directories	Displays only directories or subdirectories
Programs	Displays only files with file extensions of EXE, COM, PIF, or BAT
Docu**m**ents	Displays document files and files that have been associated with an application with the File Associate command
Other Files	Displays all other files that are not directories, applications, or documents
Show Hidden/**S**ystem files	Displays hidden files or system files

4. Choose OK or press Enter.

Changing a File's Attributes

Each file on a disk has a set of *attributes*, or descriptive characteristics. Attributes describe whether the file has been backed up, is part of the DOS system, is hidden from normal viewing, or can be read but not written over. With File Manager, you can display file attributes and change them.

You can display the file attributes in the current directory window by opening the **V**iew menu and choosing the **A**ll File Details command. If you want to see only the attributes, open the **V**iew menu and select the **P**artial File Details command; now select the attributes option.

To change a file's attributes, select the file or files you want to change and then open the **F**ile menu and choose the Properties command. The Properties dialog box appears. Select the attribute you want changed, and choose OK or press Enter. The following is a list of the attributes you can change:

Attribute	Description
Read Only	Sets the R or read-only attribute, which prevents a file from being changed or erased. Set this attribute for a file when you want to prevent someone from accidentally changing a master template or erasing a file critical to system operation.
Archive	Sets the A or archive attribute. Marks with an A any file that has changed since being backed up using the DOS BACKUP, RESTORE, or XCOPY commands. If no A appears, the file has not changed since you backed it up.
Hidden	Sets the H or hidden attribute, which prevents files from displaying.
System	Sets the S or system attribute, which prevents files from displaying. Some files that belong to DOS are hidden so that they aren't accidentally erased.

Reducing the Chance of Erasing Critical Files

If you want to ensure that a file isn't accidentally changed or erased, set the attributes to **R**ead Only and **H**idden or **S**ystem. These attributes prevent the file from being changed and hide the file from standard display.

> ### Display Hidden or System Files with the View Include Command
>
> Assigning the Hidden or System attribute to hide files is a good way to prevent tampering or accidental erasure. As an experienced Windows user, however, you may need to see these files to change, erase, or copy them. To display files with the Hidden or System attribute, open the View menu and choose the By File Type command; next select the Show Hidden/System Files check box.

Viewing the Properties of a File or Directory

You can view the properties of a file or directory in the Properties dialog box. The file name, path, file size, and the date and time the file or directory was last changed are displayed.

The Properties dialog box in File Manager in Windows for Workgroups includes more information. For example, you also will find information on the version number, copyright, and company name of a program if the selected item is a program file.

Displaying Warning Messages

During some File Manager operations, a warning message appears and asks you to confirm the action about to take place. If you select a directory and open the File menu and select the Delete command, for example, you may be asked to confirm the deletion of each file and the removal of the directory. If you find the confirmation messages annoying, you can turn the confirmation off—but remember that these warning messages appear to prevent you from making mistakes. If you turn off the messages, you have no warning for potentially hazardous actions!

Turn off warning messages by opening the Options menu and selecting the Confirmation command, and deselecting the desired options from the Confirmation dialog box (see fig. 4.21). Choose OK or press Enter after choosing an option. Turn a confirmation message back on by reselecting the option so that the check box contains an x.

Fig. 4.21
The Confirmation dialog box.

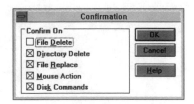

The following is a list of the options in the Confirmation dialog box and the messages whose display they control.

Option	Action Confirmed by Message
File **D**elete	Each file being erased
Directory Delete	Each directory being erased
File **R**eplace	One file being copied or moved over another
Mouse Action	Any mouse action involving moving or copying
Dis**k** Commands	Each disk being copied over or formatted

As you gain more experience and confidence with the computer, you may want to turn off these messages. If you are a beginner or have difficulty accurately positioning the mouse, you may want to leave these messages on.

Customizing the Toolbar

The toolbar comes with a default set of buttons for quickly accessing some of the more commonly used File Manager commands. However, you can add and remove buttons from the toolbar so that the commands you use most frequently are accessible from the toolbar. There is a button available for every File Manager command. You can remove buttons that you do not use, add buttons for the commands you use frequently, and move buttons around to arrange them in whatever order you want. You can also return to the default set of buttons at any time.

Adding a Toolbar Button

To add a button to the toolbar, follow these steps:

1. Double-click anywhere on the background of the toolbar.

   or

   Open the **O**ptions menu and choose Customize Tool**b**ar.

   The dialog box shown in figure 4.22 appears. All available toolbar buttons are listed in the A**v**ailable Buttons list on the left side of the dialog box. All buttons currently displayed on the toolbar are listed in the **T**oolbar Buttons list on the right.

2. Select the button you want to add from the A**v**ailable Buttons list. Use the scroll bar to find the button you want, if necessary.

Fig. 4.22
Customize your
toolbar in the
Customize Toolbar
dialog box.

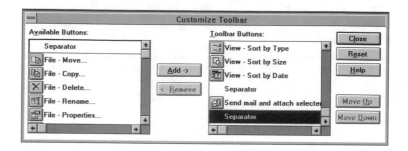

3. Click the **A**dd button. The button will be added to the **T**oolbar Buttons list on the right side of the dialog box.

   The button will be inserted immediately above the button that was selected in the **T**oolbar Buttons list when the **A**dd button was chosen. Use the Move **U**p and Move **D**own buttons to locate the button wherever you want on the toolbar.

4. Repeat steps 2 and 3 to add buttons you desire.

5. Click the **Cl**ose button.

   If you run out of room to add more buttons, you must remove buttons for commands that you use less often.

Removing a Toolbar Button

To quickly remove a toolbar button, put the tip of the mouse pointer on the button on the toolbar, hold down the Shift key, and drag the button off the toolbar. When the toolbar button is off the toolbar, release the mouse button.

To remove a toolbar button using the Customize Toolbar dialog box, follow these steps:

1. Open the **O**ptions menu and choose the Customize Tool**b**ar command, or double-click in the background of the toolbar.

   This displays the Customize Toolbar dialog box, shown in figure 4.22.

2. Select the button you want to remove from the **T**oolbar Buttons list.

3. Choose the **R**emove button.

4. Repeat steps 2 and 3 for each button you want to remove.

5. Choose the **Cl**ose button.

Rearranging Toolbar Buttons

To quickly move a toolbar button to a new location when you are using a mouse, put the tip of the mouse pointer on the button on the toolbar, hold down the Shift key, and drag the button to its new location on the toolbar, then release the mouse button.

You can arrange the buttons on the toolbar in any order you want. To move a toolbar button using the Customize Toolbar dialog box, follow these steps:

1. Open the **O**ptions menu and select the Customize Tool**b**ar command, or double-click in the background of the toolbar to display the Customize Toolbar dialog box, shown in figure 4.22.

2. Select the button that you want to move from the **T**oolbar Buttons list.

3. Choose the Move **U**p button to move the button up the list. This action will move the button to the left on the toolbar.

   or

   Choose the Move **D**own button to move the button down the list. This action will move the button to the right on the toolbar.

4. Repeat steps 2 and 3 for each button you want to move.

5. Choose the C**l**ose button.

Restoring the Default Toolbar

You can restore the default toolbar by following these steps:

1. Double-click anywhere on the background of the toolbar.

   or

   Open the **O**ptions menu and select the Tool**b**ar command.

   This displays the Customize Toolbar dialog box.

2. Choose the R**e**set button.

3. Choose the C**l**ose button.

Managing Your Work

II

Managing Files and Disks

Working with a hard disk, which can store thousands of files, can be confusing. Problems arise if you do not erase unnecessary files or do not make backup copies of files in case the hard disk fails.

In this section, you see how easy it is to erase unwanted files, copy files to other disks, or move files between directories. You also learn how to create directories so that you can organize a disk to fit your work and data.

Copying Files or Directories

Copying files is an important part of keeping work organized and secure. When organizing files, you may want to copy a file to make it accessible in two different locations. A more important reason for copying files is security.

The hard disk on which you store files is a mechanical device, and it has one of the highest failure rates among computer components. Should the hard disk fail, the cost of replacing the disk is insignificant compared to the cost of the hours you worked accumulating data on the disk. One way to prevent the loss of this data is to make a set of duplicate files on backup disks.

If you have copied files with DOS commands, you will find copying files and directories much more fun with Windows. All you do is drag the files you want to copy from one location in File Manager to another.

Note

Before you copy multiple files or a directory full of files, make sure that you have enough storage space on the destination disk. To do this, select the destination disk-drive icon, activate the directory tree area, and check the amount of available storage displayed in the status bar at the bottom of the screen. Then activate the directory window that contains the files you want to copy, and select the files. (If you are copying an entire directory, you must select all the files in the directory.) Check the status bar again to see how much storage these files occupy. Compare the amount of space occupied by the files you want to copy with the amount of space left on the destination disk to make sure that the destination disk can receive all the files.

Follow these steps to copy files:

1. Make sure that both the source and destination are visible.

   The *source* is the item you want to copy. It can be a file in the contents list or a directory from the contents list or the directory tree.

The *destination* can be a directory icon in the directory tree or the contents list. It also can be a directory icon at the bottom of File Manager window or a disk drive icon at the top of File Manager window.

2. Activate the part of the File Manager screen that contains the source file or directory. If you are copying an entire directory, you can activate the directory tree or the contents list.

3. Select the file(s) or directory to be copied.

If you want to copy more than one file, select multiple files. You can select only one directory at a time from the directory-tree area, but you can select multiple directories in the contents list. When you copy a directory, you copy all the files and subdirectories in the directory.

4. To copy the files, drag the directory or the individual files to the destination (see fig. 4.23). Press and hold down the Ctrl key if the destination is on the same disk as the source files. Do not hold down the Ctrl key if the destination is on a different disk from the source files.

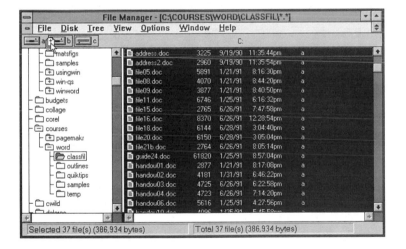

Fig. 4.23
Dragging files to a disk or directory to make copies.

Managing Your Work

You cannot drag a window to copy it, but you can use keyboard techniques to copy an entire window.

5. When the file icon is over the destination, release the mouse button; release the Ctrl key if you were using the Ctrl key.

If the destination has a file with the same name as the file you are copying, you are asked to confirm that the destination file can be replaced by the copy.

Troubleshooting

I attempted to copy to a floppy disk but got an error message saying that the disk didn't have enough room.

You can prevent this from happening by first selecting the disk you want to copy to and noticing the amount of free space. Then select the disk you are copying from, select the files you want to copy, and then look at the total number of bytes in the selected files. If there is not enough room on the disk to hold all the files to copy use a disk with more space, delete some files from the disk, or select fewer files to be copied.

Copying Many Files into Multiple Directories

A directory icon can serve as the destination for a file or files that you copy. If you want to copy files into several different directories quickly, this technique is useful. For each directory into which you want to copy the file or files, open a window by selecting the directory in the directory tree, and then choosing the Window New Window command. Minimize each new window to an icon at the bottom of the File Manager screen by clicking the Minimize button at the top right of the window. (Make sure that your original directory window is smaller than the File Manager window so that you can see the icons.) Then drag the files you want to copy onto the directory icons.

To copy files with the keyboard, follow these steps:

1. Activate the window that contains the files or directories you want to copy.

2. Select the files or directories you want to copy. If you want to select a large number of files, you can use DOS wild cards in step 4.

3. Open the **F**ile menu and choose **C**opy, or press F8. The Copy dialog box appears (see fig. 4.24).

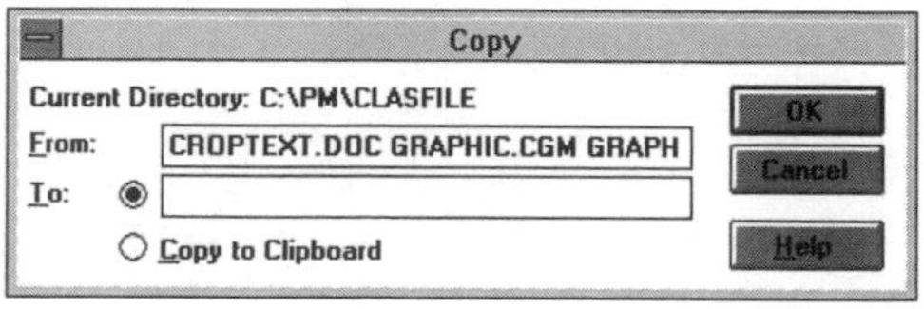

Fig. 4.24
The Copy dialog box, showing the files being copied.

4. If you want to specify a group of files to copy, type a file-name pattern in the From text box. Use the DOS wild cards * and ? to specify groups of similar file names. To specify an entire directory, type the directory path, such as **C:\BUDGET**.

5. Type the path name of the destination location in the To text box.

6. Choose OK or press Enter.

▶ "Linking Data between Applications," p. 203

▶ "Embedding Data into a Document," p. 212

If the destination has a file with the same name as the file you are copying, you are asked to confirm that the destination file can be replaced by the copy.

Use the DOS wild cards * and ? in the From text box of the Copy dialog box to copy multiple files with similar names. Remember that the * wild card matches any group of letters; the ? wild card matches any single letter in the same location. Following are some examples:

Tip
You can link a file to a different document by selecting the Copy to Clipboard option in the Copy dialog box.

File Name Pattern	Files Matched
PROJ*.XLS	PROJ05.XLS
PROJECT.XLS	PROJECTA.XLS
SM?TH.DOC	SMITH.DOC
	SMYTH.DOC but not SMITHS.DOC
*.XL?	anyname.XLS
	anyname.XLC
	anyname.XLW
.	all file names

Note

Use the Windows Recorder accessory to make a macro duplicating the keystrokes and commands you use when making backup copies of files to disk. For example, if you daily want to back up any file you have created or modified that day, use the Recorder to record each of the steps in the process. Then play back the macro at the end of each day. If you use keystrokes and commands with the Recorder rather than mouse actions, you can play back the recording no matter where or how the directory window is located.

II

Managing Your Work

Moving Files or Directories

You can move files just as easily as you can copy them. Moving files puts them in a new location and removes the originals from the old location. You move files when you need to reorganize a disk. You can move files or directories to a new directory or disk. Moving a directory moves this directory's files and subdirectories.

Selecting All Files in a Directory

If you want to move all the files in a directory, you can select all the files in the current window by opening the File menu and selecting the Move command, and then typing *.* in the From text box. Or, you can do the following:

1. Open the File menu and choose Select File.

2. Type *.* in the File(s) text box.

3. Choose Select or press Enter.

To move files or directories, follow these steps:

1. Activate the source and destination directory windows.

2. Select the files or directories you want to move.

3. To move, drag the file or directory to the destination if the destination is on the same disk. If the destination is on a different disk, press and hold down the Alt key as you drag to move a file, files, directory, or directories.

4. Release the mouse button when the icon or file is over the destination.

5. If you are asked to confirm the move, consider whether you are copying or moving and how the files will change. Then choose Yes to complete the action, No to stop a single move, or Cancel to cancel all moves.

Using the Mouse To Move or Copy Files

The following chart summarizes the mouse actions you use to move or copy files with the mouse:

Desired Action	Mouse Action
Copy to a different disk	Drag
Copy to the same disk	Ctrl+drag
Move to a different disk	Alt+drag
Move to the same disk	Drag

Creating Directories

Creating directories on a disk is like adding new drawers to a filing cabinet. It is an excellent way to reorganize or restructure the disk for new categories. After you build directories and subdirectories, you can put existing files in them using the **F**ile **M**ove and **F**ile **C**opy commands.

To make new directories, follow these steps:

1. Activate the directory-tree area. (This step is unnecessary if you want to put the new subdirectory under the currently selected directory.)

2. Select the directory under which you want a new subdirectory.

3. Open the **F**ile menu and choose the **C**reate Directory command. The Create Directory dialog box appears (see fig. 4.25).

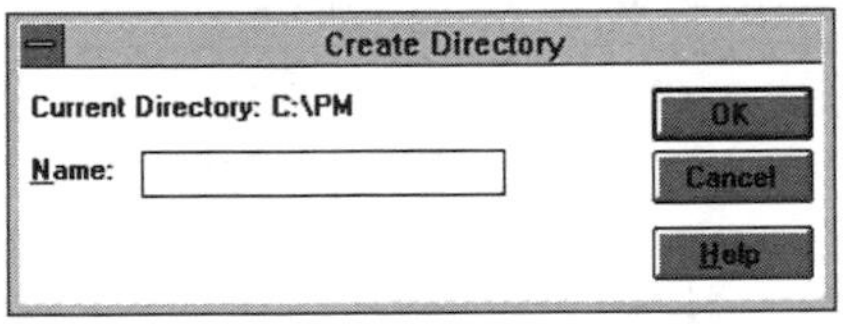

Fig. 4.25
The Create Directory dialog box.

4. Type the name of the new directory. Directory names are the same as file names; they can have eight letters in the file name and three letters in the extension.

5. Choose OK or press Enter.

Adding new subdirectories is like growing new branches on a tree—new subdirectories must sprout from existing directories or subdirectories. If you want to create multiple layers of subdirectories, first create the directories or subdirectories that precede the ones you want to add.

Create a Directory without Selecting a Directory

You can create a directory at any location without selecting the parent directory by typing the full path name in the **N**ame text box of the Create Directory dialog box.

Renaming Files or Directories

Unless you do everything perfectly the first time, sometimes you want to rename a file or directory. To rename a file or directory, select the file or directory from a directory window, open the **F**ile menu, and select the Re**n**ame command. When the Rename dialog box appears, type the new file name and choose OK or press Enter.

You can rename a group of files with a similar name or the same extension. To rename a group of files, select the files you want to rename and open the **F**ile menu and select the Re**n**ame command. Use the DOS wild cards * and ? in the **F**rom and **T**o text boxes to indicate the parts of the names you want to change. Choose OK or press Enter to rename the files. Renaming with wild cards can save you a great deal of typing, as shown by the following example:

Original File Names	From	To	Resultant File Names
ACNTAR.XLS	ACNT*.*	ACCT*.*	ACCTAR.XLS
ACNTAP.XLS	ACNT*.*	ACCT*.*	ACCTAP.XLS
ACNTTRND.XLC	ACNT*.*	ACCT*.*	ACCTTRND.XLC

Deleting Files or Directories

Delete files or directories when you want to remove old work from the disk. Deleting files gives you more available storage on a disk. Deleting directories that don't contain any files makes very little difference in storage space.

Unless you have prepared the hard disk with special software, you cannot recover files or directories after you delete them. Be very careful to select only the files or directories you want to delete. If you aren't sure about deleting files or directories, turn on the warning messages by choosing the **O**ptions **C**onfirmation command and selecting the warning messages you want.

> ### Note
>
> Be careful that you do not accidentally select a directory when you select files to be deleted. If you select a directory, open the **F**ile menu, and choose **D**elete, all the files in the directory as well as the directory itself are deleted. Deleting entire directories can be convenient, but it also can be a real surprise if it is not what you wanted to do.
>
> If you want to confirm each file or subdirectory being deleted, open the **O**ptions menu and choose **C**onfirmation; make sure that the File Delete and Directory Delete boxes are selected.

To delete files or subdirectories, follow these steps:

1. Activate the directory window that contains the files you want to delete. Activate the directory-tree area if you want to delete only directories.

2. Select the files or directories you want to delete; alternatively, use wild cards in step 4.

3. Press the Del key. The Delete dialog box appears.

4. If you did not select the files you want to delete, type their names in the Delete text box. Use DOS wild cards to select multiple files. For example, type *.* in the Delete text box to specify every file in the current directory.

5. Choose the OK button. If the Confirm File Delete dialog box appears, asking you to confirm deletions, choose **Y**es when appropriate or choose Yes to **A**ll to confirm deletion of several files.

   Use the **O**ptions **C**onfirmation command to specify the types of deletions that require a confirmation. Only by selecting options in the Confirmation dialog box will you see a Confirm File Delete dialog box in step 5.

Undeleting Files or Directories

If you are using DOS 6.0 or greater, you were asked if you wanted to install some Windows utilities that came with the new DOS versions when you upgraded to either of these versions of DOS. One of these utilities is the Microsoft Undelete program. If you installed the Windows version of this utility, it will be available both from the **F**ile menu and (if you are using Windows for Workgroups) from the toolbar.

II

Managing Your Work

It is not unusual to accidentally erase a file or an entire subdirectory. If you do this, you can open the **F**ile menu and choose Undelete to attempt to recover the files or subdirectory. Either operation requires you to start the Undelete program. This is done by either opening the **F**ile menu and choosing **U**ndelete, or clicking on the Undelete icon on the toolbar. You will then see the Microsoft Undelete window, shown in figure 4.26.

Fig. 4.26

The Microsoft Undelete program window.

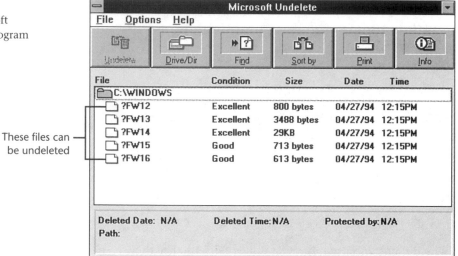

The main part of the program window indicates which files and subdirectories can be undeleted. The icon to the left of each entry indicates whether the item is a file or subdirectory. Notice that the name of the file or subdirectory begins with a question mark. This is a peculiarity of DOS; it means that the Undelete program cannot tell what the first character of the file or subdirectory name should be. To undelete the item, you need to supply the character.

The next column indicates the chances of successfully undeleting the file. Excellent is the best rating, but you could also have a prognosis of Good or Destroyed. Excellent files are those with the best chance of being recovered, although the success of the operation is not guaranteed. Files with a Good condition are those that can possibly be recovered, but there is a very good chance that one or more parts of the old file have been overwritten with new data. Files with a Destroyed condition cannot be recovered; the Undelete program will not even allow you to attempt the operation.

Notice that above the file-listing area there are several buttons that you can use to control the Undelete program. These buttons perform the same operations as menu choices under the **F**ile menu, and they should be fairly self-explanatory (they are very close in purpose to many of File Manager commands). For instance, the Drive/Dir button allows you to change the disk drive and directory on which you are working.

To undelete a file or a subdirectory, follow these steps:

1. Use the Drive/Dir button or the File Change Drive/Directory button to select the drive and directory that contains the file or subdirectory you want to undelete.

2. From the file list, select the file or subdirectory you want to undelete.

3. Click the Undelete button or open the **F**ile menu and choose **U**ndelete. Alternatively, you can open the **F**ile menu and choose **U**ndelete to undelete the file to a different drive or directory.

> **Note**
>
> Not all files can be undeleted. Your success will depend on whether the file was stored in a single place on your disk drive and whether you have done many other file operations since the file was deleted. If there is a chance that a file cannot be successfully undeleted, the Undelete program will let you know. Regardless of whether Undelete indicates it has successfully undeleted a file, you should always check the file to make sure it really is intact.

The Undelete program also offers other options that you can use to help locate deleted files. The most useful of these options is the Find capability. If you either click the Fi**n**d button or open the **F**ile menu and choose Find Deleted File, you will see the dialog box shown in figure 4.27.

Fig. 4.27
The Find Deleted
Files dialog box.

Here, you can specify both wild-card characters that are used in finding deleted file or subdirectory names, and you can specify file content you want to find. This last option is especially useful. For instance, let's say that you used to have a file that contained your list of business addresses, but you don't know the exact file name. (Was it NAMES.DAT, LIST.DOC, or NAME.TXT?) Instead of doing multiple searches, you can simply specify that you want to see all files that contain the text Barry Davidson, which is one of the names you know was in your address list. The Undelete program then displays every deleted file it finds that contains the specified information.

Copying Disks

Make duplicate copies of disks whenever you need another disk for secure storage off-site or when you need a duplicate of original program disks. To copy an entire disk to another disk, the disks must be the same size and capacity. If the original is a 3 1/2-inch high-density disk, the destination disk must be the same. To duplicate a disk, follow these steps:

1. Protect the original disk by attaching a write-protect tab on 5 1/4-inch disks or sliding the protect notch open on 3 1/2-inch disks.

2. Insert the original disk in the source disk drive.

3. Insert the disk to receive the copy (the destination disk) in the second disk drive. If you don't have a second disk drive, don't be concerned; you can switch disks in a single drive.

4. Open the **D**isk menu and choose **C**opy Disk. The Copy Disk dialog box appears. If you have only one disk drive, skip to step 7.

5. In the **S**ource In list, select the drive letter for the source drive.

6. In the **D**estination In list, select the drive letter for the destination drive (even if it is the same as the source drive).

7. Choose OK.

8. If you have only a single disk drive, you are instructed to switch the source disk and destination disk in and out of the single drive. Windows prompts you to exchange disks.

The **D**isk **C**opy Disk command formats the destination disk if it is not already formatted. If the destination disk contains data, the data is lost.

Formatting Disks

You usually cannot use new disks until you format them (some disks come already formatted). *Formatting* prepares disks for use on a computer. It is similar to preparing a blank book for use by writing in page numbers and creating a blank table of contents. If a disk contains data, formatting completely erases all existing data. Part of the process of formatting is checking for bad areas on the disk's magnetic surface   all bad areas found are identified so that data is not recorded in these areas.

To format a disk, follow these steps:

1. Put the disk to be formatted in the disk drive.

2. Open the **D**isk menu and choose **F**ormat Disk. The Format Disk dialog box appears.

3. Select the disk drive that contains the disk to be formatted in the **D**isk In drop-down list box.

4. Select the appropriate disk size in the **C**apacity drop-down list box.

5. If you want to assign a label to the disk, type the label in the **L**abel text box.

6. Select **M**ake System Disk if you want to use the disk to start the computer. Do not use this option unless it is needed because the system files use storage space on the disk that can otherwise be used for data.

7. Select **Q**uick Format to save time if the disk has been formatted and you're reasonably sure that the disk does not have bad areas.

8. Choose OK. A message box warns you that formatting will erase all data on the disk. If you're sure, choose **Y**es.

9. After this disk is formatted, you are given the chance to format additional disks.

Format an entire box of disks at one time, and put a label on each disk when it is formatted. This system lets you know that open boxes contain formatted disks; the labels confirm that the disks are formatted.

If you have a disk you want to change to a system disk (one that can start the computer), put the disk in a disk drive, open the **D**isk menu, and choose the **M**ake System Disk command. Choose the disk drive that contains the disk. Windows copies files from the hard disk onto the disk so that you can boot the computer from this disk.

Labeling Disks

Although you may be accustomed to putting a paper label on disks, both hard disks and disks can have magnetically recorded labels, known as *volume labels*. Volume labels appear at the top of the directory tree area when the drive with the volume label is active. Not all disks have or need this kind of label.

You just learned how to create a volume label when you format a disk. If you want to create or change a volume label on a previously formatted disk, select the drive icon, open the **D**isk menu, and choose the **L**abel Disk command. When the Label Disk dialog box appears, type a label name of up to 11 characters, and choose OK or press Enter.

Getting Information about a DoubleSpace Drive

DoubleSpace is a system that allows you to double the amount of information you can store on a disk. DoubleSpace is available with DOS 6 or greater. This is done through device drivers that compress and store information in a non-standard format on the disk. When you later read the information, DoubleSpace uncompresses the information. This compression and decompression are transparent to you, the user.

If you are using any DoubleSpace drives, File Manager provides a way for you to get information about the status of the drive. This is done by first clicking on the DoubleSpace drive, and then either choosing Too**l**s **D**oubleSpace or (if you are using Windows for Workgroups) by clicking the DoubleSpace icon on the toolbar. You will see an informational window similar to what is shown in figure 4.28.

Fig. 4.28
Getting information about a DoubleSpace drive.

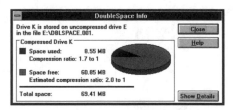

This window details how space is being used in the DoubleSpace drive. You can see, both graphically and through statistics, what is in use and what is available.

Printing Files

You can send text files directly to the printer from File Manager. For example, many software applications come with last-minute corrections and additional information stored in a text file. The information usually is not in the printed manual. These text files, which usually have the extension TXT, contain information such as helpful tips, corrections to the manual, and hardware configuration settings not covered in the manual. It often is helpful to print these files.

▶ "Adding and Configuring Printers," p. 284

When you print with File Manager, you send the file to the default printer. To change the default printer, use Control Panel.

To print a file with File Manager, the file must be associated with an application. To print a file using File Manager, follow these steps:

1. Activate the directory window that contains the file or files you want to print.

2. Select the file or files you want to print.

3. Open the **F**ile menu and choose the **P**rint command.

4. Choose OK or press Enter.

You also can use File Manager's drag-and-drop feature to print; see the section, "Using File Manager's Drag-and-Drop Feature," later in this chapter.

Protecting Your Data

If you are using DOS 6.0 or greater, you were asked if you wanted to install some Windows utilities that came with the new DOS versions when you upgraded to either of these versions of DOS. Two of these utilities allow you to proactively protect the data on your computer: Microsoft Backup and Microsoft Anti-Virus. If you installed the Windows version of these utilities, they will be available both from the T**o**ols menu and (if you are using Windows for Workgroups) from the toolbar.

Backing Up Your Files

One of the important activities that many computer users either forget or ignore is backing up files. In a sense, backing up your files is nothing but cheap insurance—you may never need your backups, but if you do, they are invaluable.

II

Managing Your Work

Microsoft Backup is a full-featured program that comes with DOS 6 or greater and enables you to perform the following tasks:

- Copy one or more files from your hard disk to another disk (usually a floppy disk).

- Restore your backed-up files to any location you choose (including their original locations).

- Compare files on your backup disks with the original files to ensure their validity.

As you already know, there is more information stored on your hard drive than you could possibly fit on a single floppy disk. Microsoft Backup automatically overcomes this problem by spreading your backup across multiple floppy disks—as many as are needed to back up your data. These floppy disks are collectively referred to as a *backup set*. During the backup operation, each disk in the set is filled to capacity before the next disk is requested.

> **Note**
>
> Before you can create backups of your data, you must first test the Backup program for compatibility with your computer hardware. This test is automatically performed the first time you run Microsoft Backup. The tests check out your floppy disk drives, as well as the speed of your processor chip and hard drive. There is really very little you need to do to complete the testing. Periodically, dialog boxes appear and ask you for permission to continue. In these cases, respond to the prompts and the Backup program will continue. When the tests are finished running, your configuration information is saved to disk so it can be used whenever you run the Backup program again.

To start the backup program, you should open the Tools menu and choose **B**ackup, or click the Backup icon on the toolbar. When you do this, the Backup program starts and the files on your hard disk are quickly scanned. Shortly, you see the Microsoft Backup program window, shown in figure 4.29.

The Backup program has five basic functions that are represented by buttons on the toolbar near the top of the screen. These functions are:

- **B**ackup copies one or more files from your hard disk to floppy disks.

- **C**ompare compares the files in a backup set to make sure they match the source files on the hard disk.

- **R**estore copies one or more files from your backup set to the hard disk or to another floppy.

- **Co**nfigure enables you to change how the program functions regarding your hardware.

- **Q**uit enables you to exit the program.

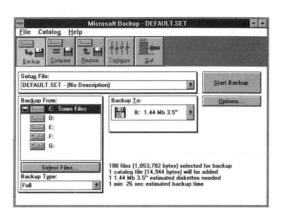

Fig. 4.29
The Microsoft Backup program window.

Besides these major functions (which are covered shortly), there are several other operations that can be accessed from the pull-down menus. For instance, the **F**ile menu enables you to load and save setup files that define settings to be used when backing up and restoring files. The **F**ile menu also enables you to print a list of files contained in a backup set. The Catalo**g** menu enables you to select catalog files (included with the backup sets) for restoring or comparison.

To perform a backup, follow these steps:

1. Click on the Backup icon on the toolbar. Your screen will appear as shown in figure 4.29.

2. Select the drive to back up from the Bac**k**up From list by double-clicking the appropriate drive. You may choose more than one drive. Each time you choose a drive, the Backup program scans the drive and adds the selected files to the totals. (Notice that the program window is updated to indicate how many floppy disks you will need to perform the backup.)

3. Choose a Backup T**y**pe. Full means that everything you select is backed up, Incremental means that everything that is new or has changed since the last backup is copied, and Differential means that everything that is new or has changed since the last Full backup is copied.

4. Click the **S**tart Backup button.

You next see a dialog box, informing you that you should not use the disk drives for anything else while Backup is working; the program expects to be the only program using them. You are prompted to insert your first floppy disk, and you will be prompted every time Backup needs a new disk. As the backup progresses, a display similar to figure 4.30 appears.

Fig. 4.30
During a backup.

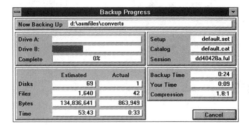

As each floppy disk is completed, remove it from the drive and label it so that you know the backup-disk number. You may also want to use a date so that you know when the backup was made.

Verifying Backup Files

The first time you use a series of disks for a backup, or any time you want to be absolutely sure of your backup, you should do a comparison. When you compare the backups to the original files, you verify that the disks are both readable and accurate. To perform a compare, follow these steps:

1. Click the Compare icon on the toolbar. The Microsoft Backup program window appears, as shown in figure 4.31.

2. Choose Bac**k**up Set Catalog, and select the setup file you used for the backup. (If you haven't saved any setup files, this will be DEFAULT.SET.)

3. Select the drive or drives from the Compar**e** From list.

4. Click the **S**tart Compare button.

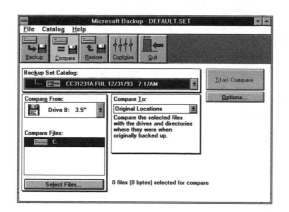

Fig. 4.31
Getting ready to
do a comparison.

As the comparison continues, you are prompted to insert each backup disk in turn, and a progress screen keeps you apprised of events. At the end of the comparison, you are informed of how many errors (if any) were found.

Restoring Backup Files

Restoring data using your backup files and Microsoft Backup is quick and easy. To do so, follow these steps:

1. Click the Restore icon on the toolbar. The Microsoft Backup program window appears.

2. Choose Ba**c**kup Set Catalog, and select the setup file you used for the backup.

3. Select the drive or drives from the Resto**re** From list.

4. Select a destination for the restored files in the Restore **T**o list.

5. Click the Start Restore button.

You are prompted to insert disks whenever one is needed by the Backup program. When the program is done, you can exit and use the restored files in any way you see fit.

Using Microsoft Anti-Virus

A computer *virus* is a program, written by unscrupulous programmers, designed to do damage to either your computer or your computer data. Viruses are designed to make copies of themselves and spread from one computer to another, as they do in people. Just as a doctor can help provide ways to protect yourself from getting sick, you can also protect your computer from a virus that may attack it.

II

Managing Your Work

The best method of protection is prevention. There are only two ways in which viruses can be transmitted between computers: loading and running infected software, or booting up with an infected floppy disk. If you don't do either of these things, your system won't acquire a virus.

Understanding that such an insulated approach to computers is virtually impossible, Microsoft provides a program called Microsoft Anti-Virus, available with DOS 6 or greater, which can detect and eliminate many different types of viruses. Used correctly, a good virus program can protect you against the vast majority of known viruses before they damage your computer.

To start the Anti-Virus program, you should open the Tools menu and choose **A**ntivirus, or click on the Anti-Virus icon on the toolbar. When you do this, the Anti-Virus program is started and the files on your hard disk are quickly scanned. Shortly you will see the Microsoft Anti-Virus program window, shown in Figure 4.32.

Fig. 4.32
The Microsoft
Anti-Virus
program window.

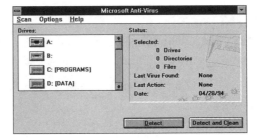

The operation of the program is very simple. All you need to do is select a disk drive you want to scan, and then click on either the **D**etect or the Detect and **C**lean buttons. The difference between the two is the action that Anti-Virus will take upon uncovering a virus. If you select **D**etect, you are only notified about the presence of a virus. Detect and **C**lean, on the other hand, attempts to eliminate any viruses that it encounters.

Starting Applications and Documents

◄ "Customizing
Groups," p. 95

Using the Program Manager and group windows is the best way to start frequently used applications. You can use Program Manager to group together a frequently used application and an associated document to make them readily accessible.

On some occasions, however, the application you want to start may not be in a group window. When this happens, start the application directly from File Manager. You can start any application from File Manager.

Starting an Application

Starting an application from File Manager is easy with the mouse: just open the directory window that contains the application and double-click on the name of the application.

Starting an application with the keyboard is almost as easy: open the directory window that contains the application, select the application name, and press Enter. Alternatively, open the **F**ile menu and choose the **O**pen or **R**un commands.

▶ "Loading and Running DOS Applications," p. 738

Application file names end with EXE or COM. You may have to start some DOS applications by double-clicking on a file with the extension BAT or PIF.

You can specify some document or data files so that they start an application. Choosing this associated document or data file starts the application and loads the document or data as well.

If an application is associated with a specific file extension, you can start an application by using the same starting procedures on a document file. Pretend that the document file is the application you want to start—Windows starts the associated application and then loads the selected document file.

If you want to start an application with a document or with special arguments that modify how the application runs, open the **F**ile menu and choose **R**un. In the Command Line text box, type the directory path and full application name. Press the space bar and type the name of the document you want the application to load. Choose OK or press Enter.

If you want the application to minimize to an icon as soon as it starts, select the Run **M**inimized check box from the Run dialog box before choosing OK.

See the section "Using File Manager's Drag-and-Drop Feature" to learn how you can start an application by dragging a document icon onto an application icon.

Associating Documents with an Application

One of the convenient features of Windows is its capacity to start an application when you choose an *associated document*, which is one that runs with a particular application. When you choose an associated document, Windows finds the application that runs the document, starts the application, and then

II

Managing Your Work

loads the document. Many Windows applications create associations for their own files by modifying the Windows WIN.INI file when the application is installed. You also can add associations to fit your applications and work habits.

Spreadsheet files with the extension XLS, for example, are associated with Microsoft Excel. This association is made automatically because installing Excel modifies the WIN.INI file. You may be in an office with people who use Lotus 1-2-3, for example. Because Excel can open and save Lotus 1-2-3 files, you can associate Lotus 1-2-3 files with the Excel application. After you associate a Lotus 1-2-3 file with Excel, you can choose this 1-2-3 file to make Excel start and load the 1-2-3 worksheet and charts.

To associate a document file with a specific application, follow these steps:

1. Activate the directory window that contains the data file (document file) you want to associate with an application.

2. Select the name of the file you want associated. Windows associates document files to applications by checking the file extension of the document file.

3. Open the **F**ile menu and choose **A**ssociate. This brings up the Associate dialog box (see fig. 4.33). The extension for the document you selected is listed in the Files with Extension text box.

Fig. 4.33
The Associate
dialog box.

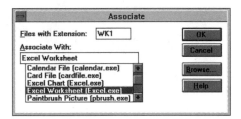

4. Scroll through the list box attached to the Associate With text box. Find the name of the application you want to associate with all files using the extension shown in the **F**iles with Extension text box. Select the application name if you find it.

   If necessary, type the full path and file name of the application. If you're unsure of the correct directory path, you can search for it by choosing the Browse button.

5. Choose OK or press Enter.

Some DOS applications, such as WordPerfect, can use any file extension for data documents. In this case, you must associate each of the different file extensions you use with WordPerfect to the WordPerfect application.

▶ "Creating and Using PIFs," p. 741

Some DOS applications may not start directly from an associated file. Other applications may start but not run with optimal configuration.

Using File Manager's Drag-and-Drop Feature

File Manager's drag-and-drop feature enables you to print files, link or embed files, create program-item icons, and start applications by dragging File Manager icons or file names with a mouse. You also drag and drop icons to copy and move files, as described in other sections in this chapter.

To use the drag-and-drop feature, you need to be able to see two things on your screen: File Manager or the source—displaying the file you want to drag, and the destination—displaying the icon or document where you want to drag the file. Before you drag and drop File Manager icons, arrange windows on your screen so that you can see both. In some cases, such as when you are starting an application, File Manager is both source and destination, so you must open two File Manager windows.

To learn how to use the drag-and-drop feature for copying and moving, see the sections in this chapter on "Copying Files or Directories" and "Moving Files or Directories."

Using Drag and Drop To Print

To print a file using the drag-and-drop feature, you must be able to see the file you want to print in File Manager, and you must be able to see Print Manager's program icon or window on your desktop. If Print Manager is not running, start it from Program Manager.

You also must be sure that the document you want to print is associated with its application. To learn how to do that, refer to the section in this chapter on "Associating Documents with an Application."

To use the drag-and-drop feature to print, follow these steps:

1. Start File Manager, if necessary, and locate the file you want to print.

2. Start Print Manager, if necessary.

3. In File Manager, position the mouse pointer over the file you want to print. Click and hold down the left mouse button and drag the file onto Print Manager's window or icon.

   As you drag, you see a changing icon. When the icon appears as a page with a plus (+) sign inside it, and you are sure that you are on top of Printer Manager's window or icon, release the mouse button.

If a message box appears telling you that no association exists for the file or that the association data is incomplete, then you must complete the association or use the application to print your file.

Using Drag and Drop To Link or Embed

▶ "Embedding
Data as
Packages,"
p. 220

One of the easiest ways to link or embed a file into a document is to drag the file name from File Manager onto the open document. Embedding a file in this way creates a package, which appears in the document as an icon. You can edit the package, or you can double-click the icon to start the application containing the embedded file.

To use the drag-and-drop feature to link or embed a file, follow these steps:

1. Start File Manager, if necessary, and locate the file you want to link or embed.

2. Start the application containing the document into which you want to link or embed a file (if you haven't already), and open the document. Display the location in the document where you want to insert the linked or embedded file.

3. In File Manager, position the mouse pointer over the file you want to link or embed. Click and hold down the left mouse button and drag the file onto the document where you want the file to be linked or embedded.

   As you drag, you see a changing icon. When the icon appears as a page with a plus (+) sign inside it, and you are sure that you are on top of the document icon into which you want to link or embed the file, release the mouse button.

Using Drag and Drop To Create a Program Item Icon

You can quickly create a program item icon in Program Manager by dragging a program file from File Manager onto Program Manager. Follow these steps:

1. Start File Manager and locate the application for which you want to create a program-item icon.

2. Activate Program Manager and display the group window in which you want to add your new program item icon.

3. Arrange File Manager and Program Manager windows so that you can see both the application for which you want to create the program item icon and the group window in which you want to create it.

4. Drag the application file name from File Manager onto Program Manager. Release the mouse button when the application name is over the group window where you want to create the program item icon.

Using Drag and Drop To Start an Application

You can quickly start an application by dragging a document file icon onto an application icon. The application starts, and the document opens. Follow these steps:

1. Start File Manager and open two windows: one displaying the directory containing the document file you want to open and one displaying the directory containing the application you want to start. Open the **W**indow menu and choose **N**ew Window to open a new window or double-click on a disk-drive icon.

2. Tile the two windows by opening the **W**indow menu and choosing **T**ile.

3. Scroll each window so that you can see both the document and the application file names.

4. Drag the document file name onto the application file name. Release the mouse button when the document file name is over the application file name.

Working with Networks in Windows for Workgroups

When you are using Windows for Workgroups on a network, you can share directories with other users in your workgroup. You can open the files in any directory that has been designated as shared by another user, and you can share any of your directories so that the files in that directory can be shared by other users. File Manager is where you connect to directories that others have shared, and where you share directories on your computer that you want others to have access to.

Connecting to Shared Directories

You can connect to any directory that has been designated as shared by any user on your network (to learn how to share a directory, see the next section, "Sharing a Directory"). You connect to a directory by using File Manager. When you connect to a directory, File Manager creates a network drive for that directory and assigns a letter to that drive. You can view the files in that directory by selecting the drive icon assigned to that directory or by selecting the drive from the drive list in the toolbar. You open files in the directory in exactly the same way you open a file on your own hard disk. Whether you can modify the file depends on the level of access the owner of the directory has granted to other users.

Connecting to a Network Directory

To connect to a shared directory, follow these steps:

1. Click the Connect Network Drive button on the toolbar.

   or

   Open the **D**isk menu and choose Connect **N**etwork Drive.

   The Connect Network Drive dialog box shown in figure 4.34 appears.

2. By default, File Manager assigns the next available drive letter on your computer to the directory you select to connect to. To assign a different letter, open the **D**rive list and select a letter from the list.

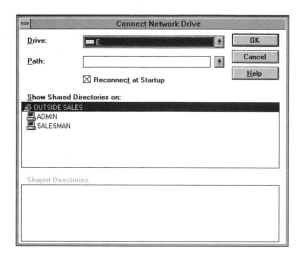

Fig. 4.34
Select the directory you want to connect to in the Connect Network Drive dialog box.

3. Enter the path for the shared directory in the **P**ath box.

   The path includes the computer name where the directory is located and the share name assigned to that directory. The computer name is preceded by double backslashes and is separated from the share name by a single backslash: for example, \\SALESMAN\SALES.

   There are three methods for entering the path:

   If you know the path for the directory, you can type it directly in the **P**ath text box.

   or

   You can open the Path drop-down list and select a path from a list of recently used paths.

   or

   Double-click on a workgroup icon in the Show Shared Directories on list (or select the icon with the arrow keys and press Enter) to expand the workgroup. Select a name from the computer names listed under the workgroup to display a list of shared directories in the Shared Directories box. When you find the directory to which you want to connect, select it.

4. If you want to automatically reconnect to this shared directory at startup, choose the Reconnect at Startup button.

5. Choose OK or press Enter.

When you connect to a shared directory, a new window for that directory will appear if the **O**pen New Window on Connect option in the **O**ptions menu is selected. To select this option, open the **O**ptions menu and choose **O**pen New Window on Connect. A check mark appears next to the command when it is turned on. If you do not want a new window to open each time you connect to a shared directory, turn this option off.

Disconnecting from a Network Drive

To disconnect from a network drive, follow these steps:

1. Click the Disconnect Network Drive button on the toolbar.

   or

   Open the **D**isk menu and choose **D**isconnect Network Drive.

   The Disconnect Network Drive dialog box, shown in figure 4.35 appears.

Fig. 4.35
Use the Disconnect Network Drive dialog box to disconnect from a shared directory.

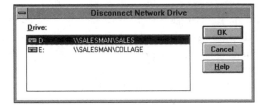

2. Select from the **D**rive list the drive you want to disconnect.

   You can select additional directories from the list if you want to disconnect from more than one directory at once. To select more than one directory, click on the first directory, hold down the Ctrl key, and click on subsequent directories. To deselect a directory, hold down the Ctrl key and click on the directory. To use the keyboard, select the first directory, press Shift+F8, use the up- and down-arrow keys to move to the next directory, and press the space bar. Move to additional directories and press the space bar. To deselect a directory and retain the other selections, move to the selected directory and press the space bar. To return to selecting a single directory at a time, press Shift+F8 again.

3. Choose OK or press Enter.

Sharing Directories

You can designate any directory on your computer as shared. When you *share* a directory, you can assign a share name and password to that directory. You can also specify what type of access users have to the shared directory. After you have shared a directory, other users have access to the files in that directory. You must be running in 386 Enhanced mode to share a directory on your computer. The computers that have the directories you want to share must be on and logged on to the network.

Caution

Be very careful when using shared directories. It is very easy to put confidential data into a shared directory so that another user in your workgroup can retrieve it. While the data is in the shared directory, however, it is accessible to everyone else in the workgroup. If you put confidential information into a directory use one of the following methods to preserve confidentiality:

■ Put a password on the data when it is saved in the application that created the data

■ Create a shared directory that has a password that you change frequently and distribute discreetly

■ Use Chat to talk with the other user as you copy the file into your shared directory and they retrieve it. As soon as they have retrieved the file, delete it.

Sharing a Directory

To share a directory, follow these steps:

1. Using the mouse or the keyboard, select the directory you want to share.

2. Click the Share As button on the toolbar.

   or

   Open the **D**isk menu and choose Share **A**s.

   The Share Directory dialog box shown in figure 4.36 appears.

3. The name of the directory you selected in step 1 is the default name of the shared directory. You can type a new name in the **S**hare Name box.

Fig. 4.36
The Share
Directory dialog
box is used
to share a
directory on
your computer.

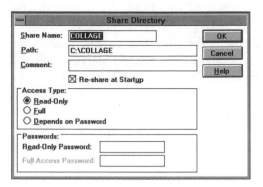

4. The path of the directory you selected in step 1 appears in the **P**ath box. If you selected the wrong directory in step 1, type in the path for the correct directory.

5. You can type a comment in the **C**omment box. This comment appears next to the share name in the Connect Network Drive dialog box, and it can be helpful for other users when those users are looking for a particular shared directory to connect to.

6. If you want to automatically reshare the directory at start up, select the Reshare at Start**u**p check box.

7. Select an access option in the Access Type group.

   You can grant users two levels of access of a shared directory. If you want users to be able only to read files and run programs in a directory, select the **R**ead-Only option. If you want users to be able to read, modify, rename, move, delete, or create files and run your programs, select the **F**ull option. If you want the level of access to depend on which password the user enters, select the **D**epends on Password option.

   If you want to limit access to the files in the shared directory to certain users, assign a password to the directory, and only give the password to those users. If you selected the **D**epends on Password option, you need to enter two passwords: one for users who have read-only access to your files, and one for users with full access. If you want all users to have access to your files, don't assign a password.

8. Type a password in one or both of the Read-Only Password or Full Access Password boxes, depending on which option you selected in step 7.

9. Choose OK or press Enter.

Unsharing a Directory

To stop sharing a directory, follow these steps:

1. Click the Stop Sharing button on the toolbar.

or

Open the **D**isk menu and choose S**t**op Sharing.

The Stop Sharing dialog box appears (see fig. 4.37).

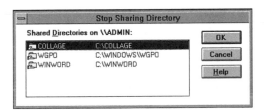

Fig. 4.37
Select the directories you want to stop sharing in the Stop Sharing dialog box.

2. Select the name of the directory you want to stop sharing in the Shared **D**irectories on list.

You can choose additional directories from the list if you want to stop sharing more than one directory at once. To select more than one directory, click the first directory, hold down the Ctrl key, and click subsequent directories. To deselect a directory, hold down the Ctrl key and click the directory. To use the keyboard, select the first directory, press Shift+F8, use the up- and down-arrow keys to move to the next directory, and press the space bar. Move to additional directories and press the space bar. To deselect a directory and retain the other selections, move to the selected directory and press the space bar. To return to selecting a single directory at a time, press Shift+F8 again.

3. Choose OK or press Enter.

Changing the Password, Share Name, or Comment for a Shared Directory

You can use the **D**isk Share **A**s command to change the password, share name, or comment for a shared directory. To change any of these properties, follow these steps:

1. Using the mouse or keyboard, select the directory you want to modify.

2. Click the Share As button on the toolbar.

   or

   Open the **D**isk menu and choose Share **A**s.

   The Share Directory dialog box, shown in figure 4.29, appears.

3. Change the entries in the **S**hare Name, **C**omment, or **P**assword boxes, as needed.

4. Choose OK or press Enter.

Viewing Workgroup Directories

You can find out which directories are being shared in the workgroups on your network. To view the directories in the workgroups on your network, follow these steps:

1. Click the Connect Network Drive button on the toolbar.

   or

   Open the **D**isk menu and choose Connect **N**etwork Drive.

   The Connect Network Drive dialog box appears.

2. Double-click the workgroup whose directories you want to view in the **S**how Shared Directories on list, or use the arrow keys to select the workgroup and press Enter.

3. Select the computer whose directories you want to view from the list of computer names under the workgroup name.

   A list of shared directories appears in the Shared Directories box.

4. In the Shared Directories box, select the shared directory to which you want to connect.

5. Choose OK or press Enter.

As an alternative to selecting a directory and choosing OK, double-click on the directory to which you want to connect in the Shared Directories list.

Your computer will probably have a specified limit to the number of local or network drives to which it can be connected. If you attempt to connect to a network drive and your computer has already used all the drives it has available, then you will get a warning message. This message says that the drive letter you specified in the Drive pull-down list is invalid.

The number of drives your computer can be connected to is specified in the CONFIG.SYS file, which is probably located in your root (C:\) directory. Using the Windows Notepad, you can open the CONFIG.SYS file and change the LASTDRIVE command to allow additional network drives. The LASTDRIVE command appears in the following form:

```
LASTDRIVE=F
```

In this case, good drive F is the last allowable drive. Change the last letter and save the CONFIG.SYS file back to its original directory. You must exit Windows and restart your computer before you can take advantage of the extra drives you can now connect.

Viewing the Users of a Shared Directory

If you are sharing directories with other users, you may want to know which of those directories are being used by other users at any time, or you may want to know which users are using specific files. For example, if someone else is using a file of yours in a directory you are sharing, you may want to find out who is using the file. You may want to know who is using one of your shared files so you can warn them if you need to turn off your computer. Some files also restrict the access or capabilities of other users while they are being shared. In that case, you may want to ask the user to stop using the file so that another user can have full access.

To view the names of users of a directory or file, follow these steps:

1. Using the mouse or keyboard, select the directory or file you want to check.

2. Open the File menu and choose Properties, or press Alt+Enter.

3. Choose the **O**pen By button to display the Open Files dialog box (see fig. 4.38). The **O**pen By button only appears in the Properties for dialog box when you have selected a shared directory or file in step 1.

Fig. 4.38
The Open Files dialog box displays a list of shared files that are in use by others.

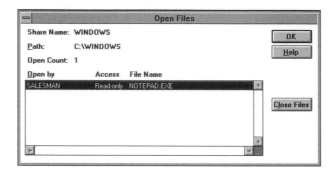

4. Choose OK twice or press Enter twice to return to the directory window.

Closing a File in a Shared Directory

If someone is using one of your files in a directory you have shared, you cannot open that file. If you want to be able to access your file, you can close the file. Be aware that the person using the file at the time you close it may lose data. Use the procedure described in the preceding section to learn who is using the file and then ask the person to close the file.

If you must forcefully close a shared file regardless of the other user, follow these steps:

1. Select the directory in which the file is located or select the file itself.

2. Open the **F**ile menu and choose Properties.

3. Choose the **O**pen By button.

4. Select the file you want to close from the **O**pen By list.

5. Choose the **C**lose button.

6. Choose OK twice or press Enter twice to return to the directory window.

Working with Non-Windows for Workgroups Networks

If the computer is connected to a network, you may have access to more than one hard disk drive. You can access those drives through Windows if you are logged on to the network. Each hard disk drive on the network shows up in File Manager window as a hard disk icon that is different from the local drive icons. When you select a network drive icon, the path to this drive displays in the status bar at the bottom of File Manager window. In a LAN environment, the computer is known as a *workstation*.

Drives on the network appear in File Manager with a special network disk drive icon (see fig. 4.39).

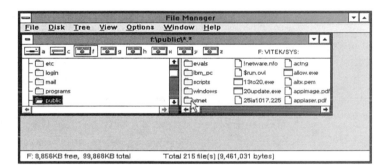

Fig. 4.39
File Manager showing a network disk drive icon.

If you want to use network drives with Windows, you must log on to the network before you start Windows. See the network administrator for the procedure on how to log on to the network. When you connect the computer to a network, you have additional disk drives available. You can use these additional drives with Windows if you know the path name to the drive and the password.

> **Note**
>
> If you connect a DOS application to a network while this application is running in Windows, disconnect from the network before quitting the application.

> **Note**
>
> If you logged on to the network before starting Windows in 386 Enhanced mode, you may not be able to log out from the network while you are in Windows. To log out from the network, exit Windows and then type **Logout** or another command, depending on your network.
>
> If you want to use network drives with Windows, you must connect to the network before you start Windows for the Windows network commands to be available. If you start Windows without first connecting to the network, the network commands are gray and therefore unavailable.

Working with Network Drives

Windows 3.1 works more seamlessly with networks than did Windows 3.0. If your computer is connected to a network, you can use any network drive, provided that you know which server the drive is connected to and that you have authorization to the server. Depending on the network you are using, you may be able to browse through the available drives.

Windows 3.1 remembers connections that you have established. If you established network connections in previous Windows sessions, they are reconnected. Connections made in File Manager are treated like any other drive or subdirectory on your local hard disk. You may start programs from the server or use the drag-and-drop feature with a file.

From Here...

File Manager plays a central role in the operation of Windows. Because of that, it is related to many other topics in Windows. For more information on working with files, refer to the following chapters:

- Chapter 3, "Controlling Applications with Program Manager," explains how to run and otherwise manage applications under Windows.

- Chapter 6, "Advanced Data Sharing," covers how to embed and link files and portions of files.

■ Chapter 9, "Printing with Windows," teaches you how to use Print Manager and other printing controls within Windows.

■ Chapter 22, "Running, Installing, and Configuring DOS Applications," discusses using DOS batch files and running other DOS programs under Windows.

II

Managing Your Work

Chapter 5

Simple Data Sharing

One of the most useful features of Windows is its capability to run multiple applications—both Windows and DOS applications—at the same time and to transfer data between those applications. Windows enables you to use different Windows applications as though they were parts of a single application. By integrating applications, you multiply their power, making your work more efficient and your results more professional.

There are several methods for transferring data between applications:

- Copying and pasting text or graphics between applications via the Clipboard. DOS applications can receive only alphanumeric (text and numbers) data

- Transferring text or graphics by saving the file from one application, and reading and converting the file into another application

- Linking text or graphics between Windows applications by using a Copy and Paste Link command

- Embedding data or graphics from a server Windows application into a client Windows application so that the data from the server document actually is stored inside the client document

- Transferring data between Windows applications with Dynamic Data Exchange under the control of a macro application

▶ "Linking Data between Applications," p. 203

▶ "Embedding Data into a Document," p. 212

In this chapter, you learn about the first two methods. The simplest method for transferring information, either text or graphics, from one application to another is to use the **E**dit **C**opy and **E**dit **P**aste commands, common to all Windows applications, to transfer data with the Clipboard. This method simply copies (or moves) the data from one application to another. The data in the application that receives the information is not linked in any way to the original data source. You can also transfer data by saving the data in one application in a format that is compatible with another application. The data file can then be opened in the second application. In Chapter 6, "Advanced Data Sharing," you learn how to link and embed data from one application to another, enabling you to integrate your applications to a much greater degree than is possible with the simple methods you learn in this chapter.

In this chapter, you learn how to:

- Transfer data with the **C**opy and **P**aste commands

- Copy between DOS and Windows applications

- Exchange data by using files

Transferring Data with Copy and Paste

Copying and pasting—the same way you move text or graphics in a document—is the simplest method of transferring small amounts of data or graphics between applications. To copy from one Windows application to another Windows application, follow these general steps:

1. Select the text, cells, or graphic in the originating document.

2. Open the **E**dit menu and choose **C**opy.

3. Switch to the receiving document—the application in which you want to paste the data.

4. Position the insertion point where you want the data to appear in the document.

5. Open the **E**dit menu and choose **P**aste.

Troubleshooting

*When I open the **E**dit menu to paste data into a document, the **P**aste command is gray.*

Before you can paste selected data from one application to another, or from one part of a document to another, you must select the data you want to transfer. Then open the **E**dit menu, and choose either **C**opy or Cu**t**. Until you do this, there is nothing in the Clipboard to paste, so the **P**aste command is grayed out.

*I opened the **E**dit command and chose **P**aste, but the data that was inserted was not the data I intended to paste in.*

When you use the **E**dit **C**opy and **E**dit Cu**t** commands, whatever data (text or graphics) is currently selected is placed into the Clipboard. The data remains in the Clipboard until you copy or cut something else, which then replaces whatever was already there. Be sure you paste the data before you cut or copy any other data.

Text pastes into the document as formatted text. Microsoft Excel worksheet cells or ranges paste in as a table. Graphics paste in as pictures. None of them are linked to the server document. If you double-click a picture, however, it loads a graphics application such as Microsoft Paintbrush or Microsoft Draw, which can be used to edit the picture.

▶ "Editing Embedded Objects," p. 215

Viewing Data in the Clipboard

Windows 3.1 transfers copied or linked data between applications using the Clipboard, which is a temporary storage area for data being transferred or linked. The Clipboard takes its name from an artist's clipboard, where cut items are stored until they can be pasted down in new locations.

▶ "Viewing and Using Data in the ClipBook Viewer," p. 626

If you need to see the information currently in the Clipboard, open Clipboard Viewer located in the Main program window. Inside the Clipboard Viewer window, you can see the contents or a description of the Clipboard's contents (see fig. 5.1).

Use the **F**ile **S**ave command and **F**ile **O**pen command to save Clipboard contents as files that can be retrieved for later use. In the **D**isplay menu, you can see the different ways in which the current contents can be pasted. When you copy a selection into the Clipboard, Windows queries the application to see which formats it supports. Windows lists all these formats in the **D**isplay menu and selects the one that gives the best copy. Normally, the **D**isplay **A**uto command is selected. If you want to paste the Clipboard contents in a

▶ "Saving the Information in the Clipboard," p. 629

Fig. 5.1
You can view the
contents of the
Clipboard with the
Clipboard Viewer.

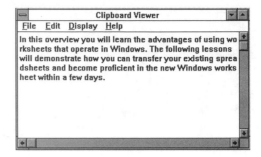

different format, you can choose a different format in the **D**isplay menu or use the **E**dit Paste **S**pecial command of the client document.

You can clear the contents from the Clipboard by selecting the Clipboard window and pressing the Del key. Choose **Y**es when the message box asking you to confirm your choice appears.

Copying between DOS and Windows Applications

Windows makes DOS applications more productive, too. You can use DOS applications under Windows to copy budget and report information from an accounting application or 1-2-3 spreadsheet, for example. You then can paste that information into a DOS or Windows application—helpful if you want to copy a column of numbers from Lotus 1-2-3 and paste them into a DOS accounting application. DOS applications can copy and paste data, but they cannot link or embed data.

Windows applications and DOS applications can exchange data in two ways: you can copy and paste data between the applications, or you can use a common file format that both applications understand. Copying and pasting data with DOS applications is easier when Windows is operating in 386 Enhanced mode. When Windows runs in 386 Enhanced mode, you can easily switch between applications, and select portions of the screen to copy and paste into another application. If Windows is running in Standard mode, Windows can copy only the entire screen of data.

DOS applications handle multiple lines of pasted data differently, depending on how the application deals with the carriage return at the end of a line. If you paste multiple lines of data into Lotus 1-2-3 for DOS, for example, all lines of text copied into the Clipboard are pasted into the same spreadsheet cell; each line is entered over the top of the preceding line. You therefore should paste cells one at a time in Lotus 1-2-3 for DOS. Word processors accept multiple lines of data and paste all the copied lines to a separate line. Each line, however, ends with a carriage return.

Capturing DOS and Windows Screens for Documentation

Windows presents you with an excellent set of tools for creating training materials and documentation. In Windows, you can run the software you want to document and the Windows software used to create the documentation simultaneously. To put a snapshot of the screen into the Clipboard, press the PrtScr key. You then can paste the screen shot into Windows-composition software, such as PageMaker, Word for Windows, or Ami Professional. You can use this technique to document Windows or DOS software.

The following technique captures a 1-2-3 for DOS screen and pastes it into PageMaker, Word for Windows, or Ami Pro (see fig. 5.2). You also can capture screens of Windows applications and easily insert snapshots of application screens into documentation or training materials. To use this technique, follow these steps:

1. Start 1-2-3 and retrieve the spreadsheet you want to document.

2. Start the Windows software that you are using to write the documentation. (In this example, you use the word processing software Word for Windows.)

3. Activate the 1-2-3 application. If the application is running in a window in 386 Enhanced mode, press Alt+Enter to expand 1-2-3 to full screen.

4. Capture an image of the 1-2-3 screen by pressing PrtScr. (If you are using an older computer, you may need to press Alt+PrtScr.)

   Windows stores the image in the Clipboard. This step captures the screen text. If the application is any Windows application, it captures the screen as a graphic.

5. Activate the Word for Windows window. Position the insertion point where you want the captured screen to appear.

6. Open the **E**dit menu and choose **P**aste.

   The 1-2-3 screen text appears in Word for Windows as though typed. If you captured a Windows or graphics screen, a picture of the screen appears.

7. If the pasted text does not align correctly, select the text and change the font to Courier, a nonproportional typeface. Alternatively, leave the font and insert tab stops on which to align columns.

Fig. 5.2
Press the PrtScr key to capture screens and paste them into Windows applications.

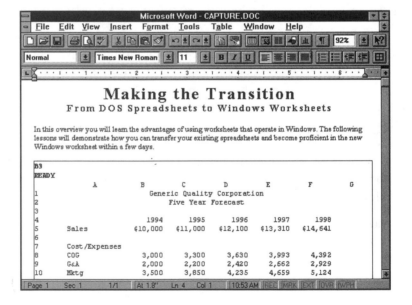

If you paste a graphic screen image into PageMaker, Word for Windows, or Ami Pro, the image appears as a picture that you can resize or crop. These Windows applications also enable you to draw lines and borders around screen images. You can send the resulting documentation to a normal printer for printing or print it to a file so that it can be typeset on a Linotronic typesetter.

Windows makes documentation easier. Because you easily can switch between applications, you can run an application you are writing about and
your Windows word processor or page layout application at the same time.
All it takes to switch between them is Alt+Tab or Ctrl+Esc.

Copying from DOS Applications into Windows Applications

You can paste text or numbers from any DOS application into another Windows or DOS application. Figure 5.3 shows how tabbed data is copied from a
memo in WordPerfect for DOS and pasted into a Microsoft Excel worksheet.
If you copy tabbed data, the data automatically separates itself into cells in
the worksheet where it is pasted.

Copying from DOS applications usually is efficient only when Windows is in
386 Enhanced mode. When Windows operates in 386 Enhanced mode, you
can copy selected portions of the DOS application screen. When Windows is
in Standard mode, however, you must copy the entire screen and edit out
any extraneous material after you paste the data into another application.

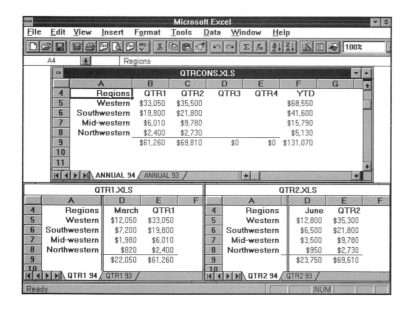

Fig. 5.3
Copy text out of
any DOS applica-
tion and paste it
into any other
application.

To copy out of a DOS application and paste into a Windows or other DOS application when you are operating in 386 Enhanced mode, follow these steps:

1. Activate the DOS application.

2. Press Alt+Enter until the DOS application displays in a window. You must display the DOS application in a window to complete the following steps.

3. Use the DOS application's movement keys to display the data you want to copy.

4. Choose the application's Control menu, and then open the **E**dit menu and choose Mar**k**.

5. With the mouse, click and drag across the portion of the screen you want to copy. With the keyboard, move the square cursor to a corner of what you want to select, hold down the Shift key, and press arrow keys to select the area to be copied. The selected area is highlighted.

▶ "Using the DOS Application Control Menu," p. 771

6. Open the document's Control menu again; open the **E**dit menu and choose Cop**y** Enter.

The text and numbers you selected are now copied into the Clipboard. To paste that information into another application, follow these steps:

1. Activate the receiving DOS or Windows application.

2. Move the insertion point or cursor to where you want to paste the text or numbers.

3. If the application is a Windows application, open the **E**dit menu and chooose **P**aste.

   or

◀ "Starting Applications," p. 48

   If the application is a DOS application, put the DOS application into a window by pressing Alt+Enter. Open the application's Control menu and choose **E**dit. Then choose **P**aste from the cascading menu.

Text and numbers copied from DOS applications are pasted in as a line of text. Each line ends with a carriage return.

Exchanging Data Using Files

The most common method of exchanging data in DOS applications is to save the file from one application, exit the application, use a second application to convert the file's data and format, exit that application, and import the data into a third application. 1-2-3 for DOS, for example, uses this method with its Translate application, and WordPerfect for DOS uses this method with its Convert utility.

Most Windows applications read or save other file formats and automatically convert or translate the file while the applications read or save. Microsoft Excel, for example, reads and writes text files, 1-2-3 files, and dBASE files. Word for Windows reads and writes files for common word processors such as WordPerfect, WordStar, MultiMate, and the IBM standard, DCA (RFT). PageMaker converts files from Word for DOS, WordPerfect, and other word processors. The translation process is invisible to you. You often can use Windows applications and the DOS applications in the same office.

From Here...

Refer to the following chapters to learn more about sharing information between applications:

- Chapter 6, "Advanced Data Sharing," explains how to use linking and embedding to share information between applications.

- Chapter 17, "Using Clipbook Viewer, Chat, and Popup," shows you how to use the Clipbook Viewer to see the contents of the Clipboard.

- Chapter 22, "Running, Installing, and Configuring DOS Applications," teaches you how to work with DOS applications from within Windows.

II

Managing Your Work

Chapter 6

Advanced Data Sharing

One of the unique advantages of Windows applications is their capability to exchange and link information easily with other Windows applications. If you are accustomed to working with one application, the value of linking or embedding data is not always immediately apparent. After you begin to link and embed data, however, you will see how much it can improve your communication.

In this chapter, you will learn:

- The advantages and disadvantages to pasting, linking, or embedding data, and when each method of data sharing is appropriate

- How to link or embed data

- How to link or embed data across a Windows for Workgroups network

- How to repair and manage links between documents

- How to *freeze* links so the linked data does not change

The following list describes examples of the way linking and embedding can work with various applications:

- Creating sales projections, financial analyses, inventory reports, and investment analyses with Microsoft Excel or Lotus 1-2-3 for Windows, and then linking or embedding them into Windows word processing documents

- Maintaining client-reminder letters and callbacks by linking a personal information manager to Word for Windows

■ Embedding drawings or schematics created in Visio in Word for Windows or Ami Pro. The drawings can be updated by double-clicking them in the document or, if they are linked, by modifying the original drawing's file

■ Linking Microsoft Excel to a Windows database or SQL Server through the use of Microsoft Query to monitor and analyze inventory

■ Creating a compound document composed of pieces of text, graphics, and other data from many users on a network. Updating the shared data in the ClipBook updates the compound document

■ Posting a changing graph or worksheet table in the Clipbook so everyone on the Windows for Workgroups network can have the most current data

Figure 6.1 shows an example of a letter that has links to a Microsoft Excel worksheet and chart.

Fig. 6.1
Compound documents can contain linked or embedded data from many other applications.

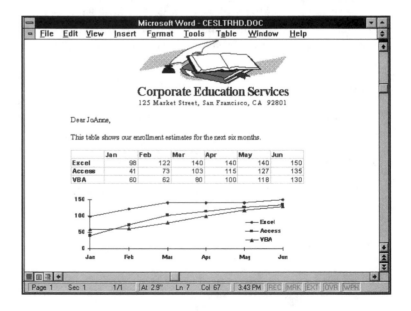

Throughout this chapter, the *server* is the application that is supplying data. The *client* is the application receiving information. Some applications function as both server and client. Other applications may be one or the other, but not both. Microsoft Write and Cardfile, for example, are clients—they only receive information. Windows Paintbrush however, is a server—it only can supply information.

Copying, linking, or embedding data between Windows applications may use the same or similar commands, and the results may appear the same on-screen or in the document. Each fits a different situation, however, and has unique advantages and disadvantages. The following table describes the different ways to transfer data, and the advantages and disadvantages of each method.

◄ "Viewing Data in the Clipboard," p. 191

Table 6.1 Transferring Data	
Copying	**Use when you do not want to update data. Data must be replaced to be updated.**

Advantages

- Data does not change when other parts of the document update.

- Less memory and storage are required to use or save the document.

- Data, such as bit maps, may be editable without having the original server application available.

Disadvantages

- Pictures may print at lower resolution if copied as a bit map.

- Updating data requires redoing each copy and paste of data.

- Copied data cannot be edited using the functionality of the original server application that created the document.

Linking	**Use when you need to update one original in the server and have the changes cascade into multiple client documents.**

Advantages

- Less memory is required than for an embedded object.

- Many client documents can be updated by changing one server document.

- Older Windows applications that cannot embed objects can still link data.

Disadvantages

- Links between the server and the client may be broken if the server file names or path names are changed or deleted.

- Automatically updated links may slow down Windows operation.

- Server data must be saved, and the name and path name must be maintained.

- User of the client document must have the same type of server application in order to edit the linked data.

II

Managing Your Work

(continues)

Table 6.1 Continued	
Embedding	Use when you have only a few client documents that may need updating, and you want to include the server data (an *embedded object*) as part of the document.

Advantages

■ Client document and server data are stored as a single file; you do not have to maintain links, path names, and server files.

■ Server data is saved as part of the client document.

■ You can stay within the client document and use the server application to update the embedded object.

Disadvantages

■ Documents containing embedded objects are larger than other documents because they contain both client and server data.

■ Documents containing an embedded object must be edited on a computer having the same application that created the embedded object if the object is to retain all of its information.

■ Each client document must be updated individually.

Two additional methods of transferring data within Windows applications are not described in this chapter. Applications such as Word for Windows and Microsoft Excel can open files created by the application, or they can use a command, such as **I**nsert Fi**l**e in Word for Windows, to link to an on-disk file created by another application.

Microsoft Excel, Word for Windows, Lotus 1-2-3 for Windows, WordPerfect for Windows, Ami Pro and most databases can open files created by other applications. Files that are opened like this become part of the document and cannot be updated except by replacing them. To open another application's file, you must install the file converters that come with the Windows application.

Applications that can link to a file on disk, such as Word for Windows, enable you to link their documents to Microsoft Excel, Lotus 1-2-3, WordPerfect, or dBASE files. When the file on disk changes, you can update the Word for Windows document to reflect the new data. Different Windows applications sometimes use different commands to implement object linking and embedding. For example, to insert an embedded object in a Word for Windows document, you choose the **I**nsert **O**bject command; to do the same in Windows Write, you choose **E**dit **I**nsert Object.

The following procedures describe the commands and active letters for some of the more frequently used applications. (Not all applications that have object linking and embedding capability have all the features described in this chapter.)

Linking Data between Applications

Linking documents together is another way to transfer data between Windows applications. Links in a client document create references to data in a server application or a server document from the same application. The actual data is still stored in the server document; a copy is sent through the link to the client document.

Changing a single-server document can update all the client documents that depend on its data. Another major advantage to linking documents is that client documents are smaller than documents containing embedded objects because the data still resides in the server document.

The disadvantage to using links is that you must maintain the links to a server document. If the location or name of the server document changes, you must update the reference by editing the link. If you give the client document to another user, you will probably want to provide the server documents to make updating possible.

Creating a Link

Creating a link between Windows applications capable of linking is as easy as copying and pasting. The command to paste in a link may vary between applications. The client document may use a command such as **E**dit Paste **L**ink or **E**dit Paste **S**pecial with a dialog box that contains a Paste **L**ink button or option. If your client application contains a Paste **L**ink command, you may not need to continue past step 6 in the following procedure.

To create a link, follow these steps:

1. Start both Windows applications—the server and the client—and open their documents. Activate the server document.

2. Save the server document using the name that it will keep during all future transactions. (If you resave the server document to a different name or directory, you have to update the link in the client document as described in the section titled "Managing Links," later in this chapter.)

Tip
If your server application does not have linking capability, the client's Link button or command may be dimmed because it is unavailable.

II

Managing Your Work

3. Select the text, range of cells, graphic, or database records that you want to link.

4. Open the **E**dit menu and choose **C**opy.

5. Activate the client document that will receive the data, and position the insertion point where you want the link to appear.

6. Open the **E**dit menu and choose Paste **L**ink to paste in the link immediately. (If your application has a Paste **L**ink command, you do not need to continue.)

   or

   Open the **E**dit menu and choose Paste **S**pecial, and select the Link option or button.

   A Paste Special dialog box may appear (see fig. 6.2). Notice that the Paste Special dialog box displays the source of the link, and presents a list of different ways in which the linked data can appear.

Fig. 6.2
The Paste Special dialog box for Word 6 for Windows shows the different forms in which you can paste link an Excel range.

7. Select the Paste **L**ink option.

8. From the **A**s list, select the form in which you want your linked data. These link types are described in table 6.2.

   Selecting some data types may disable the **L**ink option or button. If this occurs, you may be able to paste the data or insert the data as an embedded object.

9. Choose OK. Choose the Paste **L**ink button.

When you choose the Paste **L**ink option button, Windows creates an automatically updating link. To have the link update only when you manually request it, see the section called "Controlling Manual versus Automatic Updates," later in this chapter.

When you create a link, the data from the server may appear in different forms in the client document. Your data may appear as tabbed text, a formatted table, a picture, or a bit map. Each server application has different forms in which it enables its data to appear. Generally, choose the type that gives the best graphics resolution or transfers the most text formatting. Table 6.2 describes some of the types.

Table 6.2 Data Types Stored in the Clipboard	
Data Type	**Type of Link Created**
Object	Data is an embedded object. All data is stored in an object. No link is maintained with the source worksheet or chart.
Formatted Text (RTF)	Text transfers with formats. Worksheets appear formatted in tables. Data can be edited or reformatted. If Paste **L**ink was chosen, a LINK field that links to the source document is inserted. If **P**aste was chosen, the data appears as unlinked text.
Unformatted Text	Text is unformatted. Worksheets appear as unformatted text with cells separated by tabs.
Picture	Some graphics, text, database tables, and worksheet ranges appear as pictures. (A picture preserves formatting and resolution from the original application—usually resulting in a high-quality image on-screen and when printed.) They can be formatted as pictures, but text cannot be edited.
Bit map	Some graphics, text, and worksheet ranges appear as bit-map pictures. (A bit map appears at screen resolution and may be distorted if resized.) They can be formatted as pictures, but text cannot be edited in Word. Resolution is poorer than that of a picture.

Note

Some applications enable you to reformat linked data and retain the format when the linked data is updated. In Word for Windows, for example, this is done by using switches within the {LINK} field codes. An example of a {LINK} field code produced by the **E**dit Paste **S**pecial command is as follows:

```
{LINK Excel.Sheet.5 "C:\\CES\\ENROLL.XLS"
"Sheet1!R5C1:R8C7" \a \p}
```

In this example, a range of cells, R5C1:R8C7, within the Microsoft Excel worksheet was copied and pasted into the Word for Windows document as a picture. The different arguments that specify the form for the linked data are the following:

\r	Formatted Text (RTF)
\t	Unformatted Text
\p	Picture
\b	Bit map

Any manual changes to the format of the linked data are preserved by the following switch:

```
\* mergeformat
```

You do not need to type this field code into the Word document; the code is automatically pasted in, according to the selections you have made in the Paste Special dialog box.

Passing Linked Documents to Other Computer Users

To make changes in the linked data in a client document containing a link, you must have both the server application and the server document available. When you give a document containing links to someone else, make sure that they have access to the server document and application. If you must share a document with someone who does not own the server application, you can convert the link to simple pasted data by breaking the link, or you can create the document by just pasting data rather than linking.

When you know you are giving another user a client file and its server files, it is best to put all the files in the same directory, and then do the copies and paste links. The user who receives the files can then put all the files into a single directory and easily update the client document.

Some linked documents received by another user require extra work before updating. If the person receiving a client document has copied the server documents into a directory with a name that is different from the directory name used during creation, the client document cannot find the server document. When this happens the user must use the link-management techniques, described in the following section titled "Managing Links," to update the directory names used in the links.

If you want to *freeze* the data displayed by a link, you can break the link. This destroys the link to the server document but leaves the data. Breaking the link changes linked word processing and worksheet information into text—as though the text were typed in the client document. Graphics become pictures or bit maps.

Troubleshooting

After receiving a document containing linked data, I attempted to update the links, and all the linked data changed to errors.

If you do not have the source documents that created the linked data and you attempt to update the link, many applications change the linked data into an error. The best thing you can do is to close the document without saving it. This preserves the original file. You can then freeze the data so it is no longer linked to the unavailable files, but it will at least be stable and usable.

In an application like Word for Windows you can unlink data by selecting the linked area and then pressing Shift+Ctrl+F9. In Excel 5 you can copy the linked data by opening the **E**dit menu and choosing **C**opy. Keep the same range selected, and then open the **E**dit menu and choose Paste **S**pecial. Select the **V**alues option and OK to paste only the values over the links.

In the future, you should make sure that you receive the source documents and the client document if you need to update links.

To break a link, follow these steps:

1. Open the **E**dit menu and choose Lin**k**s, or open the **F**ile menu and choose **L**inks (or a similar command). The Links dialog box appears (see fig. 6.3).

Fig. 6.3

Correct lost links or freeze links using the Links dialog box.

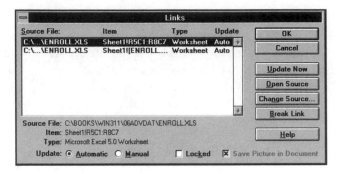

2. If you did not select the links you want to break in step 1, select the links you want to break now from the **L**inks list.

3. Choose the **C**ancel Link or **B**reak Link button.

If you want to remove linked data rather than break the link, select the linked data, and press the Del key.

Editing Linked Data

To edit linked data with a mouse, double-click the data in the client document. The server application activates and loads the file necessary to update the data. After you have made changes to the data, from within the server application, open the **F**ile menu, and choose **U**pdate or E**x**it and Return to document to update the linked data and exit the server application.

Some applications can specify that linked data does not update automatically. To edit linked text or worksheet data that does not update automatically, follow these steps:

1. Open the **E**dit menu and choose **L**inks, or open the **F**ile menu and choose **L**inks. The Links dialog box appears.

2. If you did not select the linked data in step 1, select the links you want to edit from the **L**inks list.

3. Choose the **U**pdate Now button, or its equivalent, in your application.

Linking Data between Computers

If you are connected to a Windows for Workgroups network, you can link data between computers, just as you can link data between applications on a single computer, as described in the section "Linking Data between Applications."

When changes are made to the source data stored in a ClipBook, the data updates in all client documents linked to the data.

Before you can link data from another computer, the data must be created in an application on the other computer, copied to the Clipboard on that computer, and then saved in a page in that computer's ClipBook. This page in the ClipBook must be designated as a *shared page* so that others on the network can link to it.

Linking to the Server's Clipboard

In order to link to data stored in another computer's ClipBook, you must first connect to the other computer's ClipBook.

A ClipBook window appears, listing all the shared pages in the other computer's ClipBook. To link data that is already in the ClipBook from another computer on the Windows for Workgroups network to your computer, begin by preparing your Windows application to receive linked data.

▶ "Using Clip-Book Viewer, Chat, and WinPopup," p. 625

1. Activate your Windows application and the document that you want to contain linked information. Press Alt+Tab until the application appears, or press Ctrl+Esc and select the application. If you need to start the application, activate Program Manager and start your application.

2. Position the insertion point in the document where you want the linked information to appear.

3. Activate or start ClipBook. Press Alt+Tab until ClipBook appears, or press Ctrl+Esc and select ClipBook. If you need to start ClipBook, activate Program Manager and start ClipBook.

Now, with ClipBook active, connect to another computer's ClipBook:

1. Click the Connect button, or open the **F**ile menu and choose **C**onnect.

2. Select the workgroup and computer name to which you want to connect.

3. Choose OK.

Finally, select the page in the other computer's ClipBook and link it into your document:

▶ "Connecting to the ClipBook on Another Computer," p. 632

1. Select the ClipBook page to which you want to link. Click the page or press arrow keys to select the page.

2. To copy the page contents into your Clipboard, click the Copy button on the toolbar, or open the **E**dit menu and choose **C**opy.

3. Activate the application and document that will receive the information. (The insertion point must be where you want the information to appear.)

4. Open the **E**dit menu and choose Paste **S**pecial or Paste **L**ink. The command you use depends upon how your application creates linked data.

   The Paste Special dialog box, similar to the one in figure 6.2, appears. The Paste Special dialog box displays the source of the link and lists several formats in which the linked data can be displayed.

5. From the **A**s or Data Type list, select the format you want to use for your linked data. See table 6.2 for a description of the different formats.

   Selecting some data types may disable the Paste **L**ink button or option because this data type may not be able to link. Some applications may not be able to link with any data type, in which case the Paste **L**ink button or option is disabled for all data types. If this occurs, you may be able to paste or embed the data. Pasting or embedding across the network is described in a later section, "Embedding Data from Another Computer."

6. Choose the Paste **L**ink button or option.

7. Choose OK.

The data you paste in appears in your document. For example, figure 6.4 shows a Microsoft Word 6 for Windows document containing a chart linked to a Microsoft Excel 5 chart.

Updating Linked Information

Changing the file from which the data originated, the source, updates all the links across the network. Linking data from one computer to another via the ClipBook actually creates a link to the file containing the original data. When the original file changes, any documents that contain the linked data update. Because this link references the original file name that was the source of the data, you should not move the source file or change its name.

In some Windows applications, such as Windows Write, you are unable to see where the original data is linked to. In some applications, such as Word for Windows, you can see the formula that creates the link. Figure 6.5 shows the same Word 6 for Windows document as in figure 6.1, but the **T**ools **O**ptions View **F**ield Codes command has been selected to display the code that actually tells the Word document how to go across the network and find the file containing the linked data.

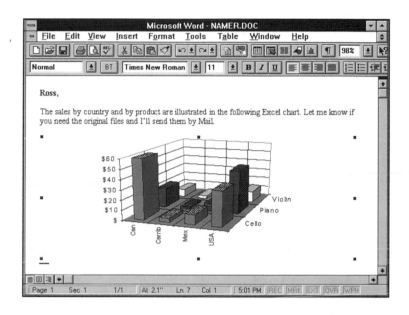

Fig. 6.4
Updating the Excel chart in another computer updates the data in this linked Word document.

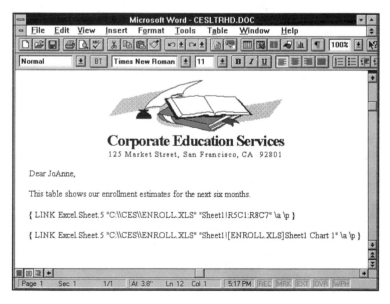

Fig. 6.5
Some applications insert a code that shows you the link between documents across the network.

If you have a document containing linked data, you can update the linked data if you can share the directory and file that created the source data. To update the linked data, start the application that created the source data, and then access the directory containing the shared file. Update the data document and resave it into the same directory with the same file name.

When you reopen a document that contains data linked across the network, you may get a dialog box asking whether you want to automatically link the document to applications outside your current application. Choose **Y**es to relink with the source document for the linked data.

You may encounter a situation in which you no longer want your client document to change when the source data changes. Some applications enable you to break a link, which then changes the linked data into pasted or embedded data. Each application has its own command or keystroke for breaking links. Once a link has been broken, you must update the data manually; it does not update when the source changes.

Embedding Data into a Document

Embedding is another method of inserting data from one application into another. Embedding enables a server document to store its data directly within a client application's document. A picture from Windows Paintbrush, for example, can be stored within a Windows Write letter.

Embedding objects gives you an alternative to pasting or linking data. It also gives applications more power because you can access one application's features from within another application. From within Word for Windows, for example, you can start Microsoft Excel and store the data from a worksheet or chart directly within the Word document.

Linking data has some advantages but also comes with inherent problems. Linked data requires you to keep track of where the server files are located, to make sure that the server file names do not change, and to make sure that anyone receiving your client document receives all the server files.

Embedding the linked data directly within the client document eliminates those file-management problems, but creates another issue. The document becomes quite large because the client document contains both server and client data.

Creating an Embedded Object

You can create embedded objects in three ways. In the first method, you insert a new embedded object into a client document, starting the server application so that you can create a new drawing, worksheet, or chart. When you close the server application, the object is embedded in the client document. In the second method, you start the server application, create or use existing data, copy the data, and embed it in the client document. The third method assumes that the data has already been created and is in a file on disk. The complete file can then be inserted as an embedded object.

Each of these methods has its advantages and disadvantages. If you need the power of another application for a single embedded object, you probably want to use the method of creating a new blank object in which to work. If you have data that you use frequently for other work and you want to only embed a portion of it, open the document, copy that portion, and use paste to embed the selected portion. And finally, if you have a document that you want to completely embed, use the file-embedding method.

To insert a new blank embedded object, follow these steps:

1. Move the insertion point to where you want the object.

2. Open the **E**dit menu and choose **I**nsert Object, or open the **I**nsert menu and choose **O**bject (or a similar command in your application). The Object dialog box, similar to the one in figure 6.6, appears, showing applications from which you can embed objects. (If the dialog box is a tabbed dialog box, select the tab to insert a new object.)

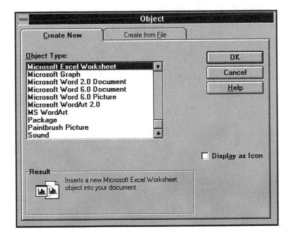

Fig. 6.6
The Object dialog box shows the types of objects you can embed.

3. From the **O**bject Type list, select the type of object you want to insert and then choose OK.

   This either starts the application that creates the type of object you requested, or it embeds a blank object in your document and changes the application's menus and toolbars to reflect those of the embedded object.

4. Create the data you want in the inserted object. You use the menus and toolbars appropriate for that object. For example, if you inserted an Excel Worksheet object, you see the Excel worksheet menus and toolbars at the top of the application that you are in.

   You can create the server data from scratch or copy existing data into the server document from the Clipboard. In many applications, you cannot open a file from the server application.

5. Embed the server data with one of the following techniques as appropriate to the application creating the object:

   Deactivate the embedded object by clicking outside the embedded object in the surrounding document. Use this technique if the embedded document stays within the client document and the client application's menus and toolbars change.

   or

   Open the **F**ile menu and choose E**x**it and Return to document (or just E**x**it) to close the application and update the embedded object. Answer Yes if a dialog box asks you whether you want to update the object in your client document.

   or

   Open the **F**ile menu and choose **U**pdate to update the embedded object but keep the application and object open.

▶ "Registering
Application
Features in the
Registration
Editor," p. 725

▶ "Solving Object
Linking and
Embedding
Problems,"
p. 1,005

For an application to appear in the **O**bject Type list, the application must be registered with Windows and must be capable of producing embedded objects. Applications capable of object linking and embedding are registered when you install them in Windows.

If you already have a document that you want to embed and you want to embed a portion of the document, you need to use the second method, described in the following steps:

1. Start the server application and create the text, chart, worksheet, or database you want to embed. (Unlike linked data, you do not have to save the data you are creating because it is stored within the client document.)

2. Select the data. Open the **E**dit menu and choose **C**opy.

3. Switch to the client application, open the document, and position the insertion point where you want to embed the object.

4. Open the **E**dit menu and choose Paste **S**pecial.

5. Select the application object item, such as Paintbrush Picture Object, from the **D**ata Type or **O**bject Type list.

6. Choose the **P**aste button.

7. Choose OK.

Editing Embedded Objects

Embedded objects are very easy to edit—just double-click the embedded object. With the keyboard, select the object and choose the **E**dit **O**bject command at the bottom of the **E**dit menu (the command may vary slightly). In order to edit an embedded object, the server application must be available to your computer and in the registration database.

When you double-click the object or choose the **E**dit **O**bject command, the object reacts in one of two ways. If either or both of the server and client application use OLE 1.0, the server application starts and loads the object. The server application with the object loaded appears in a window over the top of the client application. Figure 6.7 shows an Excel 4 worksheet object being edited within a Word 2 for Windows client document. Notice that the title of the Excel application shows that it is in a Word document. A new server application is opened to edit an object, even if the same application is already open.

Troubleshooting

After double-clicking on an embedded graphic and editing it, I notice that the graphic does not print with the fine resolution it did before editing.

If the application server that created a document is not available on the computer on which you are editing, the registration database may open an application that can handle the same file format. This other application may not be able to save the object back with the same resolution that it had originally.

Fig. 6.7

OLE 1.0 objects are edited in a window containing the server application.

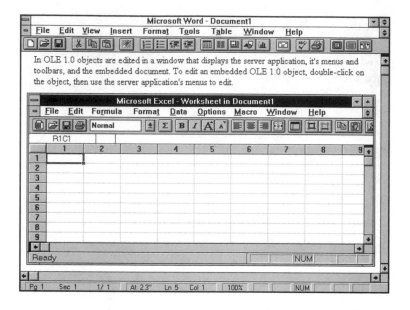

If you are using applications that are compatible with the newer OLE 2.0, you have in-place editing capability. When you edit an OLE 2.0 object, the object remains in the client document, but it displays a wide dashed border. The menus and toolbars in the client application change to the menus and toolbars of the object's server application.

Figure 6.8 shows an Excel 5 worksheet range embedded in a Word 6 for Windows document. Notice the thin border around the range and the Word 6 for Windows toolbars and menus. Figure 6.9 shows the same embedded Excel 5 worksheet range while it is being edited. The wide dashed border indicates that the object is being edited. Notice that the application title still says Microsoft Word, but the menu bar and toolbars have changed to those used in Excel.

To update the object when you are done editing or formatting it, follow one of these steps:

> If you are editing an OLE 2.0 object, select something in the client document outside the embedded object you are editing.
>
> or
>
> If you are editing an OLE 1.0 object, open the **F**ile menu and choose E**x**it and Return to document (or just E**x**it) to close the application and update the embedded object.
>
> or

If you are editing an OLE 1.0 object, open the **F**ile menu and choose **U**pdate to update the embedded object but keep the server application and object open. This enables you to preview how your changes will look in the client document.

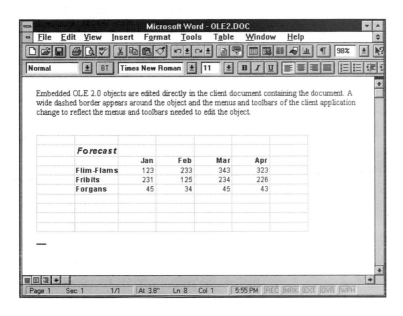

Fig. 6.8
This Excel 5 range is embedded in a Word 6 for Windows document.

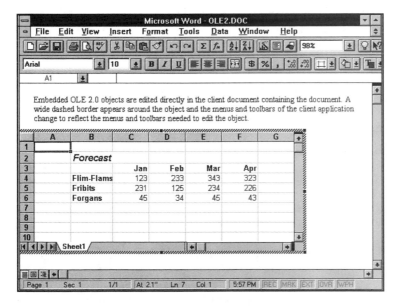

Fig. 6.9
During OLE 2.0 editing the toolbars and menus change to those of the object's applicaton.

Embedding Data from Another Computer

When you are working with Windows for Workgroups, not only can you embed data from one application into another on your computer, but you can embed data from another computer on your network into an application on your computer. Embedding objects from another computer is an advantage if you do not want your document to change whenever the source data changes. In addition, it enables the document to carry with it all the data required to create or edit the objects. For example, you may want to embed a portion of an Excel cost-estimate table into a Word document. By embedding the table in the Word document, changes to the original Excel worksheet do not appear in your document, but you can easily change the cost-estimate table with your copy of Excel, as necessary.

▶ "Sharing Pages in Your ClipBook," p. 630

Before you can embed an object from another computer, the object must be created in an application on the other computer, copied to the Clipboard on that computer, and then copied to a page in the ClipBook. The page in the ClipBook must be shared by the other user before you can proceed to embed the object in a document on your computer. Not all Windows applications are capable of creating objects that can be embedded. A Windows application must have OLE capability for embedding to work.

▶ "Connecting to the ClipBook on Another Computer," p. 632

To embed an object from another computer, you must first connect to the other computer's ClipBook. When you connect, a ClipBook window appears and lists all the shared pages in the other computer's ClipBook.

To embed data from another computer on the Windows for Workgroups network to your computer, begin by preparing your Windows application to receive the embedded data. Follow these steps:

1. Activate your Windows application and the document that you want to contain the data.

2. Position the insertion point in the document where you want the embedded data to appear.

3. Activate or start ClipBook.

Now, with your ClipBook application active, connect to another computer's ClipBook. Follow these steps:

1. Click the Connect button, or open the **F**ile menu and choose **C**onnect.

2. Select the workgroup and computer name to which you want to connect.

3. Choose OK.

Finally, select the page in the other computer's ClipBook and embed its contents into your document.

1. Select the ClipBook page whose contents you want to embed.

2. Click the Copy button on the toolbar, or open the **E**dit menu and choose **C**opy, to copy the page contents into your Clipboard.

3. Activate the application and document that will receive the object. (The insertion point must be where you want the embedded object to appear.)

4. Open the **E**dit menu and choose Paste **S**pecial, or open the **I**nsert menu and choose **O**bject. The command you use depends on the way your application creates embedded objects.

   A Paste Special dialog box appears. The dialog box displays the source of the object and lists several formats in which the selected object embedded.

5. From the **A**s or Data Type list, select the format you want to use for the embedded object. See table 6.2 for a description of the different formats.

   Some data types may not allow embedding.

6. Choose the **P**aste option.

7. Choose OK.

The object you embed appears in your document. For example, a Microsoft Excel chart embedded can be embedded as an object into a Word for Windows document. The chart still appears as it did in Excel, but it is not linked to the original file that created the chart.

An embedded object contains all the data used to create the object. If you have a copy of the application that created the object on your computer, you can edit the object, as described in the previous section.

II

Managing Your Work

Embedding Data as Packages

In addition to linking or embedding data, you can bundle data as a package and embed an icon that represents that data in your client document. The icon, a small picture, can represent part of a document or an entire document. Only applications that support object linking and embedding can support packages of embedded data. Figure 6.10 shows a document containing packaged data.

Fig. 6.10
Embedded packages can contain all or part of a file, sound, or animation.

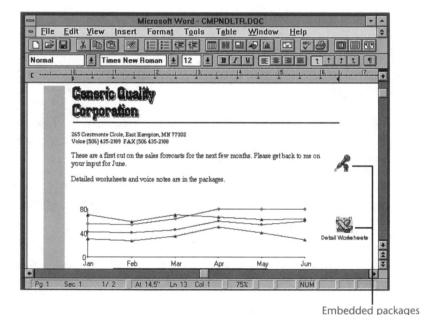

Embedded packages

Embedded packages act like embedded objects. When activated, they open the server application and display the data contained. Besides data, embedded packages can contain sound, voice, or animation, as described in Chapters 19 and 20. You also can add a label or create your own icon to represent the data.

The situations in which you may want to embed a package of data are as follows:

■ A memo refers to a previous report that you want to package with the memo so that the reader can review it. Rather than inserting a lengthy report in the memo, you embed a package containing the report. Double-clicking the package icon explodes it into the entire report.

■ A new product proposal you have written gets to the point right away, but you want to make sure that all the supporting detail is included in case there are additional questions. You package the worksheets, charts, and notes and embed them in the proposal so that readers can delve into detail only if they want.

■ A sales report has variances that you need to explain. Rather than break up the flow of the report, you package the variance report as notes. Each note is embedded at the proper location in the report.

To package objects, your application must support object linking and embedding. There are different methods of creating packages that depend upon when your application was written, and whether you want to embed or link a package. In some applications, creating an embedded package is as easy as dragging a file from File Manager and dropping it onto a document. For other applications, you may need to use File Manager or Object Packager, which is found in the Accessories group, to package embedded or linked files.

Object Packager appears in figure 6.11. The left side of Object Packager displays the icon that represents the data. The right side shows the name of the object, such as a file name or a picture of the object.

Fig. 6.11
Use Object Packager to embed icons that represent data.

Activating Package Contents

A package may contain any form of Windows document, including multimedia files containing sound or animation. To activate the package so that it delivers its contents, double-click the package icon, or select the package and then open the **E**dit menu and choose Package **O**bject (or a similar command). If a cascading menu appears, choose **A**ctivate Contents to start the application and load the embedded data. (In some applications, using the keyboard to edit a packaged object only enables you to edit the object using Object Packager.)

Packaging Entire Files

Files can be packaged and embedded using Object Packager or File Manager. The File Manager method is easy and enables you to link a package to the server document, but Object Packager offers you the chance to change the icon and add a custom label.

Packaging a File with Object Packager

To include the entire contents of a file or document in the package, follow these steps:

1. Open Object Packager, found in the Accessories application window.

2. Select the Content window by clicking or pressing Tab.

3. Open the File menu and choose Import.

4. Select the file you want to package, and choose OK.

Figure 6.11 shows how a package and its description appear in Object Packager. Notice that the default icon associated with the imported file appears on the Appearance side of Object Packager. The Content side shows a description.

At this point, you can change the appearance of the icon or the label attached to the icon. Both features are described in the section titled "Selecting or Creating an Icon for Your Package," later in this chapter.

To embed the package into a document that has object linking and embedding capability, follow these steps:

1. With Object Packager still active, make sure that the Appearance side is active by clicking it or pressing Tab until the title Appearance is selected.

2. Open the Edit menu and choose Copy Package.

3. Activate the client application, and open the document. Move the insertion point to where you want the package icon to appear.

4. Open the Edit menu and choose Paste.

    or

    Open the Edit menu and choose Paste Special. Then select Package Object as the Data Type, and choose Paste.

The package appears in the document as the icon you saw in Object Packager.

Packaging Files with the File Manager

Newer Windows applications can use the Clipboard to copy files from File Manager and paste them as objects directly into an application that supports object linking and embedding.

Some Windows applications that have object linking and embedding enable you to drag a file from File Manager and drop it into a client document. The file then becomes an embedded package.

◀ "Using File Manager's Drag-and-Drop Feature," p. 173

To use the mouse and File Manager to package a file, follow these steps:

1. Activate File Manager, and select the file you want to package.

2. Activate the client application to receive the package. Scroll the document so that you can see the place where you want to embed the package.

3. Arrange the application windows so that you can see both the file name and the client document.

4. To create an embedded package, drag the file name from File Manager onto the client document and release it.

To use the keyboard to package a file with File Manager, follow these steps:

1. Activate File Manager, and select the file name you want to package.

2. Open the **F**ile menu and choose **C**opy. The Copy dialog box appears (see fig. 6.12).

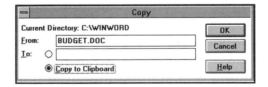

Fig. 6.12
The Copy dialog box enables you to copy a file into the Clipboard.

3. Select the **C**opy to Clipboard option, and choose OK.

4. Activate the application, and open the document to receive the package. Move the insertion point to where you want the package.

5. Open the **E**dit menu and choose **P**aste to embed a package, or open the **E**dit menu and choose Paste **L**ink (or open the **E**dit menu, choose Paste **S**pecial and then Paste **L**ink) to create a linked package.

If your application was written before object linking and embedding were completely designed, it may not work with one of the previous methods. If one of the previous methods does not work, try the following method:

1. Activate File Manager, and select the file you want to package.

2. Open the **F**ile menu and choose **C**opy.

3. Select the **C**opy to Clipboard option button, and choose OK.

Now that the file is in the Clipboard, follow these steps:

1. Activate Object Packager.

2. Select the Content side.

3. To create a linked object, open the **E**dit menu and choose **P**aste to create an embedded object, or open the **E**dit menu and choose Paste **L**ink. The object icon and its contents or description appear in Object Packager.

4. Open the **E**dit menu and choose Copy Pac**k**age.

5. Activate the application, and open the document in which you want to paste the package. Position the insertion point where you want the icon to appear.

6. Open the **E**dit menu and choose **P**aste.

Packaging Part of a Document

The procedure to package only part of a document is similar to that used with Object Packager, except that you copy into Object Packager only the part of the document you want packaged. As before, the applications must have object linking and embedding capability.

To package part of a document or graphic, follow these steps:

1. Open the document containing the data. Save the document if you want to create a linked package.

2. Select the data or graphic you want to package.

3. Open the **E**dit menu and choose **C**opy.

4. Activate Object Packager and select the Content side.

5. Open the **E**dit menu and choose **P**aste to create an embedded package, or open the **E**dit menu and choose Paste **L**ink to create a linked package.

6. Open the **E**dit menu and choose Copy Pac**k**age.

Now that the package is in the Clipboard, you can paste the package into the client document by following these steps:

1. Activate the client application and open the client document.

2. Move the insertion point to where you want the package.

3. Open the **E**dit menu and choose **P**aste.

Packaging a DOS Command Line

You can create a package icon that runs a DOS batch file or DOS application. This can be useful if you have a DOS application that you want to load or run from within an application that supports object linking and embedding.

To create a package containing a DOS command line from within Object Packager, follow these steps:

1. Open the **E**dit menu and choose Co**m**mand Line. The Command Line dialog box appears.

2. In the **C**ommand text box, type the command line as you would enter it from a DOS prompt. Include the full path name and command or application arguments.

3. Choose OK. The command line you type appears in the Content window.

4. Choose the Insert **I**con button. The Insert Icon dialog box appears. Use the technique described in the section "Selecting or Creating an Icon for Your Package," later in this chapter to select an icon for the command line package. Choose OK after you select an icon.

   The icon appears on the Appearance side of the Object Packager.

5. Open the **E**dit menu and choose Copy Pac**k**age.

6. Activate the client application, and open the client document.

7. Move the insertion point to where you want the package to appear.

8. Open the **E**dit menu and choose **P**aste.

II

Managing Your Work

Saving the Packager's Contents

If you are packaging an entire file to link or embed into your client document, you can save that file from within Object Packager (the file must have previously been saved). After you have imported the file into Object Packager, open the **F**ile menu and choose **S**ave Contents. In the Save Contents dialog box, type a name for the file in the File **N**ame text box (if necessary, select a different drive in the Dri**v**es list box or a different directory in the **D**irectories list box). Choose OK. The file is saved in its native format.

Selecting or Creating an Icon for Your Package

Normally, when you paste or import data into the Object Packager, the icon related to the data's document appears on the Appearance side. You can change that icon or create your own icon.

To change an icon while it is in Object Packager, follow these steps:

1. Select the Appearance side of Object Packager.

2. Choose the Insert **I**con button.

    The Insert Icon dialog box displays the current icon related to the data you are packaging.

3. Choose the **B**rowse button.

4. From the Browse dialog box that appears (similar to a File Open dialog box), select the name of a file containing icons. Choose OK.

    Windows applications contain an icon; you also can buy or create files that contain a library of icons. If you do not have a file containing a library of icons, choose the PROGMAN.EXE or MORICONS.DLL file from the WINDOWS directory. Figure 6.13 shows some of the icons contained in PROGMAN.EXE.

Fig. 6.13
The
PROGMAN.EXE
file contains many
icons you can use
for packages.

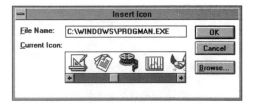

5. Select an icon from the scrolling **C**urrent Icon list shown in the Insert Icon dialog box. Choose OK.

You also can create your own icons by drawing them with the Paintbrush application. One way to do that is to modify an existing icon. When you have copied data into Object Packager and it displays an icon, follow these steps to modify an icon:

1. Select the Appearance side of Object Packager.

2. Open the **E**dit menu and choose **C**opy.

3. Activate Paintbrush.

4. Open the **E**dit menu and choose **P**aste.

   The existing icon is pasted into Paintbrush, where you can modify it. If you want to create an icon, start with step 5.

5. Use Paintbrush to modify or create an icon. Open the **F**ile menu and choose **S**ave if you want to save a copy of the icon.

   ▶ "Using the Paintbrush Tools," p. 368

6. Select the icon you have drawn, and then open the **E**dit menu and choose **C**opy.

7. Activate Object Packager.

8. Select the Appearance side, and open the **E**dit menu and choose **P**aste.

Use the procedures described previously to paste the package with its new icon into a document.

Editing an Icon's Label

Each package is labeled by the file name if you packaged a document; by the object type if you packaged part of a file. You can create your own label or file name.

To change a label while the package is in Object Packager, select the Appearance side of Object Packager, and then open the **E**dit menu and choose La**b**el. Enter a new name in the Label dialog box that appears, and then choose OK.

Editing Existing Package Icons

To change the icon or label of an existing package in a client document, select the icon, and then choose the **E**dit Package **O**bject command (or a similar command). From the cascading menu that appears, choose the **E**dit Package command. Object Packager loads the package, enabling you to use the preceding procedures to change the icon's appearance or label.

Sizing and Moving Package Icons

You can size and move a package within Windows Write and other applications in the same way that you size or move other graphic objects. For information on how to do this in Windows Write, refer to Chapter 10.

Managing Links

Keeping track of the many links that create a complex document can be difficult. The **E**dit Lin**k**s command makes the job considerably easier. When you open the **E**dit menu and choose Lin**k**s, the Links dialog box displays a list of all the links, their types, and how they update (see fig. 6.14). From the buttons and check boxes, you can update linked data, lock links to prevent changes, cancel the link, and change the file names or directories where the linked data is stored.

Fig. 6.14

The Links dialog box simplifies managing multiple links in a document.

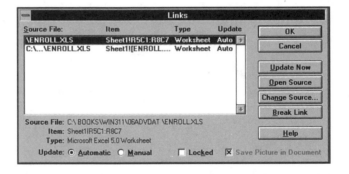

Updating Links

Tip

To select multiple adjacent links, click the first link in the Link dialog box and then Shift+click the last. To select or clear multiple nonadjacent links, hold down the Ctrl key as you click links.

To update individual links in a client document to reflect changes in the original document, select the linked data, and then open the **E**dit menu and choose Lin**k**s. When the Links dialog box appears, select the links you want to update, and then click the **U**pdate Now button.

When you want to update all the links in an entire document, select either the entire document or all the links in the Link dialog box, and choose the **U**pdate Now button. In some applications, shortcuts exist for updating links. For example, in Word for Windows, you can update a link by selecting it and pressing the F9 key.

Controlling Manual versus Automatic Updates

Some client/server applications enable you to specify whether a link should automatically update itself or should be updated manually only. You may want to use manual links if you have many links that change frequently because numerous automatic links can slow down Windows.

You also may want to use manual links if you want the client document to update selectively. This may occur if you have Microsoft Excel linked to a mainframe database, so inventory charts can be analyzed every ten minutes. A manually controlled link from Microsoft Excel into a Word for Windows document, however, updates an inventory report only when you request an update.

When you open the **E**dit menu and choose Paste **S**pecial to create a link, it is created as an automatic link. To change a link to a manually updated link, follow these steps:

1. Select the linked data or graphic.

2. Open the **E**dit menu and choose Lin**k**s. The Links dialog box appears.

3. Select the Update option that specifies when you want updates, as follows:

   Manual   Link is updated when you specify

   Automatic   Link is updated when source data changes

4. Choose OK.

To update a manual link, use the procedure described in "Updating Links," earlier in this chapter. Some applications enable you to update a link by selecting the linked data and pressing a shortcut key, such as F9. To prevent a link from updating, lock the link by using the next procedure.

Locking a Link To Prevent Accidental Changes

You may want to prevent accidental updating of a link but still want updates at your discretion. You can do this by locking or unlocking the related link. To lock or unlock a link, select the linked data, and open the **E**dit menu and choose Lin**k**s. Select the link you want to lock or unlock, and then select or clear the Loc**k**ed check box.

Unlinking Inserted Files or Pictures

To unlink the server document and change the result into normal text or graphics that do not change when the server changes, select the linked data, open the **E**dit menu and choose Lin**k**s, and then click the **B**reak Link button. A dialog box appears, asking you to confirm that you want the link cancelled. Choose **Y**es to cancel the link.

II

Managing Your Work

Editing Links when Server File Names or Locations Change

If a server document's location, file name, or the linked range within the document changes, you need to change the link. If you do not change the link, the client document cannot find the correct server document or the correct data within the document.

To update a link, open the **E**dit menu and choose Lin**k**s, select the link you need to edit, and then click the Cha**n**ge Source button. The Change Source dialog box appears, (see fig. 6.15). Within this dialog box, you can edit the **D**irectories, **F**ile Name, or **I**tem text boxes to match the path, file, and range name for the new server. (The **I**tem is the range name or bookmark that describes the linked data within the document.)

Fig. 6.15
Use the Change Source dialog box when a linked file's name or directory changes.

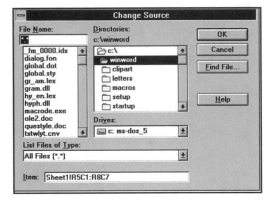

From Here...

For more information relating to linking or embedding data (or ensuring that applications are correctly installed so they can use linked and embedded objects), you may want to review the following sections of this book:

- Chapter 5, "Simple Data Sharing," describes copy, cut, and paste techniques you can use to transfer a portion of data when you do not need to create a link to the original or embed a full copy of the data.

- Chapter 21, "Installing and Configuring Windows Applications," shows you how to manually register a Windows application so that Windows knows the application's capabilities (if the registration process fails, or you move the application to another directory).

Chapter 7

Customizing with Control Panel

Control Panel gives you the power to customize Windows. You can add print-ers and fonts; change window colors, background patterns, or date and time formats; set Windows for different languages, keyboards, and date/time/cur-rency formats; add a screen saver; control how your computer interacts with a network; and so on.

In this chapter, you learn how to:

- Customize Windows' colors

- Customize your desktop

- Change your computer's date and time

- Control how your keyboard works

- Control how your mouse works

- Change international settings

Operating Control Panel

Control Panel's icon looks like a personal computer with a clock and a mouse (see fig. 7.1). The icon is in the Main group window in Program Manager.

To open Control Panel, follow these steps:

1. Open Program Manager.

2. Activate the Main group window.

3. Open Control Panel by double-clicking its icon.

Fig. 7.1
The Control Panel icon within the Main group window.

Control Panel icon

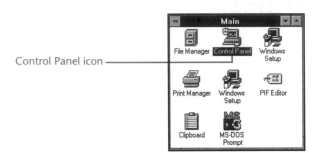

◀ "Starting Applications," p. 48

When you start Control Panel, its window shows the icons shown in figure 7.2 (or some variation of these icons). Each icon represents an application you can use to customize some feature of Windows. Although many Control Panel applications are standard with Windows, others appear only when you install certain equipment. The 386 Enhanced icon appears when Windows is running in 386 Enhanced mode, for example, and a Network icon appears if you have installed network software.

Fig. 7.2
Control Panel, showing icons that represent different applications used to customize Windows.

To use one of the Control Panel applications to customize Windows, double-click the application that fits your needs. The following table shows the icons that generally appear in Control Panel and describes what each application does. (Your system may have different icons and different capabilities.)

Table 7.1 Control Panel Icons	
Icon	**Description**
Color	Changes the colors in the desktop and other parts of the Windows environment.
Fonts	Adds or removes TrueType and other fonts; turns TrueType on or off.
Ports	Configures the printer and communication ports (COM1 through COM4) and defines how they work. Establishes IRQ interrupt settings.
Mouse	Adjusts how fast the pointer moves when you move the mouse and the speed at which you double-click, enables or disables the mouse "trails," and enables you to reverse the left and right mouse buttons.
Desktop	Changes the patterns or pictures used as the desktop background, specifies how icons align themselves on the desktop and icon title word-wrapping, and controls the operation of the screen saver.
Keyboard	Changes the keyboard's rate of repeating.
Network	Controls how you interact with your network if installed.
Printers	Adds or removes printer drivers and defines which features they use; connects printers to the appropriate port or network queue.
International	Changes display and operation between different languages, keyboards, and formats for numbers, date, time, and currency.
Date/Time	Resets the computer's date and time.
386 Enhanced	Indicates how applications run in 386 Enhanced mode, which controls the default amount of processor power each application uses and how they contend with conflicts over peripherals. This icon is visible only if Windows is running in 386 Enhanced mode. Also used to configure virtual memory.
Drivers	Installs and configures your system's multimedia drivers, including sound boards, CD Audio, and MIDI.
MIDI Mapper	Sets up MIDI devices (for details, refer to Chapter 20, "Using Windows Multimedia").
Sound	Sets the sounds used for different Windows events.

Customizing Windows with Color

After working in the drab and dreary DOS computer world, one of the first changes many Windows users want to make is to customize their screens. You can pick colors for window titles, backgrounds, bars—in fact all parts of the window. Predesigned color schemes range from the brilliant Fluorescent and Hot Dog Stand schemes to the cool Ocean and dark Black Leather Jacket schemes. You also can design and save your own color schemes and blend your own colors.

Using Existing Color Schemes

◀ "Using Menus and Dialog Boxes," p. 31

Windows comes with a set of predefined color schemes. Each color scheme maps a different color to a different part of the screen; you can select from existing color schemes, or you can devise your own schemes (described in the next section). To select one of the predefined color schemes, follow these steps:

1. Double-click the Color icon in Control Panel to display the Color dialog box (see fig. 7.3).

Fig. 7.3
The Color dialog box.

2. Select the Color **S**chemes drop-down list box by clicking the down arrow.

3. Select a named color scheme from the list. The colors in the demonstration window show how Windows will appear with these colors.

4. Choose OK if you want to use the displayed color scheme, return to step 2 to select another color scheme, or choose Cancel to close the Color dialog box without making any changes.

Creating Color Schemes

You can select all or some of the colors for the parts of your Windows desktop. For example, you can select different colors for the inactive and active title bars, for the border, for regular and highlighted text, and so on. You can use existing colors or blend your own, as described later in this chapter. To create new color schemes, follow these steps:

1. Open Control Panel.

2. Double-click the Color icon.

3. Open the Color **S**chemes list by clicking the arrow button. Select the scheme that most closely matches the color combination you want.

4. Click the Color **P**alette button to display the right side of the Color dialog box (see fig. 7.4).

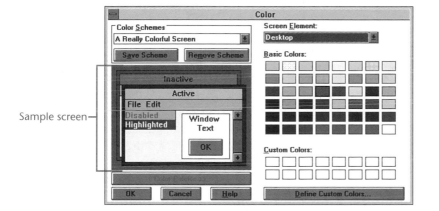

Fig. 7.4
The expanded Color dialog box to choose your own colors.

5. In the sample screen, click the window element you want to change. (Some elements require that you click more than once. For example, clicking the OK button once enables you to change the Button Shadow; clicking additional times enables you to change the Button Text, Button Face, and Button Highlight—although not necessarily in that order. To see which element you have selected, read the Screen **E**lement text box.)

   Alternatively, select the window element you want to change in the Screen **E**lement drop-down list.

6. Click the color you want in the **B**asic Colors palette. As soon as you select the color, the demonstration window shows the change.

7. Choose one of these alternatives for the colors you have selected:

■ If you want to change the color of another window element, return to step 5.

■ If you want to save these colors so that you can use them now or return to them at any time, click the Save Scheme button and assign the new color scheme a name in the Color Schemes list box.

■ If you want to use these colors now but you don't want to create a new named color scheme, click OK or press Enter.

■ If you want to cancel these color changes and return to the original scheme, choose Cancel.

To remove a color scheme, select the scheme you want to remove from the Color Schemes drop-down list and click the Remove Scheme button. Choose Yes to confirm.

Blending Custom Colors

Windows lets you blend your own colors and custom design your own color schemes. In addition to the 48 colors in the basic palette, Windows can display up to 16 additional blended colors in the custom palette. You can use the colors you create for the custom palette in the same way as you do the colors in the basic palette. Figure 7.5 shows the Custom Color Selector dialog box which you use to blend your own colors.

Fig. 7.5
Blending your own colors with the Custom Color Selector dialog box.

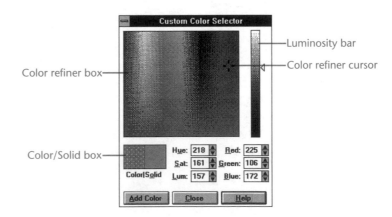

In the Custom Color Selector dialog box, you can create colors in one of two ways, described in the steps that follow. You can click the color you want and then adjust its luminosity, or you can exactly define the hue, saturation, and luminosity of the color.

Hue, Saturation, Luminosity, and Dithering

Hue. Amount of red/green/blue components in the color

Saturation. Purity of the color; lower saturation colors have more gray

Luminosity. How bright or dull the color is

Dithering. Dot pattern of colors that approximates colors that cannot be displayed—in the Color/Solid box, these are the blended colors

To blend your own colors, follow these steps:

1. Double-click the Color icon in Control Panel.

2. Click the Color **P**alette button to open the Color dialog box.

3. If you want the color you have created to appear in a specific box on the **C**ustom Colors palette, select the box by clicking it.

4. Click the **D**efine Custom Colors button. The Custom Color Selector dialog box appears.

5. Click the approximate color you want in the color refiner box. The color refiner cursor moves to the spot where you clicked, and the color you selected appears in the color/solid box.

   You also can drag the mouse pointer around in the color refiner box while holding down the mouse button; the color refiner cursor appears when you release the mouse button.

   This step selects the color's hue and saturation. Next, drag the arrowhead up or down along the side of the luminosity bar to adjust the luminosity of the color. (You can adjust the color in small increments by clicking the up or down arrows to the right of each text box.)

   To specify a particular color whose numbers you know, click the box you want to adjust (**R**ed, **G**reen, **B**lue, **H**ue, **S**at, or **L**um) and adjust the value in the box by typing new numbers or by clicking the up or down arrow on the right side of the box to increase or decrease the number.

The color refiner cursor, luminosity bar, and Color/Solid box reflect the changes you make. Continue adjusting until you have the correct set of numbers and the color looks correct in the Color/Solid box.

6. If you want a solid color (rather than blended), double-click the solid (right) side of the Color/Solid box when the color displayed there is correct.

7. Click the **A**dd Color button to add this color to the custom palette. Each time you click the **A**dd Color button, a new color is added to the next box in the **C**ustom Colors section of the Color dialog box.

8. Return to step 5 if you want to add more colors to the custom palette.

   or

   Choose **C**lose to close the Custom Color Selector dialog box.

You can assign custom colors to any part of your window by following the steps described in the preceding section, "Creating Color Schemes."

Customizing the Desktop

Changing colors is just one way you can customize the desktop. You also can change the pattern used in the desktop background, add a graphical wallpaper as a background, change the border width of windows, adjust the positioning of icons, and more.

To think of how color, pattern, and wallpaper interact on your screen, imagine the Windows desktop (screen background) as a wall. The wall can have a color selected from the Color dialog box (see the preceding section for details) and a pattern. You also can hang wallpaper over the entire wall or just a part of the wall.

You can put wallpaper over just the center portion of the desktop, or you can tile the desktop with wallpaper, with the wallpaper repeating as necessary to fill the area. Tiling wallpaper may put wallpaper pieces edge-to-edge to fill the screen. Even when wallpaper fills the screen, icon titles show through with the desktop's color and pattern.

Wallpaper options you select here can include patterns that come with Windows—including some wild and colorful ones—designs you create or modify with Windows Paintbrush or other drawing programs, or designs you obtain commercially or from computer bulletin boards.

Customizing the Background Pattern

Earlier in this chapter, you learned how to change the desktop's background color using the Color dialog box. In this section you learn how to put a pattern over the desktop's color. The *pattern* is a small grid of dots that repeats to fill the screen.

Windows comes with predefined patterns you can select; you also can create your own. The color of the pattern is the same as the color selected for Window Text in the Color dialog box.

To choose an existing desktop pattern, follow these steps:

1. Double-click the Desktop icon in Control Panel. The Desktop dialog box appears (see fig. 7.6).

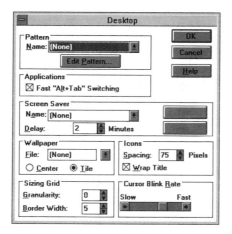

Fig. 7.6

The Desktop dialog box.

II

Managing Your Work

2. Open the **N**ame list in the Pattern section of the dialog box. Select a pattern from the list. Some of the built-in repetitive patterns you can select are 50% Gray, Boxes, Diamonds, Weave, and Scottie.

3. Choose OK to add the pattern to the desktop.

You can edit or create new patterns only if you have a mouse. To edit an existing pattern or create a new pattern, follow these steps:

1. In the Pattern section of the Desktop dialog box, choose the Edit **Pat**-tern button. The Desktop - Edit Pattern dialog box appears (see fig. 7.7).

Fig. 7.7
The Desktop - Edit Pattern dialog box. The Sample area shows how the pattern will appear when it covers the screen.

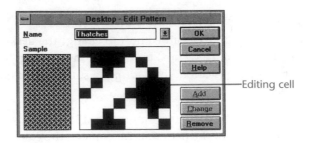

Editing cell

2. Select an existing pattern from the **N**ame drop-down list or type a new name if you want to create a new pattern.

3. To reverse a dot in the pattern to the opposite color, click the dot in the editing cell. Watch the sample box to see the overall effect.

4. Continue to click in the grid until the pattern is what you want. You also can drag the mouse pointer across multiple dots to make quick changes.

5. When you are finished creating or editing, continue with one of the following options:

   ■ If you want to replace the existing pattern with your new version, click the Change button.

   ■ If you want to add the new pattern to the list of available patterns, type a new name in the **N**ame list box and then click the **A**dd button.

6. Choose OK or press Enter.

Tip
Because the pattern appears behind program icon names, it may make the icon names hard to read, especially if you are using wallpaper as well. If you plan to use wallpaper, don't use a desktop pattern.

To remove an unwanted pattern from the list, select the pattern and click the **R**emove button. Confirm the deletion by choosing **Y**es. The **R**emove button is available only immediately after you specify a pattern name in the **N**ame text box.

Wallpapering Your Desktop with a Graphic

Using a graphic or picture as the Windows desktop is a nice personal touch. For special business situations or for custom applications, you may want to use a color company logo or pictorial theme as the Wallpaper for your desktop.

Windows comes with a collection of graphics for the desktop. You can modify these images or draw new images for the desktop with Paintbrush or other programs. For high-quality pictorials, use a scanner to create a digitized black-and-white or color image.

Figures 7.8 and 7.9 show two of the several wallpaper patterns that come with Windows. Most of the patterns must be tiled to fill the entire screen, which you learn how to do in the upcoming steps.

Fig. 7.8
The Arches wallpaper as a desktop background.

Fig. 7.9
The Tartan wallpaper as a desktop background.

II

Managing Your Work

Tip

Bit-map images displayed as the desktop wallpaper use more memory than a colored or patterned desktop. If you run low on memory, remove the wallpaper.

Wallpaper is created from files stored in a bit-map format. These files end with the BMP extension and, to be used as wallpaper, must be stored in the WINDOWS directory. You can edit BMP formats with Paintbrush. You also can read and edit files in PCX format with Paintbrush and then save them in BMP format to use as a desktop wallpaper.

To select wallpaper, follow these steps:

1. Double-click the Desktop icon in Control Panel.

2. Open the Wallpaper File drop-down list.

3. Select a wallpaper from the list.

4. Select Center to center the wallpaper in the desktop; select Tile to fill the desktop with the wallpaper. Tile uses multiple copies if necessary.

5. Choose OK or press Enter.

To remove the wallpaper from the desktop, repeat the preceding steps but select None in step 3.

Creating Desktop Wallpapers

You can create your own desktop wallpapers in one of three ways:

■ Buy clip art from a software vendor. If the clip art is not in PCX or BMP format, use a graphics-conversion application such as DoDot! to convert the image to one of these formats. Use Paintbrush to read PCX format and resave the figure in BMP format.

■ Scan a black-and-white or color picture using a digital scanner. Scanners create TIFF files with the extension TIF. Use a graphics-conversion application to convert the TIF file to a BMP file for use as a wallpaper or to a PCX file to use with Paintbrush.

■ Modify an existing desktop wallpaper or create a new one with Paintbrush. Use Paintbrush to read BMP or PCX files. After you edit them with Paintbrush, save the files with the BMP format. See Chapter 11, "Using Windows Paintbrush," for more information on working with Paintbrush.

Store your new BMP graphics files in the WINDOWS directory.

To remove a wallpaper file from the Wallpaper File list, delete or remove its BMP file from the WINDOWS directory.

Setting Up a Screen Saver

A screen saver prevents an image from burning into your screen by replacing a document screen with pictures or patterns. You can specify the delay before the screen saver activates, and you can set up various attributes—including a password—for most of the screen savers.

To select and set up a screen saver, follow these steps:

1. Open the Desktop dialog box.

2. Open the Screen Saver Name drop-down list and select the screen saver you want.

   Choose Test to see what the screen saver looks like.

3. Select Delay and enter the number of minutes after you quit using your computer that the screen saver should appear.

4. Choose Setup to set various parameters for your screen saver. The parameters for each are different; figure 7.10 shows the Setup dialog box for the screen saver Mystify. Choose OK or press Enter.

5. Choose OK or press Enter to close the Desktop dialog box.

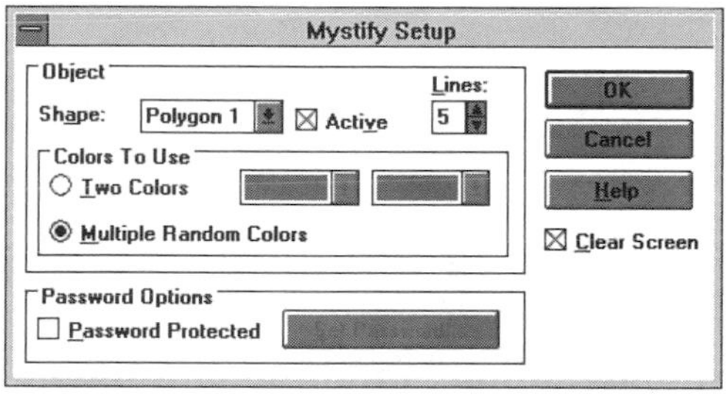

Fig. 7.10
Options for the Mystify screen saver.

Although each Windows screen saver has unique settings, all except Blank Screen have an area where you can specify password protection. This requires the correct entry of the password before the normal Windows desktop is restored.

To set the password, select the Password Protected option. Then select the Set Password button, which displays the Change Password dialog box (see fig. 7.11). In the New Password box, type your password; in the Retype New Password box, confirm your password by typing it again (both must contain the same characters). As you type in the characters for the password, an asterisk (*) is shown for each character. Passwords are not case-sensitive and can contain punctuation, but can be no longer than 20 characters. Once you have entered the password twice, choose OK. A dialog box alerts you if the passwords do not match. Use the **T**est button to test the screen saver. Then when you press a key, you can test the password before the screen is restored.

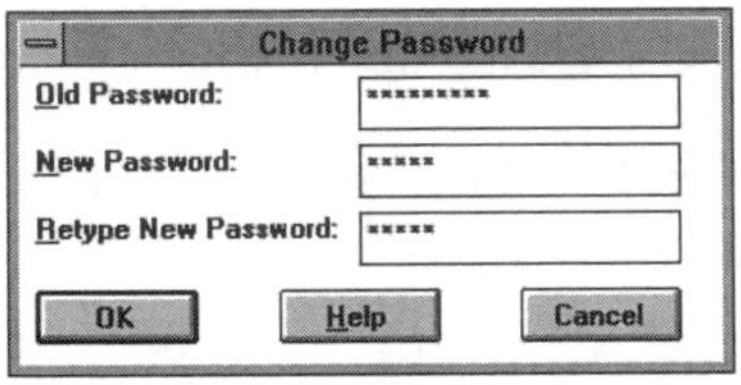

Fig. 7.11
The Change
Password dialog
box.

After you have set the password, you can change it with the same procedure. You first must correctly enter the existing password in the **O**ld Password box before you can successfully change the password. You can clear the password by leaving the password fields blank—but you need to know the old password before you can change it.

The screen saver is activated after the time-out specified in the dialog box. Any mouse movement or click, or key pressed on the keyboard restores the desktop (use the Shift key to restore your desktop so that your application isn't affected). If you have enabled passwords, a dialog box prompts you for the password, which must be correctly entered before the desktop screen is restored.

Spacing and Aligning Icons

If the names of your application or program item icons overlap, you may want to change the automatic spacing of the icons. At the same time, you also can turn on a grid that helps you align icons in a neat and orderly row.

To change the space between icons, click the **S**pacing option in the Icons section of the Desktop dialog box. Then specify the desired number of pixels (screen dots) of separation between icons. The width you specify applies to both the icon and its label. The maximum number of pixels you can specify for spacing is 512.

When your icon titles are long, you can put them on multiple text lines by selecting the **W**rap Title check box; if you want the names all on one line, deselect the **W**rap Title option.

To line up icons more easily, turn on an invisible grid that icons "snap to." With the grid on, move and then release an icon close to the desired location; the icon "snaps to" the nearest grid line. Use the grid to help put all the icons on the same line. When the grid is on, it also affects window sizing so that the window edges align with the grid.

To turn on the invisible "snap to" grid system, select the **G**ranularity option and specify the desired number of pixels between grid lines. You can specify numbers between 0 and 49; each increment of 1 moves the icons 8 pixels apart. Enter 0 to turn off the grid.

To change the border width on most windows, select the **B**order Width option and specify a new number. Widths can range from 1, the narrowest, to 50, the widest. Changing the border width to a value of 3 to 5 makes it easier to use the mouse to grab the window border for resizing.

> **Note**
>
> Windows that you cannot resize have a fixed border width you cannot change.

Setting Up Fast Switching between Applications

The Fast "Alt+Tab" Switching check box in the Desktop dialog box provides a quick method for switching between applications. When this option is enabled, pressing Alt+Tab displays a title box in the center of your screen, with the next application's name. Pressing Alt+Tab repeatedly quickly cycles through the open applications. When you see the name of the application you want to switch to, release the Alt key. Press Alt+Esc to return to your original application.

◀ "Switching between Applications," p. 63

Alt+Tab switching is selected by default when Windows is installed.

Adjusting the Cursor Blink Rate

Some people are driven frantic by a rapidly blinking cursor; others fall asleep when the cursor blinks too slowly. Whichever group you happen to fall in, remember that you can control the blink rate. To change the cursor blink rate, use the Cursor Blink **R**ate option in the Desktop dialog box. Drag the scroll box or click the left or right arrows to adjust the setting. Watch the sample cursor to see the resulting blink rate.

Managing Your Work

Changing the System Date and Time

▶ "Keeping Time with Clock," p. 501

Use Control Panel's Date/Time icon to change the date or time in your computer system. Open the Date/Time icon from Control Panel to display the Date & Time dialog box (see fig. 7.12).

To change the date or time, click the up or down arrows to scroll rapidly to the date or time you want, or type the new date or time. Choose OK or press Enter when the date or time is set correctly.

Fig. 7.12
The Date & Time dialog box.

Tip
With some Windows applications, including Word for Windows and Excel, you can create custom date and time formats different from the predefined formats.

Changing date and time formats is explained in "Customizing International Settings" later in this chapter. Often you need to select only the country to change the date and time formats accordingly.

Changing Keyboard Speed

Although changing the keyboard speed doesn't result in a miracle that makes you type faster, it does speed up the rate at which characters are repeated. You also can change the delay before the character repeats.

Change the keyboard repeat rate by double-clicking the Keyboard icon in Control Panel. The Keyboard dialog box appears (see fig. 7.13). Drag the scroll box or click the arrow buttons to change the setting for **R**epeat Rate and **D**elay Before First Repeat as desired. Test the repeat rate by clicking the **T**est box; then press and hold down one letter key to see how quickly it repeats.

Fig. 7.13
The Keyboard dialog box.

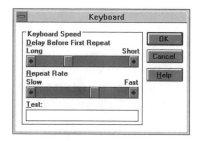

> **Note**
>
> Four of the most commonly repeated keys are the arrow keys. Use the Repeat Rate option to set the repeat rate that is most comfortable for you when you press an arrow key. To test the speed of the arrows in the **T**est text box, you first must type text in the box.

Controlling the Mouse

If you are left-handed or if you like a "hot-rod" mouse, you will want to know how to modify your mouse's behavior. Double-click the Mouse icon in Control Panel to display the Mouse dialog box (see fig. 7.14). To change the speed at which the pointer moves as you move the mouse, adjust the **M**ouse Tracking Speed option.

> **Note**
>
> Depending on which type of mouse and mouse driver you've installed on your system, the Mouse icon and Mouse dialog box may vary from the one shown in figure 7.14. Refer to the documentation that comes with your mouse or the on-line help to get information on the settings that are associated with your mouse.

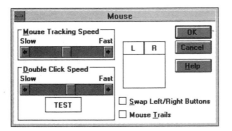

Fig. 7.14
The Mouse dialog box.

Activating the Mouse **T**rails check box causes mouse movement to leave a trail of mouse pointers on the screen. This feature is especially useful if you have an LCD screen where the mouse pointer can sometimes get lost. This option cannot be shown for video display drivers that don't support it.

Swapping Mouse Buttons

If you use the mouse with your left hand, you may find the mouse more comfortable to use if you reverse the left and right mouse buttons. Mark the **S**wap Left/Right Buttons check box. Press the left and right mouse buttons and watch the test *L* and *R* to see the result. This option takes effect immediately, so you need to use the Right mouse button to unmark the button swapping.

Changing the Double-Click Rate

◄ "Using the Mouse," p. 28

► "Getting the Mouse To Work," p. 984

Another customizable feature is the rate at which Windows recognizes double-clicks with the mouse. Some people—especially beginners—double-click the mouse slowly. As you gain experience with Windows, the speed at which you double-click increases. To change the double-click response rate, drag the **D**ouble Click Speed scroll box to the left or right. Double-click in the TEST box to test the new rate; the TEST box changes colors when you have successfully double-clicked.

Customizing International Settings

Windows has the capacity to switch between different international character sets, time and date displays, and numeric formats. The international settings you choose in Control Panel affect applications, such as Microsoft Excel, that take advantage of these Windows features.

Check with Vendors for International Software Versions

Although you can use the International dialog box to change language and country formats, doing so does not change the language used in menus or Help information. To obtain versions of Windows and Microsoft applications for countries other than the United States, check with your local Microsoft representative. Check with the corporate offices of other software vendors for international versions of their applications.

Changing the Character Set

To set up Windows with a country format, keyboard layout, measurement system, and other settings that vary from those of the United States, follow these steps:

1. Double-click the International icon in Control Panel. The International dialog box appears (see fig. 7.15).

2. Open the **C**ountry drop-down list, and select a country. The sample formats in the Date, Time, Currency, and Number boxes change to match the selected country. Changing the country also may change default paper sizes in your applications.

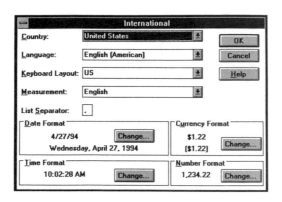

Fig. 7.15
The International
dialog box.

3. Open the **L**anguage drop-down list, and select the language you use. Changing this option enables your applications to accurately sort words that may contain non-English characters, such as accent marks. However, changing the language setting does not change the language use by Windows. You need to purchase a different language version of Windows to accomplish this.

4. Open the **K**eyboard Layout drop-down list, and select the international keyboard style you use. Changing this option enables you to use key-characters specific to your language.

5. Open the **M**easurement drop-down list, and select either English (for inches) or Metric (for centimeters).

6. In the List **S**eparator text box, type the character you want to use to separate lists. Many applications, such as Microsoft Excel, use the separator character to separate a list of arguments used in math functions.

7. Make custom changes to the **D**ate Format, **T**ime Format, C**u**rrency Format, or **N**umber Format boxes as necessary. (See the next section for details.)

8. Choose OK or press Enter.

Selecting the Number Format

If the number, currency, date, and time formats do not change to what you want when you select a **C**ountry setting, you can change their formats manually. The following instructions explain how to make these manual adjustments.

To change the number format when the International dialog box is already open, follow these steps:

1. Select the **N**umber Format box by clicking its Change button. The International - Number Format dialog box appears (see fig. 7.16).

Fig. 7.16
The International -
Number Format
dialog box.

2. Select the formatting option you want, as described in the following table.

Option	Description
1000 **S**eparator	Changes the character separating thousands
Decimal Separator	Changes the character separating decimal and whole numbers
D**e**cimal Digits	Changes the number of decimal digits displayed
Leading Zero	Specifies whether a leading zero displays in front of decimal numbers

3. Choose OK or press Enter.

4. Examine the sample format. Return to step 2 to make additional changes if desired.

5. Choose OK to accept the new format.

Change the currency format in the same way you changed the number format. Click the C**u**rrency Format Change button to display the International - Currency Format dialog box (see fig. 7.17). Then select options from the drop-down list boxes or type your entry. The following table lists the options available.

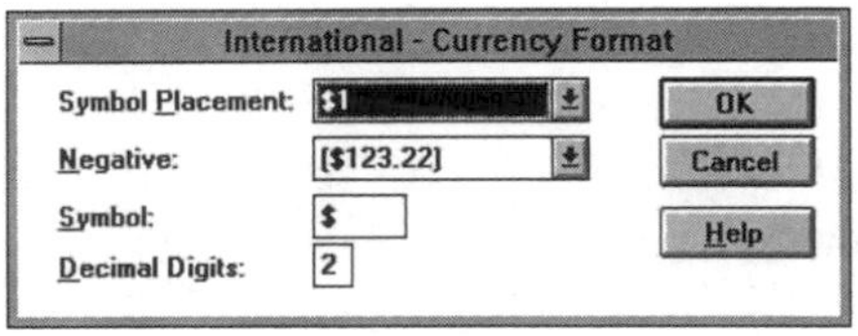

Fig. 7.17
The International -
Currency Format
dialog box.

Option	Description
Symbol **P**lacement	Selects the placement and spacing of the currency symbol.
Negative	Indicates how you want negative currency amounts to appear.
Symbol	Specifies the currency symbol (you may have to select a different keyboard to type the character you want).
Decimal Digits	Specifies the number of decimal digits you want to display by default (but note that applications such as spreadsheets can override this setting).

Changing Date and Time Formats

Changing date and time formats in the International dialog box changes the default date and time formats in most Windows applications. It also changes how they display in the Windows accessories. Choosing the country usually changes the date and time to that country's standard. To make specific changes, however, click the Change button in the **D**ate Format or **T**ime Format section of the International dialog box and select from the lists presented.

Changing the Date Format

When you click the **D**ate Format Change button, the International - Date Format dialog box appears (see fig. 7.18).

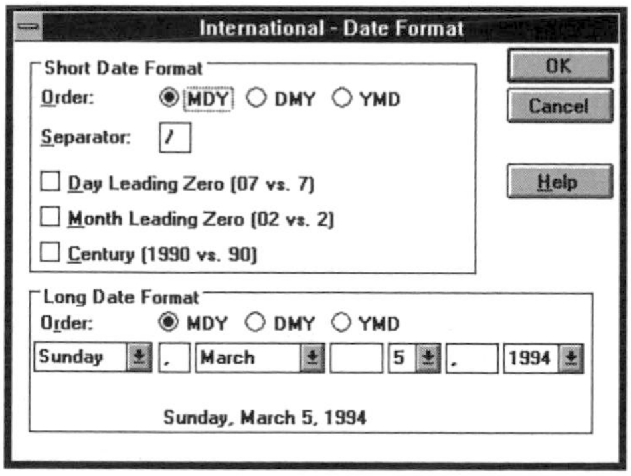

Fig. 7.18
The International - Date Format dialog box.

Notice that the formatting group at the top of the dialog box is for short dates, such as 6/12/94, and the bottom formatting group is for long dates, such as June 12, 1994. With many Windows applications, you can format dates so that they spell out the full month or day. Tables 7.2 and 7.3 list date format options.

Table 7.2 Short Date Format Options	
Option	**Description**
Order	Changes the order in which month (M), day (D), and year (Y) display.
Separator	Changes the character separating the month, day, and year (for example, the / in 6/12/94).
Day Leading Zero	Changes how day digits display (for example, 7/1/94 or 7/01/94).
Month Leading Zero	Changes how month digits display (for example, 7/1/94 or 07/1/94).
Century	Changes how years display (for example, 1994 or just 94).

Table 7.3 Long Date Format Options	
Option	**Description**
Order	Changes the order in which month (M), day (D), and year (Y) display.
Day of the week	Changes between full day name and abbreviated name.
Month	Changes between full month name, abbreviation, and numeric (with or without leading zeros).
Day of the month	Changes between numeric day formats (with or without leading zeros).
Year	Changes between numeric year formats (the last two digits or all four digits).

> **Note**
>
> When you change the long date format, watch the sample date at the bottom of the dialog box. (No sample date appears for short date formats.)

The long date format boxes are dynamic; they change order as you select different MDY orders.

Be careful not to miss the Separator text boxes. These boxes contain the character that appears between segments of long dates. Type the character you prefer to use—usually a period, a slash, or a comma.

Changing the Time Format

When you click the **T**ime Format Change button, the International - Time Format dialog box appears (see fig. 7.19). Select new time formats in the same way you did date formats. The time-format options are given in the following table.

Fig. 7.19
The International - Time Format dialog box.

Option	Result
12 hour 00:00-11:59	Displays times from a 12-hour clock.
24 hour 12:00-23:59	Displays times from a 24-hour clock.
AM/PM boxes	Specifies the 12-hour time formats you want (for example, am and pm or AM and PM). If you select the 24-hour format, use the text box to type a time zone abbreviation (such as EST for Eastern Standard Time).
Separator	Specifies the character separating time segments.
Leading Zero	Adds or removes leading zeros for times.

Setting Up Serial Ports

Serial ports are hardware connections in the computer to which you connect some printers and all modems. Unlike *parallel ports* (also called *LPT* ports), serial ports (also called *COM* ports) must be set up so that Windows knows the speed of data to be sent to the port and how to package information it sends.

Basic Port Settings

Use the Ports icon from Control Panel to set up COM ports. If you do not have a serial printer, a modem, or other serial device, you do not need to set up serial ports.

To set up a serial port, follow these steps:

1. Double-click the Ports icon in Control Panel. The Ports dialog box appears (see fig. 7.20).

Fig. 7.20
The Ports dialog
box.

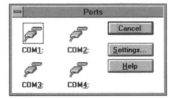

2. Click the COM port you want to set up. All ports (COM1:-COM4:) are shown, even if they are not installed on your computer.

3. Click the **S**ettings button to display the Settings dialog box (see fig. 7.21).

Fig. 7.21
The port settings
for COM1.

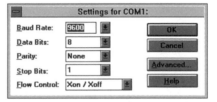

▶ "Selecting
Commun-
ications
Parameters,"
p. 430

4. Select the options needed by the device you have connected to the specified COM port. Refer to your printer, plotter, or modem manual for these settings. The options you select must be compatible with the communications parameters of the device. The options are described in the following table.

Option	Description
Baud Rate	Changes the speed at which information is sent to the port. Most modems in use are 9600 or 14400 baud. Printers generally use 9600 baud. Check your printer settings to make sure that you use the correct value.

Option	Description
Data Bits	Changes the amount of information sent in each package of data. The setting is usually 7 or 8.
Parity	Changes the type of error-checking performed. Most PC software uses None as the parity setting.
Stop Bits	Changes how data packets are marked. The setting usually is 1.
Flow Control	Changes how the computer and the device signal each other when a packet of data is received. Refer to the manual for your communication device to determine what kind of handshaking is used.

Advanced Port Settings

The Advanced Port settings enable you to specify the base input/output port address and interrupt request number used by your COM ports. These settings must match those installed in your computer. The following table shows the normal settings for the COM ports.

Port	I/O Address	Interrupt
COM1	03F8	4
COM2	02F8	3
COM3	03E8	4
COM4	02E8	3

To make changes to these settings, follow these steps:

1. Double-click the Ports icon in Control Panel. The Ports dialog box appears.

2. Click the COM port that you want to modify.

3. Click the **S**ettings button to display the Settings dialog box.

4. Click the **A**dvanced button, which displays the Advanced Settings dialog box for the port you selected (see fig. 7.22).

5. Enter the **B**ase I/O Port Address in the text box or click the down arrow to see a standard list of values, and then select the desired port address.

II

Managing Your Work

Fig. 7.22
Advanced Settings
dialog box.

6. To change the Interrupt, select the **I**nterrupt Request Line (IRQ) option and change the value.

7. Choose OK to return to the Settings dialog box; then choose OK to save your changes for that port.

8. Make any needed changes to the other ports with the same procedure; then choose Close to exit the Ports dialog box and return to Control Panel.

Configuring for 386 Enhanced Mode

◀ "Choosing an Operating Mode," p. 67

Tip
Computers with an 80386, 80386sx, 80486sx, or 80486 processor and more than 2M of memory automatically run in 386 Enhanced mode.

◀ "Using Multiple Applications," p. 63

One of the two modes that Windows runs in on an 80386 computer is 386 Enhanced mode. In 386 Enhanced mode, you can run DOS applications in a window and continue to run applications even when they are not in the active window. In standard mode, DOS applications must run full-screen—they cannot run in a window. Also, DOS applications are suspended—they are in memory but not computing—when another application is running. Both these features could cause difficulties if it were not for the control you have with Control Panel.

Setting Multitasking Options

If you run multiple applications simultaneously (DOS and Windows) while in 386 Enhanced mode, each application uses part of the processor's calculating power and the performance of all applications degrades. Processing takes longer. By using Control Panel, however, you can specify how much processor time is spent on each application. This becomes important if you are running an application such as a database report-generator in the *background* (an inactive window) and calculating a worksheet in the *foreground* (the active window). If these applications shared processing power equally, the worksheet runs significantly slower. If you don't need the database report quickly, you can schedule less computing power for the report-generator, leaving more calculating power for the worksheet.

To schedule different amounts of processing power for Windows and DOS applications, follow these steps:

1. Double-click the 386 Enhanced icon in Control Panel. The 386
Enhanced dialog box appears (see fig. 7.23).

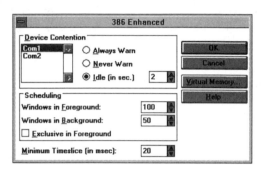

Fig. 7.23
The 386 Enhanced
dialog box.

2. Select the Scheduling options you need and type a number in the text
boxes. The options are described in the following table.

Option	Description
Windows in **F**oreground	Schedules the amount of processing time for Windows applications running in the active window relative to DOS applications running in the background. The setting can be from 1 to 10,000 for the Windows application. This setting is relative to the settings of other applications.
Windows in **B**ackground	Schedules the amount of processing time for Windows applications running in the back-ground (inactive) window relative to DOS applications running in the foreground (active) window. The setting can be from 1 to 10,000 for the Windows application.
Exclusive in Foreground	Ensures that Windows applications always get 100 percent of the processing time when in an active window. This setting leaves DOS applications on hold in the background.
Minimum Timeslice	Specifies the number of milliseconds each application runs before the processor gives control to the next application. All Windows applications share one time slice; each DOS application gets its own time slice. Use a number from 1 to 1000.

3. Choose OK or make changes in the **D**evice Contention group.
The following section provides additional information about
device contention.

II

Managing Your Work

Note

The Foreground and Background settings apply only to Windows applications; foreground and background settings for DOS applications are controlled through PIF Editor.

Managing Device Contention

When two or more Windows applications need a printer or modem at the same time, Windows automatically acts as a referee to prevent lost data or interference between the applications. The battle between applications for the use of a printer or modem is called *device contention*. DOS applications that want to use a printer or modem simultaneously are not so obliging. When multiple DOS applications attempt to print or use the modem at the same time, problems can result. With Control Panel, however, you can control how Windows solves device contention for DOS applications.

To control device contention, follow these steps:

1. Double-click the 386 Enhanced icon in Control Panel.

2. Select from the **D**evice Contention list the port that may have a scheduling problem.

3. Select the way you want Windows to handle any contention problems. The following table describes the options.

Option	Description
Always Warn	Displays a message when a problem arises. You are then given the opportunity to select which application has priority over the port. In general, this is the safest and most commonly used option.
Never Warn	Allows any DOS application use of the port at any time. This can cause contention problems; use it only when you know that only one application at a time will attempt to use the port.
Idle	Specifies how long, in seconds, the port should remain idle before the next application can use it without the warning message appearing. Specify a time of 1 to 999 seconds. Use this option if you have an application that pauses between printing, such as a Lotus 1-2-3 print macro that prints multiple but separate pages, or a communications application that logs on to a database, downloads information, and then logs on a second time for additional information.

Configuring 386 Enhanced Virtual Memory

When Windows is running in 386 Enhanced mode, the program uses *virtual memory* (in the form of a permanent or temporary *swap file* on the hard disk) to handle applications and data that are larger than the memory available in RAM. Windows swaps the data or application back into memory as needed. The virtual memory functions as an extension of memory because it enables you to run more applications at once with more data than actually fits in memory.

Several factors affect the performance of this virtual memory. The speed at which your hard disk can retrieve data is an important factor, as well as the amount of space set aside for virtual memory. Other factors include the speed of your processor and the data transfer rate of the hard disk—how fast the data can be gotten from and sent to the hard disk. The amount of contiguous disk space—space that is all in the same spot rather than scattered through-out the hard disk—also is another important factor. Finally, the size of the virtual memory area on the hard disk affects the performance of virtual memory swapping.

The TEMP DOS environment variable specifies the location of the temporary swap file. This setting, placed in your AUTOEXEC.BAT file during the installa-tion of Windows, tells Windows where to create the temporary swap file. The Virtual Memory option of the 386 Enhanced dialog box enables you to look at the existing settings and configure the temporary or permanent swap file.

> **Note**
>
> Do not place a permanent swap file on a compressed drive. The permanent swap file should always be placed on the hot (uncompressed) drive. For more information on swap files, see Chapter 24, "Installing and Optimizing Windows 3.1."

There are several steps that you should take before creating permanent swap files. Discussed in greater detail in Chapter 24, they include the following:

- Delete unnecessary files.

- Recover storage space wasted by lost file clusters.

- Compact (optimize) your hard disk so that more contiguous disk space is available.

After you have completed these preliminary steps, follow these steps to set up the virtual memory area:

▶ "Using Memory Efficiently," p. 836

▶ "Optimizing Hard Disk Performance," p. 846

II

Managing Your Work

1. Double-click the 386 Enhanced icon in Control Panel.

2. Click the **V**irtual Memory button.

   The Virtual Memory dialog box shows the current swap file settings (see fig. 7.24).

Fig. 7.24

The Virtual Memory dialog box.

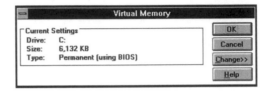

3. To change the settings, select **C**hange. Windows scans the current drive and then displays the expanded Virtual Memory dialog box (see fig. 7.25). The current settings are shown in the upper portion of the dialog box.

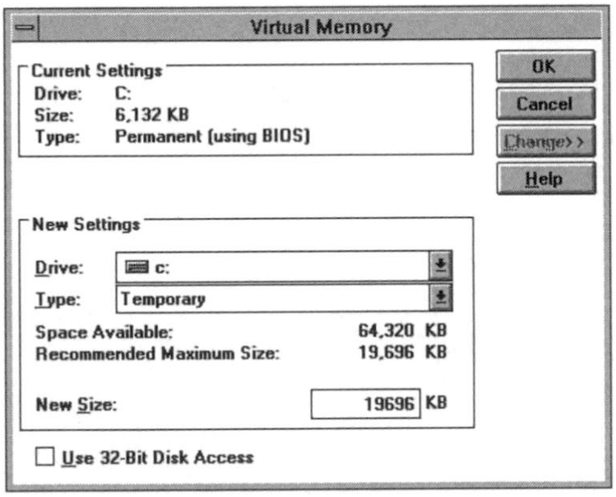

Fig. 7.25

Use the options in this dialog box to change the configuration of your swap file.

4. Select the **D**rive you want to use for the swap file. As you select each drive, Windows recomputes the space available (total amount of space on the disk) and recommended size values for that drive.

5. Change the **T**ype of swap file you want to use: Temporary, Permanent, or None. If you select a permanent swap file, the dialog box shows the maximum size (contiguous space) and recommended size.

> **Note**
>
> If you selected a network drive in step 5, the Permanent option isn't available.

6. Enter the size of the swap file you want to create in the New **S**ize box. Make this value as large as possible, but not more than the maximum size specified by Windows. (The use of noncontiguous disk space in your swap file slows down the swapping process.) The dialog box also shows the Recommended Size for Windows, which you can use as a guide to the value to enter in the Size box.

7. Some computers have the capability of 32-bit access, which increases the performance of accessing disk drives. The Windows Setup program determines if your system has this capability when Windows is installed, indicated by a check box in the Virtual Memory dialog box. To use this capability, select the **U**se 32-Bit Disk Access option.

8. Choose OK to create the swap file with the parameters specified. You are returned to the 386 Enhanced dialog box. Choose OK to exit back to Control Panel.

Using the Printers, Fonts, and Network Applets

When you first installed Windows on your computer, you were given the opportunity to set up Windows to work with your printer. If you didn't do this at the time you installed Windows, or if you purchase a new printer, you must tell Windows that you have added a printer to your system. The Printers icon in Control Panel is used to configure Windows to work with your printer. The steps for configuring a printer to work with your system are covered in detail in Chapter 9, "Printing with Windows."

When you install a new printer, Windows automatically adds the built-in fonts so that they appear in the list of fonts in your Windows applications. Later, if you purchase new software fonts or a font cartridge for your printer, you need to inform Windows that you have added these fonts so that you can display and use the fonts in your Windows applications. The Fonts application in Control Panel is used to add and remove fonts from your system. For detailed information on how to add and remove fonts in Windows, see Chapter 8, "Managing Fonts."

A Network icon appears in your Control Panel if your computer is attached to a network. You can use this icon to enable or disable network messages, to control drive mapping, and to set printing options and network warnings. For details about using Windows on a network, see Chapter 26, "Networking Windows 3.1x."

II

Managing Your Work

Working with Sound

A beeping computer is one thing when you're up playing Nintendo games after the kids have gone to bed. But it's something else entirely when you are at work and each earsplitting beep tells your coworkers you have made another embarrassing computer mistake.

You can control the way that Windows uses sound for warnings and other *events*, such as the default beep, certain dialog boxes and applications, and when you start or exit Windows. If you need more sound capability (for example, to use or create multimedia applications), you can install special sound devices such as a Sound Blaster or the Windows Sound System. The following sections describe how to use Control Panel to set up and control sound drivers and system sounds.

Where To Get a Windows Speaker Driver

You can obtain the new Microsoft Windows speaker driver, which adds more capabilities to the built-in sound that comes with Windows. You can obtain the driver by writing to the following address:

> Microsoft Customer Service
> 1 Microsoft Way
> Redmond, WA 98052-6399

If you have a modem, you can download the device driver from Microsoft's Download Service. Call (206) 936-6735 and use the following settings in your communications software:

> 1200, 2400, or 9600 baud
> No parity
> 8 data bits
> 1 stop bit

See Chapter 12, "Using Windows Terminal," for more information on setting communications parameters and connecting with an on-line service.

The file you want to download is called SPEAK.EXE. Once you have downloaded the file into a directory on your computer, go to the DOS prompt, type **SPEAK**, and press Enter. The file is self-extracting, and the files needed to install the driver are loaded onto your hard disk. One of the files is a TXT file with installation instructions, which you can read using Notepad in the Accessories program group. Follow the instructions for installing the driver.

Assigning System Sounds

To turn off the warning beep, double-click the Sound icon in Control Panel, deselect the E**n**able System Sounds option, and choose OK. This action disables all beeping for all applications used in Windows.

You use Control Panel's Drivers application to add support for any sound devices installed on your computer. This enables you to set the sounds used for various Windows events. To specify these settings, first use the Drivers application to install the sound drivers for your device. (See the next section for that procedure.) Then you can set the sounds for various Windows events by following these steps:

1. In Control Panel, double-click the Sound icon.

2. The Sound dialog box shows the available Windows events in one list box and the sound files in another list box (see fig. 7.26). Sound files normally have a WAV file extension. If your sound files are stored in another drive or directory, select the drive or directory from the **F**iles box.

▶ "Operating Sound Recorder," p. 670

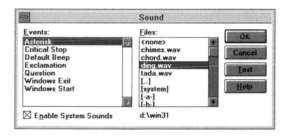

Fig. 7.26
The Sound dialog box.

3. Click the event that you want to change. The file being used for that event is selected in the **F**iles box. Click another sound file if you want to change it.

4. Click the **T**est button to see how the sound file sounds.

5. Repeat steps 3 and 4 for other Windows events.

6. When you have set sounds for all the events as desired, choose OK.

▶ "Choosing a Sound Board," p. 663

▶ "Adding Multimedia Drivers," p. 666

▶ "Using MIDI Mapper," p. 684

Configuring for Sound Devices

Windows has the capability to install *drivers* for multimedia devices, such as sound boards or CD-ROM drives. Windows comes with some sound drivers; other drivers are part of the added device. If you add a sound board, for instance, it may come with its own custom drivers but also can use the included Windows sound drivers.

> **Caution**
>
> Sounds have their limitations. If you are running a communications application in the background, a sound "task" in the foreground may cause data loss.

To install a driver, follow these steps:

1. In Control Panel, double-click the Drivers icon.

   The Drivers dialog box appears, showing a list of drivers that are standard with Windows (see fig. 7.27).

Fig. 7.27
The Drivers dialog box.

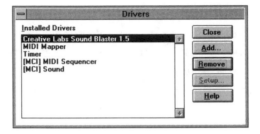

2. If you are configuring one of the listed devices, select it in the **I**nstalled Drivers list, choose **S**etup, and skip to step 5.

3. To see additional drivers, choose **A**dd to open the Add dialog box. Select the driver you want to add in the **L**ist of Drivers list box.

   To use a driver installed in a drive or directory other than your Windows directory, select Unlisted or Updated Driver and then select OK. The Install Driver dialog box asks you for the disk with the driver file. Or use the **B**rowse button to select the drive or directory that contains the driver file. Select OK to return to the Drivers dialog box.

4. Each driver installed has different settings you can select with the **S**etup button. You can select the Port and Interrupt, for example, for the Creative Labs Sound Blaster board. Configure the settings as appropriate for the device you are adding (consult your documentation for specific instructions).

   Some driver settings dialog boxes have a **T**est button for testing your settings. Some also may have a Help button or option available.

5. To complete the driver installation, choose OK as many times as necessary to get back to Control Panel.

6. As you exit, a dialog box advises that you need to restart Windows to enable most drivers. Select the Restart Now button to exit and restart Windows so that the installed drivers are available to Windows.

   Alternatively, you can continue working with the current settings and restart Windows at a later time.

If you remove a device from your computer, you should remove its driver also. The file itself is not deleted from the disk. But don't delete any *required* device driver's files, or Windows will not work properly.

To remove a device driver, follow these steps:

1. From Control Panel, select Drivers.

2. Select the driver you need to remove.

3. Choose the **R**emove button. A dialog box asks for confirmation. Choose OK until you return to Control Panel.

4. Since Windows has to be restarted for the change to take effect, choose the Restart Now button. That exits and restarts Windows so that your changes can take effect.

   If you prefer, restart Windows at a later time.

The documentation or Help files for your device should have additional information about using the device in Windows.

Managing Your Work

From Here...

To learn more about controlling how you work in Windows, see the following chapters:

■ Chapter 3, "Controlling Applications with Program Manager," explains how to use Program Manager to organize and use the applications on your computer.

■ Chapter 4, "Managing Files with File Manager," shows you how to use File Manager to manage the files on your computer.

■ Chapter 8, "Managing Fonts," explains how to install, manage, and use fonts in the Windows environments.

■ Chapter 19, "Using Windows Multimedia," introduces you to multimedia and teaches you how to add and work with sound on your computer.

■ Chapter 20, "Using Windows with CD-ROM and Video," shows you how to add full multimedia capabilities to your computer with CD-ROM.

Chapter 8

Managing Fonts

The days of limited font selections—when the one or two fonts that came with the printer were the only fonts you had—are long gone. Fortunately, with Windows 3.1 and TrueType, the days of complex solutions to the problem of limited font selections also are gone. TrueType brings you easily accessible, built-in, scalable fonts that don't care what kind of printer or display monitor you have.

Windows comes equipped with only a few TrueType fonts, but you can easily add more fonts to your system. Many font manufacturers offer TrueType fonts, so you aren't limited to using only TrueType fonts with Windows. You still can use any downloadable fonts that you may have purchased previously. You can also use the fonts built into the printer along with the TrueType fonts.

Table 8.1 describes the fonts that come with Windows.

Table 8.1 Windows Fonts	
Font	**Description**
Arial	A proportional sans serif font. Arial is a TrueType font that resembles the popular Helvetica font.
Times New Roman	A proportional serif font commonly used in newspapers and magazines. Times New Roman is a TrueType font that resembles the Times font.
Courier New	A non-proportional serif font commonly used by typewriters. Courier New is a TrueType font.

(continues)

Table 8.1 Continued	
Font	**Description**
Symbol	A proportional font containing mathematical symbols. Symbol is a TrueType font.
Wingdings	A proportional font containing desktop publishing symbols, such as arrows, boxes, circled numbers, and so on. It is used to draw attention to parts of a document. Wingdings is a TrueType font.
Roman	A proportional serif font.
Modern	A proportional sans serif font.
Script	A proportional font that looks like handwriting.

In this chapter, you learn how to:

- Manage and use fonts

- Understand the way computers use fonts

- Add and remove fonts

Understanding Fonts

Loosely defined, a *font* is a style of type, or the way the letters and numbers look—whether straight-sided *sans serif* fonts or *serif* fonts with strokes (serifs) that extend from the ends of each line (see fig. 8.1). Fonts can appear wide and rounded, or thin and condensed. Fonts can have an old-fashioned appearance or can look contemporary. Type design is an art form hundreds of years old, and thousands of type styles are available.

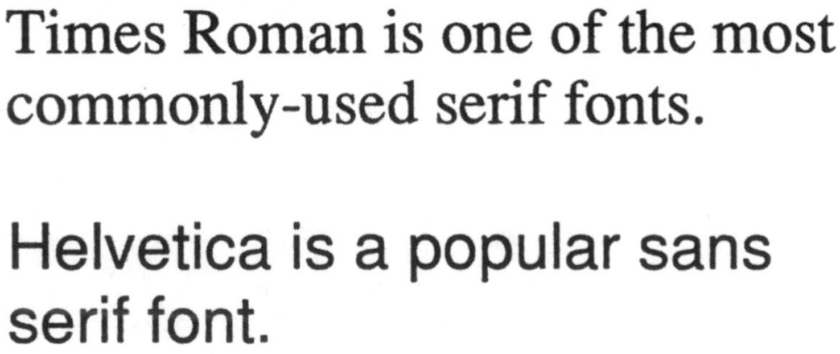

Fig. 8.1
Times Roman is one of the most popular serif fonts; Helvetica is a common sans serif font.

Times Roman is one of the most commonly-used serif fonts.

Helvetica is a popular sans serif font.

Despite the many type styles in existence, only a few basic categories of type styles exist: serif, sans serif, script, symbol, and decorative fonts are the most common styles. Serif type styles are characterized by thick and thin lines with tiny strokes (or serifs) at the ends of each line. Because these fonts are considered more readable than other fonts, you see serif type styles used in most books, magazines, and newspapers. Sans serif type styles have lines of uniform thickness and have no strokes (or serifs) at the end of each line. Because these fonts are easier to read from a distance, sans serif type styles are frequently used in signs and bold headlines. Script type styles resemble handwriting; symbol type styles replace characters with mathematical or *dingbat* symbols. Finally, decorative type styles each have a specialized appearance.

The terminology used to describe fonts and type styles can be confusing. Fonts are grouped in type families: the Times New Roman family includes Times New Roman regular, Times New Roman bold, Times New Roman italic, and Times New Roman bold italic. Most serif and sans serif type families come in four font styles: regular, bold, italic, and bold italic. Windows defines a font as a type and a style: Times regular is a font; Times New Roman italic is a font; Arial bold is a font. Each font may appear in a wide range of sizes.

Note

Symbol and decorative type styles usually include only a single font style.

Early computers used *monospace* type, which resembled an old typewriter, with each character occupying the same horizontal width on a page. A narrow *i* occupied the same space as a wide *w*. The fonts on many computers today, however, are *proportional* rather than monospace: each character's width is appropriate to the character. An *i* occupies much less horizontal space than a *w*. Although you use proportional fonts for most work, Windows also provides a monospace font (Courier New).

Non-proportional fonts, such as Courier, are measured by their width, in characters-per-inch (*cpi*). Such fonts can be measured this way because each character has the same width. Proportional fonts are measured by their height in *points* (72 points-per-inch) because each character has a different width. A typical type size for a newspaper may be 9 or 10 points. Books frequently are printed in 10- or 11-point fonts. Subheadings are larger: 12, 14, or even 18 points. Titles range from 18 points up to about 36 points. Screaming headlines in a newspaper may measure more than 100 points. In Windows applications, you see character sizes specified in a **P**oints text box or scrolling list. Remember that the larger the point size, the taller the character. A 12-point character is approximately the same size as a 10-cpi character.

Type does more than deliver words to a reader. Type makes the text easier or more difficult to read, determines how much text fits on a page, creates a mood, and sets a tone. Don't use type carelessly; pick the font best suited to the job.

Understanding How Computers Use Fonts

With so many fonts available, you may find it comforting to know that most computers have access to only a select group of fonts. This knowledge greatly simplifies the job of selecting the right font for the task. (And you can always add more fonts to the system as you become more discriminating about the fonts you use.)

Computers gain access to fonts in several ways. Fonts may be built into the operating system, for example, Windows TrueType fonts. Fonts may be built into the printer, as in many PostScript printers, some HP LaserJet models, and most dot-matrix printers. Fonts also may be added to the printer with a cartridge or added to the computer hard disk as soft fonts, which are downloaded to the printer either before or when the fonts are needed.

The fonts that reside in the computer or on the printer are stored in one of two ways, either as bit-map representations or as scalable outlines.

Bit-map fonts store a unique bit map (or graphic) image for each font in each size (see fig. 8.2).

Fig. 8.2
Bits are the on-screen pixels, or the dots, that make up a printed character.

When you want to print a 10-point Helvetica bold capital E, the computer searches for that specific bit map. Bit-map fonts can quickly consume a large amount of storage space on the computer, in the printer, or in both. Many downloadable and cartridge fonts use bit-map technology.

Scalable outline fonts store an outline of each character in a font and, when needed, scale the outline to size (see fig. 8.3).

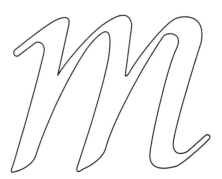

Fig. 8.3
Scalable fonts are stored as outlines rather than as bit maps.

Because only one outline is scaled to create all sizes, scalable fonts usually consume far less disk storage space than do bit-map fonts. PostScript fonts, TrueType fonts, and fonts built into the HP LaserJet III are scalable fonts.

Regardless of how you store fonts in your system, each font must fulfill two roles: it must appear on-screen and print on the printer. Before TrueType, computers needed separate screen and printer fonts because monitors have a different resolution than printers. Even scalable fonts depended on bit-map fonts for on-screen displays because these fonts could be scaled only to printer resolution.

With the introduction of TrueType, however, a single font outline fulfills both roles. The TrueType outline scales to any resolution—screen resolution, dot-matrix printer resolution, laser-printer resolution, or high-quality typesetting resolution.

TrueType fonts, therefore, have two space-saving advantages over other fonts: these fonts are scalable, so only one picture of each character is needed (instead of an image for each character in each size) and these fonts are *device-independent*, so only one version of the font must reside in the system.

Windows offers another advantage over DOS in using fonts. Some DOS applications each require separate font files, which means that you must reinstall the same font for each separate application (these duplicated font files can quickly consume a large amount of disk space). Windows, however, shares resources among applications. After you install a font in Windows, the font is available to all Windows applications that support multiple font usage.

Using TrueType Fonts

Windows comes with TrueType font technology built in, along with 14 TrueType fonts in five families. These scalable fonts are installed in Windows and are ready to use immediately.

Three of the TrueType families are Times New Roman, Arial, and Courier New (see fig. 8.4). Each family includes regular, bold, italic, and bold italic fonts. The Symbol font is made up of only a single font. The Wingdings font also is a single-font family. Times New Roman, a serif font, is similar to the popular Times Roman font. Arial, a sans serif font, is similar to Helvetica.

Fig. 8.4
Windows
TrueType fonts.

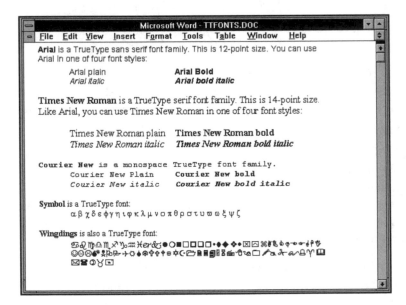

TrueType offers the following advantages over other alternatives for producing fonts on-screen and on the printer:

- *TrueType is a scalable font, so only a single version of each font is stored in the computer.* A single outline can produce a font of any size. In contrast, bit-map fonts store a different picture for each font in each size, and either consume massive amounts of storage or severely limit the number of sizes available.

- *TrueType fonts adapt to both the screen and the printer.* A single outline suffices for both and produces equally high quality on both the screen and the printer. Most other fonts, however, require separate screen and printer fonts. To save disk space, many fonts come in limited screen sizes only, rendering blocky representations of a size you request that is not stored as a screen font.

■ *Whether you use a laser printer or a dot-matrix printer, TrueType fonts print on all printers that Windows supports.* Many other fonts are printer-specific, so you're tied to using a single printer or, if you switch printers, you may switch to a different set of fonts, which results in different line breaks and page breaks. With TrueType, you can print the same fonts on all printers.

A final advantage of TrueType fonts over many downloadable fonts is that they are immediately available to all Windows applications; many downloadable fonts first must be installed for each application you use.

Because of the benefits, TrueType is a Windows default. When you start using Windows, TrueType is on. You can turn off TrueType, however.

Turning TrueType On and Off

By default, TrueType is always turned on in Windows. TrueType fonts, however, consume memory on a computer and may slow the display on-screen. They also may print somewhat more slowly than other fonts because the first time you use a TrueType font, Windows must create the screen image by scaling the outline. This process takes longer than using a bit-map font. Windows, however, remembers this font and, the next time it is used, the font is as quick to use as a prebuilt bit-map screen font. Downloading a TrueType font to the printer also takes longer than printing with a printer-resident font, so TrueType fonts may print more slowly than fonts built into the printer.

If the computer has limited memory or runs slowly, you may want to turn off TrueType. With TrueType turned off, you have access to all other fonts installed in the computer or on the printer. You can turn TrueType back on for printing, if necessary.

To use TrueType fonts exclusively, you can turn off all other fonts so that these fonts don't appear in font lists in applications.

To turn TrueType off or on, or to turn other fonts off or on, take the following steps:

1. Display the Windows Program Manager and open the Main group window.

◀ "Starting
Applications,"
p. 48

2. Choose Control Panel by double-clicking the Control Panel icon or by pressing arrow keys to select the Control Panel icon. Press Enter. The Control Panel window appears.

3. Choose the Fonts icon by double-clicking it or by pressing arrow keys to select the Fonts icon and then pressing Enter. As shown in figure 8.5, the Fonts window appears.

   Fonts currently installed are listed in the Installed Fonts list box.

Fig. 8.5
The Fonts window
shows currently
installed fonts.

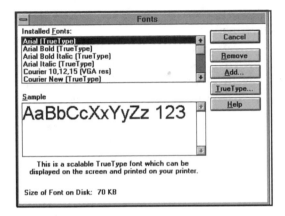

4. Choose the **True**Type button. The TrueType dialog box appears (see fig. 8.6).

Fig. 8.6
This TrueType
dialog box shows
TrueType turned
on.

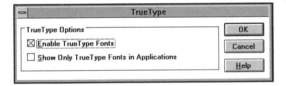

5. To turn off TrueType, deselect the **E**nable TrueType Fonts option so that no x appears in the check box.

   To display only TrueType fonts in applications, select the **S**how Only TrueType Fonts in Applications option. (This option is unavailable if you previously deselected the **E**nable TrueType Fonts option.)

6. Choose OK.

7. A dialog box advises that you must restart Windows so that the changes can take effect. To restart Windows, choose the **R**estart Now button. Otherwise, choose the **D**on't Restart Now button.

8. Choose Close if you did not restart Windows.

Using Non-TrueType Fonts

Although TrueType offers significant advantages, for some people TrueType also has a big disadvantage: Windows ships with only a few TrueType fonts. You may need more fonts and as a result, you may have already invested in non-TrueType fonts. Fortunately, you can continue to use the existing fonts and also the new TrueType fonts.

Non-TrueType fonts come in various styles and may be *built-in fonts*, which are built into the printer (as are PostScript fonts, LaserJet III fonts, and many dot-matrix fonts). Fonts may come as *cartridge fonts*, which are contained in a cartridge that you plug into a printer and act like printer fonts. Another way to add non-TrueType fonts to the system is with *soft fonts*, also known as *downloadable fonts*. Built-in fonts and cartridge fonts reside in the printer. Soft fonts reside in the computer and are downloaded to the printer as needed (this process may happen by default, or you may need to use a command to download the fonts).

Although the fonts you add may have scalable outlines to use on the printer, these fonts usually display bit-map screen fonts. This may be true of both printer and soft fonts. Screen fonts come from one of two sources. For printer fonts with no corresponding screen fonts, Windows includes a set of generic bit-map screen fonts in serif, sans serif, and symbol models, available in 8-, 10-, 12-, 14-, 18-, and 24-point sizes; a Courier screen font is available in 10-, 12-, and 15-point sizes. Some printer fonts have corresponding screen fonts that match the printer fonts, and when you install them, you decide the sizes to include. Because a bit-map font file can be quite large—especially the larger font sizes—the number of bit-map screen font sizes is limited.

Bit-map screen fonts have long presented a problem to people concerned with making a screen display closely match the printed output. Bit-map screen fonts fail to match printer output in two ways. First, if you don't have screen fonts to specifically match the printer fonts, Windows substitutes the closest generic screen font and spaces the on-screen characters as closely as possible to the actual font's print requirements. The line and page breaks may be correct, but don't count on accurate letter and word spacing. Second, if you specify a size that doesn't match an available screen-font size, Windows scales the nearest bit-map size to the size you want, which often results in a jagged-looking letter. (At large point sizes, Windows may substitute a vector font, designed for use on plotters. *Vector fonts* appear on-screen as outlines.)

You can turn TrueType on or off when using non-TrueType fonts, but leaving TrueType on can solve at least part of the problem of mismatched screen appearance and printer output. With TrueType off, Windows always uses bit-map screen fonts—either the generic Windows bit maps or bit maps specific to the font. With TrueType on, Windows creates display fonts in one of two ways. If no screen font specific to the font exists, Windows substitutes the nearest TrueType font, accurately scaling the font to size. If, for example, you choose the Bookman font (which is installed in your PostScript printer but for which you have no corresponding screen font), Windows substitutes the serif TrueType font Times New Roman for the screen display. Therefore, with TrueType turned on, fonts look better than if Windows scales a bit-map screen font to size. However, even with TrueType turned on, if Windows detects a screen font specifically designed to match the printer font, the screen font instead of the TrueType font is used for display (see the section, "Using Non-TrueType Fonts with TrueType," later in this chapter, for more information).

Another solution to the problem of mismatched screen and printer fonts is a type-management application (such as Adobe Type Manager, which scales screen fonts, or Agfa Type Director, which creates bit-map screen fonts from scalable printer fonts).

Working with Mismatched Screen and Printer Fonts

If the printer font doesn't have a matching set of screen fonts, Windows uses its own screen fonts to try to match the printer fonts. These screen fonts may not be as accurate as custom screen fonts, however, and you may see discrepancies between the text on-screen and the text as printed.

This difference between screen and printer fonts can cause the following problems:

- Words wrap at a different place on-screen than they do in print.

- Titles or sidebars extend further than expected.

- On-screen text extends past the margin set in the ruler.

- On-screen text in tables overfills cells in tables.

- Bold or italic formatting causes lines to appear longer on-screen than the lines look when printed.

Another cause of mismatched screen fonts and printer fonts arises when fonts unavailable in the printer are used on-screen. This problem can occur because selecting a font—even a font unavailable on the current printer—is possible in many applications. (Understanding this quirk can be useful if you want to create a document for printing on another printer.) If you use a font not available in the printer, Windows substitutes a font close in style and size to the unavailable font. Windows tries to find a similar typeface and size. If the requested size isn't found, Windows substitutes the next smaller size.

You can remedy these issues in one of two ways. First, if you are using soft fonts or a font manager, make sure that you generate and install the screen fonts that go with the printer's soft fonts. Second, use fonts available in the printer. You can tell if a font is in the current printer because a small printer icon appears to the left of the font name in your application's Font list.

Using Non-TrueType Fonts with TrueType Fonts

TrueType fonts work side by side with non-TrueType fonts. As discussed previously, you can turn off TrueType so that you use only non-TrueType fonts, or you can turn off non-TrueType fonts so that you use only TrueType fonts. But there is an advantage to working with both TrueType and non-TrueType fonts.

Many printer fonts don't include corresponding bit-map screen fonts. In previous versions of Windows, applications depended on the generic Windows screen fonts to supply screen fonts for these printer fonts. Windows' *font metrics* files provided information to help the application space characters and words more accurately and increase the similarity between screen display and printed output. TrueType, however, takes over the job of supplying screen fonts for printer fonts that don't have screen fonts. One advantage of using TrueType scalable screen fonts is that you can scale these fonts to any size. Bit-map screen fonts, however, are not scalable and when you request a size not included on the disk (such as 11 or 13 points), Windows fashions a rather jagged-looking font from the nearest available font size.

There is one disadvantage, however, to using TrueType screen fonts. TrueType substitutes the nearest TrueType font for the font you request.

Managing Your Work

Thus, the on-screen representation of a PostScript font, such as Palatino (for which you may not have a specific screen font), looks exactly the same as the TrueType font Times New Roman. You see the difference between the two fonts when you print. Although line and page breaks remain accurate, character and word spacing are inaccurate when Windows substitutes a TrueType screen font for the printer font you request.

To get an accurate screen display, you must either use TrueType fonts only, which look the same on-screen and on the printed page, or you must provide a screen font that matches the printer font. If you have a screen font that matches the printer font, TrueType uses this screen font instead of scaling the closest TrueType font. Therefore, you see a screen display that closely matches the printed page. The tradeoff is that bit-map screen fonts take up extra disk space, but the screen display is more accurate.

Adding New Fonts

You add or remove fonts from Windows when you add a new printer or when you purchase new fonts to give more capability to a laser printer. Normally, Windows adds fonts automatically when you install a new printer.

If you add software fonts or enhance your printer, you may need to install additional fonts after the printer is installed. For some printers, Windows needs font information to display fonts on the screen (*screen fonts*) as well as font information to print data to the printer (*printer fonts*). Some types of printers, such as dot-matrix and inkjet printers, use the screen fonts for printing.

For printers that contain their own fonts internally, Windows needs to know only how the fonts should appear on-screen. The font information for printers with internal fonts can be found on one of the original Windows installation disks, on the disk that came with the printer, or on the disk that came with the software fonts (*soft fonts*).

To install TrueType fonts, you can use the Fonts program you see in the Windows Control Panel. To install some downloadable or cartridge fonts, you may need to use special installation software that comes with the fonts. Printer-resident fonts are usually installed by default when you install a printer.

Before you add a new font, be sure that the original font diskettes are available. You need these disks during the installation process.

To add a new font to the system by using the Fonts application, follow these steps:

1. Display Windows Program Manager and open the Main group window.

2. Choose Control Panel.

◄ "Operating Control Panel," p. 231

3. Choose the Fonts icon. The Fonts window appears. Fonts currently installed are listed in the Installed Fonts list box (refer to fig. 8.5).

4. Choose the **A**dd button. The Add Fonts dialog box, shown in figure 8.7, appears.

5. In the Dri**v**es list, select the drive that contains the font you want to add.

6. In the **D**irectories list, select the directory that contains the font you want to add.

   The fonts in the directory and drive you selected appear in the List of **F**onts box.

7. From the List of **F**onts box, select the font or fonts you want to add. To select more than one font at a time, hold down the Shift key as you select the fonts. If you want to add all the fonts, choose the **S**elect All button.

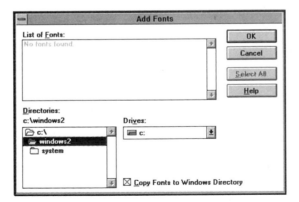

Fig. 8.7
The Add Fonts dialog box.

8. If you decide not to add the fonts to the system, but rather to use the fonts from the current drive and directory, deselect the **C**opy Fonts to Windows Directory check box.

   Use this option only if you want to use the fonts occasionally and don't want to use up disk space by storing these fonts permanently.

9. Choose OK to add the font or fonts to the system.

10. Choose Close to close the Fonts window.

When you install fonts by using the Font Installer, you install both the screen fonts and printer fonts at the same time.

▶ "Printing with Windows," p. 283

If you are adding fonts by installing a new font cartridge, you must set up the printer to recognize the new cartridge. If the fonts are built into the print driver, you need do nothing more. If, however, you don't have access to the fonts after you installed the printer and set up the cartridge, you need to install the fonts. Use the Font Installer or check the font documentation to see if you must use a special font installation application.

To set up a new font cartridge, follow these steps:

1. Turn off the printer and insert the cartridge. Turn the printer back on.

2. From the Main group in the Program Manager, choose Control Panel.

3. From Control Panel, choose Printers.

4. From the Installed **P**rinters list, select the printer into which, in step 1, you inserted the new font cartridge.

5. Choose **S**etup.

6. From the Cartridges list, select the name of the cartridge you inserted.

7. Choose OK to close the Setup dialog box. Then choose Close to close the Printer dialog box. Close Control Panel.

Using Fonts in Windows Applications

After installation, fonts become available for use in all Windows applications. Because you may have several kinds of fonts installed in Windows, special icons identify each font. By looking at these icons, which appear to the left of the font names in font list boxes, you can tell whether a font is a TrueType font, a printer font, or a Windows system font.

In the font list (from Word for Windows, a word processing application) shown in figure 8.8, you can see that TrueType fonts display a TT icon to the left of the TrueType font, and printer fonts display a printer icon.

Troubleshooting

Character formatting appeared to be correct the last time the document was opened, but now the character formatting has changed. In some cases, formatting is missing.

The currently selected printer may not be the printer that was selected during the document's original formatting. If the current printer is not capable of reproducing the fonts, sizes, or styles that you originally formatted, Windows shows you the best that the current printer can do. Correct this problem by selecting a printer that is capable of printing the formats. See Chapter 9, "Printing with Windows," for detailed information on how to install select printers.

Removing Old Fonts

You can remove a font that you no longer need from Windows. Removing fonts saves memory on a computer with limited memory or a computer running memory-hungry applications. If you remove the disk file, you also save disk space (but you must reinstall this font to be able to use the font again in future work sessions). Do not delete font files or change the WIN.INI file without first using the following procedure to remove the fonts from Windows.

Using Control Panel To Remove Fonts

Windows keeps track of the location of font files. Do not manually delete font references in the WIN.INI file or delete font files from the hard disk unless you have first used Control Panel to remove fonts from Windows. If your fonts have been "messed up," you may have to reinstall the fonts so that your system can handle the fonts correctly.

To remove a font, follow these steps:

1. Display Program Manager and open the Main group window.

2. Choose Control Panel.

3. Choose the Fonts icon. The Fonts window appears. Currently installed fonts are listed in the Installed **F**onts list box.

4. In the Installed **F**onts list box, select the font you want to remove.

5. Choose the **R**emove button.

   A dialog box confirms that you want to remove the font. To proceed with removing the font, choose **Y**es.

6. If you also want to remove the font files from the disk, select the **D**elete Font File From Disk check box.

   Do not delete font files from the disk if you deselected the **C**opy Fonts to Window Directory option when you installed the fonts (in other words, if you were using fonts from the original disks rather than copying the fonts to Windows). Doing so deletes the font files from the original font disk, and you cannot reinstall these fonts.

7. Choose **Y**es, or choose Yes to **A**ll to remove several fonts at once.

   You return to the Fonts dialog box.

8. Choose Close.

Caution

Do not remove the MS Sans Serif font. Windows uses this font for titles, menus, and dialog boxes.

From Here...

This chapter covered the basics of fonts—how to manage, use, add, and remove them. Refer to the following chapters for more information.

- Chapter 9, "Printing with Windows," shows you which available fonts can be printed.

- Chapter 10, "Using Windows Write," gives you ideas for experimenting with Windows' fonts by using Windows Write.

Chapter 9

Printing with Windows

Windows applications share more than a common graphical interface; they also share printing resources. In regular DOS applications, such as Lotus 1-2-3 and WordPerfect, printer "drivers" are built into each application. These drivers—a driver for each different printer—translate the text or data that you want to print into commands understood by the printer. But Windows applications are different. Windows applications, such as Excel and Word for Windows, have no printer drivers. Instead, these applications use the printer drivers built into Windows. (Some applications, such as WordPerfect for Windows, can use both their own printer drivers and the Windows drivers.) Windows has a special application, Print Manager, that manages printing for all Windows applications. Print Manager is initially located in the Main group window.

In this chapter, you learn how to:

- Add and configure printers
- Print a file
- Use Print Manager
- Print on a network
- Use the Windows Printing System
- Correct printer problems

Print Manager springs into action when you issue the command to print a file, causing two things to happen. First, Print Manager intercepts text or graphics output and sends it not to the printer, but to a *buffer*, or *queue*, where files waiting to be printed are lined up (or *queued*) for printing. Second, these output files are routed, in the order received, to the printer. If the application isn't maximized and you can see the lower portion of the Windows background, then you can see the Print Manager icon at the bottom of the screen while the file or files are printing (see fig. 9.1). The icon disappears after printing is complete.

Fig. 9.1
The Print Manager icon shows on the lower-left corner of the desktop when files are printing.

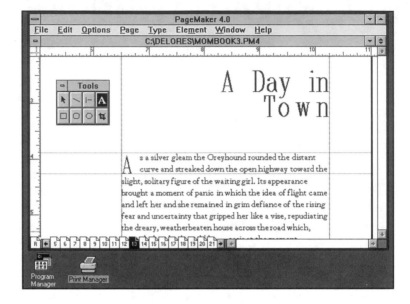

Windows gives Print Manager control over the printing rather than letting the application control printing (as happens with DOS applications) because you can continue using the application or switch to another application while Print Manager handles the print job. You don't have to wait for the document to print before you can start working on something else.

To print a Windows file, you must install the correct printer drivers when you install Windows or use the Windows Control Panel to install the printer drivers after you install Windows. Before you learn how to use Print Manager to control printing in Windows, you learn how to use the Control Panel to add and configure printers on your system.

Adding and Configuring Printers

When you buy a new printer and connect it to your computer, you must install and configure the printer to operate under Windows. Installing a printer adds a "printer driver" to Windows, enabling Windows to recognize your printer and access the printer's features. Configuring a printer tells Windows where and how the printer is connected to your computer.

Control Panel gives you a way to add printer drivers and fonts not installed initially with Windows. (A *printer driver* is software that tells Windows how to work with a family of printers. You select a specific printer model from the driver.) Most printer drivers are included on your original Windows installation disks; others are available on a disk from your dealer, the printer manufacturer, or Microsoft.

Before adding a new printer to Windows, have ready your original Windows installation disks or the disk from your printer manufacturer that contains the Windows printer driver for that printer.

The Windows installation disks contain software definitions and appropriate fonts for making most printers work with Windows applications. If your printer driver is not included, call the Microsoft telephone support line or your printer's manufacturer. Microsoft maintains a library of printer and font files for additional printers.

Follow these basic steps to install a printer driver from Control Panel:

1. Select the printer model from the list of printers supported by the driver and add the printer driver from the printer disk to your hard disk.

2. Assign a port to the printer.

3. Change the time-out settings.

4. Select printer settings for layout and features.

5. Make the printer the default printer if you want it to be the one you use most frequently.

6. Specify the network connections for the printer if you are connected to a network.

Use the Control Panel's Printers icon to perform all these installation tasks. Not all steps are required, but you do need to install the printer driver. You also can use the Printers application to turn Print Manager on or off, to choose the default printer, to change your existing printer's setup or connections, or to remove a printer.

Installing a Printer

To add a printer driver to Windows or to make changes to your existing printer driver, follow these steps:

1. Choose the Printers icon from the Control Panel window to display the Printers dialog box (see fig. 9.2).

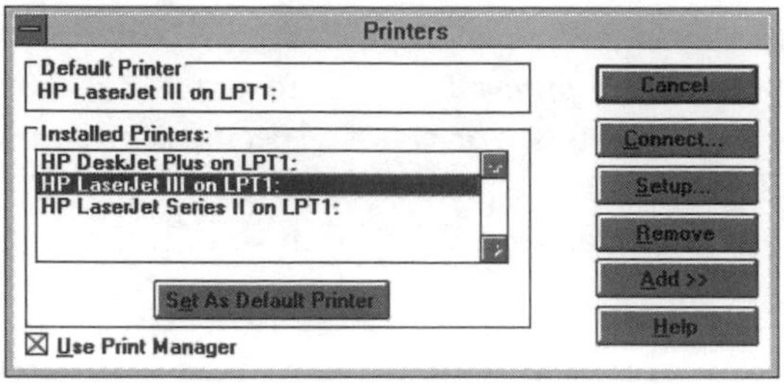

Fig. 9.2
The Printers dialog
box.

2. Choose the **A**dd button. The bottom of the Printers dialog box expands to show you a list of the drivers currently available (see fig. 9.3).

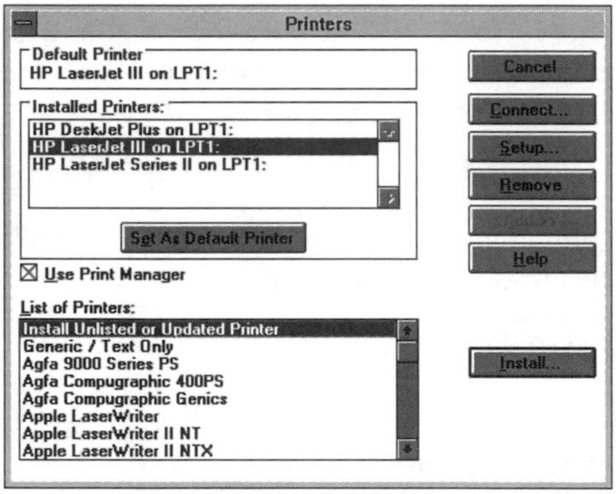

Fig. 9.3
The Printers dialog
box with the
available printer
list.

3. Select the printer you want to install from the **L**ist of Printers list box. The printer drivers in this list box came with your Windows installation disks. If you press a letter, you quickly move through the list of printers to the first printer in the list starting with the letter you press.

4. Choose **I**nstall. The Install Printer dialog box appears.

5. If you are installing a new driver, Windows prompts you to insert in drive A the disk containing the printer driver. Insert either the initial Windows installation disk or the disk you obtained from a manufacturer with a new printer driver or a new edition of the driver. If your printer files are located on another disk or directory, change the path name in the text box. Choose **B**rowse to search for the driver.

6. If Windows needs additional disks to install the fonts for the selected driver, it prompts you for additional disks. Insert the disks as prompted, and then choose OK or press Enter.

7. Windows adds the printer driver to the Installed **P**rinters list in the Printers dialog box. The printer is connected to the LPT1: port by default. To make the selected printer the printer you normally use, choose the **Se**t As Default Printer button.

◄ "Operating Control Panel," p. 231

8. Complete the rest of the installation and configuration steps as described in the following sections.

Assigning a Printer Port

When you install a printer, Windows assigns that printer to the LPT1: port by default. This is sufficient for most printer installations. If your printer is connected to another port, however, you need to change that assignment before your printer can print from Windows. You also can change the Time-out settings. To select the port assignment for your printer or to change the Time-out settings, follow these steps:

1. Choose the Printers icon from Control Panel if you are not already in the Printers dialog box.

2. Select the printer driver you want to set up from the Installed **P**rinters list box.

3. Choose the **C**onnect button. The Connect dialog box appears (see fig. 9.4).

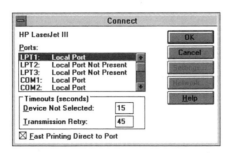

Fig. 9.4
The Connect dialog box.

4. From the **P**orts list box, select the port that is connected to your printer. Choose from LPT1: - LPT3:, COM1: - COM4, EPT, FILE, or LPT1.DOS or LPT2.DOS.

5. If your printer is connected to one of the COM ports, select the COM port and then choose the **S**ettings button to display the Settings dialog box (see fig. 9.5). Make sure that the parameters (**B**aud Rate, **D**ata Bits, **P**arity, **S**top Bits, and **F**low Control) have the same settings as your printer.

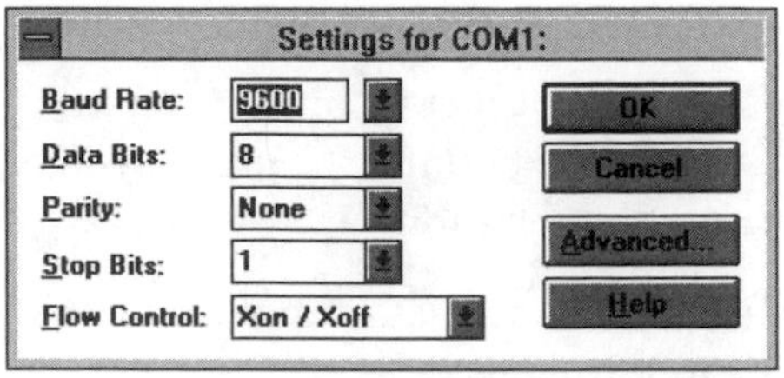

Fig. 9.5
The Settings
dialog box.

◄ "Setting up
Serial Ports,"
p. 253

6. Choose the **A**dvanced button to change the **B**ase I/O Port Address and **I**nterrupt Request Line (IRQ) if your COM ports are not set to the standard values. The Advanced Settings for the COM1: dialog box are shown in figure 9.6. Make any required changes; then choose OK until you return to the Connect dialog box.

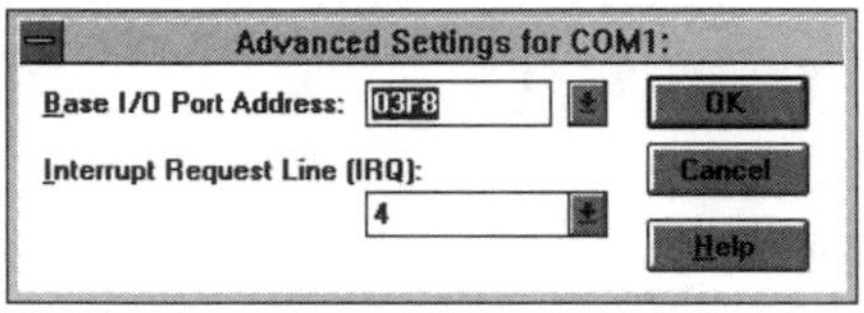

Fig. 9.6
Advanced Settings
for COM1: dialog
box.

7. The Timeouts group of the Connect dialog box enables you to set the amount of time Windows waits before sending you a message if there are problems with the printer. Windows uses the **D**evice Not Selected time when the printer is off-line or not ready. The **T**ransmission Retry value is used whenever the printer is not accepting characters, such as when the printer's buffer is full.

► "Solving
Communica-
tion and Port
Difficulties,"
p. 1,006

8. The **F**ast Printing Direct to Port check box tells Windows how to send data to the printer port. When selected, it enables Windows to send data directly to the printer port, bypassing DOS printing requests. If you are using a printer spooler or "pop-up" software that controls your printer switch box, clear the check box to enable that software to recognize text sent through normal DOS interrupts. This slows down printing, however, so choose accordingly.

9. If your printer is connected to a network, choose the **N**etwork button. Otherwise, choose the OK button to save the changes made.

Use the PRINTERS.WRI files in the Windows directory to get specific help on special settings for your printer. Use the Write application to read these files. Some printer drivers come with their own README files that also can be read with the Notepad or Write application.

Troubleshooting

I bought a new printer and installed it, but have been unable to get my applications to print.

When you installed the printer, you may have selected the wrong printer driver from the Printers dialog box. Be sure the name of the printer you selected matches your printer.

You may also have specified the wrong printer port in the Connect dialog box. Click the **C**onnect button in the Printers dialog box, and make sure the port you chose matches the port your printer is actually connected to (usually LPT1 or LPT2).

Printing without a Printer Driver

You have three alternatives if your printer is not included in the List of Printers box:

- Call Microsoft or your printer manufacturer to obtain a driver. Install your printer by selecting Install Unlisted or Updated Printer from the **L**ist of Printers list.

- Switch your printer into a printer-emulation mode so that it duplicates an industry-standard printer, such as the Epson FX-80 (dot matrix), HP LaserJet (laser printer), or Apple LaserWriterPlus (PostScript). You may have to change switches on your printer to put it into emulation mode. Select the driver for the printer being emulated.

- Select the Generic/Text Only driver as the last resort. This driver prints text and numbers but does not print graphics or enhanced text.

Changing the Default Settings for Your Printer

Selecting the **S**etup button from the Printers dialog box enables you to change many settings for your printer. These settings include paper size and source, resolution, page orientation, font cartridges, and soft fonts. You also can change other options, such as Print Quality, Intensity Control, and Dithering, depending on the printer driver. Figure 9.7 shows the dialog box for the HP LaserJet III, and figure 9.8 shows the dialog box for the Epson FX-850 printer.

Tip
If you are having trouble printing large files, try increasing the **T**ransmission Retry value.

In the HP LaserJet III Setup dialog box, for example, you can specify the Paper Size, how much memory the printer has, and which font cartridges are installed. You can select two font cartridges by clicking the first and then Shift+clicking the second. Use Ctrl+arrow and the space bar to select two

II

Managing Your Work

cartridges with the keyboard. The Epson FX-850 Setup dialog box, however, has different choices. Since each printer is unique, use the Help button to get specific information about your printer.

Fig. 9.7
The HP LaserJet III
Setup dialog box.

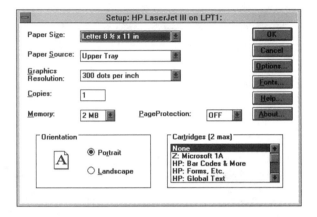

Fig. 9.8
The Epson FX-850
setup dialog box.

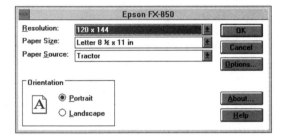

Once you have made the needed selections in the printer's Option dialog box, choose the OK button to save your changes. If you need to set up additional printers, use the same procedure as above.

Finally, if you haven't already done it, select your default printer. Just select the printer from the Installed **P**rinters list box and then select the S**e**t As Default Printer button. The printer name is then shown in the Default Printer box of the Printers dialog box. Select Close (or press the Enter key) to save the changes you have made and exit the Printers application.

> **Note**
>
> You can add memory to many laser printers. If your laser printer has more memory than is standard, be sure to increase the value in the Memory option in the Setup dialog box (see fig. 9.7).
>
> Some printers do not support downloadable fonts or are not compatible with TrueType. Other printers are not perfect in their emulation and have problems with TrueType. In these cases, you can choose Print TrueType as Graphics and have the text sent as an image, rather than as text. This method, which is how ATM works, is slower and takes more memory but usually works.

Troubleshooting

I tried to print a note with graphics on it, but I can't get the whole page to print properly.

Your printer has to have sufficient memory to print pages with graphics. Many printers come with only enough memory to print a small amount of graphics on a page. The best solution is to install additional memory in your printer; otherwise, you have to be content with printing smaller graphics.

Connecting to and Disconnecting from Network Printers with Control Panel

If you are connected to a network printer, you can print from Windows to that printer. To connect to a network printer, follow these steps:

1. Choose the Printers icon if the Printers dialog box is not open.

2. Choose the **C**onnect button.

3. Choose the **N**etwork button. This button is grayed if you are not connected to a network.

4. The dialog box displayed is dependent on the network you have installed. In general, you need to specify the network path, the port, and any required password. With some networks, you can use the Browse feature to get a list of available network printers; if not available, the Browse button is dimmed. If you have previously connected to a printer, choose the Previous button to reconnect to that printer.

   ▶ "Installing and Configuring Windows for Workgroups 3.11," p. 867

5. Choose **C**onnect to link with the network printer.

   ▶ "Installing Printers and Queues," p. 921

II

Managing Your Work

To disconnect from the network printer, repeat the preceding steps, selecting the printer from the Network Printer Connection dialog box and choosing the **D**isconnect button.

Removing Printers from Windows

Tip

Some drivers may be used by more than one printer. Do not remove a driver used by an-other printer from the same family.

Removing a printer driver saves only a small amount of disk space, but it unclutters the printer selection and setup dialog boxes. To remove a printer driver, choose the Printers icon from Control Panel, displaying the Printers dialog box. Select the printer from the Installed **P**rinters list and then choose the **R**emove button. Windows asks you to confirm whether you want to remove the printer driver.

Turning Print Manager On or Off

Print Manager enables you to print multiple files as you continue to work in an application. Using Print Manager to control the print job results in slower printing than when printing directly to the printer. If you print directly to the printer, however, you cannot continue to work as you print.

You can turn off Print Manager so that you can print faster. To do so, choose the Printers icon from Control Panel; when the Printers dialog box appears, deselect the **U**se Print Manager check box.

If you do not use Print Manager, you do not receive any error messages from local or network printers. If you are on a network, you probably will use the network printer queue and may not need Print Manager.

Troubleshooting

I installed a new font cartridge in my laser printer, but the new fonts don't appear in the font lists in my applications.

When you install a new font cartridge, you have to let Window know so it can use those fonts. To do this, open the Printers dialog box from Control Panel, click the **S**etup button, and select the name of the new cartridge from the Cartridges list. Click OK and Close to close the dialog box. The new fonts will appear in the font lists in your Windows applications.

Installing Printers from Print Manager

You can use Print Manager to add, configure, and remove a printer on your system—just as you can use the Printers application in Control Panel. Before you add a printer, be sure to have your original Windows disks on hand—they contain the printer driver that you need.

To add, configure, or remove a printer by using Print Manager, follow these steps:

1. Choose Print Manager from the Main window in Program Manager.

2. Open the **O**ptions menu and choose **P**rinter Setup. The Printers dialog box appears.

3. To add a printer, choose the **A**dd button. The Printers dialog box expands to show a list of available printers (see fig. 9.9).

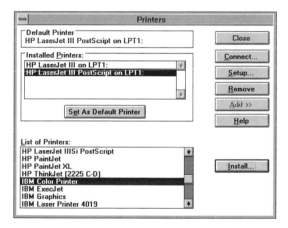

Fig. 9.9
The Printers dialog box showing a list of available printers.

4. Select the printer you want to add, and choose **I**nstall. Follow instructions for inserting the Windows disk containing the driver for the printer you want to install, and choose OK.

5. Select your newly installed printer from the Installed **P**rinters list, and choose **C**onnect to link your printer to a port or to a network. Choose OK when you are finished.

6. With your printer still selected in the Installed **P**rinters list, choose **S**etup to change the paper size and orientation. Choose OK when you are finished.

7. If you want to use your printer as the default printer, while your printer is still selected, select the Set as Default Printer option.

8. Choose Close.

> **Note**
>
> You can set the default printer without using the **P**rinter Setup command in Print Manager in Windows for Workgroups. To set the default printer, select the printer in the Print Manager window that you want to be the default printer, and choose the **P**rinter Set **D**efault Printer command.

If you want to remove a printer, select it in the Installed **P**rinters list and choose **R**emove.

Printing a File

▶ "Solving Font and Printing Problems," p. 998

The procedure for printing may vary slightly from application to application, but the basic steps remain the same when you print from a Windows application. Usually, two steps are required. First, you set up the printer you plan to use by choosing the **F**ile **P**rint Setup command. This step includes selecting the correct printer from a list of the printers previously installed in Windows and selecting printer setup characteristics, such as paper source, size, and orientation. These selections remain in effect until changed again, so you usually make this change only when you change printers or setup options.

The second step in printing from a Windows application is to print the file by choosing the **F**ile **P**rint command. Depending on the application, in this step, you identify the number of copies to print, the range of pages to print, and other choices. (For details about printing with Windows applications, refer to the application documentation or to a Que book, such as *Using Excel Version 5 for Windows*, Special Edition or *Using Word Version 6 for Windows*, Special Edition.)

◀ "Opening, Saving, Printing, and Closing Files," p. 53

After you have issued the print command from the Windows application, Print Manager takes over, transferring information and instructions to the printer as you work.

◀ "Working with Applications," p. 48

Although the Print Manager manages the task of printing, you manage Print Manager. You can open the Print Manager window to see which files are in queue to print on which printer, and you can make changes. You can, for example, pause the printing, cancel a print job, or reorder the print queue. These procedures are explained in later sections of this chapter.

You Cannot Use an Application Until the File Reaches Print Manager

While Print Manager is printing a file, you can continue working with the application. If you print a large file, however, you may wait a while for the file to reach Print Manager. You can't use the application while the application sends the file to Print Manager. Be patient; the file reaches Print Manager much more quickly than it prints!

Different Printers Produce Different Results

Printers have different characteristics and capabilities. Some laser printers print at a resolution of 300 dots per inch; some dot matrix printers print at a much coarser resolution. Some printers have built-in fonts that you may want to use; with others, you rely on Windows' TrueType technology to supply fonts. Some printers have enough memory to print a full page of graphics; others have limited memory. Before you print a document, become familiar with your printer's capabilities, possibilities, and limitations.

Using the Print Manager Window

While a file is printing from a Windows application, Print Manager is running. If the application isn't *maximized* (if the application doesn't occupy the entire computer screen), you can see the Print Manager icon at the bottom of the screen (refer to fig. 9.1). The icon represents the Print Manager application.

Activate Print Manager in the same way you activate other applications: double-click the application icon or hold down the Alt key, press Tab to highlight the Print Manager icon or display its name, and release both keys. When you activate Print Manager, the Print Manager window opens on-screen, shows the status of current print jobs, and enables you to change several things about the print job.

The Print Manager window shows the status of the *print queue*. The window shows you which printer is active, which printer is printing, which file is being printed, and which other files are in queue for printing. The window also can show you the time and date you sent the file to the printer and the size of the file. Figure 9.10 shows a sample Print Manager window.

Fig. 9.10
The Print Manager window showing the status of a print job, with the Hewlett-Packard DeskJet Plus printer selected.

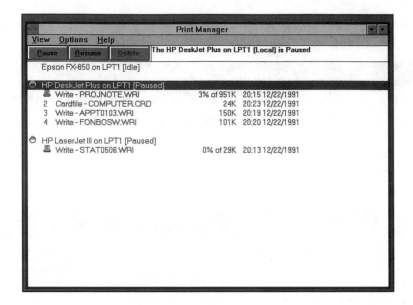

The Print Manager window contains several buttons and areas that you use to control the print job. The following chart lists these areas and uses.

Window Area	Use
Pause button	Stops printing temporarily for the selected printer
Resume button	Restarts the selected printer after pausing
Delete button	Removes the selected file from the print queue
Message box	Provides information about the currently selected printer or print job
Printer queue information line	Lists the printer name, printer port, and printer status (if you have more than one printer connected to the computer, you have more than one printer queue information line)
File information lines	Lists a file's position in the queue, the title of the print job, the file size, the percent of the file already printed, and the time and date you sent the file to the printer (if you have more than one printer, you may see more than one list of files in queue for printing)

To use the **P**ause, **R**esume, and **D**elete buttons, you must indicate the printer that you want to pause or resume or the file that you want to delete from the print queue. You perform these actions by selecting the appropriate printer or file. The selected printer or file is highlighted (in fig. 9.10, the HP DeskJet Plus printer is selected). To select a printer or file, click the printer or file with the mouse or press the up or down arrows to move the selection bar.

The file information line for each print job disappears after printing completes.

Start Print Manager from the Program Manager

Print Manager starts by default when you print a document. You can run Print Manager, however, even if you aren't printing. In Program Manager, activate the Main window. Then double-click the Print Manager icon or press arrow keys to select the Print Manager icon and press Enter. To close Print Manager, choose the **V**iew E**x**it command.

Changing the Print Order

The number to the left of each file listed in the print queue tells you the order in which the files print. Print Manager, however, makes changing your mind about this order easy. (Notice that the first file listed in the print queue isn't numbered but shows a printer icon to the left. Because this file is already printing, you cannot change its print order. You can change only the print order of the numbered files.)

To use the mouse to change the order of the files to be printed, follow these steps:

1. Point to the file you want to reorder.

2. Press and hold down the mouse button. The pointer changes to an arrow.

3. Drag the file to a new position in the queue.

4. Release the mouse button.

To use the keyboard to change the order of the files to be printed, follow these steps:

1. Press the down-arrow key to select the file you want to reorder.

2. Press and hold down the Ctrl key.

3. Press the up- or down-arrow key to move the file to the new position in the queue.

4. Release the Ctrl key.

Pausing and Resuming Printing

You can interrupt a print job temporarily by pausing the printer, and you can resume the print job when you're ready. While a printer is paused, the word [Paused] appears at the end of the printer queue information line. Note that although you paused the printer, the printer continues to print all text in the printer's buffer, so printing may not stop immediately.

To pause printing, follow these steps:

1. Select the printer queue information line. Select the line for the *printer* you want to pause; do not select the line for the file.

2. Select the **P**ause button or press Alt+P.

To resume printing, follow these steps:

1. Select the printer queue information line. Select the line for the *printer* you want to resume; do not select the line for the file.

2. Select the **R**esume button or press Alt+R.

Deleting a File from the Queue

To cancel a specific print job, you can delete a file from the print queue. To cancel all printing, you can exit Print Manager. (If you want to close the Print Manager window without canceling printing, minimize the window.)

To delete a file from the print queue, follow these steps:

1. Select the file information line. Select the line for the *file* you want to delete; do not select the printer queue information line.

2. Select the **D**elete button or press Alt+D. A dialog box appears on-screen asking you to confirm that you want to delete the print job for this file.

3. Choose OK or press Enter.

To cancel all printing, follow these steps:

1. Open the **V**iew menu and choose E**x**it command. A dialog box appears on-screen asking for confirmation.

2. Choose OK or press Enter.

You May Have To Reset the Printer

If you delete a file currently being printed, especially if the file contains graphics, you may have to reset the printer to clear the print buffer. The printer may print *buffered* information long after you delete the file currently printing. Resetting the printer stops the printer from continuing to print a file. You can reset the printer by turning it off and back on again (or, if the printer has a reset option, by selecting this option). Performing a reset is sometimes necessary for laser printers because of these printers' unusually large memories.

Changing the Printer's Priority

Because Windows can print in the background as you work in the foreground, the PC must divide resources between these two tasks. You can, however, choose which task has priority. If given the high priority, the printer prints more quickly but the application in which you are working may slow down. If given low priority, the printer prints more slowly but doesn't interrupt the application in which you're working. If the printer is given medium priority (Windows' default choice), the PC shares resources equally between the printer and application.

The printer priority you select appears with a check mark to its left in the **O**ptions Background Printing menu. The selection remains in effect—for all printing in the current Windows session and for all future sessions—until you change it again (see fig. 9.11).

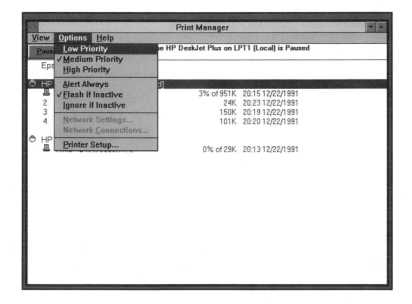

Fig. 9.11
Selecting the printing priority.

II

Managing Your Work

To change the printer priority, follow these steps:

1. Choose the **O**ptions Background menu.

2. Select one of the following options:

Option	Result
Low Priority	Printer runs slower; application runs faster
Medium Priority	Printer and application have the same priority
High Priority	Printer runs faster; application may slow down

Displaying Print Manager Alerts

Occasionally, the printer needs attention. If you're printing envelopes and you need to insert the next envelope, some printers alert you to do this. You can control whether Print Manager always alerts you with a message, whether the Print Manager icon or inactive title bar flashes to let you know a message is waiting, or whether Print Manager ignores the printer's request if Print Manager is an icon or the window is inactive.

To control printer alert messages, follow these steps:

1. Choose the **O**ptions menu.

2. Select one of the following options:

Option	Result
Alert Always	Always alerts you with a message box when the printer needs attention
Flash if Inactive	Beeps and flashes if Print Manager is an icon or if the window is inactive; you must activate the Print Manager window to see the message (this is Print Manager's default setting)
Ignore if Inactive	Ignores the printer's request if Print Manager is an icon or if the window is inactive (you might not know that the printer needs attention)

Displaying Print Time, Date, and File Size

You have the option to display (or not display) in the Print Manager window each file's size and the time and date you sent the file to the printer. Make these selections from the **V**iew menu (see fig. 9.12).

To display (or not display) the file size and the print time and date, follow these steps:

1. Open the **V**iew menu.

2. Choose one of the following options:

Option	Result
Time/Date Sent	Displays the time and date you sent a file to the printer
Print File Size	Displays the size of the files in the Print Manager print queue

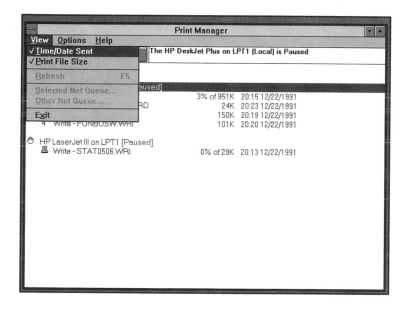

Fig. 9.12
Choosing whether to display the file size and the time and date sent to printer.

II

Managing Your Work

Using the Print Manager Window in Windows for Workgroups

The Print Manager window in Windows for Workgroups is shown in figure 9.13. The window displays a list of all the printers that are available for your use, including

■ Printers that are connected to your computer

■ Printers that are connected to your computer and designated as shared so that others on your network can use them

■ Printers that are connected to other computers on your network and designated as shared and available for your use

The *default printer*, which is the printer that is used automatically when you issue the Print command in Windows applications, is listed in bold type. Listed under each printer are the files that are currently in the *print queue* for that printer. To the left of each printer and file name are icons indicating the status of that printer or file. Table 9.1 explains the meaning of each of these icons.

Fig. 9.13
The Print Manager window in Windows for Workgroups.

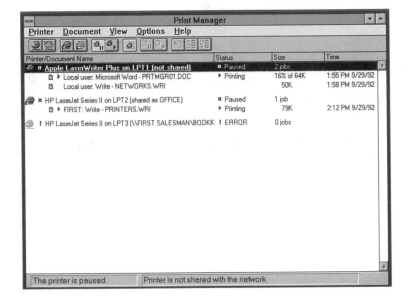

Table 9.1 Status Icons Used in the Print Manager Window

Icon	Description
	A printer connected to your computer not shared with others on your network.
	A printer connected to your computer shared with others on your network.
	A printer on your network shared and available for you to use.
	A printer or document currently printing.

Icon	Description
▌▌	A printer or document paused.
!	A printer or document stopped printing because of an error. (See status bar for message explaining the error.)

The log-on name of the person who sent a file to the printer is listed next to each file name. To the right of each printer and file name are three columns listing additional information. The first column indicates the status of the printer or file—for example, whether a printer or file is printing, paused, or stopped because of an error. The second column lists the number of jobs sent to the printer or the size of the file and what percentage of the file has been sent to the printer. The third column lists the time and date you sent a file to a printer.

At the top of the Print Manager window, just below the menu bar, is the toolbar containing several buttons that you can use to control your print jobs. Table 9.2 describes the function of each of these buttons on the toolbar. A corresponding menu command exists for each of these buttons.

Table 9.2 Toolbar Functions in Print Manager

Icon	Button Name	Function
🖧	Connect Network Printer	Connects to any shared printer on your network.
🖧	Disconnect Network Printer	Disconnects from a network printer.
🖨	Share Printer As	Shares your printer with others on your network. (Available only if you are working in 386 Enhanced mode.)
🖨	Stop Sharing Printer	Stops the sharing of your printer with others on your network. (Available only if you are working in 386 Enhanced mode.)
🖨	Pause Printer	Temporarily stops the selected printer from printing.
🖨	Resume Printer	Resumes printing for the selected printer.

(continues)

Table 9.2	Continued	
Icon	**Button Name**	**Function**
	Set Default Printer	Designates the selected printer as the *default printer,* which is the printer that is used automatically when you issue the Print command from Windows applications.
	Pause Printing Document	Temporarily stops the selected document from printing.
	Resume Printing Document	Resumes printing of the selected document.
	Delete Document	Removes the selected document from the print queue.
	Move Document Up	Moves the selected document towards the top of the printer queue.
	Move Document Down	Moves the selected document towards the bottom of the printer queue.

To use the toolbar buttons, you first must select the printer or file on which you want to carry out an action. Select the printer or file by clicking the file or printer with the mouse or by using the arrow keys to move the selection bar. Then click the appropriate button.

Changing the Print Order in Windows for Workgroups

Print Manager enables you to control the order in which documents print. You can change the print order of any document on printers that are connected to your computer. On printers that are on your network but not connected to your computer, you can change only the printing order of your own documents, and you can only move documents down the print queue. You cannot move a document while it is printing.

To move a document in the print queue using the mouse, follow these steps:

1. Move the mouse pointer to the document name you want to move.

2. Press and hold down the mouse button. The pointer changes to an arrow.

3. Drag the document to a new position in the queue.

4. Release the mouse button.

There is another alternative to using the mouse. Follow these steps:

1. Select the document you want to move.

2. Click the Move Document Up or Move Document Down button on the toolbar.

To move a document by using the keyboard, follow these steps:

1. Use the up- and down-arrow keys to select the document you want to reorder.

2. Press and hold down the Ctrl key.

3. Press the up- or down-arrow key to move the document to the new position in the queue.

4. Release the Ctrl key.

Pausing and Resuming Printing in Windows for Workgroups

When working with Windows for Workgroups, you can pause printing for any printer connected to your computer or for any of the files listed under a printer connected to your computer, regardless of whether the printer is shared. When working with a printer that is on your network but not connected to your computer, you can pause only your own documents. While a printer or document is paused, the word Paused appears in brackets in the Status column. Although you paused the printer or document, the printer continues to print all text in the printer's buffer; therefore, printing may not stop immediately.

To pause printing, follow these steps:

1. Select the printer or document you want to pause in the Print Manager window.

2. Click the Pause Printer or Pause Printing Document button on the toolbar.

   or

   Open the **P**rinter menu and choose **P**ause Printer, or open the **D**ocument menu and choose P**a**use Printing Document.

II

Managing Your Work

To resume printing, follow these steps:

1. Select the printer or document you want to pause in the Print Manager window.

2. Click the Resume Printer or Resume Printing Document button on the toolbar.

   or

   Open the **P**rinter menu and choose Resume Printer, or open the **D**ocument menu and choose Resume Printing Document.

Deleting a Document from the Queue in Windows for Workgroups

When working with Windows for Workgroups, you can delete any of the documents on your printer even if they came from another user to be printed on your shared printer. If you are printing on a shared printer that is not connected to your computer, you can delete only documents that you created.

To delete a document from the print queue, follow these steps:

1. Select the document you want to remove from the queue.

2. Click the Delete Document button on the toolbar.

   or

   Open the **D**ocument menu and choose **D**elete Document, or press Del.

3. Choose OK or press Enter when the confirmation message box appears.

> **Note**
>
> If you exit Print Manager by using the **P**rinter Ex**i**t command, a message box appears and warns you that all pending print jobs will be cancelled. Choose OK if your intention is to cancel all print jobs, including those sent to your printer by others on your network.

Changing the Printer's Priority in Windows for Workgroups

Windows has the capability to perform more than one task at a time. Therefore, you can print while you are working in one or more applications.

Each task, however, consumes some of the computer's computational power. You have the ability to balance how much of the computer's power is spent on applications and how much on printing. If you want your applications to run faster while a document is printing, you can give a low priority to printing. If you want printing to run faster, you can give a high priority to printing.

To change the printer priority in Windows for Workgroups, follow these steps:

1. Open the **O**ptions menu and choose **B**ackground Printing. The Background Printing dialog box appears (see fig. 9.14).

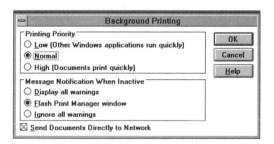

Fig. 9.14
Change the priority that your printer has in the Background Printing dialog box.

2. Select one of the following options:

Option	Result
Low	Printer runs slower; application runs faster.
Normal	Printer and application have the same priority.
Hi**g**h	Printer runs faster; application may run slower.

Displaying Print Manager Alerts in Windows for Workgroups

Your printer sends you a message if it runs out of paper, paper jams, or technical problems occur. You can decide how to receive those printer messages.

Follow these steps:

1. Open the **O**ptions menu and choose **B**ackground Printing to display the Background Printing dialog box (see fig. 9.14).

2. Select one of the following options:

Option	Result
Display all warnings	Always alerts you with a message box when the printer needs attention.
Flash Print Manager	Beeps and flashes if Print Manager is an icon or window if the window is inactive when the printer needs attention. You must activate the Print Manager window to see the message; this is Print Manager's default setting.
Ignore all warnings	Ignores the printer's request if Print Manager is an icon or if the window is inactive; you may not know that the printer needs attention.

Changing the Display in Print Manager in Windows for Workgroups

You can use several options for changing the look of Print Manager in Windows for Workgroups. You can decide how much information is displayed in the Print Manager window and you can modify the format of several of the displayed items.

You can choose whether to display the Status, Size, and Time columns in the Print Manager window. To display or not display any of these items, follow these steps:

1. Open the **V**iew menu (see fig. 9.15).

Fig. 9.15
The **V**iew menu.

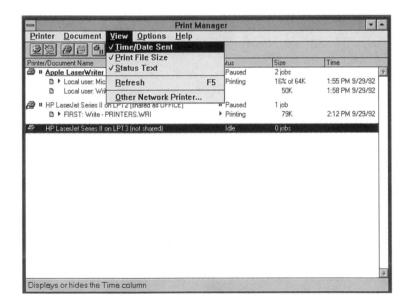

2. Select one of the following options. A check mark appears next to each selected option in the View menu.

Option	Result
Time/Date Sent	Displays the time and date you sent a file to the printer.
Print File Size	Displays the size of the files in the Print Manager print queue.
Status Text	Displays the status of printers and files.

You also can decide whether to display the status bar and toolbar. To display or not display the status bar and toolbar, follow these steps:

1. Open the **O**ptions menu (see fig. 9.16).

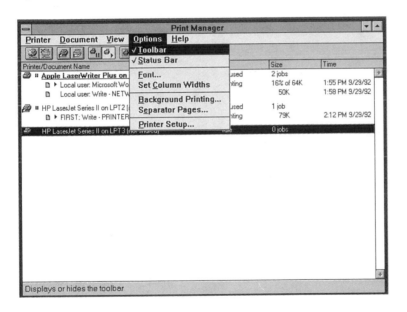

Fig. 9.16
The **O**ptions menu.

2. Select **T**oolbar to remove the toolbar from the display, or select **S**tatus Bar to remove the status bar from the display.

A check mark appears next to these options when they are selected.

Managing Your Work

To change the font, font style, and font size of displayed text, follow these steps:

1. Open the **O**ptions menu and choose **F**ont to display the Font dialog box (see fig. 9.17).

Fig. 9.17
Modify the display font using the Font dialog box.

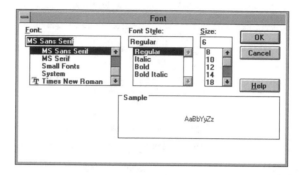

2. Select a font from the **F**ont drop-down list.

◄ "Understanding Fonts," p. 268

3. Select a style from the Font St**y**le list.

4. Select a font size from the **S**ize list.

5. Choose OK or press Enter.

You can change the widths of the Status, Size, and Time columns. To resize these columns, follow these steps:

1. Point to one of the column borders located just below the toolbar and above the Status, Size, and Time columns. The mouse pointer changes to a two-headed pointer when it is correctly positioned over a column border.

2. Drag the border until the column is the desired width.

   or

1. Open the **O**ptions menu and choose Set **C**olumn Widths, and use the arrow keys to change the width of the columns. Press the Tab key to move between columns.

2. Press Esc when you have finished setting the column widths.

Using Separator Pages

In Windows for Workgroups, you have the option of inserting separator pages between printed documents. This process can help you to identify the owner of documents on shared printers or to simply separate your documents on your own printer. You can use a simple standard separator page, or you can create a custom separator page that can include custom fonts and graphics.

To print a separator page, follow these steps:

1. Open the **O**ptions menu and choose S**e**parator Pages. The Separator Pages dialog box appears (see fig. 9.18).

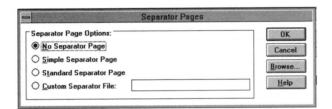

Fig. 9.18
The Separator Pages dialog box.

II

Managing Your Work

2. Choose one of the following options:

Option	Result
No Separator Page	Prints documents without pages between them.
Simple Separator Page	Prints a page using the Courier font.
S**t**andard Separator Page	Prints a separator page using a larger font.
Custom Separator Page	Prints a separator page containing a .WMF (Windows Metafile) or .CLP (Clipboard file) that you have specified. Specify the file and path to the .WMF or .CLP file in the edit box. CLP files are created by copying to the Clipboard and then saving from the Clipboard. WMF files are created by some Windows applications.

3. Choose OK or press Enter.

Closing the Print Manager Window

Print Manager may shut down when printing is complete. If Print Manager started when you selected to print from an application, Print Manager shuts down when printing is complete. However, if you started Print Manager from the Main program group, you must exit Print Manager manually after printing ends. You also can have Print Manager minimized so that you can drag and drop files from File Manager.

Be careful; if you exit Print Manager while print jobs are still outstanding in the queue, the print jobs are canceled. To close the Print Manager window without canceling print jobs, minimize the window by clicking the Minimize button (the down arrow at the top right of the window). If you use the keyboard, choose the Minimize command from the Control menu. After the window is minimized to an icon, Print Manager shuts down after printing is completed.

◀ "Controlling Windows and Icons," p. 40

To exit Print Manager, open the **V**iew menu and choose E**x**it.

> **Note**
>
> When you exit Print Manager while print jobs are still pending, not only are your print jobs canceled, but any jobs sent by other users sharing your printer are also canceled. *Be careful!* You may want to use the Chat available on Mail or send a mail message to the person who is printing before you attempt to shut down.

Printing to a File

On occasion, you may want to print to a file rather than to the printer. If you want to print a desktop-published document on a high-resolution typesetter owned by a service bureau, for example, you can more easily print from an EPS (Encapsulated PostScript) file. You create an EPS file by selecting a PostScript printer and then printing to an EPS file (by selecting a PostScript printer, you instruct Windows to create a file that is PostScript-compatible). As another example, suppose that you share a laser printer with someone down the hall. You can print the document to a file, walk down the hall with a floppy disk, and copy the file to the laser printer. In both cases, you can create the document even if you don't have the printer, and the person who prints the file can print the file even if he or she doesn't have the application that you used to create the file.

To print to a file, you must direct the printer's output to a file (rather than to the port to which the printer is connected). When you are done printing to a file, remember to redirect the printer to the correct port.

To print to a file, follow these steps:

1. If Print Manager isn't running, choose the Print Manager icon in the Main group in the Program Manager.

2. Open the **O**ptions menu and choose **P**rinter Setup. The Printers dialog box appears.

3. From the Installed **P**rinters list box, select the printer on which you (or a service bureau) eventually will print the file. The printer you select doesn't have to be connected to your computer. To create an EPS file, select a PostScript printer.

4. If the desired printer isn't the current default printer, select the printer and choose the S**e**t As Default Printer button (or press E).

5. Choose the **C**onnect button. The Connect dialog box appears.

6. From the **P**orts list, select FILE. You may need to use the scroll button to select FILE. Then choose OK to return to the Printers dialog box.

7. Choose the **S**etup button and set up the print options. For example, select the Paper **S**ource, Paper Si**z**e, and Orientation (Po**r**trait or **L**and-scape). To create an EPS file, you also must choose the **O**ptions button, select En**c**apsulated PostScript File, and enter a file name.

8. Choose OK enough times to return to the Printers dialog box; then select Close to return to Print Manager.

9. Return to the application and print as usual. Open the **F**ile menu and choose **P**rint to print the file. The Print to File dialog box asks you to name the file to which the file is going to print.

You also can access the Printers dialog box by choosing Control Panel from the Main window in the Program Manager. Then choose the Printers application.

◄ "Understanding Storage, Memory, Files, and Directories," p. 117

◄ "Managing Files and Disks," p. 152

Managing Your Work

> ### Setting Up a Bogus Printer for Printing to a File
>
> If you plan to print to a file frequently, set up a bogus printer. For example, set up a second PostScript printer to create EPS files. Use the **O**ptions **P**rinter Setup command (or the Printers application in Control Panel) to install a new printer; accept the current driver if you already have a PostScript printer installed or to add the PostScript driver if you don't have one installed. Follow the preceding procedures to direct this printer's output to an EPS file. When you're ready to print from the application, choose the **F**ile P**r**int Setup command to select the bogus printer and print.

Printing on a Network in Windows for Workgroups

If you are using Windows for Workgroups and are connected to a network, you can print on *network printers*, which are printers connected to other computers on the network, and other users on the network can use printers connected to your computer. Before you can print on a network printer, that printer must be designated as *shared* by the person using the computer to which the printer is connected. In the same way, you must *share* a printer connected to your computer before other users can print on it.

Connecting to a Network Printer

▶ "Installing and Configuring Windows for Workgroups," p. 867

Before you can connect to a network printer, you need to install the *printer driver* for that printer on your computer. See the section "Installing Printers from Print Manager" for instructions on how to install a printer from Print Manager. When you have installed the printer on your computer, follow these steps to connect to a network printer from within Print Manager:

1. Click the Connect Network Printer button on the toolbar.

   or

   Open the **P**rinter menu and choose **C**onnect Network Printer.

   The Connect Network Printer dialog box appears (see fig. 9.19).

2. Select the port that corresponds to the port you assigned to the network printer from the **D**evice Name drop-down list.

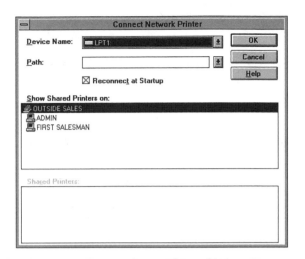

Fig. 9.19
The Connect
Network Printer
dialog box.

3. Type in the **P**ath text box the path for the shared printer.

The path includes the computer name for the computer the printer is connected to and the share name assigned to that printer. The computer name is preceded by double backslashes and is separated from the share name by a single backslash (for example: `\\ADMIN\OFFICE`).

You can use three methods for entering the path:

- If you know the path for the printer, you can type it directly into the Path text box.

- You can display the Path drop-down list and select a path from a list of recently used paths.

- Double-click a workgroup icon in the **S**how Shared Printers On list—or select the icon with the arrow keys and press Enter—to expand the workgroup. Select a name from the list of computer names listed under the workgroup to display a list of shared printers in the Sha**r**ed Printers box. When you find the printer you want to connect to, select it.

4. If you want to automatically reconnect to this shared printer at startup, mark the Reconnec**t** at Startup button.

5. Choose OK or press Enter.

II

Managing Your Work

Disconnecting from a Network Printer

To disconnect from a network printer, follow these steps:

1. Click the Disconnect Network Printer button on the toolbar.

   or

   Open the **P**rinter menu and choose D**i**sconnect Network Printer.

   The Disconnect Network Printer dialog box appears (see fig. 9.20).

Fig. 9.20
Use the Disconnect
Network Printer
dialog box to
disconnect from
other printers.

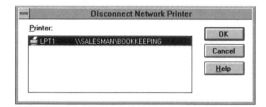

2. Select the printers in the **P**rinter list from which you want to disconnect.

3. Choose OK or press Enter.

You can select additional printers from the list if you want to disconnect from more than one printer at the same time. To select more than one printer, click the first printer, hold down the Ctrl key, and click subsequent printers. To deselect a printer, hold down the Ctrl key and click the printer. To use the keyboard, select the first printer, press Shift+F8, use the up- and down-arrow keys to move to the next printer, and press the space bar. Move to additional printers and press the space bar. To deselect a printer and retain the other selections, move to the selected printer and press the space bar. To return to selecting a single printer at a time, press Shift+F8 again.

Sharing Your Printer

If you want others on your network to be able to use your printer, you must first *share* your printer. You must be running in 386 Enhanced mode to share a printer with other users. To share your printer, follow these steps:

1. Using the mouse or keyboard, select the printer you want to share in the Print Manager window.

2. Click the Share Printer button on the toolbar.

   or

   Open the **P**rinter menu and choose **S**hare Printer As.

   The Share Printer dialog box appears (see fig. 9.21).

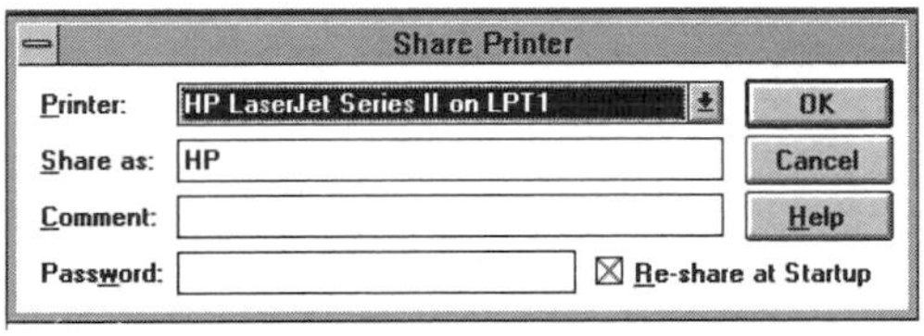

<table>
<tr><td colspan="2" style="text-align:center">Share Printer</td></tr>
<tr><td>Printer:</td><td>HP LaserJet Series II on LPT1</td><td>OK</td></tr>
<tr><td>Share as:</td><td>HP</td><td>Cancel</td></tr>
<tr><td>Comment:</td><td></td><td>Help</td></tr>
<tr><td>Password:</td><td></td><td>☒ Re-share at Startup</td></tr>
</table>

Fig. 9.21
The Share Printer
dialog box.

3. The name of the printer you select in step 1 appears in the **P**rinter drop-down list. You can select another printer from the drop-down list if you want.

4. Type a new share name in the **S**hare as text box if you do not like the default suggestion.

5. Type a comment in the **C**omment text box if you choose. This comment appears next to the share name in the Connect Network Printer dialog box and can be helpful for other users when they are looking for a particular shared printer to connect.

6. If you want to limit access to the shared printer to certain users, assign a password to the printer and only give the password to those users. Type the password in the Pass**w**ord text box.

7. If you want to automatically reshare the printer at start up, mark the **R**e-share at Startup check box.

8. Choose OK or press Enter.

To stop sharing a printer, follow these steps:

1. Click the Stop Sharing Printer button on the toolbar.

   or

   Open the **P**rinter menu and choose S**t**op Sharing Printer.

   The Stop Sharing Printer dialog box appears (see fig. 9.22).

II

Managing Your Work

Fig. 9.22
Select printers you
want to stop
sharing in the
Stop Sharing
Printer dialog box.

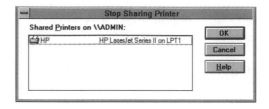

2. Select the printer you want to stop sharing from the Shared **P**rinters On
list.

You can select additional printers from the list if you want to stop sharing more than one printer at the same time. To select more than one
printer, click the first printer, hold down the Ctrl key, and click subsequent printers. To deselect a printer, hold down the Ctrl key and click
the printer. To use the keyboard, select the first printer, press Shift+F8,
use the up- and down-arrow keys to move to the next printer, and press
the space bar. Move to additional printers and press the space bar. To
deselect a printer and retain the other selections, move to the selected
printer and press the space bar. To return to selecting a single printer at
a time, press Shift+F8 again.

3. Choose OK or press Enter.

Changing the Password, Share Name, or Comment of a Shared Printer

You can change the password, share name, or comment for any printer you
are sharing with others on your network. To change the password for a
shared printer, follow these steps:

1. Using the mouse or keyboard, select the printer you want to change in
the Print Manager window.

2. Click the Share Printer As button on the toolbar.

or

Open the **P**rinter menu and choose **S**hare Printer As.

3. Change the **S**hare As, **C**omment, or Pass**w**ord entries.

4. Choose OK or press Enter.

Viewing Other Network Print Queues

The names and information for every file that is currently printing or waiting to be printed on your printers and any other printers you are connected to are listed in the Print Manager window. You can use the Other Network Printer command if you also want to view the activity on network printers you are not connected to—to decide, for example, whether you can speed up the printing of a file by connecting to another network printer. To view the queue for a printer you are not connected to, follow these steps:

1. Open the **V**iew menu and choose **O**ther Network Printer to display the Other Network Printer dialog box (see fig. 9.23).

Fig. 9.23
The Other Network Printer dialog box.

2. Type the network path name for the other network printer you want to view in the **N**etwork Printer text box.

3. Choose the **V**iew button or press Enter.

   A list of files in the queue for the designated printer is displayed in the box.

4. When you have finished viewing the files, choose Close or press Esc.

Updating Network Queue Status

Print Manager regularly updates the status of network printer queues displayed in the Print Manager window. However, you can manually update the status if you want to be sure that you have an up-to-the-minute status report. To manually update the status of network printer queues, open the **V**iew menu and choose **R**efresh, or press F5.

Printing Directly to a Network in Windows for Workgroups

When you are using Print Manager, all files that you send to print, including those you send to another printer, are managed by the Print Manager on your computer. Often, you can speed up the printing of files you are sending to a network printer by sending these files directly to the network printer, bypassing Print Manager. If you choose to do this, you can still use Print Manager to view the print queues on network printers and to control the printing of files on your printers.

To send files directly to network printers, follow these steps:

1. Open the **O**ptions menu and choose **B**ackground Printing.

2. Mark the **S**end Documents Directly to Network check box.

3. Choose OK or press Enter.

Printing on a Non-Windows for Workgroups Network

If you share printers with others on a local area network, printing with Print Manager is a little different. Additional Print Manager options, such as **N**etwork Settings and Network **C**onnections, become available in the **O**ptions menu. You also have the option to bypass Print Manager altogether, which is sometimes a faster way to print on a network.

▶ "Installing
Printers and
Queues,"
p. 921

When you print on a network, no Print Manager icon appears at the bottom of the screen.

Connecting to a Non-Windows for Workgroups Network Printer

If Windows is installed for a network and is connected to the network, you can print on a network printer. First, however, you must be sure that you are connected to the network printer you want to use—while you are installing a printer or by using the Print Manager window.

To connect to a network printer from the Print Manager window, follow these steps:

1. From the Main group, choose Print Manager. The Print Manager window appears.

2. Open the **O**ptions menu and choose Network **C**onnections. The Network Connections dialog box appears, which lists all network printers to which you are already connected (see fig. 9.24).

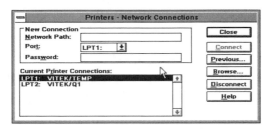

Fig. 9.24
Use the Network Connections dialog box to connect to a network printer.

3. In the **N**etwork Path box, type the name of the network.

4. Select the port you want to use from the Por**t** list.

   A network printer may already be connected to the port you want to use. Disconnect this printer before connecting a new printer (see the following section, "Disconnecting from a Network Printer").

5. If necessary, type a password in the Pass**w**ord text box.

6. Choose the **C**onnect button.

7. Choose **C**lose.

Windows remembers the network path and port settings for network printers to which you connected in the past. To quickly reconnect to a network printer you used before, open the **O**ptions menu and choose the Network **C**onnections command. Choose the **P**revious button. From the list, select the network path for the printer to which you want to reconnect. Choose **S**elect. Select the port you want to use, type a password if necessary, choose **C**onnect, and then choose **C**lose.

Disconnecting from a Non-Windows for Workgroups Network Printer

After you are finished using a network printer, you can disconnect from the printer. Do this when you need to connect a different network printer to the same port.

To disconnect from a network printer, follow these steps:

1. Open the Print Manager window.

2. Open **O**ptions and choose Network **C**onnections.

3. In the Current Printer Connections list, select the printer you want to disconnect.

4. Choose the **D**isconnect button.

5. Choose Close.

Viewing a Network Print Queue

When you print to a network printer, Print Manager lists the files you previously sent to a printer. By choosing the **S**elected Net Queue command, you can see all the files everyone on the network has sent to the same printer. Seeing this list can give you an idea of how much time will pass before the printer prints your job.

To view a network print queue, follow these steps:

1. Print the file and open the Print Manager window.

2. Select the printer queue information line.

3. Open the **V**iew menu and choose **S**elected Net Queue. Print Manager displays a list of all the files in queue for the printer.

4. Select Close or press Enter to close the dialog box.

Viewing Other Network Print Queues

If you have access to a number of printers on a network, you can view queues for all the printers before deciding which printer to use—even if this printer isn't installed or activated. (Before you can print to a printer, you must install it by using the **O**ptions **P**rinter Setup command in Print Manager or by choosing the Printers application icon in Control Panel.)

To view network queues for uninstalled printers, follow these steps:

1. Open the Print Manager window.

2. Open the **V**iew menu and choose **O**ther Net Queue. The Other Network Printers dialog box appears and asks you for the location and name of the network queue you want to view.

3. Type the network path name for the network queue you want to view in the **N**etwork Queue box.

4. Choose the **V**iew button. Information about the other print queues appears in the dialog box.

5. Type the name of another queue or click the Close button.

Updating Network Queue Status

By default, Print Manager tracks and periodically updates the status of a network queue. If you want, you can turn off automatic network queue updating so that you can update the network queue from the keyboard. By updating the network queue manually, you can make sure that you have an up-to-the-minute status report.

To turn off automatic network status updating, follow these steps:

1. Open the Print Manager window.

2. Open the **O**ptions menu and choose **N**etwork Settings. The Network Options dialog box appears (see fig. 9.25).

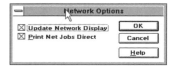

Fig. 9.25
You can use the Network Options dialog box to manage network queue updating.

3. Select the **U**pdate Network Display check box so that no mark appears in the box.

4. Choose OK or press Enter.

To update the network queue status, choose the **V**iew **R**efresh command or press F5.

Printing Directly to a Network

Usually printing is faster when you print files on a network directly, bypassing Print Manager. Because this is true, the **P**rint Net Jobs Direct option is Print Manager's default choice. Networks differ, however, so experiment with printing times on networks to determine whether printing directly or with Print Manager is faster.

When you bypass Print Manager, the information lines aren't updated to show the current status of the printers or the jobs currently printing. When you print directly to a network, the network completely controls the print job.

To print directly to a network printer, follow these steps:

1. Open the Print Manager window.

2. Open the **O**ptions menu and choose **N**etwork Settings to display the Network Settings dialog box.

II

Managing Your Work

3. Select the **P**rint Net Jobs Direct check box so that an x appears in the box. To print by using Print Manager, select this box so that no x appears in the box.

4. Choose OK or press Enter.

Using the Windows Printing System

The Microsoft Windows Printing System, which is designed to work with HP LaserJet printers, makes printing from Windows much faster and gives you far greater control over the printing of documents than you've ever had. The Windows Printing System consists of software that you install on your computer and a cartridge that you insert into the left cartridge slot of your HP LaserJet printer. The Windows Printing System establishes a dynamic communication link between your computer and printer, enabling you to know exactly what the status of your printer and print jobs is. The Windows Printing System also gives you the power to control the printed output from your Windows applications in ways that were previously unavailable. You can, for example, collate your printed output without the slowdown that is normal when you select this option in Windows applications, enlarge or reduce the size of your printed output, and produce two-sided output to save paper and give your documents a more professional look.

Opening the Setup Dialog Box

Once you have installed the Windows Printing System and established it as your default printer driver, you use the Windows Printing System Setup dialog box to control your print jobs (see fig. 9.26). There are two ways to access the Setup dialog box:

- Use the **F**ile **P**rint or **F**ile P**r**int Setup commands in your Windows applications.

- Use Control Panel or Print Manager.

If you access the Setup dialog box from a Windows application, the settings you select only affect the documents in the application you are working with. When you use the **P**rint command to open the Windows Printing System Setup dialog box, the settings you select only affect the current print job. When you use the P**r**int Setup command, if there is one in the application you are working with, the settings affect the current document whenever you print it until you change the settings. When you use Control Panel or Print Manager to access the Windows Printing System Setup dialog box, all Windows applications are affected.

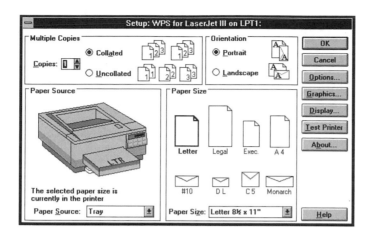

Fig. 9.26
The Windows
Printing System
Setup dialog box.

The exact steps you use to open the Windows Printing System Setup dialog box vary from application to application. The following are the steps you need to take to access the Windows Printing System Setup dialog box from three commonly used Windows applications. The steps you use for your Windows applications should be similar to one of the following procedures.

To open the Windows Printing System Setup dialog box in Word 6.0 for Windows, follow these steps:

1. Open the **F**ile menu and choose **P**rint.

2. Choose the Prin**t**er button.

3. Click the **O**ptions button.

To open the Windows Printing System Setup dialog box in Excel 5.0 for Windows, follow these steps:

1. Open the **F**ile menu and choose **P**rint.

2. Choose the P**r**inter Setup button.

3. Choose the **S**etup button.

    or

1. Open the **F**ile menu and choose Page Set**u**p.

2. Click the **O**ptions button.

When you use the first method, the choices you make in the Windows Printing System Setup dialog box affect the current print job only. When you want the Windows Printing System Setup dialog box settings to be saved with

II

Managing Your Work

the current document, use the second method to access the Windows Printing System Setup dialog box.

To open the Windows Printing System Setup dialog box in Quicken 3.0, follow these steps:

1. Open the **F**ile menu and choose Printer **S**etup.

2. Choose the **C**heck Printer Setup or **R**eport/Graph Printer Setup command from the submenu.

3. Click the **S**ettings button.

Regardless of the application you are working with, you need to be sure that the Windows Printing System is the selected printer before you can open the Windows Printing System Setup dialog box.

The other way to access the Windows Printing System Setup dialog box is to use Control Panel or Print Manager. Accessing the Windows Printing System Setup dialog box this way affects all your Windows applications until you change the settings from Control Panel or Print Manager again.

To open the Windows Printing System Setup dialog box from Control Panel, follow these steps:

1. Open Control Panel from the Main program group.

2. Choose the Printers icon to open the Printers dialog box.

3. Click the **S**etup button.

To open the Windows Printing System Setup dialog box from Print Manager, follow these steps:

1. Open the **O**ptions menu and choose **P**rinter Setup.

2. Click the **S**etup button.

Remember, when you open the Windows Printing System Setup dialog box from either Control Panel or Print Manager, the changes you make affect all your Windows applications.

Using the Windows Printing System Setup Dialog Box

The Windows Printing System Setup dialog box (see fig. 9.26), is where you make the routine settings that affect your print jobs. You can specify how many copies are printed, whether or not they are collated, the page orientation of the printed output, and the size and source of the paper. There are also command buttons for opening the Options, Graphics, and Display Options dialog boxes, which are described later in this chapter. To find out what version of the Windows Printing System you are running, choose the A**b**out button. Choose the **T**est Printer button to print a test page to verify that the Windows Printing System Windows Printing System is operating correctly and to obtain detailed information about your printer configuration. To get help with the Windows Printing System Setup dialog box, choose the **H**elp button.

To specify the number of copies to be printed, select or type the number of copies in the **C**opies text box. When you select multiple copies, only one copy of the print job is sent to the printer and that job is printed the specified number of times. With many applications, when you specify multiple copies, the print job is sent to the printer for each copy, which takes much longer than when you specify multiple copies using the Windows Printing System.

When you specify multiple copies, you can have the Windows Printing System collate your copies, that is, print the pages in the correct order for each copy. Select the Coll**a**ted option to have your copies collated or select the **U**ncollated option to print out all copies of each page together.

Select either the **P**ortrait or **L**andscape option to specify how your printed output will be oriented on the page.

You can specify the source and size of the paper that is used for a print job in the Windows Printing System Setup dialog box. To select the paper source, click one of the trays (if there is more than one for your printer) in the schematic diagram in the dialog box or make a selection from the Paper **S**ource drop-down list. You can also select Manual Feed if you want to manually feed the paper into the printer. This is useful for printing on envelopes or paper sizes for which you don't have a paper tray. When you select the manual feed option, the printer pauses and informs you when you need to insert the paper.

Select the paper size you want to use from the Paper Size group of options. You can either select one of the paper size icons or make a selection from the Paper Si**z**e drop-down list. If you select a paper size that does not match the tray that is selected as the paper source, a message alerts you to this fact.

Using the Options Dialog Box

You can make additional choices that affect your print jobs in the Options dialog box. To use the Options dialog box, follow these steps.

1. Choose the **O**ptions button in the Setup dialog box. The Options dialog box appears (see fig. 9.27).

Fig. 9.27
The Options
dialog box

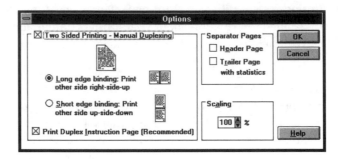

2. To print on both sides of the paper, mark the Two Side Printing - Manual **D**uplexing check box.

3. If you selected the duplexing option in step 2, select either the **L**ong Edge Binding or **S**hort Edge Binding option button.

4. Mark the Print Duplex **I**nstruction Page chec box if you want to include a page that instructs you how to reinsert the paper to print the second side.

5. Mark one or both of the H**e**ader Page and T**r**ailer Page with Statistics check boxes to print a separator before or after each print job.

   The separator pages include useful information that can help you distinguish one print job from another.

6. To reduce or enlarge your printout, type or select a specification in the Sc**a**ling box.

   You can reduce your printout to as small as one-tenth the original size and enlarge it up to four times the original size.

   The Graphics dialog box has options for controlling the printer resolution, the resolution enhancement (RET) feature of your HP LaserJet, changing the brightness and contrast of graphics output, and adjusting settings that affect grayscale images. To open the Graphics dialog box (see fig. 9.28), choose the **G**raphics button in the Setup dialog box. To learn more about using the available options, choose the **H**elp button in the Graphics dialog box.

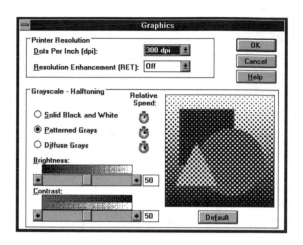

Fig. 9.28
The Graphics
dialog box.

Using the Status Window

The Windows Printing System Status window (see fig. 9.29) provides you with useful information on the status of your print jobs. When a print job is in progress, it tells you what file is being printed and what the progress of the print job is. If the Windows Printing System detects any problems with the printer (for example, a paper jam), an alert message informs you of this so that you can take corrective action. Because there is two-way communication between the Windows Printing System and your printer, you have much more information at your computer about what your printer is doing.

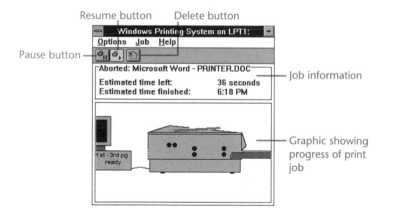

Fig. 9.29
The Status
window.

Normally, the Status window opens automatically when a print job is in progress, unless you deselect the **D**isplay Printer Status While Printing option in the Display Options dialog box (see below). When the print job is finished, the Status window closes. The Status window also opens if there are any problems with the printer during a print job that require your attention and inform you about what you need to do to correct the problem. If you reduce the Status window to an icon, the icon changes depending on the status of the print job. You can also pause, resume, and delete print jobs from the Status window, using the buttons in the toolbar shown in fig. 9.29, or the corresponding commands in the **J**ob menu.

You can change the Status window display using the Display Options dialog box. You can access this dialog box from either the **O**ptions menu in the Status window or with the **D**isplay button in the Windows Printing System Setup dialog box. You can select whether or not the Status window displays automatically when a print job starts, as described above. You can also choose whether or not to have sounds played along with the Windows Printing System messages with the Play **S**ounds With Messages option. You have three choices about what should appear in the Status window: only the Progress Bar, only the Printer Animation graphic, or both.

Correcting Printing Problems

Occasionally, problems arise when you try to print. If you run into trouble, read through the following checklist. Sometimes, the solution to printing problems is simpler than you expect. Many printer difficulties arise from installation and setup errors that you can correct by using the **O**ptions **P**rinter Setup command. (You can use the Printers application in Control Panel to do the same thing. See Chapter 7.)

■ Is the printer plugged in and turned on?

Turn off the printer, check all connections, and turn your printer back on.

■ Are you out of paper?

Reload the paper tray in your printer.

■ Do you have the proper printer cable, and is it correctly connected to the printer and the computer?

Check the connections to your printer to make sure they are secure. If this doesn't work, try a new printer cable.

■ Is the printer driver installed in Windows?

To install printers for Windows, use the **O**ptions **P**rinter Setup command in Print Manager, or the Printers application in Control Panel, and then choose the **A**dd button.

■ Did you select the correct printer name when you installed the printer?

Choose the **O**ptions **P**rinter Setup command in the Print Manager. Then choose **A**dd and check which printer is selected in the **L**ist of Printers. Make sure that you select the right printer.

■ Is the correct printer selected as the default printer?

Choose the **O**ptions **P**rinter Setup command in Print Manager or choose the Printers application in Control Panel to set the default printer. Select the printer you want to be the default in the Installed **P**rinters list; then choose S**e**t as Default Printer.

■ Is the printer connected to the correct port?

Choose the **O**ptions **P**rinter Setup command in Print Manager, or the Printers application in Control Panel and then choose the **C**onnect button to set the printer port.

■ Are the port settings correct?

Use the Ports application in Control Panel to select port settings. If the serial printer loses text, try reducing the baud rate.

■ Are the paper source, size, and orientation correct?

Check the **F**ile P**r**int Setup command in the application. You also can choose the **O**ptions **P**rinter Setup command in Print Manager or the Printers application in Control Panel and select **S**etup.

■ Is TrueType enabled?

Choose the Fonts application in Control Panel; then choose the **T**rueType button and select the **E**nable TrueType fonts option.

■ Is the font cartridge all the way in the slot?

Push the cartridge in firmly.

■ Are the soft fonts properly installed?

Check the installation manual that came with the font package, or choose the Fonts application in Control Panel and then choose the **A**dd button to add fonts.

■ Was the printer turned off after you downloaded fonts?

Download the fonts again.

■ Is the printer short on memory?

A printer that lacks enough memory may not print all the fonts or graphics you expect; printers like the HP LaserJet with 512K of memory may not have enough memory to print multiple fonts or large graphics. You must either print smaller graphics or buy more memory for the printer.

From Here...

Now that you know how to print in Windows, refer to the following chapters for additional information that complements this chapter:

■ Chapter 7, "Customizing with Control Panel," explains how to customize your Windows environment.

■ Chapter 8, "Managing Fonts," discusses what fonts are and how to use them with Windows applications.

■ Chapter 10, "Using Windows Write," teaches you how to use the word processor that comes with Windows.

■ Chapter 11, "Using Windows Paintbrush," shows you how to use Windows' painting application.

Part III

Using Windows Accessories

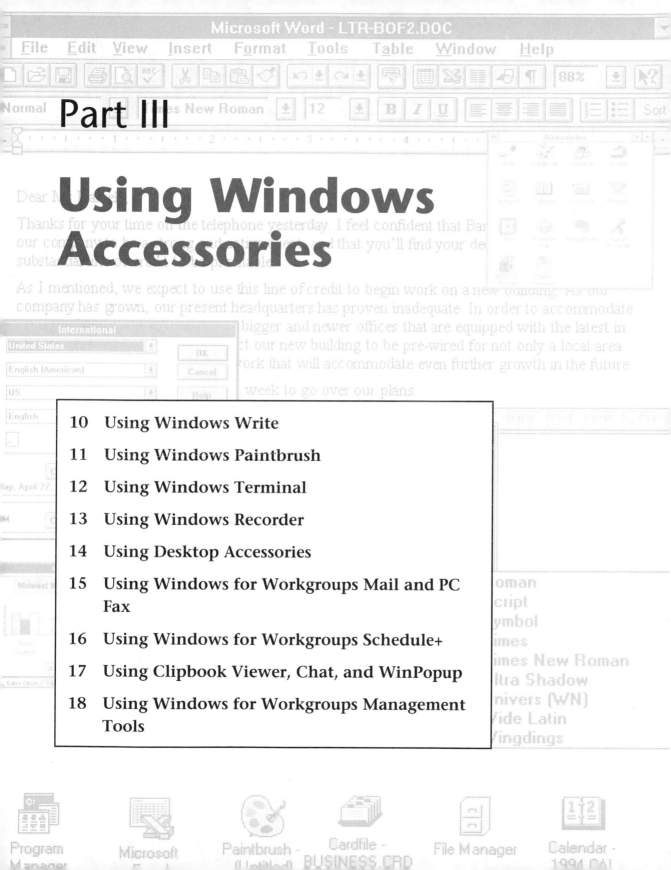

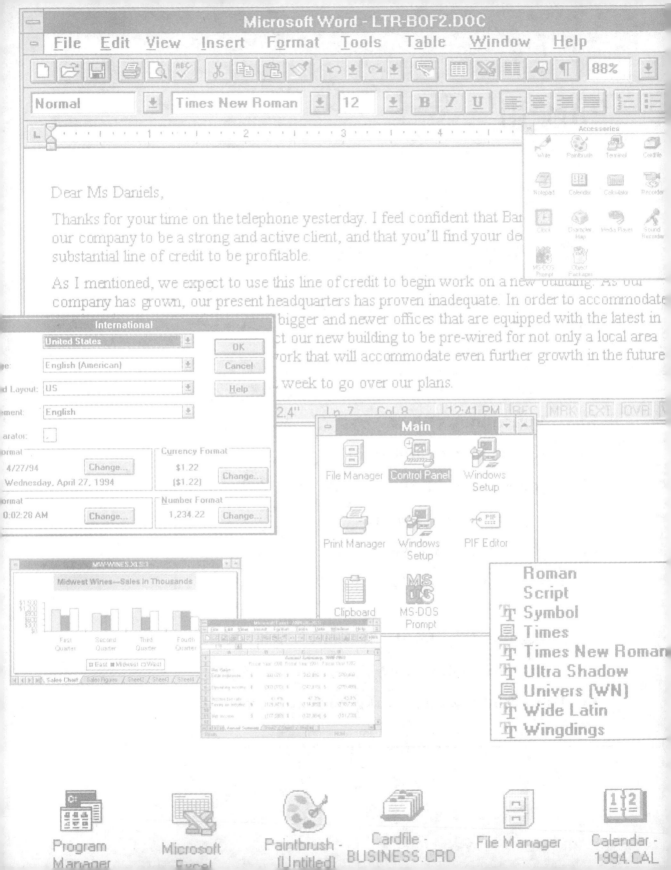

Chapter 10

Using Windows Write

Write is a simple but powerful word processor for Windows. This simple application is ideal for many day-to-day word processing needs. Although it is one of the easiest word processors to use, Write offers many of the editing and formatting capabilities commonly found in more advanced applications. Write also provides an advantage that many applications don't provide: the capability of sharing information with other applications and files. You can cut, copy, and paste text and graphics between Write documents and between Write and other applications. Another advantage of Write is that it uses the same structure of menus, commands, icons, and dialog boxes that all Windows applications use. Therefore, what you learn about managing text in Write applies to most of the Windows applications involving text.

In this chapter, you learn how to:

- Create a document
- Edit text
- Format a document
- Insert pictures into a document
- Print a document
- Save a document

Creating Documents

To start Write, open the Accessories group window from Program Manager, and double-click the Write icon. You can open an existing Write document directly from File Manager if the file ends with the extension WRI. Simply double-click the Write file or select the file and choose **F**ile **O**pen. You also can open Write and a Write document together by associating Write and the document together in a program item icon in Program Manager. To learn how, refer to Chapter 3, "Controlling Applications with Program Manager."

Creating a Write document is as simple as starting the application and typing the text. Because margins, a font, and tabs are already set, you can begin using Write as soon as you start the application. A blank Write window (the document) appears, with the name *Untitled* in the title bar (see fig. 10.1).

Fig. 10.1
The Write window.

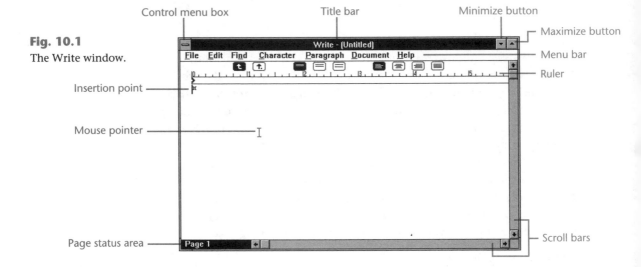

In Write, you can work on only one document at a time. You can start a new document (or open a different document) while you are working on an existing Write document, but the existing document closes. If you haven't saved changes to the existing document, the program asks whether you want to save the changes. (For details about saving, read the section "Saving and Naming the Document.")

Tip
To work with multiple Write documents, open the Write application multiple times (limited only by the amount of memory in the computer).

To view, edit, or print a file already created and saved, you must *open* the file. Follow these steps:

1. Open the **F**ile menu and choose the **O**pen command. The Open dialog box appears (see fig. 10.2).

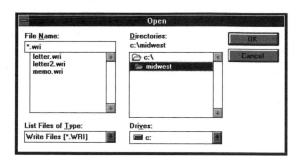

Fig. 10.2
The Open dialog
box.

2. From the Dri**v**es list, select the drive containing the file you want (if the file is on a drive different from the drive currently displayed in the **D**irectories list).

3. From the **D**irectories list, select the directory containing the file you want.

4. In the List Files of **T**ype box, select the file type you want to list in the File **N**ame list.

5. From the File **N**ame list, select the file you want to open. Or, in the text box, type the name of the file you want to open.

6. Choose OK or press Enter.

Entering Text

In the top left corner of the Write text area is a flashing insertion point followed by an end mark. The insertion point (also known as a *cursor*) is where text appears when you start typing; the end mark shows where the file ends. A new Write document is empty except for the insertion point and the end mark.

You can begin typing as soon as you open a file. (Editing techniques are explained later in this chapter.) When you reach the end of a line, continue typing. Write by default *wraps* the text to the next line. Press Enter to begin a new paragraph. Press Enter twice to leave a space between paragraphs. As you fill the page, the screen scrolls down (or left and right), keeping the insertion point in view.

Tip
The default size of the Write window may cause the text to scroll left and right as you type. To prevent left-to-right scrolling, widen the Write window.

> **Note**
>
> You can never move the insertion point beyond the end mark (if you want to move the end mark further down, position the insertion point before the end mark and press Enter as many times as you want).

III

Using Windows Accessories

Moving through a Document

Before you can edit the text, you must be able to move the insertion point through the document. You can use either the keyboard or the mouse to move the insertion point. To use the mouse to move the insertion point to a different location on-screen, move the I-beam where you want the insertion point and click the mouse button. To scroll to a different area of the document, use the scroll bars at the right and bottom edges of the window. (The scroll box in the scroll bar indicates the cursor's relative position in the document. If, for example, the box is in the middle of the scroll bar, you are near the middle of the document.)

To move with the keyboard, use the techniques listed in the following table.

Movement	Press
Single character	Left- or right-arrow key
Single line	Up- or down-arrow key
Next or previous word	Ctrl+left-arrow key or Ctrl+right-arrow key
Beginning of the line	Home
End of the line	End
Next or previous sentence	Goto (5 on the keypad)+left- or right-arrow key
Next or previous paragraph	Goto (5 on the keypad)+up- or down-arrow key
Top or bottom of window	Ctrl+PgUp or Ctrl+PgDn
Next or previous page	Goto (5 on the keypad)+PgUp or PgDn
Continuous movement	Hold any of the above keys or key combinations
One screen	PgUp or PgDn
Beginning of document	Ctrl+Home
End of document	Ctrl+End

To jump to a specific page, press F4, type the page number in the Go To dialog box, and choose OK or press Enter.

Saving and Naming the Document

As you create your Write document, you should save it periodically to avoid losing your work in case of a power failure or equipment malfunction. Write includes two commands for saving: **F**ile **S**ave and **F**ile Save **A**s. **F**ile **S**ave quickly saves a previously saved document using its current name. **F**ile Save **A**s allows you to save an unnamed file or to rename a file you already saved.

The first time you save a document, both **F**ile **S**ave and **F**ile Save **A**s call up the Save As dialog box, enabling you to enter the new file name (see fig. 10.3). Using the same dialog box, you can change the directory in which you save the file, and you can select a different file format in which to save the file.

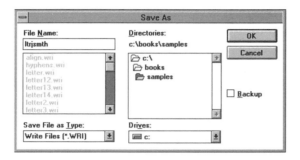

Fig. 10.3
The Save As dialog box.

The next time you save the same file, you can choose either **F**ile **S**ave (keeping the current file name and replacing the old file) or **F**ile Save **A**s (giving the file a different name and, therefore, creating a new version of the file). Unlike Save **A**s, **S**ave isn't followed by a dialog box if the document was saved previously.

After saving, the file name you assigned appears in the Write title bar.

To save and name a file, follow these steps:

1. Open the **F**ile menu and choose Save **A**s.

2. Select the drive where you want to save the file in the Dri**v**es list.

3. In the **D**irectories list, select the directory in which to save the file. By default, Write saves files in the current directory.

4. In the File **N**ame text box, type the file name.

5. If you want to save the file in some format other than Write, select a format from the Save File as **T**ype list.

6. To make a backup copy of the file (besides the saved WRI file), select **B**ackup. Note that backup Write files use the extension BKP rather than WRI. Backup Word files use the extension BAK.

7. Choose OK or press Enter.

III

Using Windows Accessories

To resave a file with its current name, choose the **F**ile **S**ave command.

Selecting and Editing Text

You can make simple edits in your Write documents by moving the insertion point and deleting or inserting text. But more complex editing requires that you first *select* the text you want to edit.

To make simple insertions, place the insertion point where you want to add text and begin typing. The new text is "threaded" into existing text. Simple deletions also are easy. To erase one character at a time, position the insertion point next to the character and press Backspace (to delete characters to the left) or Del (to delete characters to the right). By default, Write reformats the paragraph.

Undoing an Edit

Write lets you change your mind about an edit you just made or a sentence you just typed. To undo, select **E**dit **U**ndo or press Alt+Backspace or Ctrl+Z. You can restore text you just deleted, delete text you just added, or remove formatting. You can even undo an undo. If you find that **E**dit **U**ndo removes too much typing, choose **E**dit **U**ndo a second time to undo the undo.

Notice that the **E**dit **U**ndo command changes depending on the kind of edit you have made. For example, the command may appear as **U**ndo Typing, **U**ndo Formatting, or **U**ndo Editing.

Selecting Text

Many edits you need to make are more complex than simply entering or deleting one character at a time. You may want to change a word, delete a sentence, or move a whole paragraph. To do these things, you must identify the text you want to edit or format by *selecting* it. Selected text appears in reverse video on-screen, as shown in figure 10.4.

To select text with the mouse, position the I-beam at the beginning of the text, hold down the mouse button, drag to the end of the text, and release the mouse button. Write also offers time-saving selection shortcuts, such as double-clicking to select a word. The selection bar also is convenient. The *selection bar* is the white space between the left edge of the screen and the left margin of the text. (For example, in fig. 10.4, the selection bar is the blank area between the left edge of the Write window and the left edge of the text in the letter.) When you move the I-beam to the selection bar, the I-beam turns into a right-pointing arrow. You can select a line of text by pointing at the line and clicking the mouse button. Dragging the mouse pointer down the selection bar selects entire lines and paragraphs at a time.

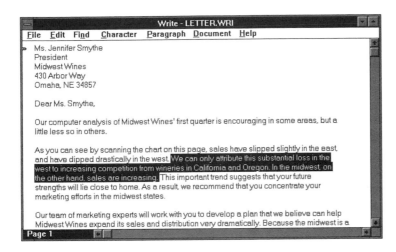

Fig. 10.4
Two sentences selected for editing.

Techniques for selecting with the mouse are shown in the following table.

Selection	Action
One word	Double-click the word.
Several words	Double-click the first word and drag to the end of the last word.
Any amount of text	Press the mouse button and drag from the beginning to the end of the text.
Between two points	Move the insertion point to the beginning, click, move to the second point, press and hold down Shift, and click at the second point.
One line	Click the selection bar (white space) to the left of the line.
Several lines	Press the mouse button and drag up or down in the selection bar.
Paragraph	Double-click in the selection bar to the left of the paragraph.
Entire document	Press Ctrl and click in the selection bar.

To deselect text with the mouse, click once anywhere in the text portion of the window. To deselect text with the keyboard, press any arrow key. Deselected text returns to its normal appearance.

To delete a block of text, select it and press Delete or Backspace or choose the **E**dit Cu**t** command. You also can replace text by selecting it and then typing; Write deletes the selected block and inserts the new words.

Moving Text

Any amount of text—a letter, a word, part of a sentence, or several pages—can be moved from one place in a document to another. Start by selecting the text; then use the **E**dit Cu**t** or **E**dit **C**opy command to cut or copy the text to the Windows Clipboard, a temporary memory space. Move the insertion point to where you want to move the text; then choose **E**dit **P**aste.

Caution

The Clipboard holds only one selection at a time. The next text you cut replaces what was in the Clipboard. When you move text, paste the text immediately after cutting so that you do not lose the information.

You can use shortcut keys instead of **E**dit Cu**t** (Shift+Del or Ctrl+X) and **E**dit **P**aste (Shift+Ins or Ctrl+V). Remembering two of these shortcut keys is easy. Just think that you want to *shift* text to a new location, so you Shift+Del (Delete) it from one location and Shift+Ins (Insert) it to a new location.

To move text with the mouse, select the text to be moved. Then, using the scroll bars, scroll the screen until you can see the point where you want to relocate the text. (Do not move the insertion point, which deselects the text.) Press and hold down Shift+Alt; click the mouse button where you want the text to appear. The selected text is cut and pasted where you clicked.

Copying Text

You can copy text from one place to another or to several other places in a document. The process is similar to moving, but the original text is left in place. Remember that cutting or copying another block of text replaces the existing contents of the Clipboard. To copy text, follow these steps:

1. Select the text to be copied.

2. Open the **E**dit menu and choose **C**opy, or press F2, Ctrl+Ins, or Ctrl+C.

3. Move the insertion point to the place in the document where you want to copy the text.

4. Open the **E**dit menu and choose **P**aste, or press Shift+Ins or Ctrl+V.

You can paste additional copies of the text in the Clipboard by moving the insertion point and choosing **E**dit **P**aste again.

You can use the mouse and these steps as a shortcut for copying text:

◄ "Copying and Moving," p. 56

1. Select the text to be copied.

2. Scroll the screen to display where you want the copied text. (Make sure that the text remains selected.)

3. Press and hold down Alt; click the mouse button where you want the text to be copied.

Finding and Replacing Text

You can search a document to find or change text—for example, to change a misspelled name or correct an old date. The **Fi**nd menu includes three commands that help you find text and make changes quickly: **F**ind, Repeat **L**ast Find, and R**e**place.

The **Fi**nd **F**ind and **Fi**nd **R**eplace commands operate through dialog boxes. After you enter the text you want to find or change, Write starts at the insertion point and searches forward through the document. It finds and selects the first occurrence of the text. At this point, you have three choices: you can move the insertion point into the document and edit the text while the dialog box remains on-screen; you can close the dialog box; or you can continue searching for the next occurrence of the text. Close the dialog box when the search is complete.

If Write cannot match the text you indicated, Write shows a dialog box with the message Text not found. If this happens, choose OK and try a different search word.

To find text, follow these steps:

1. Open the **Fi**nd menu and choose **F**ind. Figure 10.5 shows the Find dialog box. Move the dialog box if it obstructs your view of the document. (To move the insertion point between the document and the dialog box, click the document with the mouse or press Alt+F6 on the keyboard.)

2. Type the text you want to find in the **Fi**nd What text box.

3. Mark the Match **W**hole Word Only check box to match only whole words. Mark the **M**atch Case check box to match capitalization.

III

Using Windows Accessories

4. Choose the **F**ind Next button, or press the Enter key.

5. When Write is finished finding, you see a dialog box that reads `Find Complete`. Choose OK or press Enter.

Fig. 10.5

The Find dialog box.

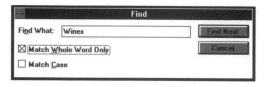

To close the Find dialog box, press Esc or choose Cancel. To repeat the last find, choose Fi**n**d Repeat **L**ast Find or press F3.

Finding Close Matches

You can use Find Find and Find Replace to find words even when you are not certain which words you want. Do this by using a wild card in the words. For example, the question mark wild card represents unknown characters. If you want to look for *Smith* or *Smythe*, but are unsure whether the name is spelled with a *y* or an *i*, you can search for *Sm?th?*. Write finds occurrences of both *Smith* and *Smythe*.

Write also enables you to make repetitive changes rapidly throughout the document with the Fi**n**d **R**eplace command. Some word processors call this a search-and-replace feature. To change text, follow these steps:

1. Choose Fi**n**d **R**eplace. The Replace dialog box appears (see fig. 10.6).

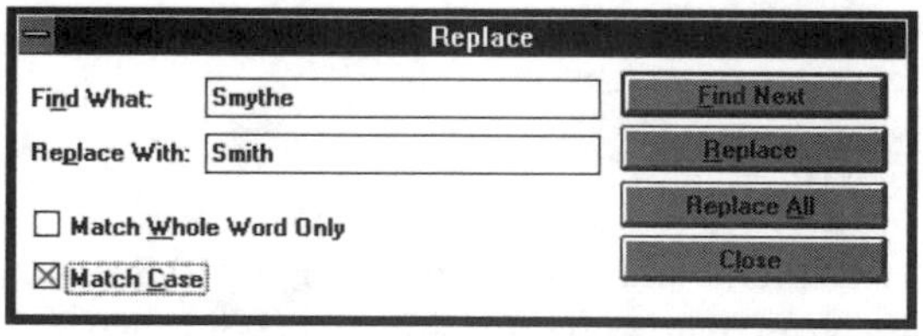

Fig. 10.6

The Replace dialog box.

2. Type the text you want to find in the Fi**n**d What text box. Type the text you want to replace the selected text with in the Re**p**lace With text box.

3. Choose other options as desired; then choose the **F**ind Next button.

4. Select the type of change you want. Following are the selections you can make and a description of the change made:

Find Next. The first time this option is used it finds the first occurrence of the text. On subsequent use, it finds the next occurrence of the text without replacing the current occurrence.

Replace. Makes the change on the found text, and then finds the next occurrence.

Replace **A**ll. Changes the specified text throughout the document.

5. When Write is finished replacing, you see a dialog box that reads Find Complete. Choose OK, and then choose the Close button.

Formatting the Document

Write offers a number of ways to customize the look of your documents. You can add emphasis to individual characters or words with boldface or italics, specify the font and point size of the text, use superscripts or subscripts for mathematical formulas, and so on. These formats are called *character formatting*. Character formatting applies to individual characters within words, and includes such options as boldface, italics, and underline.

In addition to character formatting, you can format paragraphs individually or as a group. For example, you can set up tables with special column alignment, center headings and quotations, and so on. This type of formatting is called *paragraph formatting*.

When the text of your document is finished, it's time to think about the *document formatting*. Do you want a particular header or footer to appear on every page or every other page? Do you plan to print the document on letterhead or other special paper that requires certain margins to fit correctly? Document formatting controls the overall look of the document as a whole.

The following sections describe the three types of Write formatting in detail.

Character Formatting

The **C**haracter menu controls the appearance of characters. If you already have typed the characters, you can change their appearance by selecting the text and choosing commands from the **C**haracter menu. If you have not yet typed the text, position the insertion point where you want the enhanced text to begin, choose the enhancement, and type the text.

Many of the character enhancement options, shown in the **C**haracter menu in figure 10.7, "toggle" on and off like a light switch—you turn them on the

◄ "Understanding
Fonts," p. 268

same way you turn them off: choosing the command. To make plain text bold, for example, you select the text and choose the **B**old command; to make bold text plain, do the same thing. The **C**haracter menu shows a check mark next to selected enhancements. Some enhancements, such as bold and italic, can be used together, so you see two check marks.

Fig. 10.7
The **C**haracter menu.

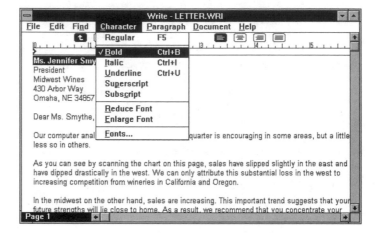

Several shortcuts exist for quickly enhancing text, as shown in the following table.

Enhancement	Function Key	Ctrl+Key Combination
Boldface	F6	Ctrl+B
Italic	F7	Ctrl+I
Underline	F8	Ctrl+U

To remove all enhancements, follow these steps:

1. Select the enhanced text.

2. Open the **C**haracter menu and choose Re**g**ular, or press F5.

Superscripts and Subscripts

Superscripts (raised text) and *subscripts* (lowered text) are useful in science, math, and footnoting: for example, H_2O or "So proclaimed the King."[4]

These features raise or lower the selected text and shrink it slightly so that the changed text fits easily between lines.

To create a superscript or a subscript, select the text to be raised or lowered. Then choose the **C**haracter Su**p**erscript command to raise the selected text or the **C**haracter Sub**s**cript command to lower the text. To remove super-scripting and subscripting, select the text and choose the Su**p**erscript or Sub**s**cript command again.

> **Note**
>
> If you try to enhance text but the enhancement doesn't change on-screen or when printed, either the printer isn't capable of printing this enhancement, or you are using a printer driver that doesn't take advantage of the printer's capabilities.

Changing Fonts and Point Size

Another use for **C**haracter menu commands is to enhance a passage by changing the size of the type. You can enlarge type to the next larger size or reduce it to the next smaller size. (Write displays only the sizes the printer can print.)

To change the size of characters you are about to type, choose **C**haracter **E**n-large Font or **C**haracter **R**educe Font and then type the characters. To enlarge or reduce text you have already typed, select the text, open the **C**haracter menu, and choose **E**nlarge Font or **R**educe Font. You can repeat this step, enlarging or reducing the text as large or small as you want.

Another way to change the font size is to use the **C**haracter **F**onts command:

1. Select the text to change.

2. Open the **C**haracter menu and choose **F**onts.

3. Select the size you want from the **S**ize list, or type the size you want in the **S**ize text box.

4. Choose OK or press Enter.

A sample of the font and font size appears in the Sample box.

The Font dialog box also enables you to change the font style and size (see fig. 10.8). The following table lists the options in the Font dialog box.

Item	Description
Font	The **F**ont text box displays the font selected in the Font list. You can select a font by choosing it from the list or by typing its name in the text box.
Font St**y**le	Lists font styles for the selected font.
Size	Lists font sizes available for the selected font.
Sample	Shows a sample of the selected font, along with a message describing the nature of the font.

Fig. 10.8
The Font dialog box.

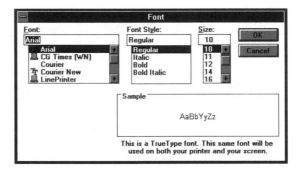

In the **F**ont list, an icon to the left of each font describes the nature of the font. TrueType fonts have a "TT" icon; printer fonts have a printer icon; screen fonts have no icon.

The font you choose is displayed in the Sample box, along with a message describing the nature of the font. For example, the message accompanying the TrueType fonts shown in the figure explains that the same font is used both on-screen and by the printer. If you choose a non-TrueType font, a message says, `This is a printer font. The closest matching Windows font will be used on your screen.` Using TrueType fonts gives you a more accurate screen representation of the final output. To learn more about TrueType, refer to Chapter 8, "Managing Fonts."

Determining Fonts and Sizes

To find out what font or size a section of text is, select the text and choose **C**haracter **F**onts. The current font and size are shown selected in the Font dialog box. If you selected text containing more than one font or size, the text boxes are empty; you should select a smaller amount of text.

Paragraph Formatting

Paragraph formatting describes the appearance of a paragraph (or of a single line that stands by itself as a paragraph). This level of formatting includes characteristics such as centering, line justification, indentation, and line spacing. Some paragraph formatting choices are made for you already: text is left-aligned, and no paragraphs are indented.

The End-of-Paragraph Mark Holds the Formatting Code

A paragraph's formatting is stored in the paragraph mark that defines the paragraph. This paragraph mark doesn't appear on-screen, but you can delete or select it. If you accidentally delete the paragraph mark, the paragraph merges with the paragraph below it, assuming the lower paragraph's formatting.

Choosing an Alignment

In Write, paragraphs can be aligned with the left margin, the right margin, both the left and the right margins, or in the center between the margins (see fig. 10.9). The alignment for the paragraph containing the insertion point is identified with a check mark in the **P**aragraph menu (see fig. 10.10).

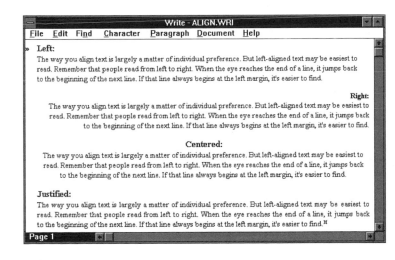

Fig. 10.9
Four ways to align paragraphs.

To change paragraph alignment, follow these steps:

1. Select the paragraphs to be aligned. (To align only one paragraph, position the insertion point anywhere inside the paragraph.)

2. Open the **P**aragraph menu and choose **L**eft, **C**entered, **R**ight, or **J**ustified.

III

Using Windows Accessories

Fig. 10.10
The **P**aragraph menu lists commands for formatting paragraphs.

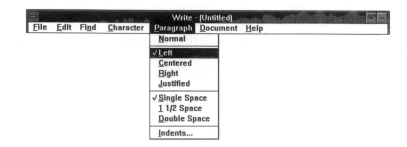

You can restore a paragraph to Write's default format choices—left-aligned, single-spaced, and unjustified with no indentations—by choosing the **P**aragraph **N**ormal command.

Spacing Lines

Lines in paragraphs can be single, one-and-a-half, or double-spaced. The spacing for the paragraph with the insertion point is shown with a check mark in the **P**aragraph menu.

To change paragraph spacing, follow these steps:

1. Select the paragraphs to be spaced. (To change the spacing of only one paragraph, position the insertion point anywhere inside the paragraph.)

2. Open the **P**aragraph menu and choose **S**ingle Space, **1** 1/2 Space, or **D**ouble Space.

Indenting Paragraphs

Paragraphs can be indented to set them off from the main body of text—for example, for long quotations. Also, the first lines of paragraphs can be indented so that you do not have to press Tab at the beginning of each paragraph.

Indentations, like all measurements in Write, are measured in inches rather than characters because Write supports different font sizes and proportional spacing.

Understanding Character Spacing

In *proportional* spacing, the widths of letters are proportional; for example, the letter *i* is narrower than the letter *m*. If margins and indentations were measured in characters, Write would not know how large to make an indentation: an inch might contain 16 *i*'s but only 12 *m*'s. Similarly, varying font sizes means that Write cannot measure the length of a page by lines.

Measurements are calculated in inches and are typed in decimals (rather than in fractions). Half an inch is typed as .5 rather than 1/2. Use a negative number for a hanging indent (a *hanging indent* makes the first line start to the left of the left margin or indent).

The **P**aragraph **I**ndents command works through the Indents dialog box (see fig. 10.11). The settings shown in the figure indent a selected paragraph three inches from the right margin, with no indent on the left margin, and the first line one-quarter inch from the indented margin.

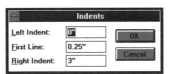

Fig. 10.11
The Indents dialog box.

To indent a paragraph using a command, follow these steps:

1. Select the paragraphs to be indented. (To change the indentation of only one paragraph, position the insertion point anywhere inside the paragraph.)

2. Open the **P**aragraph menu and choose **I**ndents.

3. Type the left indentation value in the **L**eft Indent box. Always enter indentation values in inches, using decimals for fractions of inches (one-half inch is .5).

4. In the **F**irst Line box, type the amount of space to indent the first line. Type a negative value to create a hanging indent.

5. In the **R**ight Indent box, type the value of the right indentation.

6. Choose OK or press Enter.

Removing Paragraph Formatting

You can add many different kinds of paragraph formatting to a paragraph, and you can change or remove each one individually. If, for example, the paragraph is centered, but you want it to be left-aligned, you simply select the paragraph and select the left alignment command from the **P**aragraph menu.

If you want to remove all paragraph formatting at once, select the paragraph (or paragraphs) and choose the **P**aragraph **N**ormal command. The selected paragraphs return to Write's default settings: left-aligned, no tabs or indents, and single-spaced.

III

Using Windows Accessories

Document Formatting

Document formatting affects an entire document and its appearance: headers, footers, and tab and margin settings. The **D**ocument menu controls document formatting. In a new Write document, many document formatting choices are made for you already. Margins, for example, are set to 1.25 inches on the left and right, and 1 inch on the top and bottom. Default tab settings are every .5 inch. You can change all these settings and many more.

Adding Headers, Footers, and Page Numbers

You can add one header and one footer to each Write document; headers appear at the top of every page of the printed document; footers at the bottom (you can exclude headers and footers from the first page, if you prefer). You can include automatic page numbers as part of a header or footer.

You create headers and footers using a special screen and dialog box (see fig. 10.12). The screen, where you type the header or footer text, works like any other Write screen: you can format the header or footer just as you format any Write text. Use the dialog box to specify where on the page to place the header or footer, and whether to include a page number. Headers and footers appear wherever you position them on the page, regardless of the top and bottom margins.

Fig. 10.12
The Page Footer screen and dialog box.

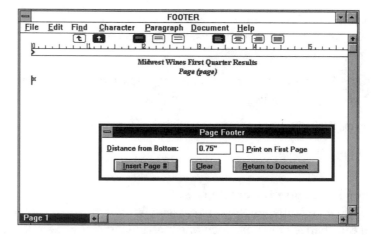

To create a header or footer, follow these steps:

1. Open the **D**ocument menu and choose either **H**eader or **F**ooter.

2. Type the header or footer text. Format the header or footer as you would any document.

3. Activate the Header or Footer dialog box by clicking it with the mouse button or pressing Alt+F6.

4. Select the **D**istance from Top or **D**istance from Bottom box and type the distance in decimal inches (1/2 of an inch is .5) for the header or footer to appear from the top or bottom of the page.

5. Select the **I**nsert Page # button to include automatic page numbering. The (page) page-number symbol appears at the insertion point, marking where page numbers will print.

6. Select the **P**rint on First Page box if you want the header or footer to print on the first page of the document. Leave the box deselected if you don't want the header or footer to appear on the first page.

7. Choose the **R**eturn to Document button.

To remove a header or footer, choose the **C**lear button in the Page Header or Page Footer dialog box and choose the **R**eturn to Document button. Pressing Esc in the header or footer dialog box acts the same as choosing the **R**eturn to Document button. If you want to undo a mistake, use the **E**dit **U**ndo command.

Note that a selection in the Page Layout dialog box controls the starting page number in headers and footers. To change the starting page number, choose the **D**ocument **P**age Layout command and type the starting page number in the **S**tart Page Numbers At text box.

Headers and footers do not appear in the document on-screen—you do not see them until you print the document.

Setting Tabs

Write's tab settings apply to the entire document. Write includes preset tabs at every half inch, but you can override these tab settings. The tab settings tell the insertion point where to go when you press the Tab key in the document.

You can choose from two kinds of tabs: left-aligned and decimal. A left-aligned tab lines up text from the left; decimal tabs align numbers by a decimal (which is useful for columns of dollar amounts). You also can use the decimal tab as a right-aligned tab, aligning entries that do not contain a decimal point so that the right edge is on the tab setting.

You can have up to 12 tabs in the document.

The Tabs dialog box is shown in figure 10.13, and its options are described in the following table. Set tabs in inches from the left margin (as shown in the figure), not from another tab setting. Press Tab to move between boxes in the dialog box. Remember that tab settings apply to the entire document.

Item	Description
Positions	Where you type how far from the left margin to set each tab (type tab settings in decimal inches; for example, a tab one-quarter inch from the left margin is typed as .25).
Decimal check boxes	Specifies that the tab above the box is a decimal tab. Click the box, or tab to the box and press the space bar to select or deselect this box.
Clear **A**ll button	Clears the tabs that you have typed, and restores the default 1/2-inch tabs.

Fig. 10.13
Entering tab measurements in the Tabs dialog box.

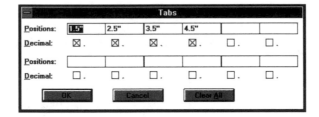

To set tabs, follow these steps:

1. Open the **D**ocument menu and choose **T**abs.

2. Type tab positions in decimal inches from the left margin in the **P**ositions text boxes. (Press Tab to move between the boxes.)

3. Select the **D**ecimal boxes to specify decimal tabs.

4. Choose OK or press Enter.

To change or remove a tab setting, follow these steps:

1. Open the **D**ocument menu and choose **T**abs.

2. Select the tab setting you want to change. (Press Tab to move between the boxes.)

3. Type a new tab setting, or press Del to remove the current tab setting.

4. Choose OK.

To restore the default tabs at every half inch, open the **D**ocument menu and choose **T**abs, choose the Clear **A**ll button, and choose OK.

If you use a mouse, you can set tabs with the ruler. The ruler contains two kinds of tab icons: left and decimal. Set tabs by selecting the icon for the kind of tab you want and then clicking the ruler where you want the tab setting. You move tab settings by dragging the tab arrows left or right. Remove tabs by dragging them down off the ruler. When you move tab settings, any tabbed text in the document moves with them.

To set tabs with the ruler, follow these steps:

1. Open the **D**ocument menu and choose **R**uler On to display the ruler.

2. Click either the left-align tab icon or the decimal tab icon to identify the kind of tab you want.

3. Click the blank bar below the numbers on the ruler to set a tab at this point.

By default, the ruler uses inches as a measurement system; if you select centimeters (cm) in the Page Layout dialog box, the ruler displays centimeters instead. To access the Page Layout dialog box, choose the **D**ocument **P**age Layout command.

Setting Margins

Write's margins are preset to 1 inch on the top and bottom, and 1.25 inches on the left and right. With the **D**ocument **P**age Layout command, you can change the margins. You also can specify a starting page number other than 1 for automatic page numbering in headers and footers and can change the measurement system from inches to centimeters.

To set margins, follow these steps:

1. Open the **D**ocument menu and choose **P**age Layout to display the Page Layout dialog box (see fig. 10.14).

2. Select the **L**eft, **R**ight, **T**op, and **B**ottom boxes in turn and type a decimal measurement for each margin.

3. Choose OK or press Enter.

III

Using Windows Accessories

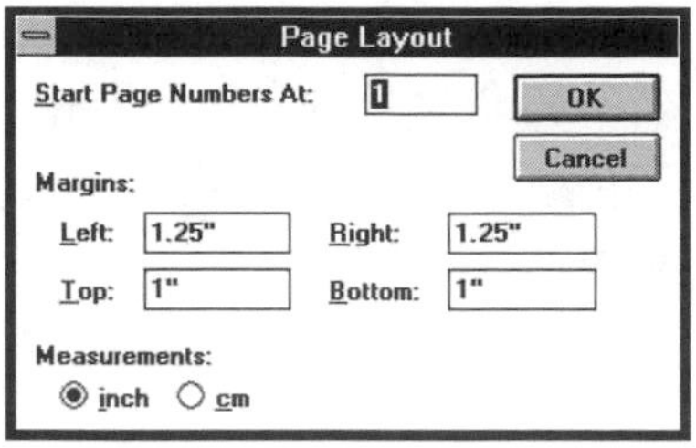

Fig. 10.14

The Page Layout
dialog box.

```
┌─────────────────────────────────────────────┐
│ ═             Page Layout                     │
│  Start Page Numbers At:  [0]      ┌────────┐ │
│                                   │   OK   │ │
│                                   └────────┘ │
│                                   ┌────────┐ │
│  Margins:                         │ Cancel │ │
│                                   └────────┘ │
│   Left:  [1.25"]      Right:  [1.25"]        │
│                                              │
│   Top:   [1"]         Bottom: [1"]           │
│                                              │
│  Measurements:                               │
│    ⦿ inch  ○ cm                              │
└─────────────────────────────────────────────┘
```

Controlling Page Breaks

When you print, Write determines by default where to end one page and
begin the next. Write inserts page breaks to start each new page. The number
of lines per page depends on line spacing, margin settings, and font size.

If you want precise control over where page breaks occur (or if you simply
want to see where page breaks will occur), you can repaginate the document
before you print, inserting page breaks where you want them.

To repaginate with page breaks, follow these steps:

1. Open the **F**ile menu and choose **R**epaginate.

2. Select Confirm Page **B**reaks if you want to confirm each page break.

3. Choose OK or press Enter.

If you didn't select Confirm Page **B**reaks in step 2, Write inserts page breaks
and then returns to the document. Page breaks appear as double arrows (>>)
in the left margin.

If you selected Confirm Page **B**reaks in step 2, Write displays a page break
mark (>>) at the first proposed page break and displays a dialog box that you
use to move or confirm page breaks (see fig. 10.15). You can move the page
break up or back, but you cannot move a page break further down than Write
originally positioned it. After you confirm a page break, Write advances to
the next proposed page break.

Another way to force a page break is to move the insertion point to the spot
where you want to start a new page and press Ctrl+Enter. The forced page
break appears on-screen as a dotted line. To delete a forced page break, move
the insertion point just below the line and press Backspace enough times to
erase the dotted line.

You also can confirm or delete a forced page break as part of the repagination
process. If you're confirming page breaks, when Write encounters a forced

page break in the document, it highlights the page break and displays a dialog box asking whether you want to keep it or remove it. Choose **K**eep to keep the break or **R**emove to remove it.

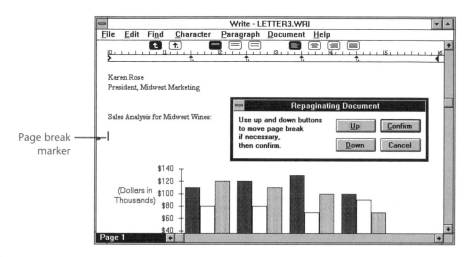

Page break —| marker

Fig. 10.15
Confirming page breaks.

After you repaginate or print a document, you see two changes in the document. Page breaks you entered by repaginating appear as double arrows (>>) in the left margin; page breaks you entered by pressing Ctrl+Enter appear as dotted lines that extend the full width of the page. Additionally, the current page number appears at the bottom left of the window in a status box.

Using Other Applications with Write

Through the Windows technology called object linking and embedding, or OLE, you can embed or link objects into a Write document. Linked objects retain their connection to the original file, and when you change the original, the linked copy in Write updates to reflect your changes. Embedded objects are updated when you update the file or exit the application. You also can copy graphics and text from other applications to Write.

To learn more about object linking and embedding, refer to Chapter 6.

Linking Objects

To link text or an object into a Write document, follow these steps:

1. Start the server application (such as Excel) and create the data you want to link into your Write document or open the file containing the data.

Tip
If you made any editing changes, the page numbers shown before repaginating may be incorrect. Repaginate before trusting page numbers or page breaks.

III

Using Windows Accessories

Tip
Whether it's copied, embedded, or linked, you can move or size a graphic after you have added it to a Write document.

2. Save the original data file.

3. Select the data you want to link into Write. Open the **E**dit menu and choose **C**opy.

4. Switch to your Write document and position the insertion point where you want the linked data to appear.

5. Open the **E**dit menu and choose Paste **L**ink.

One of two things appears in your Write document, depending on the server application. Either you see an icon representing the object in your Write document, or you see the object itself. When you link text from Word for Windows, for example, you see an icon; when you link data from an Excel spreadsheet, you see a spreadsheet (see fig. 10.16).

Fig. 10.16
A spreadsheet
chart in a Write
document.

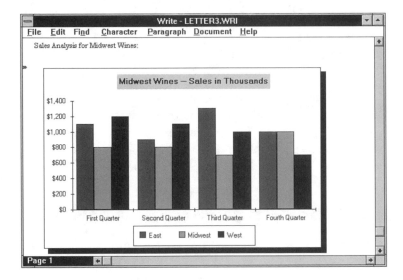

If you edit the original data file, the linked data in your Write document updates, by default, to reflect the changes. You can edit the data from within Write or in the server application.

Embedding Objects

To embed an object, you use the server application to create the object; when you update the file or exit the application, the updated object is added to the Write document. To embed an object in a Write file, follow these steps:

1. Position the insertion point where you want the object to appear in the Write document.

2. Open the **E**dit menu and choose **I**nsert Object. The Insert Object dialog box appears, listing all applications that support object linking and embedding (see fig. 10.17).

Fig. 10.17
The Insert Object dialog box.

3. Select the application you want to use to create an embedded object.

4. Choose OK or press Enter. The application opens.

5. Use the application to create the object, or open the **E**dit menu and choose **P**aste to paste in an object from the Clipboard.

6. When you're finished with the object, open the **F**ile menu and choose **U**pdate to include a copy of the object in the Write document.

7. Open the server application's **F**ile menu and choose E**x**it and Return to Document.

If you get an error telling you of a memory shortage when you choose the **F**ile **U**pdate command, resize the object to make it smaller and try again.

When you choose the **E**dit **I**nsert Object command, the Insert Object dialog box lists all the applications on your computer that support object linking and embedding. Because Paintbrush comes free with Windows, you always see Paintbrush on the list (unless you have deleted it), but you also see applets like MS WordArt and Microsoft Draw if you have installed an application such as Word for Windows, which includes these applications for free.

◀ "Creating an Embedded Object," p. 213

Copying Text and Graphics

If you want to copy text or graphics to a Write document, the simplest method is to use the Clipboard. Open the other application, select the text or graphic you want to copy, and choose **E**dit **C**opy. Switch back to Write, place the insertion point, and choose **E**dit **P**aste.

To copy from an application that supports object linking and embedding, when you do not want the text or graphics to be embedded, follow these steps:

1. Start the server application, such as Paintbrush, and create the picture or open the file containing the picture.

2. Select the picture. Open the **E**dit menu and choose **C**opy.

3. Switch to your Write document, and position the insertion point where you want the picture to appear.

4. Open the **E**dit menu and choose Paste Sp**e**cial. The Paste Special dialog box appears.

5. From the Data Type list, select Bitmap or Picture.

6. Choose **P**aste or press Enter.

Printing a Document

Printing with Write involves two steps: selecting the printer, and specifying what you want to print.

To identify and set up the default printer, follow these steps:

1. Open the **F**ile menu and choose P**r**int Setup, or open the **F**ile menu and choose **P**rint and then the **S**etup button. Once a printer is selected, it remains selected for all documents—you won't have to select a printer again unless you want to change to a different printer.

2. Select either the **D**efault Printer or another printer from the Specific **P**rinter list.

3. Select the paper orientation: Po**r**trait (vertical pages) or **L**andscape (horizontal pages).

4. Select a Paper Si**z**e and **S**ource from the lists provided.

5. Choose **O**ptions to make additional choices, depending on the printer.

6. Choose OK to close the Options dialog box; then choose OK or press Enter to close the Print Setup dialog box.

The Print Setup dialog box lists all the printers installed for Windows on the computer, as well as options for selecting paper orientation, size, and source. When you select a printer, page orientation, paper size, and paper source, the choices remain in effect until you change them—even after you start a new document. The dialog box also includes an **O**ptions button; choose it to select additional information, such as scaling on a PostScript printer. The Print Setup and Options dialog boxes are shown in figure 10.18.

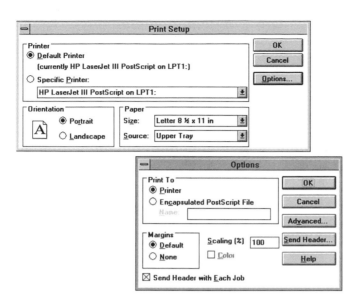

Fig. 10.18
The Print Setup
and Options dialog
boxes.

To print the document, follow these steps:

1. Open the **F**ile menu and choose **P**rint. The Print dialog box appears
   (see fig. 10.19).

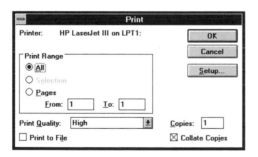

Fig. 10.19
The Print dialog
box.

2. Select the Print Range **A**ll button to print all the pages; select Print
   Range **S**election to print only the selected text, or select the **P**ages **F**rom
   and **P**ages **T**o text boxes and type a range of pages to print.

3. From the Print **Q**uality list, select the print resolution you want.

4. Mark the Print to Fi**l**e check box to print to a file rather than to the
   printer.

5. In the **C**opies box, type the number of copies you want to print.

6. To collate multiple copies of the document, mark Collate Copies (available if your printer supports collating).

7. Choose OK or press Enter.

◄ "Printing a File," p. 294

◄ "Using the Print Manager Window," p. 295

When you send a document to be printed, Write presents a dialog box that tells you the file is being printed and offers a Cancel button, in case you want to stop the print job in progress. (Notice that the currently selected printer is named at the top of the dialog box.)

Exiting Write

After you finish writing or are ready to stop for the day, exit Write and return to the Windows desktop by choosing File Exit.

◄ "Quitting Windows Applications," p. 58

If you have not saved the most recent changes, Write reminds you that the document has changed and asks whether you want to save the changes. Select Yes if you want to save the changes, No to discard the changes, or Cancel to return to the document.

From Here...

Now that you can use Write, refer to the following chapters for more information:

■ Chapter 5, "Simple Data Sharing," explains methods for transferring information from one application to another.

■ Chapter 6, "Advanced Data Sharing," shows you how to use object linking and embedding to share information between applications.

■ Chapter 8, "Managing Fonts," explains ways to work with fonts in the Windows environment.

■ Chapter 9, "Printing with Windows," describes how to install printers; you also learn how to print your documents from Windows.

■ Chapter 11, "Using Windows Paintbrush," teaches you how to use the drawing application that comes with Windows.

Chapter 11

Using Windows Paintbrush

A computer is a business tool; everyone knows that. Sometimes when you sneak up on someone who has Windows on his PC, however, you find that he is not working—he is playing Solitaire, or creating a masterpiece with Windows' fun and colorful painting application, Paintbrush.

Even though Paintbrush is a simple, easy-to-use graphics application, it may be as powerful a graphics application as you will ever need. Paintbrush is fun, but it also is a serious business tool. With Paintbrush, you can create everything from free-flowing drawings to precise mathematical charts, and you can use your creations in other Windows applications, such as Windows Write, Windows Notepad, Windows Cardfile, or Word for Windows. You can use your computer "paintings" to illustrate a story, to emphasize an important point in a report, or to clarify instructions.

The following are some of the graphic effects that you can create with Paintbrush:

- Lines in many widths, shades, and colors

- Brush strokes in a variety of styles, widths, shades, and colors

- Unfilled or filled shapes with shades or colors

- Text in many sizes, styles, and colors

- Special effects like rotating, tilting, and inverting

Windows Paintbrush is fun, but it also is a tool that you can use in your work. People are attracted to pictures. They understand pictures better than they understand text alone. Whatever type of work that you do, think about how you can communicate more effectively by using illustrations you create with Windows Paintbrush.

In this chapter, you learn to

- Use the Paintbrush tools

- Select line widths, shades, and colors

- Type text in a painting

- Edit a painting

- Create special effects

- Use Paintbrush with other applications

Starting Windows Paintbrush

Because Paintbrush is a Windows accessory, you must start Windows before you can start Paintbrush. You usually can start Windows by typing **WIN** at the DOS prompt, but your computer may be set up differently. (Your AUTOEXEC.BAT file, for example, may include a command that starts Windows when you turn on your computer.) To learn more about starting Windows, refer to Chapter 1, "Operating Windows."

The Paintbrush program item icon is located inside the Accessories group, which may be open as a window or closed as a group icon. To start Paintbrush, follow these steps:

1. If the Accessories group appears as an icon, select the icon and press Enter or double-click on the Accessories group icon. Either method opens the Accessories window.

2. Select the Paintbrush icon and press Enter, or double-click on the Paintbrush icon.

◀ "Starting Applications," p. 48

Starting Paintbrush opens a new, empty Paintbrush file. You can customize a program item icon, however, so that when you start the application, an existing file opens automatically (see Chapter 3, "Controlling Applications with Program Manager").

Getting To Know the Paintbrush Window and Tools

The Paintbrush window, like other windows, has a *title bar* across the top, a *menu bar* below the title bar, *scroll bars* on the right and bottom, and a *drawing area* in the middle. Unique to Paintbrush are its three tool areas: the *toolbox* on the left side, the *line-width box* in the bottom-left corner, and the color and shades *palette* along the bottom. Figure 11.1 shows a labeled Paintbrush screen.

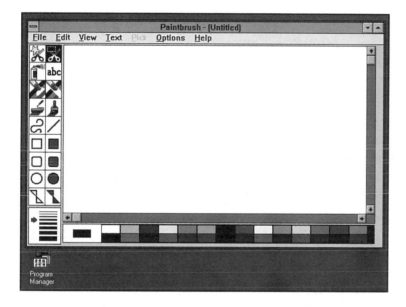

Fig. 11.1
The Paintbrush screen.

To paint, draw, fill, color or shade, write, and edit in Paintbrush, you first must select the appropriate tool, line width, and shade or color. Figure 11.2 labels the individual tools in the toolbox on the left side of the screen.

On a color system, the palette appears in color. If your system is monochrome, shades of gray are in your palette.

To select a tool, line width, shade, or color, position the pointer on the tool, line, shade, or color that you want and then click the left mouse button.

The general procedure for using Paintbrush is as follows:

1. Select from the toolbox the tool with which you want to draw.

2. Select from the line-width box the line width that you want.

3. Select from the palette the color that you want.

4. Move the pointer into the drawing area and draw a shape. (The pointer changes into a different shape in the drawing area, depending on which tool you select.)

Fig. 11.2
The Paintbrush toolbox.

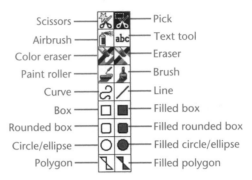

To draw an unfilled red box with a wide line, for example, select the unfilled box tool; select a wide line; select red; move the pointer into the drawing area, where the pointer turns into a crosshair; and drag the crosshair while holding down the mouse button. Release the mouse button when the box is the size and shape that you want.

Because Paintbrush is a bit-map graphics application (rather than an object-oriented application), the shapes that you create are painted on-screen in one layer. You cannot reshape a box or move an object behind another object, but you can select a box and move it somewhere else, select a picture of a house and tilt it, select a pattern and flip it, or change the colors of your painting. You also can erase your painting (or part of it) and paint something new.

Using the Keyboard with Paintbrush

Paintbrush is easiest to use if you have a mouse. The instructions in this chapter assume that you have a mouse; if you're using a keyboard, use the following keystrokes in place of the equivalent mouse action:

Mouse Action	Keyboard Equivalent
Click the left mouse button	Press Ins
Click the right mouse button	Press Del

Mouse Action	Keyboard Equivalent
Double-click the left mouse button	Press F9+Ins
Double-click the right mouse button	Press F9+Del
Drag	Press Ins+arrow keys

You also can use the keyboard to move around the Paintbrush screen. You may find that some of these techniques work as shortcuts, even if you have a mouse:

Press	To Move
Tab	Among the drawing area, toolbox, line-width box, and palette
Arrow	In the direction of the arrow
Home	To the top of the drawing area
End	To the bottom of the drawing area
PgUp	Up one screen
PgDn	Down one screen
Shift+up arrow	Up one line on the screen
Shift+down arrow	Down one line on the screen
Shift+Home	To the left edge of the drawing area
Shift+End	To the right edge of the drawing area
Shift+PgUp	Left one screen
Shift+PgDn	Right one screen
Shift+left arrow	Left one space on the screen
Shift+right arrow	Right one space on the screen

Selecting Tools, Line Widths, and Shades or Colors

When you draw a picture with Paintbrush, you draw it with the tool that you select, in the line width that you select, and in the shade or color that you select. Before you start drawing, select a tool, line width, and shade or color.

To select a tool or line width, position the pointer on the tool or line width that you want and press the left mouse button.

The palette offers two choices: foreground and background shade or color. At the left end of the palette, shown in figure 11.3, is a box within a box. The *inner* box is the *foreground* shade or color; the *outer* box is the *background* shade or color. You use the foreground shade or color to create lines, brush strokes, shapes, and text. The background shade or color has three functions: it borders a filled shape; it shadows the edges of text typed with the **S**hadow style; and it becomes the background of the next *new* Paintbrush file that you start (but not the current file).

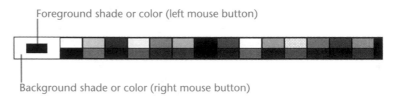

Foreground shade or color (left mouse button)

Background shade or color (right mouse button)

Fig. 11.3
The Paintbrush palette.

To select a shade or color from the palette, follow these steps:

1. Move the pointer over the shade or color that you want to select.

2. Press the left mouse button to select the foreground color; press the right mouse button to select the background color.

> **Note**
>
> If you are selecting colors with the keyboard, press Insert (Ins) to select the foreground color and press Delete (Del) to select the background color.

Using the Paintbrush Tools

  The toolbox includes tools for cutting out, airbrushing, typing text, erasing, filling, brushing, drawing curves or straight lines, and drawing filled or unfilled shapes. The process for operating most of the tools is similar: press and hold down the left mouse button, drag the mouse, and release the mouse button. (There are three exceptions: you operate the Text tool by clicking and typing, the Paint Roller tool by pointing and clicking, and the curve tool by clicking, dragging, and clicking.)

Whichever tool you use, the **U**ndo command of the **E**dit menu is a useful ally. Use it to undo your most recent action. However, keep one rule in mind when you choose **U**ndo: it undoes everything you've done since you either selected the tool that you're using, used a scroll bar, opened another application, or resized the window. Therefore, when you choose **U**ndo, you may undo one line or ten. To keep **U**ndo useful, reselect the tool each time that you draw a successful line or shape.

Several Tools Use the Right Mouse Button To Undo

Several tools—including the selection tools, the line tools, and the shape tools—use the right mouse button to undo. To cancel the line or shape that you're currently drawing, click the right mouse button *before* you release the left mouse button.

Using the Cutout Tools

With the cutout tools, you can draw an enclosure around any part of your Paintbrush drawing. Whatever is inside the enclosure is selected and can be moved, cut or copied (and then pasted), resized, tilted, flipped, or inverted. The sections "Editing the Painting" and "Creating Special Effects," later in this chapter, explain the things that you can do with a selected object or area of the painting.

The toolbox has two cutout tools: the *Scissors* is the icon on the left side of the toolbox, and the *Pick* is the icon on the right side of the toolbox. The Scissors cutout tool draws a free-form enclosure. The Pick cutout tool draws a rectangular enclosure. Both tools select everything inside the enclosure—the object and the space around it.

To use the Scissors tool, follow these steps:

1. Select the Scissors tool from the top-left of the toolbox.

2. Position the mouse pointer where you want to begin the enclosure, and then press and hold down the left mouse button.

3. Drag the mouse to draw a line that encloses the area that you want to select.

4. Release the mouse button at the same place that you started drawing the line.

III

Using Windows Accessories

> ### Press the Mouse Button To Cancel a Cutout
>
> If you make a mistake while using either of the cutout tools, click the left mouse button outside the cutout area to cancel the cutout. Then try again.

To use the Pick tool, follow these steps:

1. Select the Pick tool from the top-right of the toolbox.

2. Position the mouse pointer where you want to begin the enclosure, and then press and hold down the left mouse button.

3. Drag the mouse to draw a rectangle around the area that you want to select.

4. Release the mouse button.

Figure 11.4 shows an image selected with the Pick tool. Notice that the selection box—the box that surrounds the image—is formed of dashed lines.

Fig. 11.4
Using the Pick cutout tool to select an object or area.

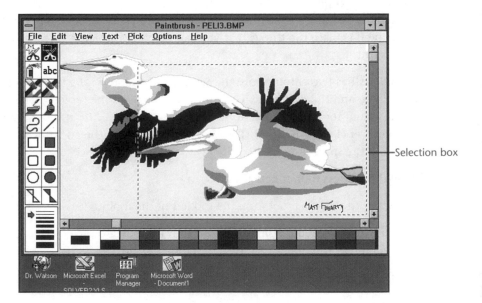

Selection box

Expanding the Paintbrush Screen

To blow up the Paintbrush screen to the full size of the monitor, double-click the Pick cutout tool in the toolbox. You cannot edit the painting in this view, but you can see more of it. To return the screen to the normal editing size, click the mouse button or press the Esc key.

Using the Airbrush Tool

The Airbrush tool works like a can of spray paint, spraying a mist of color. When selected, the Airbrush tool turns into a crosshair that produces a circular pattern of dots when you click it on-screen (to produce an airbrushed dot) or drag it across the screen (to produce an airbrushed line). The line width that you select determines the diameter of the circle of dots; the palette foreground color determines the shade or color that the Airbrush tool sprays. The speed that you drag determines the density of dots; if you drag the crosshair slowly, you get a dense pattern of dots; if you drag it quickly, the spray is lighter.

Unlike other tools, the Airbrush tool draws transparently. Any image under the airbrush spray may remain visible, depending on how densely you spray over the image (see fig. 11.5).

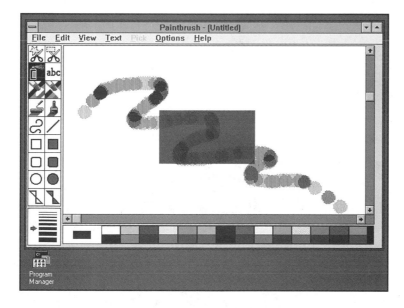

Fig. 11.5

Use the Airbrush tool to draw a circular, transparent mist of dots in the foreground shade or color.

To use the Airbrush tool, follow these steps:

1. Select the Airbrush tool from the toolbox.

2. Select a line width and foreground color.

3. Position the pointer where you want to begin the airbrush stroke, and then press and hold down the left mouse button.

4. Drag the crosshair to paint the airbrush stroke.

5. Release the mouse button.

Using the Text Tool

 With the Text tool, you can add words to your computer painting. Paintbrush has limited typing capabilities: text does not wrap from line to line; you must press Enter to begin the next line of text. You can press the Backspace key to erase a letter when you type, but after you click the mouse button, you cannot return to the text to edit it.

The following steps briefly explain how to use the Text tool; refer to the section "Typing Text in Paintbrush," later in this chapter, for details about changing the font, style, and size of the text.

To type text, follow these steps:

1. Select the Text tool from the toolbox.

2. Select from the palette the color that you want your text to be.

3. Position the I-beam where you want to start typing and click to display the insertion point.

4. Type the text. Press Backspace to erase characters; choose any command from the **T**ext menu to change the appearance of the text.

5. Press Enter to begin the next line of text.

Using the Eraser Tools

◄ "Simple Editing
Techniques,"
p. 55

Paintbrush has two eraser tools: the *Color Eraser* on the left side of the toolbox, and the *Eraser* on the right side of the toolbox.

 The Color Eraser tool is actually a color switcher. It works two ways, and both ways depend on the foreground and background color choices that you make in the palette. (The foreground color is the color in the center box at the left end of the palette. You select the foreground color by clicking the *left* mouse button on the color that you want. The background color is the border color in the palette box. You select the background color by clicking the *right* mouse button on the color that you want.)

Dragging the Color Eraser tool across an area in your painting changes every occurrence of the selected foreground color to the selected background color. Double-clicking on the Color Eraser tool in the toolbox changes every occurrence of the selected foreground color in the visible area of your painting to the selected background color. (The Color Eraser changes only the *selected* foreground color; the Eraser tool, described next, changes *all* foreground color.) Be aware that the Color Eraser tool also erases or alters custom colors blended from the foreground color.

Suppose that your screen is displaying a red square with a wide, black border. Red is the selected foreground color, and yellow is the selected background color. If you drag across the square with the Color Eraser, the red foreground color turns to yellow, but the black stays black (see fig. 11.6). (If you use the Eraser tool rather than the Color Eraser, the black also turns yellow, as does any area outside the square that you drag the Eraser across.)

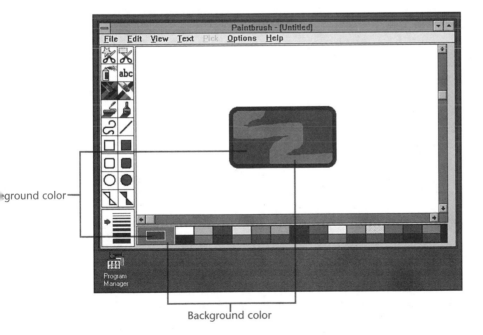

Fig. 11.6
Using the Color Eraser tool to change the selected foreground color to the selected background color.

To use the Color Eraser tool on part of your painting, follow these steps:

1. Select the Color Eraser tool.

2. Select a line width. The width of the area that this tool erases depends on the line width that you select.

3. Select a foreground color from the palette. When you drag the Color Eraser over your painting, you change this color.

4. Select a background color from the palette. When you drag the Color Eraser over your painting, the foreground color changes to this color.

5. Press and hold down the left mouse button.

6. Drag the Color Eraser tool across the part of your drawing that you want to change.

7. Release the mouse button.

> ### The Color Eraser Tool Doesn't Work with Shades
>
> You can paint with shades or colors, but the Color Eraser tool works only with colors. If you use a monochrome monitor, the Color Eraser tool works the same as the Eraser tool.

The Color Eraser tool makes it easy for you to change a color throughout your painting. Suppose that you used green in your painting and now think that the painting would look better if the green were blue. In the palette, select green as the foreground color and blue as the background color. Double-click the Color Eraser tool to change all the green to blue. (Be sure to select as the foreground color the same shade of green that you used in the original painting.)

Double-clicking on the Color Eraser changes the *displayed* portion of the painting. If the painting is larger than the screen and you want to change all the painting, scroll to display each portion and then double-click to change each displayed portion.

To change a color throughout your painting, follow these steps:

1. Display the portion of your painting that you want to change.

2. Select a foreground color from the palette. This is the color in your painting that you want to change.

3. Select a background color from the palette. You want the selected foreground color in your painting to change to this color.

4. Double-click the Color Eraser tool in the toolbox. If you don't have a mouse, move the pointer over the Color Eraser tool and press F9+Ins.

The Eraser tool (the tool on the right side of the toolbox) "erases" by changing to the background color every part of the painting that it touches (see fig. 11.7). It erases everything in the foreground.

To use the Eraser tool, follow these steps:

1. Select the Eraser tool from the toolbox. The width of the area that it erases depends on the line width that you select.

2. If necessary, select a background color from the palette. Everything in your painting changes to this background color when you pass the Eraser over it.

3. Press and hold down the left mouse button.

4. Drag the Eraser tool across the part of your drawing that you want to erase.

5. Release the mouse button.

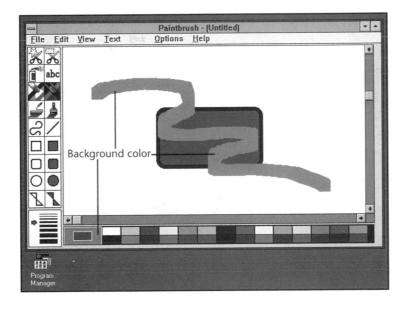

Fig. 11.7
Use the Eraser tool to change the foreground color to the selected background color.

Use the Eraser as a Brush

Because the Eraser tool works by converting foreground shades or colors into the background shade or color, you can turn the Eraser tool into a giant paint brush. Select the shade or color with which you want to paint as the *background* shade or color; select a wide line width (the wider the line width, the bigger the Eraser); and then click and drag the Eraser to draw a wide line of the background color.

Use the Eraser Tool To Erase the Entire Painting

To erase an entire painting, double-click the Eraser tool in the toolbox. Paintbrush asks whether you want to save changes (choose Yes if you do, No if you do not), closes the current file, and opens a new file. The new file has the same background color as the file that Paintbrush closed. (If you want a white background, be sure that white is the selected background color before you use this method.)

Using the Paint Roller

 The Paint Roller tool fills a closed shape with the selected foreground shade or color (see fig. 11.8). You can use it to fill a solid shape (if the shape is filled with a solid color or black or white) or an empty shape enclosed by a border.

Fig. 11.8
Using the Paint Roller tool to fill a shape with a shade or color.

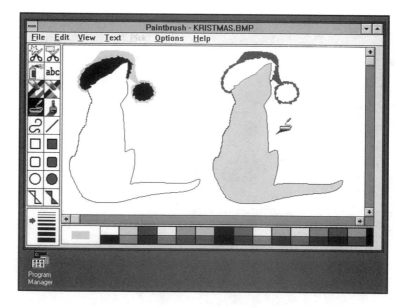

The Paint Roller tool looks like a paint roller that is spreading paint. The tip of this spreading paint is the *active* part of the tool—the part from which the selected foreground shade or color flows. Because the tip is sharply pointed, you can fill very small shapes with the Paint Roller tool.

If you fill a shape that has a gap in its border, the paint leaks out onto the entire painting. If this happens, open the **E**dit menu, choose **U**ndo, fix the gap, and try again. When patching a gap in the border, you can use the **V**iew menu's Zoom **I**n command.

Be Careful When You Use the Undo Command

The **E**dit menu's **U**ndo command undoes all edits up to the last time that you selected a tool, saved the file, used a scroll bar, or resized the window. If you're filling
many areas in a painting with the Paint Roller tool, set each successful fill by saving
the file or reselecting the Paint Roller tool. If you issue **U**ndo incorrectly, however,
you can choose to return your drawing to the way it was previous to choosing **U**ndo
the first time.

To fill a shape using the Paint Roller tool, follow these steps:

1. Select the Paint Roller tool from the toolbox.

2. Select a foreground color from the palette. This color will fill the shape.

3. Position the pointed tip of the Paint Roller tool inside the shape that you want to fill. The pointed tip of the Paint Roller tool is where the paint comes out; this tool is very precise, so you can use it to fill even a small shape.

4. Click the left mouse button. The shape fills with the selected fore-ground color.

Using the Brush Tool

The Brush tool brushes an opaque stroke of the selected foreground shade or color onto your painting (see fig. 11.9). The brush stroke appears in the line width selected in the line-width box.

To use the Brush tool, follow these steps:

1. Select the Brush tool from the toolbox.

2. Select a foreground shade or color from the palette.

Tip
The Paint Roller
tool is one of the
two tools that you
can use when you
zoom in to edit in
detail a portion of
a painting (see the
section "Getting
Different Views of
the Painting" later
in this chapter).
The other tool that
you can use is the
Brush tool.

III

Using Windows Accessories

3. Position the pointer where you want the brush stroke to begin, and then press and hold down the left mouse button.

4. Drag the brush to paint a brush stroke.

5. Release the mouse button.

Fig. 11.9

An opaque brush stroke painted with the Brush tool.

You can use the Brush tool in any of six shapes that you choose from the Brush Shapes dialog box (see fig. 11.10). The default square shape paints with a square brush; the round shape paints with a round brush. The straight-line and diagonal-line brushes paint with a thin line and can paint a variable-width brush stroke, as shown in figure 11.9 (fig. 11.9 was painted with the diagonal-line brush shape shown selected in fig. 11.10). No matter what the brush shape, the brush's width is determined by the selected line width.

Fig. 11.10

The Brush Shapes dialog box.

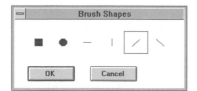

To select a brush shape, follow these steps:

1. Open the **O**ptions menu and choose **B**rush Shapes. Alternatively, double-click on the Brush tool in the toolbox.

2. Select the brush shape that you want to use from the Brush Shapes dialog box (see fig. 11.10).

3. Choose OK or press Enter. Alternatively, double-click on the brush shape that you want in the dialog box.

Using the Curve Tool

The Curve tool is probably the most unusual tool in the Paintbrush toolbox. Unlike the Brush, the Curve tool cannot be used to draw freehand shapes. Instead, you use the tool to draw very accurate curves.

To use the Curve tool, you use a series of three click-and-drag movements. Follow these steps:

1. Select the Curve tool from the toolbox.

2. If necessary, select a line width and foreground color.

3. Press, drag, and release the mouse button to draw a straight line. Notice that the line appears thin and black.

4. Move the crosshair to one side of the line that you drew.

5. Press the left mouse button and drag the pointer away from the line to pull the line into a curve. When you have achieved the shape that you want, click the mouse button to complete the line. If you want an s-shaped curve, go on to step 6.

6. Move the crosshair to the other side of the line, press and hold down the left mouse button, and drag the pointer away from the line to pull the line in the opposite direction. You now have an s-shaped curve, as shown in the flower stem in figure 11.11.

When using the Curve tool, you can use a special type of undo: any time before you complete the line, you can click the right mouse button to undo the line and start over.

III

Using Windows Accessories

Fig. 11.11
Use the Curve tool
to draw accurate
curves.

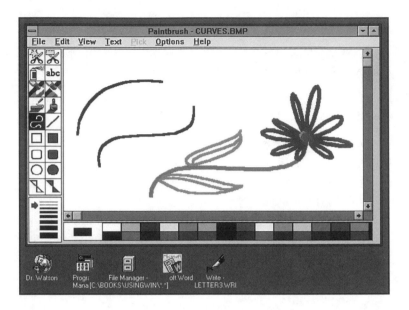

Draw a Petal Shape with the Curve Tool

To draw a petal shape with the Curve tool, click the mouse once to anchor the base of the petal, click a second time at the wide end of the petal, and then click and drag away from the wide end of the petal to form the petal shape. The petal appears as a thin, black line until you release the mouse button.

Using the Line Tool

 With the Line tool, you can draw a straight line in the foreground shade or color and in the selected line width. When you draw the line, it appears as a thin, black line. When you release the mouse button to complete the line, however, the line appears with the width and color that you selected.

Like the Curve tool, the Line tool enables you to undo an action by clicking the right mouse button. To undo the line that you're drawing, click the right mouse button before you release the left mouse button.

To draw a line that is perfectly vertical, perfectly horizontal, or at a 45-degree angle, press and hold down the Shift key as you draw (see fig. 11.12).

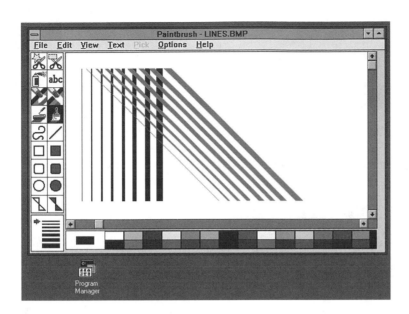

Fig. 11.12
Use the Shift key
and the Line tool
to draw perfectly
horizontal,
vertical, and
diagonal lines.

To use the Line tool, follow these steps:

1. Select the Line tool from the toolbox.

2. Select a line width and foreground color.

3. Position the pointer where you want to start the line, and then press
   and hold down the left mouse button. To draw a vertical, horizontal, or
   45-degree line, press and hold down the Shift key as you press and hold
   down the left mouse button.

4. Continue holding down the mouse button and drag the crosshair in
   any direction to draw a line. If you're holding down the Shift key, keep
   pressing it, too.

5. Release the mouse button to complete the line. Release the Shift key.

Using the Box and Rounded Box Tools

Using the Box and Rounded Box tools, you can draw rectangles or perfect
squares, either unfilled or filled. The Box tools draw rectangles and squares
with angled corners; the Rounded Box tools draw rectangles and squares with
rounded corners.

An unfilled box line is the selected foreground shade or color. A filled box
line is the selected background color, and its fill is the selected foreground
color. The border of any box is the selected line width. (If you don't want a

III

Using Windows Accessories

border, select the same foreground and background shade or color, or make sure that the selected background color is the same as your painting's background.)

To draw a perfectly square box or rounded box, hold down the Shift key as you draw.

Figure 11.13 shows a selection of rectangles drawn with the various box tools.

Fig. 11.13
Use the Box and Rounded Box tools to draw unfilled or filled rectangles or squares.

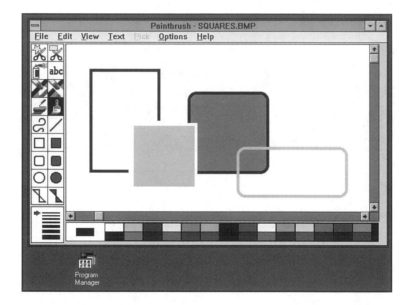

To use the box tools, follow these steps:

1. Select the Unfilled Box, Filled Box, Unfilled Rounded Box, or Filled Rounded Box tool from the toolbox. Each of these tools appears on-screen as a crosshair.

2. Select a line width, foreground color, and background color.

3. Press and hold down the left mouse button to anchor one corner of the rectangle. To draw a square, press and hold down the Shift key as you draw.

4. Continue holding down the mouse button and drag the crosshair in any direction to draw the rectangle. The rectangle appears as a thin, black line.

5. Release the mouse button when the rectangle is the shape that you want. The rectangle takes on the selected line width and shade or color.

Using the Circle and Ellipse Tools

You can use the Circle/Ellipse tools to draw ovals and circles. If you use the Unfilled Circle/Ellipse tool, Paintbrush draws the resulting shape in the selected foreground color and leaves the center empty. If you use the Filled Circle/Ellipse tool, Paintbrush draws the border in the selected background color and fills the shape with the selected foreground color. (If you don't want a border, select the same foreground and background shade or color.) With either tool, the border is the selected line width.

The circle tools draw an oval (ellipse) shape by default; if you want a perfect circle, press and hold down the Shift key as you draw.

Figure 11.14 shows a selection of circles and ellipses drawn with the circle tools.

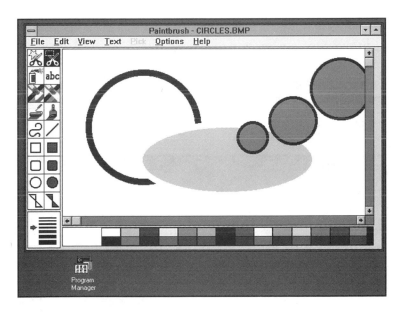

Fig. 11.14
Use the Circle/ Ellipse tools to draw ovals or circles.

To draw an ellipse or circle, follow these steps:

1. Select the Circle/Ellipse or Filled Circle/Ellipse tool from the toolbox. The Circle/Ellipse tool appears on-screen as a crosshair.

2. Select a line width, foreground color, and background color.

3. Position the pointer where you want to start the ellipse or circle; press and hold down the left mouse button. To draw a perfect circle, press and hold down the Shift key as you draw.

4. Drag the crosshair away from the starting point in any direction. The ellipse or circle appears as a thin, black line.

5. Release the mouse button to complete the circle or ellipse. If you're drawing a perfect circle, release the Shift key. The border and fill take on the characteristics that you selected.

Using the Polygon Tools

You can use the polygon tools to draw closed, multisided shapes (unfilled or filled). If you use the Unfilled Polygon tool, Paintbrush draws the polygon in the selected foreground color and leaves the center empty. If you use the Filled Polygon tool, Paintbrush draws the border in the selected background color and fills the polygon with the selected foreground color. (If you don't want a border, select the same foreground and background shade or color.) With either tool, the border is the selected line width.

Drawing a shape with a polygon tool requires three steps: to draw the first side of the polygon, you click and drag, and then release the mouse button; to define each of the polygon's remaining corners, you simply click the mouse button; and to close the polygon, you double-click the mouse button.

Figure 11.15 shows a filled polygon.

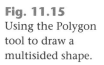

Fig. 11.15
Using the Polygon tool to draw a multisided shape.

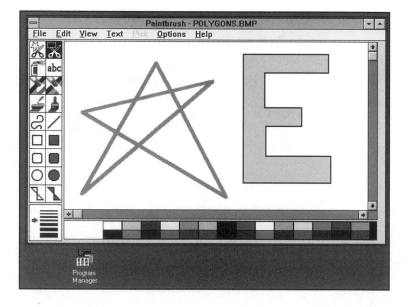

To draw an unfilled or filled polygon, follow these steps:

1. Select the Filled or Unfilled Polygon tool from the toolbox. The polygon-drawing tool appears on-screen as a crosshair.

2. Select a line width, foreground color, and background color.

3. Position the crosshair where you want to start the polygon and press and hold down the left mouse button.

4. Drag the crosshair to draw the first side of the polygon; release the mouse button when you finish drawing the line. To draw a perfectly horizontal, vertical, or diagonal line, press and hold down the Shift key.

5. Click the left mouse button to define each of the polygon's remaining corner points. The border appears as a thin, black line.

6. Double-click the left mouse button to complete the polygon. The end point joins the starting point to close the polygon, and the border and fill take on the characteristics that you selected.

Typing Text in Paintbrush

A picture may be worth a thousand words, but sometimes words can help clarify your message. You can use the Text tool to add text to your painting in any of several fonts, sizes, styles, and shades or colors.

As explained in the section "Using the Text Tool," typing in Paintbrush has some limitations. You can edit the text that you type only until you complete the typing by clicking the mouse button. The text becomes part of the picture, and the only way that you can edit the text is to erase it or paint over it. Paintbrush doesn't have a word-wrap feature; when you reach the edge of the screen, you must press Enter to move the insertion point to the next line.

When you type text, it appears in the selected font, the selected style, the selected size, and the selected foreground color. You can change any of these selections *while* you are typing to change the *current* block of text. Alternatively, you can change any of these selections *before* you start typing to set the style for the *next* block of text that you type. Each block of text, however, can have only one font, style, size, or color. The fonts available in Paintbrush are the same as those fonts installed in Windows. Figure 11.16 shows some examples of text that you can use in your drawings.

Fig. 11.16
Examples of
Paintbrush fonts
and styles.

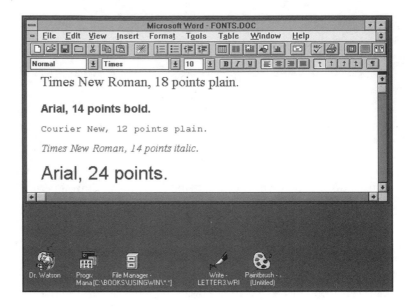

To change the font or type style before you begin typing, refer to the upcoming sections "Enhancing Text" and "Selecting a Font, Style, and Size."

To type text, follow these steps:

1. Select the Text tool from the toolbox.

2. Move the pointer into the drawing area, where it becomes an I-beam.

3. Position the I-beam where you want to start typing and then click the left mouse button. (The I-beam turns into a flashing cursor or insertion point.)

4. Type the text. Press Enter when you want to start a new line. If you make a mistake, press Backspace to erase it.

5. Click the mouse button to set the text into your painting; after you click the mouse button, you cannot edit the text.

Enhancing Text

A text enhancement is a variation of the selected font. Paintbrush offers several text enhancements: **R**egular, **B**old, **I**talic, **U**nderline, **O**utline, and **S**hadow. You can use as many enhancements as you want at the same time. For example, you can type a bold and underlined title. To delete all text enhancements, choose **R**egular. All these choices and the font, style, and size choices described in the next section are available from the **T**ext menu shown in figure 11.17.

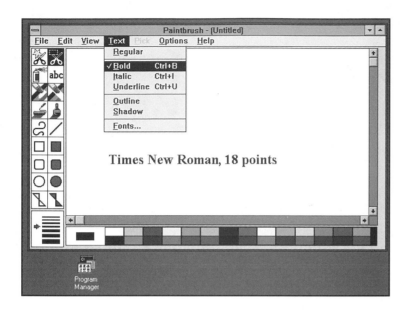

Fig. 11.17
You can select text enhancements from the **Text** menu.

Typed text appears in the selected foreground color, with two exceptions: shadow text adds a shadow in the selected background color, and outlined text adds an outline in the selected background color.

If you choose enhancements while the insertion point is flashing inside a block of text, the enhancements apply to the current block of text and to future blocks of text that you type. If you choose enhancements before you click the I-beam on the painting to begin a block of text or after you click the mouse button to end a block of text, enhancements apply to the next block of text that you type.

To select a text enhancement, follow these steps:

1. Open the **Text** menu.

2. Choose one of the following enhancements: **R**egular, **B**old, **I**talic, **U**nderline, **O**utline, or **S**hadow.

3. Repeat the process to select additional enhancements for the same text.

◄"Using Menus and Dialog Boxes," p. 31

You can select a text enhancement before you begin typing or while you are typing, but after you click the mouse button to set your text into the painting, you cannot change the text enhancement. (For information on how to erase the text and type new text, see the upcoming section "Editing a Painting.")

III

Using Windows Accessories

Selecting a Font, Style, and Size

A *font* is an alphabet of characters that have the same general characteristics. Fonts that come with Windows (if you are using TrueType) include Times New Roman, Arial, and Courier New. Your printer or font software may supply additional fonts. Using a dialog box, you can change the font, font style, and font size all at once (font styles are the same as the font enhancements listed in the **T**ext menu). You also can add strikeout and underlining.

If you are not using TrueType, the fonts that you have available to use are those fonts that are installed in your printer or those fonts that you download from your computer. In the Font dialog box (shown in fig. 11.18), the icon that appears to the left of the font name in the **F**ont list tells you whether a font is a TrueType font, a printer font, or a system font. TrueType fonts have a "TT" icon, printer fonts have a printer icon, and system fonts have no icon. The Sample box shows you how your font, style, and size will look on-screen and when you print. To learn more about TrueType, refer to Chapter 8, "Managing Fonts."

Fig. 11.18
The Font dialog box.

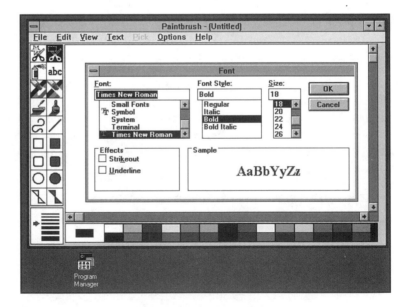

To select a font, style, and size, follow these steps:

1. Open **T**ext and choose **F**onts. The Font dialog box appears, which enables you to change font, style, and size all at once.

2. From the **F**ont list box, select the font that you want to use.

3. From the Font St**y**le list box, select the style that you want.

4. From the **S**ize list box, select the size that you want your text to be.

5. In the Effects group, select the Stri**k**eout check box if you want a line drawn through your text or select the **U**nderline check box if you want to underline your text.

6. Choose OK or press Enter.

◀ "Understanding Fonts," p. 268

When you select a font, that font applies to any new text that you type and to any text that you are currently typing, if you haven't clicked the mouse button.

Editing a Painting

With Paintbrush, you can edit a painting by using the following:

- The eraser tools (described earlier in this chapter)

- The **U**ndo command

- The **E**dit menu's Cu**t**, **C**opy, and **P**aste commands

- The **P**ick commands

- The Backspace key

- The right mouse button

As you edit, be aware that objects in a Paintbrush painting are always completed or uncompleted. Anything uncompleted is subject to edits. You can cancel an uncompleted line or curve, for example, by clicking the right mouse button; you can change the appearance of uncompleted text by making a selection from the **T**ext menu. The method that you use to complete an object depends on the object. To complete a straight line, for example, you release the mouse button; to complete text, you click the mouse button.

Using the Undo Command

Use the **U**ndo command to cancel all the work you did up until you saved the file, selected the tool that you're currently using, resized the window, or scrolled the page. For example, if you select a box tool, draw five rectangles, and choose **U**ndo, you erase all five rectangles. (To undo the **U**ndo, select **U**ndo again.) If you draw four rectangles, select the rectangle tool, draw one more rectangle, and *then* choose **U**ndo, however, you remove only the most recent rectangle.

Be careful when you use **U**ndo. You should frequently save your file or reselect the tool that you are using so that you don't lose more than you want when you use **U**ndo.

To undo your most recent work, open the **E**dit menu and choose **U**ndo. Alternatively, press Ctrl+Z.

Using Backspace as an Eraser

While working with any drawing tool, you can press the Backspace key to display a temporary eraser that looks like a square with an *X* through it. You can use this eraser to erase the work done with the current tool, but you can erase work done only from the point at which you selected the tool. When you're finished erasing, the eraser turns back into the tool that you were using before you pressed the Backspace key.

To use the Backspace eraser, follow these steps:

1. Press the Backspace key. The tool turns into an eraser that looks like a box with an *X* in it; the size of the box depends on the selected line width.

2. Press and hold down the mouse button and drag over the part of your drawing that you want to erase. Remember that the Backspace eraser removes only what you just drew; you cannot erase a completed painting.

3. Release the mouse button. The Backspace eraser changes back to a drawing tool.

Cutting, Copying, and Pasting

In Paintbrush, you cut, copy, and paste objects just as you do in any other Windows application. You start by selecting the object with one of the two cutout tools. Techniques for using the cutout tools are described in the section "Using the Cutout Tools" earlier in this chapter.

To cut or copy a portion of your painting, follow these steps:

1. Use the Scissors or the Pick cutout tool to select the area you want to cut or copy. A dashed line appears around the selected area.

2. To cut, open the **E**dit menu and choose Cu**t**; or press Ctrl+X. To copy, open the **E**dit menu and choose **C**opy; or press Ctrl+C. The selection is cut or copied to the Clipboard.

To paste the portion of the painting that you cut or copied, follow these steps:

1. Display the area of the painting where you want to paste the contents of the Clipboard.

2. Open the **E**dit menu and choose **P**aste; or press Ctrl+V.

◄ "Transferring Data with Copy and Paste," p. 190

The pasted object appears at the top-left of the screen and is enclosed by a dotted line to show that the object still is selected. You can move the selection by clicking on it and dragging. For additional information, see "Moving a Selection" later in this chapter.

Copying a Selection to a File

You can save a portion of your painting to a file by using the **E**dit menu's C**o**py To command. When you use this command, name the file and choose a file format. If you don't choose a file format, Paintbrush saves the file in its native format, which ends with the extension BMP. Files that have the extension BMP can be opened in Paintbrush.

To copy part of a painting to a file, follow these steps:

1. Use the Scissors or the Pick cutout tool to select the portion of the painting that you want to save to a file.

2. Open the **E**dit menu and choose C**o**py To. The Copy To dialog box appears.

3. Type a file name in the File **N**ame text box and select from the list in the **D**irectories box the directory in which you want to save the file.

III

Using Windows Accessories

4. In the List Files of **T**ype list, select one of the following file formats:

Format	File Extension Assigned
PCX	PCX
Monochrome bitmap	BMP
16 Color bitmap	BMP
256 Color bitmap	BMP
24-bit bitmap	BMP

If you don't select one of these formats, Paintbrush saves the file in Paintbrush bit-map format with the extension BMP.

5. Choose the **I**nfo button to see a dialog box that describes the width, height, number of colors, and number of planes in your painting. Choose OK.

6. Choose OK or press Enter.

Pasting from a File

◄ "Changing Directories in a List Box," p. 37

The **E**dit menu's Paste **F**rom command enables you to merge the contents of two or more Paintbrush files. When you choose the command, a dialog box is displayed that lists all the Paintbrush files (those files with the extension BMP). You also can list and open files with the extensions PCX and MSP. When you select one of the listed files, Paintbrush pastes it into the top-left corner of the file currently open. Because the pasted picture arrives selected (as if it were selected with a cutout tool), you easily can move it where you want it on the page.

To paste from a file, follow these steps:

1. Open the **E**dit menu and choose Paste **F**rom.

2. If necessary, select the file format of the files that you want to list and open. The available selections are BMP, MSP, PCX, and All Files.

3. From the File **N**ame list, select the file that you want to open. (If necessary, first select a different directory from the **D**irectories box.) Alternatively, type in the File **N**ame box the name of the file that you want to open.

4. Choose OK or press Enter. The file is pasted in the top-left corner of the screen.

Moving a Selection

You can move an object or area on-screen after you select it with the Scissors or Pick cutout tool. (The object already is selected if you just pasted it.) Paintbrush has several tricks for moving selections. You can move a selection and make it transparent or opaque. You can move a selection and leave a copy of the selection behind. You can *sweep* a selection across the screen and leave a trail of copies of the selected image behind.

To move a selection, follow these steps:

1. Use the Scissors or Pick cutout tool to select an object or area of the drawing. A dashed line encloses the selection.

2. Move the crosshair over the selection (so that the crosshair is inside the dashed line that defines the edges of the selection). The crosshair turns into an arrow.

3. Press and hold down the left mouse button to drag the selection to its new location and make it a transparent object. Press and hold down the right mouse button to drag the selection to its new location and make it an opaque object.

4. Release the mouse button.

5. Click the mouse button outside the selection to fix the selection in its new location.

If you move a selection transparently, the space between the object and the dashed selection line—usually a white border around the outside edge of the object that you want to move—is transparent. If you move opaquely, the white space between the object and the selection line is also opaque and erases whatever is underneath it when you release the mouse button.

To copy a selection, follow the preceding steps for moving a selection, but press and hold down the Ctrl key as you drag the object to its new location. You can copy the selection and make it a transparent object (by holding down Ctrl and dragging with the left mouse button) or an opaque object (by holding down Ctrl and dragging with the right mouse button).

To sweep an image, follow the preceding steps for moving a selection, but press and hold down the Shift key as you sweep the image to its new location and leave a trail of images behind. You can sweep the selection and make it a transparent or opaque image. The faster you sweep the selection, the fewer copies of the image it leaves behind. Figure 11.19 shows an example of sweeping a transparent object.

III

Using Windows Accessories

Fig. 11.19
Sweeping an object by holding down the Ctrl key as you drag.

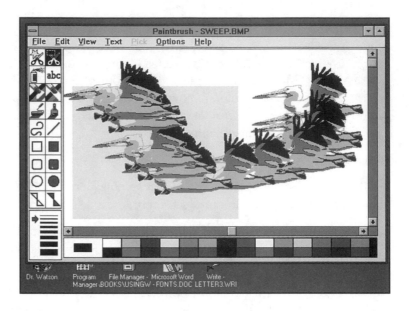

Getting Different Views of the Painting

 You can zoom in to get a closer look at your painting or zoom out to see the whole page. Zoom In mode shows you the pixels, or tiny squares of color, that make up your painting. You can paint pixels in the selected foreground color by clicking the dots with the left mouse button and in the background color by clicking the right mouse button. You can use the Paint Roller tool in Zoom In mode, or you can click and drag the mouse to change all the pixels in a selected area. (Click with the left mouse button to change all selected pixels to the foreground color; click with the right mouse button to change all selected pixels to the background color.) The upper-left corner of the Zoom In view shows a normal view of the Zoom area.

To zoom in for a close-up view of your painting, follow these steps:

1. Open the **V**iew menu and choose Zoom **I**n; or press Ctrl+N. A zoom box appears to help you define where you want to zoom in.

2. Position the zoom box over the spot on which you want to zoom in.

3. Click the mouse button to zoom in. Paintbrush displays a close-up view of your painting on-screen (see fig. 11.20).

To zoom back out to regular editing view, open the **V**iew menu and choose Zoom **O**ut (or press Ctrl+O). When you are in the regular view, you also can choose the Zoom **O**ut command to display a reduced picture of the entire page. To return the display to normal size, open the **V**iew menu and choose Zoom **I**n.

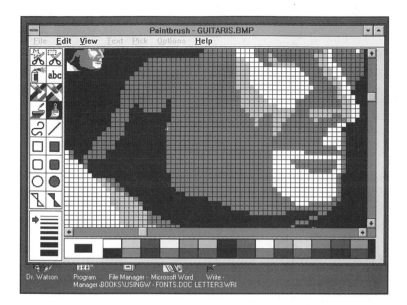

Fig. 11.20
Zooming in to get a
closer look at your
work.

You Can Do Some Editing in the Zoom Out View

When you zoom out to see your whole painting, you can cut, copy, and paste selections. You can rearrange a painting that is larger than your screen. You can only paste, move, or sweep the selection as an opaque object, however. To paste, move, or sweep transparently, zoom in to the regular editing view.

If your painting is larger than your computer screen, you can see more of it by using the **V**iew Picture command. When you choose **V**iew Picture, all toolboxes, menus, and scroll bars disappear, and your picture expands to fill the window. You can only view in this mode; you cannot edit your painting in Picture mode.

To view more of your painting, follow these steps:

1. Open the **V**iew menu and choose **V**iew Picture, or press Ctrl+P.

2. Return to the normal editing view by clicking the mouse button or by pressing the Esc key.

Another option that you have for viewing more of the image on the screen is to turn off the display of the toolbox and line size box, using the **V**iew menu's **T**ools and Linesize command. When you choose this command, the toolbox and line size box disappear and you can see more of the current image. Even though the toolbox and line size box are not on-screen, you still can edit the picture. Whatever tool and line width were selected before you chose the **V**iew menu's **T**ools and Linesize command, will still be in effect.

To remove the tools and line size box from the screen, open the **V**iew menu and choose **T**ools and Linesize. To display the tools and line size box, open the **V**iew menu and choose **T**ools and Linesize again.

You also can remove the color palette from the screen to make more room. Be sure to select the foreground and background colors that you want to use before you remove the palette.

To remove the color palette, open the **V**iew menu and choose **P**alette. To re-display the color palette, open the **V**iew menu and choose **P**alette again.

When you draw lines or shapes that must align accurately on-screen, the **V**iew menu's **C**ursor Position command is helpful. This command displays a small window at the top-right corner of the screen. In the window are two numbers that tell you the position on-screen of the insertion point or drawing tool. The position is given in XY coordinates, measured in pixels, from the top-left corner of the painting. The left number is the X-coordinate (the position relative to the left edge of the painting); the right number is the Y-coordinate (the position relative to the top of the painting). If the numbers in the Cursor Position window read 42, 100, for example, the cursor is 42 pixels from the left edge of the painting and 100 pixels down from the top of the painting.

To display the Cursor Position window, follow these steps:

1. Open the **V**iew menu and choose **C**ursor Position. The window appears as shown in figure 11.21.

2. Hide the Cursor Position window by choosing the **V**iew **C**ursor Position command again. Alternatively, double-click the control bar at the top left of the Cursor Position window.

If the Cursor Position window is not conveniently located, you can move it to another place on-screen. With the mouse, drag the window by its title bar to a new location. Press Alt+F6 to activate the window; press Alt+space bar to open that window's Control menu; and then choose the **M**ove command to display the four-cornered move arrow. Press the arrow keys to move the window; press Enter to anchor the window in its new position.

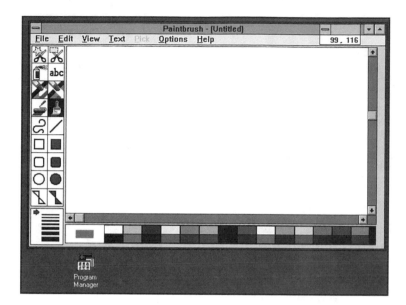

Fig. 11.21
The Cursor
Position window
appears at the right
end of the title bar.

Creating Special Effects

Using the **P**ick menu, you can flip, invert, shrink, enlarge, or tilt objects that
you select with the Scissors or Pick cutout tool. These special effects can help
you refine your Paintbrush painting by altering selected objects in subtle or
not-so-subtle ways.

Flipping a Selection

You can flip a selection in two ways: horizontally (left to right) or vertically
(top to bottom). Flipping horizontally reverses an image from left to right;
you can use this technique to create mirror images by copying the selection
and then flipping the pasted copy, as shown in figure 11.22. Flipping vertically flips an image from top to bottom, making it upside-down.

To flip a selection, follow these steps:

1. Use the Scissors or Pick cutout tool to select the object or area that you
   want to flip.

2. Open the **P**ick menu. To flip the object or area horizontally, choose Flip
   Horizontal; to flip the image vertically, choose Flip **V**ertical.

III

Using Windows Accessories

Fig. 11.22
You can create mirror images by flipping a copy of your selection horizontally.

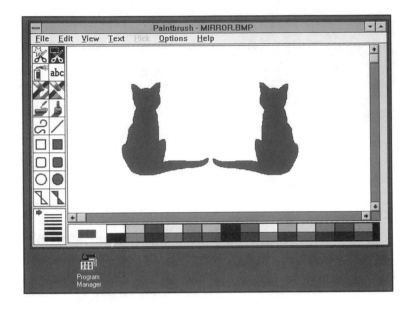

Inverting Colors

You can invert the colors in your painting, changing them to their opposite on the red/green/blue color wheel. In an inverted black-and-white painting, for example, black becomes white, and white becomes black; in an inverted green-and-yellow painting, green becomes purple, and yellow becomes blue. (Any white border area turns black.) Use this technique to *reverse* a selected object.

To invert colors, follow these steps:

1. Use the Scissors or Pick cutout tool to select the object or area that you want to invert.

2. Open the **P**ick menu and choose **I**nverse.

Shrinking and Growing a Selection

You can use the **P**ick menu's **S**hrink + Grow command to reduce or enlarge a selection. After you select the object and choose the command, you drag the mouse to draw a box the size in which you want the resized image to fit. When you release the mouse button, the object fills the box that you drew, and the box disappears.

If you choose the **P**ick menu's **C**lear command before you choose the **S**hrink + Grow command, Paintbrush erases the original selection after resizing the image. (If you choose the **C**lear command, make sure that the selected background color in your palette matches the background color in your painting—the area that you select is filled with the background color when you shrink or grow the selection.) If you don't choose the **C**lear command, you create a resized duplicate of the original.

To shrink or grow a selection, follow these steps:

1. Use the Scissors or Pick cutout tool to select the object or area that you want to shrink or grow.

2. Open the **P**ick menu and choose **S**hrink + Grow.

3. Position the crosshair where you want the new resized image.

4. Press and hold down the mouse button, then drag the mouse to draw a box the same size as you want the new, duplicated image. To keep the new image proportional to the original, hold down the Shift key while you press and hold down the mouse button, drag the mouse, and release the mouse button.

5. Release the mouse button. Release the Shift key if you used it.

When you finish shrinking or growing your selection, select a tool to cancel the **S**hrink & Grow command. Otherwise, you may shrink or grow your image again and again.

Tilting a Selection

Drawing an angled polygon is a precise science. Fortunately, Paintbrush makes it easy with the **P**ick menu's **T**ilt command. The **T**ilt command works a little like the **S**hrink + Grow command: after you select the object and choose the command, you drag the mouse to draw a box at the angle at which you want the tilted image to appear. When you release the mouse button, the object appears—tilted—in the box that you drew, and the box disappears.

If you choose the **C**lear command before you choose the **T**ilt command, Paintbrush erases the original selection after tilting the image. If you don't choose the **C**lear command, you create a duplicate of the original. If you choose the **C**lear command, make sure that the background color in your painting matches the background color selected in your palette.

To tilt a selection, follow these steps:

1. Use the Scissors or Pick cutout tool to select the object or area that you want to tilt.

2. Open the **P**ick menu and choose **T**ilt.

3. Position the crosshair where you want the tilted object to appear.

4. Press and hold down the mouse button; drag left or right to create a tilted box that is the same shape that you want your tilted object to be. Notice that the box you're drawing has a dashed-line border.

5. Release the mouse button. The selected object fills the tilted box that you drew, and the box disappears.

Figure 11.23 shows an image before and after it was tilted.

Fig. 11.23
Tilting an image.

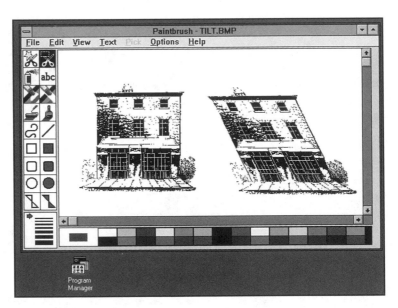

Working with Color

Color is a tremendously important component in daily life, giving meaning to what you see. Psychologists have studied colors' effects on people; advertisers use color carefully to attract attention; artists use color as one of their most important tools. If you have a color monitor, you can use color in your Paintbrush paintings, and you can use your colorful paintings in applications such as Windows Write, Word for Windows, and Aldus PageMaker. If you are lucky enough to have a color printer, you can print your painting in color.

Computer color is different from pigment color because computer color is made of light. In Paintbrush, colors are blended from three primary colors— red, green, and blue—each of which has 255 degrees of shading. Black is no light: zero red, zero green, and zero blue. White is pure light: 255 red, 255 green, and 255 blue.

Paintbrush has 28 colors in its palette, including black and white. All these colors are blended from the three primary colors. You can customize the Paintbrush palette by blending your own colors. If you create a palette of colors that you like, you can save it and retrieve it to use in another Paintbrush painting. (You can retrieve palettes from Microsoft Draw if they have no more than 28 colors and end with the extension PAL.)

To customize colors in Paintbrush, start with an existing foreground color and modify it by adding or subtracting amounts of the three primary colors. A sample box at the right side of the Edit Colors dialog box shows you the color that you are creating.

To create a custom color, follow these steps:

1. Select from the palette the foreground color that you want to alter.

2. Open the **O**ptions menu and choose **E**dit Colors. Alternatively, double-click on the color in the palette that you want to customize. The Edit Colors dialog box appears (see fig. 11.24).

3. Increase or decrease the amount of each color (**R**ed, **G**reen, and **B**lue) by clicking the left or right arrows in the scroll bars. The color in the sample box on the right side of the dialog box changes when you alter the amount of each color.

4. Choose OK or press Enter to add your custom color to the palette, replacing the color that was there before. Alternatively, choose the R**e**set button to restore the color to what it was originally.

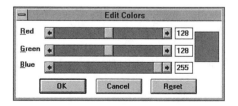

Fig. 11.24
The Edit Colors dialog box.

The colors that you customize don't change the current painting, but they make different colors available on the palette. Your custom palette remains in effect when you start a new Paintbrush painting; unless you save the custom palette, the colors are gone when you close the Paintbrush application. If you save a custom palette, you can retrieve it into any Paintbrush file.

◄ "Blending Custom Colors," p. 236

To save a custom palette, follow these steps:

1. Open the **O**ptions menu and choose **S**ave Colors. The Save Colors As dialog box appears.

2. Type a name in the File **N**ame box. If necessary, select a different directory in the **D**irectories box or a different drive in the Dri**v**es list box.

3. Choose OK or press Enter.

When you save a palette, Paintbrush assigns the extension PAL, but you can specify a different extension if you want.

To retrieve a custom palette, follow these steps:

1. Open the **O**ptions menu and choose **G**et Colors.

2. Select a palette file from the File **N**ame list box. (If necessary, first select a directory from the **D**irectories box.) If you know the file name of the palette that you want to retrieve, you can type its name in the File **N**ame box.

3. Choose OK or press Enter.

Remember that you can reset a custom color to its original palette shade by selecting the color and choosing the R**e**set button in the Edit Colors dialog box. You can reset a color to its original color even if you have changed it more than once or have saved the palette.

If you customize your palette, the customized version appears in any new document that you create until you restart Paintbrush—at which time you revert to the default 28-color palette.

Setting Up the Page

Page-setup choices affect your printed paintings. Margins, for example, determine where your painting is positioned on the page. You add headers and footers to the top and bottom of your printed pages. (Table 11.1 lists the commands that you can use in headers and footers.)

To set up your page for printing, follow these steps:

1. Open the **F**ile menu and choose Page Se**t**up. The Page Setup dialog box appears.

2. Select the **H**eader box and type a header to appear at the top of your printed page. Headers appear inside the top margin.

3. Select the **F**ooter box and type a footer to appear at the bottom of your printed page. Footers appear inside the bottom margin.

4. In the Margins box, select the **T**op, **L**eft, **B**ottom, and **R**ight boxes and type the margins that you want. Paintbrush warns you if your margins are too large for your painting.

5. Choose OK or press Enter.

When you type the text of the headers and footers, you can include any or all the commands listed in table 11.1.

◀ "Formatting the Document," p. 345

Table 11.1 Commands for Headers and Footers	
Command	**Function**
&d	Includes the current date.
&p	Numbers the pages.
&f	Includes the file name.
&t	Includes the current time.
&l	Aligns the header/footer to the left margin.
&r	Aligns the header/footer to the right margin.
&c	Centers the header/footer between the margins. (This command is the default choice.)

Controlling Screen Size and Appearance

Paintbrush determines the capabilities of your computer monitor and the amount of memory that your computer has available for printing graphics. With this information, Paintbrush creates an appropriately sized drawing area. You can override the default image area by resizing the image area to make it smaller or larger.

III

Using Windows Accessories

To resize the Paintbrush image area, follow these steps:

1. Open the **O**ptions menu and choose **I**mage Attributes.

2. In the **W**idth box, type the width that you want for the image area.

3. In the **H**eight box, type the height that you want for the image area.

4. In the **U**nits group, select in (inches), cm (centimeters), or pels (pixels).

5. Choose OK or press Enter.

If you plan to expand the size of your painting, remember that a larger paint-ing (or one with colors) uses more of your computer's memory and takes more memory to print. If you expect to print at printer resolution rather than screen resolution (see the section "Printing Paintbrush Files" later in this chapter), enter the height and width dimensions in pels (pixels, or picture elements) in proportion to the current screen dimensions.

To return to the default image area size, select the **D**efault button. In the same dialog box, you can select whether the palette appears in black and white or color (and hence whether your drawing is in black and white or color). The changes that you make in this dialog box don't affect the current Paintbrush document; they take effect when you open a *new* Paintbrush document and remain in effect for all new documents until you change them again.

Saving Paintbrush Files

When you save a Paintbrush file, Paintbrush assigns the extension BMP to the file name and saves the file in Windows bit-map format. If you prefer, you can save the painting in a different format so that you can use it in an-other application. For example, you can save a file in PCX format to use with several PC painting applications.

To save a Paintbrush file, follow these steps:

1. Open the **F**ile menu and choose Save **A**s. The File Save As dialog box appears.

2. Type a file name in the File**n**ame text box; select from the **D**irectories box the directory where you want to save the file.

3. Select the **O**ptions box to select one of the following file formats:

Format	File Extension Assigned
PCX	PCX
Monochrome bit map	BMP
16 Color bit map	BMP
256 Color bit map	BMP
24-bit bit map	BMP

If you don't select one of these formats, Paintbrush saves the file in Paintbrush bit-map format with the extension BMP.

4. Select the **I**nfo box to see a dialog box that describes the width, height, number of colors, and number of planes in your painting.

5. Choose OK or press Enter.

To resave your file later without changing its name, open the **E**dit menu and choose **S**ave.

◄ "Opening, Saving, Printing, and Closing Files," p. 53

Working with Other Applications

The paintings that you create in Paintbrush make wonderful illustrations that you can use with many other applications. If the other application does not support object linking and embedding, you can include a Paintbrush painting by copying the painting. (Such a painting remains static in your other application—you cannot change it.) You also can link or embed it in an application that supports object linking and embedding. You can edit linked and embedded paintings from within the other application.

To copy a Paintbrush painting into another application, follow these steps:

1. Select the painting, or portion of the painting, that you want to copy to another application.

2. Open the **E**dit menu and choose **C**opy.

3. Start the other application, open the document in which you want to copy the painting, and position the insertion point where you want the painting to appear.

4. Open the **E**dit menu and choose **P**aste.

III

Using Windows Accessories

◄ "Transferring
Data with
Copy and
Paste," p. 190

With some applications, you can insert a Paintbrush file without opening Paintbrush. In PageMaker, you can choose the **F**ile menu's **Pl**ace command. In Word for Windows, you can choose the **I**nsert menu's **P**icture command.

Applications such as Windows Write, Word for Windows, and PageMaker include commands that you can use to move and resize illustrations that you paste into your documents.

When you copy a Paintbrush painting onto the Clipboard (or copy part of a painting), the painting is stored in various formats so that you can paste the painting into documents in other applications. Some applications, however, cannot paste those formats. For those applications, you must remove the formatting before you copy the painting or selection onto the Clipboard.

To remove formatting, follow these steps:

1. Open the **O**ptions menu and choose **O**mit Picture Format. A check mark appears next to the command.

2. Select the portion of the painting that you want to copy.

3. Open the **E**dit menu and choose **C**opy.

Remember to choose the **O**ptions menu's **O**mit Picture Format command a second time, if necessary, to turn it off for future copies.

Embedding and Linking Paintbrush Paintings

Besides being a stand-alone painting application, Paintbrush also is an OLE server application. *OLE* stands for object linking and embedding. A *server* is an application that can create objects that you can embed inside or link to documents created in other applications. Paintbrush can create objects that you can embed or link to documents created by applications such as Windows Write and Word for Windows.

For example, you can embed or link a Paintbrush painting (or part of one) inside a letter created in Windows Write or a report created in Word for Windows. When you embed or link objects inside a document, the application used to create that document functions as an OLE client. Applications besides Write and Word for Windows also can function as OLE clients.

When you embed or link a Paintbrush object in a document, you can start Paintbrush—with the object displayed in its drawing window—from within that document. For example, if you create a bar chart in Paintbrush and embed or link that chart in a letter that you create in Write, you can start Paintbrush and edit the bar chart from within your Write document.

Embedding and linking differ in three ways: in the way that you get the embedded or linked object from the server document into the client document; in the way that the client application stores the object; and in the way that you update the object.

Embedding a Paintbrush Object

You can use two different methods to embed a Paintbrush painting inside a document created by an application that supports OLE: you can either copy the painting into the client application's document, or you can use a command in the client program to insert the object. Each way has advantages. If you copy the painting, you can use an existing painting; if you create a painting, you can save it to a separate file that you can embed in other documents. If you embed a painting from within the client document, you cannot use an existing painting, and you cannot save the painting as a stand-alone file, but you can create the painting without leaving the client document.

When you embed an object inside a document, the client application stores the entire object with the client document. For example, you can give other users a disk that contains a Write file with an embedded Paintbrush picture, and as long as their computers have Paintbrush on it, they can view, edit, and update the picture. Similarly, if someone gives you a Word for Windows file that contains an embedded object created by a graphics application that you do not own, you still may be able to view, edit, and update the picture—because Windows has all the information about the picture, it will use another graphics application (such as Paintbrush) to display, edit, and update it.

To embed a Paintbrush painting by copying, follow these steps:

1. Start the client application (into which you want to embed your Paintbrush painting) and Paintbrush.

2. In the client application, open the document into which you want to embed the Paintbrush painting. Scroll to display the exact place where you want to embed the painting.

3. In Paintbrush, open the document that contains the painting that you want to embed in the client document. Or, you can create the painting. (Save the painting if you want to use it again later.)

4. Select the Paintbrush painting (or part of it) that you want to embed.

III

Using Windows Accessories

5. Open the **E**dit menu and choose **C**opy.

6. Switch to the client application and position the insertion point in the document where you want to embed the painting.

7. Open the **E**dit menu and choose **P**aste.

The commands for embedding a Paintbrush painting from within a client application vary. In the following example, you see the command for embedding a painting into a Windows Write document. Using this technique, you must create the painting from within your Write document, and you cannot save the painting to use in any other document. (You also can use the same technique to embed many other types of objects besides Paintbrush paintings.)

To embed a Paintbrush painting from within Windows Write, follow these steps:

1. Start Windows Write and open the document into which you want to embed a painting. Position the insertion point where you want the painting.

2. Open the **E**dit menu and choose **I**nsert Object. The Insert Object dialog box appears.

3. From the **O**bject Type list, select Paintbrush Painting. Choose OK or press Enter. Paintbrush then appears on your screen with a new, blank painting window.

4. Create your painting.

5. To add your painting to your Write document without closing Paintbrush, open the **F**ile menu and choose **U**pdate. When you are ready to close Paintbrush and return to your document, open the **F**ile menu and choose E**x**it & Return.

   Or, to add your painting to your Write document and at the same time close Paintbrush, open the **F**ile menu and choose E**x**it & Return command. When a dialog box appears asking whether you want to update your Write document, choose **Y**es.

◄ "Creating an Embedded Object," p. 213 To embed a Paintbrush painting into a Word for Windows document, open the **I**nsert menu and choose **O**bject. From there, the steps are the same as for Write. If you have a different application, check the menus to see which command will work; although the command may not be exactly the same as the commands in Write or Word for Windows, it is likely to be similar.

To save your Paintbrush painting, be sure to save your Write or Word for Windows file.

After embedding a Paintbrush object inside a client application's document, you can edit the object from within that document. In almost any application, you can do that by double-clicking on the object to start Paintbrush. You also can use keyboard commands to edit embedded objects in most applications, but the commands vary. In Write, select the object, open the **E**dit menu, and choose Edit Paintbrush Picture **O**bject. In Word for Windows, select the object, open the **E**dit menu, choose Paintbrush Picture **O**bject, and then choose **E**dit. Look for a similar command if your application is different.

To update an embedded Paintbrush object, follow these steps:

1. Start Paintbrush from within the client document by double-clicking on the Paintbrush picture or by choosing the appropriate command from the client application's menu.

2. Change the Paintbrush object.

3. Open the **F**ile menu and choose **U**pdate.

4. Open the **F**ile menu and choose E**x**it & Return to exit Paintbrush and return to your document.

◄ "Editing Embedded Objects," p. 215

To learn more about object linking and embedding, see Chapter 6, "Advanced Data Sharing."

Linking a Paintbrush Object

Linking an object from Paintbrush into a client document is similar to embedding. There is only one way to do it, however: you must use a special command to copy a saved picture into the client document.

A linked picture is not stored as a complete file inside the client document, as is an embedded picture. Instead, the client document stores a link to the original file. If you give someone a disk with a Write file that contains a linked Paintbrush picture, therefore, you also should include the Paintbrush picture on disk.

The advantage to linking is that when you change the original picture, the picture in the client document updates to reflect your changes. Because the client document stores a link to the original instead of storing the original, you can create a single original picture and link it to many client documents (even if they are created by different applications). All the client documents update to reflect changes to the original.

III

Using Windows Accessories

To link a Paintbrush picture to a client document, follow these steps:

1. In Paintbrush, create or open the picture that you want to link to the client document. If you make any changes, you must save the file.

2. Select the portion of the picture that you want to link.

3. Open the **E**dit menu and choose **C**opy.

4. Start the client application and open the document where you want to link the picture. Position the insertion point where you want the picture.

5. Open the **E**dit menu and choose Paste **L**ink.

◄ "Creating a Link," p. 203

◄ "Editing Linked Data," p. 208

Most client documents link objects so that they update automatically when the original object changes. However, you can edit the link in many ways: you can set it for manual update, you can update the link to reflect a new location for an original file that you have moved, or you can link the picture to a different original file.

You can edit a linked object, like an embedded object, from within the client document. The technique for starting the server application is the same as for embedding: you can double-click on the linked picture, or you can select the picture and choose an editing command. After you start the application, you edit and save the picture.

To learn more about linking, read Chapter 6, "Advanced Data Sharing."

Printing Paintbrush Files

Paintbrush gives you great flexibility in printing paintings. You can print all or part of a painting, in draft or final quality, scaled smaller or larger. Before you print, be sure that you have the correct printer selected and set up.

To select and set up a printer, follow these steps:

1. Open the **F**ile menu and choose P**r**int Setup. The Printer Setup dialog box appears.

2. Select a printer from the Printer group. You can select the **D**efault printer or any other printer from the Specific **P**rinter list.

3. Select an option from the Orientation group: Po**r**trait prints your painting vertically on the page; **L**andscape prints it horizontally.

4. If necessary, choose options from the Paper group. To change the paper size, select an option from the Si**z**e list; to change paper source on your printer, select an option from the **S**ource list.

5. Choose OK or press Enter.

You set up a printer in Paintbrush the same way that you do with any Windows application. Remember that the printer setup choices that you make in one Windows application apply to *all* Windows applications. For details about printer setup, refer to Chapter 7, "Printing with Windows."

To print the Paintbrush painting on the selected printer, follow these steps:

1. Open the **F**ile menu and choose **P**rint. The Print dialog box appears (see fig. 11.25).

◄ "Adding and Configuring Printers," p. 284

◄ "Printing a File," p. 294

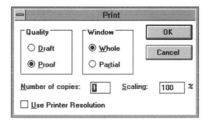

Fig. 11.25
The Print dialog box.

2. In the Quality box, select either the **D**raft or **P**roof radio button. **D**raft prints an unenhanced version of the painting quickly; **P**roof prints an accurate version of the painting. (On some printers, such as laser printers, there is no difference between **D**raft and **P**roof printing.)

3. In the Window box, select either **W**hole or Pa**r**tial radio button. **W**hole prints the entire painting; Pa**r**tial displays the painting on-screen and enables you to drag a crosshair to enclose the part of the painting that you want to print.

4. In the **N**umber of Copies box, type the number of copies of the painting that you want to print.

5. In the **S**caling box, type a percentage at which you want to print the painting. Actual size is 100 percent, half size is 50 percent, double size is 200 percent, and so on.

6. Select the **U**se Printer Resolution check box to print the painting at printer resolution rather than Paintbrush screen resolution. Printer and screen resolution may differ. If you do not select this check box, Paintbrush stretches a painting to make it print the same as it appears on-screen.

7. Choose OK or press Enter.

From Here...

You can learn how to use Windows' other applications and how to use Paintbrush together with these applications by referring to the following chapters.

- Chapter 5, "Simple Data Sharing," shows simple ways to transfer information from one application to another.

- Chapter 6, "Advanced Data Sharing," discusses advanced techniques for sharing with other Windows applications.

- Chapter 10, "Using Windows Write," explains how to use the word processor that comes with Windows.

Chapter 12

Using Windows Terminal

Webster's Dictionary defines *communication* as the giving or exchanging of information. This definition provides a good start toward explaining what a communications application does. It enables a user to give information to or get information from a variety of sources, such as a mainframe, a public bulletin board, or another PC. The information may be as varied as corporate manufacturing data, medical or literary information, on-line airline information, budget worksheets, or messages sent to other users of a bulletin board.

Personal computers provide a wonderful, quick way to create letters, track business data, and generate financial information. But users need to share the information created. Information from a mainframe may help create a management report. To transfer the information from place to place—from an office computer to a home computer, for example—you need communications software, such as the Terminal application.

Communications applications use software and hardware components to link computers. The software component translates computer information into a signal that can be transmitted quickly and accurately over telephone lines. The hardware component may be a modem that converts computer signals into telephone signals and connects the computer to the telephone line. The hardware and software components of both your PC and the other computer must use the same methods of communication and the same *protocol* (communication language).

For computers to communicate, they must use the same communication settings, including type of communications port, memory parity (a checking method), stop bits (the bit that indicates the end of a word), and baud rate (the transmission rate). If you are dialing through a modem, you also may need a telephone number. Once the settings are in place, you can start the communications process.

In this chapter, you will learn how to:

- Create settings files

- Copy data into Terminal

- Customize Terminal

- Make a call with Terminal

- Send and receive files

Starting and Exiting Terminal

Suppose that you and a coworker in the same office—or across the country—want to use Terminal to send and receive files. Although you cannot communicate directly from terminal to terminal, you can leave messages for each other in a public database such as CompuServe, or upload and download information from your company's computer.

Many people enjoy using on-line databases and mail services. Companies such as CompuServe offer business information, access to buying services, discussions on many topics, and even games.

Normally, to communicate with another computer, you follow this procedure:

1. Start the Terminal application by opening the Accessories group in Program Manager and double-clicking the Terminal icon.

2. Use the **S**ettings menu to change settings, if necessary, or open the **F**ile menu and choose **O**pen to open and load settings that you saved previously.

3. Use the **P**hone menu to dial the phone line of the other computer.

4. Enter log-on information. Then either interact with an on-line computer service, or receive or send files in text or binary format.

5. Disconnect from the other computer.

6. Using the **P**hone menu, hang up the phone line.

7. If you have changed your settings or if you want to use them again, save the settings by opening the **F**ile menu and choosing **S**ave or Save **A**s.

8. Exit the Terminal application by opening the **F**ile menu and choosing E**x**it.

Terminal Cannot Connect to Another Terminal Application

Designed to send or receive information to and from a host communication program, Terminal cannot act as a host itself. Instead, you can connect Terminal to a corporate database system, to a public service such as CompuServe, or to another personal computer that uses a communication program that can act as a host.

If you have made any changes to the settings (as described in the following sections), Terminal asks whether you want to save the changes before you exit.

Remember To Hang Up

If you are currently connected with a modem, Terminal asks whether you want to hang up. If you fail to hang up the phone when you exit, you may leave your computer connected to a remote computer system and be billed for unused connect time. Don't worry about being billed for days of use, however; most systems automatically hang up if you have not made an entry in the last few minutes.

◀ "Starting Applications," p. 48

Creating and Using Settings Files

If you frequently use Terminal to connect to the same source of information, you may want to save the settings for this communication. This makes reconnecting quick and easy. Settings files contain the information that you select in the **S**ettings menu. All commands in the **S**ettings menu are saved except the last three menu items: Printer **E**cho, T**i**mer Mode, and Show **F**unction Keys.

Creating a Settings File

To reset Terminal settings to their default, or normal state, open the **F**ile menu and choose **N**ew. This command deletes any phone number that you entered, clears the Terminal scroll buffer, and resets the communications port to 1,200 baud, 8 bits, 0 stop bits, and no parity. If you made changes before choosing **N**ew, Terminal asks whether you want to save the existing settings before it resets all options to their default states.

Saving a Settings File

To save any changes made to the currently loaded settings file, open the **F**ile menu and choose **S**ave. **S**ave automatically overwrites the existing settings file and saves all currently selected settings options. If the current file is un-named, the **S**ave command automatically defaults to the Save **A**s command so that you can name the settings file.

To save the current settings under a new file name, open the **F**ile menu and choose Save **A**s. The previous settings file remains unchanged. Save **A**s displays the dialog box shown in figure 12.1.

Fig. 12.1
The Save As dialog box.

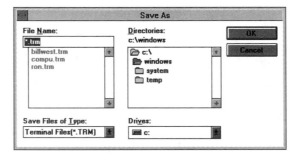

If you enter the name of an existing file, Terminal displays a dialog box that asks whether you want to replace the existing file with your new Terminal settings file.

Tip

If you save a settings file with the name TERMINAL.TRM, Terminal loads this file as the default when you start the application.

Troubleshooting

I opened Terminal and changed all the settings to get Terminal working with my modem. When I returned to use Terminal the next day, I couldn't get Terminal to work.

Whenever you alter the settings in Terminal, you must save the settings file. When you close Terminal, the settings will return to what they were before you made the changes if you don't save the settings file. Use the **F**ile **S**ave command to save the file.

Opening a Settings File

To load a previously saved settings file, open the **F**ile menu and choose **O**pen. When you choose this command, the dialog box shown in figure 12.2 appears. If you have made changes to the currently loaded settings file, Terminal asks whether you want to save any current settings before loading the new settings file.

◀ "Opening, Saving, Printing, and Closing Files," p. 53

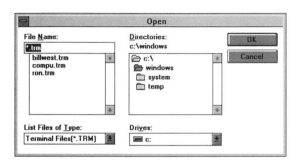

Fig. 12.2
The Open dialog box.

As shown in figure 12.2, Terminal defaults to the file extension TRM. You can change this extension to anything you want.

To speed up the setup process, you can create a special Terminal program item icon. Then associate a particular settings file with this icon so that, when you start Terminal, it automatically loads with all the options saved in the settings file.

Copying Data into Terminal

The **E**dit menu enables you to copy information from an application and paste the information into the Terminal window. You then can send what you paste to the computer to which you are connected.

Suppose that you have written a note in Windows Notepad and want to send it as though you were typing directly into the Terminal program. Make the Notepad window active, select a block of text, and copy it to the Clipboard. Next, activate Terminal, and when the computer to which you are connected requests that you type your message, open the **E**dit menu and choose **P**aste. Although you are pasting information into Terminal, the computer to which you are connected assumes that you are typing the message from the keyboard.

III

Using Windows Accessories

◄ "Transferring
Data with Copy
and Paste,"
p. 190
To copy text or numbers into the Clipboard, use the normal copying procedures for Windows or non-Windows applications. Terminal purges all blanks
at the end of each selected line and ends each line with a carriage return and
line feed.

To send text directly to another computer without copying and pasting, wait
until the computer to which you are connected requests your message. Then
select the text, open the **E**dit menu and choose Se**n**d, or press Ctrl+Shift+Ins.
Terminal copies the text that you pasted to the Clipboard and sends it to the
remote computer. This option is particularly useful when you are replying to
electronic mail and want to forward part of a message that you have received.

If you want to send graphics through Terminal, you need to send them as a
binary file. See the section called "Sending Binary Files," later in this chapter.

Working with Terminal's Buffer

Terminal stores the information it receives in an area of memory called a
buffer. To select the entire contents of Terminal's buffer, open the **E**dit menu
and choose Select **A**ll. Choosing this command has the same effect as using
the mouse or keyboard to select all of Terminal's received messages.

To clear the contents of Terminal's scroll buffer and window, open the **E**dit
menu and choose Cl**e**ar Buffer. This command clears the data displayed in
the Terminal window.

Customizing Terminal

You can tailor most of Terminal's options to your needs through the **S**ettings
menu, where you configure Terminal to match the communications requirements of other computers. The **S**ettings menu enables you to select the default phone number, terminal emulation, terminal preferences, function keys,
text transfers, binary transfers, communications parameters, and modem
commands. Each operation is described in the following sections.

Connecting to CompuServe

CompuServe is one of the most widely used public databases. For a low membership fee, anyone can join CompuServe. You then can connect to many
different types of information services at rates of $8.95 per hour and up. The
information services to which you can connect cover a wide range of topics:

■ Help for Windows and Windows applications

■ Libraries of free programs and sample files

■ On-line airline guides that help you find and schedule the lowest
air fares

■ Dow Jones stock quotes

■ *Wall Street Journal* articles and analyses

■ News reports that have been filed but not yet published

■ Medical and legal databases

■ Engineering and technical databases

■ Games

To connect to CompuServe, select the following settings from the
Settings menu:

Phone Number	The local CompuServe access phone number (call CompuServe for this number)
Binary Transfers	**X**Modem/CRC (remember this setting; every time that you download files, CompuServe asks for this information)
Communications:	
Baud Rate	1,200, 2,400, 9,600, or 14,400 (call Compu-Serve for baud rates supported by your local access number)
Data Bits	8
Stop Bits	1
Parity	None
Flow Control	Xon/Xoff
Connector	The COM port to which your modem is connected

Chapter 2, "Getting Help," lists some of the CompuServe forums related to
Windows and Windows applications. These forums are an excellent source
of software updates, shareware and freeware programs, access to technical
support from Microsoft engineers, and more.

III

Using Windows Accessories

For information on how to join CompuServe, contact Customer Service at (800) 848-8990.

Entering a Phone Number

To specify the phone number that you want Terminal to dial, open the **S**ettings menu and choose Phone **N**umber. The dialog box shown in figure 12.3 appears when you select this option.

Fig. 12.3
The Phone Number dialog box.

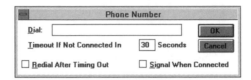

Tip
If you find that Terminal consistently times out before establishing a connection with a remote computer, increase the timeout setting in the Phone Number dialog box. Some systems may take longer than the default 30 seconds to connect.

In the **D**ial text box, type the phone number that you want to use. The phone number can contain parentheses and dashes. A comma placed anywhere in the text field causes the modem to pause for two seconds before dialing any remaining digits. Use this option when you need to dial 9 to get an outside line and must pause briefly.

In the **T**imeout If Not Connected In text box, enter the time (in seconds) that you want Terminal to wait before assuming that the remote computer is not answering the phone. The minimum time allowed is 30 seconds.

Select the **R**edial After Timing Out check box to make Terminal automatically redial the phone number after the time limit is reached.

When you have selected the **S**ignal When Connected check box, your computer beeps whenever a connection is made. This feature can be very useful when you are working on several tasks and want Terminal to signal you when it connects with the remote computer.

Selecting a Terminal Emulation

To specify which type of terminal you want to emulate, open the **S**ettings menu and choose **T**erminal Emulation. The dialog box shown in figure 12.4 appears.

Fig. 12.4
The Terminal Emulation dialog box.

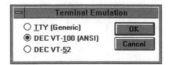

Terminal emulation makes the Terminal program act like one of three industry standard hardware terminals used with most computers: TTY, VT 52, and VT 100. The TTY emulation recognizes only ASCII text, and responds to carriage returns and line feeds. The VT 100 and VT 52 emulations are based on the popular DEC VT 100 and DEC VT 52 terminals. When you select either of these terminal emulations, Terminal responds to all the display requests that these terminals have, such as bold, underline, and the DEC line-drawing character set.

Using Arrow and Function Keys During Terminal Emulation

When Terminal emulates VT 52 or VT 100 terminals, your PC keyboard can emulate the VT 52 or VT 100 keyboard. To switch from the Windows keyboard to the terminal keyboard, press the Scroll Lock key. When your keyboard emulates that of a terminal, the arrow keys work the same, the function keys F1 through F4 become the PF1 through PF4 keys, and the numeric and punctuation keys are the same. Press the + key on your keyboard for the VT 52 or VT 100 Enter key.

Choosing Terminal Preferences

To modify local terminal parameters, open the **S**ettings menu and choose Terminal **P**references. When you choose this command, the Terminal Preferences dialog box appears (see fig. 12.5). In this dialog box, you can specify the way your personal computer accepts the characters that it receives—for example, how it wraps lines of text and whether it double-spaces lines.

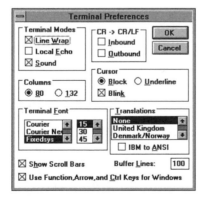

Fig. 12.5
The Terminal Preferences dialog box.

III

Using Windows Accessories

Select the Line **W**rap check box if you want Terminal to wrap characters that pass the last character column displayed in Terminal. Do not select this option if you want Terminal to lose and not display characters that exceed the width of the Terminal display. For example, if Terminal is set to display 80 columns, but the computer to which you are connected sends 132 columns, you can ensure that the data is not lost by selecting the Line **W**rap option.

Select the Local **E**cho check box if you want Terminal to *echo* (repeat on your screen) keystrokes that you are sending. Otherwise, Terminal displays outgoing keystrokes on the remote system only, and you cannot see them on your screen.

In some hardware, the remote system echoes the transmitted keystrokes back to you (a condition called *remote echo*). In this instance, deselect Local **E**cho to avoid displaying each keystroke twice on your screen. If the remote system is not configured for remote echo or if you are not currently connected, select Local **E**cho to display the outgoing keystrokes as you type them. By default, the Local **E**cho setting is deselected.

Select the **S**ound check box to direct Terminal to sound warning bells (^G characters) coming from the remote system. Disable the bell by deselecting the **S**ound check box. By default, this setting is selected.

Select the **I**nbound check box to display incoming carriage returns as carriage returns followed by line feeds. Deselect the **I**nbound check box to display incoming carriage returns as carriage returns only. By default, the **I**nbound setting is deselected. If your computer receives the transmission with double-spacing, change this setting.

Select the **O**utbound check box to display outgoing carriage returns as carriage returns followed by line feeds. Deselect the **O**utbound check box to display outgoing carriage returns as carriage returns only. By default, the **O**utbound setting is deselected. If the other computer receives the transmission with double-spacing, change this setting.

Select the width of the scrolling region for your window by specifying in the Columns group the desired number of columns (one character per column). You can select a width of either 80 or 132 characters. If the width that you specify is too wide to display in the Terminal window, you may have to scroll right to view the entire document. The default number of columns is 80.

Depending on the type of display monitor you have, you may find that one type of insertion point or cursor is more visible than another. To find the best cursor type, you may have to experiment a little, particularly if your computer is portable. To display the cursor as a block, select the **B**lock radio button; to display the cursor as an underscore character, select the **U**nderline radio button. If you want the cursor to blink, select the Blin**k** check box.

Deselect the Blin**k** check box if you want the cursor to display without blink-ing. By default, the Blin**k** setting is selected.

Like any good Windows application, Terminal enables you to select the font and point size used for on-screen characters. Select fonts and sizes for the Terminal window from the scrolling list in the **T**erminal Font group. All Win-dows display fonts are available for use in the Terminal window. The fonts you select only affect the Terminal display and have no effect on the remote computer.

If you use Terminal in an international environment, you may need to use international-character sets. Select the desired character translation from the **T**ranslations scrolling list. By default, Terminal selects the country specified in Country Settings in the WIN.INI file. You can see and change these set-tings by using the International option in the Control Panel window. Modi-fying the **T**ranslations setting in this dialog box does not permanently alter the WIN.INI file.

If your message is long or its characters exceed the screen width, you need to scroll the window. To scroll with the mouse, use the scroll bars. If you work with the keyboard exclusively, however, you may want to remove the scroll bars so that you can see more of the screen. Select the **Sh**ow Scroll Bars check box to direct Terminal to display the scrolling lists in the Terminal window. To remove the scroll-bar display, deselect the **Sh**ow Scroll Bars check box. This choice is valid, whether or not the Terminal window is maximized.

You can specify the size of Terminal's buffer. In the Buffer **L**ines text box, enter the number of lines for the buffer. If you enter a number smaller than 25, Terminal allocates a scroll buffer that contains 25 lines. The default num-ber of buffer lines is 100. If you often have occasion to scroll back through several screens of data, you need to increase the size of the buffer. Otherwise, keep the size small to save memory. Scroll backward and forward through the buffer to display the text that you typed and received.

If you know that you want to save all the lines that you send and receive, use the techniques described in the section called "Receiving Text Files," later in this chapter.

If you want to use the function, arrow, and Ctrl keys to perform Windows tasks—for example, using Ctrl+Esc to open the Task List—select the Use Func-tion, Arrow, and **C**trl Keys for Windows check box. If you want to use these keys to control the software on the remote computer, deselect this option.

Tip

If the information that you are receiving includes characters from the extended-character set—such as accented letters, for ex-ample—and the remote computer is using the IBM extended charac-ter set, they will not display prop-erly on the screen. You must select the IBM to **A**NSI option in the Terminal Prefer-ences dialog box to convert IBM extended charac-ters to the ANSI extended charac-ters used in Windows.

◄ "Scrolling Windows," p. 39

III

Using Windows Accessories

After you specify the Terminal Preferences settings, you can use them, discard them, or save them to a settings file.

Creating On-Screen Function Keys

The function keys provide an easy way to automate the communications process. Instead of using the menu items, for example, you can program a function key to dial a number, send your user ID, or hang up. You can display function keys as buttons at the bottom of the Terminal window, as shown in figure 12.6. To display or hide function keys, open the **S**ettings menu and choose either Show **F**unction Keys or Hide **F**unction Keys.

Fig. 12.6
Function keys displayed as buttons at bottom of the Terminal window.

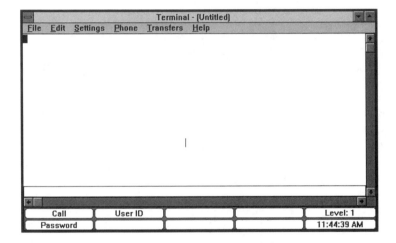

You can create up to 32 function keys. Because the function keys have other purposes in Windows, you must press Ctrl+Alt+*function key* to activate the custom keys.

The 32 possible function keys appear in four *levels* of eight keys. At the bottom of figure 12.6 you see the first level of keys. For convenience, put the keys that you use most often in level 1. You can access level 1 function keys without additional mouse clicks or key presses.

Switch between levels with the mouse by clicking on the level-indicator button at the far right of the banks of buttons. (In fig. 12.6, this indicator is labeled Level:1.) To switch between levels with the keyboard, create a function key in each level that takes you to the next level. The code that you use to define such a key is described later in this section.

To customize function keys, follow these steps:

1. Open the **S**ettings menu and choose Function **K**eys. The dialog box shown in figure 12.7 appears.

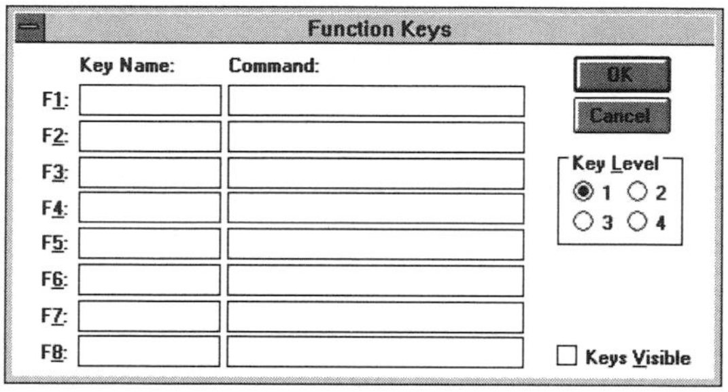

Fig. 12.7
The Function Keys
dialog box.

As you can see in figure 12.7, a function key definition has two parts: the function key name and the function key command.

2. Select a Key **L**evel of 1 through 4 to specify the group of function keys that you want to create. Usually, you start with level 1.

3. Select the function key that you want to customize. In the Key Name text box for that key, type the text that you want to appear in the button (the *label* of the button). Press Tab to move to the Command text box for that key.

4. In the Command text box, type the text or commands that you want the key to perform. A table later in this section describes those commands.

5. Repeat steps 3 and 4 to customize any other function keys in this level.

6. Select the Keys **V**isible check box to display the function keys.

7. Choose OK or press Enter.

The Command text boxes can contain any combination of text and codes from the following chart. The chart lists the actions that you may want a function key to perform and provides the appropriate commands to achieve those actions.

◄ "Using Menus and Dialog Boxes," p. 31

III

Using Windows Accessories

Action	What To Type in the Command Text Box
Send Ctrl+A through Ctrl+Z (note that these commands do not include a $).	**^A through ^Z**
Send a break code (each *number* is a unit equal to 117 milliseconds).	**^$B*number***
Open the **P**hone menu and choose **D**ial.	**^$C**
Delay Terminal for *number* of seconds (use this command while waiting for password or log-on response).	**^$D*number***
Open the **P**hone menu and choose **H**angup.	**^$H**
Change to the level of the key group indicated by *number* (1 through 4). This enables you to use the four groups of eight function keys.	**^$L*number***
Send a caret (^) to the remote computer.	**^**
Send a NULL character to the remote computer.	**^@**
Send *number* escape code sequences to remote computer.	**^[*number***

Press Shift+6 to type the ^ that precedes these codes. The caret represents the control code.

You can assign the key name MyLogin to F1, for example, and type the following commands in the Command text box:

^$C^$D10LOGIN^M^$D10PASSWORD^M

When you press F1 or click the on-screen button that contains this command, Terminal executes the ^$C command and calls the number specified in the active settings file. Terminal waits 10 seconds as specified by ^$D10, sends the string LOGIN and a carriage return (^M), waits 10 more seconds, sends the string PASSWORD, and sends another carriage return (^M).

If you want a key that changes between function-key levels, use a code like the following in that key's Command box:

^$L3

When you press Ctrl+Alt+*function key* (in which *function key* is the key to which this command is assigned), the display changes to show the function keys on level 3.

Displaying Function Keys On-Screen

To display the function keys on-screen when you open a settings file, check the Key **V**isible check box in the Function Keys dialog box and save the settings file. If you want to toggle between displaying and hiding the on-screen function keys, open the **S**ettings menu and choose Show Function **K**eys. This command toggles between Show **F**unction Keys and Hide **F**unction Keys.

Changing How Terminal Sends Text

You use text transfers to transmit text files. Text files are usually word-processing or mainframe files that do not contain formatting. (To transfer other types of files, see the next section, "Selecting Binary Transfers Options.") To set the text-transfer protocol and the text margins, open the **S**ettings menu and choose Te**x**t Transfers. The dialog box shown in figure 12.8 appears.

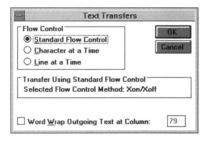

Fig. 12.8
The Text Transfers dialog box.

To transfer text in XON/XOFF mode, select the **S**tandard Flow Control radio button. In this mode, the receiving system sends an XOFF message to the transmitting system when the receiving system's input buffer is nearly full. The transmitting system then halts transmission until it receives from the receiving system an XON message, which indicates that the input buffer has been cleared.

Select the **C**haracter at a Time radio button to transfer text one character at a time. Notice that when you select this option, the dialog box changes, as shown in figure 12.9.

III

Using Windows Accessories

Fig. 12.9
The **C**haracter at a
Time option in
the Text Transfers
dialog box.

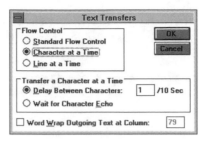

Select the **D**elay Between Characters radio button to specify the delay between characters. Enter in the text box the desired delay in tenths of a second. Changes are sent at even intervals, regardless of whether they have been received correctly.

Select the Wait for Character **E**cho radio button to instruct Terminal to wait until the receiving computer echoes back its response. In this mode, the transmitting system waits for the transmitted character to be returned by the receiving system before it sends the next character. The transmitting system compares the two characters to verify that the correct character was received.

To transfer one line at a time, select the **L**ine at a Time radio button from the Flow Control group. The dialog box options change, as shown in figure 12.10. To specify the delay between lines, select the Delay **B**etween Lines radio button. Enter in the text box the desired delay in tenths of a second. Lines are sent at even intervals, regardless of whether they have been received correctly.

Fig. 12.10
The **L**ine at a Time
option in the Text
Transfers dialog
box.

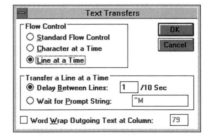

Select the Wait for **P**rompt String radio button to prompt Terminal to wait to receive a line from the remote system before sending the next line. The suggested end-of-line character is ^M. Use this method when you have difficulty with character transmission.

If the text that you are sending can be formatted wider than the width of the receiving screen, select the Word **W**rap Outgoing Text at Column check box.

(You often need this option when you send text files from a word processor.) In the text box to the right of the option, you then can specify the column number at which you want the text to wrap. For example, if the receiving terminal has a 132-column screen, enter **131** in the text box. This setting leaves one character position for the ^M end-of-line code. If you do not select this option, text is sent as it is formatted.

Selecting Binary Transfers Options

Use a binary transfer when you want to transfer a file in its native format— for example, an Excel XLS or XLC file, a Lotus WK1 file, a formatted Word for Windows file, a graphics file, or a compressed PKZIP or archived file.

To specify the binary transfer protocol, open the **S**ettings menu and choose **B**inary Transfers. The dialog box in figure 12.11 appears. You can choose either the **X**Modem/CRC or **K**ermit protocol; the default binary-transfer protocol is XModem/CRC. Make sure that the sending and receiving communications applications are using the same protocol. Some computers or services to which you connect, such as CompuServe, ask you which method of transmission you want to use.

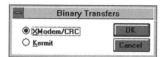

Fig. 12.11
The Binary Transfers dialog box.

Transmitting Application Files

If you want to use Terminal to send a Microsoft Excel, Word for Windows, or 1-2-3 file from one PC to another, make sure that both computers are transmitting at the same baud rate and with the same file-transfer protocol—either XModem or Kermit. After you connect with the other PC, test the connection by typing some text in your Terminal window. The text that you type should appear on the other PC's screen. When text is typed on the other PC, that same text should appear on your screen.

When you know that you have established the connection, open the **T**ransfers menu and choose Send **B**inary File, select from the scrolling list the file that you want to send, and then choose OK.

If the user of the other PC opens the **T**ransfers menu and chooses Receive Binary **F**ile, you can view the progress of the transfer in the status bar. You also can make Terminal an icon and watch the background color of the icon change as the transfer progresses. While the transfer is proceeding, you can work in other applications. The icon flashes when the transfer is complete.

Selecting Communications Parameters

An important aspect of using your computer to exchange information is setting the communications *parameters*. These communications characteristics ensure that two computers "talk" at the same rate, use the same bundles of information, and use the same dialect. If you are connecting to a commercial database service such as CompuServe, or with a local bulletin board system, call the service to find out what settings you should use. (Settings for CompuServe are listed in an earlier section in this chapter.) To change or set parameters, open the **S**ettings menu and choose **C**ommunications. The dialog box shown in figure 12.12 appears.

Fig. 12.12

The Communications dialog box.

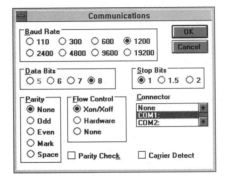

Select the speed at which you want data to be sent and received by specifying the **B**aud Rate. The maximum baud rate at which you can communicate depends on many factors, such as the type of modem and the quality and length of the communications line. The default **B**aud Rate setting is 1,200. With the current generation of modems, baud rates of 9,600 or even 14,400 are common.

Use **D**ata Bits setting to specify the number of data bits to be transmitted in each character packet. The default **D**ata Bits setting is 8.

To specify the number of stop bits to be transmitted, use the **S**top Bits setting. The default setting is 1.

Select the **P**arity type. Parity is used for detecting errors during transmission. If you selected 8 for the **D**ata Bits setting, then select None for the **P**arity setting. If you select Mark parity, the eighth bit is set to on. If you select Space parity, the eighth bit is set to off. Odd and Even parities calculate the total of the first seven bits; Terminal then sets the eighth bit to make the total of the eight bits either always odd or always even.

Select the **F**low Control. If you select Xon/Xoff, the receiving system sends an XOFF message to the transmitting system when its input buffer is nearly full. The transmitting system halts transmission until it receives from the receiving system an XON message, which indicates that the input buffer has been cleared. If you select Hardware, the pins on the RS-232 serial cable handle flow control. If you select None, no flow-control method is used. Unless you have a specific reason to change this setting, leave Xon/Xoff selected.

Your modem connects your computer to another computer's telephone line, or directly to a minicomputer or mainframe computer. To send information to the modem, Terminal must know which communication port the modem is connected to. If the serial ports in the back of your computer are not labeled, check with your dealer or support representative to find out which one the modem is connected to. Select the desired communications port from the **C**onnector scrolling list. In Windows 3.1, you can use COM1 through COM4. When the modem is disconnected, select None, because you're using its serial port for a printer or other device.

Select the Parity Chec**k** check box to direct Terminal to replace with a question mark (?) characters that do not match the specified parity. Characters may not match because of transmission errors or noise in the telephone line. To ignore parity errors, deselect the Parity Chec**k** check box. By default, this check box is deselected.

Hayes-compatible modems have a hardware-connect signal that is set to TRUE when a communications connection is made. To enable Terminal to use this signal to determine whether the Receive Line Signal Detect (RLSD) is set, select the Ca**r**rier Detect check box. If you select this check box, Terminal automatically hangs up if the carrier is lost, so that you don't have to open the **P**hone menu and choose **H**angup before dialing. Deselect the Ca**r**rier Detect check box if you do not want Terminal to hang up automatically or if your modem's RLSD is unreliable. By default, the Ca**r**rier Detect setting is deselected.

Changing Modem Options

To modify the commands that Terminal sends to your modem, open the **S**ettings menu and choose **M**odem Commands. The Modem Commands dialog box shown in figure 12.13 appears. The correct modem commands for the modem type selected (Hayes is the default) are displayed in the text boxes. You can use these commands "as-is" or modify them to accommodate the codes used by nonstandard modems. Be sure to check your modem manual for the appropriate commands. In most cases, you need only select from the **M**odem Defaults group the type of modem that you are using; you need not enter your own commands.

Fig. 12.13

The Modem Commands dialog box, showing Hayes commands.

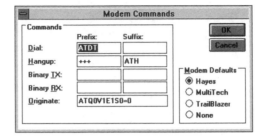

Table 12.1 lists the various text boxes in the Modem Commands dialog box and the kind of information expected by each.

Table 12.1	Text Boxes in the Modem Commands Dialog Box
Text Box	**Description**
Dial	The prefix and suffix appended to the phone number that direct the modem to dial
Hangup	The prefix and suffix that direct the modem to hang up
Binary **T**X	The prefix and suffix necessary for initiating a binary file transfer
Binary **R**X	The prefix and suffix necessary for receiving a binary file transfer
Originate	How Terminal directs the modem to exit answer mode

Consult your modem manual before you modify these commands. If you make a mistake, choose one of the **M**odem Defaults options to reset the settings.

Viewing Text Files from Disk

◄ "Opening, Saving, Printing, and Closing Files," p. 53

Before you send a text file, you may want to view its contents. To see in the Terminal window the file that you request, open the **T**ransfers menu and choose **V**iew Text File. The dialog box shown in figure 12.14 appears. The *.txt in the File **N**ame text box appears by default, listing all text files with the extension TXT. Select the file that you want to view. You can display a file in this fashion when you want to review a file before sending it or when you want to add to the file or replace it with an incoming text file.

To view the file, enter the desired file name in the File **N**ame text box and choose OK or press Enter.

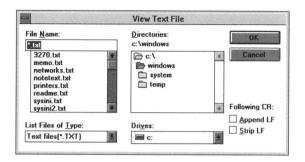

Fig. 12.14
The View Text File dialog box.

Select the **A**ppend LF check box to add a line feed after each carriage return in the file, producing a new line after each paragraph. To leave carriage returns as they appear in the file, deselect the option. By default, **A**ppend LF is deselected.

Select the **S**trip LF check box to strip line-feed characters after carriage returns. By deselecting the **S**trip LF check box, you leave carriage returns and line feeds as they appear in the file. The default **S**trip LF status is deselected.

After specifying the options in the View Text File dialog box, choose OK or press Enter. The file that you specified is displayed on-screen, as shown in figure 12.15.

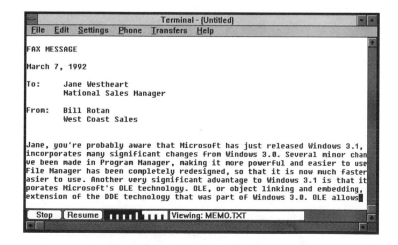

Fig. 12.15
A text file before it is replaced or sent.

III

Using Windows Accessories

A status bar appears in the lower portion of the Terminal window as you view the text file. To stop the text file from scrolling past the text in which you are interested, either choose the Stop button or open the **T**ransfers menu and choose St**o**p. To pause the scrolling text temporarily, either choose the Pause button or open the **T**ransfers menu and choose **P**ause. After you click on the Pause button, it changes to a Resume button. To restart the suspended file display, either choose the Resume button or open the **T**ransfers menu and choose R**e**sume. Terminal displays the name of the file being viewed, and the scale at the bottom changes to indicate the portion of the text that has been displayed.

Printing Incoming Text from Terminal

To print all data received in the Terminal window, open the **S**ettings menu and choose Printer **E**cho. When active, this option is preceded by a check mark in the **S**ettings menu. To exit Printer Echo mode, choose the Printer **E**cho command again. When you exit Printer Echo mode, Terminal sends the printer a form feed to eject the current sheet of paper.

You also can paste information from the Terminal window into a word processing application or Notepad, in which you can edit, save, or print copy. To print information that has already been received, select the information in the Terminal window and copy and paste it into Windows Write or Notepad. You can then print the information by opening the **F**ile menu and choosing **P**rint.

If you receive a large amount of text data, a much more efficient method of printing is to save incoming text to a file. To learn how to save received text directly to a file, see the section called "Receiving Text Files," later in this chapter. Open this file into a word processing application when you want to edit or print it.

Keeping Track of Time with Timer Mode

If you connect with a commercial database, you are charged by the amount of time you are connected, by which database you access, and by your transmission rate (baud rate). Dawdling while you are connected to one of these databases can cost you money, so watch the time. You can have Terminal's clock function as a timer. Just open the **S**ettings menu and choose T**i**mer Mode, and the digital timer is displayed at the lower right when the function keys are visible. Choose the **S**ettings Show **F**unction Keys command to display the function keys. To reset the timer to zero, deselect and reselect the T**i**mer Mode command from the **S**ettings menu.

Displaying and Hiding On-Screen Function Keys

To see the function keys displayed as buttons at the bottom of your screen, open the **S**ettings menu and choose Show **F**unction Keys. Once the function keys are displayed, the menu option changes to Hide **F**unction Keys. Select this option to remove the function-key display.

Figure 12.6 showed you how the function keys appear when they are displayed. To program your own function keys, refer to the section called "Creating On-Screen Function Keys," earlier in this chapter.

Making a Call with Terminal

After you have set all the settings necessary to connect to another computer, open the **P**hone menu and choose **D**ial to dial the other computer's modem and make a connection. The **P**hone menu's commands dial a telephone number or hang up from the current connection. The **D**ial command directs Terminal to dial a phone number. By default, Terminal dials the phone number specified in the settings file. If no phone number is in the active settings file, the **D**ial command displays a dialog box in which you can enter the number.

To send the hang-up prefix and hang-up suffix specified in the Modem Commands dialog box, open the **P**hone menu and choose **H**angup.

Sending Text Files

To send a text file, open the **T**ransfers menu and choose **S**end Text File. This command sends the text file that you select, whether created by Notepad or a word processor. When you choose the **S**end Text File command, the dialog box shown in figure 12.16 appears.

Fig. 12.16

The Send Text File dialog box.

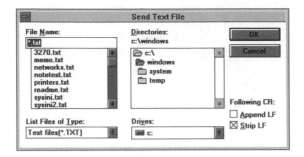

If you want to remove line feeds from the end of each line sent, you can choose one of the Following CR check boxes. If the information that you receive has overlapping lines (that is, no line feed was sent), select **A**ppend LF. If the information that you receive has double-spaced lines, select **S**trip LF. If you are in doubt about how the receiving terminal handles lines, transmit with these boxes cleared. Check the message received by the receiving terminal and then select one of these check boxes so that the text is received the way that you want it.

While you send a text file, a status bar appears in the lower portion of the Terminal window. To cancel the **S**end Text File command, click on the Stop button or open the **T**ransfers menu and choose St**o**p. To suspend the file transfer temporarily, click on the Pause button or open the **T**ransfers menu and choose **P**ause. When you click on the Pause button, it changes to a Resume button. This procedure is equivalent to using the **T**ransfers menu's R**e**sume command to restart the suspended file transfer.

Troubleshooting

When I tried to transfer a file that I had created in a word processor to a colleague, the file was trashed.

Although you may think the file is a text file because that is what it looks like to you, it is a binary file from the computer's point of view. Any file created by a Windows application is a binary file unless you specifically save it as a text file. For this reason, when you send the file using Terminal, you must send it as a binary file, not as a text file.

Terminal also displays the name of the file being sent. The scale changes to display the portion of the text file that has been sent.

Receiving Text Files

To receive a text file, open the **T**ransfers menu and choose **R**eceive Text File. The dialog box shown in figure 12.17 appears. You can use this command either to receive a text file from the remote system or to capture text coming into the Terminal window and save it to a file.

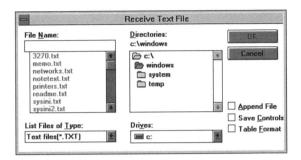

Fig. 12.17
The Receive Text File dialog box.

Use the **D**irectories list box to specify the directory in which you want the incoming file saved. In the File **N**ame text box, enter the file name under which you want the text stored.

Select the **A**ppend File check box to save incoming text to the end of the specified file without clearing the current contents of the file. To replace the current file contents with the incoming text, deselect the **A**ppend File check box. By default, the **A**ppend File check box is deselected.

To save incoming control characters, select the Save **C**ontrols check box. Some applications use control characters to format text, set options, and so on. If you are unfamiliar with control characters, try both settings and then open the files with a word processing application and check the results. To strip incoming control characters, deselect the Save **C**ontrols check box. The default Save **C**ontrols status is deselected.

To save incoming text in tabular format, select the Table **F**ormat check box. Terminal puts tab characters between incoming text fields, separated by two or more consecutive spaces. Use this setting when you want to receive a Lotus 1-2-3 print file (which contains only characters and spaces) or a Microsoft Excel TXT file (which uses tabs to separate cell values). Clear the Table **F**ormat check box to save the file in its current format. By default, Table **F**ormat is cleared.

Control buttons appear in the lower portion of the Terminal window as you receive a text file. To cancel the **R**eceive Text File command, click on the Stop button or open the **T**ransfers menu and choose St**o**p. To stop storing the incoming text to the specified file temporarily, click on the Pause button. After you click on the Pause button, it changes to a Resume button, and the **T**ransfer menu's **R**esume command becomes available. To resume storing the incoming text to the specified file, choose the Resume button or open the **T**ransfer menu and choose R**e**sume.

> ### Caution
>
> When you choose the Pause button or the **T**ransfer menu's **P**ause command to stop storing incoming text temporarily, you do not prevent the remote system from sending text. Instead, while the **R**eceive Text File command is paused, the incoming text is simply not saved. Although the option is useful for saving (or not saving) parts of a file, you can miss data if you select the option at the wrong time.

At the bottom of the screen, Terminal displays the name of the file in which the incoming text is stored. The Bytes indicator changes to reflect the number of bytes received.

Sending Binary Files

If you are sending formatted word processing files, database files, worksheets, programs, graphics, or compressed files of any type, you probably want to send them as binary files. To send a file in binary format, open the **T**ransfers menu and choose Send **B**inary File. The dialog box shown in figure 12.18 appears. By default, the File **N**ame text box displays *.*, so that all the files in the current directory are listed. The file is sent according to the binary transfer protocol that you specified in the Binary Transfers dialog box.

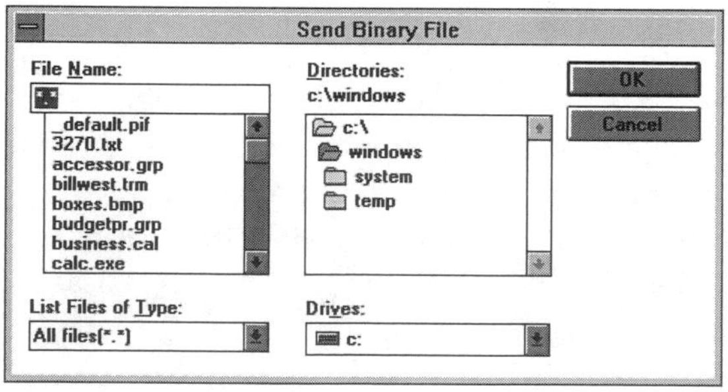

Fig. 12.18
The Send Binary
File dialog box.

To send a binary file, use the **D**irectories list box to select the directory that contains the file. Type the file name in the File **N**ame text box or select the file from the **F**ile Names scrolling list.

While you send a binary file, a status bar appears in the lower portion of the Terminal window. To cancel the Send **B**inary File command, click on the Stop button.

Occasionally, a communications error occurs, preventing the transfer of a packet of data in the binary file. When an error occurs, Terminal tries to send the data packet again. After making the maximum number of unsuccessful retries, Terminal cancels the file transfer. The Retries indicator displays the number of times that Terminal tried to resend the data packet.

If an error occurs, check with the receiving party to ensure that you are using the same settings. Line noise or static also can cause the problem. If the problem is telephone noise, try sending the file later.

Terminal displays the name of the binary file being sent. The scale at the bottom of the screen shows the portion of the file that has been sent.

Receiving Binary Files

To receive a file in binary file format, open the **T**ransfer menu and choose Receive Binary **F**ile. The file is received according to the binary-transfer protocol that you specified in the Binary Transfers dialog box.

Check to make sure that you are using the same settings as the computer sending the information. Complete the steps necessary to prepare the remote computer for sending the file, open the **T**ransfer menu, and choose Receive Binary **F**ile. The dialog box in figure 12.19 appears. Enter the name of the file that you want to receive. To receive the file, click on the OK button or press Enter.

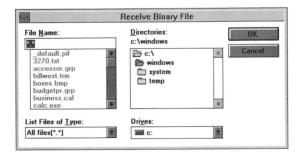

Fig. 12.19
The Receive Binary File dialog box.

As you receive a binary file, a status bar appears in the lower portion of the Terminal window. Clicking on the Stop button or opening the **Terminal** menu and choosing St**o**p instructs Terminal to cancel the Receive Binary **F**ile command.

Occasionally, a communications error occurs, preventing the transfer of a packet of binary data. When an error occurs, the remote system tries to send the data again. After the remote system makes the maximum number of unsuccessful retries, Terminal cancels the file transfer. The Retries indicator at the bottom of the screen displays the number of times that the remote system tried to resend data packets. With the XModem/CRC protocol, the maximum number of retries is 20; with the Kermit protocol, the maximum number of retries is 5.

◄ "Working with Applications," p. 48

Terminal also displays the name of the binary file being received. The scale changes to display the portion of the file that has been received.

From Here...

Now that you have learned how to use Terminal, you can learn to use some of the other applications that come with Windows by referring to the following chapters:

- Chapter 7, "Using Windows Paintbrush," teaches you how to use the drawing application that comes with Windows.

- Chapter 10, "Using Windows Write," explains how to use the word processor that comes with Windows.

Chapter 13

Using Windows Recorder

Windows Recorder enables you to automate many repetitious tasks that you now perform manually. Recorder tracks the keystrokes that you type, the shortcut keys that you press, and the mouse actions that you make, and then saves them in a macro that you can later replay. When you replay the macro, Windows repeats the keystrokes and mouse actions exactly.

You can use Recorder with any Windows application. Even with powerful applications such as Excel and Word for Windows, which have built-in macro recorders, you may find Recorder useful. Recorder can make your work easier in many ways:

- Automates any long procedure that you perform frequently or that takes multiple keystrokes

- Types repetitive words, phrases, titles, or boilerplate text in Windows word processing or other applications

- Creates macros that produce the same actions even when they run in applications that have macro recorders

- Automates data exchanges between Windows applications that do not support object linking and embedding

- Opens multiple applications and loads multiple documents with one command

You create macros by running the application, displaying a document, turning on Recorder, and then performing the actions that you want Recorder to remember. When you finish, turn off Recorder.

Macros are stored in Recorder files. You can store as many macros as you want in one file. When you want to replay a macro, you start Recorder, open the file that contains the macro that you want to replay, and run the macro. In most cases, all your frequently used macros are in one Recorder file; when the file is open, you need only press a shortcut key or execute a command to replay the macro that you want.

In this chapter, you will learn how to:

- Record a macro

- Play back a macro

- Troubleshoot macros

- Create some useful macros

Recording and Using Macros

Recording a macro with Recorder is no more difficult than recording sound with a simple portable tape recorder. When you create a macro, all your keystrokes, shortcut keys, and mouse actions are recorded and given the name and shortcut key that you assign. The recording is called a *macro*. Unlike macros in applications such as Excel and Word for Windows, Recorder macros cannot be edited. To change a macro, you must record the macro again.

The macro that you record is stored in a Recorder file. Each Recorder file can contain more than one macro. When you display Recorder and open a file, you see all the macros in the file in a scrolling list, such as that shown in figure 13.1.

Fig. 13.1

A Recorder files list of macros.

Recorder - BASIC.REC	
File Macro Options Help	
ctrl+shift+Scroll Lock	My Signature Block
ctrl+shift+B	List all BAK files in current drive
ctrl+F7	Resume the current Printer
alt+F7	Pause the Current Printer

Although macros can be very simple, you can make them longer to handle complex tasks. When you create complex macros, you should make and test smaller macros before linking them in one master macro.

Setting Up and Recording Macros

Before you begin recording a macro, you should have a good idea of what you want it to do. Try practicing the procedure that you want to record. You may find that each time you practice a procedure, you think of a shorter or better way to do it.

If the process that you want to record is very long, you may want to divide the process into segments and record the segments as separate macros. After you confirm that each of the separate, smaller macros works correctly, you can create a master macro that runs all the smaller ones in the correct sequence.

To prepare your applications for a recording, follow these steps:

1. Open the applications and documents that you need for the recording.

2. Practice the task that you want to record, if necessary.

3. Position the applications and documents where you want them to be when the macro starts.

To prepare Recorder, follow these steps:

1. Open the Accessories group window, as shown in figure 13.2.

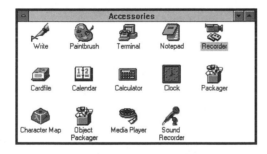

Fig. 13.2
The Recorder icon in the Accessories group window.

2. Start Recorder by clicking on the Recorder icon.

3. Minimize Program Manager, if necessary, to get it out of the way of the applications and documents with which you want to work.

4. Position the insertion point in the application's document or select the text or graphics that you want the macro to work on.

III

Using Windows Accessories

◄ "Starting
Applications,"
p. 48

5. Activate the Recorder window (that is, make the Recorder window the current window), as shown in figure 13.1. If you have not recorded other macros, the Recorder window is blank.

For example, if your macro copies an address block from a Cardfile document into Write, you must meet the following conditions before you create or play back the macro:

- You must start the Write and Cardfile applications.

- You must open the Write and Cardfile files.

- The format of the address block must be consistent: the macro should take into account the possibility that an address can contain three or more lines.

- You should place the cursor at the beginning of the Cardfile document's address block.

- Cardfile must be the current (active) window.

For the macro to perform properly, each of these conditions is important. The key to creating a successful macro is to ensure that the macro actions are repeatable. This advance planning is important when you create a macro, because you cannot edit a macro after you have created it. To prevent errors, you also should keep the following rules in mind:

- Don't use a Recorder macro with DOS applications.

- When you record a macro for use with the Terminal application, the macro should control the application only up to the point that Terminal connects to the other computer.

Selecting Options That Don't Have Active Letters

Some dialog boxes—for example, the one shown in figure 13.3—have options that you cannot select directly with an Alt+*key* combination because they do not have underlined letters. To select options in these cases, press Alt+*letter* to select the group. Watch for the enclosing dashed line that indicates which option is the *focus*. Move the focus by pressing Tab or Shift+Tab. Select or deselect the option by pressing the space bar. Open a drop-down list box by moving the focus to the list and then holding down Alt while pressing the down-arrow key.

To record a macro, follow these steps:

1. To add the macro that you are going to record to an existing file of macros, open the **F**ile menu and choose **O**pen, select the file from the scrolling list, and choose OK or press Enter.

2. Open the **M**acro menu and choose Re**c**ord. The dialog box shown in figure 13.3 appears.

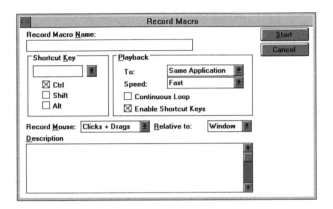

Fig. 13.3
The Record Macro
dialog box.

3. Enter a macro name of up to 40 characters in the Record Macro **N**ame text box.

4. Select options to control the playback:

◀ "Selecting Options from Dialog Boxes," p. 34

Option	Description
Shortcut **K**ey	Specifies the key or key combination that you press to activate the macro. Type a letter in the text box or choose a special key from the drop-down list. Select Ctrl, Shift, or Alt to use in combination with the shortcut key. You can also use combinations of these keys; for example, Ctrl+Shift.
Playback **T**o	Determines which applications the macro runs in. Select Same Application to run the macro in only the application in which it was recorded. Select Any Application to run the macro in any application.
Playback **S**peed	Determines the speed of the macro. Select Fast to play back the macro at maximum speed. Select Recorded Speed to play back the macro at the speed at which you recorded it. The Fast playback can cause problems if the macro operation must wait for the keystrokes to be processed. For example, use Recorded Speed when creating a macro that looks for a group of files in File Manager. This option ensures that the search operation is completed before the macro does the next step.

III

Using Windows Accessories

(continues)

Option	Description
Playback Continuous Loop	Repeats the macro continuously. Press Ctrl+Break to stop the macro.
Playback Enable Shortcut Keys	Enables you to press shortcut keys that run other macros while you record a new macro. This procedure enables you to nest one macro inside another.
Record Mouse	Determines the type of mouse actions that are recorded, as described later in this chapter.
Relative To	Determines how mouse movements appear in the macro. Select Screen to make mouse movements relative to the screen position. Select Window to make mouse movements relative to the active window.
Description	Provides room for you to type a description of what the macro does and which applications the macro works with.

5. Choose the **S**tart button.

6. Perform the procedure that you want to record.

7. Stop Recorder by clicking on the blinking Recorder icon, pressing Ctrl+Break, or Alt+Tab until the Recorder's title box appears and then releasing both keys. You can also press Alt+Tab to switch back to Recorder. The dialog box in figure 13.4 appears.

Fig. 13.4
The Macro
Recording
Suspended
dialog box.

8. Choose one of the options in the dialog box:

Option	Description
Save Macro	Saves the macro that you have recorded (you also must save the file to keep your macro)
Resume Recording	Continues recording from where you stopped
Cancel Recording	Cancels the recording; does not record what you have done

9. Choose OK or press Enter.

While you are recording, the Recorder application has minimized itself into an icon at the bottom of the screen. While you are recording, the icon flashes, which you can see if your application windows are sized to show the bottom of your desktop.

◀ "Controlling Windows and Icons." p. 40

If you want your macro to work on text or graphics that you select, select a representative piece of text or graphics before you start Recorder. This procedure enables you to use the macro with any text or graphics that you select. If you wait to select text or graphics until after Recorder is on, Recorder always tries to select the same text or graphics that you selected in the original recording.

Note

In the **Description** text box, include the names of the applications that you must have open in order to use the macro, along with any necessary conditions (for example, that text must be selected). If you have trouble running the macro, you can check this box to see whether you have missed any of these necessary preconditions. (You can read the **Description** box by selecting the macro, opening the **Macro** menu, and choosing **Properties**.)

Mouse Actions, Keystroke Commands, and Shortcut Keys

Recorder can record mouse actions and keystrokes. Recording mouse actions, however, can cause problems if you run the macro in an application when the windows are in locations that are different than when you originally recorded the macro, or if you run the macro on a computer with screen resolution (the number of dots) that differs from that of the original screen. Mouse actions are recorded in units of the current screen. A mouse movement on an EGA screen is a different distance than one on a SuperVGA screen.

When Recorder records mouse actions, it actually records the mouse pointer's position on-screen at the time that you click, drag, select, and so on. If application or document windows are in different locations when the macro runs (which is likely), the macro may miss the command, option, or object on which the mouse was supposed to work. If you run the macro on a computer with a different screen resolution, the relative location of the pointer is different. Therefore, use keystrokes and shortcut keys if you want a macro to run in different situations.

III

Using Windows Accessories

Tip
Careful plan-
ning of the
macro can save
time. After you
record a
macro, you
cannot edit it.

In many cases, if you make a mistake during a recording, you can correct the mistake and continue; the macro records the correction. For example, if you choose an italic font instead of bold, return to the normal font and then choose bold. When you play back the macro, it may operate so quickly that you do not see the correction taking place. You cannot correct some mistakes, such as deleting files.

Pausing during Recording

You can pause during a recording and continue when you are ready. To pause Recorder, click on the Recorder icon, press Ctrl+Break, or press Alt+Tab until the Recorder title box appears and then release both keys. When Recorder stops, you see the Macro Recording Suspended dialog box (see fig. 13.4). Move the Recorder window out of the way, if necessary, and go on to another task. When you are ready to continue, select the Recorder window, select the **R**esume Recording option in the dialog box, and choose OK to continue recording.

Recording with Mouse Actions

Recording macros of mouse movements can cause difficulty if windows are in different positions when you play back the macro than they were when you recorded the macro. One way to reduce this problem is to record the mouse pointer's position relative to the *application window* and not relative to the *entire screen*. To record relative to the window, choose the **R**elative To drop-down list box from the Record Macro dialog box and select Window (the other option is Screen).

You can choose the mouse actions that you record. If you select the Record **M**ouse drop-down list box from the Record Macro dialog box, you see the following choices:

Mouse Option	Description
Ignore Mouse	Records only keystrokes. Use this option if the macro is to be used in multiple applications with windows in varying positions or if the macro will be copied to computers with different graphics resolutions.
Everything	Records keystrokes and mouse actions even if you don't press the mouse button. To stop recording when using this option, press Ctrl+Break.
Clicks + Drags	Records keystrokes and mouse actions that result in a command choice.

Using Macros To Run Other Macros

If you need to create large macros or macros that perform similar tasks, you can make your job easier by creating macros that run other macros. Smaller macros that act as building blocks for other macros are known as *subroutines* in programming language. Creating macros from subroutines makes sense and can save you time. Subroutine macros have several advantages:

- Small subroutines are easier to troubleshoot than large, complex macros.

- You can use a subroutine in more than one macro.

- You can replace (but not edit) subroutines without damaging the larger macro that they run within.

Before creating a macro that runs other macros, analyze how you can divide tasks so that many other macros can use the subroutine macro that you are creating. For example, you may want a macro that changes the printer setup to landscape mode for sideways printing. That macro can be used within many other macros that print reports or charts.

Macros to be run by other macros *must* be activated by a shortcut key. You use the shortcut key to activate the subroutine macro during recording.

You can *nest* macros inside other macros up to five levels deep. You can, for example, use the macro to change the printer setup to landscape mode (described in the previous paragraph). This change is done inside another macro, creating a two-level macro. When you use your macros together, they must be stored in the same Recorder file.

To use an existing macro within the macro that you are recording, follow these steps:

1. Ensure that the **S**hortcut Keys option is selected on the **O**ptions menu. (A check mark appears next to the command when selected.)

2. Open the **M**acro menu and choose Re**c**ord. The Record Macro dialog box is displayed.

3. In the **P**layback group of options, select the **E**nable Shortcut Keys check box.

4. Record the macro up to the point where you want to use a subroutine macro.

5. Press the shortcut key that activates the subroutine macro.

III

Using Windows Accessories

6. Continue recording the macro, adding other shortcut keys for subroutine macros if needed.

7. Stop and save the recording when you are finished.

The subroutine macro can be used as a normal macro even though you nest it within another macro. If you record over the subroutine macro and use the same shortcut key name, the new subroutine macro runs as the nested macro.

To record a macro that cannot use subroutine macros, deselect the **E**nable Shortcut Keys check box in the Record Macros dialog box.

Changing the Default Recorder Settings

You can change the default settings in the Record Macro dialog box by opening the **O**ptions menu and choosing **P**references. The dialog box shown in figure 13.5 appears, enabling you to change the default settings for the **P**layback To, **P**layback Speed, Record **M**ouse, and **R**elative To options. The choices and their meanings are the same as those described for the Record Macro dialog box earlier in this chapter. If most of the macros you create use different defaults than those already selected, change the settings in this dialog box so you don't have to change them each time you start a new recording.

Fig. 13.5
The Default
Preferences dialog
box.

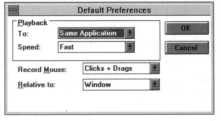

Saving Macros

Tip
If you share your
computer, or if
your Recorder
files are stored in
a common directory on your
network, use an
extension other
than REC.

When you record a macro, the recording is placed in the current Recorder file along with other macros. If you do not save this file, you lose the macros you have made since the last time that you saved the file. Files containing macros normally use the extension REC, although you can specify any extension to hide your macro files.

To save your new macros, follow these steps:

1. Open the **F**ile menu and choose Save **A**s.

2. From the Dri**v**es list, select the drive in which you want to save your macro file. From the **D**irectories list, select the directory.

3. Type a name (from one to eight characters) in the File **N**ame box. Recorder adds the extension REC.

4. Choose OK or press Enter.

If you have added macros to an existing file and want to save the file without changing its name, open the **F**ile menu and choose **S**ave.

Playing Back Macros

You can play back any of the macros in the file currently open in Recorder. Recorder must be running, and the file containing the macro that you want to run must be open. To replay a macro, press the shortcut key or choose the macro's name from the list in the Recorder file.

Opening Macro Files

After you save a file that contains macros, you can retrieve the file and use the macros. You can have only one file at a time open in Recorder, so you can use only the macros in the open file.

To open a file, follow these steps:

1. Activate Recorder.

2. Open the **F**ile menu and choose **O**pen. (If a file is already open, the file closes, and you are prompted to save the file if you haven't already.)

3. If necessary, select from the Dri**v**es list the drive that contains your macro file and select the directory from the **D**irectories list.

4. To see a list of all file types, select All Files (***.***) from the List File of **T**ype list. Otherwise, select Recorder Files (*.REC) to list just the files that end with the extension REC.

5. Select from the File **N**ame list the file that you want to open.

6. Choose OK or press Enter.

◀ "Opening, Saving, Printing, and Closing Files," p. 53

◀ "Opening, Saving, Printing, and Closing Files," p. 53

> **Note**
>
> If all the macros that you use are combined in a single Recorder file, associate that file with the Recorder program item icon in Program Manager. When you start Recorder, therefore, you automatically open your macro file. (To learn how to associate a file and application, see Chapter 4, "Managing Files with File Manager.")

III

Using Windows Accessories

Replaying Macros from a File

You can replay a macro in two ways: by pressing its shortcut key or by choosing its name from a list in Recorder. When you replay a macro, the Recorder window minimizes (if you have selected the **M**inimize on Use command from the **O**ptions menu) or moves behind the window that is just below the Recorder window. Recorder reacts in one of two ways with the currently loaded applications in Windows:

■ If the macro is the type that runs with any application, the macro replays in the current window. If more than one window is open, the macro replays in the foreground window.

■ If the macro is the type that replays only in a specific application, Recorder activates that application's window when the macro replays. If the application has not been started or is minimized to an icon, the macro does not replay, and an error dialog box is displayed.

To use a shortcut key to replay a macro, follow these steps:

1. Open the **F**ile menu and choose **O**pen to open the file that contains the macro, if necessary.

2. Activate the application in which you want the macro to play; position the insertion point or select text or graphics, whichever the macro expects.

3. Press the shortcut key assigned to the macro that you want to play back.

You can assign a new shortcut key to a macro if the current shortcut key interferes with the shortcut keys in an application. The section "Editing and Changing Macros," later in this chapter, explains how to change the properties of a recorded macro.

> **Note**
>
> If one of your Recorder macros uses a shortcut key that conflicts with an application's shortcut key, you can turn off Recorder's shortcut key by opening the **O**ptions menu and choosing the **S**hortcut Keys command so that no check mark appears next to it. You can run the Recorder macro by selecting its name, opening the **M**acro menu, and choosing **R**un.

Macros that operate when you choose their names are useful if you have more macros than you can conveniently assign to shortcut keys or if your macros are complex and you need a reminder about their actions. To make a macro replay when you choose its name, follow these steps:

1. Open the **F**ile menu and choose **O**pen to open the file that contains the macro, if necessary.

2. Activate the application in which you want the macro to play; position the insertion point or select text or graphics, whichever the macro expects.

3. Activate Recorder.

4. Choose the name of the macro that you want to play back by double-clicking on the name or by selecting the name with the arrow keys. Then open the **M**acro menu and choose **R**un.

> **Note**
>
> You can print a list of your Recorder macros and their corresponding shortcut keys. First, open the macro file that you want a listing of and press Alt+PrintScreen. Then open Windows Write from the Accessories group. Finally, to print the listing, open the Edit menu and choose Paste, and then open the File menu and choose Print.

Troubleshooting Macros

If you run a macro that cannot properly carry out its recorded instructions, the macro stops and Windows displays the Recorder Playback Aborted dialog box shown in figure 13.6.

Fig. 13.6
The Recorder Playback Aborted dialog box.

In the dialog box, the Error text box indicates the probable reason that the macro stopped. In figure 13.6, the macro was recorded specifically for the Write application, using mouse movements and mouse actions. The messages in the text boxes are as follows:

- Error box. `Playback window does not exist` indicates that when the macro was run, Write wasn't running.

- At instruction. This text box shows where the macro broke down. In this case, Recorder was trying to execute the first instruction in the macro, accessing the Write menu.

- In Macro. The name of the macro being executed.

To correct this macro error, you must start the Write application. If a macro fails, check to see whether it runs when you correctly position the windows. If the macro continues to fail, re-record the macro using keystrokes and note which applications the macro uses. When you play back the macro, make sure that these applications are in active or inactive windows. The first application that the macro uses does not have to be in the active window, because the macro activates windows as it needs them. The applications must be running, however.

If a long macro fails, consider re-recording it as subroutine macros. You can troubleshoot each subroutine macro and then link them together under the control of the large macro. If a subroutine macro later has trouble or must be changed, you need to change only that subroutine, not the entire large macro. Subroutine macros are described earlier in this chapter in the section "Using Macros To Run Other Macros."

Looking at the Contents of a Macro

Although you cannot edit a macro, you can look at the keystrokes, mouse clicks, and movements that are part of the macro. Looking at the contents of an improperly working macro may help you create a macro that *does* work.

To view a macro's contents, follow these steps:

1. Activate Recorder. Open the **F**ile menu and choose **O**pen to load the macro file.

2. Select the macro with the mouse or by using the arrow keys.

3. Hold down the Shift key while opening the **M**acro menu and choosing **P**roperties.

The Macro Events dialog box appears, as shown in figure 13.7. Each mouse movement or keystroke is shown, along with the window application name and the amount of time used by the keystroke or mouse clicks and movements. You can use the scroll bars to see additional commands. For example, figure 13.7 shows that the Ctrl+F7 macro that pauses the printer consists of the following keystrokes:

- Pressing the Alt key

- Pressing the P key

- Releasing the P key

- Releasing the Alt key

To close the Macro Events dialog box, choose OK.

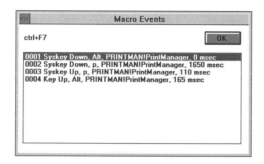

Fig. 13.7
The Macro Events dialog box showing the contents of a macro that pauses the current printer in Print Manager.

Stopping Macros

To stop most macros from running, press Ctrl+Break. You can specify that your macros not be stopped with Ctrl+Break by opening the **O**ptions menu and choosing **C**trl+Break Checking. If no check mark appears next to the command, you cannot turn off a macro by pressing Ctrl+Break; you must wait for the macro to finish. Make sure that the macro is working correctly before you disable the Ctrl+Break checking option.

> **Note**
>
> Beware of creating continuously playing macros that you cannot turn off by pressing Ctrl+Break. If you turn off Ctrl+Break checking for a continuously running macro, you must restart the computer to stop the macro. To do this without turning off the electricity, press Ctrl+Alt+Del; press Enter to close only the current application. Stopping a macro this way can be dangerous, because you may lose data in other open applications if Windows cannot successfully close the current window that is running the macro.

III

Using Windows Accessories

Creating Continuously Playing Macros

To create a demonstration, a tutorial, or an action that replays repeatedly, you need to know how to make macros repeat continuously. To make a macro repeat continuously, select the Continuous Loop check box in the Record Macro dialog box's **P**layback group before you record the macro.

If you already have recorded the macro, you can use the **P**roperties command of the **M**acro menu to change a normal macro to one that loops by enabling the Continuous Loop option.

Stop a continuously playing macro by pressing Ctrl+Break. If Ctrl+Break checking has been turned off (see the preceding section for details), you must restart your computer to stop the macro.

Editing and Changing Macros

You cannot change the steps that a recorded macro performs (although you can look at the macro commands as described in the preceding section). But you can change some properties of a recorded macro, such as its shortcut keys, whether it works with only one application or with any application, and whether it plays back continuously.

Figure 13.8 shows the Macro Properties dialog box, which enables you to change settings for a macro you already have recorded.

Fig. 13.8
The Macro
Properties dialog
box.

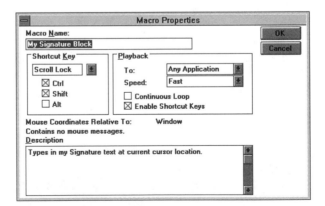

To change a macro's properties, follow these steps:

1. Activate Recorder.

2. Select the name of the macro that you want to change.

3. Open the **M**acro menu and choose **P**roperties. The Macro Properties dialog box is displayed.

4. Select and change a property.

5. Choose OK or press Enter.

6. Save the changed macro into its Recorder file by opening the **F**ile menu and choosing **S**ave or Save **A**s.

The properties of macros are described earlier in this chapter in the section "Setting Up and Recording Macros." Notice that you cannot change the Mouse Coordinates Relative To property. If you didn't record any mouse actions, then you also see a message saying Contains no mouse messages. If you did record mouse actions, you see a message telling you the type of monitor on which the actions were recorded. (This information indicates whether the macro is compatible with a different display.)

Managing Macros

Macros are like files; they seem to expand and grow on their own. One moment, you have only 2 on your disk; the next time you look, you have 176. Before incalculable volumes of macros swamp your sea of serenity, learn to manage them.

Deleting a Macro from a File

To delete a macro from a Recorder file, load the file that contains the macro, select the macro name, open the **M**acro menu, and choose **D**elete. When you are asked to confirm that you want to delete the macro, choose OK. Then save the Recorder file again.

Merging Files

To use one macro in multiple files, you can merge Recorder files. Merging files brings the macros from a file on disk into the active file in Recorder. If the macros have duplicate shortcut keys, the duplicate key is removed, but the macro remains. The shortcut keys assigned to macros in the active file in Recorder are retained.

To merge the macros in two files, follow these steps:

1. Open an existing Recorder file by opening the **F**ile menu and choosing **O**pen, or create a file by opening the **F**ile menu and choosing **N**ew.

2. Delete unwanted or duplicate macros from the file.

3. Open the **F**ile menu and choose **M**erge.

4. In the File **N**ame list, select the name of the file that you want to merge into the existing file (change the drive and directory to locate the file, if necessary).

5. Choose OK or press Enter.

The file in Recorder now contains the combined set of macros. You can save this file under the same name as the original active file by opening the **F**ile menu and choosing **S**ave, or you can save the file under a new file name by opening the **F**ile menu and choosing Save **A**s.

Creating Some Useful Macros

After you work with a few common macros, you probably will think of different macros to create that can help save you time. To get you started, the following list contains a few useful macros that you can create. You may find that a few extra commands in a macro will give you even more flexibility.

When you start creating macros, you may find it hard to stop. Many of the following macro ideas take advantage of the fact that most Windows applications use the same keystrokes for the same types of commands.

- *To print the current document.* This simple macro contains only the Alt+F, P, and Enter keys. Because most Windows applications use this standard for printing the entire document, you may want to set the **P**layback To setting to Any Application. Also, for quick printing, assign a shortcut key to this macro. Place the macro in your default macro file.

- *To create a common header or footer.* If you always want the page number to appear at the bottom of each page, this macro sets up the footer for you. You may have to make a customized one for each type of word processing application (Write, Notepad, or other Windows applications) or generalize the macro enough so that you are placed in the Header or Footer editing screen.

- *To pause/resume Print Manager.* One macro can pause the printer (through Print Manager) and one can restart the printer. To use these macros, you must ensure that Print Manager is running; one way that you can do this is to place a Print Manager program item icon in the StartUp group.

- *To start bulletin board systems (BBSs).* If you regularly log onto several different BBSs, create a macro that does this for you. The steps required in the macro depend on your communications application. With Terminal, for example, you want the macro to load the configuration file name, dial, and log on. You can create a group of macros that have start-up commands for different BBSs. Then place this macro group in a Recorder file that contains communications macros.

- *To start your fax board application or to print faxes.* If you have a fax board in your computer, a macro to print the current faxes is useful. Enter the commands that the application requires to print any unread faxes. You also can create a macro that starts up your fax board application.

- *To perform start-up tasks.* This complex macro may use several subroutine macros. For example, create a macro to check your electronic mail, another macro to print your calendar page for the current day, and other macros to do other start-up functions. Then combine these macros into a master macro that performs each macro subroutine.

- *To maintain an address book.* If you write many letters to people, you can store their addresses in Cardfile or a similar application. Create a macro that copies the current card into your word processing application. For new people, create another macro that copies the address block into a new entry in your Cardfile application. This macro may require a bit of advance planning, because you need to have the Cardfile application running when you run these macros. You also need to select the address block before you start the macro.

- *To print an envelope.* Set up a Write document that contains the proper formatting commands to print an envelope. Then create a macro that takes the address block from your word processing application, copies the block to the Clipboard, and pastes the block into the Write document. Then continue the macro with a Print command. You also can use your Print macro as a macro subroutine by assigning it a shortcut key and using the shortcut key in your envelope macro. This macro requires a bit of advance planning so that you can specify the exact Write commands required to set up the envelope document properly. After you set up that document, select the address block and then record the macro. After you build the macro, select the address block in any application and then start it. Make sure that the Write window is open.

As you can see, Recorder has many uses. A little advance planning is important when you create the macros. Try to make your macros as general as possible so that they can be shared among applications.

Setting Up a Windows Start-Up Macro

You can set up your Windows environment so that your Recorder file is loaded when you start Windows. Then your standard macros are available to you as needed.

◀ "Adding Applications and Documents to a Group," p. 98

Follow these steps:

1. Open or create the StartUp group from the Program Manager window.

2. Hold down the Ctrl key and drag a copy of the Recorder program item icon into the StartUp group window.

3. Select the new icon, open the **F**ile menu and choose **P**roperties.

4. In the **C**ommand Line box, move the cursor to the end of the command line and type a space followed by the name of the Recorder file you want to open on start-up.

5. If you want, assign a working directory and a shortcut key. Choose the Change **I**con option if you want to select a different icon. Select the **R**un Minimized option to start Recorder and to minimize Recorder to an icon every time that you start your computer.

6. Choose OK to save the new program item.

Tip

You can use Recorder to create a macro that runs automatically when you start Windows, in the same way that the AUTOEXEC.BAT batch file runs when you start your computer. You can create such a macro so that it automatically opens up applications and arranges windows the way that you want them.

The next time that you start Windows, Recorder opens; your macro file automatically is loaded. If you selected the **R**un Minimized option, the Recorder icon is minimized at the bottom of the screen. All the macros in the macro file that loads on start-up are available for you to use.

To run a macro automatically when Windows starts, first create the macro, making sure to assign a shortcut key to the macro. Next, you create a DOS batch file that includes the WIN command line. To ensure that the macro runs automatically when Windows starts, you must add several parameters to the WIN command line. For example, if your macro's shortcut key is Ctrl+Shift+F1, your WIN command line would look like this:

```
WIN RECORDER -H ^+F1 C:\WINDOWS\MYMACROS.REC
```

By including RECORDER in the command, you ensure that Recorder opens when you open Windows. The -H parameter tells Recorder to run the macro that is invoked by the shortcut keys that follow -H; because Ctrl is designated with a caret (^), Shift with a plus sign (+), and Alt with a percent sign (%), this command line runs the macro when you press with Ctrl+Shift+F1. The last part of the command line tells Recorder which Recorder file to open and where it is located. (Substitute the name of your macro file for MYMACROS.REC.)

◄ "Starting and Exiting Windows," p. 18

From Here...

Now that you know how to create macros, you can learn how to run the applications that come with Windows, and use macros to automate tasks with these applications. To learn how to use these applications, refer to:

- Chapter 10, "Using Windows Write," explains how to use the word processor that comes with Windows.

- Chapter 11, "Using Paintbrush," teaches you how to use Windows drawing applications.

- Chapter 12, "Using Windows Terminal," explains how to use Windows telecommunications application.

- Chapter 14, "Using Desktop Accessories," teaches you how to use the necessary applications that come with Windows.

III

Using Windows Accessories

Chapter 14

Using Desktop Accessories

The desktop accessories that come with Windows can help you perform special tasks related to a current project without leaving the application. You may be working in Excel, for example, and need to make a quick note; the Windows Notepad is the perfect companion. When working in Word for Windows, you may need to make a quick calculation; the Windows Calculator can do the job. If you are using Windows for Workgroups, you will be interested in the WinMeter and NetWatcher accessories. They help you manage your computer while it is on the network.

These desktop accessories take advantage of one of Windows' most powerful features: the capability of running several applications simultaneously. As you work in the main application, you can keep the Windows desktop applications running at the same time. Because so little of the computer's memory is used, the desktop accessories don't slow you down.

The Write, Paintbrush, Terminal, and Recorder applications were discussed in previous chapters. PIF Editor, which helps you specify how DOS applications run, is discussed in Chapter 22, "Running, Installing, and Configuring DOS Applications." Media Player and Sound Recorder are described in Chapter 19, "Using Windows Multimedia." Object Packager is discussed in Chapter 6, "Advanced Data Sharing."

In this chapter, you learn how to:

- ■ Use Notepad
- ■ Use Cardfile
- ■ Use Calendar

■ Use Calculator

■ Play Windows games

Keeping Notes with Notepad

Notepad is a miniature text editor. Just as you use a notepad on the desk, you can use Notepad to take notes on-screen while working in other Windows applications. Notepad uses little memory and is useful for editing text that you want to copy in a Windows or DOS application that lacks an editing capability.

Notepad retrieves and saves files in text format. This feature makes Notepad a convenient editor for creating and altering the Windows WIN.INI file, MS-DOS batch files, CONFIG.SYS files, and other text-based files. Because Notepad stores files in text format, almost all word processors can retrieve Notepad's files.

Another handy use for Notepad is to hold text you want to move to another application. Clipboard can hold only one selection at a time, but the Notepad can serve as a text scrapbook when you are moving several items as a group.

As a bonus, Notepad also includes a feature for logging time, so you can use Notepad as a time clock, which enables you to know when you opened a file or to monitor the time you spend on a project. Notepad files cannot hold graphics.

Starting Notepad

◀ "Starting Applications," p. 48

Open Notepad by double-clicking the Notepad icon in the Accessories window in Program Manager. A blank Notepad appears (see fig. 14.1).

You can open a new or existing file from within the Notepad application by choosing the **File New** or **File O**pen command. To open the file, choose the **File O**pen command to display the Open dialog box, select the directory and file you want to open, and choose OK. Notepad can open files with the extensions BAT, SYS, INI, and files with the extension TXT.

As an alternative, you can open an existing text file that has the extension TXT in Notepad directly from the Windows File Manager. To do so, double-click the file name in File Manager. Notepad opens and loads the TXT file.

You can close a Notepad file in two ways: open a new file or close the Notepad application. To close the Notepad application, choose **File Exit**.

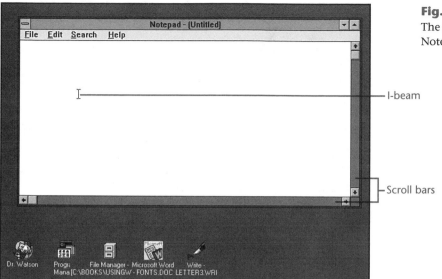

Fig. 14.1
The initial blank
Notepad file.

I-beam

Scroll bars

Caution

Be careful when you edit with Notepad. Because Notepad creates text files, you can open and edit important system, application, and data files. To avoid loss of data or applications, make sure that you open only files with which you are familiar or that have the file extensions TXT, BAT, or INI.

◄ "Opening, Saving, Printing, and Closing Files," p. 53

When you open a new file in Notepad, the currently open file closes. If your file has changed, a dialog box asks whether you want to save the current changes. Choose **Y**es to save or **N**o to discard the changes. Choose Cancel to return to the original file.

Immediately after you open a new Notepad file, you can begin typing. Each character you type appears to the left of a blinking vertical line known as the *insertion point*.

Unlike most word processing applications, Notepad doesn't by default wrap text to the following line. You must either choose the **E**dit **W**ord Wrap command or press Enter at the end of each line. With Word Wrap turned on, text wraps to fit the width of the Notepad window, no matter how wide the window is. If you change the size of the window, the text rewraps to fit (see fig. 14.2).

III

Using Windows Accessories

Fig. 14.2
Two examples of
text wrapping to
fit the Notepad
window.

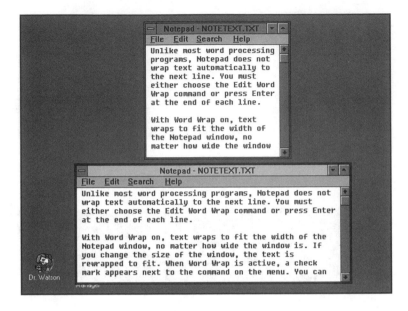

You can activate Word Wrap at any time. When Word Wrap is active, a check mark appears beside the command on the menu. If you choose the **E**dit **W**ord Wrap command again, the Word Wrap feature turns off, and text stretches out until it reaches a hard return. Without automatic word wrap, lines can reach up to 160 characters long (if you type beyond the right edge of the window, the page scrolls to the left).

Moving and Scrolling in the Notepad Window

Although Notepad pages scroll through the window, the best way to think of this action is as a Notepad window that moves down a long strip of document. The horizontal and vertical scroll bars along the left and bottom edge of the Notepad window move the window around on this strip of paper. The length and width of the scroll bars represent the entire Notepad document and the scroll box represents the Notepad window's current position on the document. To scroll by line, click the arrows on the scroll bars. To move one full screen at a time, click in the gray area of the scroll bar. For larger moves, drag the scroll box to a new vertical or horizontal location. With the keyboard, press the page up key to scroll up one screen at a time; press the page down key to scroll down one screen at a time.

> **Note**
>
> The horizontal scroll bar appears only when the **W**ord Wrap command is selected in the **E**dit menu.

You can move the insertion point by using either the mouse or the keyboard. To move the insertion point with the mouse, position the *I-beam*, (the text-screen mouse pointer) where you want the insertion point and click the mouse button. With the keyboard, use the arrow keys to move the insertion point. As in any word processing application, the insertion point in Notepad travels only where typed characters appear, even if these characters are spaces or Enter characters. You cannot move the insertion point beyond where you already typed.

Keyboard shortcuts for moving the insertion point and scrolling are listed in the following table:

Key	Action
End	Move to end of line
Home	Move to beginning of line
Ctrl+Home	Move to beginning of document
Ctrl+End	Move to end of document
PgUp	Scroll one screen up
PgDn	Scroll one screen down

Editing Notes

You select and edit text in Notepad the same way you select and edit text in Write. (See Chapter 10, "Using Windows Write," for details.)

◄ "Scrolling Windows," p. 39

Notepad enables you to perform limited formatting by using the File Page Setup command. When you select this command, the Page Setup dialog box appears (see fig. 14.3), which is where you can change the margins and add a header or footer to the note. In Notepad, you cannot format characters or paragraphs in any way, although you can use Tab, the space bar, and Backspace to align text. Tab stops are preset at every eight characters.

A handy shortcut for selecting a single word is to double-click the word. To select a large block of text, click at the beginning of the selection, use the scroll bars to scroll to the end of the selection, and then hold down the Shift key as you click at the end of the selection. All text between the original insertion point and the Shift+click is selected.

III

Using Windows Accessories

Fig. 14.3

Set margins and insert header/ footers in the Page Setup dialog box.

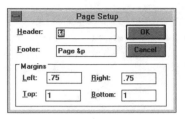

With Notepad's Edit commands, you can cut, copy, and move selected text from one place in a file to another. As in any Windows application, text you cut or copy is stored in the Clipboard. When you paste text, this text is copied from the Clipboard to the document at the insertion point.

To cut, copy, and paste text, follow these steps:

1. Select the text you want to cut, copy, or move (see fig. 14.4).

Fig. 14.4

Selected text in reverse type.

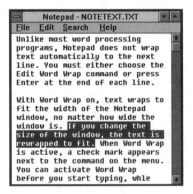

2. To move text, open the **E**dit menu and choose Cu**t**; to make a duplicate of the text and leave the original in place, open the **E**dit menu and choose **C**opy.

3. Move the insertion point where you want to paste the text.

4. Open the **E**dit menu and choose **P**aste. The text is copied from the Clipboard to the location of the insertion point.

You can use keyboard shortcuts: cut using Ctrl+X, copy using Ctrl+C, and paste using Ctrl+V. (If you select text and press Del, text is deleted without being copied to the Clipboard. The only way to retrieve this kind of deletion is to immediately choose the **E**dit **U**ndo command.)

Searching through Notepad

Notepad's Search command finds and selects any word or phrase. You can search forward or backward through a document, beginning at the insertion point. You can specify whether to search for an exact uppercase or lowercase match or whether to search for any match.

◀ "Copying and Moving," p. 56

◀ "Viewing Data in the Clipboard," p. 191

To search for text, follow these steps:

1. Open the **S**earch menu and choose **F**ind. The Find dialog box appears (see fig. 14.5).

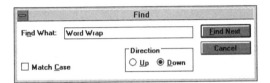

Fig. 14.5

The Find dialog box.

2. In the Fi**n**d What text box, type the text you want to find.

3. To find text that exactly matches the text you typed in uppercase and lowercase letters, mark the Match **C**ase check box.

4. Select **D**own to search forward from the insertion point; select **U**p to select backward from the insertion point.

5. Choose **F**ind Next or press F3.

The application selects the first occurrence of the word or phrase. The dialog box remains open so that you can continue the search by choosing **F**ind Next again. To return to the document, choose Cancel. If Notepad cannot find the word or phrase, a message box appears and tells you that it cannot find the text. Choose OK to acknowledge the message and then choose Cancel to return to the document. To continue the search after you close the dialog box, choose **S**earch Find **N**ext (or press F3).

Creating a Time-Log File with Notepad

By using a simple command, .LOG, you can have Notepad enter the time and date at the end of a document each time you open the file. This feature is convenient for taking phone messages or for calculating the time spent on a project. An example of Notepad with a time log is shown in figure 14.6. As an alternative to the .LOG command, you can choose the **E**dit Time/**D**ate command to insert the current time and date at the insertion point.

III

Using Windows Accessories

Fig. 14.6
You can track times in a Notepad document in two ways.

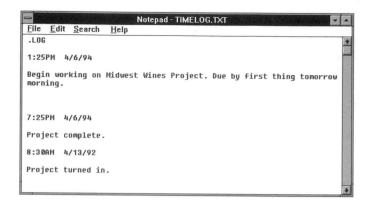

To create a time log by default in a document, follow these steps:

1. Move the insertion point to the left margin of the first line in the Notepad document.

2. In capital letters, type the command **.LOG**.

3. Save the file.

4. Reopen the file.

When you reopen the Notepad file, the time and date are inserted by default. Type notes as desired.

5. Save the file again.

6. After you finish the project, reopen the file.

Again, the time and date are entered by default. Type a log entry that states that the project is finished.

To insert the time and date from the keyboard, follow these steps:

1. Move the insertion point where you want to enter the time and date.

2. Open the **E**dit menu and choose Time/**D**ate, or press F5.

Saving and Printing Notepad Files

To save and name a Notepad document, follow these steps:

1. Open the **F**ile menu and choose Save **A**s.

Tip
Notepad takes the time and date information from the computer's internal clock. Use the International Application of Control Panel to set the time and date accurately, as described in Chapter 7.

2. From the **D**irectories list box, select the directory in which you want to save the file.

   By default, Notepad saves the file in the current directory.

3. In the File **N**ame text box, enter a name.

4. Choose OK or press Enter.

◀ "Changing Directories in a List Box," p. 37

◀ "Opening, Saving, Printing, and Closing Files," p. 53

If you previously saved a file but want to save it again with the same file name, choose **F**ile **S**ave. The current file replaces the original version.

If you don't enter a file extension, Notepad adds the extension TXT. To save a different kind of file, enter the file name and add the desired extension.

You can print a Notepad file on the currently selected printer. If you want to select a different printer, follow these steps:

1. Open the **F**ile menu and choose P**r**int Setup.

2. From the Specific **P**rinter list, select the printer you want to use.

3. Make the selections that pertain to the printer you use: the paper size, orientation, source, and so on. Depending on the printer you select, these selections vary.

4. Choose the **O**ptions button to display a dialog box containing additional Print Setup options, depending on what type of printer you selected. Select the options you want.

5. Choose OK or press Enter.

6. Choose OK or press Enter a second time to close the Print Setup dialog box.

To print a Notepad file on the selected printer, follow these steps:

1. Open the file to be printed.

2. Open the **F**ile menu and choose **P**rint.

Although you don't see a dialog box when you issue the **F**ile **P**rint command, a message box appears that tells you the document is printing. To cancel the print job, select the Cancel button in the dialog box.

III

Using Windows Accessories

Inserting Symbols with Character Map

The Character Map accessory gives you access to symbol fonts and ANSI characters. *ANSI characters* are the regular character set that you see on the keyboard and more than a hundred other characters, including a copyright symbol, a registered trademark symbol, and many foreign language characters.

One symbol font, Symbol, is included with most Windows applications. Other symbol fonts may be built into the printer. Most PostScript printers, for example, include Zapf Dingbats. When you set up and indicate the model of the printer, font cartridges, and so on, the printer tells Windows what symbol fonts are available. (Printer fonts appear in character map only when they include a matching screen font.)

To use the Character Map accessory, you first must start the application from Program Manager. You then can select any characters or symbols from the Character Map dialog box and, by using the Clipboard, insert these items in any Windows application.

Open Character Map by double-clicking the Character Map icon in the Accessories window in Program Manager. The Character Map dialog box appears (see fig. 14.7). The dialog box includes a drop-down list box, from which you can select any of the available fonts on the system. After you select a font, the characters and symbols for this font appear in the Character Map table.

Fig. 14.7

Select characters from the Character Map dialog box for use in Windows documents.

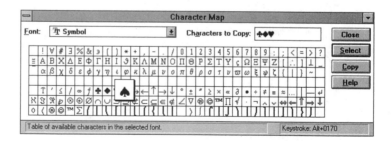

To insert characters and symbols in a Windows application, you copy the characters you selected from the Character Map dialog box to Clipboard and then paste the characters in the application by using standard Windows copy-and-paste procedures.

To insert a character in a Windows application from Character Map, follow these steps:

1. From Program Manager, open the Character Map accessory.

2. Select the font you want to use from the **F**ont list.

   Character Map displays the characters for the selected font. Each set of fonts may have different symbols. Some fonts, such as Symbol and Zapf Dingbats, contain nothing but symbols and special characters.

3. To see an enlarged version of the character, click it or use the arrow keys to move the character.

4. Double-click the character you want to insert or choose the **S**elect button to place the current character in the Ch**a**racters text box.

5. Repeat steps 2 through 4 to select as many characters as desired.

6. Choose the **C**opy button to copy the characters from the Ch**a**racters to Copy text box to the Clipboard.

7. Open or switch to the application in which you want to copy the character(s).

8. Place the insertion point where you want to insert the character(s), open the **E**dit menu, and choose **P**aste.

If the characters don't appear as they did in Character Map, you may need to reselect the characters in the application and change the font to the same font in which the character originally appeared in Character Map.

> **Tip**
> If you plan to use Character Map frequently, add this application to the StartUp group in Program Manager so that Character Map opens when you start Windows.

◄ "Understanding Fonts," p. 268

Tracking Appointments with Calendar

Calendar is a computerized appointment book that records appointments, marks special dates, and even sets an alarm to remind you of important events. Calendar operates in two views: daily and monthly. When you open Calendar for the first time, you see the daily view (see fig. 14.8). This calendar is marked in hourly intervals; you can scroll through the times and type appointments for each hour. To view an entire month, switch to the monthly view. In this view, you can scroll through the months and add notes to any date. The notes you type in the monthly view also appear in the daily view for this date.

III

Using Windows Accessories

Fig. 14.8
Calendar's daily
view.

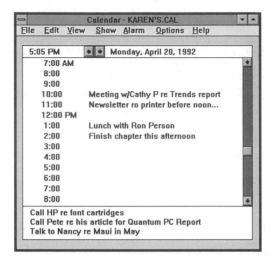

Calendar creates and stores files like any other application. After you open
Calendar, you see a new, blank calendar. You can save as many different
calendar files as you want. For example, you may want to create a separate
calendar file for each of several projects.

Note

◄ "Customizing
International
Settings,"
p. 248

The date formats shown in Calendar are those selected by using the International
application in Control Panel.

If you are using Windows for Workgroups, you may want to use the Schedule+ application instead of Calendar. Schedule+ is more functional as both a personal scheduling system and for scheduling meetings that involve other people in your workgroup.

Opening and Closing Calendar in Program Manager

Open the Calendar application by double-clicking the Calendar icon in the
Accessories window in Program Manager. You also can open a new or existing file from within the Calendar application by choosing the File New or
File Open command. In the Open dialog box, select the directory and file you
want to open. Calendar files have the extension CAL.

If you want to open a file without being able to edit it (when you're opening
someone else's Calendar file, for example) select the Read Only option in the
Open dialog box. Choose OK to open the file. Alternatively, you can open an
existing Calendar file directly from File Manager by double-clicking the file
name.

When you open a new file from within Calendar, the currently open file is closed. A dialog box asks whether you want to save the current changes (this dialog box appears only if changes were made). Choose **Y**es to save the changes, choose **N**o to discard them, or choose Cancel to return to the original file.

You can close a Calendar file in only two ways: open a new file or close the Calendar application. To close the Calendar application, open the **F**ile menu and choose E**xit**.

At the top of the Calendar window are a title bar and a menu bar listing all of Calendar's commands. Below the menu bar is a status bar that shows the current time and date (if they're wrong, reset them using Control Panel). The title, menu, and status bars appear in both the daily and monthly views of Calendar. At the bottom of the Calendar window is a scratch-pad area where you can enter up to three lines of notes for each day. Like the status bars, the scratch pad appears in both the monthly and daily views. Figure 14.9 shows the Calendar in monthly view.

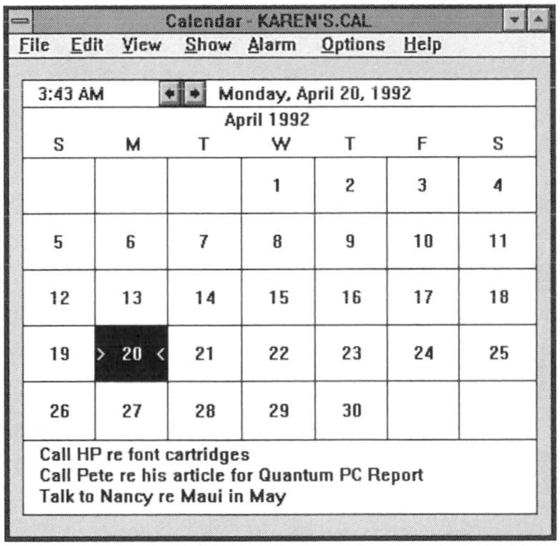

Fig. 14.9
Calendar's
monthly view.

Switching between the two views is easy. Just choose the **View M**onth command or press F9 to switch to the monthly view. Choose the **View D**ay command or press F8 to switch to the daily view. If you have a mouse, double-click the date in the status bar to switch between monthly and daily views (in the monthly view, double-click any day to switch back to this date in the daily view).

Entering Appointments

After you open Calendar, you see the daily view for the current time and date. On the left of the calendar window are listed times; to the right of the times is room to enter appointments.

Although only part of the day is displayed in the Calendar window, all 24 hours are available. To enter an appointment at a time not displayed, use the scroll bar on the right side of the calendar to scroll up or down to the time you want. From the keyboard, use the up and down arrows and PgUp and PgDn to scroll up and down. Take a shortcut to the original starting time by pressing Ctrl+Home; go to the time 12 hours after the starting time by pressing Ctrl+End.

To enter an appointment, follow these steps:

1. Scroll to display the time you want.

2. Move the insertion point to the time of the appointment. To move the insertion point to a time with the mouse, click the I-beam where you want to type. To move the insertion point with the keyboard, press the arrow keys.

3. Type the appointment. You can type about 80 characters on each line; if you type beyond the right margin, the Calendar window scrolls to the right so that you can see all the text.

4. Press Enter to move the insertion point to the next line.

5. If desired, enter a note for that date in the scratch pad. To move between the scratch-pad area and the appointment area, click in the area you want or press Tab. Once in the scratch-pad area, type and edit using normal Windows procedures. A note stays attached to its date; whenever you turn to this date, the note appears in the scratch pad.

If you want to enter an appointment at a time not displayed on Calendar (for example, 1:45), you must insert this "special" time. Refer to "Changing the Starting Time and Intervals," later in this chapter, for more information.

Editing and Moving Calendar Appointments

You can edit Calendar appointments and scratch-pad notes in the same way you edit text in other Windows applications. You can insert and delete text for any date, and you can select, cut, copy, or paste appointments from one location to another between days, months, and even years. Using the Clipboard, you can move text not only between times and days but also between applications. Moving an appointment in this way is a convenient way to update the schedule.

To move appointments or notes to other dates, follow these steps:

1. Select the text you want to move.

2. Open the **E**dit menu and choose **C**opy (Ctrl+C), or open the **E**dit menu and choose Cu**t** (Ctrl+X).

3. Move the insertion point to the new date.

4. Open the **E**dit menu and choose **P**aste (Ctrl+V).

Removing Appointments from the Calendar

Because old appointments use disk space, you probably don't need these notations on the calendar. Fortunately, you can remove appointments for an individual day or for a range of days. You can remove appointments only from the active Calendar file. To remove appointments from other Calendar files, you first must open the files.

To remove appointments from the current Calendar file, follow these steps:

1. Open the **E**dit menu and choose **R**emove. The Remove dialog box shown in figure 14.10 appears.

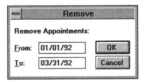

Fig. 14.10
The Remove dialog box.

2. In the **F**rom and **T**o boxes in the dialog box, enter the range of dates you want to remove. To remove a single date, type the date in the **F**rom text box.

3. Choose OK or press Enter.

Displaying Different Dates, Times, and Views

After you open a new or existing Calendar file, you always see the current date in the daily view, but you can move between dates, times, and views by using the techniques listed in table 14.2.

III

Using Windows Accessories

Table 14.2 Moving in the Calendar	
Location To Move To	**Actions**
Previous day (daily view)	Choose **S**how **P**revious
Previous month (monthly view)	Press Ctrl+PgUp Click the left arrow in status bar
Next day (daily view)	Choose **S**how **N**ext
Next month (monthly view)	Press Ctrl+PgDn Click the right arrow in status bar
Today's date	Choose **S**how **T**oday
A specific date	Choose **S**how **D**ate or press F4; then type desired date in mm/dd/yy format and press Enter
A different time (daily view)	Press the up or down arrow Press PgUp or PgDn Click the scroll-bar arrows
Monthly view	Choose **V**iew **M**onth Press F9 Double-click the date in status bar
Daily view	Choose **V**iew **D**ay Press F8 Double-click the date in status bar Double-click the day in monthly view

Setting an Alarm

To be reminded of an important appointment, you can set an alarm in Calendar's daily view, with or without sound. You can set alarms for as many appointments as you like.

To turn on the alarm, move the insertion point to the time you want the alarm to sound and choose **A**larm **S**et or press F5. (To remove the alarm, repeat this procedure.) After you set the alarm, a small bell appears to the left of the appropriate time on the calendar (see fig. 14.11).

When this time arrives, the computer beeps (unless you deactivate the sound), and a dialog box flashes on-screen to remind you of the appointment (see fig. 14.12).

To continue working, you must respond to the Alarm dialog box. To turn off the Alarm dialog box, choose OK. If Calendar is minimized to an icon when the alarm goes off, the title bar or icon flashes. You must activate the

Calendar window to display and respond to the Alarm dialog box. If you plan to use the Calendar alarm feature, keep Calendar running so that the alarm can sound to warn you of imminent appointments and deadlines.

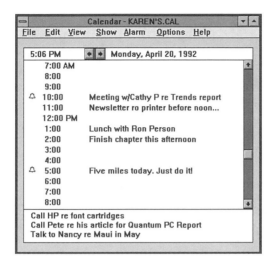

Fig. 14.11
Alarm bells to the left of certain appointment times.

Fig. 14.12
The dialog box that reminds you of appointments.

You can control the alarm in two ways: by setting the alarm to ring from 1 to 10 minutes early and by turning off the alarm sound so that you get a silent alarm (the on-screen reminder) rather than a beep.

To control the alarm options, follow these steps:

1. Open the **A**larm menu and choose **C**ontrols. The Alarm Controls dialog box appears (see fig. 14.13).

2. If you want the alarm to sound before the scheduled time on the Calendar, select **E**arly Ring and enter a number from 1 to 10.

3. To turn off the alarm beep (for a silent alarm), deselect the **S**ound check box. Leave this check box marked if you want the alarm to beep.

4. Choose OK or press Enter.

Tip
If you use alarms, add Calendar to the StartUp group to start Calendar each time you start Windows.

III

Using Windows Accessories

Fig. 14.13
The Alarm
Controls dialog
box.

Changing the Starting Time and Intervals

When you open a new Calendar file, the times are set at one-hour intervals; the day begins at 7:00 a.m. You can change these intervals, and you can set the calendar to display a different first hour if your day typically starts at a different time than 7:00. You also can change the hour format to a 24-hour clock rather than the conventional 12-hour clock. You always have a full 24 hours for appointments, no matter what changes you make to Calendar's appearance.

To change the day settings, follow these steps:

1. Open the **O**ptions menu and choose **D**ay Settings. The Day Settings dialog box appears (see fig. 14.14).

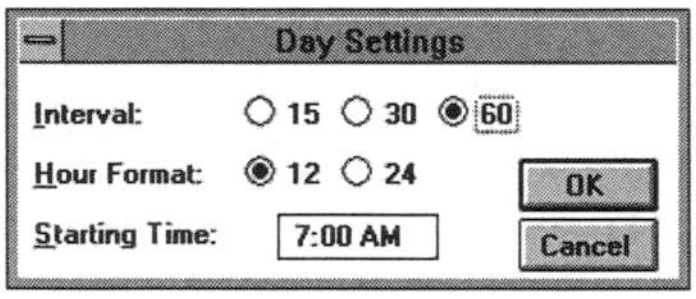

Fig. 14.14
The Day Settings
dialog box.

2. Choose **I**nterval, and select a 15-, 30-, or 60-minute time interval for the display of the appointment calendar.

3. Choose **H**our Format, and select a 12- or 24-hour format.

4. In the **S**tarting Time text box, enter a different time to change Calendar's first displayed hour.

5. Choose OK or press Enter.

Occasionally, appointments don't fall exactly on Calendar's preset time intervals. For this kind of appointment, you can insert special times. In figure 14.15, the time intervals were changed to 30 minutes, and a special time was inserted at 2:40 p.m.

To add a special time, follow these steps:

1. Open the **O**ptions menu and choose **S**pecial Time or press F7. The Special Time dialog box appears (see fig. 14.16).

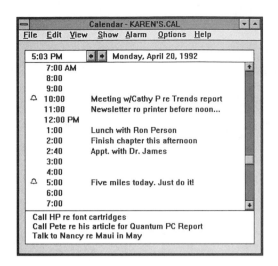

Fig. 14.15
Adding a special
time to Calendar.

Fig. 14.16
The Special Time
dialog box.

2. Select **S**pecial Time and enter the special time you want to insert.

3. Select **A**M or **P**M. (If Calendar is set to the 12-hour format, Calendar
   assumes a.m. unless you specify p.m.)

4. Choose the **I**nsert button.

To delete a special time, follow these steps:

1. Move the insertion point to the special time you want to delete.

2. Open the **O**ptions menu and choose **S**pecial Time or press F7.

3. Choose the **D**elete button.

Viewing the Calendar by Month

After you start Calendar, you see the daily view; you can switch to a monthly
view (refer to fig. 14.10). As in the daily view, the current time and date in
the monthly view always appears in a status bar below the menus. The day
selected in the monthly view is the same day you were on when you
switched from the daily view. The current date (today's date) appears on the
monthly calendar enclosed in angle brackets (> <).

III

Using Windows Accessories

Marking Important Days

In the monthly view, you can mark a date to remind you of a special event, such as a report due, a project-completion date, or a sister's birthday. In figure 14.17, dates are marked with Calendar's different marker symbols.

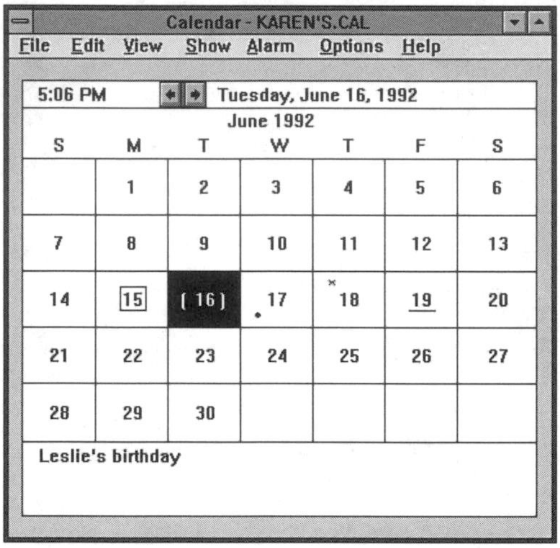

Fig. 14.17
Using five
different symbols
to mark dates in
the monthly view.

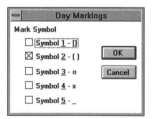

Tip
Switch from
daily to
monthly view
by clicking the
status bar at
the top of the
window. After
the monthly
view appears,
double-click
the day that
contains the
appointment
list you want to
see.

To mark a date in Calendar's monthly view, follow these steps:

1. Select the date you want to mark by clicking it or by pressing the arrow keys until it is highlighted.

2. Open the **O**ptions menu and choose **M**ark, or press F6. The Day Markings dialog box appears (see fig. 14.18).

Fig. 14.18
The Day Markings
dialog box.

3. Select the desired mark symbol.

4. Choose OK or press Enter.

Saving and Printing Calendar Files

You can save as many different Calendar files as you like so that you can have separate files for different projects, resources, clients, and so on. The first time you save a file, you must assign the file a name.

To save a new Calendar file, follow these steps:

1. Open the **F**ile menu and choose **S**ave **A**s.

2. In the File **N**ame text box, enter a file name.

3. From the **D**irectories list box, select the directory in which you want to save the file. By default, Windows saves the file in the current directory.

4. Choose OK or press Enter.

◀ "Opening, Saving, Printing, and Closing Files," p. 53

To save an existing Calendar file without changing the name, choose the **F**ile **S**ave command.

The new version of the file replaces the existing version on the disk.

> **Note**
>
> Giving an important file a new name each time you save is a good practice. This way, if the current version of a file is lost or destroyed, you have a backup. Name the business-calendar files, for example, BUSCAL01, BUSCAL02, and so on. Use File Manager to delete old and no longer needed files.

You can print appointments for a day or for a range of days from the current calendar by using the Print dialog box (see fig. 14.19).

Fig. 14.19
The Print dialog box.

III

To print a range of appointments, follow these steps:

1. Open the **F**ile menu and choose **P**rint.

2. In the **F**rom text box, enter the first appointment date you want to print; in the **T**o text box, enter the last date you want to print. If you want to print a single date, type the date in the **F**rom text box.

3. Choose OK or press Enter.

◀ "Printing a File," p. 294

◀ "Adding and Configuring Printers," p. 284

Using Windows Accessories

On the printed calendar, you can include headers and footers, and you can print within specified margins. You specify headers, footers, and margins in the Page Setup dialog box (see fig. 14.20).

Fig. 14.20
The Page Setup dialog box.

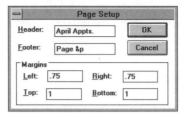

Follow these steps to create headers and footers and set margins for the printed calendar:

1. Open the File menu and choose Page Setup.

2. Select the Header text box, and type the text of the header you want to print.

3. Select the Footer text box, and type the text of the footer you want to print.

4. Select the Left, Right, Top, and Bottom Margins boxes, and type, in decimal numbers, the margins you want. Remember that Windows uses a default measurement of inches.

5. Choose OK or press Enter.

Calendar prints on the currently selected printer. To select a printer, choose the File Print Setup command and select the printer you want, Default Printer or Specific Printer, as well as the paper Orientation (select Portrait or Landscape), the Paper Size, and the Paper Source. Choose the Options button to make additional selections specific to your printer. Choose OK to close the Options dialog box; choose OK again to close the Print Setup box.

Storing and Retrieving Information in Cardfile

Cardfile is like a computerized stack of three-by-five index cards that gives you quick reference to names, addresses, phone numbers, and all other information stored—even graphics—in the cardfile. Cardfile is an excellent way to store free-form information that you may need to retrieve quickly.

Each *card* in Cardfile has two parts: a single index line at the top and an area for text or graphics below. Cards always are arranged alphabetically by the index line (see fig. 14.21). The active card is the top card on the stack.

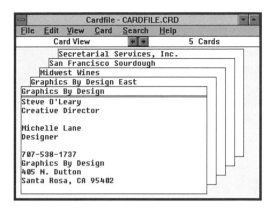

Fig. 14.21
Cards in Cardfile store information you can get at quickly.

You can have as many cards in a Cardfile file as the computer's memory can hold, and you can use as many Cardfile files as the disk can hold.

> **Note**
>
> Cardfile is convenient for handling small amounts of simple information. While it can function to keep track of clients or mailing lists you will be more efficient and less frustrated if you use a true mailing list manager, personal information manager (PIM), or database to handle large or related lists of information.

Opening and Closing the Cardfile

You open the Cardfile application from the Accessories window in Program Manager by double-clicking the Cardfile icon. After you open the application, a new, untitled cardfile appears on-screen.

You also can open new or existing files from within Cardfile by opening the **F**ile menu and choosing **O**pen or **N**ew. When you open a new file from within Cardfile, the currently open file closes. If you made changes to this file, a dialog box asks whether you want to save the changes. Choose **Y**es to save current changes, **N**o to discard the changes, or Cancel to return to the file.

You also can simultaneously open a Cardfile file and the Cardfile application by double-clicking a data file from File Manager. Cardfile data files have the extension CRD.

You can close a Cardfile file only by opening a new file or by closing Cardfile. To close Cardfile, open the Control menu and choose **C**lose, or open the **F**ile menu and choose E**x**it.

Entering Information

After opening a new cardfile, you see a single blank card (see fig. 14.22). The insertion point flashes in the top left corner of the card, just below the double line. This location is where you type information, such as names, addresses, and phone numbers, in the body of the card. To enter information in the card, just begin typing. Use Tab, Backspace, and the space bar to arrange the text. If you reach the right edge of the card, the text wraps to the next line.

Fig. 14.22
A new cardfile, displaying only a blank card.

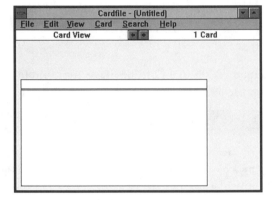

The index line at the top of the card is important: Cardfile arranges cards alphabetically by index lines. After you type the body of the first card, you are ready to enter an index line.

To type text in the index line, follow these steps:

1. Open the **E**dit menu and choose **I**ndex, or press F6. The Index dialog box appears (see fig. 14.23).

Fig. 14.23
The Index dialog box.

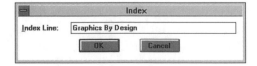

2. In the **I**ndex Line text box, type the text that identifies the contents of the card. Remember that cards are arranged alphabetically by index lines.

3. Choose OK or press Enter. The insertion point returns to the body of
   the card.

Like the cards in a rotary card file, Cardfile cards always stay alphabetized—
even when a card in the middle of the stack is on top. If you want to arrange
the Cardfile alphabetically by last name, type the last name first in the index
line. You can begin an index line with a number; numbers are listed before
letters in alphabetical order.

To edit existing index lines, select the card and choose the **E**dit **I**ndex command or press the F6 key.

Inserting Pictures in a Card

You can paste pictures of all kinds in Cardfile cards: graphs from Microsoft
Excel or 1-2-3, sketches from Paintbrush or Draw, clip art from files of graphics, and even scanned images of photographs.

Three ways are available to insert a picture in a card:

- The simplest way is to copy and paste into the card a picture from a
  graphics application that does not support object linking and embedding. After pasting, you cannot edit this picture; you must replace it
  with another picture.

- You can *embed* a picture. The picture must be created by a graphics
  application that supports object embedding, such as Paintbrush or
  Draw. The advantage of embedded pictures is that these images contain
  all the information needed to recreate and edit the picture. Embed a
  picture when you don't need to update many copies of the picture and
  when you want the data in the picture to go with the cardfile so that
  the receiver of the cardfile can make changes.

- You can *link* the image. The picture must come from an application
  that supports object linking. By default, Cardfile updates linked graphics when you change the original picture in the original file. Linking is
  useful when you have one original picture or chart that feeds into multiple documents. By updating the single original, all the documents that
  use this picture are also updated. A disadvantage of linking is that if you
  want to send the cardfile to another user, you should send copies of all
  the linked pictures used in the cardfile.

To learn more about object linking and embedding, read Chapter 6,
"Advanced Data Sharing."

III

Using Windows Accessories

You can include only one picture in a card.

Figure 14.24 shows a map that was copied from Paintbrush and pasted in a Cardfile card.

Fig. 14.24
Applications such as Paintbrush can create unlinked pictures, embedded objects, or linked pictures.

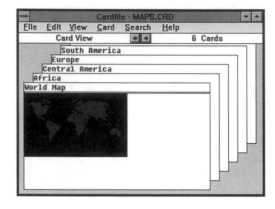

If you attempt to edit a picture that isn't linked or embedded, an alert box appears with the message `Cannot activate static object`.

Adding Cards

◀ "Linking Data between Applications," p. 203

To add a new card, follow these steps:

1. Open the **C**ard menu and choose **A**dd or press F7. The Add dialog box appears.

2. In the **A**dd text box, type an index line for the new card.

3. Choose OK or press Enter.

The new card with the index line you just typed is displayed on top of the stack. The insertion point is at the top left of the card, ready for you to type the contents of the card.

Searching through the Cards

Cardfile provides several ways to search through the stack of cards and bring the card you want to the front of the stack. You can scroll through the cards, as described in this section, or you can search through the cards to find a card with specific information, as described in the following section.

In the status bar of the Cardfile window, you see a pair of arrows. You can scroll through the cards, one card at a time, by clicking these arrows. To scroll back one card, click left; to scroll ahead one card, click right. The PgUp and

PgDn keys on the keyboard perform the same tasks. These and other ways of scrolling in Cardfile are summarized in the following table.

Direction To Scroll	Action
Backward one card	PgUp Click the left arrow
Forward one card	PgDn Click the right arrow
To a specific card	Click the card's index line
To first card	Ctrl+Home
To last card	Ctrl+End
To card with index, beginning with *letter*	Shift+Ctrl+*letter*

You can search through the cards in a Cardfile by the index line or by the information in the body of the card. Both searches use a menu command and a dialog box to locate the card that contains the word or phrase you want to find. A third menu command enables you to quickly repeat the most recent search.

To search through index lines in Cardfile, follow these steps:

1. Open the **S**earch menu and choose **G**o To or press F4. The Go To dialog box appears.

2. In the **G**o To text box, type any portion of the index line you want to find—even a partial word works (see fig. 14.25). Because the search isn't case-sensitive, you can type either upper- or lowercase letters.

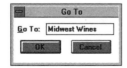

Fig. 14.25
Using the Search Go To command to search through index lines.

3. Choose OK or press Enter.

After you select OK, the first card with the specified text in the index line is brought to the top of the stack.

> **Note**
>
> To quickly bring up the first card with a specific beginning letter in the index line, press Shift+Ctrl+*letter*. Press Shift+Ctrl+M, for example, to bring to the top of the stack the first card that has *M* as the first letter of the card's index line.

To search through information in the body of the cards, follow these steps:

1. Open the **S**earch menu and choose **F**ind. The Find dialog box appears (see fig. 14.26).

Fig. 14.26
Using the Find dialog box to search through text in the cards themselves.

2. In the Fi**n**d What text box, type any portion of the information for which you want to search (a partial word also works with this search).

3. From the direction options, select **U**p or **D**own and the Match **C**ase option if you want to make the search sensitive to upper- and lowercase.

4. Choose the **F**ind Next button.

Cardfile finds and selects the first occurrence of the word. To continue the search, choose **F**ind Next. To close the dialog box, choose Cancel. To repeat the most recent search after closing the dialog box, choose the **S**earch Find **N**ext command (or press F3).

> **Note**
>
> In the Find dialog box shown in figure 14.26, choosing OK or pressing Enter brings to the top of the stack the next card that contains the letters *ted* anywhere in the body of the card. The search may bring up a card that contains the word *interested*. If you are looking for the name Ted and want the search to ignore the letters ted within words, use the space bar to enter a space before and after the search word: <space>**ted**<space>.

Duplicating and Deleting Cards

Often, the information on two cards is so similar that duplicating the current card and making minor changes to the duplicate is faster than typing a new card. You may want, for example, two separate cards for two people in the same company—the names and phone numbers are different but the company name and address are the same.

To duplicate a card, follow these steps:

1. Bring the card you want to duplicate to the top of the stack.

2. Open the **C**ard menu and choose Du**p**licate.

Using normal Windows text-editing procedures, edit the duplicated card text. (Choose the **E**dit **I**ndex command or double-click the index line to edit the index line.)

You can delete from Cardfile all cards you no longer need. To delete a card, follow these steps:

1. Bring the card you want to delete to the top of the stack.

2. Open the **C**ard menu and choose **D**elete. A message box appears, asking for confirmation.

3. Choose OK or press Enter.

Caution

After you delete a card, you cannot use the **E**dit **U**ndo command to undo the deletion. Be absolutely certain that you no longer need the information on a card before you delete it.

You can retrieve an important card that you deleted, provided you have not saved Cardfile to disk after deleting the card. Open a new Cardfile application from the Accessories window and reopen the same file on which you are currently working. A copy of the unedited Cardfile on the disk loads into memory. From the unedited file, copy the card you accidentally deleted and paste it in the file where the card is missing.

Another way to recover from an accidental deletion is to choose the **F**ile **O**pen command and reopen the current file. This method closes the current file. Do not save the changes. Use care when performing this procedure and

III

Using Windows Accessories

use this method only when you don't mind losing all changes made since the last time you saved the file.

Editing and Moving Cardfile Text

You can change, add, or delete text from a card or the index line, move text or graphics from one card to another, transfer data from Cardfile to another application (such as Notepad or Write), or transfer text or graphics to Cardfile from another application (such as Write or Paintbrush).

To edit the text on a Cardfile card, display the card you want to change. The insertion point flashes at the top left of the card. Use normal editing techniques to edit the text: move the insertion point where you want to make a change by positioning the I-beam and clicking the mouse button or by pressing the arrow keys. Then press Backspace or Del to delete text or just type to insert text. Select longer blocks of text to edit by dragging the mouse across the text or by holding down the Shift key and pressing the arrow keys. Just type to replace selected text or press Del or Backspace to remove the text.

If you want to edit an index line, you must display the card and choose the **E**dit **I**ndex command. If you have a mouse, double-click the index line of the top card. The Index Line dialog box appears, in which you make the changes.

You can move a single picture in a card anywhere in the lower area. To move a picture with a mouse, open the **E**dit menu and choose Pictur**e**, and then drag the picture to the new location. To move a picture with the keyboard, open the **E**dit menu and choose Pictur**e**, and then press the arrow keys to move the picture.

◀ "Transferring Data with Copy and Paste," p. 190
Two more useful editing commands are **U**ndo and **R**estore. Cardfile *remembers* and can undo the most-recent edit—if you use **U**ndo before you make another change. Cardfile also remembers the information on the card before editing began and can restore the card to original condition if you do not turn to another card after editing the first card.

To undo the most recent edit, open the **E**dit menu and choose **U**ndo, or press Ctrl+Z. To restore a card to original condition, open the **E**dit menu and choose **R**estore.

Viewing an Index List

After you first open Cardfile, you view the entire first card. You can see all the information on the top card but cannot see more than a few cards at a time. For a quick review of a file's contents, you can look at only the index lines (see fig. 14.27).

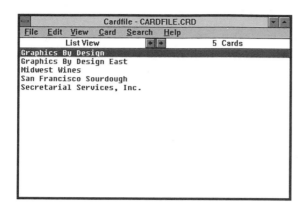

Fig. 14.27
A list of the index
lines in Cardfile.

To view a list of the index lines, open the **V**iew menu and choose **L**ist. To
restore the full view of the cards, open the **V**iew menu and choose **C**ard.

As a shortcut, you can double-click any index line listed in the List View
window. The Index dialog box appears with the selected index line highlighted and ready for changes.

Dialing a Phone with Cardfile

If your computer is connected to a Hayes or Hayes-compatible modem, you
can use Cardfile to dial a phone number that appears on a card. You must be
in the Card view.

When you choose the **C**ard Au**t**odial command or press F5, Cardfile dials the
first number that appears on the top card. Figure 14.28 shows Cardfile just
after the **C**ard Au**t**odial command has been chosen. Notice that the phone
number in the dialog box is the same as the phone number on the top card.
To dial another number on the card, select this number before you choose
the **C**ard Autodial command. To change the number after choosing Au**t**odial,
type the new number in the **N**umber text box in the Autodial dialog box.

Fig. 14.28
Dialing numbers
with Cardfile's
Autodial
command.

If you select the **U**se Prefix box, Autodial dials the number in the Prefix box
before dialing the phone number on the card, which is helpful for long-
distance dialing. After you type a prefix in the Prefix box, the prefix remains
until you enter a new prefix.

When you type a phone number on a card, be sure that you include the area code (if different from your area code). Leave no spaces between numbers; spaces cause some or all of the phone number to be ignored. Remove parentheses from around the area code; numbers between parentheses are ignored. Hyphens don't interfere with autodialing, so a good format for phone numbers is (707) 555-4247.

The first time you use Autodial to dial a number, check the dial settings (choose **S**etup in the Autodial dialog box). All settings, the dial type, port, and baud rate, stay set and don't have to be changed. After you select Setup, a dialog box appears, from which you make the following choices:

1. Depending on the kind of phone line you have, from the Dial **T**ype box, select Tone or Pulse.

2. From the **P**ort box, select COM1, COM2, COM3, or COM4, depending on the port to which the modem is connected.

3. From the **B**aud Rate box, select 110, 300, 1200, 2400, 4800, 9600, or 19200, depending on the modem's baud rate.

Tone or Pulse Phone?

If you don't know what kind of phone line you have, try the following experiment. Pick up the phone and dial a few numbers. If you hear different tones when you dial, you have a touch-tone phone. If you hear clicks, you have a pulse phone.

◄ "Selecting
Communications
Parameters,"
p. 430

To dial a phone number with Autodial, follow these steps:

1. Display the card with the phone number you want to dial. If the number you want to dial is not the first number listed on the card, select the number you want to dial.

2. Open the **C**ard menu and choose Au**t**odial, or press F5.

3. Select Pre**f**ix and type a dialing prefix if necessary.

4. Select **U**se Prefix if you want Autodial to begin dialing with the prefix (usually not needed for local calls).

5. If necessary, choose **S**etup and make the appropriate dialog-box selections.

6. Choose OK or press Enter. The computer dials and displays a message box with instructions.

7. Pick up the phone receiver when instructed to do so by the dialog box.

8. Choose OK or press Enter to complete the connection.

To make Autodial pause or wait during dialing, insert a comma. For example, type a comma after a prefix to add a 5-second delay after the prefix.

Merging Cardfile Data Files and Counting the Cards

You can have as many different Cardfile files as you want. You can have one file for business contacts, one file for personal friends, a file for pictures you use frequently, and so on. On certain occasions, however, you may want to merge multiple Cardfile files into a single file.

A special command appends the contents of an unopened Cardfile to the open Cardfile. The application then alphabetizes all the cards. The unopened file is preserved in original form, and the open file includes both files.

To merge two Cardfile files, follow these steps:

1. Open the Cardfile you want to contain both files.

2. Open the **F**ile menu and choose **M**erge.

3. From the File **N**ame list, select the file you want to merge in the open file.

4. Choose OK or press Enter.

5. If you want to preserve both original files, save the resulting Cardfile file under a new name.

Saving and Printing Cardfile Documents

To print the top card in the stack, choose the **F**ile **P**rint command. To print all the cards in a Cardfile, choose the **F**ile Print A**l**l command. No dialog boxes appear after you select the command; the cards just print on the se-lected printer. You can cancel printing by selecting the Cancel button that appears in the on-screen status box during printing. The cards are printed as actual card representations, which you can cut out and tape to cards on a rotary file.

To select a printer, choose the **F**ile **P**rint Setup command. In the Print Setup dialog box, select **D**efault Printer or Specific **P**rinter and then select the printer you want from the list of installed printers.

Tip

Before you choose the **F**ile Print All com-mand, you can check how many cards are in the file by looking at the right-hand side of the status bar (immediately below the menu bar).

III

Using Windows Accessories

When Cardfile documents are saved, they receive the default extension, CRD. You can use a different extension, but if you do, Cardfile doesn't list the file in the Open dialog box, and you can't open the file directly from File Manager.

To save and name a Cardfile, follow these steps:

1. Open the **F**ile menu and choose Save **A**s.

2. Type a name in the File **N**ame box.

3. From the **D**irectories list box, select the directory in which you want to save the file. By default, Cardfile saves files in the current directory.

4. Choose OK or press Enter.

To save an existing Cardfile with the same name, open the **F**ile menu and choose **S**ave. The new version of the file replaces the existing version on disk.

If, when you save a file, you assign a file name already in use, Cardfile asks whether you want to replace the original file with the new file. If you do, choose **Y**es; if not, choose **N**o and type a different name.

Performing Desktop Calculations with Calculator

Calculator performs all the calculations common to a standard calculator. Calculator, however, has added advantages: you can keep this calculator on-screen alongside other applications, and you can copy numbers between Calculator and other applications.

Calculator works so much like the pocket version that you need little help getting started (see fig. 14.29).

Fig. 14.29
The Standard
Calculator.

Calculator's keypad, the on-screen representation, contains familiar number keys, along with memory and simple math keys. A display window just above the keypad shows the numbers you enter and the results of calculations. If your computational needs are more advanced, you can choose a different view of the calculator, the Scientific view (see fig. 14.30).

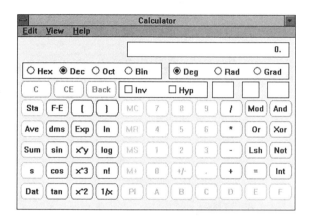

Fig. 14.30
The Scientific Calculator.

Calculator has only three menus: **E**dit, **V**iew, and **H**elp. The **E**dit menu contains two simple commands for copying and pasting, the **V**iew menu switches between the Standard and Scientific views, and the **H**elp menu is the same as in all Windows accessories.

Although you cannot change the size of Calculator (as you can other Windows applications), you can shrink Calculator to an icon for easy availability when working in another application.

Opening, Closing, and Operating the Calculator

You open the Calculator application by double-clicking the Calculator icon in the Accessories window in Program Manager. Calculator opens in the same view (Standard or Scientific) that was displayed the last time Calculator was used.

You close Calculator by choosing **C**lose from the Control menu, double-clicking the Control menu box, or pressing Alt+F4.

To use Calculator with the mouse, just click the appropriate number and sign keys like you press buttons on a desk calculator. Numbers appear in the display window as you select them, and the results appear after the calculations are performed.

Operating Calculator with the keyboard also is easy. To enter numbers, use either the numbers across the top of the keyboard, or you can use the numeric keypad (although you first must activate NumLock). To calculate, press the keys on the keyboard that match the Calculator keys. If the Calculator button reads +, for example, press the + key on the keyboard (press either the + key near the Backspace key or the + key on the numeric keypad). Table 14.3 shows the Calculator keys for the keyboard.

Table 14.3 Calculator Keys		
Calculator Key	**Function**	**Keyboard Key**
MC	Clear memory	Ctrl+L
MR	Display memory	Ctrl+R
M+	Add to memory	Ctrl+P
MS	Store value in memory	Ctrl+M
CE	Delete displayed value	Del
Back	Delete last digit in displayed value	Backspace
+/−	Change sign	F9
/	Divide	/
*	Multiply	*
−	Subtract	-
+	Add	+
sqrt	Square root	@
%	Percent	%
1/x	Calculate reciprocal	R
C	Clear	Esc
=	Equals	= or Enter

Working with the Memory Function

You can use Calculator's memory to total the results of several calculations. The memory holds a single number, which starts as zero; you can add to, display, or clear this number, or you can store another number in memory. After the number in memory appears in the display window, you can perform calculations on the number, just as you can on any other number. When a number is stored in memory, the letter M appears in the box above the sqrt key on the Calculator.

Copying Numbers between Calculator and Other Applications

When working with many numbers or complex numbers, you make fewer mistakes if you copy Calculator results to other applications rather than re-typing the result. To copy a number from the Calculator to another application, follow these steps:

1. In the Calculator display window, perform the math calculations required to display the number.

2. Open the **E**dit menu and choose **C**opy (Ctrl+C).

3. Activate the application you want to receive the calculated number.

4. Position the insertion point in the newly opened application where you want the number copied.

5. In the newly opened application, open the **E**dit menu and choose **P**aste (or its equivalent).

You can copy and paste a number from another application to Calculator. After the number is in the calculator, you can perform calculations with the number and then copy the result back in the application.

A number pasted into Calculator erases the number currently shown in the display window.

To copy a number from another application to Calculator, follow these steps:

1. In the other application, select the number.

2. Open the **E**dit menu and choose **C**opy (or its equivalent) from the application.

3. Activate Calculator, and open the **E**dit menu and choose **P**aste or press Ctrl+V.

If you paste a formula in Calculator, the result appears in the display window. If you copy 5+5 from Write and paste the calculation into Calculator, the resulting number 10 appears. If you paste a function, such as @ for square root, Calculator performs the function on the number displayed. If, for example, you copy @ from a letter in Write and paste in a Calculator displaying the number 25, the result 5 appears.

Numbers and most operators (such as + and –) work fine when pasted in the Calculator display, but Calculator interprets some characters as commands. The following table lists the characters that Calculator interprets as commands.

Character	Interpreted As
C	Ctrl+L (clears memory)
E	Scientific notation in decimal mode; the number E in hexadecimal mode
M	Ctrl+M (stores current value in memory)
P	Ctrl+P (adds value to memory)
Q	C button or Esc key (clears current calculation)
R	Ctrl+R (displays value in memory)
:	Ctrl if before a letter (:m is Ctrl+M); function-key letter if before a number (:2 is F2)
\	Data key

Using the Scientific Calculator

If you have ever written an equation wider than a sheet of paper, you're a good candidate for using the Scientific Calculator. The Scientific Calculator is a special view of the Calculator.

To display the Scientific Calculator, open the **V**iew menu and choose **S**cientific.

The Scientific Calculator works the same as the Standard Calculator but adds many advanced functions. You can work in one of four number systems: hexadecimal, decimal, octal, or binary. You can perform statistical calculations, such as averages and statistical deviations. You can calculate sines, cosines, tangents, powers, logarithms, squares, and cubes. These specialized functions aren't described here but are well documented in Calculator's Help command. To learn more about using Help, refer to Chapter 2, "Getting Help."

Keeping Time with Clock

Windows comes equipped with a standard clock, which you can display on-screen in different sizes (see figs. 14.31 and 14.32). Even after you shrink the clock to an icon at the bottom of the screen, the hands still are readable in Analog view.

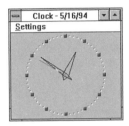

Fig. 14.31
The Clock in Analog view.

Fig. 14.32
The Clock in Digital view.

Start Clock by double-clicking the Clock icon in the Accessories window in Program Manager. Close Clock by choosing **C**lose from the Control menu or pressing Alt+F4. By minimizing the application instead of closing it, you can keep Clock visible on-screen; even as a small icon at the bottom of the screen, the time is readable. You can also resize the clock face by dragging the Clock window's edges or corners.

Clock has one menu—**S**ettings. From this menu you choose whether to display the clock in **A**nalog or **D**igital view. Analog view shows a round clock face with ticking hands; Digital view shows a numeric readout of the time. You also can change the font used in the Digital view, remove the title bar, and choose whether or not to display seconds and the date (in the title bar). Windows remembers the settings you choose and uses these settings every time you start Clock.

The time displayed by Clock is based on either the computer's internal clock (if the computer has an internal clock) or on the time you type when you start the computer. If the time on Clock is inaccurate, use Control Panel to

III

Using Windows Accessories

reset the computer's date/time, as described in Chapter 7, "Customizing with Control Panel."

Note

To display just the clock—with no title or menu bar—double-click the clock face or choose the **S**ettings **N**o Title command. (Repeat the procedure to redisplay the title and menu bars.) This technique works in either Analog or Digital view.

To change the font used for the Clock display, choose the **S**ettings Set **F**ont command and select the font you want to use from the **F**ont list. Choose OK.

Developing Strategic Skills with Minesweeper, Solitaire, and Networked Hearts

A good reason exists to include Minesweeper and Solitaire at the end of this chapter: many Windows users stay up until the late hours of the evening, trying to beat the computer at a challenging game of Minesweeper or Solitaire! Now you have a good excuse for playing these games: you can claim that you're developing strategic skills and honing your hand-eye coordination. And if you use Windows for Workgroups, you can develop a closer working relationship with members of your workgroup while learning about workgroup applications by playing Hearts against people on other computers.

To open the game applications, double-click icons in the Games window (they are not located in the Accessories window). Close either game by choosing E**x**it from the **G**ame menu.

Playing Solitaire

After you start Solitaire, you see a screen like the one shown in figure 14.33.

The Solitaire screen has three active areas: the deck in the upper left corner of the playing area; the four suit stacks in the upper right corner of the playing area (which start out empty); and the seven row stacks in the bottom half of the screen. The number of cards in each row stack increases from one to seven, from left to right. The top card in each row stack is face up; all other cards in each stack are face down.

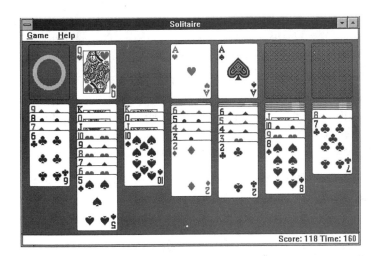

Fig. 14.33
Playing Solitaire.

The object of the game is to move all the cards from the row stacks into the suit stacks at the top right of the screen. You must build the stack upwards, in sequential order, from Ace to King, one suit per stack. To start the stack, you need an Ace.

To get an Ace, you must either display this card in the lower stacks or turn over an Ace from the deck. The lower stacks build from high cards downward, in suits of alternating colors. You can build a lower stack, for example, starting with the King of Diamonds, the Queen of Spades, the Jack of Hearts, the Ten of Clubs, and so on. When you get an Ace, you can move the card to an upper suit stack and start building the suit stack there.

In the lower stacks, you can move cards between the stacks or from the deck to the stacks. You can move a single card at a time or a group of cards. After all the upturned cards are moved from a lower stack, you can turn over the top card on the stack. To turn a card, click it with the mouse button or move the arrow to the card (by using the arrow keys) and press the space bar.

To deal from the deck, select the deck (by clicking the deck or by pressing the arrow keys to move to the deck and pressing the space bar). The dealt card appears to the right of the deck. If you can, move this card to a stack. You can move, for example, a King onto a blank space in the lower stack area.

To move a card (or cards), click and drag with the mouse. (You can move a card quickly from the lower stacks to the upper suit stacks by double-clicking the card you want to move.) You can use the left and right arrow keys to move the selection arrow to the card you want to move: press Enter, use the arrow keys to move the card where you want, and press Enter to complete the move. If you want to move more than one card in a stack, press the up-arrow key to select a card higher up in the stack before you press Enter. If you make an illegal move, Solitaire moves the card to its original location.

Solitaire offers several options. Choose the **G**ame **De**ck command to choose a different deck illustration. Choose the **G**ame **O**ptions command to select the number of cards in each draw (one or three cards) and scoring options. Solitaire even has a **G**ame **U**ndo command to undo the last action.

When you finish playing and want to start a new game, choose the **G**ame **D**eal command.

To learn the rules of Solitaire, browse through the **H**elp command.

Watch the Dealer's Hand!

If you're playing with the deck that shows a hand full of aces, watch what the dealer has up his sleeve! Give it time and you may see amazing things. Other decks also show interesting animation when you use the **T**imed setting.

Note

Undoubtedly, when you have played a few games of Draw Three solitaire, you will have the experience of seeing the one card you need just below the top card in the drawing deck. Once you've started a Draw Three game, you can't switch to a Draw One game. But you can cheat!! Choose the **G**ame **U**ndo command and then hold down the Ctrl, Alt, and Shift keys all at once. As long as you hold down these keys, you can turn over one card at a time. Good luck!!!

Playing Minesweeper

Minesweeper is a game of analysis and tension, requiring a totally different flair than Solitaire.

When you open Minesweeper, you are faced with a grid of squares that represent a mine field (see fig. 14.34). The goal of this game is to mark all the mines; if you step on a mine, the game is over. When you step on a square, three outcomes are possible: the square contains a mine that "blows up," and the game ends; the square contains no mine, and the minesweeper indicates that no mines exist in the surrounding eight squares; or the square contains no mine, and the minesweeper indicates that a certain number of mines exist in the surrounding eight squares (the number that appears in the square).

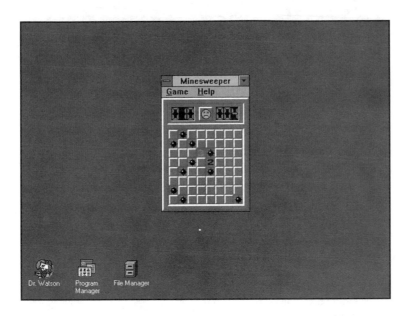

Fig. 14.34
Minesweeper is a game of analysis and tension.

As you successfully uncover squares without stepping on a mine, the information provided by your minesweeper helps you deduce which squares contain mines. When you know a square contains a mine, you can mark this square, which effectively deactivates this mine. The object of the game is to mark all mines *before* stepping on one.

To uncover a square, click it. If the square contains no mine, either a number appears in the square, indicating the number of mines in the surrounding eight squares, or a blank space appears. If the square contains a number, you can try to deduce and mark which of the surrounding squares contains a mine or mines. To mark a mine, click the square with the right mouse button.

Watch for patterns in the numbers. Once you play a few games, you will begin to see repeating patterns of numbers on the mine field. From those numbers, and the mines you can see, you can deduce where it is safe to take your next step.

Three predefined skill levels, which you select from the **G**ame menu, are available in Minesweeper: **B**eginner, **I**ntermediate, and **E**xpert. The levels differ in the size of the minefield and in the total number of mines per minefield. You also can define custom minefields with the **G**ame **C**ustom command. For more information on the rules of Minesweeper and some strategic hints on playing the game, choose the **H**elp command.

Win Every Single Time!

This tip gives you the secret weapon you need to win every time—a mine detector! To turn on the mine detector, follow these steps:

1. Change your Desktop color to black, using Control Panel.

2. Minimize all open applications except Minesweeper so that you can see the upper left corner of your desktop.

3. Start Minesweeper.

4. With the mouse pointer anywhere in the playing area, type xyzzy and press Enter.

5. Hold down the Shift key as you move the mouse pointer over the squares in Minesweeper.

A single white pixel appears in the upper left corner of your Desktop whenever the mouse pointer is over a square that doesn't cover a mine. You can't lose!

Starting and Playing Networked Hearts

Hearts is a card game that many people know. Many college grades have been marked down due to the affect of late night games of hearts and poker. Now you can bring the same productivity and late nights to your group at work by playing hearts over the network. Hearts is available only in Windows for Workgroups.

To start or join an open game of Hearts:

1. Double-click the Hearts icon in the Game group window in Program Manager.

   The Microsoft Hearts Network dialog box appears (see fig. 14.35).

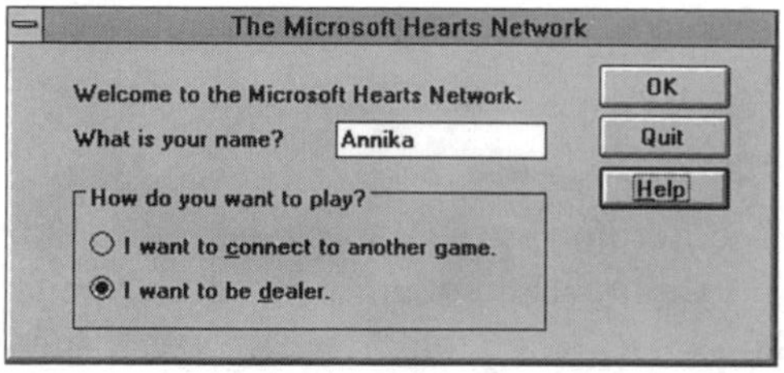

Fig. 14.35
You can start a game as a dealer or join a game as a player.

The Microsoft Hearts Network
Welcome to the Microsoft Hearts Network.
What is your name? Annika
How do you want to play?
○ I want to connect to another game.
● I want to be dealer.
OK Quit Help

2. Type the name you want to be identified with to the group in the What Is Your Name? text box.

3. Select the hand that you want to play from the How Do You Want To Play? group. If you want to start the game and be dealer, select the I want to be **d**ealer option button. If you want to join a game as a player, select the I want to **c**onnect to another game option button.

4. Choose OK or press Enter.

The Hearts card table and dealt hands appear, as shown in figure 14.36.

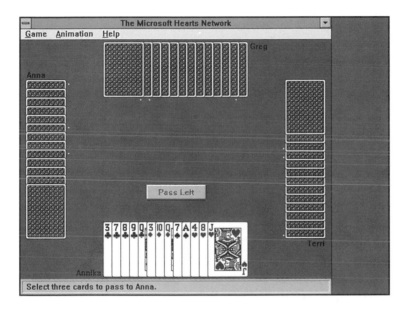

Fig. 14.36
You can play hearts against others in your workgroup or against the computer.

It takes four card hands to play Hearts, but if you don't have enough players to play, the computer plays for the absent players. If you play by yourself against the computer, you must play the dealer's hand. If someone quits during the game, the computer continues to play his or her hand.

As you play Hearts, the appropriate card hands display on each player's screen. To learn how to play Hearts and learn about the options available in the game, choose the **H**elp **C**ontents command and select from such topics as Keep Score, Play the Game, Start the Game, Understand the Rules, or Use Strategy.

From Here...

You can learn how to use the other applications that come with Windows by referring to the following chapters.

- Chapter 10, "Using Windows Write," explains how to use the word processor that comes with Windows.

- Chapter 11, "Using Windows Paintbrush," teaches you how to use the painting application that comes with Windows.

- Chapter 12, "Using Windows Terminal," explains how to use the Window's telecommunications application.

Chapter 15

Using Windows for Workgroups Mail and PC Fax

A workgroup can accomplish far more when everyone can communicate easily. Mail is a program that enables you and others in your workgroup to send and store *messages*, which are text notes that you send to or receive from other users on your network. You also have the option of attaching files to a message—for example, a word processing document or spreadsheet file. Mail is a stripped-down version of Microsoft's full-featured mail application. Although it lacks some of the more high-powered electronic-mail features, Mail's design meets the needs of small groups of users who work together.

In some ways, Mail offers features more powerful than mail applications not designed specifically for use on a Windows network. You can accomplish the following tasks (among others) with Mail:

- Send messages to coworkers
- Receive messages
- Attach files to messages
- Work with messages and files away from the office
- Create linked files across the network
- Embed objects in messages and files

PC Fax is an application that comes with Windows for Workgroups 3.11. PC Fax enables you to send or receive faxes in Windows. You can send a fax from within a Windows document or from within Mail. Faxes that you receive show up as a Mail message in the Mail in box, even if you are not on a network. You can use Fax Viewer, a separate application, to view, save, or print faxes that you receive.

This chapter shows you how to use Mail and PC Fax to become more efficient in working with others.

In this chapter, you will learn how to:

- Set up a new Postoffice for Mail

- Send a Mail message and attach files to a message

- Read and manage your mail

- Manage a mail system

- Send a fax from within your workgroup

- Receive faxes and documents embedded in a fax

Starting Mail

Mail is a message system built around a Postoffice. The Mail Postoffice can be set up on any workgroup member's computer. The workgroup member whose computer stores the Postoffice directory administers the mail system. For details on creating and maintaining Postoffice, see "Administering the Postoffice" later in this chapter.

Before any workgroup member can begin to send and receive mail, the member must set up a user account with the Postoffice (see the following section, "Creating Your User Account"). Either the administrator or the member can set up the account. After the member has a user account, the Postoffice acts as a collective mail drop with an Inbox folder and an Outbox folder for the member, as well as a Sent Mail folder that holds copies of the messages the user sends.

You don't need to be logged on to the network (*on-line*) to work with your messages and their attached files. If you work off-line, you don't have to deal with mail interruptions; you can even work with messages off-site. The "Using Mail Off-Line" section later in this chapter describes how to work with your messages off-line.

To start Mail, you first must start Windows. You normally start Windows by typing **win** at the DOS prompt. Your system may start Windows automatically, or you may have some other arrangement. For more information on starting and setting up Windows and Windows applications, see Chapter 1, "Operating Windows," Chapter 3, "Controlling Applications with Program Manager," and Chapter 24, "Installing and Optimizing Windows 3.1."

> **Note**
>
> A Postoffice must be created before the first person in a workgroup can use Mail. If no one has set up a Postoffice, refer to the section "Administering the Postoffice" near the end of this chapter for information on how to set up a Postoffice.
>
> If you have created a user account and only need to sign-in and check your mail, refer to "Signing In to Mail" later in this chapter.

The first time you start Mail, you must connect to an existing Postoffice, and you must create a user account if the Postoffice administrator hasn't already created one for you. See the following section, "Creating Your User Account," for details on how to set up a user account.

To start Mail and connect to a Postoffice, follow these steps:

1. Open the Network group window within Program Manager.

2. Choose the Mail icon, which looks like a gold-plated mail slot (see fig. 15.1).

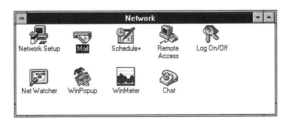

Fig. 15.1
The Mail icon in the Network program group.

The first time you execute this step, Mail displays the Welcome to Mail dialog box (see fig. 15.2).

3. Choose the **C**onnect to an Existing Postoffice option; then choose OK. The Network Disk Resources dialog box opens (see fig. 15.3).

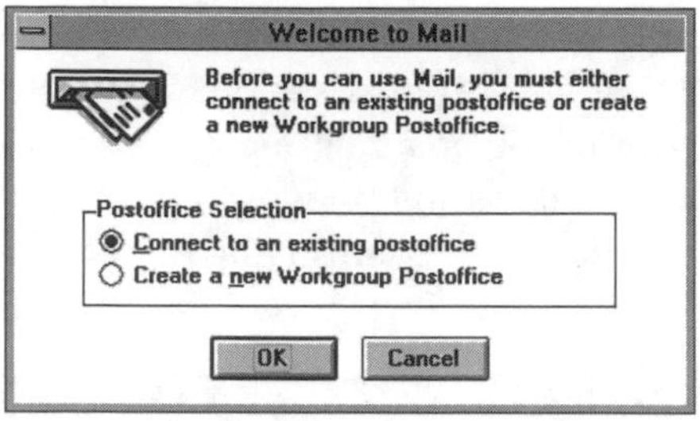

Fig. 15.2
Windows for
Workgroups
greets new users
and invites them
to connect to an
existing
Postoffice.

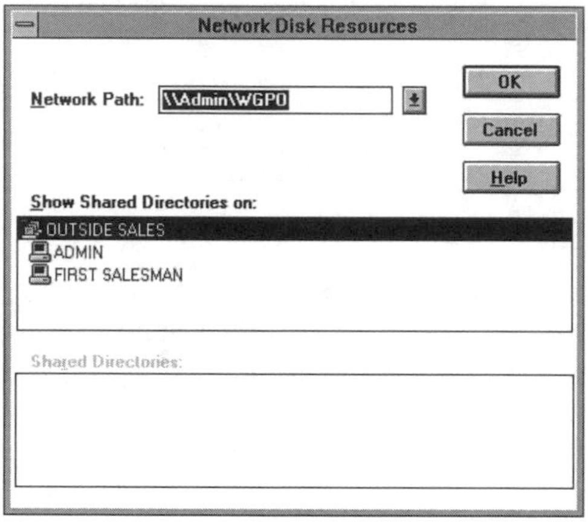

Fig. 15.3
The Network
Disk Resources
dialog box.

4. If you know the location of your workgroup's Postoffice, type the path in the **N**etwork Path text box. Use the following format:

   *computername**sharename*.

   (The term *computername* refers to the name of the computer and the drive on that computer where the Windows for Workgroups software is installed. The term *sharename* refers to the directory in *computername* that contains your workgroup's Postoffice.)

   If you are unsure of the path of the Postoffice, select the name of the computer containing the Postoffice in the **S**how Shared Directories On list box. The Shared Directories list box displays the shared directories contained on the selected computer. Select the shared directory containing your workgroup's Postoffice. The selected directory name appears in the **N**etwork Path text box.

5. Choose OK.

If the Postoffice directory is password-protected, Mail displays the Enter Shared Directory Password dialog box (see fig. 15.4). Type the password in the text box (the characters appear as asterisks), and then choose OK.

If the Postoffice directory isn't password-protected, this dialog box doesn't appear.

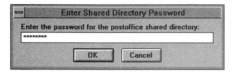

Fig. 15.4
The Enter Shared Directory Password dialog box.

6. Mail displays a dialog box that asks whether you have an account (see fig. 15.5).

Choose **Y**es if the administrator has created an account for you.

Click **N**o if you need to set up your account. See the following section for details on how to set up an account.

Fig. 15.5
The dialog box that asks whether you have an account.

Creating Your User Account

If you do not already have a user account when you connect to a Postoffice, as described in the preceding section, and if you click No when you are asked whether you have an account in the Postoffice, the Enter Your Account Details dialog box appears, as shown in figure 15.6.

Fig. 15.6
The Enter Your Account Details dialog box.

III

Using Windows Accessories

Tip
Because Postoffice is indifferent to case, you can use any combination of upper- and lowercase letters for your name, mailbox name, and password. Be sure to use words that are simple and easy to re- member.

To set up your user account, enter your name in the **N**ame text box, a name for your mailbox in the **M**ailbox text box, and a password in the **P**assword text box. All other entries are optional. After you complete the information in the dialog box, choose OK.

In the Enter Your Account Details dialog box, you must enter the following information:

- **N**ame. Enter a name of up to 30 characters.

- **M**ailbox. Enter a mailbox name of up to 10 characters.

- **P**assword. If you don't want to use the default password (PASSWORD), type a unique password of up to eight characters.

The following entries in the dialog box are optional:

- *Phone #1 and Phone #2.* Enter one or two phone numbers (for example, enter your office phone number and your fax number). You can use up to 32 characters for each number.

- **O**ffice. Enter up to 32 characters describing your office location (for example, *fourth floor, room 12*).

- **D**epartment. Enter up to 32 characters identifying your department name (for example, *Packaging* or *New Sales*).

- *Notes.* Enter a note of up to 128 characters.

> **Note**
>
> After you establish your user account, Mail creates the MSMAIL.INI file and the MSMAIL.MMF message file in your WINDOWS directory. The MMF file records all your messages and addresses (MSMAIL.MMF is the default file name). Every user should have a uniquely named MMF file.

Signing In to Mail

You need to connect to the Postoffice and create your user account only once. Subsequently, you can sign in to Mail each time you start Windows, using one of the following methods:

- Go through the normal sign-in and password procedures.

- Set up the Mail icon's properties to bypass the normal sign-in procedure.

To use the normal Mail start-up and sign-in procedures, follow these steps:

1. Choose the Mail icon in Program Manager's Network group window. The Mail Sign In dialog box appears (see fig. 15.7).

Fig. 15.7
The Mail Sign In dialog box.

2. Make sure that your mailbox **N**ame is correct.

3. In the **P**assword text box, type your password (Mail displays asterisks in place of the characters you type), and then choose OK. The Mail Inbox window opens (see fig. 15.8).

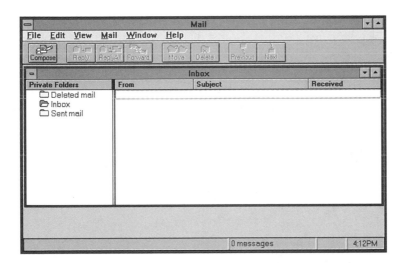

Fig. 15.8
The Mail application window and Inbox window at start-up.

Note

If security is a concern in your business or organization, be sure to create a password. Don't use the default password (PASSWORD).

To skip the sign-in procedures when you start Mail, follow these steps:

1. Choose the Mail icon in the Network group window in Program Manager.

Tip
You can automatically start Mail when Windows starts by dragging a copy of the Mail icon to Program Manager's StartUp group window. (For details on using Program Manager, see Chapter 3, "Controlling Applications with Program Manager.")

2. Open the **F**ile menu and choose **P**roperties, or press Alt+Enter, to display the Program Item Properties dialog box.

3. In the **C**ommand Line text box, at the end of the path statement, type a space, your mailbox name, another space, and then your password.

4. Choose OK to start Mail.

> **Note**
>
> If you are concerned about the security of your data, don't type your password in the command line.

Using Help

Like most Windows applications, Mail comes with its own Help file and on-line Help system. To access Help, you can open the **H**elp menu and choose the **C**ontents command or the **I**ndex command. You also can press F1 to access Help. If you access Help from a dialog box or while a command in the menu is selected, Mail displays Help for that dialog box or command. If you choose **H**elp **C**ontents, the Mail Help Contents window opens. In this window, expansion buttons reveal topic lists (see fig. 15.9). See Chapter 2, "Getting Help," for a detailed explanation of how to use the Help system.

Fig. 15.9
The Mail Help Contents window with a topic selected.

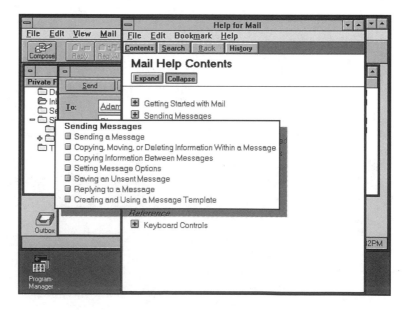

Quitting Mail

Quitting Mail is slightly different from quitting other applications. You can exit and sign out of Mail, or you can exit without signing out. If you exit and sign out, applications that require the Postoffice (such as Scheduler+) close when Mail closes, and you must sign in again if you restart Mail. To quit and sign out of Mail, open the **F**ile menu and choose Exit and Sign Ou**t**.

If you exit without signing out, other applications that depend on the Postoffice can run, and you don't have to sign in again when you restart Mail. To quit without signing out of Mail, open the **F**ile menu and choose E**x**it, open the Mail window's Control menu and choose **C**lose, or press Alt+F4.

> **Note**
>
> If no applications that depend on the Postoffice are running when you exit Mail, opening the **F**ile menu and choosing E**x**it signs you out of Mail.

Sending Messages with Mail

Sending messages to group members is a two-step operation. First, you compose and address your message; then you send the message. Mail gives you some options to consider, but sending a message can be as simple as making a phone call.

Composing the Message

To prepare a message, you first must display the Send Note window (see fig. 15.10). You display the window in one of three ways: by choosing the Compose button in the toolbar (refer to fig. 15.8), by opening the **M**ail menu and choosing Compose **N**ote, or by pressing Ctrl+N.

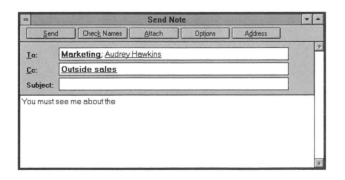

Fig. 15.10
The Mail Send Note window.

III

Using Windows Accessories

When composing your message, you first address the message by specifying the recipient in the **T**o text box. If you want to copy the message to other recipients, use the **C**c text box. You can type the address of the recipient or select the address from a list of addresses. The next two sections describe manual and automatic addressing of messages.

Addressing Mail Automatically

Mail contains an address list. New addresses are automatically added to the address list when you send a message to an address to which you have not sent a message before. The address list enables you to keep a list of people or groups to which you frequently send messages, reducing typing and the number of incorrect addresses. To address your message by using the address list, follow these steps:

1. Choose the A**d**dress button in the Send Note window, or open the **M**ail menu and choose A**d**dress. The Address dialog box appears (see fig. 15.11).

Directory button

Fig. 15.11
Use the Address dialog box to select addresses for your messages.

Personal Address Book button

Search button

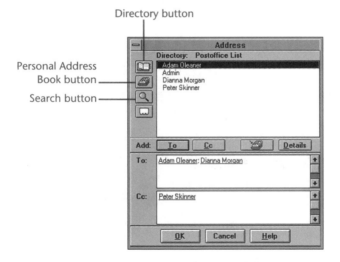

2. In the Postoffice List, select the names of people or groups to whom you want to send the message. Then choose the **T**o button. The names appear in the To text box.

3. In the Postoffice List, select the names of people or groups to whom you want to send copies of the message. Then choose the **C**c button. The names appear in the Cc text box.

4. Choose **O**K.

A later section of this chapter, "Sending the Message," describes other features of the Address dialog box.

The selected names appear in the **T**o and **C**c text boxes of the Send Note window. Mail underlines the names that match names in its records.

Addressing Mail Manually

If you decide to address your message by typing addresses in the **T**o and **C**c text boxes, you need to type only the first few characters of an address; then press Alt+K. Mail completes the entry from its address list.

To address the message manually, follow these steps:

1. In the **T**o text box, enter the name of the person(s) or group(s) to receive the message. To include multiple names, type a semicolon and a space between the names.

2. To send a copy of the message to another person or group, type the name(s) in the **C**c text box. To include multiple names, type a semicolon and a space between the names.

3. If you want to check your entries in the **T**o and **C**c text boxes, choose the Chec**k** Names button.

   If the entries don't match the names in Mail's address list of users, an information box appears, instructing you to check the names you typed.

   If the entries match Mail's address list, the names appear underlined in the **T**o and **C**c text boxes.

Completing the Message

After you address the message, click the Sub**j**ect text box or press Tab to move to that box. Then type the subject, using up to 480 characters (a brief subject is more considerate than a long one). You don't need to list a subject, but a subject listing helps workgroup members sort and prioritize incoming mail. After you finish typing the subject, move to the text-editing area. Your subject text appears in place of Send Note in the title bar of the Send Note window.

In the text-editing area, you can type and edit text as you do in many Windows text-editing or word processing programs, such as Write and Notepad. You can perform any of the following tasks:

Tip

You can cancel a message in the Send Note window at any time by pressing the Esc key.

III

Using Windows Accessories

- Enter letters, numbers, and symbols from the keyboard.

- Select and then delete text by opening the **E**dit menu and choosing **D**elete or by pressing Del.

- Change fonts. You have only two choices: the Windows default (Times New Roman) or a nonproportional typewriter typeface. Open the **V**iew menu and choose Change **F**ont to toggle between these fonts.

- Select and copy text to the Windows Clipboard by opening the **E**dit menu and choosing Cu**t** or **C**opy.

- Insert text copied from other Windows applications or other messages (that is, any text stored in the Clipboard) by placing the insertion point where you want to insert the text and then opening the **E**dit menu and choosing **P**aste. To copy between messages, you must close the message you copied from and open the message you are copying to; you cannot have two Send Note windows open at one time.

- Insert special characters from the Windows Character Map.

Saving or Storing the Message

After you finish entering the message, you can send the message immediately, as described in the following section. Occasionally, however, you may want to save the message as a text file (for example, if you want to use the message text in another application), or you may want to store it in a folder to be sent later.

To save a message as a text file, open the **F**ile menu and choose **S**ave As to display the Save Message dialog box. A truncated version of the text you entered in the Sub**j**ect box is used as the default file name that appears in the File **N**ame text box. The extension TXT is added to the file name.

You can store your message to send later by moving or copying it to a folder. Mail comes with three default folders: Deleted Mail, Inbox, and Sent Mail. You also can create your own folders (see "Creating and Using Folders" later in this chapter). You can store your message temporarily in a folder and then open and send the message later.

To store a message in a folder, follow these steps:

1. To copy the message, open the **F**ile menu and choose **C**opy. The Copy Message dialog box appears.

To move the message, click the Move button in the toolbar, or open the **F**ile menu and choose **M**ove. The Move Message dialog box appears.

The Copy Message and Move Message dialog boxes are identical except for the name in the title bar (see fig. 15.12).

Fig. 15.12
The Move Message and Copy Message dialog boxes are identical except for their names and functions.

2. Select a folder in the Move **T**o or Copy **T**o list box.

   As in any list, you can scroll the list to find a name that does not appear in the box. You cannot scroll horizontally to see beyond the right side of the box.

3. Choose OK. Mail moves or copies the message to the new folder and displays your Inbox window. When you select the folder to which the message was moved or copied, the listing of the message appears, with a gray envelope and note icon next to it.

Sending the Message

You can send a Mail message immediately after you compose it, or you can retrieve and send messages from any folder that is available to you. The Inbox window displays folder icons (Deleted Mail, Inbox, Sent Mail, and any folders you created) to the left of the message listing. (To learn how to create a folder, see "Creating and Using Folders" later in this chapter.)

Note

If you frequently send a message to the same addresses, copy a version to a new folder called Templates. (For a description of how to create a new folder, see "Creating and Using Folders" later in this chapter.) When you need to send that message, drag its template to the Outbox, adjust the text and address information as necessary, and send the message. Mail sends the message, but the template copy remains intact in the Template folder.

To send a message immediately, choose the **S**end button in the message's Send Note window after you finish addressing and composing the message. Mail delivers the message to the Inbox of the addressee(s).

To send a stored message from the Inbox window, open the folder in which you stored the message. The title bar displays the name of the new folder, and Mail lists the stored messages by priority, addressee, subject, and date and time sent.

From the folder, you can send a message in the following ways:

■ Double-click the message name, or select it and press Enter. You can change the addresses, if necessary.

■ Drag the message name to the Outbox (see fig. 15.13). Mail opens the Send Note window with the message title in the title bar. You can change the addresses, if necessary.

Fig. 15.13
To send the selected message, drag it to the Outbox.

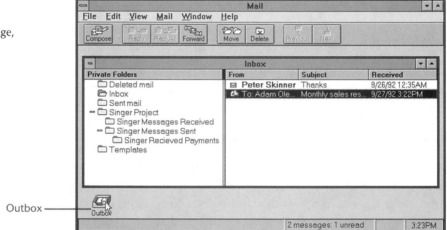

Outbox

Finding Addresses

Remembering all the names of all the users on the network and the many different groups may be difficult. Mail gives you a way to remember all the names and find them easily.

If you are familiar with the name, you will want to use the first method. In the **T**o text box of the Send Note window, begin typing a name; then press Alt+K. Mail completes the name if it finds a matching name in the address list. (For a description of this process, refer to "Composing the Message" earlier in this chapter.)

For other methods of entering addresses, use the Address dialog box. With the Send Note window or any message open, choose the **A**ddress button, or open the **M**ail menu and choose A**d**dress Mail to display the Address dialog box (refer to fig. 15.11). Then use one of the following methods:

■ Type the first letter of the name you want to find. The displayed list of users scrolls to the names beginning with that letter. Typing **S**, for example, could scroll the list to *Sales Group*, which may be followed by *Sam Taylor, Scot*, and any other names that fit in the list box. Select the desired name in the list box.

■ Click the Search button (a magnifying-glass icon) in the Address dialog box, or press Ctrl+F. The Name Finder dialog box appears, as shown in figure 15.14. In the text box, type as much of the name as you remember; then choose **F**ind. Name Finder searches for all occurrences of the specified characters. When the search is complete, Mail lists the matching names in the address list box; select the name you want. If the address you want doesn't appear, modify your entry in the Name Finder dialog box and try again.

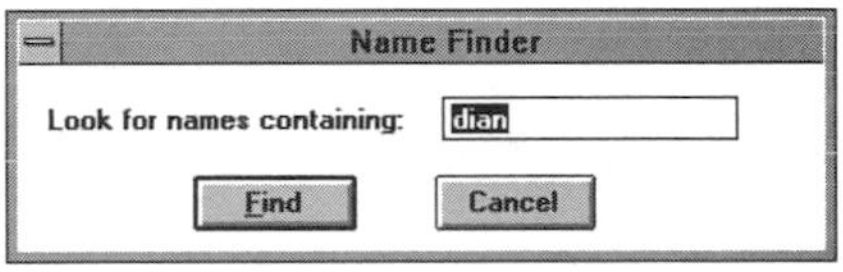

Fig. 15.14
Use the Name Finder dialog box to find and select users.

■ Click the Directory button (an address-book icon) in the Address dialog box, or press Ctrl+L. The Open Directory dialog box appears, listing two directories: your Personal Address Book and the Postoffice list. Select the directory you want to use, and choose OK. The list of users in the selected directory appears in the Address dialog box.

■ Click the Personal Address Book button (an index-card-file icon) in the Address dialog box, or press Ctrl+P. This address book records all users to whom you have sent a message and all personal groups that you have created. Search for names alphabetically, select the users, and choose the **T**o or **C**c button in the Address dialog box to add these names to the **T**o or **C**c text box.

You can select more than one user from the list in the Personal Address Book. To select more than one user, click the first user, hold down the Ctrl key, and click subsequent users. To deselect a user, hold down the Ctrl key and click the user. To use the keyboard, select the first user, press Shift+F8, use the up- and down-arrow keys to move to the next user, and press the space bar. Move to additional users and press the space bar. To deselect a user and retain the other selections, move to the selected user and press the space bar. To return to selecting a single user at a time, press Shift+F8 again.

Getting Details on a User

Even if Mail finds a name that matches your search criteria, you may not be sure that you have found the right address. If you are unsure, you can look at the detail information provided by the user when he or she first set up the account. To display the detail information, follow these steps:

1. Open the Address dialog box by clicking the **A**ddress button in the toolbar or by opening the **M**ail menu and choosing A**d**dress.

2. Find a potential addressee by using any of the methods described in the preceding section, "Finding Addresses."

3. Choose the **D**etails button in the Address dialog box. An information dialog box appears, with the addressee's name in the title bar.

Reading and Working with Messages

All your incoming messages are stored in your Inbox folder. At your convenience, you can read your messages. You then have several options: you can store the messages in a folder, forward them to other users, reply to them, print them, or delete them. You can accomplish each of these tasks easily in Mail, which enables you to use your electronic-mail system to streamline communications with your co-workers.

Reading Messages

Mail notifies you in a couple of different ways when you receive an incoming message. If you are working in another Windows application, your computer may beep to indicate that new messages have come in. You can control the way Mail notifies you (and how frequently it checks for new mail) by opening the **M**ail menu and choosing the **O**ptions command, as described in "Managing Messages with Mail" later in this chapter.

If you are viewing your Inbox in Mail when a message from another user arrives, your computer beeps, your mouse pointer briefly changes to an envelope icon, and the new message appears in the Inbox folder's list of messages. An icon of a closed envelope appears next to the listing, indicating that the message has not been read.

If Mail is reduced to an icon on your desktop when a message arrives, your computer beeps, and the icon changes to show an envelope popping out the mail slot. If you want to know when a message arrives while you are working in another application, you can minimize Mail (that is, reduce it to an icon on your desktop) and arrange your application windows so that you can see the Mail icon on your desktop. When a message arrives, you see the Mail icon change (and hear a beep), and you can quickly restore Mail to a window and read the message.

To read a message, follow these steps:

1. Switch to Mail and open the Inbox folder.

2. Select the message you want to read. The message appears in a window, as shown in figure 15.15.

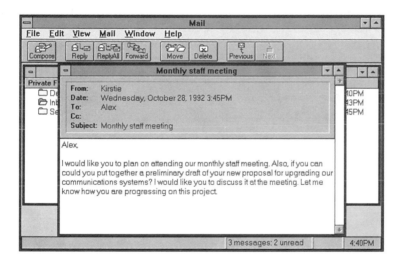

Fig. 15.15
When you open a message, it appears in its own window.

After you read a message, you can reply to the message, forward it to another address, print it, store it in a folder, save it as a text file, or delete it.

Replying to Messages
Replying to a letter is cordial but not always expedient. In the electronic-mail environment, replying to a message may lead to problems in disk storage space and may slow the network. Replying to every message you receive also may prove to be too great a task or one of low priority. If you need confirmation that an addressee received your message, Mail offers a Return Receipt option (see "Setting Message Options" later in this chapter).

Nevertheless, you may need to send a reply to workgroup members. You can reply to only the sender of a message or to every recipient of the message. To reply to a message, follow these steps:

1. If you are viewing the message to which you want to reply, click the **R**eply or Reply to **A**ll button in the toolbar, or open the **M**ail menu and choose **R**eply or Reply to **A**ll.

   or

   Open the folder that contains the message to which you want to reply. Select the message; then click the **R**eply or Reply to **A**ll button in the toolbar, or open the **M**ail menu and choose **R**eply or Reply to **A**ll.

   A Reply window appears (see fig. 15.16). The addressee(s) are listed in the **T**o and **C**c text boxes, and RE appears at the beginning of the Sub-ject text box, indicating that this message is a reply to another message. RE also appears in the title bar, followed by the text from the Subject box. The text-editing area contains a copy of the original message.

Fig. 15.16
Mail automatically inserts the addressee and subject fields into a reply.

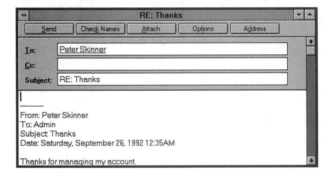

2. Compose your reply in the text area.

3. Add or delete names in the **T**o and **C**c text boxes as necessary. Separate the names with semicolons.

4. Choose the **S**end button. Mail sends the reply to all the addressees.

Forwarding Messages

In this information-driven age, the ability to pass information to others quickly is a great advantage. Because your workgroup may depend on shared information, you can easily forward to any name or group in your address list any message that you can access.

To forward a Mail message, follow these steps:

1. With the message displayed in its Send Note window or selected in the folder's list of messages, choose the Forward button in the toolbar, or open the **M**ail menu and choose **F**orward. Mail displays the message in a Send Note window, and FW appears at the beginning of the Subject text box.

2. Change addresses, change the subject, or modify the text as necessary.

3. Choose the **S**end button. Mail sends the message.

Deleting Messages

If you have no reason to save a message, you should delete it to conserve disk space and reduce the clutter in your Mail folders. You can move files to the Deleted Mail folder at any time. When you quit Mail, the program deletes these messages.

To delete a message or messages, use one of the following techniques:

■ While viewing the message (or with the message selected in a folder), choose the Delete button in the toolbar, open the **F**ile menu and choose Delete, or press the Del key. Mail moves the message to the Deleted Mail folder.

■ Select the folder that contains the message you want to delete, and select the message you want to delete from the list. Then click the Delete button in the toolbar, drag the message to the Deleted Mail folder, or open the **F**ile menu and choose **D**elete.

You can select several messages and delete them with one command. To select more than one message, click the first message, hold down the Ctrl key, and click subsequent messages. To deselect a message, hold down the Ctrl key and click the message. To use the keyboard, select the first message, press Shift+F8, use the up- and down-arrow keys to move to the next message, and press the space bar. Move to additional messages and press the space bar. To deselect a message and retain the other selections, move to the selected message and press the space bar. To return to selecting a single message at a time, press Shift+F8 again. When you have selected all the messages you want to delete, click the Delete button in the toolbar, drag the message to the Deleted Mail folder, or open the **F**ile menu and choose **D**elete.

If you mistakenly delete a message, you can open the Deleted Mail folder and move the message back to its former folder or to any other folder. When you exit Mail, the program deletes the messages in the Deleted Mail folder; at that point, you cannot retrieve them.

Printing Messages

You can print a message easily, either as you view it or by selecting from the list of messages in a folder. To print a message, follow these steps:

1. If you are viewing the message, open the **F**ile menu and choose **P**rint, or press Ctrl+P.

   or

   Select the folder that contains the message you want to print, and select the message you want to print. Then open the **F**ile menu and choose **P**rint, or press Ctrl+P.

   The Print dialog box appears (see fig. 15.17).

Fig. 15.17
Mail's Print
dialog box.

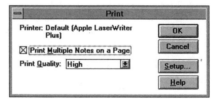

You can select two or more messages from the list of messages in a folder and print them with one command. To select multiple messages, click the first message, hold down the Ctrl key, and click subsequent messages. To deselect a message, hold down the Ctrl key and click the message. To use the keyboard, select the first message, press Shift+F8, use the up- and down-arrow keys to move to the next message, and press the space bar. Move to additional messages and press the space bar. To deselect a message and retain the other selections, move to the selected message and press the space bar. To return to selecting a single message at a time, press Shift+F8 again.

2. If you selected more than one message to print, choose the Print **M**ultiple Notes on a Page option if you want the messages to print continuously, one after another. Deselect this option if you want a new page for each message.

3. Select the desired print quality from the Print **Q**uality drop-down list.

4. Choose OK.

> **Note**
>
> Embedded objects in a message will print, but you can print attached files only from their original application (see "Attaching Files to a Message" later in this chapter). You must use Excel, for example, to print an Excel worksheet, even if you received it as part of a message.

Finding Messages

Mail provides a convenient way to find messages that you need to reference, forward, copy, or otherwise use in your work. Using the Message Finder, you can specify the criteria that are used for finding messages, based on the text in the To, From, Subject, and Text fields of the message. For example, you can search for all messages sent to a specific person or for messages containing a particular word or phrase. You can search all folders for a message or limit the search to a particular folder. When the search is complete, the headings for all the messages that meet the criteria you specified are listed in the Message Finder window. From this list, you can select messages to read, reply to, forward, print, or delete. You can run the Message Finder as many times as you want, specifying different search criteria each time, and you can reduce a Message Finder window to an icon on your Mail desktop so that you can rerun a search at a later time, using the original criteria that you specified in that Message Finder window.

To search for a message, follow these steps:

1. Open the **F**ile menu and choose Messa**g**e Finder. The Message Finder window opens (see fig. 15.18).

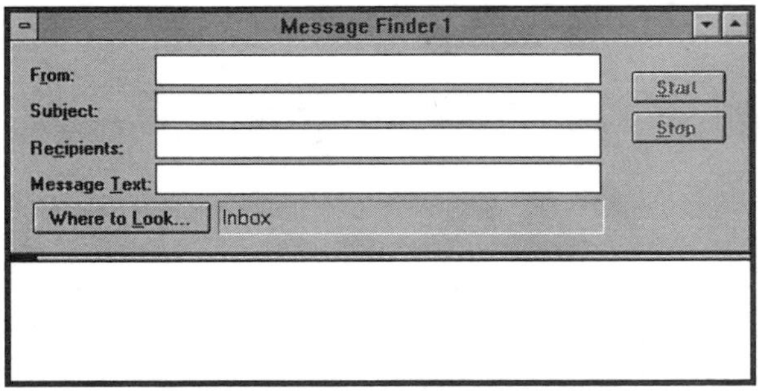

Fig. 15.18
The Message Finder locates messages by using search criteria that you specify.

When you first open a Message Finder window, the title bar displays the words Message Finder and a number indicating what instance of the Message Finder this window is.

2. In each text box, enter as much information about the message as you know. In the From text box, type the name of the sender; in the Subject text box, type the subject; and in the Recipients text box, type the names of the To and Cc workgroup members.

   If you type criteria in more than one of the text boxes, Message Finder finds only messages that meet all those criteria. For example, if you type **Peter** in the From text box and **Budget Reports** in the Subject text box, Message Finder locates only messages that are from Peter and about budget reports.

3. If you know which folder may contain the message, choose the Where To Look button in the Message Finder window. The Where To Look dialog box opens. Choose the Look in All Folders option, or select a specific folder in which you want to search. Then choose OK to close the Where To Look dialog box.

4. Choose the Start button in the Message Finder window. The Message Finder searches all the folders or the folder you specified for any match of the specified criteria.

   Mail lists the titles of the matching messages in the Message Finder window. If you see the message you are looking for before the search is complete, you can choose the Stop button to end the search.

You can select any message from the list of message titles in the Message Finder window and then read, reply to, forward, print, move (to any folder), or delete it, using the methods described in the previous sections.

> **Note**
>
> When you delete a message from the Message Finder, Mail also deletes the message from its folder.

> **Note**
>
> If you often use the same criteria to search for messages, you can set up a Message Finder window for those particular criteria only once. When you finish searching for messages with these criteria, minimize the Message Finder window to an icon on your Mail desktop. When you need to repeat a search with these criteria, double-click the icon, or press Ctrl+Tab until the icon is selected and then press Enter, to restore the Message Finder window. Then choose the Start button. Message Finder icons on the Mail desktop are saved when you exit Mail so that they will be available whenever you use Mail. You can set up as many Message Finder windows as you want, each with different search criteria.

Attaching Files to a Message

Mail allows you to attach a file to a message so that the recipient of the message receives an actual copy of the file along with the message. For example, if you want to distribute a copy of a document you have been working on to several co-workers, you can address a message to those co-workers, explaining what the document is about, and attach the document file to the message. Each addressee will receive the message and a copy of the file. Think how much quicker and easier this method is than hand-delivering the file on floppy disks.

You can use any of three methods to attach a file to a message. The first method works well if you are already working on a message in Mail. With this method, you can select the file(s) that you want to attach to the message as you compose the message text. The second two methods use File Manager. If File Manager is already open, using one of these methods may be to your advantage. For example, if you need to use File Manager to find a file that you want to attach to a message (see Chapter 4, "Managing Files with File Manager"), you can find the file and then attach a message, all from within File Manager.

Attaching Files to Messages in Mail

If you are working in Mail, and you know what file you want to attach to a message and where it is located, attaching the file from Mail is the easiest method. To attach a file to a message as you compose the message in Mail, follow these steps:

1. While composing the text in the Send Note window, position the insertion point at the point in the text where you want to insert a file or files.

2. Choose the **A**ttach button. The Attach dialog box appears (see fig. 15.19).

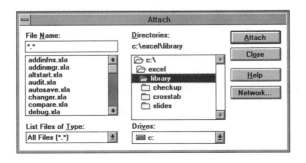

Fig. 15.19
In the Attach dialog box, you can select a file to attach to a message.

3. Select the file you want to attach to your message.

4. Choose the **A**ttach button or double-click the file name. The Attach dialog box remains on-screen, and an icon corresponding to the type of file you selected (for example, the Paintbrush icon for BMP files or the WinWord icon for Word DOC files) appears at the insertion point in the text.

5. Repeat steps 3 and 4 for as many files as you need to attach, and then choose the Cl**o**se button in the Attach File dialog box.

6. When you finish composing the message, send it as you would any other message.

Attaching Files to Messages with File Manager

You can use two methods in File Manager to attach files to a message. If you are working on a message in Mail and want to use File Manager to locate and attach a file to the message, use the first method. On the other hand, if you are working in File Manager and decide that you want to send a file to another user with a message attached, use the second method. In the end, the result of using any of the methods described here or in the preceding section is the same: the addressee receives the message and the attached file or files in his or her Inbox. The recipient can open an attached file with the application in which the file was created.

To attach a file to a Mail message on which you are working, using File Manager, follow these steps:

1. Switch to Program Manager, and open File Manager in the Network program group. (For details on how to open File Manager, refer to Chapter 4, "Managing Files with File Manager.")

2. Arrange your File Manager and Mail windows so that you can see both at the same time (see Chapter 1, "Operating Windows").

3. In File Manager, select the file or files you want to attach to the message.

4. Drag the files from File Manager to the locations in the Mail message where you want them to appear. A file icon appears in the text to mark the location of the embedded file or files.

5. Finish composing the message, and then send it as you would send any other message.

Tip
Drag a file or group of files from File Manager directly to your Outbox. A Send Note window appears, displaying the attached files in the text box. Add explanatory text, addresses, and a subject.

You also can attach a message to a file while you are working in File Manager without switching over to Mail. To attach a message to a file from within File Manager, follow these steps:

1. In File Manager, select the file or files you want to send.

2. Click the Attach Message button (an open envelope with a note clipped to it), or open the **M**ail menu and choose **S**end Mail. The Attached Files window opens (see fig. 15.20).

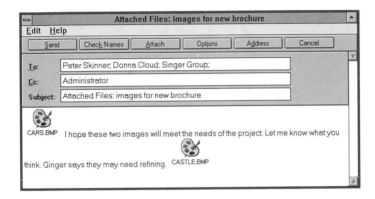

Fig. 15.20
The Attached Files window.

3. Compose the text, indicate the address or addresses, set the message options, and change the Sub**j**ect text as necessary to complete the message.

4. Choose the **S**end button. Mail delivers your message.

Viewing and Saving Attached Files

When you receive a message with attachments, you probably want to view the attached files. Mail cannot display these files; you must have an application that can display the attachment's contents. To display a picture created in Paintbrush, for example, you must have the Paintbrush application installed on your computer. You can open a text file in most text-editing, word processing, or desktop publishing applications, however.

To view an attached file, you can use either of two methods. The first technique is to double-click the attachment icon, or select it and then open the **F**ile menu and choose **O**pen. If the file's extension is associated with its application, Windows starts the application, and the application loads the attached file. If the file is not associated with an application, you can create an association (see Chapter 4, "Managing Files with File Manager"), or you can use the following method to view the file. Follow these steps:

1. Select the attachment's icon, and then open the **F**ile menu and choose Save **A**ttachments. Mail displays the Save Attachment dialog box. The message attachments are listed in the A**t**tached Files list box (see fig. 15.21).

Fig. 15.21
Saving attachments from Mail.

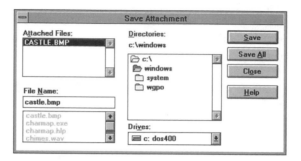

2. Select the attached file or files you want to save. If desired, change the drive, directory, and/or file name in the Dri**v**es and **D**irectories list boxes and the File **N**ame text box. Then choose the **S**ave button. Alternatively, you can choose the Save A**ll** button to save all attachments.

   Mail changes the Cl**o**se button to the **D**one button and saves the file or files in the current directory.

3. Choose the **D**one button. The Save Attachment dialog box closes.

4. Open the file by using File Manager or by loading the file into an application that can display it.

> ### Note
>
> Create a file-naming scheme for your workgroup, indicating what iteration each modification represents and who was the last worker to modify the file. The file name FBUDGT17.XLS, for example, may indicate that Fred was the last to modify the spreadsheet for a project called Budget and that this version of the worksheet is the 17th.

Embedding an Object in a Message

To embed an object in a message, follow these steps:

1. In the application that contains the data you want to embed, select the data and copy it to the Clipboard. (Usually, you perform this step by opening the **E**dit menu and choosing **C**opy.)

2. Switch to the Send Note window in Mail, and place the insertion point where you want to embed the object.

3. Open the **E**dit menu and choose Paste **S**pecial. The Paste Special dialog box appears (see fig. 15.22).

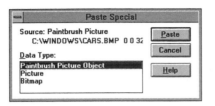

Fig. 15.22
Use the Paste Special dialog box to embed an object in a message.

4. In the **D**ata Type list box, select a form for your linked data. (See Chapter 6, "Advanced Data Sharing," for more information on data types.)

5. Choose the **P**aste button. Mail returns to the Send Note window and displays an object in the text at the insertion point.

Embedding a File in a Message

When you need to embed an entire file from an application that has Object Linking and Embedding (OLE) capability, follow these steps:

◄ "Embedding Data into a Document," p. 212

1. Save the file you want to embed.

2. In the Send Note window, place the insertion point where you want to insert the object. Then open the **E**dit menu and choose Insert from **F**ile. The Insert from File dialog box appears (see fig. 15.23).

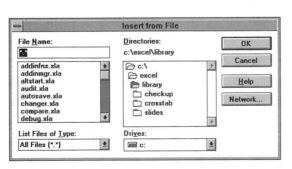

Fig. 15.23
The Insert from File dialog box.

3. Select the file.

4. Choose OK.

The object (that is, its icon) appears at the insertion point.

III

Using Windows Accessories

Creating an Object for Embedding

Occasionally, you may need to create objects to illustrate a point. When you need a chart, picture, or other object, you can use Mail to create it. Follow these steps:

1. In the Send Note window's text area, place the insertion point where you want to insert the object. Then open the **E**dit menu and choose **I**nsert. The Insert Object dialog box appears, listing the available Windows OLE applications (see fig. 15.24).

Fig. 15.24
The Insert Object
dialog box.

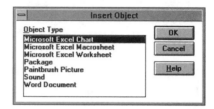

2. Select the application you want to use to create the new object.

3. Choose OK. The application opens.

4. Create the object, and then choose the originating application's file-updating command or simply close the application. The object appears at the insertion point in the Send Note window.

Managing Messages with Mail

Just as you manage the files on your hard disk with File Manager, you can manage the messages you send and receive with Mail. Mail provides several options that can help you keep track of your messages.

Setting Message Options

Mail can reduce interruptions and the time you spend on the phone or in conferences. To reduce interruptions and help focus time effectively, you can assign a priority to Mail messages, telling the receiver how important the message is and whether it should be handled immediately. (When you set a priority on a message, don't forget the tale about the boy who cried wolf too many times.)

If you just need a quick acknowledgment that someone has received your message, don't force the recipient to write a note back; instead, send your message with return receipt requested. As soon as the recipient opens your message, Mail sends you a postcard telling you that your message was opened.

To set these message options in the Send Note window, choose the Options button. Mail displays the Options dialog box (see fig. 15.25).

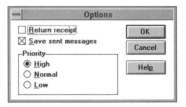

Fig. 15.25
Message options can save you time and effort.

In this dialog box, you can set the following options:

- *Priority.* Select the name of an addressee in the Send Note window; then specify a priority of **H**igh, **N**ormal, or **L**ow in the Options dialog box. The priority rating appears in the addressee's Inbox message list. Repeat this action for each addressee.

- ***Return Receipt.*** If you choose this option, the message displays a yellow sealed-envelope icon and a red exclamation point to the right of the folder's From column. When the addressee opens the message, Mail sends you a postcard message, confirming delivery (see fig. 15.26).

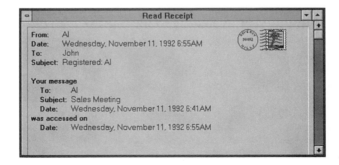

Fig. 15.26
You get a postcard when an addressee opens a return-receipt message.

- ***Save Sent Messages.*** Choose this option to retain (in your Sent Mail folder) a copy of the messages you send.

III

Using Windows Accessories

Creating and Using Folders

A workgroup may exchange hundreds of messages per week and thousands in a month. Keeping track of this electronic paper can be a nightmare without an orderly filing system. Mail provides folders for storing and organizing messages, as described in the following sections.

Adding Folders

When you open your account, Mail provides three folders: Deleted Mail, Inbox, and Sent Mail. The Inbox and Sent Mail folders may overflow, because Mail brings into the Inbox folder every message you receive, and it stores in the Sent Mail folder a copy of every message you send. You can add folders to handle this overflow. The folders can be private folders for your exclusive use or shared folders. For example, use shared folders for messages concerning a shared project.

Mail displays folders as yellow-folder icons, with names below each icon, on the left side of the Mail window. To add a folder, follow these steps:

1. Open the **F**ile menu and choose New **F**older. The New Folder dialog box appears (see fig. 15.27).

Fig. 15.27

The New Folder dialog box.

2. In the **N**ame text box, type a name for the folder. (You can use any combination of characters, including spaces.) For efficiency, keep the names of your folders brief.

3. In the Type section, choose the **P**rivate or **S**hared option:

   Private messages stored in a private folder can be viewed only by you.

   Shared messages stored in a shared folder are accessible to other users in your Postoffice. To set other users' access to a shared folder, choose the **O**ptions button in the New Folder dialog box, and then select or deselect the **R**ead, **W**rite, and **D**elete options in the Other Users Can group.

4. Choose OK. An icon of a folder appears next to the name of the folder in the Mail window. Folders are listed alphabetically by name.

By default, the folder is a top-level folder—that is, it is not subordinate to any other folders. The following section shows you how to add subfolders.

Adding Subfolders

A single-level filing system may not handle all your messages. Mail enables you to create multiple levels of subfolders. You can gather messages from general to specific categories. For example, you may have a folder named Projects that contains messages sent by all project managers. You can add subfolders, subordinate to the Project folder, for each specific project.

To create a subfolder, you normally select the folder to which you want to add the subfolder and then follow the steps for creating a new folder. The new folder is created as a subfolder of the selected folder (the *parent folder*). To create a subfolder with no parent folder selected, follow these steps:

1. In the New Folder dialog box, choose the **O**ptions button to expand the dialog box.

2. Type the name of the subfolder in the **N**ame text box.

3. In the Level section, choose the Su**b**folder Of option. (The **T**op Level Folder option creates a folder independent of all other folders.)

4. In the Su**b**folder Of file list, select the name of the parent folder.

5. Choose OK. An indented listing for the new folder appears below the listing for the parent folder.

You have the option of displaying or not displaying the subfolders of a parent folder. When the subfolders are not displayed, a plus sign appears next to the parent folder. To expand the listing to show the subfolders, click the plus sign or press the Tab key to move to the folders list, use the arrow keys to select the parent folder you want to expand, and press the plus key (+) on the keyboard. To collapse a listing, click the minus sign next to the parent folder, or select the parent folder with the keyboard and press the minus key (–).

III

Using Windows Accessories

Moving, Renaming, and Deleting Folders

Essentially, anything you can do with a message, you can do with a folder. This section describes how to manage your folders.

To move a folder or subfolder to another folder, drag the folder from its existing location to the new location. Alternatively, with the folder selected, open the **F**ile menu and choose **F**older Properties, or press Alt+Enter. The Folder Properties dialog box appears, displaying the settings for that folder (see fig. 15.28). Choose the Su**b**folder Of option, and specify the folder that you want to use as the parent of the selected folder.

Fig. 15.28
Use the Folder Properties dialog box to change the properties of a folder.

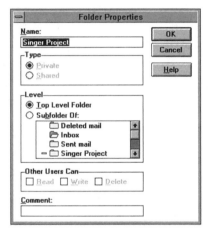

To rename a folder, type the folder's new name in the **N**ame text box. Then choose OK. The folder's new name appears below the selected folder.

> **Note**
>
> You cannot change the names of the Inbox, Sent Mail, or Deleted Mail folders.

To delete a folder, select the folder and then open the **F**ile menu and choose **D**elete, press Del, or press Ctrl+D. A message box appears, warning you that deleting a folder also deletes the folder's contents, including messages, attachments, embedded objects, and subfolders. If you still want to delete the folder, choose the **Y**es button in the warning box; if you don't want to delete the folder, choose the **N**o button.

Backing Up Message Files

Electronic messaging eliminates excessive use of paper, but it increases the number and kind of messages sent. Mail keeps all your messages in folders and keeps all the folders in the MSMAIL.MMF file. (You can rename your MMF file; MSMAIL.MMF is the default name.) Your Personal Address Book, generated as you add addressees to your messages, also is part of the MMF file. You should *back up* (make a copy of) your MMF file regularly to protect the data stored in it.

To back up your MSMAIL.MMF file (the message file), follow these steps:

1. Open the **M**ail menu and choose **B**ackup. Mail displays the Backup dialog box (see fig. 15.29).

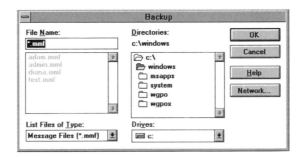

Fig. 15.29
The Backup dialog box.

2. In the File **N**ame text box, type the name you want to use for the backup of the MMF file.

3. Specify the drive and directory in which you want to save the backup file.

4. Choose OK.

If the Mail file you normally use becomes corrupted, Mail displays a dialog box, asking you to locate your backup file. When you select your backup file, Mail re-creates your Mail contents as they existed when you created the backup file.

Controlling the Mail System

Most people use an address book to organize their mail and telephone systems at home. In the office, many people used index-card files and Rolodex thumb files until computers came along. These methods have one thing in

III

Using Windows Accessories

common: you must establish a protocol for using the system, especially when a group of people depends on the accessibility and integrity of the information. A *protocol* is a set of procedures—in this case, for using your Personal Address Book and setting common rules for your workgroup. This section explains how you can modify and organize your Mail options to enhance your productivity.

Setting Up Your Personal Groups

Mail enables you to define groups of addresses for easy message addressing. This procedure makes it convenient to send a message to a task team or to all the people who work for you. To set up groups, follow these steps:

1. Open the **M**ail menu and choose Personal **G**roups. The Personal Groups dialog box appears (see fig. 15.30).

Fig. 15.30
The Personal
Groups dialog box.

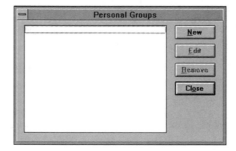

2. Choose the **N**ew button. The New Group dialog box appears (see fig 15.31).

Fig. 15.31
The New Group
dialog box.

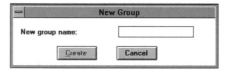

3. Type the name of the new group in the New Group Name text box. Then choose the **C**reate button in the dialog box. You return to the Personal Groups dialog box (see fig. 15.32). The name of the dialog box changes to reflect the name of the group you typed at the beginning of this step. This dialog box resembles the Address dialog box that you can access when you are composing a message. You can use this dialog box to search for and select group members' names and to get detail information.

Fig. 15.32
Selecting groups
of users.

4. Choose the **A**dd button for each member or group you selected. The group members' names appear in the Group Members list box. (If you prefer, you can type the names you want to add in the Group Members text box.)

5. Choose OK.

To edit an existing personal group, follow these steps:

1. Open the **M**ail menu and choose Personal **G**roups.

2. In the Personal Groups dialog box, select the group you want to edit.

3. Choose the **E**dit button.

4. Add and remove group members, using the **A**dd and **R**emove buttons.

5. Choose OK, and then choose Cl**o**se.

To delete a personal group, follow these steps:

1. Open the **M**ail menu and choose Personal **G**roups.

2. Select the group you want to remove.

3. Choose the **R**emove button.

4. Choose the Cl**o**se button.

III

Using Windows Accessories

Building Your Personal Address Book

Each time you send a message, Mail adds the addressees of the message to your Personal Address Book. Mail saves this address book in your MMF file. You can add addresses to your Personal Address Book even if you are not sending a message to those addresses.

Adding an Address

To add a name to your Personal Address Book, follow these steps:

1. Open the **M**ail menu and choose A**d**dress Book. The Address dialog box appears (see fig. 15.33).

Fig. 15.33
Use the Address dialog box to maintain your Personal Address Book.

2. Choose the Open Directory button, which looks like an open address book, to display the Open Directory dialog box.

3. Select Postoffice List From, and choose OK. The Address Book directory now lists all the users in your Postoffice.

4. Select the names that you want to add to your Personal Address Book.

To select more than one name from the list at one time, click the first name, hold down the Ctrl key, and click subsequent names. To deselect a name, hold down the Ctrl key and click the name. To use the keyboard, select the first name, press Shift+F8, use the up- and down-arrow keys to move to the next name, and press the space bar. Move to additional names and press the space bar. To deselect a name and retain the other selections, move to the selected name and press the space bar. To return to selecting a single name at a time, press Shift+F8 again.

To search for a name in the Postoffice list, click the Search button, which looks like a magnifying glass, or press Tab until the Search button is selected and press Enter. Type the name (or part of the name) in the Name Finder dialog box that appears, and choose Find. Every name that contains the text string that you typed in the dialog box will be listed in the Address dialog box. You then can select the name or names you want to add to your Personal Address Book.

5. Click the Add Names button at the bottom of the dialog box (this button looks like a Rolodex file with an arrow pointing into it), or press the Tab key until the Add Names button is selected and press Enter.

    If you need to find out more about a name that you selected before you add it to your Personal Address Book, choose the Details button to display the detailed information associated with that name. If you decide to add the name, choose the Add Names button at the bottom of the dialog box. Then choose the Close button to return to the Address dialog box.

6. When you finish adding names, choose the Personal Address Book button, which looks like a Rolodex file (without an arrow pointing into it). The names you added to your Personal Address Book appear in the list of names.

7. Choose Close.

Shortcut keys make maintaining your Personal Address Book easier and faster. The following table describes these keys.

Action	Keys
Open a new directory	Ctrl+L
Open your Personal Address Book	Ctrl+P
Find a name	Ctrl+F
Enter a new address	Ctrl+N
Add a name to your Personal Address Book	Ctrl+A
Close the Personal Address Book	Esc

III

Using Windows Accessories

Creating a Custom Address

If your Windows for Workgroups network has a gateway connecting your workgroup to electronic-mail systems on other computers or networks, you can add to your address book the addresses of the people on those other mail systems. Follow these steps:

1. Choose the New Address button (it looks like an index card) in the Address dialog box. The New dialog box appears (see fig. 15.34).

Fig. 15.34
Use the New dialog box to create custom addresses.

2. Select Custom Address in the Create What Kind of Entry list, and then choose OK. The New User dialog box appears (see fig. 15.35).

Fig. 15.35
Adding a user from another network.

3. Type the new user's name in the Name text box (the dialog box title bar adopts the name of the new user). Type the E-mail address and E-mail type in the appropriate text boxes; then choose the Add User button, which shows an index file with an arrow pointing to it. Mail adds the new user to your Personal Address Book.

4. Choose Cancel or press Esc to return to the Address dialog box, and then choose Close.

Setting Mail Options

You can set Mail options for sending, receiving, and deleting messages.

To access these global settings, open the **M**ail menu and choose **O**ptions. The Options dialog box appears (see fig. 15.36). All options in the dialog box are selected by default; the user in figure 15.36 has specified that he or she wants to receive mail only once a day.

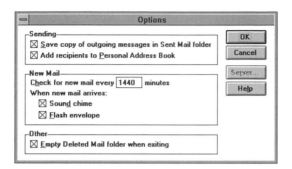

The following list describes the options in the dialog box:

Option	Function
Save Copy of Outgoing Messages in Sent Mail Folder	Saves a copy of each message you send in the Sent Mail folder.
Add Recipients to **P**ersonal Address Book	Adds all the addressees to whom you send a message to your Personal Address Book.
Check for New Mail Every *XXXX* minutes	Specifies how frequently Mail should check for new messages. Type the number of minutes in the text box.
When New Mail Arrives	Controls how Mail notifies you of new message arrivals. Choose Soun**d** Chime if you want Mail to sound a chime or beep from the computer's sound system. Choose **F**lash Envelope if you want Mail to change its desktop icon from a plain mail slot to a mail slot with letters sticking through it.
Empty Deleted Mail Folder When Exiting	Mail automatically empties the Deleted Mail folder when you exit the program.

Controlling the Way You View Folders

Mail gives you several options for controlling the way you view folders and sort their contents. Many of these options are available in the **V**iew menu (see fig. 15.37) or by using the buttons along the top of the folder window (see fig. 15.38). Some viewing options are available only by using the mouse.

Fig. 15.37

The **V**iew menu.

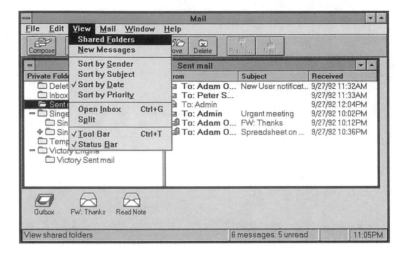

Fig. 15.38

The folder window showing the sort buttons From, Subject, and Received.

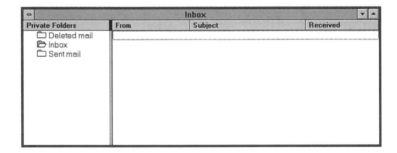

The following table summarizes Mail's folder-viewing options.

Action	View-Menu Command	On-Screen Option
Choose private or shared folders to toggle between these two views	Shared **F**olders or Private **F**olders	Click the Shared Folders or Private Folders button bar.
Open a folder	none	Select a folder and press Enter or double-click a folder.
Search for new messages	**N**ew Messages or Open **I**nbox	Open the Inbox folder (Ctrl+G).
Sort messages by sender	Sort by **S**ender	Click the From button bar.
Sort messages by subject	Sort by Sub**j**ect	Click the Subject button bar.

Action	View-Menu Command	On-Screen Option
Sort messages by date and time	Sort by **D**ate	Click the Received button bar.
Sort messages by priority	Sort by Priorit**y**	none
Redistribute window space for folder and message lists	S**p**lit selects the vertical line between the folder list and the Messages list, which you control with the arrow keys or the mouse.	Place mouse pointer on the black line between the Folders button bar and the From button bar. When the pointer changes to a white line with black arrows pointing left and right, click and drag the line.
Redistribute window space among messages	none	Place mouse pointer on the black line between the From and Subject or the Subject and Received button bars. Click and drag the line.
Display or remove the toolbar from below the menu	**T**ool Bar	Press Ctrl+T.
Display or remove the status bar* from the bottom of the window	Status **B**ar	no equivalent

The status bar displays an explanation of a menu command, the number of messages in a selected folder (and the number that are unread), the time of day, and a disconnected network icon if you are working off-line. If you are working on-line when a message arrives, the status bar displays the incoming-message icon.

Changing Your Password

You can change your Mail password. Changing your password on a regular basis is advisable because security systems depend on limited access to your data and passwords may be spread around.

To change your password, follow these steps:

1. Open the **M**ail menu and choose **C**hange Password. The Change Password dialog box appears (see fig. 15.39).

2. Type your old password in the **O**ld Password text box. Mail displays asterisks in place of the characters you type.

Fig. 15.39
The Change
Password
dialog box.

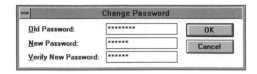

3. Type your new password in the **N**ew Password text box, and then type the new password again in the **V**erify New Password text box. If the characters typed in the **V**erify New Password text box match the password typed in the **N**ew Password text box, the OK button becomes available for selection. Retype your new password in the **V**erify New Password text box if the OK button remains gray.

4. Choose OK. Write your password down and keep it somewhere safe in case you forget it.

If you forget your password, see your Postoffice administrator, who can change your password (see "Controlling User Accounts" later in this chapter).

Using Mail Off-Line

Mail assumes that you do all your work at a single computer and on the network, but sometimes, you may need to work when the Postoffice server computer isn't available (for example, on weekends and holidays, and after work hours). You also might use a portable computer to work away from the network. In these cases, Mail enables you to work off-line.

By default, Mail stores your MSMAIL.MMF (or other MMF) file in your computer's WINDOWS directory. The MSMAIL.INI file also must be in the WINDOWS directory. In some situations (for example, to conserve local disk space), you may choose to rename and store your MMF file on the Postoffice server computer. Before you can work off-line, however, you must move your MMF file to a directory on your local computer.

To move your MMF file to your local drive, use Windows File Manager. You cannot use the Mail **B**ackup command in Mail, because it leaves a copy of your MMF file intact and other users may send messages to this MMF file while you are off-line. For information on moving files, see Chapter 4, "Managing Files with File Manager."

To work off-line, follow these steps:

1. With your computer disconnected from the network, start Mail. A message box appears, telling you that Mail didn't find your network files. Choose OK.

2. Another message box asks whether you want to work off-line. Choose OK again. The Mail Sign In dialog box appears.

3. Type your password and choose OK. If Mail cannot find your MSMAIL.MMF file, it displays a dialog box, asking you to type the path and name of your message file.

4. Type or otherwise designate the path (usually, C:\WINDOWS) and file name for your MMF file; then choose OK. Mail displays your Inbox folder as usual, and you can begin working with messages.

You may work on both a desktop computer and a laptop, and may want to maintain the same message files on both. If both computers have Windows for Workgroups installed, you can maintain your Mail files on your laptop while you travel and update your desktop when you return. To use this method of working off-line with Mail, follow these steps:

1. Delete or move the MSMAIL.MMF file (or your MMF file with a personalized name) from your laptop's WINDOWS directory. This action will later force the laptop to ask you for the directory of your MMF file.

2. Copy the MSMAIL.INI file from your desktop computer to the WINDOWS directory of your laptop.

3. Copy your MSMAIL.MMF file (or your MMF file, with a personalized name) from your desktop computer to a floppy disk, which you will use as your Postoffice while you are on the road.

4. Do not run Mail on your desktop computer while you are using Mail on your laptop. Doing so will cause you to lose messages when you return and copy the laptop's MMF file back to the desktop computer.

5. When you are ready to work with mail on your laptop, start Mail on your stand-alone system, inserting the floppy disk that contains the MSMAIL.MMF file into the floppy disk drive.

6. When Mail asks for the path to your MSMAIL.MMF file, specify the floppy disk drive.

7. Work with Mail on the laptop as usual.

8. When you return to your networked desktop computer, copy the current version of your MSMAIL.MMF file from the floppy disk you used with the laptop into the WINDOWS directory on your desktop computer. Do this before you start Mail on your desktop, or you will lose any messages that people sent to you while you were gone.

While working off-line, as you send, reply to, and forward messages, Mail places these messages in your Outbox, where they become part of your MSMAIL.MMF file. The next time you start Mail on-line, Mail sends these messages immediately.

Importing and Exporting Folders

Workgroups by definition must share information—sometimes, whole folders of information. When creating a folder, if you choose to share it, the whole workgroup has access privileges to that folder. You control the access by giving users read, write, or delete capabilities for the folder (refer to "Creating and Using Folders" earlier in this chapter). Sometimes, however, you may need to give all the messages you have in a folder to another workgroup member. In this case, you can export the folder to another member's MMF file, or that member can import the folder from your MMF file.

To import or export a folder, follow these steps:

1. To import a folder, open the **F**ile menu and choose **I**mport Folder. The Import Folders dialog box appears (see fig 15.40).

   or

   To export a folder, open the **F**ile menu and choose **E**xport Folder. The Export Folders dialog box appears (similar to fig. 15.40).

Fig. 15.40
In the Import Folders dialog box, select the MMF file name from which you want to import folders.

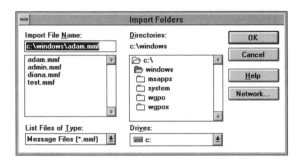

2. Specify the drive, directory, and MMF file name for the target folder (if you are importing a folder) or the destination folder (if you are exporting a folder).

3. Choose OK. Mail displays a modified version of the Import Folders dialog box (see fig. 15.41) or the Export Folders dialog box (similar to fig. 15.41). This version of the dialog box lists the folders for the MMF file that you selected in step 2.

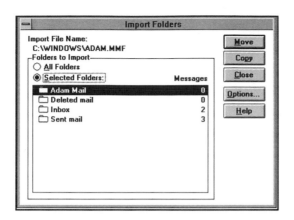

Fig. 15.41
After choosing an MMF file, you can select the folders you want to import.

4. In the Folders To Import or Folders To Export list, select **A**ll Folders or **S**elected Folders. If you choose **S**elected Folders, specify the folder or folders you want to import or export. (To select multiple folders, click the first name, press the Shift key, and click the last name to select a sequential range, or Ctrl+click individual names.)

5. Choose the **O**ptions button. The Options dialog box appears (see fig. 15.42).

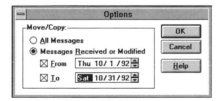

Fig. 15.42
You can import all messages or only those for a range of dates.

6. Select **A**ll Messages or Messages **R**eceived or Modified. If you choose the latter option, specify beginning and ending dates in the **F**rom and **T**o text boxes.

7. Choose OK to close the Options dialog box.

8. Choose the **M**ove or Co**p**y button. Mail moves or copies the folder and files to the appropriate MMF file. If you are importing the folder, it appears in your list of folders.

III

Using Windows Accessories

Administering the Postoffice

Any member of the workgroup can be the Postoffice administrator, but these responsibilities usually go to a member whose computer system offers the most storage space and the fastest performance features. The administrator must have this computer turned on for the workgroup to use Mail on-line. More minor administrative tasks are covered in the Microsoft Windows for Workgroups manual; this section presents the basic administrator skills.

Creating the Postoffice

The first task of the Postoffice administrator is to create the Workgroup Postoffice (WGPO). You may recognize this task as a variation on creating a user account. To create a Postoffice, follow these steps:

1. Check the hard disk storage space available for applications and tools. You need 360K disk space for an empty Postoffice and 16K disk space for each user account. In addition, each user must have enough disk space to hold the size and number of messages that he or she expects to send and receive. Remember that a large Postoffice could require tens of megabytes of storage.

2. Start Mail. This must be the first time you start Mail anywhere on the network. Mail displays the Welcome to Mail dialog box. In this version of the dialog box, you specify whether you want to connect to an existing Postoffice or create a new one (see fig. 15.43).

Fig. 15.43
The Welcome to
Mail dialog box.

3. Choose the Create a **N**ew Workgroup Postoffice option.

4. Choose OK. A message box appears, reminding you of your responsibilities as a Postoffice administrator and advising you that only one Postoffice per workgroup should exist.

5. Mail then asks whether you want to create a new Postoffice. Choose **Y**es. The Enter Your Administrator Account Details dialog box appears (see fig. 15.44). Notice that the details for the administrator are the same as those for the user accounts.

Fig. 15.44
The administrator
is the first user
defined on the
system.

6. In the dialog box, enter your name in the **N**ame text box, a name for
   your mailbox in the **M**ailbox text box, and a password in the **P**assword
   text box. All other details are optional.

7. Choose OK. Mail displays a reminder to share the WGPO directory.
   Other users must have full access to the WGPO directory that Mail
   creates on the Postoffice administrator's computer. (The procedure for
   sharing the WGPO directory is explained in the following section.)

8. Choose OK. Mail creates the new Postoffice as the subdirectory \WGPO
   in the directory C:\WINDOWS (WGPO is the default directory name).

Sharing the WGPO

Immediately after creating the WGPO directory, you must share this directory
so that other users have full access to it. Until you do, other users will be
unable to create an account on the Postoffice. To share the WGPO directory,
follow these steps:

1. In File Manager, select the Postoffice directory (the default directory is
   C:\WINDOWS\WGPO).

2. Open the **D**isk menu and choose Share **A**s. The Share Directory dialog
   box appears (see fig. 15.45).

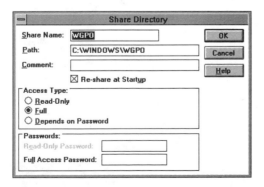

Fig. 15.45
The Share
Directory dialog
box in File
Manager.

III

Using Windows Accessories

3. Type a different name for the Postoffice or keep the default WGPO in the **S**hare Name text box.

   The *share name* is the name Windows assigns to a directory that you share with other users. It does not have to have the same name as the directory.

4. Choose the Re-Share at Start**u**p option, which instructs Windows for Workgroups to share this directory automatically each time you start your computer.

5. In the Access Type section, choose **F**ull. This option allows other users to open, read, and write to files in the WGPO directory. Other users need this level of access to the files stored in the WGPO directory to connect to and use the Postoffice.

6. If you choose to have a password, type it in the Fu**l**l Access Password text box. (Notify users of this password.)

7. Choose OK.

Controlling User Accounts

The Postoffice administrator should control the creation and removal of user accounts. To remove a user account, follow these steps:

1. Open the **M**ail menu and choose **P**ostoffice Manager. Mail displays the Postoffice Manager dialog box (see fig. 15.46). The dialog box lists the users by drive and path (specified above the list box).

Fig. 15.46
You can add or delete users in the Postoffice Manager dialog box.

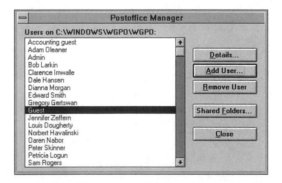

2. Select the name of the user you want to delete, and choose the **D**etails button. A user-details dialog box appears, with the user's name in its title bar. The dialog box shows the information that the user or administrator provided when creating the account (refer to fig. 15.6).

3. Look over the information to be sure that this is the account you want to delete, and then choose OK.

4. In the Postoffice Manager dialog box, choose the **R**emove User button. A confirmation box appears. Choose **Y**es if you are sure you want to remove this user; choose **N**o if you don't want to remove this user from the mail system.

To add a user, follow these steps:

1. In the Postoffice Manager dialog box, choose the **A**dd User button. An Add User dialog box appears, showing the details for the user (refer to fig. 15.6).

2. Specify the user's name, mailbox name, and password in the **N**ame, **M**ailbox, and **P**assword text boxes. The rest of the information in the dialog box is optional.

3. Choose OK. The new user's name appears in the user list in the Postoffice Manager dialog box.

Note

This procedure doesn't create an MMF file for the new user. Mail creates the MMF file when the user first signs in to Mail.

To modify user-account information, follow these steps:

1. In the Postoffice Manager dialog box, select the name of the user whose information needs to change; then choose the **D**etails button. The user's details dialog box appears.

2. In the details dialog box (the user's name appears in the title bar of the dialog box), change any or all of the information fields (for example, change the password if the user needs a new one).

3. Choose OK. Be sure to inform the user of the changes you made.

III

Using Windows Accessories

Compressing the Size of the Postoffice

You can recover hard disk storage space on the Postoffice administrator's computer by monitoring shared folders and compressing them when additional space is needed. Any user can create shared folders, and any user can access the messages in a shared folder.

To monitor and compress shared folders, follow these steps:

1. Open the **M**ail menu and choose **P**ostoffice Manager. Mail displays the Postoffice Manager dialog box.

2. Select a user-account name, and choose the Shared **F**olders button. Mail displays the Shared Folders dialog box, which shows the current status of shared folders. This information includes the number of shared folders, the number of messages in the shared folders, the collective byte count of the shared folders, and the number of bytes you can recover by compressing the shared folders.

3. Choose the Compress button. Mail compresses the files.

> **Note**
>
> Before you compress a shared folder, make absolutely certain that no users are using it. Warn all users before you attempt to compress the folder.

4. Choose Close to return to the Shared Folders dialog box.

Renaming, Moving, or Removing the Postoffice

Occasionally, you may need to re-create, relocate, or remove the Postoffice. Other workgroups may need to network with yours, which means that the two Postoffices must share information and folders. If both Postoffices have the same name, one name must change. Sometimes, when disk space becomes sparse, relocating the Postoffice is a temporary solution. If you forget your administrator password, you must remove the old Postoffice, create a new one, and reestablish user accounts in the renamed Postoffice system. For all these tasks, you use File Manager.

To rename a Postoffice, select the Postoffice directory (WGPO by default), and then open the **D**isk menu and choose Share **A**s. Type a new name in the **S**hare Name text box. Then share the directory with the new name, as described in "Sharing the WGPO" earlier in this chapter.

If you need to move the Postoffice to a new computer or to a different drive on your current computer, follow these steps:

1. Inform all users that they must exit and sign out of Mail.

2. Open File Manager, and select the WGPO directory.

3. Open the **F**ile menu and choose **M**ove.

4. Type the new path name for the WGPO directory in the Move **T**o text box.

5. Choose OK.

6. Share the new directory, as described in "Sharing the WGPO" earlier in this chapter.

7. Using Notepad or another text editor, modify the following line in the Postoffice administrator's MSMAIL.INI file:

   ```
   ServerPath=DRIVE:\DIRECTORY
   ```

   In this example, DRIVE is the letter designator for the drive on which the directory is located (for example, D:\), and DIRECTORY is the path name for the relocated WGPO (for example, \WINDOW\WGPO).

8. Instruct all users to modify the following line in the Microsoft Mail section of their MSMAIL.INI file, using Notepad or another text editor:

   ```
   ServerPath=\\COMPUTERNAME\SHARENAME
   ```

   In this example, COMPUTERNAME is the name of the computer on which the WGPO directory is located, and SHARENAME is the share name that you assigned to the WGPO directory in step 6.

> **Note**
>
> Do not attempt to move your Postoffice unless you feel comfortable with each of the preceding steps; seek help from a more experienced user, if necessary. You may want to assist other users with step 8 if they are not familiar with working with text files.

To remove a Postoffice, select the Postoffice directory; then open the **F**ile menu and choose **D**elete, or press Del.

III

Using Windows Accessories

Sending Faxes with PC Fax

Faxes have become almost as important to communication as the telephone. Unlike the telephone, a printed fax leaves less room for misinterpretation and provides written documentation of the communication. Windows for Workgroups 3.11 now includes PC Fax, so that sending a fax from within a Windows application is as easy as printing from an application or sending a Mail message.

When you install PC Fax, a new Fa**x** menu appears in the Mail menu bar. Some Windows applications, such as Microsoft Excel and Word for Windows, automatically display a Sen**d** command in their File menu. This command makes faxing a document as easy as printing.

Sending a Fax from an Application or from Mail

You can send a fax from within most Windows applications or from within Mail. Applications that are designed to work with Microsoft Mail can send a fax directly from the application menu. You can tell whether your application is Microsoft Mail-enabled if it has a Sen**d** command that displays a Send Note dialog box used with Microsoft Mail. Applications that are not Mail-enabled can send a fax by specifying the fax/modem as the printer through the Printer section of Control Panel.

To send a fax of a document (such as a Word for Windows document), follow these steps:

1. Ensure that Microsoft Mail is running.

2. Open the application; then open the document you want to send.

3. Open the **F**ile menu, and choose Sen**d**. The Send Note dialog box appears (see fig. 15.47).

> **Note**
>
> Alternatively, if you chose the fax/modem on the COM port as your printer, open the **F**ile menu and choose **P**rint.

4. Type the name and phone number in the **T**o and **C**c text boxes, using one of the following examples,

    [fax: *name @ phonenumber*]

    [fax: *phonenumber*]

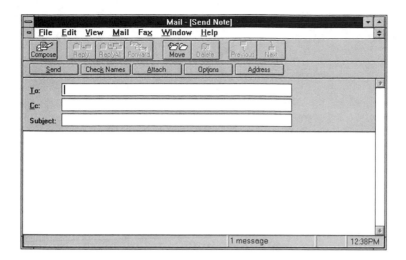

Fig. 15.47
Enter the tele-
phone number
and message
to accompany
your fax.

If you do not want to send to a specific name, use the example that shows just a phone number. Make sure that you enclose the entry in square brackets and follow the word *fax* with a colon.

Figure 15.48 shows a fax that is being sent from within Word 6 for Windows. Notice the attached Word document icon. This icon will print as the Word document when it is received by a fax machine.

Caution

If you make an incorrect entry in the **T**o or **C**c box, a Mail alert box warns you that names could not be matched against the address list. This message means that the names and phone numbers were invalid or that the structure of the entries was incorrect. If this happens, make sure that you correctly typed names that are in the Mail address list, correctly typed phone numbers, enclosed the line in square brackets, and followed the word *fax* with a colon.

---

5. Choose the **S**end button. The Send Message dialog box closes, and the application from which you sent the fax runs in the background of Windows as it spools the fax message to Mail and out to the fax/ modem.

Attaching a Document to a Fax

When you are working in Microsoft Mail, you can send a fax and attach a document. For example, you may want to send a combination of Excel worksheets and Word for Windows documents as a fax. You can attach the file to a note in Mail and then send the note. As long as your computer contains applications that can print these attached files, Mail can send the attached files and print them in the fax.

To attach a file to a fax, follow these steps:

1. Start the Mail application.

2. Complete the **T**o, **C**c, and Sub**j**ect text boxes as you would for a fax.

3. Enter any text messages you want to include in the body of the note.

4. Choose the **A**ttach button to display the Attach dialog box, which looks like the Open dialog box.

5. From the File **N**ame list, select the file that you want to attach to the note. The application that created this file must be available on your computer so that the file can be printed to the fax.

6. Choose the **A**ttach button.

   Figure 15.48 shows a note with one file attached.

Fig. 15.48
You can attach entire files to a fax note while you are in Mail.

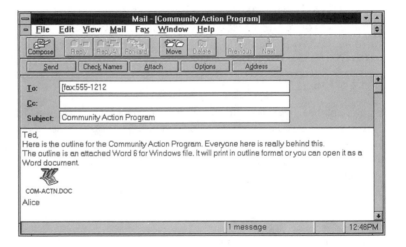

7. Return to step 5 if you want to attach additional files. If you are finished, choose Cl**o**se.

8. Choose the **S**end button to send the fax.

If you want to delete a file from the note before sending the fax, select the file icon and then press Del.

> **Note**
>
> While a fax is being set up to print, your Windows applications may slow significantly. This slowdown occurs because the application that created the document you are faxing is starting, loading the document, and printing the document to the fax software.

Receiving a Fax

A dedicated fax machine receives a fax sent from PC Fax in the same way it receives a fax sent from another fax machine. Files that are attached to a Mail note are printed out in the fax.

> **Note**
>
> If you know that someone will be sending you a fax, and you have your fax machine and telephone on the same line, you can pick up a fax call by opening the **Fax** menu and choosing the **A**nswer Now! command.

If you have PC Fax set up to accept incoming faxes, each new fax that PC Fax receives is treated like a new Mail message. The new fax appears as an item in the Mail Inbox.

To see the fax contents, choose the Fa**x V**iew New Faxes! command; then double-click the New Fax Message line in the Inbox. (For a discussion of displaying the message in a fax, refer to "Reading and Working with Messages" earlier in this chapter.) If the fax was sent from another PC Fax, you will be able to read the message as though it were sent from Mail.

A fax may contain an attached document. If the attached document was sent to you as a Mail message with an attached document, and you have a copy of the application that created the document, you can open and edit the attached document by double-clicking the document's icon. The document opens in the application, where you can edit or save it.

If the attached document was sent to you as a fax, you need to use Fax Viewer to see the document. Fax Viewer is a separate application that can save, reopen, scale, rotate, and print the fax documents you receive.

To display the attached document, double-click the icon that represents the document. Fax Viewer starts and displays the fax. Figure 15.49 shows a document in Fax Viewer.

III

Using Windows Accessories

Fig. 15.49

View, scale, print, or save attached documents with Fax Viewer.

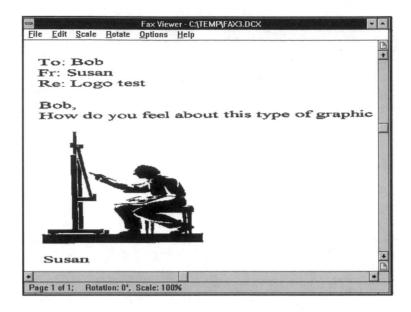

> **Note**
>
> To start Fax Viewer and load a fax into it, using the keyboard, move the insertion point to one side of the fax object in the message; then press Shift+arrow key to move across and select the object. Open the **E**dit menu and choose the Edit Attached File **O**bject command.

Manipulating Faxes in Fax Viewer

Fax Viewer is an application that displays faxes you receive. It also can scale a fax, enhance it so it is easier to read, print it, rotate it, and save it. Figure 15.49 in the preceding section shows a fax in Fax Viewer. Figure 15.50 shows the same fax at a smaller scale with black enhancement.

To manipulate the fax that is displayed in the viewer, choose the following commands:

Command	Result
File **O**pen	Opens DCX files of previous faxes you may have saved.
File **S**ave As	Saves the displayed fax as a DCX file.
File **P**rint	Prints the fax as it was received. The scaling, rotation, or enhancement you apply does not affect printing.

Command	Result
Scale	Choose scaling values ranging from 12.5% to 100%. This option does not affect printing.
Rotate	Rotates the fax for viewing in 90-degree increments. This option does not affect printing.
Options **S**tatus	Displays a status bar at the bottom screen, showing page number, scale, and rotation.
Options **R**everse Image	Reverses the black and white in the image.
Options **E**nhance Image	Smoothes and joins the image, making it easier to read. Options are **N**o Enhancement, Enhance **B**lack, and Enhance **W**hite.

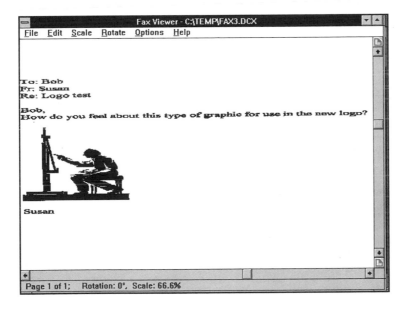

Fig. 15.50
Scaling and enhancing a fax can make it easier to read.

Setting Options To Control Your Fax

Although PC Fax does not have the multitude of features available in many dedicated fax applications, it does have a number of options that make it more versatile than it appears to be at first. To see the fax options, open the Fa**x** menu and choose **O**ptions. The Default Fax Options dialog box appears (see fig. 15.51).

Fig. 15.51
Control how
faxes are sent
with the Default
Fax Options
dialog box.

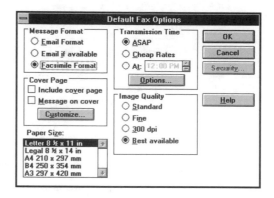

The way in which your fax is received depends on whether it is received by a
dedicated fax machine or by Microsoft Mail. The receipt format also depends
on the settings in the Message Format group. The following table shows the
different combinations of settings and receiver. In most cases, you will want
to use Email **If** Available to send documents.

Table 15.1 Fax Receipt Formats		
Option	**Fax-Machine Receipt**	**Microsoft Mail Receipt**
Email Format	Bitmap graphic	E-mail message with attachments
Email **If** Available	Bitmap graphic	E-mail and attachments if Microsoft Mail available; otherwise, bitmap graphic
Facsimile Format	Bitmap graphic	Bitmap graphic

When you are sending a broadcast message to many recipients, you probably
will want to include a cover page. A cover page can include a graphic, such as
your company logo. If you choose the Include Co**v**er Page option, the
recipient's name, address, and telephone number appear in the cover page
along with the names and numbers of other recipients, the date, the subject,
and the number of pages.

If you want to include a message in the cover page, choose the **M**essage On
Cover option. To include a graphic, choose the C**u**stomize button. The
Change Logo dialog box appears. In this dialog box, you can enter the file

name for the logo and specify the logo's height. If you do not know the path and name of a BMP (bitmap) file, choose the **B**rowse button and select the bitmap file you want to use as a logo. You can specify the logo's maximum height by entering it in the **M**aximum Height box.

Specify the size of paper and the quality of the image in the Paper Size and Image Quality areas. **S**tandard quality is 100 dots per inch (dpi)—fast, but poor quality. The Fi**n**e option produces 200 dpi. The **3**00 dpi setting is the resolution of most laser printers. You probably will want to leave the setting at **B**est Available. This option enables PC Fax to select the best-quality image available on the receiving equipment.

You can save money and work time by setting up your faxes to be sent at night. At night, telephone time is cheaper, and you probably won't be working and competing with the processor as it attempts to print faxes.

To control the printing time, choose the **A**SAP option if you want to print a fax immediately. If you want to send a fax when phone rates are low, follow these steps:

1. Choose the **O**ptions button to display the Transmission Options dialog box.

2. Select the start and end times for cheap transmissions.

3. Specify the number of times PC Fax should attempt to resend the fax if a problem occurs, indicating the amount of time between attempted transmissions.

4. Choose OK. You return to the Default Fax Options dialog box.

5. Choose the **C**heap Rates option.

6. Choose OK.

If you want to send a fax at a specific time, choose the **A**t option and enter the time.

Installing and Configuring a Fax/Modem

Before you can use the fax that comes with Windows for Workgroups, you must connect your fax/modem and configure the fax software. After you connect your fax/modem hardware, you may want to test the modem by connecting to an on-line information service such as CompuServe or America Online. You must be a subscriber to these services to be able to connect to them.

To configure your fax software for a new modem, follow these steps:

1. Start the Fax application located in Control Panel in Windows for Workgroups. The Fax Modems dialog box appears (see fig. 15.52).

Fig. 15.52
You must configure the fax software before you can send or receive a fax.

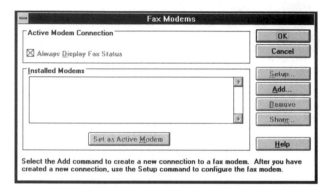

2. Choose the **A**dd button to display a list of fax/modems and the port to which each is connected. If you will be sharing the modem across the Windows for Workgroups network, choose Shared Network Fax from the **T**ype List.

3. Choose OK to display the Fax Phone Number dialog box (see fig. 15.53).

Fig. 15.53
Enter your country code, area code, and phone number.

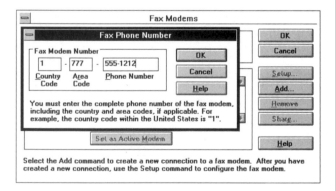

4. Enter your country code (1 in the United States), area code, and phone number.

5. Choose OK to return to the Fax Modems dialog box.

6. If you have more than one modem installed and you want the modem you are configuring to be the one that the fax software uses, choose the Set As Active Modem button.

7. Choose the **S**etup button to display the Setup dialog box (see fig. 15.54). Choose the **S**peaker button to specify when sound is used. Choose the **D**ialing button to specify international prefixes, access codes, time delays used in corporate phone systems, and the line type (tone or pulse).

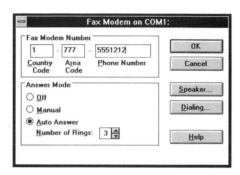

Fig. 15.54
Set up specifications for when and how the fax dials.

8. If you want to share the modem with others in your workgroup, choose the Shar**e** button from the Fax Modem dialog box. The Share Local Fax Modem dialog box appears. In this dialog box, you must do the following things:

- Type the directory name in the **D**irectory text box. Windows proposes the directory C:\WINDOWS\MSFAX.

- Choose the **C**reate Directory button to create a directory for faxes waiting to be sent.

- Choose the Create **S**hare button, and then choose OK to share the directory you just created.

9. Choose OK after preparing to share your modem.

10. Choose OK in the Fax Modems window.

III

Using Windows Accessories

From Here...

Microsoft Mail and PC Fax are two valuable applications that can improve communication and make everyone in your workgroup more productive. To make sure that your Mail system is working most effectively and files are transferred correctly, check the following chapters:

- Chapter 4, "Managing Files with File Manager," shows how to create a shared directory on your disk so that people you specify can retrieve files from that directory without bothering you.

- Chapter 18, "Using Windows for Workgroups Management Tools," discusses ways to see how much actual CPU power your applications are receiving if you monitor your computer with the WinMeter.

Chapter 16

Using Windows for Workgroups Schedule+

Schedule+ is a tool for keeping track of your appointments, meetings, and tasks. Schedule+ can improve the ways you and the people around you work. You can use Schedule+ to manage your own time, making sure you get back to people on time and don't miss appointments or deadlines. You can even use its Task List to set priorities for all the things you have to do. If you are the type of person who is on the go and can't be tied to a scheduler in your desktop computer, then you can copy Schedule+ to your portable or laptop computer, or even print pages that fit in most standard personal time-management books or schedulers.

Everyone in your workgroup can take advantage of Schedule+ and stop wasting time doing the "meeting-room shuffle." Schedule+, combined with Mail's capability to send and acknowledge messages, enables you to check the times when key people can meet. You can also see which meeting rooms and other facilities are available. Schedule+ uses Mail to notify attendees when the meeting will be held. You can even request a return receipt that acknowledges the meeting.

In this chapter, you will learn how to:

- Use the Appointment Book
- Use the Task List
- Schedule a meeting
- Work with another user's Appointment Book and Task List
- Customize Schedule+

Introducing the Features of Schedule+

Schedule+ consists of three features—the Appointment Book, the Task List, and the Planner—that help you to manage your own schedule and to coordinate your schedule with those of other members of your workgroup.

The Appointment Book (see fig. 16.1) is your place in Schedule+ for assigning time-specific events, such as your appointments and meetings. In the Appointment Book, you can schedule one-time-only events or events that occur at regular intervals, such as a weekly staff meeting. For recurring events, you need to enter the event into your Appointment Book only once and specify the time interval for its recurrence. Schedule+ then fills in the appropriate slots in your Appointment Book for all subsequent occurrences of the event.

Fig. 16.1

The Schedule+ window, showing the Appointment Book.

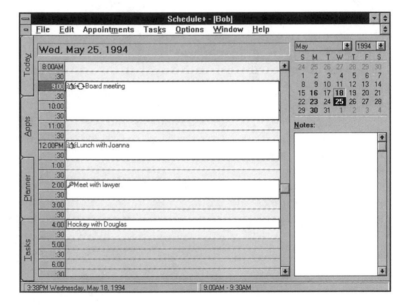

Schedule+ also acts as a scheduling tool for a group. You can examine the schedules of others in your workgroup, and if they have slots open in their calendars, you can schedule meetings during those times. After you schedule these meetings, Schedule+ sends a message to those people that you have requested to attend. Those group members can accept or decline your proposed time and use Schedule+ to send back to you their responses to your request.

The Task List (see fig. 16.2) is the place in Schedule+ to list anything that you must accomplish that is not necessarily assigned to a specific time period, such as an appointment. Essentially, the Task List is a "to-do" list of all the tasks that you need to complete, either by a specific date or whenever you can.

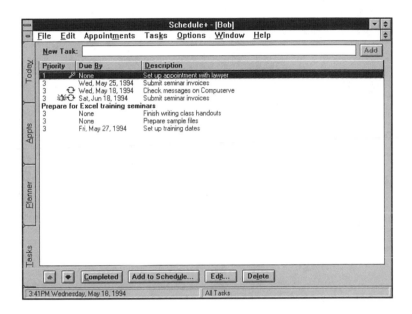

Fig. 16.2
The Schedule+ window, showing the Task List, with the last item in the list selected.

Items in the Task List remain listed until you complete the task and delete the item from the list. You also can specify the starting and due dates for each task on the list. After you specify its starting and due dates, the task appears on your to-do list on the starting date; overdue tasks—those tasks that you fail to complete by the due date—are highlighted in red in the Task List. You can also assign a priority to each task and sort your tasks by those priorities.

The Schedule+ Planner (see fig. 16.3) displays the busy and free times in your schedule in a day-by-time grid, which enables you to view several days at a time. If you are working *on-line*—that is, if you are connected to the mail server on your network—you can view the busy and free times of others in your workgroup as well. The *mail server*, which is the computer on which the Postoffice is located, enables computers collected together in a workgroup to communicate among each other. (See Chapter 15, "Using Windows for Workgroups Mail and PC Fax.") The primary function of the Planner is to help you schedule meetings with others in your workgroup at times that do not conflict. You can also use the Planner to get an overview of your time

III

Using Windows Accessories

commitments for a period of several days. (The section "Scheduling a Meeting" explains in detail how to use the Planner.)

Fig. 16.3
The Schedule+
window, showing
the Planner.

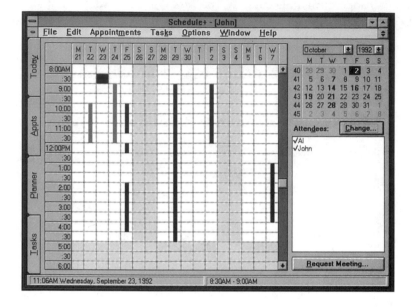

Starting Schedule+ from Program Manager

◄ "Creating Your
User Account,"
p. 513

◄ "Signing in to
Mail," p. 514

You start Schedule+ from the Network group in the Windows Program Manager. Unless you are already signed in to Mail, you must sign in to Schedule+. To sign in, you must have a user account with Mail and know your mail box name and password.

To start and sign in to Schedule+, follow these steps:

1. Open Program Manager, choose the Network icon. The Network group appears (see fig. 16.4).

2. Choose the Schedule+ icon by double-clicking on the icon or selecting the icon with the arrow keys and pressing Enter. The Mail Sign In dialog box appears (see fig. 16.5).

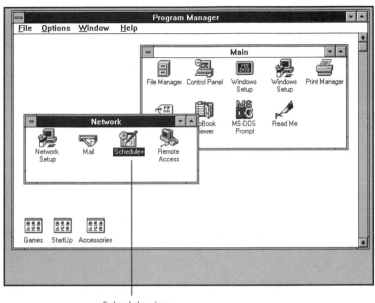

Fig. 16.4
Select the
Schedule+ icon in
the Main program
group to open
Schedule.

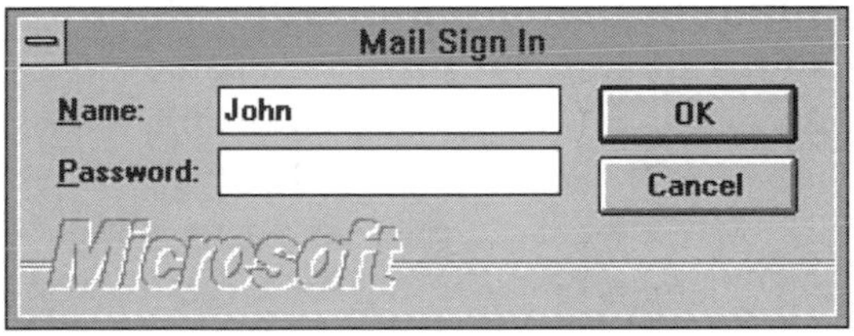

Schedule+ icon

Fig. 16.5
The Mail Sign In
dialog box.

3. Type your mailbox name in the **N**ame text box of the Mail Sign In dialog box, as shown in figure 16.5.

4. Press the Tab key or click **P**assword, and type your mailbox password in the **P**assword text box. (As you type, asterisks rather than alphabetical characters appear in the text box, to prevent anyone else from reading your password.)

5. Choose OK or press Enter.

After Schedule+ opens, the Schedule+ window displays the Appointment Book with the current date, as shown in figure 16.1. You perform most of your work with Schedule+ within the Schedule+ window. The title bar of the window displays your name, and tabs along the left side of the window list

III

Using Windows Accessories

the Appointment Book (**A**ppts), the **P**lanner, and the Task List (**T**asks). Clicking on a tab or pressing Alt+*letter* takes you to the appropriate feature. The Toda**y** tab enables you to return immediately to your Appointment Book schedule for the current day. When you view or respond to meeting requests, you work in a different window and do not see your name in the title bar or tabs along the side of the window. Also, if you are viewing someone else's schedule (as you will learn to do later in this chapter), you see that person's name in the title bar.

After you sign in to Schedule+, you work with Schedule+ *on-line*, which means that you are connected to your network's mail server and can use the features of Schedule+ that take advantage of your network. You can view the schedules of others in your workgroup, for example, and schedule meetings based on your coworkers' available time (see the sections "Working with Another User's Appointment Book and Task List" and "Scheduling a Meeting," later in this chapter).

Working with Schedule+ Off-Line

You also can work *off-line*, which simply means working with Schedule+ without being connected to your Postoffice. Normally, when you work on-line, your scheduling information is saved in a *local file*, which is located on your computer, and in a *network file*, which is located on the same computer as the Postoffice. If the computer serving as the network's mail server is temporarily off-line, for example, or you want to work on your portable or home computer, working off-line is your only option.

If you want to work on a *stand-alone* computer (that is, a computer, such as a portable computer, that is not connected to your network), you must copy to that computer the file that includes your scheduling information. Then you must copy the file back onto the *networked* computer (that is, the computer that is connected to the network) so that the information on the network file can be updated.

If you neglect to copy the file back to a networked computer, other members of your group who try to view your schedule (to schedule a meeting, for example) will not see any appointments that you made while working with Schedule+. Keep in mind that when you work with Schedule+ off-line, whether on a networked or stand-alone computer, you cannot access anyone else's schedule or use the workgroup scheduling features.

If you want to work with Schedule+ on a stand-alone computer, follow these steps:

1. Copy the file SCHDPLUS.INI from the networked computer's C:\WINDOWS subdirectory to the stand-alone computer's C:\WINDOWS directory.

   ◀ "Copying Files or Directories," p. 152

   The SCHDPLUS.INI file contains information on your setup of Schedule+. Unless you make changes in how Schedule+ is set up on your networked computer—for example, if you make changes in the General Options dialog box—you need only copy this file once to your stand-alone computer.

2. Log on to Schedule+ on your networked computer.

3. Insert a disk into your floppy drive.

4. Open the **F**ile menu and choose Move **L**ocal File.

5. Select the correct drive designation from the Dri**v**es drop-down list and, if necessary, change the directory in the **D**irectories list.

6. Choose OK or press Enter. Your Schedule+ file—which contains all the information from your Appointment Book, Task List, and Planner—is moved onto the disk that you inserted in the floppy drive. The name of the file is your mailbox name with the extension CAL.

7. Log on to Schedule+ on your stand-alone computer, and insert the disk into that computer's floppy drive.

8. When prompted for the location of your local file, specify the floppy drive.

9. Work with your schedule as usual. You can do everything but group scheduling.

10. When you next log on to Schedule+ on your networked computer, insert the disk in the computer's floppy drive, open the **F**ile menu, and choose Move **L**ocal File to move your scheduling file back to your networked computer's C:\WINDOWS directory. Alternatively, use File Manager to copy the file from the disk to your networked computer's C:\WINDOWS subdirectory.

When you open Schedule+ on your networked computer while working on-line, your Schedule+ file is updated automatically on the mail server.

III

Using Windows Accessories

To work off-line on your networked computer, open the **F**ile menu and choose **W**ork Offline. To return to working on-line, open the **F**ile menu and choose **W**ork Online. You may want to work off-line while using your networked computer, particularly if you receive many Mail or Chat messages and want to prevent interruptions for a period of time, or if you want to prevent others from using files on your drives.

If you are working on-line (that is, on a networked computer that is connected to your mail server), as described in Chapter 10, you can display a Messages window (see fig. 16.6). In this window you can receive and view replies to your requests for meetings, or requests from others in your workgroup for meetings. Later in this chapter, the sections "Reading Responses to a Meeting Request" and "Responding to a Meeting Request," explain in detail how to use the Messages window.

Fig. 16.6
The Messages window in Schedule+.

Using the Appointment Book

The Schedule+ Appointment Book is where you assign your appointments and meetings to specific time slots. A time slot can contain up to six appointments or tentative appointments. Each appointment is listed in its own section of the time slot. When you fill in a time slot in the Appointment Book, that time period is blocked out on the Planner as busy time so that you or others viewing your Planner know not to schedule anything else during that time. Tentative appointments do not show up on your Planner as busy time, however, so when others look at your schedule, they see that time as open.

If you need to schedule an appointment that recurs at regular time intervals, you can enter the appointment once in your Appointment Book and specify the intervals and how long you want that event to appear on your schedule. You also can attach a reminder to any or all appointments so that a pop-up message box appears on-screen to remind you of an appointment.

Adding an Appointment

Adding appointments to your Appointment Book involves several steps. You must designate the date on which the appointment takes place. You also must indicate on the appropriate page of your Appointment Book the starting and ending times of the appointment. Finally, you must include a description of the appointment. You also may want to designate the appointment as tentative or private and set up a reminder of the appointment to appear at a specified time beforehand.

To add an appointment to your Appointment Book, you can choose two methods:

- Select the time slot and enter a text description of the appointment directly on the page of your Appointment Book. This method is the quickest and works well if you do not need to designate certain options, such as making the appointment private or tentative or setting a reminder for the appointment.

- Open the Appointments menu, choose **N**ew Appointment, and describe the appointment in the Appointment dialog box. This method is slower but more powerful, because it offers several options that are not available with the first method. You can select a time slot for your appointment from a display that shows several days of your schedule at a glance, and you can designate the appointment as private or tentative and set a reminder from the Appointment dialog box.

To add an appointment to your schedule, your Appointment Book must be on-screen in the Schedule+ window that displays your name in the title bar. If you are not in that Schedule+ window, open the **W**indow menu and select your name by clicking with the mouse or by using the arrow keys and pressing Enter; alternatively, you can type the number that appears next to your name on the menu. Your personalized Schedule+ window then appears. If your Appointment Book is not currently displayed in your personalized Schedule+ window, choose the **A**ppts tab along the left side of the window.

III

Using Windows Accessories

Adding an Appointment Directly in Your Appointment Book

To add an appointment in your Appointment Book, you must first display the page for the date of the appointment. You can use the small calendar located in the upper-right corner of the Appointment Book (refer to fig. 16.1) to select the appointment date by following these steps:

1. Click the arrow to the right of the month box in the calendar. A drop-down list of months appears; click the desired month. The name of the month that you chose from the drop-down list appears in the month box, and the calendar changes to show the dates of that month in the year that appears in the year box. The Appointment Book also changes to display whatever date is selected in the calendar.

2. If you need to change the year, click the arrow to the right of the year box to display a drop-down list of years. Click the year in which the appointment is to take place. The year that you selected appears in the year box and the dates in the calendar change to those of the chosen month in that year.

3. To set the exact day of the appointment, click that date in the month calendar. The date that you chose appears at the top of your Appointment Book, including the exact day of the week on which the appointment is to take place.

You also can use the calendar to set the date of your appointment by pressing Alt and then using the arrow keys to select the desired day in the calendar. The date that you select in the calendar appears in color and the schedule changes to that date. To select a different month, press Shift+Alt and use the arrow keys to select the desired month. As you press Shift+*arrow key*, the month shown in the drop-down list and the month in the schedule change.

◄ "Using Menus and Dialog Boxes," p. 31

Another method of setting the date for your appointment uses the Go To Date dialog box. To set an appointment date with the Go To Date dialog box, follow these steps:

1. Open the **E**dit menu and choose **G**o To Date, or press Ctrl+**G.** The Go To Date dialog box appears (see fig. 16.7).

Fig. 16.7
The Go To Date dialog box.

2. Type the desired date in the **G**o To box. Alternatively, you can use the right- and left-arrow keys to move to different parts of the date in the **G**o To box and then type the numbers of the new date. (You also can click on the up or down scroll arrows to the right of the date box until the correct date appears in the **G**o To box.)

3. After you enter the correct date, choose OK or press Enter. The correct day and date appears at the top of the page in your Appointment Book.

After you set the date for your appointment, you must set the beginning and ending times of the appointment and enter a description of the appointment. (After you set these times, the total time of the appointment is blocked off in your Planner.) Enter the time and description for the appointment by following these steps:

Tip

To quickly move to a date and time in the Appointment Book, double-click the square for the date and time in the Planner.

1. Choose the time that the appointment begins by clicking on one of the half-hour time periods listed in the column along on the left side of the Appointment Book. Then drag the mouse pointer down to the ending time for the appointment and release the mouse button. The entire time for the appointment is highlighted.

   Alternatively, you can press Shift+Tab to move to the column of time periods. Use the up- or down-arrow keys to move to the beginning time of the appointment, press the Shift key and use the down-arrow key to move to the ending time, and release the Shift key. The time period for the appointment is highlighted.

2. Type a description for the appointment. As soon as you start typing, the highlighted time slot is displayed with a white background, with green lines before and after the time. The text description for the appointment appears inside the box. If you type beyond the limits of the box, the box scrolls so that you can continue adding text. When you select another time slot or appointment, the green borders disappear from this time slot. When you finish typing the description, you need not press Enter.

Adding an Appointment with the Appointment Dialog Box

If you want to designate any appointment as tentative or private (or both), or set up a reminder for an upcoming appointment, you must use the Appointment dialog box. Just as when you add an appointment directly to your Appointment Book, you can select the time for your appointment and enter a description for it. The Appointment dialog box also enables you to view, at a

III

Using Windows Accessories

glance, the time slots for several days; you simply choose the Choose **Time** button and then select from the display of time slots the time for your appointment.

To set an appointment using the Appointment dialog box, follow these steps:

1. Open the Appoint**m**ent menu and choose **N**ew Appointment, or press Ctrl+**N**. The Appointment dialog box appears, as shown in figure 16.8.

Fig. 16.8
The Appointment
dialog box.

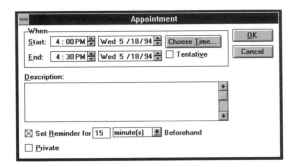

2. Set the starting and ending times and dates for the appointment in the **S**tart and **E**nd boxes.

   To set the times and dates using the mouse, select the part of the time or date that you want to change by clicking on it; then type in a new number, or click on the up or down arrows on the right side of the time and date boxes to change the entry in the selected slot.

   To set the times and dates using the keyboard, press the Tab key to move to the starting or ending time or date that you want to change, and then use the right- and left-arrow keys to select the part of the time or date that you want to change. Then type in a new entry or use the up- and down-arrows keys to select a new entry.

   If you chose the date and the time slot for a new appointment as described at the beginning of the previous section, using the small calendar in the upper-right corner of the Appointment Book, the date and the beginning and ending times for the appointment appear in the **S**tart and **E**nd boxes of the Appointment dialog box. If the dates and times that appear in the **S**tart and **E**nd boxes are correct, you can skip this step.

   To view the time slots for several days of your schedule at a glance, choose the Choose **T**ime button. The Choose Time dialog box, shown in figure 16.9, appears. You can select a time slot for the new appointment with the mouse by clicking on the starting time on the day that you want to schedule the appointment and dragging to the ending time. To use the keyboard to select a time, use the right- and left-arrow keys to select the day for the appointment, and then use the up- and down-arrow keys to select the starting time, press the Shift key, and use the down-arrow key to select the ending time. If you want to schedule the appointment for a date that is not displayed in the dialog box, follow steps 1 through 3 at the beginning of the previous section to select the date from the small calendar in the upper-right corner of the dialog box. When you finish selecting a time, choose OK to return to the Appointment dialog box.

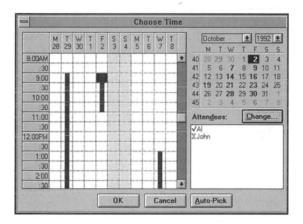

Fig. 16.9
The Choose Time dialog box displays several days of your schedule at a glance.

3. Enter a description of the appointment in the **D**escription text box.

◄ "Editing Text in Text Boxes," p. 39

4. You can select the Tentati**v**e check box. When you designate an appointment as tentative, it appears against a gray, rather than white, background in your Appointment Book, and the appointment is not blocked out in your Planner. When you or others in your workgroup view your schedule in the Planner, this time slot appears open. Designate an appointment as tentative if you want to get the appointment down in your Appointment Book so that you won't forget it, but are not ready to make a final commitment to the time for the appointment and don't want to eliminate that time slot for others who are trying to schedule meetings.

5. To set a reminder for the appointment, select the Set **R**eminder check box and enter the amount of time that you want to be reminded before the appointment. (For details on how to set reminders for appointments,

III

Using Windows Accessories

see the section "Setting Appointment Reminders" later in this chapter.) After you set a reminder for an appointment, a bell icon appears next to that appointment in your Appointment Book (refer to fig. 16.1).

6. To designate an appointment as private, select the **P**rivate check box. When you designate an appointment as private, others in your workgroup cannot view the appointment in your schedule (see the section called "Viewing or Modifying Another User's Appointment Book or Task List"). After you make an appointment private, a key icon appears next to the appointment in your Appointment Book (refer to fig. 16.1).

7. Choose OK or press Enter.

The appointment now appears in your Appointment Book on the scheduled date, and also in the Planner (if the appointment is not tentative), just as you described it in the Appointment dialog box.

After you enter an appointment in your Appointment Book, you can edit that appointment or designate it as a recurring appointment.

Editing an Appointment

As often happens, you may need to change the details of an appointment after you have recorded the appointment in your Appointment Book. Schedule+ enables you to make such changes with a few easy edits, whether the changes involve the appointment's description, a complete change in day or time, or the selection of one of the options described earlier, such as setting up a reminder or making the appointment private.

To change the description of an appointment, follow these steps:

1. Display the page in your Appointment Book for the date of the appointment that you want to edit. Follow steps 1 through 3 at the beginning of the section "Adding an Appointment Directly in Your Appointment Book" to select the date from the small calendar in the upper-right corner of the Appointment Book.

2. Double-click the time slot that contains the appointment you want to edit or select the appointment by using the Tab key.

3. Open the **E**dit menu and choose **E**dit Appt, or press Ctrl+E. The Appointment dialog box appears (refer to fig. 16.8).

4. Edit the text that appears in the **D**escription text box of the Appointment dialog box as you would edit the text in any dialog box, using the Backspace, Del, and arrow keys.

5. If necessary, change the time for the appointment. See the previous section for details on how to change the time.

6. Choose OK or press Enter.

You can also select or deselect the Tentati**v**e, **P**rivate, or Set **R**eminder check boxes in the Appointment dialog box. (See the section called "Adding an Appointment with the Appointment Dialog Box," earlier in this chapter, and "Setting Appointment Reminders," later in this chapter, for information on these options.)

> **Note**
>
> You can change the description and time slot for an appointment without using the Appointment dialog box. To change the description, you select the appointment and then edit the text in the time slot the same way you usually edit text. To change the beginning time for the appointment, click on the top edge of the time slot and drag the appointment to the new starting time. The duration of the appointment remains the same; only the starting time changes. To extend the time slot for the appointment, click on the bottom edge of the appointment and drag the edge to the new ending time.

Moving an Appointment

Moving an appointment to a new date and time is easy. Simply follow these steps:

1. Display the page in your Appointment Book for the date of the appointment that you want to move. Follow steps 1 through 3 at the beginning of the section "Adding an Appointment Directly in Your Appointment Book" to select the date from the small calendar in the upper-right corner of the Appointment Book.

2. Click on the time slot for the appointment that you want to move, or select the appointment with the Tab key.

3. Open the **E**dit menu and choose Mo**v**e Appt, or press Ctrl+O. The Move Appointment dialog box appears (see fig. 16.10).

Fig. 16.10
The Move Appointment dialog box.

4. Set the new time and date for the appointment.

   To set the time and date using the mouse, select the part of the time or date that you want to change. Then change the entry in the selected slot by typing a new number or by clicking on the up or down arrows on the left side of the time and date boxes.

   To set the time and date using the keyboard, press the Tab key to move to the starting or ending time or date that you want to change. Then use the right- or left-arrow keys to select the part of the time or date that you want to change. To select a new entry, type it or use the up and down arrows.

5. Choose OK or press Enter.

Schedule+ moves the appointment to the new day and time in your Appointment Book.

Copying an Appointment

When entering an appointment in your Appointment Book, you don't have to describe an entirely new appointment. In fact, you can often save time by copying an existing appointment to another time slot and then editing that appointment as necessary. To copy an appointment, follow these steps:

1. Display the page in your Appointment Book for the date of the appointment that you want to copy. Follow steps 1 through 3 at the beginning of the section "Adding an Appointment Directly in Your Appointment Book" to select the date from the small calendar in the upper-right corner of the Appointment Book.

2. Click on the time slot for the appointment that you want to move or use the Tab key to select the appointment.

3. Open the **E**dit menu and choose **C**opy Appt, or press Ctrl+Y.

4. Select the new date and time for the appointment as described at the beginning of the section "Adding an Appointment Directly in Your Appointment Book."

5. Open the **E**dit menu and choose **P**aste, or press Ctrl+V.

A copy of the original appointment appears at the new day and time in your Appointment Book.

Deleting an Appointment

If you want to delete an appointment from your Appointment Book, follow these steps:

1. Display the page in your Appointment Book for the date of the appointment that you want to delete. To select the date from the small calendar in the upper-right corner of the Appointment Book, follow steps 1 through 3 at the beginning of the section "Adding an Appointment Directly in Your Appointment Book."

2. Click on the time slot for the appointment that you want to delete, or use the Tab key to select the appointment.

3. Open the **E**dit menu and choose **D**elete, or press Ctrl+D.

Schedule+ removes the appointment from your Appointment Book and from your Planner.

Setting Appointment Reminders

You can tell Schedule+ to notify you in advance of any or all appointments listed in your Appointment Book by setting up a reminder. This reminder displays a pop-up message box that appears on-screen at a designated time interval before the specified appointment. You can set a reminder when you create a new appointment, or you can add a reminder to an existing appointment. You also can choose an option that sets reminders for all new appointments as you add those appointments to your Appointment Book.

To set a reminder for an existing appointment, follow these steps:

1. Display the page in your Appointment Book for the date of the appointment for which you want a reminder. Select the date from the small calendar in the upper-right corner of the Appointment Book by following steps 1 through 3 at the beginning of the section "Adding an Appointment Directly in Your Appointment Book."

2. Double-click the appointment, or select the appointment by using the Tab key.

3. Open the **E**dit menu and choose **E**dit Appt, or press Ctrl+E. The Appointment dialog box appears (refer to fig. 16.8).

4. Select the Set **R**eminder check box. This option's text box and Beforehand field list the amount of time and the time interval before the reminder appears.

Tip

If you have a recurring appointment, use the Recurring Appointment feature in Schedule+ to set an appointment that repeats at a consistent interval. For more details on setting up recurring appointments, see the section "Creating a Recurring Appointment."

III

Using Windows Accessories

5. To set a different interval for the length of time before the appointment reminder appears on-screen, type a new number in the text box immediately to the right of the Set **R**eminder check box. If necessary, you can change the unit for this interval to minutes, hours, days, weeks, or months by clicking the down-arrow box.

6. Choose OK or press Enter.

To set a reminder for a new appointment, use the method described in "Adding an Appointment with the Appointment Dialog Box" to add the new appointment. Follow steps 4 and 5 while you are in the Appointment dialog box to set the reminder.

After you set a reminder for an appointment, a bell icon appears next to the appointment in your Appointment Book.

Note

To set reminders for all new appointments, open the **O**ptions menu, choose **G**eneral Options, and, in the General Options dialog box, select the Se**t** Reminders Automatically check box. Specify the length of time before the appointment that you want the reminders to appear, and then choose OK or press Enter. If you set this option, every new appointment automatically has a reminder set for it. To turn off all reminders, open the **F**ile menu and choose Turn Off Reminders. The command then toggles to the Turn On Reminders command, which turns all reminders back on. You can toggle back and forth between these two options by successively selecting these commands.

Creating a Recurring Appointment

If a certain appointment recurs regularly, you can save time by entering the appointment once in your Appointment Book and designating that appointment as a *recurring appointment*. Schedule+ enters the recurring appointment in your Appointment Book at the designated times for as long a time period as you specify.

To create a recurring appointment, follow these steps:

1. If the appointment that you want to make recurring already exists, select that appointment using the techniques described in previous sections. If you have not already entered the appointment in your

Appointment Book, select the time slot for the appointment using the techniques described in the section "Adding an Appointment."

2. Open the Appointments menu and choose New **R**ecurring Appt, or press Ctrl+R. The Recurring Appointment dialog box appears as shown in figure 16.11.

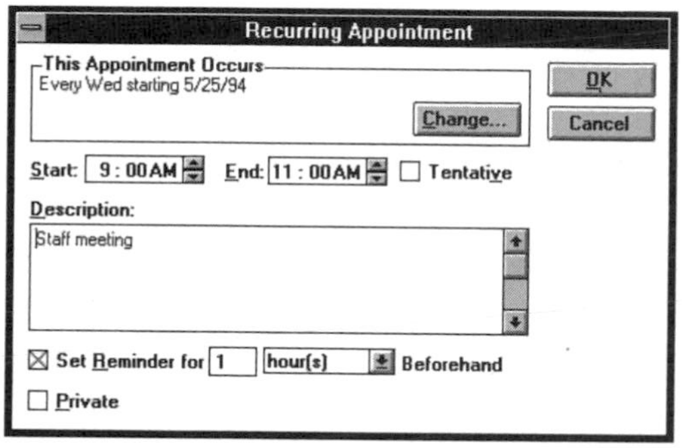

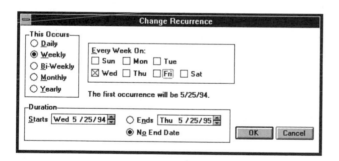

Fig. 16.11

The Recurring Appointment dialog box.

3. Choose the **C**hange button to display the Change Recurrence dialog box (see fig. 16.12).

Fig. 16.12

The Change Recurrence dialog box.

4. Select one of the options in the This Occurs group. After you select one of these options, the group of check boxes to the right change immediately. In figure 16.12, these check boxes appear as days of the week because the **W**eekly option button is selected. The following table lists the different collections of check boxes that appear for each This Occurs option:

Option	Check Boxes
Daily	**E**very day or E**v**ery weekday
Weekly	**E**very Week On (specify which days of the week)
Bi-Weekly	**E**very Other Week On (specify which days of the week)
Monthly	Specify which day of every month; for example, the first Monday or day seven of every month
Yearly	Specify a date (for example, March 1 of every year) or a particular day (for example, the first Monday of March)

5. Select from the check boxes to the right of the This Occurs group to specify the frequency of the recurring appointment.

6. To specify starting and ending dates for the recurring event (that is, the first date that the event occurs and the last date that it occurs), select the **S**tarts and E**n**ds options in the Duration box and edit the date entries in the two fields.

   To set the times and dates using the mouse, select the part of the time or date that you want to change by clicking on it, and then type a new entry or click on the up or down arrows on the right side of the date boxes to change the entry in the selected slot.

   To set the times and dates using the keyboard, press the Tab key to move to either the **S**tarts or E**n**ds date, and then use the right- or left-arrow keys to select the part of the date that you want to change. Type a new entry or use the up- and down-arrow keys to select a new entry.

   If you select the E**n**ds option but do not change the end date, the appointment is automatically set to recur for one year from the date of the page currently displayed in the Appointment Book. Alternatively, you can select the N**o** End Date check box, in which case the appointment is set to recur indefinitely (until you change the E**n**ds date or delete the recurring appointment).

7. Choose OK or press Enter to return to the Recurring Appointment dialog box.

8. If necessary, change the starting and ending times for the appointment using the **S**tart and **E**nd boxes.

To set the times using the mouse, select the part of the time that you want to change by clicking on it; then type in a new entry or click on the up or down arrows on the right side of the time boxes to change the entry in the selected slot.

To set the times using the keyboard, press the Tab key to move to the starting or ending time that you want to change, and then use the right- or left-arrow keys to select the part of the time that you want to change. Type a new entry or use the up- and down-arrow keys to select a new entry.

9. If you are working with an appointment that you have not previously entered, type a description of the appointment in the **D**escription text box. If the appointment is already described, skip to the next step.

10. Select any or all Tentati**v**e, **P**rivate, or Set **R**eminder check boxes, as described in detail in the "Adding an Appointment" and "Setting Appointment Reminders" sections earlier in this chapter.

11. Choose OK or press Enter.

The appoinment is now entered in your Appointment Book for every date that falls within the criteria designated in the Change Recurrence dialog box. A circular arrow icon is displayed next to recurring appointments in your Appointment Book. You can see this icon in figure 16.1.

Editing or Deleting a Recurring Appointment

You can edit or delete any particular occurrence of a recurring appointment in your Appointment Book by using the same method that you use to edit or delete a regular appointment. (See the section "Editing an Appointment," earlier in this chapter, for details.) You also can edit or delete *all* occurrences of a recurring appointment.

To delete all occurrences of a recurring appointment, follow these steps:

1. Open the Appoint**m**ents menu and choose Edit Re**c**urring Appts. The Edit Recurring Appointments dialog box is then displayed as shown in figure 16.13. This dialog box lists all the recurring appointments currently entered in your Appointment Book.

Fig. 16.13

The Edit Recurring
Appointments
dialog box.

2. Select the recurring appointment that you want to delete by clicking it, or press the up- or down-arrow keys until the item is selected.

3. Choose the **D**elete button. Schedule+ removes the selected recurring appointment from the appointment list in the dialog box.

4. Choose the **C**lose button. Schedule+ removes the recurring appointment from your Appointment Book and your Planner.

To edit all occurrences of a recurring appointment, follow these steps:

1. Open the Appointments menu and choose Edit Recurring Appts. This displays the Edit Recurring Appointments dialog box (refer to fig. 16.13).

2. Select the recurring appointment that you want to change, either by double-clicking the appointment in the dialog box list, or by using the arrow keys to select the item and choosing the **E**dit button.

   The Recurring Appointment dialog box is displayed (refer to fig. 16.11).

3. Make the desired changes in the Recurring Appointment dialog box, as described in the preceding section, "Creating a Recurring Appointment." To change the time interval for the recurring appointment, choose the **C**hange button, make the desired interval changes in the Change Recurrence dialog box (refer to fig. 16.12), and then choose OK or press Enter to return to the Recurring Appointment dialog box.

4. Choose OK or press Enter to return to the Edit Recurring Appointments dialog box.

5. Select another appointment to edit or choose the **C**lose button. Schedule+ makes the appropriate changes in all the occurrences of the recurring appointment in your Appointment Book and Planner.

Adding Notes to Your Appointment Book

Sometimes you may want to make a note for a particular day that is not associated with an appointment in the Appointment Book. To accommodate
such a need, Schedule+ enables you to add notes to the pages of your Appointment Book. These notes are displayed in the **N**otes box in the lower-
right corner of the Appointment Book. Notes apply to a specific day but need
not be associated with a particular time slot.

To add a note to your Appointment Book, follow these steps:

1. Change to the date in your Appointment Book to which you want to
    add your note, if that date is not the current one. See the steps de-
    scribed at the beginning of the section "Adding an Appointment Di-
    rectly in Your Appointment Book" for details on how to select the date
    in your Appointment Book.

2. Click inside the **N**otes text box, or press Alt+N. The Notes text box is in
    the lower-right corner of the Appointment book, as shown in figure
    16.1. An insertion point appears inside the Notes box where you can
    start entering text.

3. Type in the **N**otes box the text for your note. If you need more room for
    notes than appears in the box, just keep typing. The text scrolls up as
    you continue to type, just as with any text that you type. You can use
    the scroll bar to the right of the **N**otes box to move up and down
    within the box, just as with other Windows programs. Press Enter to
    start a new paragraph.

Just as you can add notes to your Appointment Book, you can edit your notes
or delete them altogether, as you can with any text. To edit or delete a note,
click inside the **N**otes box or press Alt+N, and then edit or delete the text of
your notes as you would edit text in any Windows application, using the Del,
Backspace, and arrow keys.

You can set an option to display a pop-up reminder message on days that
have notes. The reminder message appears on-screen when you first open
Schedule+ on a day that has notes associated with it. Although you can see
the notes in your Appointment Book when you open Schedule+, adding a
reminder to your notes can bring those notes to your attention immediately.
When you select this option, it applies to all days that have notes associated
with them. Open the **O**ptions menu, choose **G**eneral Options, select the Set
Reminders for Notes option, and choose OK or press Enter.

III

Using Windows Accessories

If you need to locate any particular appointment or note within your Appointment Book, you can search for strings of text by using the **E**dit menu's **F**ind command. This command is especially helpful if you know that you have scheduled an appointment regarding a specific topic or with a person that you remember, but you cannot remember the day for which you scheduled the appointment.

To find text in your Appointment Book, follow these steps:

1. Open the **E**dit menu and choose **F**ind, or press Ctrl+F. This displays the Find dialog box (see fig. 16.14).

Fig. 16.14
The Find
dialog box.

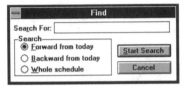

2. In the Se**a**rch For text box, type the text string that you want to locate.

3. Choose one of the three search options: **F**orward from Today, **B**ackward from Today, or **W**hole Schedule. The first two search options search through your Appointment Book in the stated direction from the current date only. The last searches the entire Appointment Book.

4. Choose the **S**tart Search button.

If the text that you specified is found, the Appointment Book page for the day in which the text occurs is displayed and the text is highlighted. The Find dialog box stays open and the **S**tart Search button changes to the Find **N**ext button. You can then choose that button to continue searching for the same text string. After you locate the appointment or note that you want, choose the Cancel button or press Esc.

If the Find dialog box covers text that you want to see, you can move it. With the mouse, you can click on the title bar and drag the dialog box to a new location. With the keyboard, you can press Alt+space bar, choose **M**ove from the control menu, use the arrow keys to move the dialog box, and press Enter.

Using the Task List

The Task List in Schedule+ is where you can list tasks that you need to accomplish but that, unlike an appointment, are not necessarily associated with a specific block of time. You can keep in this list a running collection of what you want to accomplish, removing items as you complete each task. You can designate a starting time and due date for a task. The *starting time* determines when the task becomes active in your Task List. If you have selected the Show Active Tasks command (see the section "Sorting Projects and Tasks," later in this chapter), only those tasks that are active are displayed. The *due date* is when the task is noted as overdue. When a task becomes overdue, it continues to be listed in your task list but is highlighted with red type.

You can create recurring tasks that are added to your Task List at specific time intervals. You can even attach a reminder to a task so that a pop-up message box appears on-screen to remind you to start the task. You can assign a priority to a task, according to the importance of the task's completion. You then can sort tasks by priority, due date, or description.

You also can create a project and add tasks to it, and then view all the tasks associated with a particular project. A *project* is simply a grouping of all tasks associated with a particular job, such as all the tasks associated with creating a budget or opening a new office.

Adding a Task to Your Task List

As you work with your Task List, you are certain to discover that, as you finish certain tasks, you need to add others to the list. To add a new task to your Task List, follow these steps:

1. If you are not already in the Schedule+ window that bears your name, open the **W**indow menu and select your name (or type the number listed next to your name).

2. If the Schedule+ window does not display your Task List, choose the **T**asks tab along the left side of the window. The Task List appears on-screen (refer to fig. 16.2).

3. Open the **T**asks menu and choose New **T**ask, or press Ctrl+T, to display the Task dialog box (see fig. 16.15).

III

Using Windows Accessories

Fig. 16.15

The Task
dialog box.

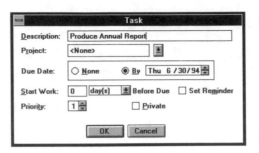

4. Type a description of the task in the **D**escription text box.

5. To add the task to a specific project that you have created, select the project from the **P**roject drop-down list by clicking the arrow to its right. (See "Adding a Project" later in this chapter.) If you do not want to add the task to a project, select None from the list.

6. To specify a due date for the task, select the **B**y option in the Due Date box. Select **N**one if you do not want to specify a due date. (If you select **N**one, skip to step 10.)

   If you select the **B**y option, you must change the date in the date field to the desired due date. (If the correct due date already appears in the date field, skip to step 8.)

7. To change the date, click in the date field and edit the date by using the arrow, Del, and Backspace keys. Alternatively, you can click the up and down arrows to the right of the date field until the desired date is selected.

   After you specify a due date for a task, the **S**tart Work and Set Re**m**inder options are enabled. You can use these options to designate a starting date for your work on the task and to set a reminder for yourself to start the task on the designated starting date.

8. To specify a starting time for the task in the **S**tart Work box, type a number in the text box and then click on the arrow to the right of the Before Due field. Select a unit of time—days, weeks, or months—from the Before Due drop-down list. (If you do not want to specify a starting time, type **0** in the Start Work text box; the unit of time is then unimportant.)

   The time interval that you specify in the **S**tart Work box and Before Due field determines how long before the due date the task is actually displayed in your Task List and thus becomes active.

9. Select the Set Reminder check box if you want Schedule+ to display a pop-up message box that reminds you of the task on the starting date. (Before you can select this option, you must set a starting date.) The pop-up message box appears on-screen in whatever Windows application you happen to be working.

   After you set a reminder for a task, a bell icon appears next to the task in the Task List (refer to fig. 16.2).

10. If you do not want to assign a default priority to a new task, select a new priority level from the Priority box by clicking the up and down arrows to the right of the box.

    Priority levels range from 1 to 9 or from A to Z (if you prefer to use letters). The highest priority level is 1, or A if you are using letters. If you use both numbers and letters to prioritize your tasks, numbers have higher priority than letters; therefore, 9 has higher priority than A. The default level is 3 or C.

    For the best time management in your day, you should have one to three A or 1 level tasks. These are tasks that must get done because they are necessary to achieving your most important goals. You might have three to five B or 2 level tasks. These are supporting tasks or daily tasks. Frequently, they are the mundane but necessary tasks to keep your job functioning, but they may not advance your career.

    Finally, there are the C or 3 level tasks and the tasks at even lower levels. These tasks are the ever-present "administrivia" that can clutter your day and keep you from advancing your career, spending time with your family, or meeting personal goals. Such tasks include returning non-mandatory phone calls, attending meetings in which you are not a contributor, cleaning out filing cabinets, and so on. Everyone needs an occasional level C or 3 task to give their brain or body a moment to unwind, but try to avoid them until you are forced to move them into the level B or 2 priority.

11. To prevent other users from viewing this task, select the **P**rivate check box. After you designate a task as private, a key icon appears next to the task in the Task List (refer to fig. 16.2)

12. Choose OK or press Enter. The new task now appears in your Task List.

III

Using Windows Accessories

Adding a Project

Just as you can create and add new tasks to your Task List, you can create projects and add to them those tasks associated with each project. After you add tasks to projects, you can choose to view the tasks grouped by project in the Task List.

To add a project to your Task List, follow these steps:

1. With the Task List displayed, open the Ta**s**ks menu and choose New **P**roject. The Project dialog box appears, as shown in figure 16.16.

Fig. 16.16

The Project dialog box.

2. Type a name for the project in the **N**ame text box.

3. To make the project private, select the **P**rivate check box. After you make a project private, other users cannot view that project. A key icon is displayed in the Task List next to projects that you have designated as private.

4. Choose OK or press Enter.

The new project appears in your Task List. The title for a project appears in bold in the Task List (refer to fig. 16.2). If you group tasks by project (as described in the next paragraph), all the tasks for a given project are listed under the project's title.

You assign tasks to a project by selecting the project's name from the P**r**oject list in the Task dialog box for that task, as described in the section "Adding a Task to Your Task List" earlier in this chapter. You can also add existing tasks to a new project by clicking the task name on the Task List and then dragging and dropping the task under the new project's name on the list, as discussed in the following section, "Editing Tasks and Projects."

Tasks assigned to a project are listed under the project name on the Task List only after you turn on the the Ta**s**ks menu's **V**iew by Project option. To turn on this option, open the Ta**s**ks menu and choose **V**iew by Project. When this option is selected (or turned on), a check mark appears next to it. To deselect (or turn off) the **V**iew by Project option, choose the command again. If the option is not turned on, all tasks are listed together on the Task List and project names do not appear in the Task List.

Editing Tasks and Projects

Sometimes you must change the description of a task or project or alter other aspects of a task in your Task List. You may even need to delete a task or project altogether—especially if you have completed it. Schedule+ enables you to edit or delete any existing tasks or projects in your list.

To edit or change a task, follow these steps:

1. With the Task List displayed, double-click the task that you want to edit, or select the task by clicking it (or by using the arrow keys to highlight it) and pressing Enter. The Task dialog box appears.

2. Edit the task **D**escription in the Task dialog box by using the arrow, Del, and Backspace keys and adding any new text necessary.

   In this dialog box, as discussed in the section "Adding a Task to Your Task List," earlier in this chapter, you also can change the task's due date and starting date, set a reminder for the task, change the priority level, or designate the task as private.

3. Choose OK or press Enter.

Changes that you make in the Task dialog box are reflected in the task's listing in the Task List after you choose OK or press Enter.

You can edit a project name the same way that you edit a task name. To edit a project name, follow these steps:

1. Double-click the project name in the Task List, or select the project by clicking it (or using the arrow keys to highlight it) and pressing Enter. The Project dialog box appears.

2. Edit the text in the **N**ame text box of the Project dialog box.

3. Choose OK or press Enter to transfer the changes to the project name from the dialog box to the Task List.

To delete a task, follow these steps:

1. With the Task List displayed, select the task that you want to delete.

2. Choose the De**l**ete button at the bottom of the Task List. The task is removed from the Task List.

After you complete a task, you may want to keep a reminder that the task is finished. Schedule+ enables you to insert a note about the completed task in your Appointment Book at the same time that you remove the task from your Task List.

Tip

To change the priority level of a task without using the Task dialog box, select the task in the Task List and click the up or down arrow at the bottom of the Task List.

III

Using Windows Accessories

To remove a completed task from the Task List and insert a note in your Appointment Book about the completed task, select the task and choose the **C**ompleted button at the bottom of the Task List. Schedule+ inserts the description of the task in the **N**otes section of your Appointment Book for the day on which you completed the task.

You can delete a project and all its associated tasks simultaneously. To delete a project and its tasks, follow these steps:

1. Select the project in the Task List and choose the De**l**ete button. A message box informs you that the project and all its tasks will be deleted.

2. Choose OK.

The project and all its tasks are removed from your Task List.

To delete a project without deleting its tasks, you must first move all the tasks from that project on the Task List. You can perform this operation by clicking on each task and then dragging and dropping them in an area of the Task List that lists tasks that are not associated with the project. You also can double-click on the task, or select the task and press Enter, to display the Task dialog box. Then select None from the P**r**oject drop-down list, and choose OK or press Enter. After you have moved all the tasks from the project, select the project name and choose the De**l**ete button to remove it from the Task List.

To copy a task from one project to another, first select from the Task List the task that you want to copy. Holding down the Ctrl key, drag and drop the task on or under the name of the project to which you want to copy the task.

Adding a Task to Your Appointment Book

You may need to complete some tasks at specific times or on specific dates. To ensure that you don't forget this type of task, you can add a task to a time slot in your Appointment Book.

To add a task to your Appointment Book, follow these steps:

1. Choose the **T**asks tab to select the Task List.

2. Select the task that you want to schedule, either by clicking on it or by pressing the up- or down-arrow keys.

3. Choose the Add To Sched**u**le button. This displays the Choose Time dialog box.

4. Select from the calendar and the time slot the date to which you want to assign the task.

5. Choose OK or press Enter.

The tasks still appear in your Task List, but are also displayed in the Appointment Book.

Adding a Recurring Task

If you must complete a certain task regularly, you can save yourself time by entering the task once in your Task List and then designating the task as a recurring task. Schedule+ then enters the task at the designated times for as long a time period as you specify.

To create a recurring task, follow these steps:

1. Open the Task menu and choose New **R**ecurring Task to display the Recurring Task dialog box (see fig. 16.17.)

Fig. 16.17
The Recurring Task dialog box.

2. Type a description of the task in the **D**escription text box of the Recurring Task dialog box.

3. To add the recurring task to a specific project that you have created, select from the **P**roject drop-down list the project to which you want to assign the task. Select None from the list if you do not want to add the task to any project.

4. Choose the **C**hange button to display the Change Recurrence dialog box (refer to fig 16.12).

5. Refer to the section called "Creating a Recurring Appointment," for details on how to set up the recurring task.

6. Choose OK or press Enter to return to the Recurring Task dialog box.

III

Using Windows Accessories

7. Follow the steps outlined in the section called "Adding a Task to Your Task List," to finish creating the recurring task.

8. Choose OK or press Enter.

The recurring task now appears in your Task List for every day that falls within the criteria designated in the Change Recurrence dialog box. A circular arrow icon is displayed next to each listing of a recurring task in the Task List (refer to fig. 16.2).

Editing a Recurring Task

You can edit or delete any occurrence of a recurring task in your Task List by using the same method as for editing or deleting a regular task. (See the section "Editing Tasks and Projects," earlier in this chapter, for details.) You also can edit or delete all occurrences of a recurring task.

To delete or edit all occurrences of a recurring task, follow these steps:

1. Open the Tasks menu and choose Edit Recurring Tasks. This command displays the Edit Recurring Tasks dialog box (see fig. 16.18). The dialog box lists all the recurring tasks currently entered in your Task List.

Fig. 16.18

The Edit Recurring Tasks dialog box.

2. Select, delete, or edit the task by following the steps described in the section called "Editing or Deleting a Recurring Appointment."

3. Choose the Close button. Schedule+ makes the appropriate changes in all occurrences of the recurring task in your Task List.

Sorting Projects and Tasks

You can arrange tasks in several ways on your Task List. You can display your tasks arranged by project, for example, and you can sort tasks by priority, due date, or description. You also can restrict your Task List to displaying only *active* tasks (that is, tasks with no starting or due dates or tasks with a starting date that has arrived), or you can display all tasks, including tasks that have not yet become active.

To view your tasks organized by project on the Task List, open the Ta**s**ks menu and choose **V**iew By Project, or press Ctrl+Shift+**V**. Then you can return to viewing your tasks ungrouped by project by once again opening the Ta**s**ks menu and choosing **V**iew By Project or pressing Ctrl+Shift+**V**. If you group your tasks by project, they are sorted within each project. Tasks that are not part of a project are grouped and sorted together, separate from tasks assigned to projects.

You can sort your tasks by priority, due date, or description:

- To sort your tasks by priority, choose the P**r**iority button at the top of the Task List, or open the Ta**s**ks menu and choose Sort By Prior**i**ty.

- To sort your tasks by due date, choose the Due **B**y button at the top of the Task List, or open the Ta**s**ks menu and choose Sort **b**y Due Date.

- To sort your tasks by description, choose the **D**escription button at the top of the Task List, or open the Ta**s**ks menu and choose Sort By **D**escription.

To view only your active tasks on the Task List, open the Ta**s**ks menu and choose Show **A**ctive Tasks. To return to viewing all your tasks, open the Ta**s**ks menu and choose Show **A**ctive Tasks again.

Scheduling a Meeting

One of the most powerful and useful features of Schedule+, when you are connected to the mail server in Windows for Workgroups (or working *on-line*), is that Schedule+ enables you to schedule meetings with others in your workgroup without ever leaving your desk or making a phone call. When you work on-line with Schedule+, everyone in a workgroup can access the schedules of the others in that workgroup. This accessibility enables anyone in the workgroup to schedule a meeting at a time that does not conflict with the appointment times for the others who are to attend the meeting.

When you schedule a meeting, you can select who you want to attend and suggest a date and time for the meeting, based on times that appear to be open in the schedules of the people you want to attend. After you have scheduled a meeting, a request is sent to each invited group member.

III

Using Windows Accessories

◀ "Sending Mes-
sages with
Mail," p. 517

◀ "Reading and
Working with
Messages,"
p. 524

You can attach to this request a message. Such a message might explain more about the agenda for the meeting. The request appears as a message in the Schedule+ Messages window as well as in the Inbox in Mail. Each invited group member can then reply to your request by declining, accepting, or tentatively accepting the proposed meeting time. Those people responding also can attach a text message to their reply. Responses to meeting requests appear in your Schedule+ Messages window and in your Inbox in Mail.

Schedule+ provides several options for designating how much other users can access your schedule. You can designate any of the following levels of access:

- Users who have no access to your schedule

- Users who can view your free and busy time slots without actually viewing your appointments

- Users who can actually read your appointments and tasks

- Users who can create or modify your appointments and tasks

You can also assign an assistant, who has complete access to your schedule and can act for you in scheduling meetings and responding to meeting requests.

You can schedule a meeting from your Appointment Book or from your Planner. The Planner (refer to fig. 16.3) displays blocks of time for several days at a glance in a day-by-time grid. When you or other group members have an appointment, that appointment is indicated in the Planner by a vertical line running through the time slot allotted for the appointment. Your appointments are indicated by a blue line, and the appointments of others in your workgroup are indicated by a gray line. A calendar in the upper-right corner of the Planner window, similar to the one in the Appointment Book, enables you to change the days displayed in the Planner.

Not only can you view the schedules for everyone in your workgroup, including your own, but you can also mark a block of time in which you want to schedule a meeting, select the people that you want to attend, and send each of them a meeting request that can include a message. If the people that you have asked to attend a meeting reply affirmatively, the meeting time is marked in the Planners of all the invited attendees.

Just as you can schedule a meeting, so can you schedule a resource, such as a meeting room or slide projector. To schedule a resource, the Postoffice Administrator must set up on the Postoffice a Mail account for that resource (see Chapter 10, "Using Windows for Workgroups Mail and PC Fax"). If you then grant full access privileges to other users for that account, anyone can view the schedule for that resource and book the resource during any open time slot. Alternatively, you can designate someone as the assistant for the resource, who must then confirm all requests for the resource.

Scheduling a Meeting with the Planner

To use your Planner to schedule a meeting, follow these steps:

1. If you are not already in your schedule window, open the **W**indow menu and select your name (or type the number next to your name).

2. If your Planner is not already displayed, choose the **P**lanner tab along the left side of the window.

3. Note who is already listed in the Atten**d**ees list in the lower-right corner of the Planner window. To select additional attendees, choose the **C**hange button. The Select Attendees dialog box appears (see fig. 16.19).

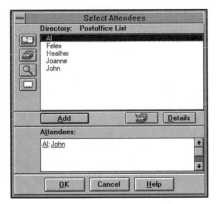

Fig. 16.19
The Select Attendees dialog box.

4. From the list of names in the Directory box at the top of the dialog box, select the people you want to attend the meeting.

   If the list does not include the names of the people to whom you want to send a request, click on the Directory button (the icon that looks like an open book) or press Ctrl+L and then, in the Open Directory dialog box, select a new directory. To make the directory that you have se-lected the default directory, choose the Set **D**efault button. Choose OK or press Enter. You then return to the Select Attendees dialog box.

5. Choose the **A**dd button. The names of the people you selected appear in the At**t**endees box.

6. After you finish selecting the attendees, choose OK.

   If the Planner's Attendees box includes people you don't want to attend, you can click on their names in the Attendees box. Then the schedules for these people are not shown in the Planner, and these people are not sent a meeting request.

7. Click on the beginning time for the proposed meeting in the Planner and drag to the ending time for the meeting. Alternatively, you can use the arrow keys to select the beginning time, hold down the Shift key, and use the arrow keys to move to the end time.

   Be sure to select a time when everyone you want to attend is available.

> **Note**
>
> To find quickly a time when everyone in your attendees list is available, select a time slot in the grid equal to the length of time for which you have scheduled the meeting. Then open the Appointments menu and choose **A**uto-Pick, or press Ctrl+A.

8. Choose the **R**equest Meeting button to display the Send Request dialog

Fig. 16.20
The Send Request dialog box.

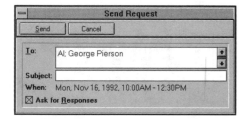

box (see fig. 16.20).

9. In the Subject text box, type the subject of the meeting. What you type in the Subject text box is also used as the description of the appointment in everyone's Appointment Book.

10. By default, the recipients of your request are asked to respond. If you don't want a response, deselect the Ask for **R**esponses check box.

11. Press the Tab key or click in the message area, and type a message1 to accompany the request. You do not have to include a message.

12. Choose the **S**end button.

A message box informing you that the meeting was successfully booked appears. Click on OK or press Enter to return to the Planner. A hand-shaking icon is displayed next to meetings in your Appointment Book.

The following are some tips for selecting names from your Personal Address Book in Mail:

- To view the names in your Personal Address Book, click on the Personal Address button (the index file icon) or press Ctrl+P in the Select Attendees dialog box (refer to fig. 16.19).

- To search for a name in the names list, click on the Find button (the magnifying glass icon) or press Ctrl+F, type the name in the Name Finder dialog box, and choose the **F**ind button.

- To select two or more names listed consecutively in the names list, click the first name (or use the arrow keys to select the first name), hold down the Shift key, and click on the last name (or use the arrow keys to select the last name).

- To select two or more names *not* listed consecutively, click on the first name (or use the arrow keys to select the first name), hold down the Ctrl key, and click on the other names that you want to select (or use the arrow keys to select a name and press the space bar).

- To deselect a name in the list, hold down the Ctrl key and click on the name (or hold down the Ctrl key, use the arrow keys to select the name, and press the space bar).

◀ "Building Your Personal Address Book," p. 544

◀ "Adding an Address," p. 544

◀ "Creating a Custom Address," p. 546

Scheduling a Meeting with the Appointment Book

To use your Appointment Book to set up a meeting, follow these steps:

1. If you are not already in your schedule window, open the **W**indow menu and select your name or type the number next to your name.

2. If your Appointment Book is not already displayed, choose the **A**ppts tab along the left side of the window.

3. Select a proposed time for the meeting. You can change this time after you view the schedules of the other people you want to attend the meeting.

4. Open the Appoint**m**ents menu and choose **N**ew Appointment, or press Ctrl+N, to display the Appointment dialog box (refer to fig. 16.8).

III

Using Windows Accessories

5. Choose the Choose **T**ime button to display the Choose Time dialog box (see fig. 16.21). In this dialog box, you can view the free and busy times of the people you want to invite to the meeting.

Fig. 16.21
The Choose Time
dialog box.

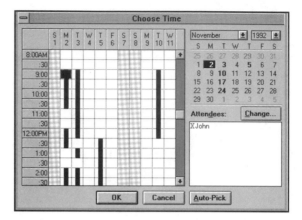

6. Choose the **C**hange button to display the Select Attendees dialog box (refer to fig. 16.19).

7. Complete steps 4 through 6 as described in the section called "Scheduling a Meeting with the Planner," earlier in this chapter.

8. If conflicts arise with the time that you originally selected in your Appointment Book, select a new time in the Choose Time dialog box.

> **Note**
>
> To find quickly a time at which everyone in your attendees list is available, select a time slot in the grid equal to the length of time for which the meeting is scheduled and choose the **A**uto-Pick button. If you do not like the scheduled time that **A**uto-Pick chooses, continue to choose the button to see other times that fit into everyone's schedule.
>
> If you do not need to view the busy and free times of the attendees, you can choose the **I**nvite button in the Appointment dialog box to go directly to the Select Attendees dialog box.

9. Choose OK to return to the Appointment dialog box.

10. Type a description of the meeting in the **D**escription text box of the Appointment dialog box.

11. Choose OK or press Enter. The Send Request dialog box is displayed (refer to fig. 16.20).

12. Complete steps 9 through 12 as described in the section "Scheduling a Meeting with the Planner" earlier in this chapter.

Scheduling a Resource

You can use Schedule+ to schedule a resource, just as you would schedule a meeting. For example, you may need to schedule a meeting room, a portable computer, or an overhead transparency projector. Before you can schedule a resource, the Postoffice Administrator must create a Mail account for that resource and someone must open Schedule+ and set up the resource so that either all users have access to it or an assistant is assigned to handle the scheduling for the resource.

To add a resource, follow these steps:

1. Ask your Postoffice Administrator to create a Mail account for the resource.

2. Sign into Schedule+ by using the name and password for the resource.

◄ "Creating Your User Account," p. 513

3. Open the **O**ptions menu and choose **G**eneral Options.

4. Select the option This **A**ccount Is for a Resource.

5. Choose OK or press Enter.

6. Open the **O**ptions menu and choose Set **A**ccess Privileges.

7. Choose one of the following options:

Select **C**reate Appointments & Tasks to enable all users to schedule the resource themselves. If you select this option, any user can schedule a resource using the methods described in the section "Working with Another User's Appointment Book and Task List" later in this chapter.

Select the Assis**t**ant option and assign an assistant to manage the resource. See "Assigning an Assistant for Your Schedule" later in this chapter for details on how to designate an assistant. If you assign an assistant to the resource, only that person can actually schedule the resource; all requests for the resource go to the assistant.

Reading Responses to a Meeting Request

After others respond to your meeting requests, their responses appear in the Schedule+ Messages window as well as in your Mail Inbox.

To read these responses, follow these steps:

◀ "Reading and
Working with
Messages,"
p. 524

1. Open the **W**indow menu and choose Messages to display the Messages window (refer to fig. 16.6).

2. Select the response that you want to read by doubling-clicking it, and then choose the **R**ead button.

3. To delete a response, select the response using the mouse or keyboard and then choose **D**elete.

Rescheduling a Meeting

To reschedule a meeting, follow these steps:

1. If you are not already in your schedule window, open the **W**indow menu and select your name or type the number next to your name.

2. If your Appointment Book is not already displayed, choose the **A**ppts tab along the left side of the window.

3. Find the meeting in your Appointment Book and move the meeting to the new proposed time. (See the section "Editing an Appointment," earlier in this chapter.)

4. At this point, Schedule+ displays a dialog box that asks whether you want to notify the meeting's attendees of the change. Choose **Y**es to display the Meeting Request window.

5. If you want, you can add a message to the request. Then choose the **S**end button.

Attendees receive a new meeting request with the new time, to which they can respond as with any meeting request.

Canceling a Meeting

To cancel a meeting, follow these steps:

1. If you are not already in your schedule window, open the **W**indow menu and select your name or type the number next to your name.

2. If your Appointment Book is not already displayed, choose the **A**ppts tab along the left side of the window.

3. Select the meeting in your Appointment Book.

4. Open the **E**dit menu and choose **D**elete Appt, or press Ctrl+D.

5. A message box asks whether you want to notify the meeting's attendees of the cancellation. Choose **Y**es to display the Cancel Meeting window.

6. Type a message in the message area and choose the **S**end button.

All attendees of the meeting receive a message that notifies them of the cancellation, and the meeting is removed from everyone's Appointment Books and Planners.

Responding to a Meeting Request

If someone else in your workgroup sends a request asking you to attend a meeting, you receive the request in your Schedule+ Messages window as well as in your Mail Inbox. You can read and respond to such requests in the Messages window.

To read and respond to meeting requests, follow these steps:

◀ "Replying to Messages," p. 525

1. Open the **W**indow menu and choose Messages.

2. Double-click the request to which you want to respond, or select the request and then choose the **R**ead button. The Meeting Request window appears, as shown in figure 16.22.

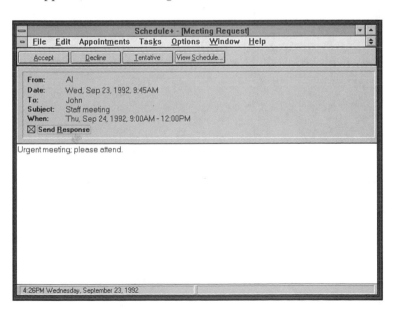

Fig. 16.22
The Meeting Request window.

3. Choose the View **S**chedule button to view your schedule. To return to the Meeting Request window, open the **W**indow menu and choose Meeting Request.

III

Using Windows Accessories

4. Choose the **A**ccept button, the **D**ecline button, or the **T**entative button. If you choose to accept or tentatively accept the request, Schedule+ enters the meeting into your Appointment Book. After you choose the **A**ccept or **T**entative button, the Send Response window appears, as shown in figure 16.23.

Fig. 16.23
The Send
Response window.

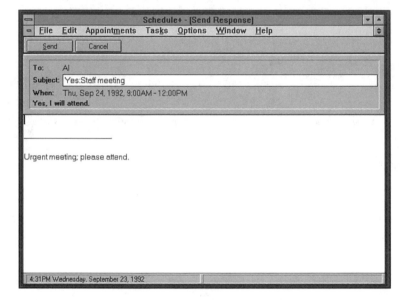

5. In the upper portion of the message area, type any message you might want to add to your response.

6. Choose the **S**end button.

Assigning an Assistant for Your Schedule

Schedule+ enables you to designate another user on your network as an assistant. That person can then view and change your Appointment Book as if the book were his own. The assistant also receives meeting requests and responses to meeting requests for the *owner* of the Appointment Book. Responses that the assistant makes to the owner's meeting requests are logged in the owner's Appointment Book.

You can even have meeting messages sent only to your assistant. Open the **O**ptions menu, choose **G**eneral Options, select the Send **M**eeting Messages Only to My Assistant check box, and choose OK or press Enter.

Designating an Assistant

To designate another user as your assistant, follow these steps:

1. Open the **O**ptions menu and choose Set **A**ccess Privileges. This command displays the Set Access Privileges dialog box (see fig. 16.24).

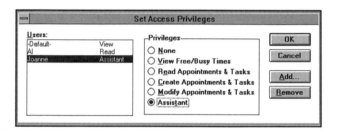

Fig. 16.24
The Set Access Privileges dialog box.

2. Select the user's name from the **U**sers box if the name is listed, or choose the **A**dd button and select the user's name from the names list.

   If the list does not include the name of the person you want to designate as your assistant, click on the Directory button (the icon that looks like an open book) or press Ctrl+L and select a new directory in the Open Directory dialog box. After you select the name for which you were looking, choose the **A**dd button and then choose OK or press Enter.

   You can designate only one assistant for your schedule at a time.

3. Choose the Assis**t**ant option from the Privileges group.

4. Choose OK or press Enter.

Removing or Changing Your Assistant

To change your assistant, you must first remove your current assistant and then designate a new assistant, because you can have only one assistant.

To remove an assistant, follow these steps:

1. Open the **O**ptions menu and choose Set **A**ccess Privileges.

2. Choose the assistant's name from the **U**sers box.

3. Select a new access privilege for your assistant by choosing from Privileges group an option other than Assis**t**ant.

III

Using Windows Accessories

> **Note**
>
> You can remove the assistant status and assign the default access privilege to your assistant in one step by selecting the assistant's name from the **U**sers list and choosing the **R**emove button. The default access privilege is applied to all users except those who have specifically been assigned another access privilege. (See the section "Designating Specific Privileges to a User" later in this chapter.)

Working as an Assistant for Another User

If you are acting as the assistant for someone else's schedule, you must open that person's Appointment Book before you can work with that schedule.

To open up the owner's Appointment Book, follow these steps:

1. Open the **F**ile menu and choose **O**pen Other's Appt. Book. The Open Other's Appt. Book is displayed (see fig. 16.25).

Fig. 16.25
The Open Other's Appt. Book dialog box.

2. Choose the name of the owner from the names listed at the top of the dialog box. If the list does not include the name of the person whose Appointment Book you want to open, click on the Directory button (the icon that looks like an open book) or press Ctrl+L and select a new directory in the Open Directory dialog box.

3. Choose the **A**dd button.

4. Choose OK or press Enter.

After you open the owner's Appointment Book, you can schedule meetings and respond to meeting requests just as you do with your own Appointment Book. You receive responses to meeting requests that you have sent, and Schedule+ logs the responses in the owner's Appointment Book.

You can act as an assistant for a resource in the same way that you assist another user. If you are in charge of scheduling for a conference room, for example, you must be assigned assistant privileges for that resource. You then receive all requests for the resource. After you receive a request, you check for the availability of the resource at the time requested by opening the **F**ile menu and choosing **O**pen Other's Appt. Book to open the Appointment Book for the resource. You can then respond to the request, just as with a meeting request.

Working with Another User's Appointment Book and Task List

In Schedule+, you can view another user's Appointment Book or Task List if the user has granted you that privilege. You can assign several levels of access privileges to a user. These levels range from no access to the privilege to view and modify another user's Appointment Book or Task List. Each user can designate the level of access that any other user has to his Appointment Book and Task List.

Designating Default Access Privileges

If you fail to assign specific access privileges to a user, that user is granted the default access privilege. You can change the default access privilege, which is the privilege granted to all users except those specifically granted another access privilege.

To set the default access privilege, follow these steps:

1. Open the **O**ptions menu and choose Set **A**ccess Privileges to display the Set Access Privileges dialog box (refer to fig. 16.24).

2. In the **U**sers box, select Default if that option is not already selected.

3. Select one of the access privilege options from the Privileges group. Table 16.1 describes the access privilege options.

4. Choose OK or press Enter.

III

Using Windows Accessories

Table 16.1	User Access Privileges
Option	**Description**
None	The user has no access.
View Free/Busy Times	The user can view the times when you are free or busy but cannot view the descriptions of your appointments.
Read Appointments & Tasks	The user can read your appointments and tasks but cannot modify them.
Create Appointments & Tasks	The user can add new appointments and tasks to your Appointment Book and Task List.
Modify Appointments & Tasks	The user can modify your appointments and tasks.
Assistant	The user can act as your assistant, and thus can view and modify your schedule, schedule meetings, and reply to meeting requests.

Designating Specific Privileges to a User

To designate a specific privilege other than the default privilege to a user, follow these steps:

1. Open the **O**ptions menu and choose Set **A**ccess Privileges.

2. Select the user's name from the **U**sers box if the name appears there. Otherwise, choose the **A**dd button and select the user's name from the names list. If the list does not include the name of the person whose access privilege you want to set, click on the Directory button (the icon that looks like an open book) or press Ctrl+L and select a new directory in the Open Directory dialog box.

3. Choose the **A**dd button, and click OK or press Enter.

4. Select the user's name from the **U**sers box.

5. Select from among the options in the Privileges group. Table 16.1 describes each option.

6. Choose OK or press Enter.

> **Note**
>
> You can determine which access privileges a user has to your schedule by opening the **O**ptions menu, choosing Set **A**ccess Privileges, selecting from the **U**sers box the user whose access privileges you want to view, and looking in the Privileges group to see which privilege is selected. To close the Set Access Privileges dialog box, choose the Cancel button.

Viewing or Modifying Another User's Appointment Book or Task List

If other users grant you access privileges to their schedules, you can work with their schedules. You may be restricted to viewing other users' schedules, but even this privilege can help you schedule a meeting at a time available to everyone you want to invite. If your access level is more extensive, you may have the privilege not only of viewing another user's appointments or tasks but even of adding to or modifying that user's appointments or tasks. Your level of access to another user's schedule depends on what access privilege the user has granted you. (See the section "Designating Specific Privileges to a User," earlier in this chapter, for details on how access privileges are assigned to a user.)

To work with another user's schedule, you must open that user's Appointment Book. To open another user's Appointment Book, follow these steps:

1. Open the **F**ile menu and choose **O**pen Other's Appt Book. The Open Other's Appt. Book dialog box appears, as shown in figure 16.25.

2. Select the user's name from the Directory box if the name is listed. If the list does not include the name of the person whose Appointment Book you want to open, click on the Directory button (the icon that looks like an open book) or press Ctrl+L and select a new directory in the Open Directory dialog box.

3. Choose the **A**dd button, and choose OK or press Enter.

The user's Appointment Book appears in your Schedule window. If you do not have access to that user's Appointment Book, Schedule+ informs you of that restriction.

After you open a user's Appointment Book, you can work with it in the same way as you work with your own Appointment Book, except that you can

III

Using Windows Accessories

perform only those operations for which you have been granted access. To access the user's Task List, choose the **T**asks tab on the left side of the Appointment Book.

Taking Your Appointments, Tasks, and Notes with You

Schedule+ would be of limited value if it restricted you to viewing your Appointment Book, Task List, and notes only on-screen. Fortunately, Schedule+ enables you to print your appointments, tasks, and notes in various formats so that you can carry them in your briefcase, insert them in your personal scheduling notebook, or post them on your wall.

Printing Your Appointments and Notes

To print your appointments and daily notes, follow these steps:

◀ "Opening, Saving, Printing, and Closing Files," p. 53

1. If you are not already in your schedule window, open the **W**indow menu and select your name (or type the number next to your name).

2. If your Appointment Book is not already displayed, choose the **A**ppts tab along the left side of the window.

3. Open the **F**ile menu and choose **P**rint, or press Ctrl+P, to display the Print dialog box (see fig. 16.26).

Fig. 16.26
The Print dialog box.

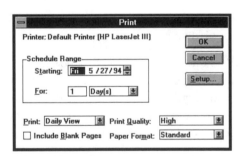

4. In the S**t**arting box, select a starting date for the printout. In the **F**or box, specify how many days you want the printout to include.

5. In the **P**rint drop-down list, select how you want your printout organized, as follows:

Daily View	Prints one day's schedule per page
Weekly View	Prints one week's schedule per page
Monthly View	Prints an entire months schedule per page
Text View	Prints just text (dates, times, and events) with out any calendar formatting
Task View	This option is used when you are printing your Task List

6. In the Print **Q**uality drop-down list, select the print quality that you want.

7. In the Paper For**m**at drop-down list, select the size of your printout. These paper formats are designed to fit many personal and desktop scheduling or time-management systems.

8. If you want to change the margins of your printout, choose the **S**etup button to display the Print Setup dialog box (see fig. 16.27). Change the settings in the Mar**g**ins edit boxes, and then choose OK or press Enter. You can also make other changes related to your printer in this dialog box.

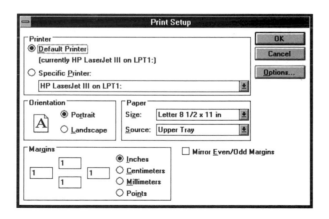

Fig. 16.27
The Print Setup dialog box.

9. Choose OK or press Enter.

Printing Your Tasks

To print your tasks, follow these steps:

1. If you are not already in your schedule window, open the **W**indow menu and select your name or type the number next to your name.

2. If your Task List is not already displayed, choose the **T**asks tab along the left side of the window.

3. Display all your tasks or just your active tasks on the Task List by opening the Tas**k**s menu and choosing Show **A**ctive Tasks. This command toggles between displaying all tasks or only your active tasks. (See the section "Sorting Projects and Tasks," earlier in this chapter.)

4. If you want to display your tasks by project, open the Tas**k**s menu and choose **V**iew By Project, or press Ctrl+Shift+V. (See the section called "Sorting Projects and Tasks.")

5. Sort your tasks by priority (choose the **P**riority button or open the Tas**k**s menu and choose Sort By Priority), due date (choose the Due **B**y button or open the Tas**k**s menu and choose Sort **b**y Due Date), or description (choose the **D**escription button or open the Tas**k**s menu and choose Sort By **D**escription). (See the section "Sorting Projects and Tasks.")

6. Open the **F**ile menu and choose **P**rint.

7. Choose Tasks from the **P**rint drop-down list.

8. Choose OK or press Enter.

Customizing Schedule+

Several options are available for customizing the way that Schedule+ looks and behaves. You can change the colors used in displaying Schedule+ by using the **O**ptions menu's **D**isplay command. You can change the password that you use to log into Schedule+ by using the **O**ptions menu's **C**hange Password command. You can control several other options by using the **O**ptions menu's **G**eneral Options command.

Changing Schedule+ Colors

To change the colors used in Schedule+, follow these steps:

1. Open the **O**ptions menu and choose **D**isplay. This command displays the Display dialog box (see fig. 16.28).

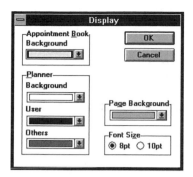

Fig. 16.28
The Display
dialog box.

2. Select the colors that you want to use for the different elements of
   Schedule+ and change the font size for the display, if necessary.

3. Choose OK or press Enter.

Changing Your Password

To change your password, you must be working on-line, because the mail
server maintains passwords. (See the section "Starting Schedule+ from Program Manager" earlier in this chapter for details on how to work on-line.)

To change your password, follow these steps:

1. Open the **O**ptions menu and choose **C**hange Password. This command
   displays the Change Password dialog box.

2. Type your current password in the **P**assword text box.

3. Choose OK or press Enter.

4. Type the new password in the **P**assword text box.

5. Choose OK or press Enter.

6. Type the new password again, to verify your new password.

7. Choose OK or press Enter.

Note

This password is the same password that you use to sign into Mail, so after you
change your password in Schedule+, you must use this new password when you sign
into Mail.

III

Using Windows Accessories

Changing Other Schedule+ Options

To select other options that affect how Schedule+ works, follow these steps:

1. Open the **O**ptions menu and choose **G**eneral Options to display the General Options dialog box (see fig. 16.29.)

Fig. 16.29
The General
Options dialog
box.

2. Change whatever options you want. Table 16.2 describes each of the options that you can change.

Table 16.2	Options You Can Change in the General Options Dialog Box
Option	**Description**
Startup **O**ffline	Starts Schedule+ in the off-line mode and creates a local file for your schedule. This option is useful when you install Schedule+ on a portable or home computer.
Set **R**eminders for Notes	Pops up a reminder on days that have a note attached.
Se**t** Reminders Automatically	Sets a reminder for all new appointments, using the default reminder settings.
Sound A**u**dible Alarm	Sounds an audible alarm when a reminder message pops up.
Day **S**tarts at	Determines the starting hour for your workday.
Day **E**nds at	Determines the ending hour for your workday.
Week Starts On	Determines what day your working week starts on.

Option	Description
Show Week Numbers in the **C**alendar	Displays the number for each week along the left side of the calendar in your Appointment Book.
Send **M**eeting Messages Only to My Assistant	Specifies that only the user you have designated as your assistant receives meeting requests and responses to meeting requests.
This **A**ccount Is for a	Designates an account as a resource.
Resource	See the section "Scheduling a Resource."

Exiting Schedule+

You can exit Schedule+ in one of two ways: you can quit Schedule+ but stay logged onto Mail, or you can exit Schedule+ and Mail with one command.

To exit Schedule+ only, open the **F**ile menu and choose E**x**it. To exit both Schedule+ and Mail, open the **F**ile menu, choose Exi**t**, and Sign Out.

From Here...

Now that you have learned how to use Schedule+, you can refer to the following chapters to learn about other topics that will help you to use Schedule+:

■ Chapter 1, "Operating Windows," teaches you how to work in the Windows environment.

■ Chapter 3, "Controlling Applications with Program Manager," explains how to use Program Manager to work with your applications.

■ Chapter 15, "Using Windows for Workgroups Mail and PC Fax," discusses ways to use Microsoft Mail and PC Fax to communicate with other users on your Windows for Workgroups network.

■ Chapter 25, "Using Windows for Workgroups," teaches you how to work with Windows for Workgroups.

III

Using Windows Accessories

Chapter 17

Using ClipBook Viewer, Chat, and WinPopup

A Windows for Workgroups network makes it easy to share information with others on your network. When you need to share a piece of data, such as a worksheet, chart, or document, you can put it in the Clipbook Viewer so that others can link their documents to it. If you need to talk back and forth over the network, you can use Chat. This feature is like having a text-based telephone conversation; both of you can send messages at the same time and see each other's responses. And with Windows for Workgroups 3.11, you can even pop up a message on someone's screen. WinPopup enables you to send a message that appears on top of someone else's Windows application like a stick-on note.

The ClipBook Viewer, Chat, and WinPopup will make your work within a workgroup much easier. This chapter will show you how to:

- View and save data with the ClipBook
- Share data that is stored in the ClipBook with others in your workgroup
- Using Chat, carry on a telephone-like interactive conversation over the network
- Send an urgent message to someone on the network using WinPopup

III

Using Windows Accessories

Viewing and Using Data in the ClipBook Viewer

When you use Windows for Workgroups, you have a Clipboard available for transferring cut or copied information between applications on your computer. But you have an additional tool at your disposal: the ClipBook.

The ClipBook serves two purposes. First, the ClipBook serves as a personal scrapbook that stores multiple clippings. Each clipping can be on a separate page in the ClipBook. In the ClipBook, you can see a table of contents, thumbnail views, or a full-window view of each clipping. From the collection of clippings, you can choose the one you want to use. The second way to use the ClipBook is as a shared scrapbook. If you designate a page as shared, others in your workgroup can use the data on the page.

Your workgroup can use data, such as text, tables, and graphics, in shared ClipBook pages, which reduces everyone's workload. For example, you can draw a company logo and copy that logo to a shared page in your ClipBook. Others in your workgroup can use that logo at any time by pasting or embedding the logo in their documents; you don't have to give everyone a copy.

The ClipBook also enables workgroup members to link to a shared page in a ClipBook. Suppose that you create a timetable and chart with Microsoft Excel. Three people need your timetable and chart for reports that they must update each week. The workload for your workgroup can be reduced significantly if you copy the timetable and chart into shared pages of your ClipBook. The three people in your workgroup then can paste linked copies of the timetable and chart from your ClipBook into their reports. Each week, when you update your Excel timetable and chart, their reports automatically update.

Displaying the ClipBook

Windows for Workgroups displays the Clipboard and ClipBook in the same ClipBook application, which is located in the Main program group window of Program Manager.

The Clipboard is where data is temporarily stored when it is being transferred within or between applications. This is where data is stored when you cut or copy data. You can view the information currently stored in your Clipboard in the Clipboard window of the ClipBook Viewer application, shown in figure 17.1.

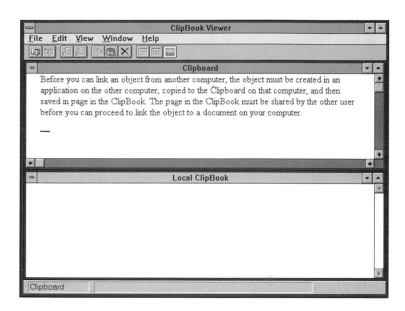

Fig. 17.1
The ClipBook
Viewer has a
Clipboard window
and a ClipBook
window.

The contents of the Clipboard remain there until you cut or copy new data to the Clipboard or until you clear the contents by opening the **E**dit menu and choosing the **D**elete command. The ClipBook viewer also has a ClipBook window. If you need to store information and retain it when you cut or copy other information, you can copy the contents of the Clipboard into a page in the ClipBook. The contents of a ClipBook page can be copied back to the Clipboard at any time. You also can share pages in your ClipBook so that other users on your network can connect to your ClipBook and transfer the information from shared pages into documents on their computers. ClipBook pages, therefore, can be a shared resource, just like a printer or directory.

To view the contents of your Clipboard and ClipBook, choose the Main group in Program Manager and then double-click the ClipBook Viewer icon. You also can use the arrow keys to select the icon and then press Enter.

Tip
To view all the windows at the same time, open the **W**in-dow menu and choose the Tile **H**orizontally or **T**ile Vertically command.

III

Using Windows Accessories

> **Note**
>
> You can start the ClipBook or Clipboard from within some applications by opening the application's Control menu and choosing the Run command. The application Control menu appears as a long dash at the top-left edge of each application's title bar. Click the long dash or press Alt+space bar to open the menu. After you choose the Run command, a Run dialog box appears. Use this dialog box to choose the Clipboard or ClipBook option, and choose OK to run the ClipBook or Clipboard.

The ClipBook Viewer screen appears (refer to fig. 17.1), with a Local ClipBook window and a Clipboard window. You can minimize one or both of these windows to icons at the bottom of the screen. To restore icons to windows, double-click the icon, or press Ctrl+Tab to select the icon and then press Enter.

The ClipBook Viewer's menu bar contains commands for carrying out various operations. If you are using a mouse, you may prefer to use the toolbar, which is just below the menu bar in figure 17.1. The toolbar gives you ready access to many of the most frequently used commands. Table 17.1 describes the buttons in the toolbar; the buttons' functions are discussed in the following sections.

Table 17.1	**Toolbar Functions**	
Button	**Name**	**Function**
	Connect	Connects you to the ClipBook on another user's computer
	Disconnect	Disconnects you from the ClipBook on another user's computer
	Share	Shares the selected ClipBook page with other users
	Stop Sharing	Stops sharing the selected ClipBook page with other users
	Copy	Copies the selected ClipBook page to the Clipboard
	Paste	Pastes the contents of the Clipboard into a new page in the ClipBook
	Delete	Deletes the contents of the Clipboard or the selected ClipBook page
	Table of Contents	Displays a list of ClipBook page titles in the ClipBook window

Button	Name	Function
	Thumbnails	Displays small graphical representations of each page in the ClipBook window
	Full Page	Displays the contents of the selected page in the ClipBook window

Saving the Information in the Clipboard

You can save information stored in the Clipboard in two ways: as a file on disk or as a page in the ClipBook.

To save the contents of the Clipboard in a file, open the ClipBook's **F**ile menu and choose the Save **A**s command to name and save the file. (Windows for Workgroups automatically adds the extension CLP to Clipboard files.) You then can open the ClipBook application's **F**ile menu and choose **O**pen to retrieve the contents of a file and place the contents back in the Clipboard. After you place information in the Clipboard, you can paste, link, or embed it as you would any Clipboard contents.

The second way to save the contents of the Clipboard is to store the data as a page in the Local ClipBook. Viewing and using ClipBook pages is much easier and quicker than working with Clipboard files. You also can share ClipBook pages so that other users can use the information in those pages—something you cannot do with Clipboard files.

> **Note**
>
> If others in your workgroup will be linking to shared pages in your ClipBook, save the source document before you copy its data to the ClipBook. Linked data refers to the source document by referencing its file name. When you change the data in the source document, all documents that contain linked data are updated.

To store data as a page in the ClipBook, follow these steps:

1. Save the original document if others in the workgroup will be linking to the data. Use a file name and directory that will not change.

2. Select the data (text, table, graphics, and so on), and copy it to the Clipboard. (In most applications, you open the **F**ile menu and choose **C**opy.)

III

Using Windows Accessories

3. Activate the ClipBook application, located in the Main group of Program Manager.

4. Activate the Local ClipBook window by clicking it or pressing Ctrl+Tab.

5. Click the Paste button in the toolbar, or open the **E**dit menu and choose **P**aste. The Paste dialog box appears (see fig. 17.2).

Fig. 17.2
The Paste dialog box, where you name a page for the ClipBook.

6. In the **P**age Name box, type a name for the page.

7. If you want to share the page with others in your workgroup, choose the **S**hare Item Now option.

8. Choose OK. The data that currently is in the Clipboard is pasted into a page in the ClipBook.

If you chose the Share Item Now option, the Share ClipBook Page dialog box appears at this point. In this dialog box, you specify the way others will share the page. (See "Sharing a ClipBook Page," later in this chapter, for more information on this dialog box.) When you finish making selections, choose OK.

Sharing Pages in Your ClipBook

You can share pages in your ClipBook if you want other users to have access to the information in those pages. For example, you may have financial data or standard-contract text that others in your workgroup can use in their own documents to save time. The ClipBook offers a simple and convenient way of sharing this common information across a network.

When you share a page in your ClipBook, the contents of that page become a shared resource, no different from a shared printer or shared directory. These contents are available to workgroup members who are connected to your ClipBook. You can limit the type of access to shared pages with a password, which can determine whether users have read-only permission or permission to modify the contents.

Two steps are involved in sharing pages in your ClipBook with other users. First, you must designate the pages as shared. You can specify that a page is shared when you create the page, or you can specify that a page is shared at any later time. When a page is shared, anyone who wants to use it must connect to your ClipBook.

Sharing a ClipBook Page

This section describes how to share a page. If you chose the **S**hare Item Now option when you created a page in the ClipBook, begin the following procedure at step 3. If you want to identify an existing ClipBook page as shared, begin with step 1.

To indicate that a page in your ClipBook is shared, follow these steps:

1. Using the mouse or keyboard, select the page you want to share.

2. Click the Share button on the toolbar, or open the **F**ile menu and choose the **S**hare command. The Share ClipBook Page dialog box appears (see fig. 17.3).

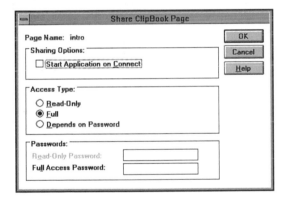

Fig. 17.3
The Share ClipBook Page dialog box describes how the clipping will be shared.

3. Choose the Start Application on **C**onnect option if you want the application that created the data in the shared page to start automatically when the page is transferred to another computer.

4. Choose an access option in the Access Type group.

   You can grant users of a shared page two levels of access. If you don't want users to be able to modify the contents of the page, choose the **R**ead-Only option. Choose the **F**ull option if you want users to be able to change the contents of the page. If you want the level of access to depend on which password the user types, choose the **D**epends on Password option.

5. If you chose the **D**epends on Password option, type a password in one or both of the **R**ead-Only Password or **F**ull Access Password boxes, depending on the options you chose in step 4.

6. Choose OK. In the table of contents view of the ClipBook, a hand now appears below the icon for the page you just shared.

Unsharing a ClipBook Page

You can stop sharing a page so that it is unavailable to others on the Windows for Workgroup network. Follow these steps:

1. Using the mouse or keyboard, select the page that you want to stop sharing in the ClipBook window's table of contents.

 2. Click the Stop Sharing button in the toolbar, or open the **F**ile menu and choose the S**t**op Sharing command.

Pages that are not shared do not display the sharing hand icon when viewed in table of contents view.

Connecting to the ClipBook on Another Computer

If you want to use information from someone else's ClipBook, you first must connect to that ClipBook. You then have access to all shared pages in that ClipBook. When you are connected to another user's ClipBook, you can paste that user's shared data, link to the data, or copy the data to your ClipBook.

Before you can connect to another workgroup member's ClipBook, that person must be connected to the network. That person must specify which ClipBook pages he or she will share.

To connect to the ClipBook of someone in your workgroup, follow these steps:

1. Choose the Main group in Program Manager. Then double-click the ClipBook Viewer icon, or use the arrow keys to select the icon and press Enter. The ClipBook Viewer window appears (see fig. 17.4), displaying your pages in the Local ClipBook area. You may see the contents of your last cut or copy operation in the Clipboard.

 2. Click the Connect button in the toolbar, or open the **F**ile menu and choose the **C**onnect command to display the Select Computer dialog box (see fig. 17.5).

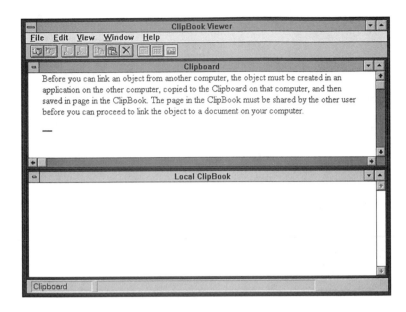

Fig. 17.4
The Clipbook Viewer is shared with others in your workgroup.

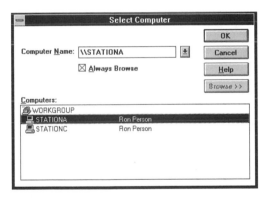

Fig. 17.5
In the Select Computer dialog box, you must select the computer that has the ClipBook you want to share.

If the **A**lways Browse check box was selected, the Select Computer dialog box opens as shown in figure 17.5. If this check box was not selected, the dialog box opens without showing the **C**omputers list. To display the **C**omputers list when it is not displayed, choose the Browse button. To make sure that the **C**omputers list always displays, select the **A**lways Browse check box.

3. In the Computer **N**ame box, specify the computer to which you want to connect, using any of the following methods:

   ■ If you know the name of the computer, type the name in the Computer **N**ame box.

■ Select the name from the Computer **N**ame list by clicking the down arrow next to the box or by pressing the down-arrow key. Then select a computer from the list of computers to which you connected recently.

■ Double-click a workgroup icon in the **C**omputers list (or press Alt+C, select the icon with the arrow keys, and press Enter) to expand the workgroup. Select a name from the list of computer names listed below the workgroup. The name appears in the Computer **N**ame box.

4. Choose OK. A ClipBook window appears, displaying a list of pages in the ClipBook on the other computer (see fig. 17.6).

Fig. 17.6
When you connect to another computer's ClipBook, you can choose the page you want to share.

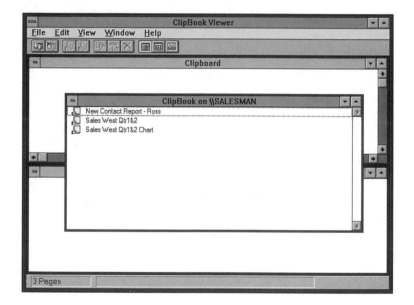

Now that you can see the shared pages in the other ClipBook, you can use them just as you would pages from your own Local ClipBook.

When you want to disconnect from the shared ClipBook, activate the window containing the shared ClipBook from which you want to disconnect; then open the **F**ile menu and choose the **D**isconnect command.

Using ClipBook Pages

To use the contents of a page in your Local ClipBook or in the ClipBook to which you are connected, you first must copy the contents of the page to your Clipboard. In the Local or connected ClipBook window, select the page whose contents you want to use. Then click the Copy button in the toolbar, or open the **E**dit menu and choose **C**opy. The contents of the page appear in the Clipboard window. You now can paste this information into any of your Windows applications by opening the application's **E**dit menu and choosing the **P**aste or Paste **S**pecial command.

To learn how to link or embed ClipBook items from the ClipBook, see "Linking Data between Computers," later in this chapter.

◀ "Passing Linked Documents to Other Computer Users," p. 206

◀ "Linking Data Between Computers," p. 208

Viewing ClipBook Pages

You can view ClipBook pages in three ways:

- To view a list of all the pages in the ClipBook, open the **V**iew menu and choose the Table of **C**ontents command. Shared pages appear, with the sharing hand displayed below them.

- The Thumbnails view, shown in figure 17.7, displays a small picture for each page, with the name of the page below the picture. Shared pages also have a small hand below the picture. To see this view, open the **V**iew menu and choose the Thumb**n**ails command.

- To view the contents of the selected page, open the **V**iew menu and choose the **F**ull Page command, or press Enter.

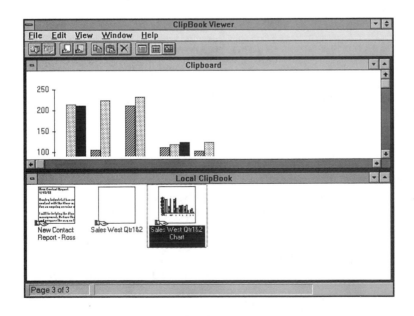

Fig. 17.7
You can view ClipBook contents as a table of contents, thumbnails, or full page.

III

Using Windows Accessories

Tip
You can toggle between views by clicking the ClipBook window or the table of contents view.

Deleting from the Clipboard or ClipBook

You can clear the contents of the Clipboard by selecting the Clipboard window and then pressing the Del key or opening the **E**dit menu and choosing the **D**elete command. Choose **Y**es when the message box appears, asking you to confirm your choice.

To delete a page from the ClipBook, select the page you want to delete; then press the Del key, or open the **E**dit menu and choose the **D**elete command. Choose **Y**es when you are asked to confirm your choice.

Chatting with Others in Your Workgroup

When you use Windows for Workgroups, you can send Mail messages to a single person or a group. An organization that uses Mail correctly can cut down on unnecessary meetings and games of phone tag. But there are occasions when you may not want to use Mail; you want to chat with someone immediately and directly. You can ask questions of anyone else on the network—questions like the following:

> "Susan, can you save this shared file to your local drive so we can shut down the computer the shared file is on?"

Or you can send a dreaded message like this one:

> "Alrich, where are you? Everyone else is in the boardroom is waiting for your presentation."

When you need to chat with someone in your workgroup, use Chat. Chat is an application in the Accessory group (its icon looks like a telephone) that works almost exactly like a telephone.

With Chat, you talk by typing with anyone in your workgroup who is logged on. When you call someone, that person is notified of an incoming call. When the person activates his or her Chat application, both of you can talk back and forth by typing in separate portions of the Chat screen.

Figure 17.8 shows the Chat screen. The top portion shows what the sender is typing; the bottom portion shows what the receiver is typing. Both people can type and receive messages at the same time. Chat is as interactive as a telephone.

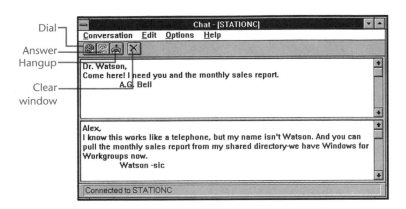

Dial
Answer
Hangup
Clear
window

Fig. 17.8
You can use the
Chat accessory to
chat with someone
else in your
workgroup.

Making a Call

Remember how to use a telephone, and you'll know how to use Chat. You
can chat with anyone in your workgroup who is logged on. To call someone,
follow these steps:

1. Click the Dial button in the toolbar, or open the **C**onversation menu
   and choose the **D**ial command. The Select Computer dialog box, shown
   in figure 17.9, appears. Notice that the Dial button (the button at the
   left end of the toolbar) looks like a rotary dial from an old phone.

   If the **A**lways Browse check box was selected, the Select Computer
   dialog box opens, as shown in figure 17.9. If this check box was not
   selected, the dialog box opens without showing the **C**omputers list.
   To display the **C**omputers list, choose the Browse button. To make sure
   that the **C**omputers list always displays, select the **A**lways Browse check
   box.

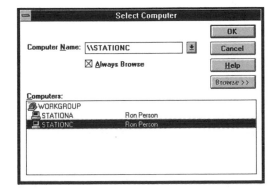

Fig 17.9
Select the com-
puter of the person
with whom you
want to chat.

III

Using Windows Accessories

Tip
Chat works
with text and
numbers.
If you need
to transmit a
formatted word
processing file,
a spreadsheet,
a chart, or
graphic, attach
the file to a
Mail message.

2. Select the computer name of the person with whom you want to chat.

3. Choose OK.

The status bar at the bottom of the Chat window shows you when the other person is connected. As soon as the status bar shows that you are connected, you can begin typing in the top window. As you type, your message appears in the receiver's bottom window.

Answering a Call

The person receiving a call is alerted to an incoming call in one of two ways. If Chat is not running, the incoming call starts as a telephone icon at the bottom of the desktop of the person receiving the call. You see the telephone's handset bounce as the telephone rings. If you have sound turned on, you also hear the ring sound that you designated. If Chat is active in a window, a message that someone is calling appears in the status bar at the bottom of the screen. You also see the computer name of the person who is calling you.

To answer a call, click the Answer button in the toolbar, or open the **C**onversation menu and choose the **A**nswer command. If Chat is an icon, you need to activate the application before you answer the call. Activate Chat by double-clicking the Chat icon, or by selecting it and pressing Enter. You can begin typing as soon as you answer the call.

Editing, Copying, and Saving Conversations

Chat uses all the Windows editing conventions to which you are accustomed. Use the editing keys with which you are familiar from Windows Write or most word processors. The receiver sees corrections as you make them. You also have the cut, copy, and paste commands available so that you can transfer text and numbers into Chat.

The undo command is not available because your conversational partner watches everything you type and correct, so there is no reason for after-the-fact editing.

To save a Chat message for later reference, open the **E**dit menu and choose the Select **A**ll command; then choose the **C**opy command. This procedure puts the entire message in the Clipboard. You then can paste the message into Windows Write or a word processor, where you can save it. You must select and copy your portion of the window and the receiver's portion separately. To switch between the portions of the screen, click the portion you want or press the F6 key.

Ending Your Conversation

A conversation in Chat ends when you hang up. To hang up, click the Hangup button, or open the **C**onversation menu and choose the **H**angup command. The Hangup button looks like a phone receiver coming down on the phone cradle.

Clearing the Chat Window

To clear the entire Chat window, click the Clear Window button in the toolbar, or open the **E**dit menu and choose the Clea**r** All command.

Changing Chat's Appearance and Sound

Like most Windows applications, Chat offers numerous features that you can customize. For example, you can change the background color, change the ring sound, turn the sound on or off, or change the font.

To change the background color in your portion of the Chat screen (the top), follow these steps:

1. Open the **O**ptions menu and choose the Background **C**olor command.

2. In the **B**asic Colors list, select the color you want.

3. Choose OK.

The **C**ustom Colors option is not available in Chat, even though it appears in the Color dialog box; this dialog box is shared by different applications, some of which have custom-color capability.

To change the font that your Chat screen uses, follow these steps:

1. Open the **O**ptions menu and choose the **F**ont command.

2. Select or type the font name in the **F**ont box.

3. Select a style in the Font St**y**le list.

4. Select a size in the **S**ize list.

5. Check the Stri**k**eout or **U**nderline check box if you want to use either of these effects.

6. Select a character color in the **C**olor combo list.

7. Choose OK.

Tip

You can select a patterned color in the **B**asic Color group, but Windows for Workgroups will use the closest solid color. In some cases, you may see no change or a black screen.

III

Using Windows Accessories

You can use the same font that the person on the other end of the conversation is using. Open the **O**ptions menu and choose the **P**references command; then choose the Use **P**artner's Font or Use **O**wn Font option.

You may want to display your screen in the side-by-side display shown in figure 17.10. To toggle your chatting windows between vertical and horizontal, open the **O**ptions menu and choose the **P**references command; then choose the **T**op and Bottom option or the **S**ide by Side option.

Fig. 17.10
Side-by-side window display makes a Chat conversation easier to follow.

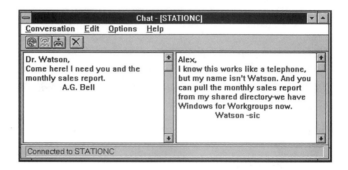

▶ "Assigning Sounds to Events," p. 675

Chat rings at both the caller's and receiver's personal computers. The sound of the ring depends on whether your computer has a sound board and on which sound you selected to serve as the ring sound. If you do not have a sound board, you hear a beep.

If you are a very popular person, you may want to turn the sound off so that your officemate isn't disturbed during his or her afternoon nap. To toggle the sound between on and off, open the **O**ptions menu and choose the Sou**n**d command. Each time you choose this command, the sound status changes.

Like most Windows applications that have toolbars and status bars, you can turn those elements on or off if you need more screen area, or if you do not use them. To toggle the toolbar on and off, open the **O**ptions menu and choose the **T**oolbar command. To toggle the status bar on or off, open the **O**ptions menu and choose the Status **B**ar command. If you want to reverse the current condition of the toolbar or status bar, just open the **O**ptions menu and choose the **T**oolbar or Status **B**ar command again.

Sending a Note with WinPopup

When you need to send a short message to people in your workgroup, and you want that message to get to them *now*, even while they are working in

Windows applications, use WinPopup. WinPopup, available in Windows for Workgroups 3.11, enables you to send a message from your computer to any computer or all computers on the Windows for Workgroups network. When the message arrives, it pops up on top of the application that the person is using, almost as though you walked up and slapped a stick-on note on the screen. Figure 17.11 shows the WinPopup window that displays an incoming message.

Send Message
Discard Message
View Previous Message
View Next Message

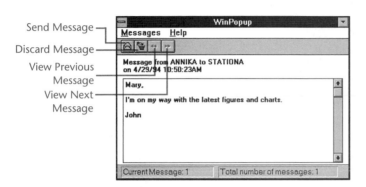

Fig. 17.11
Use WinPopup to send a message that pops up on top of the current application.

Starting WinPopup and Sending a Message

WinPopup must be running for you to enter a pop-up message or for you to receive a pop-up message from someone else in your workgroup. To start WinPopup for the current session in which you are working, double-click the WinPopup icon in the Network group of Program Manager. (The WinPopup icon looks like a jack-in-the-box.)

To make sure that WinPopup starts whenever you are connected to the network, follow these steps:

1. Choose the Network icon in Control Panel. (Control Panel is located in the Main group window.)

2. In the Network dialog box, choose the Startup button in the **O**ptions section.

3. In the Startup Settings dialog box, check the Enable **W**inPopup check box.

4. Choose OK twice to return to Control Panel.

You can send a pop-up message to one person in your workgroup or to everyone in your workgroup. To send a message, follow these steps:

Tip
WinPopup works within a Windows for Workgroups network. Other networks may not recognize it.

III

Using Windows Accessories

1. Click the Send Message button, or open the **M**essages menu and choose the **S**end command. The Send Messages dialog box appears.

2. Choose the **U**ser or Computer option to send a message to one person, or choose the **W**orkgroup option to send a message to everyone in your workgroup. (If you are unsure what person or computer name to enter, choose the **B**rowse button and select the computer or name.)

3. Type your message in the **M**essage box.

   Figure 17.12 shows a completed Send Message dialog box.

Fig. 17.12
Send a message to one person or broadcast to everyone in the workgroup.

4. Choose OK to send the message.

Viewing and Deleting Messages

If you have WinPopup running, you will be notified when you receive a pop-up message. The way in which you are notified depends on how you set your WinPopup options. When a message appears on-screen, you see it in the WinPopup window (refer to fig. 17.11).

To scroll through the pop-up messages you have received, click the View Previous Message or View Next Message button in the toolbar.

To delete the displayed message, click the Discard Message button in the toolbar, or open the **M**essages menu and choose the **D**iscard command. To delete all the messages you have received, open the **M**essages menu and choose the **C**lear All command.

Setting WinPopup Options

You can specify different ways to be notified when your computer receives a WinPopup message. To set the options for how you are notified and how the WinPopup window behaves, follow these steps:

1. Open the **M**essages menu and choose the **O**ptions command.

2. Choose one or more of the following options:

   - **P**lay Sound When New Message Arrives

   - **A**lways on Top

   - WinPopup on **M**essage Receipt

3. Choose OK.

If you want Windows for Workgroups to play your beep sound when a pop-up message arrives, choose **P**lay Sound When New Message Arrives. To get the message to pop up in a window, choose the WinPopup on **M**essage Receipt option. If you want the message to pop up on the top of the application in which you are working, you also should choose the **A**lways on Top option.

To make WinPopup unobtrusive, deselect all these check boxes. You will not be notified of incoming messages, but the title of the WinPopup icon on the desktop will include a message showing how many messages are in your WinPopup queue. To read your messages, double-click the WinPopup icon. Scroll through messages by clicking the View Previous Message and View Next Message buttons.

From Here...

For information related to copying information to the Clipboard or sending messages to others in your workgroup, you may want to review the following chapters of this book:

- Chapter 5, "Simple Data Sharing," describes how to cut information from one location and move it to another, and how to copy information from one location and paste it in another.

III

Using Windows Accessories

- Chapter 6, "Advanced Data Sharing," teaches you how to link data between documents or applications, and how to embed information from one application into another application's document.

- Chapter 15, "Using Windows for Workgroups Mail and PC Fax," describes ways to send long documents or documents that contain embedded data via electronic mail.

Chapter 18

Using Windows for Workgroups Management Tools

The introduction of Windows for Workgroups provided an inexpensive and relatively painless way for Windows users to enter the world of networking. Along with the introduction of a network, however, comes the need to manage all the resources that are spread out across the network.

This chapter discusses the management tools available under Windows for Workgroups 3.11: the NetWatcher accessory, WinMeter, and Remote Access. All three tools make it easier to use the Windows for Workgroups networking features. In this chapter, you learn how to:

- Monitor network activity
- Monitor the network's share of your computer
- Log on and off
- Communicate with Remote Access

Monitoring Network Activity

When you work with Windows for Workgroups, you can share directories, printers, and ClipBook pages with other users. When you share resources like directories, printers, and your ClipBook with others, you want a way to see which of the resources are being used and who is using them. NetWatcher, an accessory located in the Network group window, enables you to do exactly that. Not only can you learn who is using which resource, but you can also disconnect other users from your computer or close a file that another user has opened.

Monitoring Network Activity on Your Computer

To monitor the activity of users connected to your computer, choose the Network group in Program Manager and then double-click on the NetWatcher icon or use the arrow keys to select the NetWatcher icon and press Enter. The NetWatcher icon is shown in figure 18.1.

Fig. 18.1
Use the NetWatcher program to see how others on the network are using your local resources.

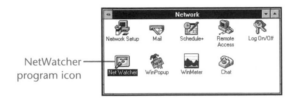

NetWatcher program icon

The NetWatcher window shown in figure 18.2 appears when you start NetWatcher. The left side of the window lists the computer names of every user connected to your computer. When you select a user from the list, the directories, printers, and ClipBook pages that the selected user is using are listed on the right side of the window. Any files that the user has opened are listed under the directories for those files. Directories and files with read-only access are designated with an eyeglasses icon; those with full access are designated with a pencil icon.

Fig. 18.2
The NetWatcher window lists the users connected to your computer and shows the resources that they are using.

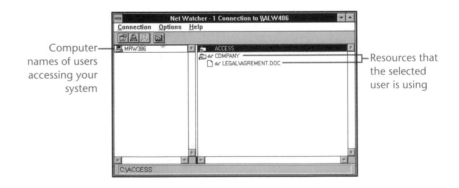

Computer names of users accessing your system

Resources that the selected user is using

◀ "Sharing Directories," p. 179

The information in the NetWatcher window updates every 20 seconds. If you want to update the information manually, open the **O**ptions menu and choose **R**efresh, or press F5.

The toolbar, located below the menu bar, gives you ready access to four of the NetWatcher commands that you use most frequently; these four commands are also available from the **C**onnection menu. The following table describes the functions of the toolbar's four buttons. See the following sections to find out how to use each of these commands.

Button Name	Function
Properties	Display additional information for the selected user
Disconnect	Disconnect the selected user from your computer
Close File	Close the selected file
View Event Log	View the event log for your system

If you don't use the toolbar, or if you need to make more room for displaying users, you can hide the toolbar. To hide the toolbar, open the **O**ptions menu and choose **T**oolbar; to redisplay the toolbar, choose the same command again. When the **T**oolbar command is selected, a check mark appears next to it in the **O**ptions menu.

You can also choose whether to display the status bar that runs along the bottom of the NetWatcher window. The status bar displays additional information about the selected item in the NetWatcher window. To remove the status bar, open the **O**ptions menu and choose **S**tatus Bar; to redisplay the status bar, choose the command again. When the **S**tatus Bar command is selected, a check mark appears next to the command in the **O**ptions menu.

If you want to make more room on one side or the other of the NetWatcher window, you can move the split bar that divides the window. Use the mouse to drag the split bar to the right or left; alternatively, you can open the **O**ptions menu, choose Split **W**indow, use the arrow keys to move the split bar, and press Enter when the split bar is located where you want it.

Displaying Information about a User

You can display additional information about any user connected to your computer. To find out more about a user, follow these steps:

1. Click the name of the user in the left side of the NetWatcher window; alternatively, you can use the Tab key to move the cursor to the left side of the window (if the cursor isn't already there) and then use the arrow keys to select the user.

III

Using Windows Accessories

2. Click the Properties button on the toolbar, open the **C**onnection menu and choose **P**roperties, or press Alt+Enter. The Properties dialog box appears, as shown in figure 18.3.

Fig. 18.3
The Properties dialog box shows information about connected users.

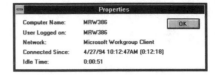

The Properties dialog box lists the name of the computer that you selected, the name of the user logged on to that computer, the name of the network to which the user is connected, at what time and for how long the user has been connected to your computer, and how much time has passed since the user last accessed resources on your computer.

Disconnecting a User

You can disconnect any user connected to your computer. To disconnect a user, follow these steps:

1. Click the user in the list on the left side of the NetWatcher window; alternatively, you can press the Tab key to move the cursor to the left side of the window (if the cursor is not already there) and then use the arrow keys to select the user.

2. Click the Disconnect button on the toolbar, or open the **C**onnection menu and choose **D**isconnect. A message box warning you that the user may lose data appears. Choose Yes to disconnect the user; choose No if you change your mind.

> **Note**
>
> When you disconnect users from your computer, they may lose data in files that they are using on your computer. Therefore, before you disconnect users, you should notify them and give them time to disconnect from your computer or to save files. If the user is accessing only read-only files on your system, no data is lost when you disconnect that user.

Closing a File

You can close a file that another user has opened on your computer. When you close a file on which another user is working (rather than having that user close the file), he or she may lose file information.

To close a file, follow these steps:

1. Click the file in the right side of the NetWatcher window; alternatively, you can press the Tab key to move the cursor to the right side of the window (if the cursor is not already there) and then use the arrow keys to select the file.

2. Click the Close File button on the NetWatcher toolbar, or open the **C**onnection menu and choose **C**lose File. A message box warning you that the user may lose data appears. Choose Yes to disconnect the user, or choose No if you change your mind.

Viewing the Event Log

An *event log* is a record of activity on your computer system. Windows for Workgroups 3.11 enables you to specify several different events that can be tracked. Before the events can be logged, you must enable the event log. You do this from the Control Panel.

To enable the event log, follow these steps:

1. Double-click on the Control Panel icon in the Main program group.

2. Double-click on the Network icon within the Control Panel.

3. Choose the Event Log option button, which displays the Event Log Settings dialog box shown in figure 18.4.

4. Select the **E**nable Event Log check box at the top-left corner of the dialog box.

Now you can use the two lists shown in the Event Log Settings dialog box to specify which events should be logged and which shouldn't. Windows for Workgroups 3.11 enables you to log any of the following events:

■ Server start-up and shutdown

■ Server connect or disconnect

Tip

You should always notify the user before you close a shared file with which the user is working.

Fig. 18.4
The Event Log Settings dialog box.

III

Using Windows Accessories

■ Unsuccessful connection attempts

■ When a print job has been spooled (submitted), paused, resumed, deleted, or completed

In addition, you may be able to monitor other events, depending on the type of network that you are using with Windows for Workgroups.

After you finish specifying what you want to log, you can close the Event Log Settings dialog box (choose OK or press Enter) and continue with your other work. Later, when you want to see what is happening on your computer, you can view the event log simply by clicking the View Event Log button on the NetWatcher toolbar or by opening the Connection menu and choosing View Event Log. You then see the View Event Log window, as shown in figure 18.5.

Fig. 18.5
The View Event Log window shows you which activities have occurred on your system.

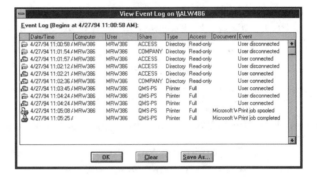

The information shown in an event log differs, depending on which events you have specified to be logged and what has actually happened. The first column in the window indicates the type of activity that occurred, and each additional column provides additional information.

You can use your mouse to adjust the width of each column. Simply position the mouse cursor over the dividing lines between columns (in the column-heading area). Hold down the mouse button and drag the mouse to affect the width of the column. When you release the mouse button, the column width remains at the new setting.

You can use the buttons at the bottom of the View Event Log window to affect the display. To close the window, click on the OK button; to erase the entire event log, choose the Clear button; to save the event log to a text file, choose the Save As button.

Note

When your event log becomes larger than the space that you allocated to it in the Network portion of the Control Panel, the oldest events are eliminated from the log to make room for more recent events. If you have a busy network and you want to keep longer event histories, you should increase the space allocated to the event log.

Monitoring the Network's Share of Your Computer

WinMeter, an application located in the Network group window (the icon is shown in fig. 18.6), uses a graph to show you how your computer is sharing its power between your work and the network's work. You can change how much of your computer's time is shared so that your computer applications run faster, or so that the network applications, such as resource sharing and Mail, run faster.

WinMeter
program icon

Fig. 18.6
The WinMeter allows you to see how your CPU is being used.

Note

If you don't like the way that your computer is sharing its time with the network, you can change the sharing percentage by dragging the Performance Priority slide bar to a new percentage. You can find this slide bar within the Network option in the Control Panel.

To use WinMeter, choose the Network group in Program Manager and then double-click the WinMeter icon, or use the arrow keys to select the icon and press Enter. The WinMeter window appears, as shown in figure 18.7.

As shown in the WinMeter window, the percentage of CPU time allocated to your applications and to the shared resources on your computer are represented by two different colors. You can change the colors by opening the **S**ettings menu and choosing **A**pplication Color and Server **C**olor. You can

Tip
If your WinMeter window is small, you cannot see all the detail that WinMeter has to offer. To see more, enlarge the window by dragging a corner of the WinMeter window to the desired size.

also control how frequently the readings are updated by opening the **S**ettings menu and selecting the time interval you want to use. To hide the title bar, open the **S**ettings menu and choose **H**ide Title Bar; to redisplay the title bar, press Esc.

Fig. 18.7
The WinMeter window shows how your computer's time is shared with the network.

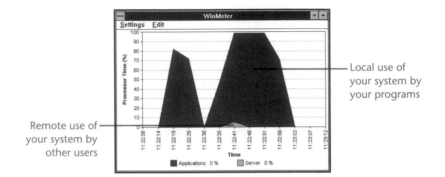

Local use of your system by your programs

Remote use of your system by other users

Logging On and Off

If you are using Windows for Workgroups, you are probably already familiar with the procedure for starting Windows. First you see a welcoming screen, and then you are asked to enter your name (which may already be displayed) and your password. This process is called *logging in*.

Sometimes you may want to log in and out of your system while you are using Windows. For instance, suppose that you are using a computer that has a good laser printer attached. Other members of your workgroup use your printer through the network. If you are leaving for lunch, you might not feel comfortable leaving open access to your computer system. Yet if you turn your system off, others cannot use your laser printer.

In such situations, the Log On/Off utility comes in handy. You can use this utility to log off of your system. This means that you (or anyone else at your system) cannot take advantage of shared resources on other systems in your workgroup. However, others can still access shared resources on your system, which provides minimal security for the resources of the workgroup.

To use the Log On/Off utility, select the program icon from the Network program group, as shown in figure 18.8.

This program detects whether you are already logged on. If you are, you are asked whether you are sure that you want to log off. When you click on the Yes button, you are logged off the system. If you use Log On/Off when you are logged off the system, the program displays the log-in dialog box that you normally see when you first start Windows for Workgroups.

— Log On/Off
program icon

Fig. 18.8
The Log On/Off
program enables
you to control
some access to
your workgroup's
resources.

Communicating with Remote Access

Networking has many different advantages. Perhaps the biggest advantage is that you can share resources—files, printers, and other devices—with other people connected to the network. But what if you aren't close to the other people in the network? What if you are located in another building or another city?

Depending on the type of network that you have installed in your company, you can use Remote Access to connect with a network over the phone lines. After your network is connected, you can access the network resources as if you were physically connected to the network. For instance, you can access files or print information on the network printer all over the phone lines. Remote Access takes care of the details, all behind the scenes.

To use Remote Access, two conditions must be met. First, the network with which you want to connect must be using Windows NT or Microsoft LAN Manager, and the network must have the RAS (Remote Access Service) capability installed. Second, you must have a modem installed in your computer.

RAS enables one of the computers on the remote network to function as a communications server. When the communications server receives a phone call, RAS establishes the connection and transfers information as your system requires.

Using Remote Access is easy, but you must install it first. When you first install Windows for Workgroups, a Remote Access icon is visible in the Network program group, as shown in figure 18.9.

When you double-click on the Remote Access icon, you are asked whether you want to install the program. If you continue with the installation, you need to have your Windows for Workgroups 3.11 installation disks handy. As the installation proceeds, you are prompted to insert each of these disks at the appropriate time to copy the program files to your hard drive.

III

Using Windows Accessories

Fig. 18.9
Remote Access
connects your
computer to a
remote network.

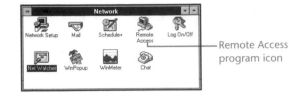

Remote Access
program icon

Note

As you install Remote Access, you need to know your modem type and how your
modem is configured in your computer. The installation program contains a lengthy
list of modems, so you simply select your modem type and model from the list of
available modems. However, you also need to know which COM port your modem is
configured as. This is perhaps the most difficult part of the installation. Still, installing
Remote Access is much simpler than installing other communications programs.

After you install Remote Access, you can start the program at any time by
double-clicking on the Remote Access program icon. When it is running, the
program seems very simple on your screen, which displays two windows, as
shown in figure 18.10.

Fig. 18.10
The two windows
opened by Remote
Access.

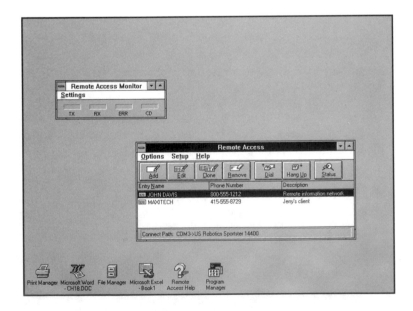

The top window, the Remote Access Monitor, represents your modem. If you
have ever used an external modem, the contents of this monitor probably

look familiar. The window has four indicators, each of which reflects the status of your communication session:

TX   Indicates when your system is transmitting information to the remote system.

RX   Indicates when your system has received data.

Err   Indicates whether a communications error has occurred.

CD   Indicates when a connection is established with the remote modem. If this indicator is off, there is no connection. *CD* stands for *carrier detect*.

The bottom window is called Remote Access. This is the main window that you work with as you try to establish a connection.

Near the top of the Remote Access window is a toolbar that indicates various operations that you can perform. The four leftmost tools—**A**dd, **E**dit, **C**lone, and **R**emove—enable you to modify what is often called a *dialing directory*. This directory records phone numbers and other information about the systems to which you can connect. These four tools enable you to do the following:

■ Add an entry. If you receive a phone number of a system to which you want to connect, use the **A**dd tool to add the phone number to the dialing directory. When you click on this tool, you see the simple dialog box shown in figure 18.11.

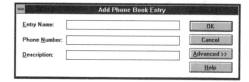

All you need to do is provide the phone number, the name, and any optional description. This new entry then appears in your dialing directory.

■ Edit an entry. With the **E**dit tool, you can edit whichever dialing directory entry you selected. The information is displayed in the same dialog box shown in figure 18.11. You can make changes that Remote Access then saves.

Fig. 18.11

The Add Phone Book Entry dialog box.

III

Using Windows Accessories

■ Clone an entry. Using the **C**lone tool is similar to using the **A**dd tool, except that you start with the information already filled in. The information in the selected dialing directory entry is copied to the dialog box, where you can make changes. When you close the dialog box, the information is saved as a new entry in the dialing directory.

■ Remove an entry. After you confirm your action, the **R**emove tool deletes an entry from the dialing directory.

After these four tools, the toolbar provides two tools—**D**ial and Hang-**U**p—that you can use to connect and disconnect from remote systems. To connect, you need only select the dialing directory entry that you want and then choose the **D**ial tool. You then see the Authentication dialog box shown in figure 18.12.

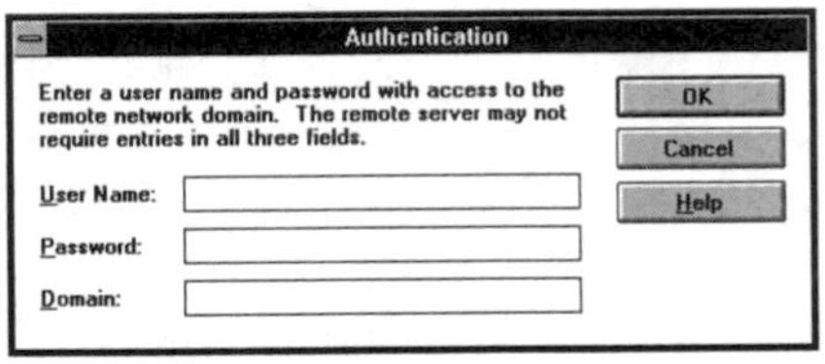

Fig. 18.12
The Authentication dialog box.

Enter a user name and password with access to the remote network domain. The remote server may not require entries in all three fields.

User Name:
Password:
Domain:

OK
Cancel
Help

In the Authentication dialog box, provide your log-in name, password, and domain (or workgroup). These are used when establishing the connection with the remote system. When you click on OK, Remote Access attempts to establish the connection.

Tip
At any time during a connection, you can use the **S**tatus tool of the Remote Access toolbar to determine information about the connection; however, this tool does not work unless you are connected to another system.

Note

If you run into problems establishing a connection with or logging onto a remote server, you should contact the administrator for the remote network. This person will be the one most capable of providing timely and accurate help. Each network to which you are connected is configured a bit differently than every other network, so talking to the network administrator is the most productive approach for troubleshooting problems.

Once you are connected with the remote system, the icon to the left of the dialing directory entry changes to a telephone. You can proceed to use Windows and access remote resources as you would at any other time. Remember, however, that if you dial long distance, your phone charges will continue to mount as long as you are connected. When you finish using the remote system, open the Remote Access program icon and choose the Hang-**U**p tool.

You are asked whether you really want to disconnect, after which the connection is broken and you are returned to Windows.

From Here...

In this chapter, you learned about the management tools available with Windows for Workgroups 3.11. For more information, refer to the following chapters:

- Chapter 15, "Using Windows for Workgroups Mail and PC Fax," discusses how to communicate with others on your network and send information by using a fax/modem.

- Chapter 16, "Using Windows for Workgroups Schedule+," teaches you to schedule your appointments and compare them with others' in your workgroup.

- Chapter 17, "Using Clipbook Viewer, Chat, and Popup," discusses how these network utilities can improve the productivity of your workgroup.

- Chapter 26, "Configuring Windows 3.1 and NetWare," teaches you how to properly configure your network.

III

Using Windows Accessories

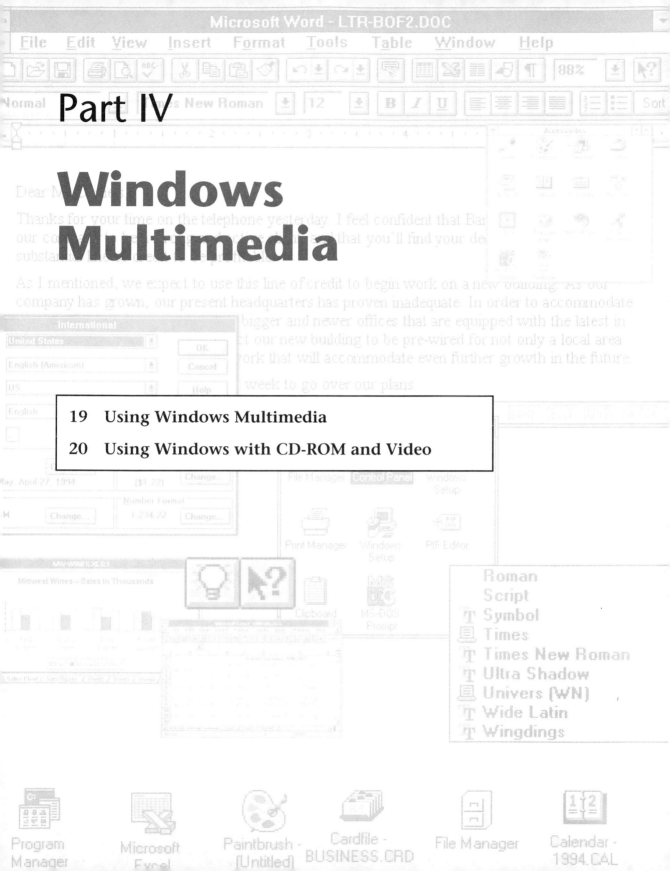

Part IV

Windows Multimedia

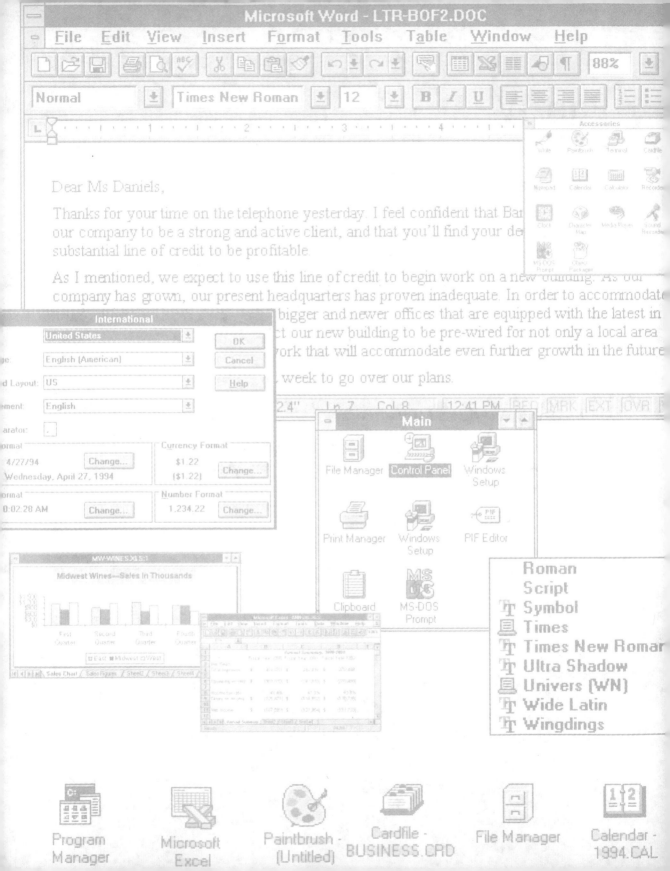

Chapter 19

Using Windows Multimedia

As computers edge into more and more aspects of everyday life, they take on new roles. Consider these roles: musician, storyteller, business presentation tool, educational tool, and research assistant.

Multimedia plays a part in each of these roles because it combines two familiar communications media—sound and sight—in a single package and gives you control over producing and delivering sound and visual effects.

You can use multimedia in several ways. With the right equipment, you can play all of the many multimedia packages available commercially. Included are games, stories, full encyclopedias, and complete reference texts. You can record simple messages, tunes, or motion pictures and embed them in documents that you create in Windows applications. If you are adventurous, you can move beyond the simple applications that come with Windows to a multimedia authoring application and create original multimedia presentations and applications.

Multimedia requires the right equipment. You need a CD-ROM player, speakers, and a sound board. All hardware must comply with the MPC-2 standard developed by Microsoft and the Multimedia PC Marketing Council. You can supply the equipment you need in either of two ways: by upgrading your current PC or by buying a special multimedia PC equipped with everything you need.

In this chapter, you learn how to choose and install a sound card and how to work with the multimedia applications that come with Windows: Sound Recorder, Media Player, and MIDI Mapper. You also learn how to embed sound and video in your Windows applications. In the following chapter, you learn everything you need to know to work with CD-ROMs, which deliver sound and video to your computer.

In this chapter, you learn how to do the following things:

- Upgrade your equipment to use multimedia

- Choose and install a sound board

- Operate Sound Recorder

- Operate Media Player

- Embed sound and video

- Use MIDI Mapper

Upgrading Your Equipment to Multimedia Standards

To take advantage of multimedia, you need the right equipment. Basically, you need a powerful PC, VGA graphics, a sound board, speakers, and a CD-ROM drive. You can add many optional pieces of equipment, including VCRs, microphones, joysticks, MIDI synthesizers, and music keyboards.

▶ "Understanding the MPC Level 2 Standard," p. 696

To ensure compatibility among all multimedia software and equipment, the Multimedia PC Marketing Council established standards for multimedia PC hardware. (See the next section, "Choosing a Sound Board," for a discussion of MPC-2 specifications for sound boards, and see Chapter 20, "Using Windows with CD-ROM and Video," for the MPC-2 specifications for CD-ROM drives.)

You can get the right equipment in either of two ways. You can purchase an MPC Level 2-compliant computer, ready to play. Several manufacturers sell these MPCs, which include all the hardware (and, often, the software) you need. The second way to get the proper equipment is to upgrade your current system by adding a sound board, a CD-ROM drive, and (if necessary) VGA graphics. Make sure that the equipment you choose conforms to this standard. The best way to accomplish this task is to look for the MPC-2 logo, which ensures compliance; another way is to understand the hardware requirements and to purchase equipment that conforms to these standards.

Choosing a Sound Board

An essential component of a multimedia computer system is a sound card. Without a sound card and speakers, you will be unable to hear the audio part of your multimedia software. As is true of most hardware components, you face a wide variety of choices when it comes time to purchase a sound card. In this section, you learn about some of the most important features you should look for when you search for a sound card, so that you won't be disappointed when you get your multimedia system up and running.

Several characteristics are an absolute minimum for any sound card you consider. Fortunately, most mainstream sound cards meet the following minimum requirements:

- *Compliance with the MPC (Multimedia PC) Level 2 standard.* The most important characteristics of the MPC standard are that the board must record and play back 16-bit stereo sound with a sampling rate of 44.1kHz and that it must support the WAV file format. The 16-bit specification refers to the size of each sound sample. With inexpensive 16-bit boards on the market, there is no reason to buy an older 8-bit board. The sampling rate refers to how often (times per second) a sound sample is taken. The standard format for Windows sound files is the WAV format, so it is essential that the board be able to process WAV files.

- *Sound Blaster compatibility.* Another de facto standard is compatibility with Sound Blaster boards, which are manufactured by Creative Labs. Compatibility with Sound Blaster boards is important, because much of the multimedia software on the market is written to work with Sound Blaster boards. Make sure that the board you purchase is compatible with Sound Blaster.

- *Wavetable lookup capability.* Besides being able to handle WAV files, which actually store digitized sounds, many sound boards can play back MIDI files. MIDI files store the instructions for playing back music, rather than the digitized sounds themselves, and are used in conjunction with MIDI devices. If you are using your sound card with MIDI devices and want to be able to play back MIDI files, or if you simply want more realistic sound from your multimedia software, you should consider how the sound card processes MIDI files. Low-end sound cards use the *FM synthesis* method to process MIDI files—a relatively crude approach that results in unrealistic sounds. Some of the better sound cards use the *wavetable lookup* method, in which actual samples of instruments are used to reproduce music, resulting in much more realistic sound. If you will be using your sound card to work with MIDI files, you should consider purchasing a card that has wavetable lookup capability.

- *Inclusion of CD-ROM drive controller.* Another consideration is whether the sound card has a controller for a CD-ROM drive, which will save you the expense (and an expansion slot in your computer) of buying a separate controller card for your CD-ROM drive. Some cards come with controllers for SCSI CD-ROM drives; others have controllers for specific non-SCSI drives, such as Sony and Panasonic. Make sure that the sound card you purchase has a controller for the drive you intend to use, or be prepared to buy a separate controller card for your drive.

> **Note**
>
> Unfortunately, the microphone jacks that are built into sound cards do not use a standard impedance, so if the board you select does not come with a microphone, make sure that you purchase a microphone with a matching impedance. And unless the card comes with built-in speakers (which will not do justice to your multimedia sound anyway), you will need to buy a pair of speakers. Speakers with built-in amplification overcome the limitations of the low-wattage amplifiers that are standard in most cards.

The following table lists some of the leading sound cards on the market. Contact the manufacturer for detailed specifications on the listed sound cards. You also can speak to a knowledgeable salesperson or look for articles in computer magazines for additional information on sound boards.

Card Number	Manufacturer	Phone
Creative Labs Sound Blaster 16 Basic Edition & Creative Labs Sound Blaster 16 SCSI-2	Creative Labs, Inc. 1901 McCarthy Blvd. Milpitas, CA 95035	(800) 998-5227 (408) 428-6600
Diamond SonicSound LX	Diamond Computer Systems, Inc. 1130 East Arques Ave. Sunnyvale, CA 94086	(408) 736-2000
IBM WindSurfer Communications Adapter	IBM Personal Computer Co. 3039 Cornwallis Rd. Dept. W32/B205 Research Triangle Park, NC 27709	(800) 426-2968 (914) 766-1900
Logitech SoundMan 16	Logitech Inc. 6505 Kaiser Dr. Fremont, CA 94555	(800) 231-7717 (510) 795-8500

Card Number	Manufacturer	Phone
Media Vision Pro Audio 16 Basic & Media Vision Pro	Media Vision, Inc. 47300 Bayside Pkwy. Fremont, CA 94538	(800) 348-7116 (510) 770-8600
Microsoft Windows Sound System 2.0	Microsoft Corp. One Microsoft Way Redmond, WA 98052	(206)882-8080
Turtle Beach MultiSound	Turtle Beach Systems 52 Grumbacher Rd. York, PA 17402	(800) 645-5640 (717) 767-0200

▶ "Installing CD-ROM Drives," p. 704

Installing a Sound Card and Drivers

Before you can use a multimedia device, such as a sound board or a CD-ROM player, you first must physically plug the device into the computer, then you must install the device driver in Windows, and finally, you must set up the hardware. The process is similar to installing a new printer on the system. Plugging in the hardware establishes the physical connection, installing the driver tells Windows that the device exists, and setting up the device tells Windows how to communicate with the device.

Installing a Sound Card

Plugging in a device—whether that device is a sound board or a CD-ROM player—isn't difficult. If the device is internal, such as a sound board, turn off the power, remove a few screws from the sides of the *system unit* (the computer box that holds the CPU), and slide off the cover. (You also may have to remove a port cover from the back of the PC to provide external access to the new board's ports.) Boards plug into an area of the PC reserved for boards. Turn to Chapter 20, "Using Windows with CD-ROM and Video," for detailed information on installing a CD-ROM drive.

Look at the boards already installed in the PC to see how these circuit boards are attached. Then look at the new board. You can see that one end of the board has ports that must point toward the back of the PC for external access and that one side of the board has a wide tab that pushes into any of the available slots in the PC. Although you need firm pressure to push the tab into the slot, the process is neither complex nor dangerous. When you finish, slide the cover back on the PC and replace the screws. (Just think how impressed your colleagues will be when you casually mention that you installed a new board in your PC.)

You also need to attach your sound card to speakers. (If you have a stereo system, you can connect the sound board to the amplifier and use the stereo's speakers.) The documentation tells you how to make this connection.

Sound boards often include connectors that simplify adding a microphone or joystick and connecting to your CD-ROM player. Most sound boards also include a connector for a MIDI musical synthesizer or keyboard, but you may need an additional converter box to operate the MIDI equipment. Check the sound-board documentation or contact the manufacturer.

After you plug in a sound card, run a test to determine whether the board is successfully connected to both the PC and the speakers. If the test is successful, you hear music that you never thought could come from a computer. From the test, you learn that the speakers are correctly attached and that the PC and the board are communicating. If the test is unsuccessful, you may have to change the setup. (For more information about changing the setup, see "Setting Up a Device Driver" later in this chapter.)

Write down all information about the installation that the test application gives you. The Sound Blaster test, for example, may tell you that the board currently is using I/O address 220 and Interrupt 7. You may need this information when you install the driver in Windows.

Adding Multimedia Drivers

For Windows to recognize and communicate with the multimedia equipment that you install, you must install the correct device driver in Windows. Windows comes with many multimedia equipment drivers, which you find listed in Windows but which are not yet installed. You know whether Windows includes a driver for the equipment when you display a list of existing drivers (step 4 in the following instructions). If the driver that you need isn't included, you may be able to use the generic driver that comes with Windows. If you learn that the generic driver doesn't work for the equipment, check the new equipment's documentation (or call the manufacturer) to find out whether a Windows driver is available.

To install the driver, you must have the original Windows installation disks (or the disks that came with your device, if you are using the manufacturer's driver). The Windows disks contain the driver you need for the device.

◀ "Operating Control Panel," p. 231

After the multimedia device is successfully attached, follow these steps to install the driver and set up the device in Windows:

1. In Windows Program Manager, open the Main window and choose Control Panel. The Control Panel window appears (see fig. 19.1).

Fig. 19.1
Control Panel
contains the
Drivers icon.

Drivers icon

2. Choose the Drivers application. The Drivers dialog box appears
   (see fig. 19.2).

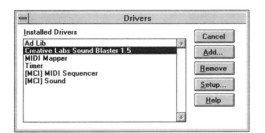

Fig. 19.2
The Drivers dialog
box shows a list of
the drivers already
installed in
Windows.

3. Choose the **A**dd button. The Add dialog box appears (see fig. 19.3).

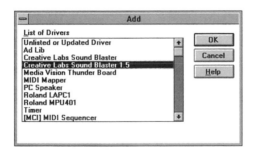

Fig. 19.3
The Add dialog
box shows all
the drivers that
Windows supplies.

4. Select the equipment's name in the **L**ist of Drivers list, and choose OK.
   If the equipment isn't listed, select Unlisted or Updated Driver. A dialog
   box appears, prompting you to insert the disk that contains the device
   driver (see fig. 19.4).

Fig. 19.4
The message tells you exactly which disk to insert.

5. Insert the disk that contains the driver into drive A. If the driver is located on a different drive or directory in the PC, type the drive and directory names (but not the driver's file name).

   If you don't know where the driver is located, choose **B**rowse to open the Browse dialog box (see fig. 19.5). Then select the drive and directory that contain the device driver, and choose OK.

Fig. 19.5
To locate the driver, you can browse through drives and directories.

6. When you return to the Add dialog box, choose OK. A Setup dialog box may appear, requesting configuration information (see fig. 19.6).

Fig. 19.6
The Setup dialog box already may show the correct setup information.

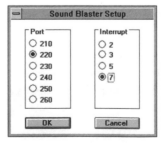

7. After referring to the notes you took when you tested the device, select the necessary setup information and choose OK.

8. If Windows requires more drivers to go with the driver you installed, Window installs them by default and may ask you for more setup information. Respond to any dialog box that appears and choose OK.

   If the installation is complete, however, a dialog box advises you that you must restart Windows for the installation to take effect.

9. Choose **R**estart Now to restart Windows so that you can use the driver. (If you don't restart, you can use the driver the next time you use Windows.)

Setting Up a Device Driver

Windows communicates with devices, such as sound boards and CD-ROM players, through a limited number of channels. When you install and set up the new device, you must make sure that the settings you choose don't conflict with settings already in use by other devices.

◄ "Configuring for Sound Devices," p. 263

Testing after you connect the equipment to your PC is the best way to ensure that no conflict exists. If, however, you have trouble using the device after connecting, installing, and setting up the system, a conflict may exist. To determine where the conflict lies, refer to the device's documentation. You also can call the manufacturer or the Microsoft support line (this number is included in Chapter 27, "Troubleshooting Windows").

Finally, you can check the setup for other equipment installed on the PC to see whether a port or IRQ interrupt is in conflict. If you suspect a printer, check by choosing the Printers application in Control Panel and choosing the **C**onnect Button. Choose OK and then Close after you change the connection. If you need to change an IRQ interrupt, choose the Ports application in Control Panel, select the COM port to change, choose **S**ettings, choose **A**dvanced, and select a different IRQ number from the **I**nterrupt Request Line list. Finally, choose OK twice and then choose Close.

◄ "Setting up Serial Ports," p. 253

To make changes to the driver setup, follow these steps:

1. Choose the Drivers icon in Control Panel. The Drivers dialog box appears.

2. From the **I**nstalled Drivers list, select the driver you want to set up.

3. Choose the **S**etup button. (If the driver requires no settings, the **S**etup button is dimmed.) The Setup dialog box appears.

4. Select the setup options you need, referring to the device's documentation.

5. Choose OK.

6. When the System Setting Change dialog box appears, choose **R**estart Now to force the changes to take effect immediately, or choose **D**on't Restart Now and choose Close to close the Drivers dialog box.

Removing a Driver

You can remove a driver you no longer use from the Installed Drivers list. Removing a driver doesn't remove the file from the hard disk, so you can reconnect the driver if you subsequently find that you need it. Do not remove drivers that Windows installed (just to be safe, don't remove any drivers you don't recognize).

To remove a driver, follow these steps:

1. In Control Panel, choose the Drivers icon. The Drivers dialog box appears.

2. Select the driver you want to remove from the **I**nstalled Drivers list.

3. Choose the **R**emove button. A dialog box appears, asking you to confirm removal of the driver.

4. Choose **Y**es.

5. Choose **R**estart Now to force the removal to take effect immediately.

Operating Sound Recorder

To use sound on a PC, you must add a sound board that conforms to the Multimedia Personal Computer specifications for the PC. You must install the board after adding it, as described in "Adding Multimedia Drivers" earlier in this chapter. If you use high-level MIDI sound or a synthesizer, you also must install the drivers for these devices.

◄ "Embedding Data as Packages," p. 220

To record sound, you also need a microphone; the sound board probably has a microphone jack (or port), but you should check the documentation to find out the connector you need. You also need to be sure that the microphone is powerful enough to replicate your voice adequately; check the documentation for specifications.

Using the Sound Recorder application, you can play, record, and edit sounds that have the WAVE format (designated by the file extension WAV). You can play these sounds on the speakers, assign sound to events, and embed sounds in applications that support object linking and embedding (OLE). You can embed a spoken message, for example, inside an Excel worksheet file or a Word for Windows document. (To learn more about object linking and embedding, refer to Chapter 6, "Advanced Data Sharing.")

Sound Recorder appears on-screen as a small window with a menu across the top, buttons on the bottom, and an oscilloscope-like display in the center. You use the menus to open, edit, and save sound files. You watch the wave-like display to monitor the sound file's progress. You use the buttons to start and stop Sound Recorder, just like a tape recorder.

Starting Sound Recorder

To start Sound Recorder, follow these steps:

1. In Program Manager, open the Accessories window (see fig. 19.7).

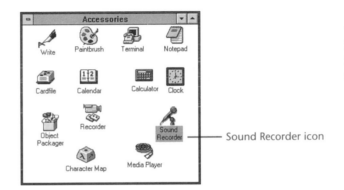

Fig. 19.7
The Sound Recorder icon is among the accessories.

Sound Recorder icon

2. Choose Sound Recorder. The Sound Recorder window appears (see fig. 19.8).

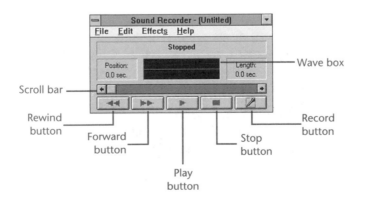

Fig. 19.8
The Sound Recorder window gives you a visual display of sound-wave forms.

Wave box

Scroll bar

Rewind button

Forward button

Play button

Stop button

Record button

◄ "Opening, Saving, Printing, and Closing Files," p. 53

Opening and Playing Sounds

On a PC, sound is stored as a file, just like other documents. To play a sound, you first must start Sound Recorder (see the preceding section) and open a sound file recorded in the WAVE format (a file with the extension WAV). Windows includes several sound files that use the WAVE format, and you can use Sound Recorder to record, edit, or mix sounds that you create.

To open and play a sound file, follow these steps:

1. Open the **F**ile menu and choose the **O**pen command. The Open dialog box appears (see fig. 19.9).

Fig. 19.9
Use the Open dialog box to locate the WAV file you want to open and play.

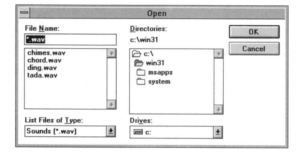

2. In the Dri**v**es list (if necessary), select the drive that contains the file, and in the **D**irectories list, select the directory. In the File **N**ame list, select the file you want to open.

3. Choose OK to open the sound file.

   The Length message on the right side of the Sound Recorder dialog box tells you the playing length, in seconds, of the file you opened.

4. Choose the Play button.

   The Position message on the left side of the Sound Recorder dialog box tells you the current position, in seconds, of the sound you are playing.

You see a visual representation of the sound waves in the Wave box (see fig. 19.10). You also see the scroll box move to the right as the file progresses.

Each time you choose the Play button, the sound plays from beginning to end. To stop the sound file before the file ends, choose the Stop button. You can resume by choosing Play again.

Fig. 19.10
Sound Recorder
with waves visible.

IV

Windows Multimedia

You also can move around in a sound file. To move forward by one tenth of a second, click the right arrow in the scroll bar; to move backward, click the left arrow. To move one second at a time, click the shaded part of the scroll bar in the direction in which you want to move. Alternatively, press the Tab key to select the scroll bar and then press the left- or right-arrow key to move forward or backward by tenths of a second.

You can move to the end of a sound file quickly by choosing the Forward button or pressing the End key; you can move to the beginning by choosing the Rewind button or pressing Home.

Creating a Sound File

You can create a sound file by recording the sound, by adding to an existing sound file, by inserting one sound file into another, or by mixing two sound files. To record a voice, you need to attach a microphone. Check the device documentation to learn how.

You can record up to one minute of speech. To record a voice, follow these steps:

1. Open the **F**ile menu and choose the **N**ew command.

2. Choose the Record button.

3. To record the message, speak into the microphone.

4. Choose the Stop button when you finish.

To record from a stereo, plug the stereo's output attachment into the microphone input port on the sound board (this procedure may require a special connector; check with an electronics store). If you find that recording exactly what you need is difficult, record a little more than you need and delete the extra (described in the following paragraphs of this section).

To record in an existing file, open the file, and use the Play and Stop buttons (or the scroll bar) to move to the position where you want to add the new sound. Choose the Record button and speak into the microphone. Choose Stop when you finish, and save the file.

You also can merge two sound files. Open the sound file in which you want to add another sound file, and use the Play and Stop buttons to move to the place where you want to add another sound file. Open the **E**dit menu and choose the **I**nsert File command. Select the file you want to insert and choose OK. Save the new file.

Another option is to mix two files so that the sounds of both files play simultaneously. One file may be music; the other file, a voice. Open one of the files, and use Play and Stop (or the scroll bar) to move to the place where you want to mix in another file. Open the **E**dit menu and choose the **M**ix With File command. Select the file you want to mix in and choose OK. Save the new file.

To delete part of a sound file, move to immediately before or after the point at which you want to delete the sound. Then open the **E**dit menu and choose either the Delete **B**efore Current Position or the Delete **A**fter Current Position command.

Before you save the sound file, you can undo changes at any time by opening the **F**ile menu and choosing the **R**evert command.

Editing a Sound File

You can edit a sound file by adding special effects, changing the volume, speeding or slowing playback, adding an echo, or reversing the sound. (If you reverse the file, make sure that you don't include offensive subliminal messages.)

To edit a sound file, follow these steps:

1. Open the **F**ile menu and choose the **O**pen command.

2. Select the file you want to edit and choose OK.

3. Open the Effec**t**s menu and choose one of the following commands:

Command	Effect
Increase Volume (by 25%)	Make the sound file 25% louder
Decrease Volume	Make the sound file 25% softer
In**c**rease speed (by 100%)	Double the speed of the sound file

Command	Effect
Decrease Speed	Halve the speed of the sound file
Add Echo	Add an echo to the sound
Reverse	Play the sound file backward

By opening the **F**ile menu and choosing the **R**evert command, you can undo changes at any time before you save the sound file.

Saving a Sound File

Be sure to save after you create or edit a sound file. To save a sound file, follow these steps:

1. Open the **F**ile menu and choose the Save **A**s command.

   > **Note**
   >
   > If you decide not to rename the file, choose **S**ave instead of Save **A**s.

◄ "Opening, Saving, Printing, and Closing Files," p. 53

2. In the Dri**v**es list, select the drive where you want to save the file.

3. In the **D**irectories list, select the directory in which you want to save the file.

4. Type a file name in the File **N**ame box. Include the file extension WAV to make the file easier to open at a later time.

5. Choose OK.

Exiting Sound Recorder

When you finish using Sound Recorder, open the **F**ile menu and choose the E**x**it command.

Assigning Sounds to Events

The simplest form of sound on a computer is the sound you can assign to computer-related events, such as pressing the asterisk key or question mark, or starting or stopping Windows. Windows comes with several sound files that you can assign to these events (and you can use Sound Recorder to create custom sounds). You also can turn off system sounds so that the PC operates more discreetly.

◄ "Assigning System Sounds," p. 263

To assign sounds to computer events, follow these steps:

1. In Control Panel, choose the Sound icon. The Sound dialog box appears, showing the available Windows **E**vents in one list box and the sound **F**iles in another list box (see fig. 19.11). Sound files usually have the WAV file extension.

Fig. 19.11
Use the Sound
dialog box to
assign sounds
to events.

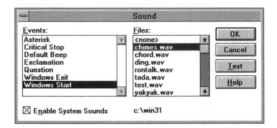

2. If the sound files are stored in another drive or directory, select the drive or directory from the **F**iles text box.

3. From the **E**vents list, select the event that you want to change. The sound file currently assigned to this event is selected in the **F**iles text box. To assign a different sound to the event, select another sound file.

4. Choose the **T**est button to see how the sound file sounds.

5. Repeat steps 3 and 4 to assign sounds to other Windows events.

6. After you set the desired sounds for the events, choose OK.

To turn off the PC's warning beep, check the **E**nable System Sounds check box and choose OK. This action disables beeping in all Windows applications.

Operating Media Player

Using the Media Player application, you can play Windows-compatible multimedia voice, animation, and music files. Whereas Sound Recorder plays only WAVE-format sound, Media Player can play animated video files and MIDI-based music files.

Before you use Media Player, you must connect the multimedia device (usually, a CD-ROM player, VCR, or MIDI synthesizer) to the PC, and you must install the device in Windows and set up the driver to run with Windows.

For more information, refer to "Adding Multimedia Drivers" earlier in this chapter, and see Chapter 20, "Using Windows with CD-ROM and Video."

Media Player is a small window that contains menus, a scroll bar, and buttons. The menus enable you to open files, select the device to play on, and switch between time and tracks. The scroll bar follows the progress of the file you play. The buttons play, pause, stop, and eject the medium, just like a VCR or CD-ROM player.

Unlike Sound Recorder, Media Player cannot create custom files. To create multimedia files, you must purchase a multimedia authoring kit, such as Multimedia ToolBook from Asymetrix or Guide Media Extensions from Owl International.

Starting Media Player

Media Player is a Windows accessory and, therefore, is located in the Accessories window.

◀ "Starting Applications," p. 48

To start Media Player, follow these steps:

1. Activate the Accessories window in Program Manager. You see the Media Player icon (see fig. 19.12).

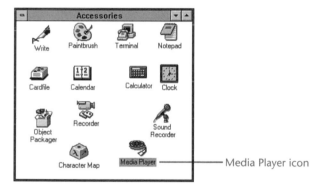

Fig. 19.12
Use the Media Player icon to start the Media Player application.

Media Player icon

2. Choose Media Player. The Media Player window appears (see fig. 19.13).

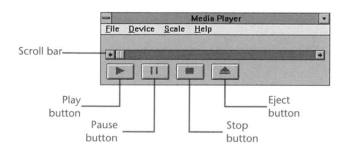

Scroll bar

Play button

Pause button

Stop button

Eject button

Fig. 19.13
Media Player enables you to open and play multimedia files.

IV

Windows Multimedia

Choosing a Media Device

Before you can play a multimedia game, movie, or story, you must specify the device on which you plan to play the game, movie, or story. Two kinds of devices exist: simple and compound. *Simple* devices play whatever is physically loaded into the device. To play a *compound* device, you must choose the device and then open the file you want to play. The listed devices reflect the equipment and drivers that you previously installed.

To choose a media device, follow these steps:

1. Open the **D**evice menu (see fig. 19.14).

Fig. 19.14

The devices listed in the Device menu depend on what is installed on the system.

2. Select the device that you want to play. Simple devices are not followed by a dialog box.

   Compound devices (such as **S**ound and **M**idi Sequencer in fig. 19.14) are followed by a dialog box.

3. If you selected a compound device, select the file that you want to play and choose OK.

If you installed a sound board and attached speakers, you can open and play one of two 2-minute music files included in the Windows directory: CANYON.MID and PASSPORT.MID.

Opening a File

After you specify a compound device and open a file, you can open a different file to play on the same device, without choosing that device again.

To open a file, follow these steps:

1. Open the **F**ile menu and choose the **O**pen command. The Open dialog box appears.

2. From the Dri**v**es list, select the drive where the file is located.

3. Select the kind of file you want to list in the List Files of **T**ype list. (Select MIDI Sequencer, for example, to list files with the extensions MID and RMI.)

4. In the **D**irectories list, select the directory that contains the file.

5. In the File **N**ame list, select the file that you want to open.

6. Choose OK.

Playing a Media File

After you select a device and either insert the medium (if you selected a simple device) or open a file (if you selected a compound device), Media Player is ready to play. The buttons in the Media Player window enable you to play, pause, stop, and eject the medium (if the device supports ejecting).

Choose the following buttons to operate Media Player:

Button	Action
Play	Begin playing the medium in the simple device or begin playing the file in the compound device
Pause	Pause the medium (choose Pause or Play to restart)
Stop	Stop the medium (choose Play to restart)
Eject	Eject the medium (if the device supports this action)

The scroll box in the scroll bar moves to the right as the medium or file plays.

Changing the Scale and Moving to a Different Position

By default, no scale appears above the scroll bar in Media Player, but two scales—Time and Tracks—are available. The Time scale shows your progress through the media or file by time. The Track scale counts the tracks as the medium or file plays. Because these scales appear above the scroll bar, you can move to a specific position in the file by watching the scale as you move the scroll box in the scroll bar.

To change the scale, follow these steps:

1. Open the **S**cale menu.

2. Choose the **Ti**me command. The Time scale appears (see fig. 19.15).

Fig. 19.15
The Time scale
enables you to
watch the progress,
by time, of the file
you are playing.

You also can choose the Tracks command. The Tracks scale appears
(see fig. 19.16).

Fig. 19.16
The Tracks scale
enables you
to watch the
progress, by tracks,
of the file you are
playing.

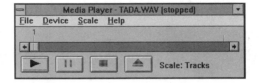

You can move to a different spot in the file by clicking the left or right arrow
in the scroll bar; dragging the scroll box; clicking the scroll bar; or pressing
the left-arrow, right-arrow, PgUp, or PgDn key.

Exiting Media Player

After you finish playing the multimedia file or device, open the File menu
and choose the Exit command. If the multimedia file or device is not finished
playing when you exit, a simple device continues playing, and you must turn
off the actual device.

Embedding Sound and Video in Applications

One of the promises of multimedia is that you can integrate pieces from different applications into a unified presentation. In its simplest form, a multimedia
presentation may consist of a file that contains embedded sound or video.

You can embed sound and video in a file by using one of two methods. The
first—and preferable—method is to use the Object Packager accessory to package a sound or video object together with the related application and then
embed the object in a file, which places a microphone icon in the file. This
method is preferable because you can play the embedded sound or video
quickly.

The other way to embed sound is to choose an insert command to embed a sound object within the file. (When you use this technique, you cannot embed a Media Player object—only a Sound Recorder object.) This method also places a microphone icon in the file but, rather than playing the sound, starts the Sound Recorder window with no file loaded. To play a sound, you first must load the sound file.

Because the second method of embedding sound seems less useful than using Object Packager, this method isn't discussed in this chapter. To learn how to use this method, refer to Chapter 6, "Advanced Data Sharing."

◄ "Embedding Data into a Document," p. 212

To embed sound or video in a file, all the applications involved must support object linking and embedding (OLE). Sound Recorder and Media Player are OLE servers; the application in which you want to embed a sound or video object must be an OLE client.

After Object Packager embeds a sound or video file in a document, an icon appears in the document. The icon for a Sound Recorder object is a microphone; the icon for a Media Player object is a reel of film. If the embedded object is a WAVE-format sound file, you can double-click the microphone icon to play the sound or display the Sound Recorder with the sound file loaded. (Whether you play the sound or display the Sound Recorder depends on how you packaged the object; in this section, you learn both ways.) If the embedded object needs Media Player (as do MIDI files), when you double-click the film-reel icon, Media Player appears on-screen with the file loaded, and you must click the Play button to play the file.

◄ "Embedding Data as Packages," p. 220

To embed a multimedia object so that the Sound Recorder or Media Player window appears when you double-click the icon, the file already should be created and saved. (This technique is the only one that works with Media Player files; a second technique, described later in this section, is available for Sound Recorder files.)

To package and embed a multimedia object in a file so that double-clicking the icon displays either the Sound Recorder window or the Media Player window, follow these steps:

1. In the Accessories window, choose Object Packager. The Object Packager window appears, as shown in figure 19.17.

Fig. 19.17
Use Object
Packager to embed
sound and video
objects in a file.

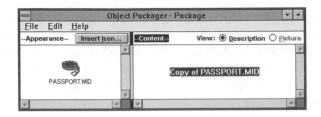

2. Select the Content window (on the right side); then open the **F**ile menu and choose the **I**mport command. When the Import dialog box appears, select the multimedia file you want to embed and choose OK. A copy of the file is added to Object Packager.

   To change the text below the icon before you copy the package and paste the icon in the document, open the **E**dit menu, choose the La**b**el command, and type new text. You may want to include a call to action, such as Double-click here, so that whoever uses the file knows exactly what to do to play the sound or video file.

3. Open the **E**dit menu and choose the Copy Pac**k**age command.

4. Position the insertion point in the document where you want to embed the package.

5. Open the **E**dit menu and choose the **P**aste command. An icon appears in the document, as shown in figure 19.18.

6. Save the document.

Fig. 19.18
A film-reel icon
identifies an
embedded Media
Player object.

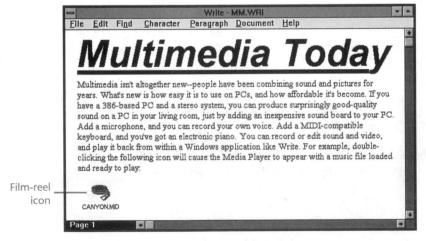

Film-reel
icon

When you double-click the icon in the document, the Sound Recorder or Media Player window appears (depending on the kind of file you embedded). The sound or video file loads, and all you have to do is click the Play button.

◀ "Transferring Data with Copy and Paste," p. 190

To package a sound to embed in a file so that the sound plays when you double-click the icon, follow these steps:

1. Open Sound Recorder.

2. Create the sound that you want to embed, or open the file that contains the sound.

3. Open the **E**dit menu and choose the **C**opy command, which copies the sound to the Clipboard.

4. Activate Object Packager and select the Content window (right side).

5. Open the **E**dit menu and choose the **P**aste command. The sound is copied from the Clipboard to Object Packager.

   To change the text below the icon before you copy and paste the package in the document, open the **E**dit menu and choose the La**b**el command, and type the new text.

6. Open the **E**dit menu and choose the Copy Pac**k**age command. The package is copied.

7. Activate the application, open the file, and position the insertion point in the document where you want to embed the package.

8. Open the **E**dit menu and choose the **P**aste command. A microphone icon appears, as shown in figure 19.19.

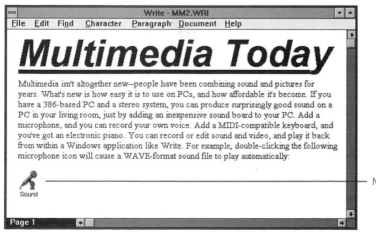

Fig. 19.19
A microphone icon indicates that a Sound Recorder object is embedded.

Microphone icon

If you use this second technique—copying the sound directly from Sound Recorder and pasting the sound in Object Packager, rather than using the **I**mport command in Object Packager—when you double-click the icon in the file, the sound plays without displaying Sound Recorder.

In many applications, you can play an embedded multimedia object by double-clicking or by selecting the object and choosing a command such as **E**dit Package **O**bject, **A**ctivate Contents in Write.

Using MIDI Mapper

When you install a device that supports MIDI, such as the Sound Blaster sound card, an application for controlling MIDI devices is added by default. The application, MIDI Mapper, appears as a new icon in Control Panel. You can use MIDI Mapper to choose a preconfigured MIDI setup for the MIDI device or to create custom setup specifications.

Choosing a MIDI Setup

When you installed Windows, some predefined MIDI settings designed to work with common MIDI devices were included. A new device probably will conform to one of these settings and, therefore, will work flawlessly with Windows. You can change the settings, however, by using the MIDI Mapper application in Control Panel. You may need to change these settings if you use a nonstandard MIDI setup or if the device doesn't include a MIDI setup.

To alter a MIDI setting, follow these steps:

1. In Program Manager, open the Main window and choose Control Panel. You can see the MIDI Mapper icon if you installed a MIDI device (see fig. 19.20).

Fig. 19.20
MIDI Mapper
enables you to
map the MIDI
device to Windows.

MIDI Mapper ———

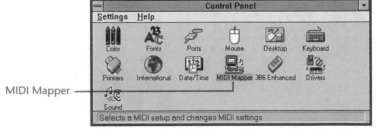

IV

2. Choose the MIDI Mapper icon. The MIDI Mapper dialog box appears (see fig. 19.21).

Fig. 19.21
Use the MIDI Mapper dialog box to choose a different MIDI setup.

3. Make sure that the Show **S**etups option is selected. Then, from the N**a**me list, select the setup you want to use.

4. Choose Close.

If no setting for the device is listed, first call the manufacturer to see whether an updated MIDIMAP.CFG setup file, which includes a setup for this device, is available. If an updated file is available, make a backup of the existing MIDIMAP.CFG file and copy the new file to the Setup subdirectory in the Windows directory. If no setup file is available, you may need to create a custom file.

Creating a Custom MIDI Setup

All MIDI devices conform to certain musical specifications, but the output is not mapped in a standard way, which is why different MIDI setups are available for different pieces of equipment. Choosing the correct mapping is like using computer keyboards from different manufacturers, each of which uses a proprietary key layout. To get a κ on-screen, you have to know where the K key is, and the PC also has to know.

Similarly, Windows must know which key and which channel the MIDI device uses for each sound. The process is known as *mapping*, which means that you map the PC keys and channels to the corresponding keys and channels in the device. This way, when you press a key that is supposed to play a middle-octave C from an acoustic grand piano, you get a middle-octave C that sounds like an acoustic grand piano, rather than a high D that sounds as though the note is being played by an oboe.

This procedure is complex and requires you to know a great deal about the device. Check the documentation to see whether information about key, patch, and channel mapping is included; if not, call the manufacturer to get the information. (First, however, read this section so that you understand what information you need.) Also be aware that the application you use to play the device must be Windows-compatible to take advantage of the settings you create in MIDI Mapper.

To set up a MIDI device, you need to know whether the device is a base-level or an extended-level synthesizer. *Base-level* synthesizers meet the minimum MIDI requirements; *extended-level* synthesizers can play more notes simultaneously than base-level synthesizers, which produce richer sounds.

Four basic steps are involved in setting up a MIDI device:

1. You must set up the device to receive MIDI messages on multiple MIDI channels. Refer to the device's documentation to learn how to perform this procedure.

2. You must create a key map for both percussion instruments and melodic instruments that play in the wrong key.

3. You must create patch maps for both the percussion and melodic instruments. A patch defines a sound and all the sound's voices.

4. You must create the channel map for the synthesizer.

Creating key, patch, and channel maps are similar processes. First, you name the map (if you are creating a map). Then, a table-like chart appears, listing possible specifications. The information in the left columns describes the MIDI source; you cannot change this information. In the remaining columns (which are identified with an underlined letter in the column headings), the information pertains to the destination: the sound device. You can change the settings in these columns. To change the settings, select the box in the same row as the corresponding sound or channel at the left. When you change information in a destination column, you map the instructions going out from the computer to the appropriate sounds on the device.

Creating a Key Map

Create a key map for the synthesizer if the synthesizer doesn't conform to MIDI standards that specify that certain keys play certain sounds or a particular octave. MIDI Mapper provides up to 2,048 key maps for each of 128 patch entries for the 16 allowable patch maps.

If the synthesizer plays certain melodic sounds at registrations different from MIDI standards, you may need to create two types of key maps: a map for percussion sounds and a map for melodic sounds.

To create a key map, follow these steps:

1. Choose the MIDI Mapper application in Control Panel. The MIDI Mapper dialog box appears.

2. Choose the **K**ey Maps option.

3. Choose the **N**ew button. The New MIDI Key Map dialog box appears, as shown in figure 19.22.

Fig. 19.22

To create a new MIDI map, you must supply a name and description.

4. In the **N**ame text box, type a name (up to 15 characters) for the new MIDI key map. In the **D**escription text box, type a description (up to 28 characters).

5. Choose OK. The MIDI Key Map dialog box appears (see fig. 19.23), with the following columns:

Src Key	*Source Key Number.* The MIDI-specified keys; you cannot change these keys.
Src Key Name	*Source Key Name.* The names of the instruments associated with the keys, as specified by MIDI standards; you cannot change these names.

Dest Key

Destination Key Number. The key on the synthesizer that plays when you press the source key; you can change this number to any number from 0 to 127.

6. Select the **D**est Key that you want to change, which causes up and down arrows to appear at the right side of the text box. Click the up arrow to raise the destination key number, or click the down arrow to lower the number. You also can press the Tab key to select the existing destination key number and type a new number.

   To show the key you want to change, you may need to scroll the window. Click the up or down arrow in the scroll bar, or press PgUp or PgDn.

7. Choose OK. A dialog box appears, confirming the changes.

8. Choose **Y**es to confirm or **N**o to discard the changes (or choose Cancel to return to the MIDI Key Map dialog box).

9. To close the MIDI Mapper dialog box, choose Close.

Fig. 19.23
The MIDI Key Map dialog box lists the sounds for keys 35 through 81 (the MIDI-specified percussion keys).

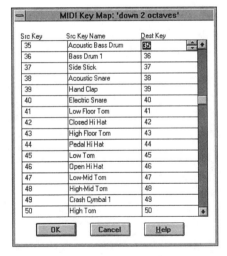

Src Key	Src Key Name	Dest Key
35	Acoustic Bass Drum	35
36	Bass Drum 1	36
37	Side Stick	37
38	Acoustic Snare	38
39	Hand Clap	39
40	Electric Snare	40
41	Low Floor Tom	41
42	Closed Hi Hat	42
43	High Floor Tom	43
44	Pedal Hi Hat	44
45	Low Tom	45
46	Open Hi Hat	46
47	Low-Mid Tom	47
48	High-Mid Tom	48
49	Crash Cymbal 1	49
50	High Tom	50

MIDI Key Map: 'down 2 octaves'

OK   Cancel   Help

Creating a Patch Map

A patch describes a sound, such as an acoustic grand piano or a dulcimer. If the synthesizer uses patches that differ from the MIDI specifications, you must create a set of patches for percussion instruments and for melodic instruments.

To create a patch, follow these steps:

1. Choose the MIDI Mapper in the Control Panel.

2. Select the **P**atch Maps option, and choose the **N**ew button. The New MIDI Patch Map dialog box appears.

3. In the **N**ame text box, type a name (up to 15 characters) for the new MIDI key map. In the **D**escription text box, type a description (up to 28 characters).

4. Choose OK. The MIDI Patch Map dialog box appears.

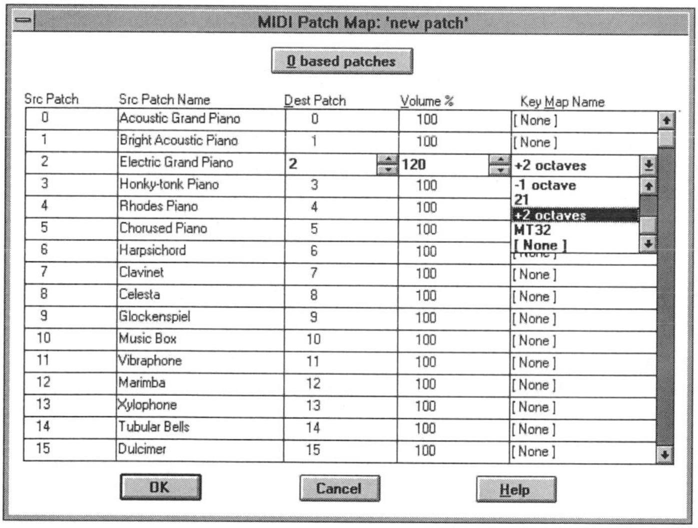

Fig. 19.24
The MIDI Patch Map dialog box enables you to create or edit a patch map.

The Patch Map dialog box contains the following columns:

Src Patch	*Source Patch Number.* MIDI-specified patch numbers; you cannot change these numbers. Some synthesizers number patches 0 through 127; others number from 1 through 128. Select the sequence the synthesizer uses by choosing a button at the top of the dialog box.

Src Patch Name	*Source Patch Name.* Names of sounds or instruments associated with the source patch numbers, specified by MIDI standards; you cannot change these names.
Dest Patch	*Destination Patch.* Patch numbers the synthesizer plays to create sounds described in the Source Patch Name column. If the synthesizer confirms to MIDI standards, these numbers are the same as Source Patch numbers. Otherwise, you must change these numbers.
Volume %	*Volume by Percent.* Volume at which the destination plays the sound. The default, 100, means that the sound plays at 100 percent. To play louder, set a **V**olume % greater than 100; to play softer, set a number less than 100.
Key **M**ap Name	Links the patch to the correct key map—a custom or an existing key map. Choosing this option shows a list of all existing key map names. Several predefined key maps exist, such as *–1 Octave*, which you can use to map a melodic patch to an octave lower.

5. If the synthesizer's patch numbers start at 0 rather than 1, choose the **0** Based Patches button; if the numbers start at 1 rather than 0, choose the **1** Based Patches button.

6. To change the destination patch number (the patch number in the synthesizer that maps to the existing source patch number), select the appropriate box in the **D**est Patch column, which causes an up and down arrow to appear at the right side of the box. Click the up arrow to increase the number, click the down arrow to decrease the number, or press the Tab key enough times to select the patch number you want to change and type a new number. If the patch you want to change isn't visible, use the scroll bar to show more numbers, or press Tab enough times to scroll to the number you want to change.

7. To change the destination patch volume, in the **V**olume % column, select the volume box in the same row as the patch you want to change. Click the up or down arrow to change the number, or select the existing number and type a new number.

8. To map the patch to a different key map, in the Key **M**ap Name column, select the key map name box in the same row as the patch you want to map differently. A list of all existing key maps appears. Select the name of the key map that you want the patch to use.

9. Choose OK. A dialog box appears, asking you to confirm the changes.

10. Choose **Y**es to confirm or **N**o to discard the changes (or choose Cancel to return to the MIDI Patch Map dialog box).

11. Choose Close to close the MIDI Mapper dialog box.

Creating a Channel Map

If the channels on the synthesizer don't map to the standard MIDI channels, you need to create a channel map. Sixteen MIDI channels are available. A base-level synthesizer uses channels 13 through 15 for melodic sounds and 16 for percussion sounds; an extended-level synthesizer uses channels 1 through 9 for melodic sounds and 10 for percussion.

To create a channel map, follow these steps:

1. Choose the MIDI Mapper icon in Control Panel.

2. Select the **S**etups option and choose the **N**ew button. The New MIDI Setup dialog box appears.

3. In the **N**ame text box, type a name (up to 15 characters) for the new MIDI key map. In the **D**escription text box, type a description (up to 28 characters).

4. Choose OK. The MIDI Setup dialog box that appears (see fig. 19.25) contains the following columns:

Src Chan	*Source Channel.* MIDI channels specified by the application; you cannot change these numbers.
Dest Chan	*Destination Channel.* Channel the synthesizer uses to play the sounds in the source channel. If the synthesizer supports the MIDI standard, this channel is the same as the source channel. If not, change the channel number.

Port Name   Port you want the channel to use. When
                                 you select a box in the **P**ort Name column,
                                 a drop-down list appears that shows all the
                                 MIDI device drivers connected to ports in
                                 the computer. Select the driver for the
                                 channel to use (not all channels must use
                                 the same port).

Patch **M**ap Name   Name of the patch map to use with the
                                 specified channel. When you select a Patch
                                 Map Name box, a list of existing patch map
                                 names appears; select the patch you want to
                                 use. For melodic source channels, select a
                                 melodic patch map; for percussion source
                                 channels, select a percussion patch map.

Active   Activates or deactivates the selected port
                                 (available only if you selected a **P**ort Name).
                                 If you select the **A**ctive option (an x appears
                                 in the check box), sound from the channel
                                 is sent to the selected port; if deselected,
                                 sound *isn't* sent.

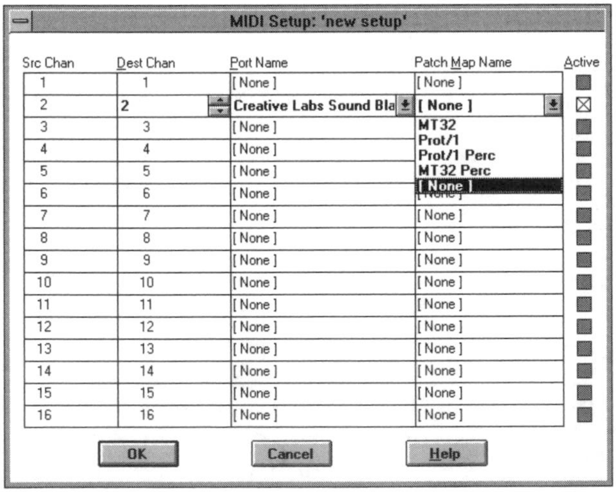

Fig. 19.25

Use the MIDI
Setup dialog box
to map MIDI
channels to the
correct channels
on the synthesizer.

	MIDI Setup: 'new setup'			
Src Chan	Dest Chan	Port Name	Patch Map Name	Active
1	1	[None]	[None]	■
2	2	Creative Labs Sound Bla ±	[None] ±	⊠
3	3	[None]	MT32	■
4	4	[None]	Prot/1 Prot/1 Perc	■
5	5	[None]	MT32 Perc	■
6	6	[None]	[None]	■
7	7	[None]	[None]	■
8	8	[None]	[None]	■
9	9	[None]	[None]	■
10	10	[None]	[None]	■
11	11	[None]	[None]	■
12	12	[None]	[None]	■
13	13	[None]	[None]	■
14	14	[None]	[None]	■
15	15	[None]	[None]	■
16	16	[None]	[None]	■

[OK]   [Cancel]   [Help]

5. If necessary, change the destination channel by using the **D**est Chan option and selecting the appropriate box in the **D**est Chan column, which causes up and down arrows to appear at the right end of the box. Click the up or down arrow to change the number, or select the existing channel number and type a new number. You can press the Tab key to move between the boxes in the **D**est Chan column.

6. If necessary, change the name of the port you want the selected channel to use by selecting from the list that appears when you select a box in the **P**ort Name column.

7. If necessary, select the patch map you want each channel to use. To perform this step, select the box in the Patch **M**ap Name column adjacent to the channel whose patch map you want to change.

8. If necessary, activate or deactivate the port by selecting or deselecting the **A**ctive option.

9. Choose OK or press Enter. A dialog box appears that confirms the changes.

10. Choose **Y**es to confirm or **N**o to discard the changes (or choose Cancel to return to the MIDI Setup dialog box).

11. Choose Close to close the MIDI Mapper dialog box.

Editing and Deleting Maps

Besides creating maps, you also can edit existing maps. The process is the same as the methods you used to create a map (see the preceding sections), but rather than choosing the **N**ew button, you choose the **E**dit button in the MIDI Mapper dialog box, and you don't have to supply a name or description.

Similarly, you can delete an existing map by selecting the appropriate category from the Show group (**S**etups, **P**atch Maps, or **K**ey Maps), selecting the map name from the N**a**me list, and then choosing the **D**elete button.

From Here...

Refer to the following chapters for more information related to using multimedia in Windows:

■ Chapter 5, "Simple Data Sharing," explains simple methods of transferring information in Windows.

■ Chapter 6, "Advanced Data Sharing," teaches you more advanced techniques for sharing information between applications.

■ Chapter 7, "Customizing with Control Panel," explains how to use Control Panel to customize your Windows environment, including how to assign system sounds and configure sound devices.

■ Chapter 20, "Using Windows with CD-ROM and Video," explains how to use CD-ROM and video to give your system full multimedia capability.

Chapter 20

Using Windows with CD-ROM and Video

Today's Windows multimedia is the forerunner of tomorrow's information superhighway. This chapter defines *multimedia* as the process of combining digital audio, the subject of Chapter 19, with still pictures, text, animated graphics, and full-motion digital video.

In this chapter, you learn how to:

- Determine whether your computer can handle the new multimedia

- Choose the right CD-ROM drive for your use of multimedia

- Install and set up a CD-ROM drive

- Display images from Kodak's new Photo CDs

- Get the most from full-motion digital video

The primary means of delivering multimedia *content* (the CD-ROM publishing's term for data) today is the CD-ROM (Compact-Disc Read-Only Memory) because only CD-ROMs presently are capable of storing the exceedingly large files associated with digital audio and especially digital video data. A standard 4 1/2-inch CD-ROM can hold about 640M of multimedia content and costs between about $1 and $3 to manufacture, depending on quantity. By the year 2000, the information superhighway may be a reality; an article called "Digital Pioneers" in the May 2, 1994 issue of *Business Week* magazine called CD-ROMs "training wheels" for interactive television content providers.

The acceptance of multimedia for home education and entertainment, as well as business training and presentation purposes has caused sales of CD-ROMs and CD-ROM drives to skyrocket. According to Dataquest, Inc., a San Jose, California market research firm, worldwide sales of CD-ROM drives are expected to reach 6.4 million units in 1994 and 8.6 million in 1995, up from the scant 240,000 drives sold in 1990.

To gain the benefits of multimedia computing, you need the right combination of computer hardware and software. This chapter gives you the background you need to make an informed purchasing decision for a CD-ROM drive, describes how to install a CD-ROM drive, and gives you tips on how to take best advantage of new multimedia features, such as digital video.

Understanding the MPC Level 2 Standard

When Microsoft added the multimedia extensions to Windows 3.0 in 1992, the firm also established a set of hardware requirements that defined the original Multimedia PC (MPC). Microsoft designed an MPC logo to identify computer systems and CD-ROM upgrade kits that complied with the early MPC standard. Shortly afterward, Microsoft and several multimedia product suppliers formed the Multimedia PC Marketing Council to administer the specification and to license suppliers to use the MPC trademarked logo. In the fall of 1993, the Council released a Level 2 specification that established the hardware standards for the second generation of multimedia PCs. At the same time, the Council established a certification process to ensure that hardware bearing either the original MPC (now called Level 1) or the new MPC-2 (Level 2) logo complies with the corresponding standard. The Council also extended certification to sound cards and CD-ROM drives, which previously had not been eligible to carry the MPC logo unless combined in a CD-ROM upgrade kit.

The original MPC Level 1 specification for MPC required a minimum of an Intel 80286 CPU, but the specification quickly was altered to require at least an 80386SX CPU. The lowest-performance CPU allowed by Level 2 is a 25-MHz 80486SX processor, a minimum 4M RAM, and a 160M or larger fixed disk drive is required. Level 2 also requires audio adapter cards (also called sound cards) to provide 16-bit resolution and video display units (VDUs) and their adapter cards to display 65,536 colors in standard VGA mode (640 by 480 pixels). Level 2 CD-ROM drives must be double-speed, provide a sustained 300K/second data throughput, and have an average access time of 400 ms or less.

Using the CD-ROM drive must consume, at most, 60 percent of the microprocessor's resources during sustained 300K/second read operations, and no more than 40 percent of the CPU's resources at 150K/second. The specification recommends, but does not require, a 64K read-ahead memory buffer in the CD-ROM. Level 2 CD-ROM drives also must be capable of reading Kodak's Photo CD format, including multisession Photo CDs, and provide the ability (or be upgradable) to read CD-ROMs that use the Extended Architecture (XA) format. The Photo CD and XA formats are described later in this chapter. An analog audio cabling standard has been added to the Level 2 specification to assure that conforming CD-ROMs and sound cards are interchangeable with respect to playing audio CDs through the sound card's mixer and amplifier.

All of the major suppliers of IBM-compatible PCs, multimedia upgrade kits, sound cards, and CD-ROM drives offer products that conform to Level 2 of the MPC specification. If the multimedia upgrade kit or CD-ROM drive you purchase carries the MPC-2 logo, you are assured that it meets the MPC specifications, but your computer also must meet the preceding specifications to take advantage of the new features of MPC Level 2.

> **Note**
>
> The MPC-2 logo does not guarantee that a CD-ROM drive is compatible with the CD-ROM connector of your MPC-2 sound card. The "SCSI versus IDE and Proprietary CD-ROM Interfaces" and "Internal Audio Connections" sections, later in this chapter, describe the connections between sound cards and CD-ROM drives.

Tip

Make sure that you look for PC2 on the logo of the MPC components you purchase. The original MPC (Level 1) logo does not display a level number.

IV

Windows Multimedia

Using CD-ROMS with Windows 3.11

Using a CD-ROM drive with Windows is simple, once you've installed and tested the drive. A CD-ROM drive appears as the next drive in sequence after your local physical and logical fixed disk drive(s). The most common designator for a CD-ROM drive is D:, but if you have more than one logical drive, the drive may be designated as E: or higher. Connected network drives appear after the CD-ROM drive. Figure 20.1 shows Windows for Workgroups 3.11's File Manager displaying part of the root directory of a CD-ROM. In figure 20.1, the D: drive is compressed with Stacker 3.1, which adds an E: partition; the F: drive is the CD-ROM drive; and the G: drive is a shared directory of the network server. The symbol for a CD-ROM drive is an image of a half-ejected CD-ROM.

Fig. 20.1

File Manager's drive designators for fixed disk, CD-ROM, and shared network drives.

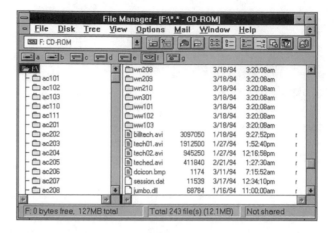

Note

Make sure the LASTDRIVE= entry in your CONFIG.SYS file specifies a letter higher in alphabetic sequence than the number of logical drives installed. If LASTDRIVE=D and you have two logical fixed disk drives, you can't install the CD-ROM drive software.

CD-ROM drives behave identically to fixed disk or floppy disk drives, but the data throughput of CD-ROM drives is considerably slower than today's fixed disk drives. You can execute applications from CD-ROM drives, and use the files containing data with the appropriate Windows or DOS application. You cannot, of course, save any changes you make to the data files to the CD-ROM, unless you have a writable CD-ROM drive.

Before you reach this point, however, you need to acquire and install the CD-ROM drive. Neither DOS nor Windows was originally designed to accommodate CD-ROMs, so you also must install the driver software that makes the format of the directory files on the CD-ROM compatible with the file allocation table (FAT) system of DOS. The sections that follow provide guidance on choosing a CD-ROM drive and how to install the driver and the software required to make CD-ROMs act like very large, write-protected floppy disks. If you have an operating CD-ROM installed, you may want to skip to the "Playing CD-ROM Digital Video" section.

Choosing a CD-ROM Drive

Conventional, read-only CD-ROM drives come in a wide variety of types and styles, and range in price from less than $200 to more than $1,000. You need to decide on the speed and style (internal or external) of the drive and the type of the interface used to connect the output of the drive to your computer's internal bus. The sections that follow interpret the nomenclature used to describe CD-ROM drives so that you can determine which features you need for your multimedia applications.

High-Speed 2x, 3x, and 4x CD-ROM Drives

High-speed CD-ROM drives that meet or exceed the MPC Level 2 requirements are variously described as multi-speed, multi-spin, double-speed (2x), triple-speed (3x), and quadruple-speed (4x). The speed at which a CD-ROM drive delivers data to your computer is determined by the speed of the spindle that rotates the CD-ROM. As noted in the preceding section on the MPC Level 2 specification, a double-speed drive delivers data at 300K/second. A quadruple-speed drive provides a throughput of 600K/second. To be able to play audio CDs on your CD-ROM drive, the CD-ROM drive must be capable of either reducing the spindle speed to the "single-speed" audio CD standard (called CD-DA, Compact Disc-Digital Audio or Redbook audio), or provide a means to store Redbook audio data in memory and send it to the digital-to-analog converter (DAC) at the standard Redbook audio speed.

When this edition was written, the street (discounted) prices of CD-ROM drives were approximately proportional to their speed. Thus double-speed CD-ROM drives are roughly twice as expensive as single-speed drives, and quadruple-speed drives are at least twice as expensive as double-speed drives. A double-speed drive is satisfactory to display partial-display, compressed digital video at the U.S. standard of 30 frames/second. You need a triple- or quadruple-speed drive and at least an 80486DX2-66 computer to display full-screen digital video images at 30 frames per second.

> **Tip**
>
> If you want to play audio CDs on your CD-ROM drive, make sure that the audio feature is included in the drive specification. Not all high-speed CD-ROM drives include audio capability.

> **Tip**
>
> Make sure the CD-ROM drive has an audio connector on the back if you want to play CD audio through your sound card's mixer and amplifier. Otherwise, CD audio requires use of the line input connector.

> **Note**
>
> If the package or specifications for a CD-ROM does not include one of the descriptions in the preceding paragraph, such as 2x or 3x, the CD-ROM drive is undoubtedly a "single-speed" drive whose spindle RPM is the same as that of an audio CD player. Such drives are no longer considered adequate for multimedia applications, especially those that involve digital video or the less common 16-bit, 44.1-KHz stereo sound. "Single-speed" drives are adequate for less demanding applications, such as installing software distributed on CD-ROMs, and displaying titles, such as encyclopedias and dictionaries. These drives now are available at bargain prices of $175 or less.

"Caddyless" CD-ROM Drives

Caution

Handle CD-ROMs with great care. Unlike audio CDs, a scratch on the active side of the CD-ROM can render all of a CD-ROM, not just a track, useless. Excessive dust on a CD-ROM can render the drive inoperable without cleaning.

The first CD-ROM drives required a special case, called a *caddy*, in which you placed the CD-ROM before inserting it into the drive. Many low-cost drives, mostly of the "single-speed" variety, now have a drive mechanism similar to audio CD players that does not require a caddy. Caddyless drives are suitable for occasional users of CD-ROMs, but storing frequently-used CD-ROMs in their own caddies makes changing CD-ROMs much quicker and assures that the CD-ROMs are protected at all times. Caddies cost about $5 each at computer stores and minimize problems with fingerprints and resulting dust accumulation inside your CD-ROM drive.

CD-ROM Changers

Windows software developers and multimedia addicts rapidly acquire a large number of CD-ROMs. If you want to minimize juggling discs, CD-ROM changers are similar to audio-CD changers except that they use cartridges with stacked CD-ROMS rather than the more common turntables for audio CDs. When this edition was written, 6-disc CD-ROM changers were about twice the price of CD-ROM drives of equivalent speed. As an example, Pioneer's DRM-602X, a double-speed changer, has a street price of about $700, and the quadruple-speed version, the DRM-604X, sold for about $1,000. Pioneer also offers an 18-disc, quadruple-speed changer (DRM-1804X) for about $2,000.

Kodak Photo CD Compatibility and "Multisession" Drives

Eastman Kodak's Photo CD format originally was intended for photographic enthusiasts to display their pictures on home TV sets. Sales of Photo CD players, like Philips' CD-I (CD-Interactive) players, did not even come close to their marketers' sales volume estimates. Professional photographers and stock photographic agencies, however, rapidly adopted the Photo CD itself as a means of distributing or advertising their commercial images.

To create a Photo CD, you send undeveloped film or 35mm film positives or negatives to a Photo CD processing center, usually run by a photofinisher. The photographic images are scanned, color-corrected, and then encoded on the Photo CD disc in a write-once CD format called *Green Book*, a combination of the CD-ROM XA and CD-I formats. Photo CDs for consumer pictures and general business photography store up to about 100 images. Typically, the cost of a conventional 36-exposure Photo CD is in the range of $35 to $75. If you have a Photo CD with an initial 24 or 36 exposures, the processing center can add additional images, but you can only display the added pictures if your CD-ROM drive has *multisession* capability.

Each image on standard and professional Photo CDs includes a small, thumbnail picture for cataloging, plus copies of the image in a variety of sizes. The largest image, 3,072-by-2,048 pixels (16Base), requires about 3M to 6M of disk space in compressed format, depending on the content of the image, and expand to about 18M in your computer's RAM and in a Windows swap file. Loading and displaying one of the large images from a double-speed CD-ROM can take several minutes. The standard Photo CD Master disc has a gold reflective layer, which Kodak claims prolongs the life of a Photo CD to 100 years or more.

Kodak now offers a variety of commercial Photo CD formats, as described in the following list:

- *Pro Photo CD Master* discs accommodate large photographic formats, including 2 1/4- by 2 1/4-inch and 4- by 5-inch negatives.

- *Print Photo CD* also includes the ability to store CMYK-encoded images that are created by high-resolution drum scanners to produce four-color printing plates. CMYK is an abbreviation for cyan, magenta, yellow, and black, the standard four printing ink colors.

- *Photo CD Portfolio* adds multimedia capability, including ADPCM-compressed audio, conventional Redbook audio, and graphics animation, to the Photo CD format. Many Photo CD centers provide workstations with Kodak's Build-It software to create Portfolio discs. ADPCM is an abbreviation for adaptive-differential pulse-code modulation, the standard format for sound on CD-ROX XA discs.

- *Photo CD Medical* is newly-introduced format designed for storing large x-ray and CAT-scan images.

- *Photo CD Catalog* disks can store up to about 4,400 images in a format with less resolution than is offered by the standard and Pro Photo CD master discs.

You need special software to display images in Kodak's .PCD format. Kodak offers a range of Windows-compatible applications for manipulating .PCD files: Kodak ShoeBox serves as an image database and PhotoEdge is a simple image editor. Most commercial imaging editing applications, such as Micrografx Picture Publisher 4.0, Adobe Photoshop, Aldus PhotoStyler, and Corel PhotoPaint (a component of CorelDRAW! 5.0) offer .PCD compatibility. You need a Photo CD compatible (MPC-2) CD-ROM drive, preferably with multisession capability and a display adapter that can handle at least 65,536 colors to use Photo CDs effectively. A Windows video accelerator card with at least 2M of RAM can speed up screen redraw operations greatly with images of substantial color depth. (Color depth is the number of bits required to display each pixel; 256-color displays require 8 bits/pixel and showing 65,536 colors uses 16 bits per pixel.)

Internal versus External Drives

If you have a laptop or notebook computer, or plan on purchasing one, consider an external CD-ROM drive. You must use an external drive if you don't have an available 5 1/4-inch drive bay in your computer. External drives include a power supply (usually a plug-in "wall wart") and plug into an SCSI or parallel port of either a desktop or portable computer. You won't be able to use the CD-ROM connector of an sound card with an external CD-ROM drive unless you purchase a special adapter cable with a ribbon cable that provides a standard SCSI connector into which to plug the drive. Connecting CD-ROM drives is the subject of a section that follows shortly. If you want to use an external CD-ROM drive to play audio CDs through your sound card, you connect the headphone output of the drive to the line input of your sound card.

Recordable CD-ROM Drives

CD-ROM drives that include the capability to create your own CD-ROMs are called CD-R (Compact Disc-Recordable), writable, or WORM (write-once-read-many) CD-ROM drives. Rewritable CD-ROM drives that use a combination of magnetic and optical method (CD-ROM MO, magneto-optic) also are available. In early 1994, the Pinnacle Micro RCD-202 CD-R drive broke the $3,000 street price barrier. The RCD-202 drive handles conventional (ISO-9660) CD-ROM and Redbook audio formats but not CD-ROM XA, CD-I, or Photo CD discs.

Eastman Kodak offers a somewhat more expensive but faster (6x) CD-R drive, the PCD Writer 600, which supports CD-DA, CD-ROM, CD-ROM XA, CD-I, and Photo CD standards. The PCD Writer 600 lets you record a full-length,

63-minute (640M) CD-ROM in about 10 minutes. Media cost is about $20/disc to $30/disk for both the Pinnacle Micro and Kodak systems.

SCSI versus IDE and Proprietary CD-ROM Interfaces

One of the most important decisions involved in purchasing a CD-ROM drive is the interface (connection) to your computer. Originally, all CD-ROM drives used small computer system interface (SCSI) connectors and required a dedicated SCSI controller card that occupied an expansion slot. The SCSI interface is the primary expansion method for Apple Macintosh computers. A variety of other computer peripherals use SCSI, including fixed disk drives, tape backup drives, and optical scanners. SCSI-II is an advanced version of the original SCSI version, and ASPI (advanced SCSI programming interface) is the standard for writing drivers to provide connectivity to SCSI-II systems.

Most sound card manufacturers include on-board CD-ROM connectors so that installing a multimedia upgrade kit requires only a single expansion slot. Some manufacturers, primarily Creative Labs, employ proprietary CD-ROM interfaces; the original Sound Blaster card has a Mitsumi interface. Media Vision provides a Sony CD-ROM connection on its standard Pro Audio Spectrum boards. *Proprietary interfaces* are less costly to implement than the SCSI standard, but limit you to attaching a drive of the brand chosen by the sound card supplier. The majority of sound card manufacturers now offer single-device SCSI connectors, either as a standard feature or as an extra-cost option. If you want to connect additional SCSI devices to your computer, however, you'll usually need to purchase a dedicated SCSI adapter.

Recently, CD-ROM drives that use the IDE interface, the most common method of interconnecting fixed disk drives to the PC bus, have appeared. Standard IDE controllers accommodate two floppy disk and two fixed disk drives, so if you have only one fixed disk, you can plug an internal IDE CD-ROM drive into the connector reserved for the second disk. Thus, you can install a CD-ROM drive in a computer with no free expansion slots, if your sound card doesn't have a CD-ROM connector. Low-cost IDE adapter cards with the ability to connect up to four fixed disk drives also are available.

If you're planning to upgrade to Windows NT, intend to use an external CD-ROM with a portable computer, or want an external interface to add other peripheral devices without occupying additional internal expansion slots, a drive with a SCSI interface is your best choice. Windows NT is oriented almost exclusively to SCSI fixed disk and CD-ROM drives and peripheral devices. The Trantor T348 MiniSCSI Plus is an example of a parallel port-to-SCSI adapter for both desktop and portable PCs.

Installing CD-ROM Drives

Installing a CD-ROM drive is a two-step process that involves connecting the CD-ROM drive to your computer's internal bus and installing the software to make the CD-ROM behave as if it were a another fixed disk or floppy disk drive. The sections that follow describe the basic installation procedure for both external and internal drives.

Connecting an External Drive

Installing an external CD-ROM drive to a SCSI adapter card usually involves the following steps. The installation instructions supplied with SCSI adapter card and the external CD-ROM drive provide additional details that are specific to the devices. If you already have a SCSI adapter card installed, skip the first two steps.

1. Set the adapter card's interrupt level (IRQ) to an unused IRQ. The default interrupt for many SCSI cards is IRQ5, which also is used by LPT2, the second parallel printer port. It is unlikely that you need to change the base address (input/output or I/O port address) of the card.

2. Turn the power off to your computer, open your computer and install the SCSI adapter card in an empty expansion slot. You may want to leave your computer open until you complete and test the installation, so you can change the IRQ setting or base address, if necessary.

3. Set the CD-ROM drive's SCSI ID, usually with a rotary selector switch located at the back of the drive, to an unused value between 1 and 6 (the 7 SCSI ID usually is reserved for the adapter card itself.) If you have a SCSI fixed disk it is likely to be set to SCSI ID 6. Check the address settings of any other devices on the SCSI bus to avoid a conflict.

4. If an external SCSI terminator (a collection of resistors inside a SCSI plug with no cable or in the form of a small plastic strip with pins that plug into an in-line connector on the CD-ROM drive or other SCSI devices) device is used, remove the terminator connector from the last device presently connected to the adapter. If you have no other devices connected to the card, the card is considered the last device. Connect the SCSI cable supplied with the CD-ROM drive between the last device and the CD-ROM drive, and install the terminator at the CD-ROM connector.

5. If internal termination is used in your SCSI setup and you have existing SCSI devices, connect your CD-ROM drive between the adapter card and the other SCSI devices. The last device in the chain provides the

termination. Make sure that you set the terminator switch of the CD-ROM to off.

6. Leave the computer's cover off, and turn the computer's power on. Install the driver software for the CD-ROM, and verify that the drive appears when you launch File Manager. (Installing the CD-ROM drivers is the subject of a section later in this chapter.) Insert a CD-ROM into the drive and make sure you can read the directory; then turn the power off and reinstall the cover.

Using a parallel port adapter, such as the Trantor T348 MiniSCSI Plus described in the preceding section, is a much simpler method of connecting a single SCSI device to a desktop computer, and usually is the only method of connecting a CD-ROM to an IBM-compatible portable computer. You simply set the device address of the CD-ROM drive, make sure the internal terminator is set on or the external terminator connector is plugged into the connector at the CD-ROM, and plug the other end of the SCSI cable into the parallel port adapter, usually connected to the LPT2 connector of desktop and the LPT1 port of portable computers. The Trantor adapter has a connector that lets you use the same printer port for printing.

> ### Note
>
> You need a three-foot stereo mini-plug (1/8-inch diameter male connectors on both ends) cable connected between the headphone output of the external CD-ROM drive and the line input connector of your sound card to play audio CD through your sound card's mixer and amplifier. These cables are available at most Radio Shack stores. If the CD sound volume from the headphone connector is not adequate, purchase a stereo-to-mono mini-plug adapter cable and try the microphone input of the adapter card.

Troubleshooting

The computer recognizes the CD-ROM drive (its icon appears in File Manager), but the computer can't read from the drive.

The most common causes of inability to read from the drive, or intermittent read failures, are improper termination and interrupt conflicts. If the SCSI bus is not terminated, or the terminator is located in the middle rather than at the end of the chain of SCSI devices, reflections occur in the SCSI cabling. These reflections cause read errors. Double-check the terminator. Interrupts are triggered only when you read

(continues)

(continued)

from the drive or another device is active. As an example, you might not discover an interrupt conflict with a sound card until you use the sound card and the CD-ROM drive at the same time. Remove accessory cards one-by-one to determine which card causes the conflict. Two cards sharing the same base address can cause similar problems, but this is a less likely occurrence.

Setting up an Internal Drive

Tip

Bring the manual for your sound card with you when you purchase a CD-ROM so that the dealer can confirm the type of CD-ROM drive interface required.

Connecting an internal CD-ROM drive to the CD-ROM connector of an sound card is a simple process, if the interface of your CD-ROM drive matches that of the adapter card and you have the correct ribbon cable to connect the two devices. You won't have compatibility or cabling problems if you purchase a multimedia upgrade kit. If you purchase a CD-ROM drive separately, however, make sure that the dealer includes the required ribbon cable. (Internal CD-ROM drives seldom include ribbon cables as a standard item.) If you do not have a free power connector (extending from your computer's power supply), you also need to purchase a Y-connector (also called a "power splitter") to provide the necessary power to the internal drive.

Following are the steps commonly required to connect a CD-ROM drive to a sound card.

1. Turn off the power to your computer and remove the outer covering.

2. Mount the CD-ROM drive in an open 5 1/4-inch drive bay with the mounting screws provided. Older computer cases require that you install plastic slides on the side of the drive. If you have such a case, be sure to purchase a set of slides from the dealer; slides are seldom included with internal CD-ROM drives.

3. Connect the power cable to the four-pin connector at the back of the drive.

4. Connect the ribbon cable between the multi-pin connector at the back of the CD-ROM drive and the similar connector on the sound card. Make sure you observe proper orientation of the cable: the edge of the cable with the red or blue stripe aligns with the pin marked 1 on both the CD-ROM and the adapter card.

5. Leave the computer's cover off, and turn the computer's power on. Install the driver software for the CD-ROM, and verify that the drive

appears when you launch File Manager. Insert a CD-ROM into the drive and make sure you can read the directory; then turn the power off and reinstall the cover.

Caution

To connect an internal SCSI CD-ROM drive with a ribbon cable to the internal connector (set of pins) of an SCSI adapter card, follow the preceding steps. However, you must also observe the termination rules for SCSI devices described in the preceding section. This is especially important if you have an SCSI fixed disk already connected to the internal SCSI connector. If you do not observe proper SCSI termination procedures, your computer is likely to fail on booting because of data errors resulting from reflections in the SCSI cabling.

Making Internal Audio Connections

If the CD-ROM drive you install has an internal (rear-panel) audio connector, you can take advantage of the CD-ROM audio input of your sound card, leaving the line input open for other uses. The standard internal CD audio connector is a four-pin connector (also called a *header*) on the sound card. Many CD-ROM drives have an identical four-pin header on the rear panel, but the pin assignments (left output, right output, and common or ground) may not be identical. If you're not installing a multimedia upgrade kit and the CD-ROM drive has an internal audio connector, make sure you obtain an interconnecting cable from the dealer.

Note

Some CD-ROM drives use two 1/4-inch phonograph (RCA) connectors for audio output. The MPC Level 2 standard specifies the pin assignment for internal audio connections, but many pre-Level 2 cards differ. Unless you are handy with a soldering iron, you'll need to have a service person make the cable for you.

Troubleshooting

The internal audio connection between the CD-ROM drive and sound card appears correct, but I can't hear my audio CDs.

The most likely cause of this problem is that the orientation of the internal audio cable is reversed. Try reversing the orientation of one end of the cable. If this doesn't

(continues)

> (continued)
>
> work, you've probably encountered a mismatched connector set. If you're technically inclined and have a soldering iron, refer to the manuals for the card and the drive and change the cabling to suit. The other alternative is to pay a service person to do this for you.

Installing MSCDEX.EXE and CD-ROM Device Drivers

As mentioned earlier in this chapter, the directory of CD-ROMs is different from DOS's file allocation table (FAT) system. Thus, you need an intermediary program to make DOS recognize the CD-ROM as a drive. Microsoft's MSCDEX.EXE, a DOS terminate-and-stay-resident (TSR) application provides the required translation. MSCDEX.EXE also specifies the device driver required by the SCSI or sound card. You need a CD-ROM device driver and MSCDEX.EXE, so SCSI and sound cards provide a copy of MSCDEX.EXE, licensed from Microsoft, and the device driver for the SCSI or proprietary CD-ROM interface on the card. (You cannot purchase MSCDEX.EXE directly from Microsoft Corp.; however, it is included with MS-DOS 6.) SCSI management software, described in the next section, also includes MSCDEX.EXE or an equivalent DOS TSR application.

Tip

Add a / v parameter to the end of the MSCDEX line of your AUTOEXEC.BAT file to have MSCDEX report free memory and the memory it consumes.

All SCSI adapter cards and sound cards that include a CD-ROM drive connector include a CD-ROM drive installation application. This application performs the following functions:

- Adds a line to your CONFIG.SYS file to load the device driver, such as `device=c:\tscsi\tslcdr.sys d:\TSLCDR` for a Trantor SCSI adapter card.

- Adds a `lastdrive = x` line to CONFIG.SYS, where *x* is the next higher letter after the current `lastdrive =` entry, or *d* if no `lastdrive =` entry is found. (Not all installation programs do this for you.)

- Adds a line to your AUTOEXEC.BAT file to load MSCDEX.EXE, for example, `c:\tscsi\mscdex d:/TSLCDR`. TSLCDR is the alias for the `tslcdr.sys` driver.

You need to reboot your computer to cause the new entries in CONFIG.SYS and AUTOEXEC.BAT to take effect. During the boot process, a message created by the driver, similar to the following, appears on your display:

```
SCSI host adapter detected at address cc00h
Device 0, Read-Only Optical Drive (Removable media)
1 CD ROM Drive found
```

If you are using an ASPI driver with a SCSI-II adapter card, the message structure differs, but the content is similar. When your AUTOEXEC.BAT file loads MSCDEX.EXE in memory, a message like the following appears:

```
Drive D: = Driver TSLCD unit 0
```

This message indicates the drive assignment of the CD-ROM to a drive letter (logical drive). The first drive connected to a SCSI adapter always is identified as logical unit number (LUN) 0.

> ### Note
>
> Early versions of MSCDEX.EXE (version 2.21 and lower) do not operate if loaded into high memory by DOS 5+'s `loadhigh` command. MSCDEX.EXE does not recognize some device drivers if they are loaded high with a `devicehigh` instruction in your CONFIG.SYS file. Test your installation with MSCDEX.EXE and the driver in conventional memory, before attempting to load either MSCDEX.EXE or the drivers into high memory.

Troubleshooting

The computer doesn't recognize the CD-ROM drive; its icon doesn't appear in File Manager.

Open AUTOEXEC.BAT in the DOS EDIT application and add a temporary pause instruction after the line that loads MSCDEX.EXE; then reboot your computer. MSCDEX reports `Drive not found` or a similar message, depending on the version of MSCDEX. The most common cause of this problem is failure to include a `lastdrive = x` statement in CONFIG.SYS that provides for the added CD-ROM drive. Use the DOS EDIT application to check the content of CONFIG.SYS. A less common problem is failure of the install program to properly update your CONFIG.SYS file, in which case you receive a `Driver not found` message when MSCDEX executes. The manual for your adapter card usually includes sections that describe the proper entries for your AUTOEXEC.BAT and CONFIG.SYS files. Compare the entries in EDIT, and make the necessary changes.

SCSI Software for Windows

If you plan on making extensive use of SCSI devices, SCSI management software, such as Corel Systems, Inc.'s CorelSCSI! application is a worthwhile investment. CorelSCSI! supports a variety of products, such as CD-ROM, CD-R, WORM, and tape backup drives. Applications for DOS, Windows, and OS/2 are included. Corel's lower-cost CD PowerPak 1.0 for SCSI CD-ROM drives includes a collection of applications that automate CD-ROM driver installation, provide troubleshooting help, and let you create CD-ROM memory caches to speed up CD-ROM operations. Corel's Photo CD Lab application creates slide shows from your photo CDs.

Sharing CD-ROM Drives on a Windows Network

Applications that support Microsoft Windows Network, which includes Windows 3.11, Windows for Workgroups 3.11, and Windows NT 3.x, let you share CD-ROM drives connected to a peer-to-peer or a network server. You need special software, however, to share CD-R and WORM drives because Windows interprets these drives as read-only. (Windows NT supports a limited number of recordable and rewritable optical drives.) Other network operating systems (NOSs), such as Novell NetWare 3.x, require special software to mount CD-ROM drives as volumes. NetWare 4.x has built-in CD-ROM support.

Another approach to sharing CD-ROM drives on Novell networks is Microtest's (Phoenix, Arizona) Discport. Discport is an adapter that connects a SCSI CD-ROM drive directly to Ethernet cabling at any point in your LAN. You can chain up to seven CD-ROM drives to a single Discport adapter. The CD-ROM drives appear as Novell volumes to network users. A SCSI-to-Ethernet device removes the CD-ROM workload from conventional network server computers, which often are running at full capacity with normal file-sharing and print-serving duties.

Playing CD-ROM Digital Video

If you're interested in digital video, which is becoming an increasingly important element of computer games and business presentations, installing a CD-ROM drive is a must. Digital video, even when small-size images are compressed, requires about 80K of storage per second of display time. Thus, a minute of 160 by 120 pixel (1/8 window), 256-color digital video in Microsoft's AVI (Audio-Video Interleaved) format requires a 5M file. Displaying 1 minute of full-screen, 24-bit color, TV-quality video requires about 1.6G (more than is held by two CD-ROMs), and your computer's internal bus would have to be able to process the video data at over 30M/second. Thus, digital video data must be compressed to achieve manageable storage size and processing rate. The sections that follow describe how digital video works and how you use Windows 3.11's Media Player to view digital video clips. A brief description of Microsoft's Video for Windows 1.1 software also is included.

Understanding Video Compression and CODECs

Scaling down storage requirements and data processing rates is possible by limiting the number of colors displayed to Super VGA's 256-color palette and then reducing the size of the image displayed to 320 by 240 pixels (1/4-window). Even with these limitations, displaying a standard 30 frames/second to achieve "full-motion" digital video requires about 140M/minute of storage space and a data processing rate (called *bandwidth*) of over 2M/second. What's more, the preceding figures don't include sound, which requires at least 660K/minute of storage for low-quality monophonic, 8-bit recording at 11.025 KHz.

A variety of compression methods have been adopted by software and hardware suppliers to compress both the video and audio components of digital video. Compression (en*co*ding) and decompression (*deco*ding) of signals is accomplished by a *codec* (which may be implemented in software), dedicated hardware, or a combination of the two. There are two types of codecs:

- *Symmetrical codecs* require about the same time to encode data for storage as to decode data for display. Thus, you can record compressed digital video from analog sources, such as camcorders and VCRs, but usually at less than 30 frames/second, the standard rate for U.S. (NTSC) broadcast TV. With a double-speed CD-ROM and a 80486 computer, you can achieve a display rate of about 10-15 frames/second with a software codec. Hardware codecs, which require installing an adapter card or 32-bit video drivers that are expected to be included in Chicago, can provide read/write rates of 30 frames per second with 1/4-window images.

- *Asymmetrical codecs*, which usually provide increased compression ratios, use off-line compression methods. Special VCRs play back analog video one frame at a time at a rate that the asymmetrical codec can compress it. The encoding process is expensive because it requires special hardware, and decoding is most commonly accomplished by hardware methods.

Most accomplish the compression by a combination of methods that results in *lossy* compression. Lossy compression sacrifices some color fidelity to reduce storage and bandwidth requirement. *Interframe* compression records only the changes in images from frame-to-frame; *intraframe* compression uses pattern-matching methods on each frame. The most common lossy compression schemes are:

- *Microsoft's Audio-Video Interleaved* (AVI) actually is a file format, not a specific codec. Several third parties can provide AVI-compatible codecs. AVI, however, usually is associated with Video 1, the original Microsoft compression method for creating AVI files. The new 32-bit Video 2 codec provides substantially improved performance, but you'll need to install Windows NT 3.5 or wait for Chicago to use it. The AVI file format uses ADPCM-2 audio compression, which also is enhanced in Video 2.

- *Apple's QuickTime* also is a file format, rather than a codec. You need Apple's QuickTime for Windows to play QuickTime "movies" on IBM-compatible PCs. The default codec supplied with QuickTime is comparable in performance to Indeo.

- *Intel's Indeo* codec is a more efficient software codec than Video 1, and you can purchase the Smart Video Recorder board, a moderate-cost hardware codec that uses the Intel i750 processor, to provide improved performance.

- *SuperMac Technologies' Cinepak* is an asymmetrical codec that can provide better playback performance at the expense of slower recording rates.

- *The Moving Pictures Experts Group's* (MPEG) codec is very asymmetrical and requires hardware for both encoding and decoding the compressed image. MPEG offers the most efficient compression, but implementing even read-only MPEG presently is quite expensive.

- *The Joint Photographic Experts Group's* (JPEG) Motion-JPEG codec encodes each frame with a lossy compression method. JPEG playback also requires a hardware codec.

Each of the codecs in the preceding list has its own advantages and drawbacks. You can compare the performance of several codecs with Doceo Publishing, Inc.'s (Norcross, GA) Video Compression Sampler, two CD-ROMs containing several codecs and sample files that you can play side-by-side with Doceo's VCS-Play application to compare the quality of the images.

Using Media Player for AVI files

The updated Media Player 3.11 application of Windows 3.11 and Windows for Workgroups 3.11 is an OLE 1.0 server that accommodates a variety of multimedia file types, including digital video (Video for Windows), MIDI, and sound files in .WAV format. Both the Microsoft Video 1 and Intel Indeo software codecs are included.

Figure 20.2 shows Microsoft's Bill Gates in the standard, 1/8-window (160[ts]120 pixels) frame provided by Media Player in edit mode, as displayed in S-VGA (256-color) mode. To use edit mode, you first launch Media Player,and then open the .AVI file you want to play by opening the **F**ile menu and choosing **O**pen.

Fig. 20.2
The standard, 1/8-window display of Media Player 3.11 in edit mode.

You also can launch Media player in play mode by embedding media player's icon in a compound document created by an OLE 1.0 or 2.0 client application, or by double-clicking an .AVI file's icon in File Manager. Figure 20.3 shows Media Player's 1/4-window play mode, created by pixel-doubling. Pixel-doubling creates a 2 by 2 pixel element from each pixel in the original 160 by 120 pixel window. Pixel-doubling creates a blocky (pixelated) image.

Fig. 20.3
A 1/4-window, 256-color display created by pixel-doubling of a Media Player 3.11 image in play mode.

Figure 20.4 shows the image of figure 20.3 displayed in 16-color, standard VGA. Fortunately, almost all users of Windows have at least 256-color capability and Windows 3.11 includes standard S-VGA drivers for both 640 by 480 and 800 by 600 pixel displays.

Fig. 20.4
The image from the
.AVI file of figure
20.4 displayed in
the 16 standard
VGA colors.

Using Video for Windows 1.1

Tip
If your digital
video images have
the strange appear-
ance of figure 20.4,
launch Windows
Setup, open the
Options Change
System Settings
command, and
select SuperVGA
(640×480, 256
colors) from the
Display drop-
down list.

Microsoft introduced Video for Windows (VfW) 1.1, which is now a product
intended for developers and not for retail distribution, in late 1993. The earlier version did not fare well in the retail market, perhaps because it arrived
before its time. Video for Windows 1.1 includes both the Microsoft Video 1
and Cinepak codecs, plus the following applications:

■ VidCap, a simple video-capture program

■ VidEdit, which has limited editing functions and lets you select the
compatible codecs you want to use

■ WaveEdit for editing ADPCM-compressed sound files

■ PalEdit for creating special Windows palettes to optimize the appearance of 256-color video clips

■ VidTest for testing the capability of PCs to play digital video clips

■ A screen-capture utility

■ Visual Basic custom controls for capturing, editing, and playing back
video clips in Visual Basic 3.0 applications

If you're serious about exploring the capabilities of today's digital video, purchasing Video for Windows 1.1 offers one of the lowest-cost methods to do
so. Video for Windows 1.1 is included with several analog video display and
capture boards, such as Creative Labs' Video Blaster.

From Here...

For further information, refer to the following chapters:

- Chapter 11, "Using Windows Paintbrush," discusses Windows Paintbrush, a fun and colorful painting program you can use to create illustrations in a rainbow of colors and shades.

- Chapter 19, "Using Windows Multimedia," introduces two accessory programs that you can use with your multimedia equipment: Sound Recorder and Media Player.

IV

Windows Multimedia

Part V

Running and Customizing Applications

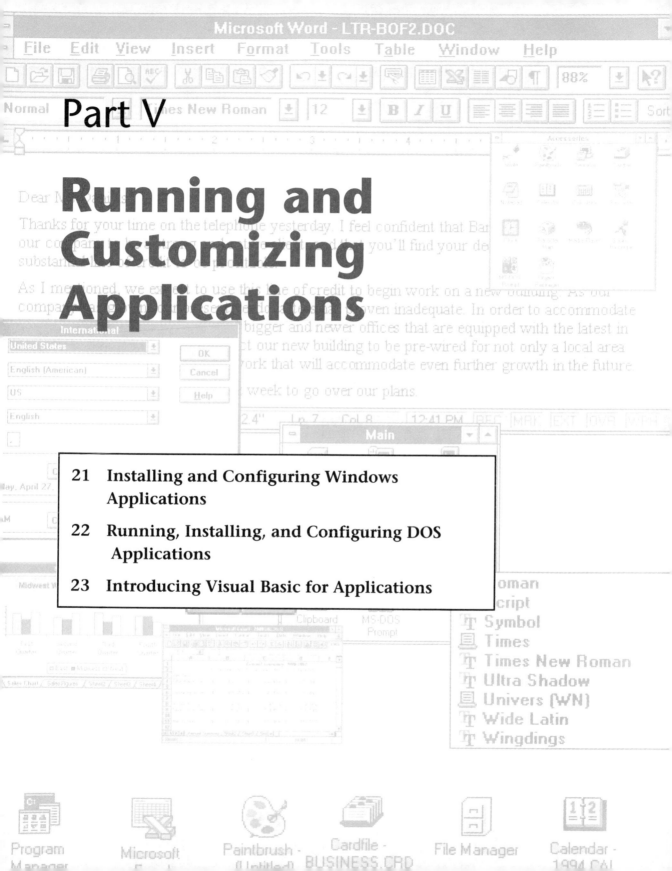

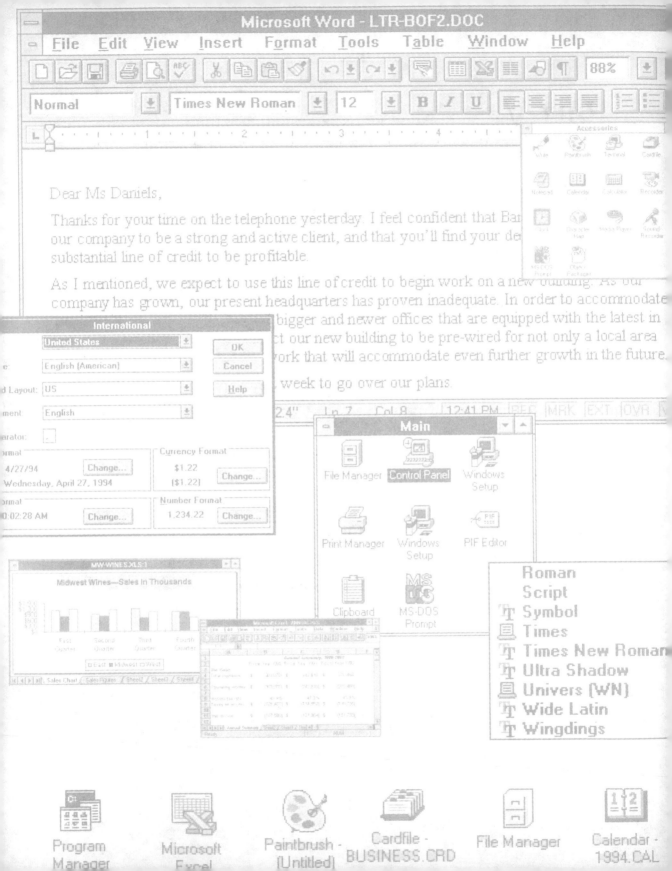

Chapter 21

Installing and Configuring Windows Applications

If you are like the majority of Windows users, you probably have a suite of Windows applications as well as many individual applications. Before you install those applications you may want to do some preparation that insures that they run with the best performance possible. Later, you may find the need to add or remove different features from applications or completely remove an application from your hard disk.

In this chapter, you will learn how to:

- ■ Prepare to install Windows applications

- ■ Install or reinstall Windows applications

- ■ Install parts of an application

- ■ Register applications in the Registration Editor

- ■ Remove Windows applications

Preparing to Install Your Windows Applications

Preparing your computer prior to installing a Windows application requires nearly the same type of preparation as that required prior to installing Windows. While the following steps are not mandatory or even necessary, they will make your applications run faster and will probably save room on your hard disk.

1. Remove lost clusters, files that have become broken and scattered. They are not accessible by their original programs and waste space on your disk. Exit Windows. Type **CHKDSK /F** at the DOS prompt and press Enter. When asked if you want to recover lost allocation units, type **Y** and press Enter. The lost files are renamed and accumulated in the root directory; delete them.

2. Erase old files you no longer need. Use a compression program to compress files you may need infrequently. Exit Windows and delete files with the .TMP extension found in the TEMP directory. (Do not delete temporary files while Windows is running or you may destroy data or Windows operating files.)

3. Use a defragmentation utility, such as the defrag command that comes with DOS 6, to reorganize files on your hard disk so each file is stored in a single contiguous area of the disk. This enables DOS and Windows to read information much more quickly from disk. Because applications read some of their program from disk as they run, the process of defragging speeds up your application and the opening and saving times for documents. (Most degragmentation utilities should be run after exiting Windows.)

4. Save backup copies of important files that a poorly written application may change or corrupt. If the installation does not work correctly you may be able to restore your system by copying these files back to their original locations. Files that you may want to create backups of are the following:

File	Location
CONFIG.SYS	Root directory (C:\)
AUTOEXEC.BAT	Root directory (C:\)
REG.DAT	Windows directory
WIN.INI	Windows directory
SYSTEM.INI	Windows directory

5. Run MemMaker, a DOS 6 program, if you have not already run it. MemMaker makes adjustments to your AUTOEXEC.BAT and CONFIG.SYS files to optimize the use of memory.

Installing New Applications

New applications often modify the AUTOEXEC.BAT and CONFIG.SYS files. Try to keep a record of the modifications each application makes in case one application causes problems or is incompatible with other applications. In many newer applications, there is a custom installation method that gives you the opportunity to see and accept or reject changes to the AUTOEXEC.BAT and CONFIG.SYS files. The usual two dangers incurred by poorly written installation applications are writing items into these files in the wrong order and changing or removing settings required by other applications. In the first case, an application may write a DEVICE= line into the CONFIG.SYS before the HIMEM line or before a driver with larger memory requirement. Either of these can mean a poorer memory configuration. In the second type of error, an installation may change an argument, such as FILES=50 to a lesser argument such as FILES=30.

Many installation programs save the original AUTOEXEC.BAT and CONFIG.SYS files with backup file names. If a backup is made, the backup file name is shown during installation. If you keep these backups or make your own backup before installing to the original AUTOEXEC.BAT and CONFIG.SYS files, you can install new applications and then use Notepad to compare the old and new versions of the files to see where changes occurred. Note these changes to see whether they are in an incorrect position or whether they change a setting required by Windows. Changes you don't want to accept can be remarked out so that they do not work by typing the letters REM at the beginning of the line. REM stands for REMark. Adding back a remarked line is easy; just remove the REM at the beginning of the line.

Some changes you must watch for are detailed in the following list:

Unnecessary Drivers	Windows comes with drivers to handle the mouse, memory, monitors, and other devices. Because these drivers were created for Windows, use them rather than third-party drivers. Comment out unneeded drivers, leaving only those required by the system, network (if necessary), and Windows. DO NOT remove HIMEM.SYS or SMARTDRV.EXE from the CONFIG.SYS file. Windows needs these drivers for optimum performance. If you are unsure whether to remove a driver, do not remove it.

Terminate-and-Stay-Resident Applications

TSRs (Terminate-and-Stay-Resident applications) are applications that stay in memory until activated by pressing a keystroke combination. TSRs loaded into memory prior to starting Windows consume valuable memory and are incompatible with Windows in some situations. If the AUTOEXEC.BAT contains statements to load TSRs, comment these out by using the REM statement. When needed, you always can load these applications from Windows.

Installing Your Windows Applications

Most Windows applications are installed using the same procedure, insert the first installation disk, and then choose **F**ile **R**un from Program Manager or File Manager. In the Run dialog box, type the following and press Enter:

A:SETUP

In the dialog boxes that appear, you can use the mouse to select options and choose the buttons. If you are using the keyboard, move between options with the Tab key, and select or deselect the option with focus by pressing the space bar.

Well-designed installation programs give you the option for different types of installations. Figure 21.1 shows one of the first dialog boxes during an Excel installation. The dialog box lists the three levels of installation recommended by Microsoft to software developers. Choose the level of installation that best fits your needs. Don't be concerned that you only get one chance to install the application. Most applications allow you to rerun the installation program and add or remove items.

The types or levels of installation used by most applications are shown in table 21.1.

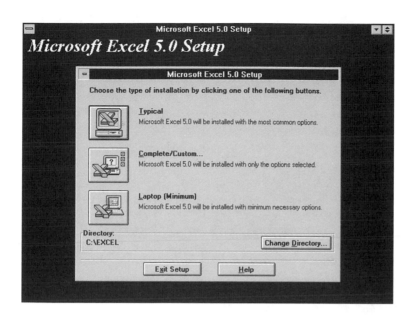

Fig. 21.1
Well-designed
applications enable
you to select
different levels of
installation.

Table 21.1   Levels of Installation

Installation	Result
Express or Typical	The application installs the components used by the majority of people using a desktop computer in their office. If there is not enough disk space to install the application, it may not install any of the application, but it does warn you.
Custom	The application displays additional dialog boxes that enable you to select which of the application's features, software drivers, and add-ins you want installed. As you select or deselect features and add-ins, the required and available disk space is shown. Figure 21.2 shows a dialog box used to select specific features during an Excel installation.
Minimal or Laptop	The application installs only the minimum features. This consumes the least amount of disk space and is usually used on laptop computers. If you want a minimum install but need to include one or two special features, such as a spelling checker, drivers or data converters, use the Custom install and deselect all the features you do not need.

Fig. 21.2
In a custom installation, you can select the features you want installed.

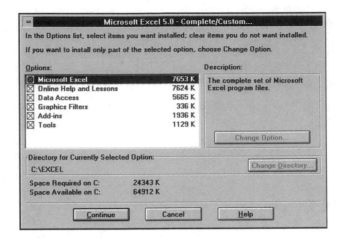

Reinstalling or Adding New Application Features

Most applications let you install features, drivers, or add-ins that were not installed during the original installation, and you don't have to reinstall the entire application. Applications that use Microsoft's recommended installation procedure created a Setup icon for the application in Program Manager. Choosing the Setup icon displays a reinstallation dialog box similar to the one shown in figure 21.3. You can use this dialog box to reinstall the application if it has become corrupted, install features that were left out during the original installation, or remove features you no longer need.

Fig. 21.3
During a reinstallation, you can install the entire application or selected features.

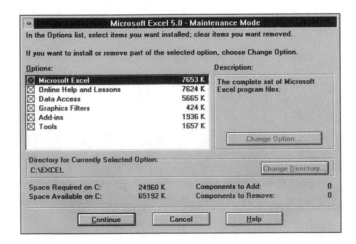

If the application uses one of the older installation methods, insert the first installation disk, choose **F**ile **R**un from Program Manager or File Manager. At the DOS prompt, type **A:SETUP** and press Enter. The installation program should detect that the program is already installed and display a dialog box similar to figure 21.3.

Registering Application Features in Registration Editor

When you install a Windows application that was created after the Fall of 1993, Windows records information about that application and its capabilities in a special registration database. (This has nothing to do with registering your software with the manufacturer.) Windows uses the information in the registration database to find the directory an application is stored in, the object linking and embedding capabilities, dynamic data exchange capabilities, and so forth. Prior to 1994, applications wrote the same type of information into the WIN.INI file.

In some rare cases, an application may not register or the registration database may be damaged. If this happens you may have problems with your application.

> **Caution**
>
> If an application is not registered or the REG.DAT file is corrupted or destroyed, you get an error when you attempt to use an **I**nsert **O**bject command or objects created by an application do not appear in the Insert Object dialog box.

Checking an Application's Current Registration

A corrupted registration database or an application that did not register in the database can cause problems. These problems usually appear when you attempt to link or embed between applications. (Applications that were written prior to Fall 1993 did not register in the database but instead wrote their application details into the WIN.INI file.)

If your application displays an error dialog box when you attempt to link or embed, or an application does not appear in the Insert Object dialog box, you should check the registration database. To check the registration database, follow these steps:

1. Choose **F**ile **R**un from File Manager or Program Manager, type **REGEDIT**, and then choose OK. The Registration Info Editor dialog box appears (see fig. 21.4).

Fig. 21.4
Check whether an application is registered with the Registration Info Editor dialog box.

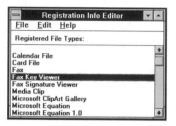

2. Scroll through the list of objects and applications that are registered to see if the application that gave you problems is in the list. If the list cannot be read or the list does not exist, you need to re-create the entire registration database. If the application is missing from the list, you may need to register the application.

Re-creating a Corrupted Registration Database

If the entire registration database is corrupted or deleted, you need to re-create it. This is a two part process. You must first re-create the REG.DAT file for those applications and files that are part of Windows, and then you must manually register the applications you installed in Windows.

To automatically re-create the REG.DAT file, follow these steps:

1. Rename the existing REG.DAT file.

2. Open the **F**ile menu and choose **R**un from File Manager or Program Manager.

3. In the Command Line text box, type the following:

   REGEDIT /U C:\WINDOWS\SYSTEM\SETUP.REG.

   Choose OK.

4. Choose the **F**ile **A**ssociate command from File Manager.

5. Type **REG** in the Files with Extension text box. Type **C:\WINDOWS\REGEDIT.EXE** in the Associate With text box or use the **B**rowse button to select the REGEDIT.EXE file. The Associate dialog box should look like figure 21.5.

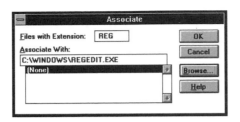

Fig. 21.5
Associate all REG
extensions with
the REGEDIT.EXE
file.

6. Choose OK.

7. Exit and restart Windows.

Windows displays a message box telling you when the REG.DAT database has
been successfully re-created.

Registering an Individual Application

Some applications may not successfully register themselves, or the registration database may become corrupted. In that case, you need to re-register the
application. To register an application, follow these steps:

1. Open the **F**ile menu and choose **R**un from File Manager or Program
   Manager and type **REGEDIT**, and choose OK.

2. Open the **F**ile menu and choose **M**erge Registration File. The Merge
   Registration File dialog box appears. This dialog box looks like the Open
   dialog box except the pattern in the File Name box is *.reg.

3. Change to the directory containing the application you want to
   register.

4. Select the application's REG file from the application's directory.

5. Choose OK. If there is no REG file for the application, choose Cancel.

6. If you choose OK, the application should appear in the registration list.

If the application's directory does not contain a REG file, the application
probably stores its information in an INI file. In this case, you should reinstall
the application or check with the application's manufacturer.

Deleting an Application's Registration

When you manually remove an application from your computer, you want to
remove the application's registration from REG.DAT. To do this, follow these
steps:

1. Start the Registration Editor, as described in the previous steps.

2. From the list, select the application whose registration you want to delete.

3. Open the **E**dit menu and choose **D**elete.

4. Return to step 2 if you need to delete other objects registered by the applications, such as charts, worksheets, pictures, and so forth. Open the **F**ile menu and choose E**x**it to quit.

Removing or Moving Windows Applications

Removing newer applications (those produced after the Fall of 1993) can be as simple as choosing a button. Removing older applications can be a tedious and error-filled process. In either case, deleting an application takes more work than just deleting the application's icon from Program Manager.

Removing Applications or Features Automatically

Applications that have a remove utility usually run the remove utility from the application's Setup icon located in Program Manager. Figure 21.6 shows the Setup dialog box that displays when you choose the Excel Setup icon when Excel 5 is already installed. Notice the Re**m**ove All button. Choosing this button removes the appropriate files, directories, dynamic link libraries, registrations, entries in INI files, and unshared components.

If you choose this button, you may be asked if you want to remove shared components (usually, you should respond with **N**o). *Shared components* are objects, utilities, or shared files that can be used by more than one application. For example, Microsoft Excel 5 and Word 6 for Windows both use the same spell checking program.

Removing Applications Manually

Just deleting an application's icons from Program Manager does not delete the application. Deleting an application is really a multistep process.

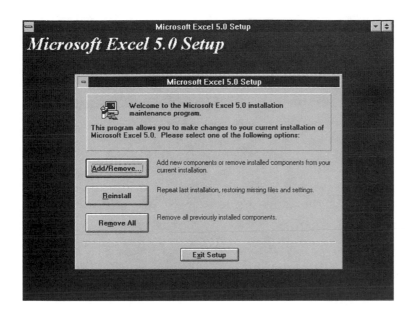

Fig 21.6
Many applications
enable you to
remove the
application from
the setup
program.

First, delete the files in the application's directory. Make sure you do not have data files or a data subdirectory located under the application's directory. Check in the WINDOWS directory for files with the HLP or INI file extension that you are sure belonged to the application, delete them. (Older Windows applications sometimes stored files in the WINDOWS directory.) Never delete a file you are unsure of.

Don't delete DLL files in the WINDOWS directory or subdirectories. You may misinterpret a file name and delete a file used by another program, or you may delete a DLL that was shared between applications. Delete the application's directories and subdirectories.

Activate Program Manager and delete the group window and icons for the application. The easiest way to do this is to reduce the application's group window to an icon, and then press the delete key. Choose **Y**es in the dialog box that asks if you really want to delete.

Start Notepad, and open the WIN.INI file. Look for sections that start with [applicationname]. These sections contain information about the application that was deleted. Remove the section, but no more than that section. Save the WIN.INI.

Delete the application's registration by following the procedure outlined in the section called "Deleting an Application's Registration," earlier in this chapter.

> **Note**
>
> The easiest and safest way to remove Windows applications that do not have their own remove utility is to purchase the UnInstaller 2 program from MicroHelp, Inc. This program is $69. Contact MicroHelp at the following address:
>
> MicroHelp, Inc.
> 4359 Shallowford Industrial Parkway
> Marietta, GA 30066-1135
> (800) 922-3383
> (404) 516-0899

Moving an Application to a Different Directory or Drive

It is safest not to try to move a Windows application to a new drive or directory. Instead, remove the application from its current location and reinstall the application at its new location.

From Here...

If you are interested in topics related to installing Windows applications, refer to these chapters:

- Chapter 22, "Running, Installing and Configuring DOS Applications," shows you how to get optimum performance for your DOS applications.

- Chapter 24, "Installing and Optimizing Windows 3.1," explains ways to tune Windows to give its best performance (and also improve the performance of Windows applications).

- Chapter 25, "Installing Windows for Workgroups 3.11," gives you tips on running Windows applications on a network.

Chapter 22

Running, Installing, and Configuring DOS Applications

When you use Windows, you don't need to give up MS-DOS applications. In fact, you will find that Windows adds new dimensions to MS-DOS applications.

With Windows, you can load more than one application, whether the applications are DOS applications or Windows applications. In 386 Enhanced mode, you can run multiple DOS and Windows applications simultaneously. In Standard mode, you can run multiple Windows applications simultaneously. You can copy text or graphics from one DOS application and paste the text into another DOS application, or paste text or graphics into a Windows application. In 386 Enhanced mode, you can run DOS applications in a window just like a Windows application. In 386 Enhanced mode, multiple DOS and Windows applications can continue working, even when they are in the background (that is, not in the topmost window).

When you start a DOS application, Windows looks for the application's Program Information File (PIF). A *PIF* is a file that provides Windows the information needed to run the DOS application, such as how much memory the application needs and what video mode is required. If Windows finds the PIF, it uses the information within this file rather than the standard settings in the default PIF. Many popular DOS applications can use the default PIF without problems. By default, PIFs are created for most DOS applications during installation.

If you dislike the configuration used in the default PIF settings, you can use PIF Editor to create or modify existing PIFs. This tool is covered later in this chapter.

Standard vs. 386 Enhanced Mode

In Standard mode, all DOS applications run in a full-screen display; a DOS application cannot run within a window. Windows doesn't try to *multitask* (run simultaneously) DOS applications. Instead, only one DOS application is active in memory at any time. Until you close the DOS application or switch back to Windows, the DOS application receives all the computer's resources. Although it constantly monitors the activities of the DOS application, Windows doesn't interfere with the application's use of computer resources. If you return to Windows without first quitting the DOS application, Windows suspends all further activity within the DOS application until you return to it.

In 386 Enhanced mode, Windows can multitask DOS applications. During multitasking, each application that runs shares a portion of computer resources by taking advantage of the 80386 and 80486 processor's capability to make virtual computers (simulating two or more computers within your machine). Each DOS application receives a portion of memory and a portion of processing power. In 386 Enhanced mode, the computer has more memory than it does when running DOS. In 386 Enhanced mode, Windows treats all memory—conventional, extended, and virtual (disk-based) memory—as one large pool of memory. When a DOS application requests a block of conventional memory, Windows satisfies this request by giving the application a block of memory from the pool. A DOS application running in 386 Enhanced mode shares both memory and CPU time with all other active applications and now is one application among many sharing the computer's resources, which Windows governs. You can run a DOS application in 386 Enhanced mode in a window or as a full-screen display.

In this chapter, you learn how to:

- Load and run DOS applications

- Create and use PIFs

- Edit PIFs

- Control DOS applications while they are running

- Run a DOS batch file

- Improve the performance of DOS applications

Understanding How Windows Handles DOS Applications

Windows manipulates memory, applications, and disk storage to load or run multiple Windows and DOS applications simultaneously. If you understand how this process works, you can get better performance from the computer.

Running DOS Applications in a Window or Full-Screen

Windows runs in two different modes: Standard and 386 Enhanced. The mode used depends on the computer processor and available memory. In 386 Enhanced mode, Windows runs DOS applications in a window or full-screen. In Standard mode, you can run DOS applications only in full-screen display. In Standard mode, you can start with one DOS application and switch to another, but Windows suspends all DOS and Windows applications that are not displayed.

In 386 Enhanced mode, you can have multiple DOS applications running in separate windows or full-screen and switch quickly between the applications. Figure 22.1 shows Lotus 1-2-3 Release 3.1 and WordPerfect 5.1 running in separate windows.

Fig. 22.1

Lotus 1-2-3 and WordPerfect in separate windows in 386 Enhanced mode.

Applications designed for Windows use memory differently from those designed for DOS. Windows distributes memory efficiently among Windows applications because Windows applications use memory cooperatively. DOS applications, however, don't have the memory-management capabilities of Windows applications. Most DOS applications, unlike Windows applications, aren't designed for multitasking. A DOS application, due to design, thinks that it is the only application running; therefore, it hogs memory and CPU time, and doesn't share data easily. In Standard mode, you can multitask multiple Windows applications, but DOS applications will be suspended when a Windows application is active, and Windows applications will be suspended when a DOS application is active. Windows in 386 Enhanced mode expands the horizons of a DOS application by controlling certain properties of the application—such as memory, CPU time, and video mode—and thereby gives DOS applications multitasking capabilities. In 386 Enhanced mode, Windows can have both multiple Windows applications and multiple DOS applications active.

When a DOS application runs in a full screen under Windows, the computer display appears as though only the DOS application is running. Appearances, however, can deceive. Pressing Ctrl+Esc returns you to the Windows Task Manager; you then can choose a different DOS or Windows application from Task List. The Windows Task Manager lists all open applications. Windows keeps the DOS application open but shrinks the application to an icon at the bottom of the screen, similar to the icons shown at the bottom of figure 22.2.

Fig. 22.2
DOS applications minimized to icons when not in use.

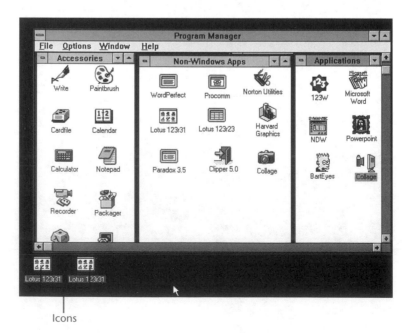

Icons

If your DOS applications are running in a window in 386 Enhanced mode and you press Ctrl+Esc, Task List appears above the DOS-application window. You can always switch to a DOS application by pressing Ctrl+Esc to display Task List and then selecting the application. You also can press Alt+Tab to switch among applications.

During the Windows installation process, Setup builds PIFs for the DOS applications on which Setup has information. This setup information is stored in the APPS.INF file. When Windows Setup creates a PIF, full-screen mode is selected as the default. To have a DOS application start in a window (in 386 Enhanced mode only), use PIF Editor to edit the application's PIF. Choose the Windowed option from the Display Usage group.

Loading More DOS Applications Than Memory Can Hold

In Windows, you can load multiple DOS applications, even if the combined applications use more memory than is available in the computer. When you start a DOS application in Standard mode, Windows creates a temporary application swap file for the application. The *temporary application swap file* is a reserved area on the hard disk for application information that is too large to fit in memory. When you switch from the application, Windows moves some or all of the DOS applications from memory to the temporary application swap file. This process makes the computer's available memory seem larger. When you exit the DOS application, Windows deletes the swap file.

Windows doesn't use application swap files while running in 386 Enhanced mode. Instead, in 386 Enhanced mode, you must have sufficient extended memory to run all the DOS applications you load. This memory is necessary in 386 Enhanced mode because each DOS application continues to run even when it is not in the active window. To run, applications must be in memory, not in a swap file on the hard disk. (If you need to run Windows in Standard mode on your 80386 computer, start Windows by typing **WIN/S** at the DOS prompt. Later in this chapter, in "Enhancing DOS Application Performance," you learn special techniques to increase the memory available for DOS applications.

Because Windows in Standard mode swaps parts of inactive DOS applications to and from memory and disk, the hard disk must have storage space available for the swap. If you have a fast disk or use SMARTdrive, a disk-caching application that comes with Windows, you can significantly improve Windows' performance when running multiple applications. (SMARTdrive and other disk-performance enhancements are described in "Enhancing DOS Application Performance" later in this chapter.)

Tip

If you are running Windows in 386 Enhanced mode and want to switch a DOS application between full-screen and window modes, press Alt+Enter. Pressing Alt+Enter at any time toggles the display between full-screen and windowed.

Tip

You may not be able to load or switch from a DOS application if the hard disk lacks available storage space to create a temporary application swap file for the DOS application you want to load or from which you want to switch.

DOS applications designed to use expanded memory still require expanded memory when running under Windows. In systems with an 80286 microprocessor, you must provide as much expanded memory as the DOS application requires. You also must use an expanded-memory manager to use this memory. Usually, you can tell whether the computer has an expanded-memory manager by looking in the CONFIG.SYS file for a reference to a file with a name such as REMM.SYS or CEMM.SYS.

In systems with an 80386 or 80486 microprocessor, Windows can use extended memory to emulate expanded memory. Because extended memory is much faster and more efficient than expanded memory, you should use only extended memory in 80386- and 80486-based systems. If you are using DOS applications that require expanded memory, use EMM386.SYS, the expanded-memory manager that comes with Windows, to emulate expanded memory from extended memory.

Note

Even when running under Windows, DOS applications use the DOS screen and printer drivers. You must install the DOS application and the print and screen drivers as described in the application's installation instructions. The DOS application doesn't use the printer drivers available in Windows. Neither does the application use the special printing features available through Windows (such as Print Manager) or the enhanced formatting capabilities of Windows applications.

Running the DOS Prompt in a Window

To run DOS commands (internal or external) from within Windows, choose the DOS Prompt icon from the Main group window in Program Manager. The icon appears as the stacked letters MSDOS. Usually, the DOS prompt appears in a full screen when DOS is started. Figure 22.3 shows the DOS prompt running in a window. From the DOS prompt, you can issue DOS commands, such as DIR and FORMAT. To quit the DOS prompt, type **EXIT** and press Enter.

Caution

Never run a DOS command or application that modifies the hard disk while Windows is running, even from the DOS-prompt window. Running the DOS command CHKDSK /F, for example, defragments the hard disk, but this command also destroys temporary files used by Windows. Use commands like CHKDSK /F only when Windows isn't running. If your system has DOS Version 5.0 installed, you cannot run CHKDSK /F, so you cannot accidentally destroy the files used by Windows.

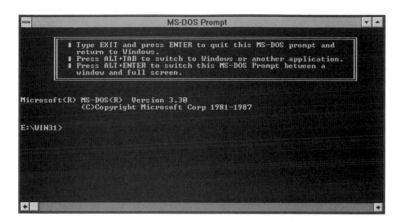

Fig. 22.3
Running the DOS
prompt from
Windows.

Running DOS Memory-Resident Applications

Some DOS applications are designed to load into memory simultaneously with other DOS applications. These resident applications then can be called up over the top of the active DOS application. These applications are referred to as pop-up or terminate-and-stay-resident (TSR) applications. One of the more familiar DOS TSR applications is SideKick.

DOS TSR applications aren't designed to run with Windows; TSRs were designed before Windows gave you the capability of running multiple applications. If you must run a DOS TSR, start the TSR directly from Windows. You then can switch to and from the application as you switch between any DOS applications.

Don't load a DOS TSR before you start Windows. Be aware that your AUTOEXEC.BAT file may load TSRs on start-up. You can use Windows Notepad to open the AUTOEXEC.BAT file and remove TSRs (by placing the term REM at the start of the appropriate batch file lines).

If you load a TSR before you load Windows, you may not be able to access the TSR from the Windows desktop or from any Windows application. You also may be wasting memory. When you load a DOS TSR before loading Windows, the memory that the TSR occupies becomes unavailable to Windows. When you start a DOS TSR and then enter Windows in 386 Enhanced mode, Windows reserves memory for the TSR each time you start a new DOS application or DOS prompt, which prevents Windows (and DOS applications) from using a large portion of the memory.

You can start the DOS TSR application by creating a program-item icon for the TSR in Program Manager and then double-clicking the icon. You also can set up a PIF for the TSR so that the TSR pops up with the same keystroke that activates the TSR in DOS. Some TSRs require a key combination that Windows reserves (such as Alt+Esc). In such a case, you must create a PIF by using PIF Editor and choosing the Reserve Shortcut Keys option for this key combination. After you create the PIF and reserve the shortcut key, pressing this key combination activates the TSR application rather than performing the usual Windows function.

Depending on whether you are operating in Standard or 386 Enhanced mode, and depending on whether you load the TSR from Program Manager (using a program-item icon) or from the DOS prompt, Windows behaves differently. When you are operating in Standard or 386 Enhanced mode and load the TSR from Program Manager, the TSR is loaded, and Windows displays a message that tells you to press Ctrl+C when you finish using the TSR.

When you press Ctrl+C, Windows removes the TSR from memory and ends that DOS session, returning you to Windows. When you load the TSR from the DOS prompt while operating in Standard mode, the TSR is loaded, but no message is displayed. To close the TSR and end the DOS session, you must type **EXIT** at the c:/ prompt, which results in a message telling you to press Ctrl+C to return to Windows. When you load the TSR from the DOS prompt while operating in 386 Enhanced mode, again, the TSR is loaded but no message is displayed. To close the TSR and return to Program Manager, you must type **EXIT** at the c:/ prompt, which immediately returns you to Program Manager; you don't have to press Ctrl+C.

You also can switch to a TSR application by using standard Windows methods rather than pressing the key combination that usually activates the application. Use Task Manager to activate a TSR, or press Alt+Tab until the TSR is activated and then release the Alt key.

Often, you may want to use a DOS TSR with a specific application and therefore want the TSR to load only when the application loads. You can do this by creating a DOS batch file that loads the TSR and the DOS application. You then create a PIF that runs the batch file. Use PIF Editor to create the PIF, and put the batch file's name in PIF Editor's Program file-name text box.

Loading and Running DOS Applications

You can start DOS applications in four ways:

- Choose an application icon from a group window, such as the DOS Application group in Program Manager.

- Choose the application file name from the directory window in File Manager.

- Choose the application PIF name from the directory window in File Manager.

- Choose **R**un from the **F**ile menu in Program Manager or File Manager, and then enter the path, file name, and all arguments for the application.

Because Windows must understand the special requirements of some DOS applications, however, Windows needs to use PIFs.

Understanding PIFs

When it starts a DOS application, Windows looks for an application's PIF. If a PIF cannot be found for an application, Windows starts the application with standard default settings. Most DOS applications run correctly when these standard settings are used; many DOS applications don't need special PIFs. If a DOS application doesn't run correctly or as you prefer when you use the default PIF or the PIF created by Windows, create or modify the application's PIF with PIF Editor.

Usually, you can start a DOS batch file (a file with the extension BAT) the way you start any DOS application. Windows also runs DOS applications started and controlled by a batch file. Occasionally, DOS applications do not run when started from a batch file under Windows, because the combined memory requirements of the batch file and the application exceed the memory limits set by the application's PIF. In this case, you should create a PIF for the batch file and increase the memory required in the application PIF to make room for the batch file. If you create a PIF for a batch file, give the PIF the same name as the batch file; for example, call the two files DOWNLOAD.BAT and DOWNLOAD.PIF.

Starting a DOS Application from Program Manager

You can install DOS applications in Windows during the Windows installation process or at a later time. If you install DOS or Windows applications at a later time, you may want to run the Windows Setup application from the Main group of Program Manager. (Chapter 24, "Installing and Optimizing Windows 3.1," describes in detail how to run Windows Setup to install applications.)

When you use Setup to install a DOS application and the SETUP.INF file contains information on that application, Setup creates and adds an application icon to the DOS Application group. If a DOS Application group doesn't exist, Setup creates one. Setup also installs a PIF for the application in the WIN-DOWS directory.

You can start a DOS application from a program-group window in Program Manager by choosing the application icon in the same way you start Windows applications: double-click the icon, or press an arrow key to select the icon and then press Enter. (Chapter 3, "Controlling Applications with Program Manager," describes in detail how to start applications from icons.)

Figure 22.4 shows the WordPerfect application icon selected in the DOS Applications group in Windows Program Manager. In this figure, the four DOS applications have different icons. Chapter 3 also explains how to select alternative icons to represent program items you create or modify.

Fig. 22.4
Starting the WordPerfect application from the icon.

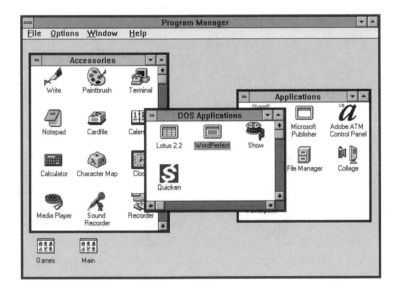

Starting a DOS Application from File Manager

You can start a DOS application by choosing either the application or PIF from Windows File Manager. Double-click the file name, or select the application file (or PIF) and press Enter. Application file names are recognizable because the file extensions are COM, EXE, or BAT.

Figure 22.5 shows the WordPerfect file name, WP.EXE, in the WP51 directory. The bottom directory window shows the PIF that starts WordPerfect—WP.PIF—in the Windows directory. You can start WordPerfect by double-clicking either the PIF or the WP.EXE file.

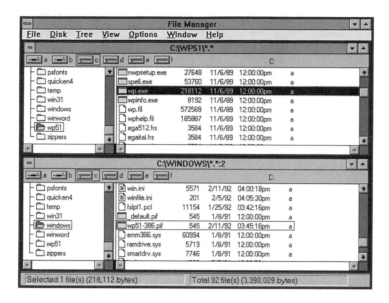

Fig. 22.5
You can start DOS
applications from
either the file
name or PIF in
File Manager.

> ### Do Not Run Applications That Modify the File Allocation Table
>
> From Windows, don't run any utility or application that modifies files or the File Allocation Table (FAT). Utilities you should not use include applications that unerase or undelete files and those that defragment or compact the disk. When they run, such applications modify temporary files that Windows leaves open for its own use. If these temporary files are destroyed or modified, Windows may freeze, and you may lose data. You may even need to reinstall Windows. Such applications are very useful, but they must be run from the DOS prompt without Windows running.

Creating and Using PIFs

When you start a non-Windows (DOS) application, Windows looks for a PIF designed for that application. If Windows finds the PIF, the application uses that information instead of the standard settings in the default PIF. Windows uses the default PIF, _DEFAULT.PIF, unless it locates a specific application PIF.

You can set up a PIF in three ways:

- Have the Windows Setup application create a PIF for you.

- Use or modify the default PIF.

- Use the PIF that came with the DOS application.

> **Note**
>
> PIFs created by the Windows Setup application are stored in the directory containing Windows. After a PIF is created, you can move it anywhere on disk. For example, you may want to locate the PIF for a particular application in that application's directory to reduce the number of files stored in the Windows directory.

The Windows Setup application creates a PIF for your DOS application when you install Windows or when you run Windows Setup to install an application. Windows Setup searches your hard disk for the Windows applications and DOS applications listed in the APPS.INF file. Windows can create PIFs for any DOS applications listed in the APPS.INF file.

If an application PIF is not created or if an application does not come with a PIF, Windows uses the default PIF. If settings need to be changed in the default PIF so that the application works correctly with Windows, you can use PIF Editor to modify the default PIF.

Many DOS applications provide a PIF. When you install Lotus 1-2-3 Release 3.1, for example, a 122.PIF is installed. Generally, you should use the PIF that comes with an application, because its settings are optimized.

Creating a PIF with Windows Setup

When you install Windows, the Windows Setup application is used to find and create PIFs and program-item icons for applications on disk. You also can run the Windows Setup program at any later time to install additional applications. The Windows Setup program-item icon is located in the Main group window.

When you use Windows Setup to install a DOS application, Setup creates and sets up a PIF for that application in the Windows directory (usually C:\WINDOWS). The Setup application searches the drives that you specify and lists any applications it finds. Setup lists only the DOS applications on which the APPS.INF file provides PIF information. When you install Windows, APPS.INF is placed on your hard disk in the C:\WINDOWS\SYSTEM directory. APPS.INF contains the recommended settings for many of the most popular DOS applications. If an application is not listed in the APPS.INF file, Windows does not provide a PIF for that application when SETUP is run.

> **Note**
>
> The Windows Setup application reads the APPS.INF when it executes. APPS.INF is located in the SYSTEM directory below the directory in which you installed Windows.
>
> APPS.INF contains a series of sections that provide information to the Windows Setup application. One section is the [pif] section. When you open APPS.INF in Notepad and view the contents of the [pif] section, you see a list of DOS applications for which Setup can create PIFs. Each line in the list includes the name of a DOS application, the name of the application's executable file (EXE or COM), and several other settings. If a DOS application is not in this list but the application is on your hard disk, Windows does not create a PIF for the application when Setup is run.

Windows makes creating PIFs easy if you use the Windows Setup application. Although most DOS applications run well with the default PIF, you may need more memory or a special feature available only if the application runs with a custom PIF. In that case, you can use PIF Editor to modify the PIF that Windows Setup creates.

To run Windows Setup and create a PIF after you install Windows, follow these instructions:

1. Activate the Main group window in Program Manager.

2. Start the Windows Setup application. The Windows Setup dialog box appears.

3. Open the **O**ptions menu and choose the **S**et Up Applications command.

4. Choose Search for Applications if you want Windows to search for applications on your hard disk(s).

   or

   Choose Ask to specify an application option if you know the path and file name of a particular application that you want to set up.

5. If you chose the Search for Applications option, select the drive to search, or choose to search the current path from the list box. Then choose the Search Now command.

   or

V

Running and Customizing

If you chose to specify an application, type the application path and file name, select the program group to add a program item to, and choose OK.

6. If Windows cannot determine the application that matches an EXE or COM file name, you can select the application from a list of possible matches. For example, WP.EXE may be the EXE file name for more than one word processor.

7. When the Setup Applications dialog box appears, select (from the list box on the left) the DOS applications for which you want PIFs.

8. Choose the Add button to add the applications to the list box on the right side of the dialog box. Setup creates PIFs for these applications.

   Figure 22.6 shows the Setup Applications dialog box with two applications selected for setup.

Fig. 22.6
Using the Setup Applications dialog box to set up applications in Windows.

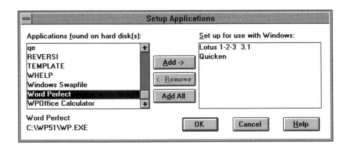

9. Choose OK if you want Windows to create PIFs for the DOS applications in the list on the right side of the dialog box.

10. Close the Windows Setup window.

If you did not have a DOS Application group before, Setup creates one for you. In addition to the PIF created and stored in the WINDOWS directory, Setup creates a program-item icon to match your application.

If you select applications to be set up that already have been set up, you may get more than one program-item icon for an application. To delete unwanted program-item icons, select them in Program Manager and press the Del key.

Open the DOS Application group in Program Manager and run the added DOS application by choosing its program-item icon. If the application does not run or does not run with a feature you desire (such as running in a window if you are in 386 Enhanced mode), modify the PIF, using the procedures described later in this chapter.

Creating a PIF by Dragging and Dropping

One of the easiest ways to create a PIF is through dragging and dropping. This easy technique works with DOS application files that Windows recognizes and for which Windows has PIF information.

To create a PIF and program-item icon by dragging and dropping, follow these steps:

1. Arrange Program Manager and File Manager side by side on-screen.

2. In Program Manager, open the group window in which you want to create a program-item icon.

3. In File Manager, display the DOS application file for which you want to create a PIF.

4. Drag the application's file folder from File Manager to the group window.

   If more than one DOS application uses the same file name, a scrolling list appears (see fig. 22.7).

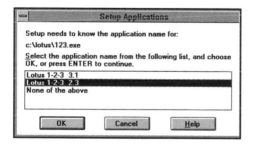

Fig. 22.7
Windows asks you to select the application when applications have the same file name.

5. If the scrolling list appears, select the name of the DOS application and then choose OK.

In the group window in which you released the file-folder icon, a generic DOS application icon appears. If Windows cannot find an existing PIF for the application, it creates a PIF in the WINDOWS directory.

You can change the generic DOS icon to an icon designed for that application. From the Program Item Properties dialog box, you can add a specific icon by completing the following steps:

1. Choose the Change Icon button. The Change Icon dialog box appears.

2. In the File Name box, type the name of the file containing icons and then choose OK. You also can use the Browse button to search for files containing icons.

Default icons are located in C:\WINDOWS\PROGMAN.EXE. Icons specifically designed for many DOS applications and generic tasks are located in C:\WINDOWS\MORICONS.DLL. Files that contain icons use the extensions EXE (for Windows applications), DLL, and ICO. Not all EXE or DLL files contain icons. You can buy libraries of icons as a file and save them to your WINDOWS directory for use with any application.

When you choose an icon file, the Current Icon list displays the available icons, as shown in figure 22.8.

3. Select an icon from the Current Icon list.

4. Choose OK twice.

Fig. 22.8
Select application-specific icons from the moricons.dll file.

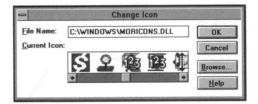

If you have created a program-item icon for any Windows or DOS application, you can change the program-item icon in Program Manager by selecting the icon and then opening the File menu and choosing Properties. When the Program Item Properties dialog box appears, choose the Change Icon button and follow the preceding steps.

Creating a PIF Manually

If you need to edit or create a PIF and want to have control of the settings, use PIF Editor. PIF Editor is located in the Accessories group if you installed Windows 3.1 over Windows 3.0 or in the Main group if you installed Windows 3.1 as a new application. The icon for PIF Editor looks like a luggage tag.

> **Note**
>
> Many popular DOS applications use the default PIF and run without a problem. In most cases, however, you want to create a PIF because the default PIF operates with settings that fit the widest range of applications. Creating a PIF that is specific to your DOS applications increases their speed and improves their memory use when operating under Windows.

When you start PIF Editor, a window displays a new, untitled PIF with the standard settings. Every PIF has two sets of options that match the different modes in which Windows runs. When you edit a PIF, you see the options available for the current Windows mode:

- Standard mode options for running the application in Standard mode

- 386 Enhanced mode options for running the application in 386 Enhanced mode

Usually, PIF Editor displays the PIF settings for the current mode in which Windows is running. You may want to choose PIF options for a mode that is not the current Windows mode. For example, you may want to create a PIF for an application in Standard mode, even though you currently are running Windows in 386 Enhanced mode. To switch modes in PIF Editor, open the **M**ode menu and choose the mode you want to use.

The PIF Editor window changes slightly, depending on which mode is being displayed. Figure 22.9 shows the default settings of the PIF Editor window that appears when Windows is operating in Standard mode, and figure 22.10 shows the default settings of the PIF Editor window that appears when 386 Enhanced is the current mode. The Advanced button on-screen in 386 Enhanced mode has a second window available for advanced options, shown in figure 22.11. Most PIF options apply only in the mode in which they are selected.

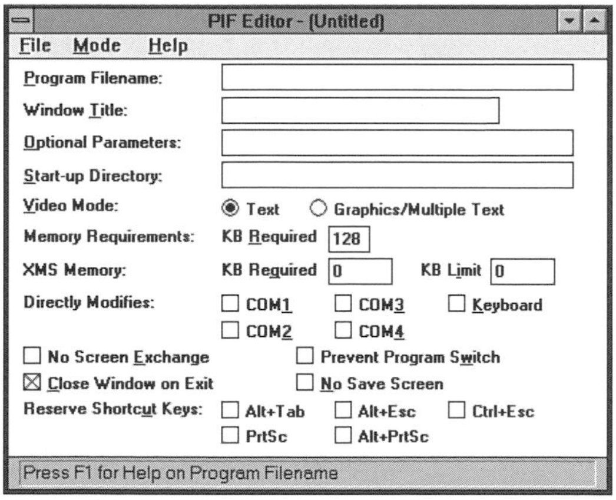

V

Running and Customizing

Fig. 22.9
The PIF Editor options and defaults for Windows in Standard mode.

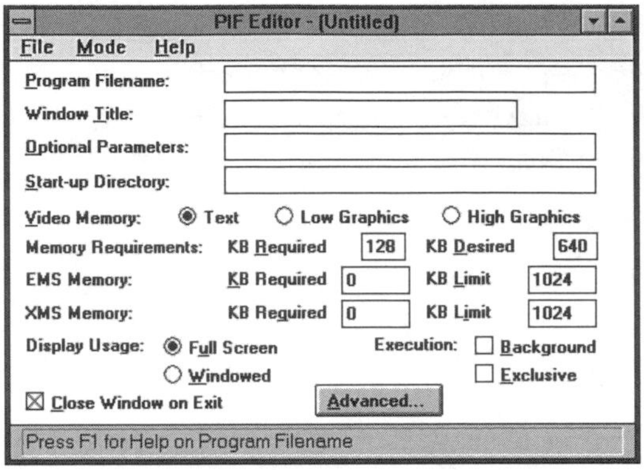

Fig. 22.10

The PIF Editor options and defaults for Windows in 386 Enhanced mode.

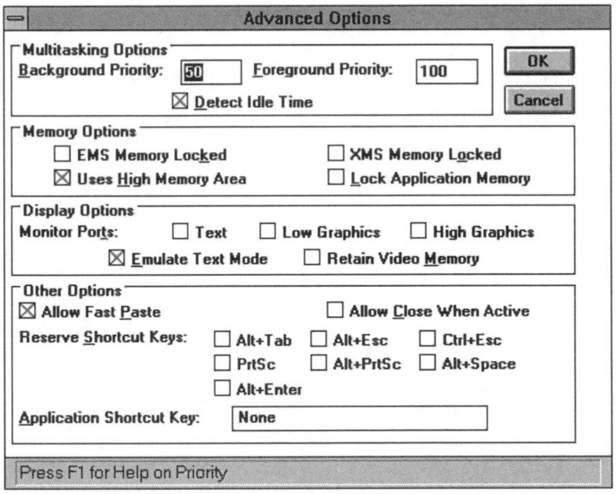

Fig. 22.11

The advanced PIF Editor options and defaults for Windows in 386 Enhanced mode.

To create a PIF, follow these steps:

1. Choose PIF Editor from the Main group window in Program Manager to start the application.

2. Fill in the appropriate text boxes and options, as described in "Understanding PIF Editor Options" later in this chapter.

3. Open the **F**ile menu and choose **S**ave, name the file, and save it.

4. Open the **F**ile menu and choose **N**ew to start a new PIF, or choose E**x**it to close PIF Editor.

> **Note**
>
> Before you test a PIF, close all other applications in Windows. If you encounter a problem, you can restart the computer without losing data in another application. After the application runs by itself, test it while running other applications.

When you start a DOS application for which Windows cannot find a PIF, Windows starts the application with the default PIF options for the current mode. You can override these default options by modifying the default PIF. The default PIF is named _DEFAULT.PIF and is in the \WINDOWS\SYSTEM directory. In 386 Enhanced mode, for example, Windows always starts DOS applications in full-screen mode. You can modify the _DEFAULT.PIF and change the Display Usage option so that applications start in a window instead of in a full screen.

Make sure that you make a backup copy of _DEFAULT.PIF before you modify it. If your new default PIF does not work as planned, you can return to the original default PIF settings by copying your backup file over the modified file.

When you change _DEFAULT.PIF, leave the Windows Title option blank. You must provide a Program Filename, however, because PIF Editor checks to make sure that this text box is filled before it enables you to save the PIF. Type **DEF.BAT** (you can use whatever program file name you like, but it must have an EXE, COM, or BAT extension) in the Program Filename box. Type over this file name when you make a new PIF.

Editing a PIF

You may have to edit a PIF in the following circumstances:

- The application runs with the _DEFAULT.PIF, but it needs operating-memory or speed improvements.

- The application is in a different directory from the one listed in the Program Filename text box of the PIF.

- The start-up directory, which specifies the data directory, is different from the directory you want or the directory that the application expects.

- You want to start an application with a special parameter.

V

Running and Customizing

■ You want to ensure that an application swaps to disk when not in use, freeing more memory for additional applications (the Prevent Program Switch option).

■ An application has been upgraded and requires more memory or uses additional graphic memory.

Naming and Running Applications from a PIF

Before you edit a PIF, make a backup copy of the original PIF, using an extension such as PAK instead of PIF. If the edited PIF gives you trouble, return to the original settings by renaming the PAK file PIF.

If you start the application by choosing the application file name from File Manager or from within a program item, the PIF name must have the same name—WP.EXE and WP.PIF, for example. If the PIF has the same name as the application file name, when you choose an application file name, the corresponding PIF is executed. If you have several WordPerfect PIFs (all for the same version of WordPerfect), each with unique settings, start the application by choosing the PIF, or create a program-item icon in Program Manager for each of the PIFs.

> **Note**
>
> If you start the application by choosing the application file name, Windows looks for the PIF file name that matches the application's name. For example, if you are in File Manager and click WP.EXE to launch WordPerfect, Windows looks for WP.PIF. Windows looks for the PIF in two places: the Windows directory and the directory associated with the application (such as WP51 for WordPerfect). Windows does *not* search the directories in your PATH statement.

Tip
To get help specific to any item in the PIF Editor window, select the item and then press the Help key (F1). A Help window displays information about the item you selected. Press Alt+F4 to close the Help application.

Editing a PIF

To edit a PIF, follow these steps:

1. Choose the PIF Editor application from the Main or Accessories group.

2. Open the **F**ile menu and choose **O**pen, and change to the directory containing the PIF to be edited.

   Windows Setup stores PIFs in the \WINDOWS directory. The default PIF, named _DEFAULT.PIF, is in the \WINDOWS\SYSTEM directory. PIFs have the extension PIF.

3. Select and open the PIF you want to edit. The PIF Editor window appears, showing the current PIF settings (see fig. 22.12). Open the **F**ile

menu and choose Save **A**s, and save a backup copy of the PIF with an extension such as PAK.

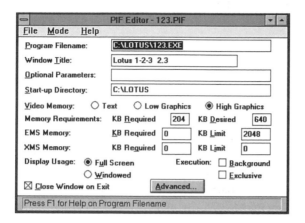

Fig. 22.12
The 123.PIF in PIF Editor shows the settings for 1-2-3 in 386 Enhanced mode.

4. Make changes to the text boxes or selections in the PIF Editor window. If you are in 386 Enhanced mode, choose the Advanced button to see additional PIF options. (For a detailed discussion of all the PIF options, see "Understanding PIF Editor Options" later in this chapter.)

5. Open the **F**ile menu and choose Save **A**s, and name the PIF with a PIF extension.

6. Open the **F**ile menu and choose E**x**it to quit PIF Editor, or minimize it to an icon so that it is readily accessible for further editing after you test the application.

Starting an Application in a Data Directory

To specify an active directory after the application starts, type that directory name in the Start-up Directory text box in that application's PIF. Because you can have multiple PIFs for the same application, you can make each PIF start the application in a different directory. Be aware, however, that some applications require the start-up directory to be the same as the application's directory. Some applications look in the application directory for additional files needed at start-up so that the application can successfully locate those files; the current directory must be the application's directory.

V

Running and Customizing

Understanding PIF Editor Options

The PIF Editor text boxes are nearly the same for Standard and 386 Enhanced modes (although each mode does have some different text boxes). The boxes also are similar in design.

PIF Options Common to Standard and 386 Enhanced Mode

The following paragraphs describe the PIF Editor text boxes that are similar for the two modes.

The Program Filename text-box entry specifies the name of the application's executable file or start-up file. You type this file name from the DOS prompt to start the application. Type the full path name and application name, including the file extension. Most application file names have the extension EXE or COM. Batch files that run commands or start applications have the extension BAT. An entry for WordPerfect 5.1, for example, would be C:\WP51\WP.EXE; an entry for Lotus 1-2-3 Release 2.2 would be \123R2\122.EXE.

If you included the directory associated with the application in your DOS path statement (located in the AUTOEXEC.BAT file), you do not need to enter the complete path in the text box. For example, if C:\WP51 is in your path, instead of entering C:\WP51\WP.EXE, you can enter WP.EXE. Generally, however, you should enter the full path name in PIF Editor.

The Window Title text-box entry is the text that appears in the application window's title bar (when the application displays in a window) and below the application's icon (when the application is minimized). Type the name you want to appear in the application window title bar and below the icon. If you leave the Window Title text box blank, Windows uses the application name (for example, WordPerfect) for the window title bar and for the icon name when you minimize the application. The title entered in the Window Title text box is used only if you start the application by opening the **F**ile menu and choosing **R**un (with the PIF file name), or from File Manager. (If you associate the PIF with an icon, the icon name entered in the Description text box in the Program Item Properties dialog box overrides the description in the PIF's Window Title text box. The icon description, therefore, appears in the application's window title bar when the application displays in a window and as the title below the application's icon when the application is minimized.)

In the Optional Parameters text box, type any parameters you want added to the application when it starts, such as which file to open. These parameters or arguments are the ones you type after the file name when you start an application from the DOS prompt. If you frequently use different parameters, type a question mark in this box, and Windows will prompt you for the optional parameter when you run the PIF. Parameters can be up to 62 characters long.

Following are some examples of optional parameters:

- `templet.let` loads the file templet.let when WordPerfect 5.1 starts

- `/m-macroname` starts the specified macro when WordPerfect 5.1 starts

- `/C` puts Microsoft Word in character mode

- `file name.set` loads a different set of drivers for Lotus 1-2-3

If you launch an application by typing the application's file name after opening the **F**ile menu and choosing **R**un (within either Program Manager or File Manager), and if the PIF has the same name as the application file, any parameters you supply in the command line automatically override those supplied in the Optional Parameters box for this PIF.

The Start-up Directory text-box entry defines the drive and directory made current before the application starts. For example, you may keep all your word processing files in a directory called \WPDOCS, but the word processor itself may be located in \WP. If you want the word processor to have \WPDOCS as the file directory when it starts, enter **C:\WPDOCS** in the Start-up Directory box.

You also can specify a start-up directory in a program-item icon by opening Program Manager's **F**ile menu, choosing **P**roperties, and entering a directory in the Working Directory box. Settings made in Program Manager override settings made in PIF Editor.

If the application has a default-settings file that includes a default start-up directory (like WordPerfect and Lotus 1-2-3), the start-up directory in the PIF or the working directory in a program-item icon are overruled.

If your application must locate additional files on start-up (as is the case with Lotus 1-2-3), do not enter a start-up directory.

PIF Options for Standard Mode

The following sections describe the Standard-mode PIF Editor settings (refer to fig. 22.10). The Memory Requirements options specify how much memory the application uses. The Directly Modifies options, Prevent Program Switch option, and No Screen Exchange option affect how much memory is left for other applications to use.

Video Mode

Option	Description
Text	Choose this option when the application uses only text mode. This video-mode option tells Windows to set aside only enough memory to save an application's text display so that you can switch back and forth between the application and Windows. The Text option reserves the smallest possible amount of memory for saving the display. You cannot display graphics screens when this option is set.
Graphics/Multiple Text	Choose this option when the application displays graphics. This option causes Windows to set aside more memory for saving the screen because the application is using video data. You should choose this option in most cases.

Memory Requirements

Setting	Description
KB Required	Type the amount of memory (in kilobytes) that the DOS application needs to run. This setting tells Windows the minimum conventional memory that must be available to load the application. The KB Required setting is less than the amount listed in the application's user manual, because the amount listed includes memory required for DOS and other parts of the system. Usually, you should start with the default setting of 128. Start the application with no other applications running to see whether it starts. If the application does not start, raise the KB Required setting in increments of 64 until the application does run. If you try to start a DOS application and the required amount of memory is not available to the system, Windows displays an error message, and you cannot start the application.

XMS Memory. These options tell Windows how much extended memory to use for applications that require XMS memory specification. Because Windows enables the use of extended memory as long as it is available, you can leave these options at the standard settings of 0.

Setting	Description
KB Required	Type the number of kilobytes of extended memory recommended by the application manual, if your application uses extended memory that conforms to the Lotus/Intel/Microsoft/AST Extended Memory Specification Version 2.0 or later. This setting is the minimum amount needed to start the application. Unless you are positive that the application for which you are creating the PIF uses extended memory, leave this setting at 0. The 0 setting prevents applications from using XMS memory. Few DOS applications use extended memory. For DOS applications that do use extended memory, such as Lotus 1-2-3 Release 3.1, enter **512** and increase the setting as necessary.
KB Limit	Type the maximum amount of extended memory needed by the application. This setting prevents the application from taking all extended memory for itself by setting an upper limit. Leave the setting at 0 to prevent the application from gaining access to any extended memory, or set the option to –1 to give the application all the extended memory it requests. Use the –1 setting only if the application requires large amounts of extended memory, because this setting slows the system significantly.

Directly Modifies. Some applications cannot share resources with other applications. The Directly Modifies settings group defines which resources cannot be shared. You cannot switch back to Windows without quitting the application if you choose these options.

Setting	Description
COM1, COM2, COM3, COM4	Check one of these check boxes if the application uses COM1, COM2, COM3, or COM4. Choosing an option prevents other applications from using the COM port selected for this application. An application that uses a PIF with this selection does not swap from memory to a hard disk, so you cannot fit as many additional applications in Windows.
Keyboard	Choose this option if the application directly controls the keyboard.

No Screen Exchange. Choose this option to prevent copying and pasting between DOS applications with the Clipboard. If you choose this option, you cannot copy screens with the Print Screen or Alt+PrtScrn key. Choosing this option conserves memory.

No Save Screen. Choose this option so that Windows does not save the screen information when you switch to another application. When you choose the No Save Screen option, Windows no longer retains in memory the screen information for the application, and the memory becomes available. Use this option only when the application has the capability to retain its own screen information and has a screen-redraw command.

Prevent Program Switch. Choose this option to prevent switching from the application back to Windows. Checking this check box prevents you from using Alt+Tab, Alt+Esc, or Ctrl+Esc to switch back to Windows. You must exit the application to return to Windows. This option conserves memory.

Close Window on Exit. Choose this option to close the window in which the DOS application is displayed when you exit the DOS application.

Reserve Shortcut Keys. Choose any of these options to indicate the key combinations you want to use for carrying out functions in the application. These key combinations then are reserved for your application instead of Windows.

Setting	Description
Alt+Tab	Choose this option to reserve the Alt+Tab shortcut key for this application. Windows uses Alt+Tab to toggle between applications.
Alt+Esc	Choose this option to reserve the Alt+Esc shortcut key for this application. Windows uses Alt+Esc to switch to the next application.
Ctrl+Esc	Choose this option to reserve the Ctrl+Esc shortcut key for this application. Windows uses Ctrl+Esc to switch to Task List.

Setting	Description
PrtSc	Choose this option to reserve the PrtSc shortcut key for this application. Windows uses Print Screen to copy a full screen to the Clipboard.
Alt+PrtSc	Choose this option to reserve the Alt+PrtSc shortcut key for the application. Windows uses Alt+PrtSc to copy a full screen (or active Window) to the Clipboard.

PIF Options for 386 Enhanced Mode

The 386 Enhanced options appear in two dialog boxes (refer to figs. 22.11 and 22.12). The basic PIF options are similar to the PIF options in Standard mode. The advanced options fine-tune the application for running in 386 Enhanced mode.

Many of the Standard-mode PIF options are duplicated for 386 Enhanced mode. For example, if you set the Program Filename option in Standard mode and then use a Mode command to switch to the settings for 386 Enhanced mode, Windows duplicates those settings in 386 Enhanced mode. This duplication is especially helpful when you run Windows frequently in Standard or 386 Enhanced mode and you need to set PIF options for both modes. The most notable exception, however, is the Optional Parameters setting, which you use to supply command-line parameters to an application when you start it. You must set this option independently for each mode.

V

Running and Customizing

Use 386 Enhanced Mode If You Have an 80386 Computer and Run DOS Applications

386 Enhanced mode enables you to run multiple DOS applications at one time. The advantages of this type of operation are that you can continue processing a mail merge or a database search while you work in a different application. If you run only Windows applications and you have an 80386 computer, performance and memory management are better in Standard mode.

386 Enhanced mode gives you greater control of DOS applications. For example, Standard mode enables you to run DOS applications only in a full screen; 386 Enhanced mode enables you to run most DOS applications in windows, making switching between windows and copying and pasting portions of a screen much easier. You can copy small sections of a DOS application from a window in 386 Enhanced mode. If you run the same application in Standard mode, the application runs full-screen; you can copy only the entire screen contents.

Windows and DOS applications view conventional memory very differently. Windows, when running in 386 Enhanced mode, treats all memory—conventional, extended, and virtual memory—as one large pool of memory. DOS is a single-tasking operating system, and a DOS application assumes that it is the only application running and that it can use unlimited conventional memory (0K to 640K). When a DOS application makes a request for a block of conventional memory, Windows satisfies that request by giving it a block of memory from the pool. The Memory Requirements PIF settings enable you to specify the upper and lower limits of memory that a DOS application receives.

The previous sections describe the 386 Enhanced mode basic options (default settings are shown in fig. 22.10). The following few sections describe the 386 Enhanced mode advanced options (default settings are shown in fig. 22.11). The descriptions of Program Filename, Window Title, Optional Parameters, and Start-up Directory are listed in "PIF Options Common to Standard and 386 Enhanced Mode" earlier in this chapter.

Video Memory. These options determine the video mode for the program. Different methods of displaying graphics require different amounts of memory, and these options ensure that Windows sets aside enough memory for the video mode used by the software. These modes are Text, Low Graphics, and High Graphics. Use the lowest memory mode possible so that more memory is available for Windows. If the application does not have sufficient video memory, it does not start, and a warning message appears. If you switch from a graphics mode to one that requires less memory, Windows releases the video memory that is no longer needed. You are prevented from switching back to graphics, however, if another application is using the memory. To ensure that video memory is reserved for your application so that this does not happen, choose the High Graphics option and (in the Advanced Options dialog box) the Retain Video Memory check box. This means that your applications always will be able to switch memory modes, but less memory will be available for other applications.

Setting	Description
Text	Requires the least amount of memory. Graphics will not display. Use this mode if the DOS application will not be displaying graphics. This mode makes more memory available for Windows.
Low Graphics	Low-resolution graphics will display.

Setting	Description
High Graphics	Requires the largest amount of memory. Choose this option and the Retain Video Memory option in the Advanced Options dialog box to ensure that high-resolution memory always is available for the application.

Memory Requirements

Setting	Description
KB Required	Type the minimum amount of conventional memory that must be free for the application to start. Windows does not start the application if available memory is less than the amount specified in the KB Required text box. If you are unsure what to enter, leave the setting at 128. Do not enter the amount of memory recommended by the user manual; this figure is inflated to account for drivers and DOS. Generally, you should use a KB Required setting just high enough to load the application without causing Windows to issue an insufficient-memory error message, but low enough that you can load the application when memory is tight. If the application does not run due to insufficient memory, close all other applications and increase the KB Required setting in 64K increments until the application runs. Enter **–1** to give the application all available conventional memory up to 640K. You should avoid using this setting; in most cases, using a setting of –1 sets aside a full 640K, which is too much for most applications.

Setting	Description
KB Desired	Type the maximum amount of memory you want the application to use if the memory is available. The default 640K is the maximum; most applications use much less. Use –1 to give the application as much memory as possible up to 640K. Most applications run more efficiently with more memory, but remember that Windows shares a pool of memory; you do not want one application taking more memory than it uses. Be frugal with this setting if you know that your application will not need the upper limit of 640K. If you decrease the KB Desired amount to 512K, you conserve 128K for other applications, because this application cannot use more than 512K of memory.

V

Running and Customizing

EMS Memory. When running in 386 Enhanced mode, Windows uses only extended memory; however, Windows simulates expanded memory for applications that need the memory or that perform better when expanded memory is available.

Setting	Description
KB Required	This setting is the minimum amount of memory required for the application to run. Leave this setting at 0 (no expanded memory) for most applications. Entering a required amount does not limit the amount of expanded memory used, but if less memory is free than the KB Required setting specifies, the application does not start and displays a warning message.
KB Limit	Enter the maximum amount of expanded memory you want the application to use. Windows gives the application as much expanded memory as it needs, up to the limit you specify in this text box or until no more memory is available. The default setting is 1024. Use 0 to prevent the application from using any expanded memory. A setting of –1 gives the application unlimited memory, but this setting can slow the performance of other applications.

XMS Memory. These settings configure Windows for an application that uses the Lotus-Intel-Microsoft-AST Extended Memory Specification (XMS). Few applications use XMS; generally, you can leave these options at their default settings. Lotus 1-2-3 Release 3.1 uses XMS memory.

Setting	Description
KB Required	Type the minimum amount of extended memory recommended by the user manual for the application. If the application uses XMS memory, the computer must have the amount of memory specified by this option, or the application will not start. Leave this setting at 0 for most applications.
KB Limit	Type the maximum amount of extended memory you want the application to use. The default setting of 1024 gives the application as much extended memory as it requires, up to 1024K or until no more memory is available. Leave this setting at 0 to prevent the application from using extended memory. Few DOS applications use extended memory. Lotus 1-2-3 Release 3.1 uses extended memory.

Display Usage

Setting	Description
Full Screen	Choose this option to start the application in a full-screen display rather than in a window. Running an application in a full screen saves memory and is required for some applications running in high video modes. You can switch between full-screen applications and Window applications quickly by pressing Alt+Tab.
Windowed	Choose this option to start the application in a window. Running in a window enables you to activate other applications easily and to copy and paste data portions of a screen.

You can switch from a window to a full-screen display quickly by pressing Alt+Enter; and the application reverts to its set color scheme. You can toggle between windows and the full screen by pressing Alt+Enter.

Execution. In 386 Enhanced mode, Windows is a multitasking environment for DOS applications. Although Windows appears to be running multiple applications, Windows really can run only one application at a time. Windows must divide the computer time among all running applications by using time slicing. Each application gets a portion of the total processor time. To run multiple DOS applications simultaneously, with all those applications continuing to run while you are working in one of them, the DOS PIFs must be set up so that one application runs in the foreground, where it is active, and the other application runs in the background. The PIFs that Windows Setup and the installation application create ensure that all DOS applications run in the foreground and background. You can change the proportion of time that each application receives by modifying the Execution Settings options in an application's PIF.

Setting	Description
Background	Check this check box to enable the application to run in the background while you use another application. For example, a mail-merge application or database search can run in the background while you complete a letter with a word processor in the foreground. You set the amount of processor time allocated to the application in the background with one of the advanced PIF options.

(continues)

Setting	Description
Exclusive	Check this check box to suspend all other applications while this application is in the foreground. All other applications are halted, even if the applications have their Background option selected. This option gives an application all the processor time. Usually, this option can be left unchecked. If you want to run the DOS application exclusively, you can change its exclusive setting while it is running. To do so, open the application window's Control menu and choose the Settings command; then check the Exclusive check box in the Tasking Operations group.

Close Window on Exit

Choose this option to close the window when you exit the DOS application.

Advanced

Choosing the Advanced button displays the Advanced Options dialog box for additional 386 Enhanced mode PIF options (refer to fig. 22.11).

Advanced PIF Options for 386-Enhanced Mode

By using the advanced options in 386 Enhanced mode, you can modify a PIF to provide better memory use and performance for the DOS application. To display the Advanced Options dialog box, choose the Advanced option button at the bottom of the basic PIF Editor window. This button displays only when PIF Editor is in 386 Enhanced mode. Use the Mode menu to switch to the 386 Enhanced PIF Editor if the Advanced button does not appear. (Although you can edit a 386 Enhanced PIF while running Standard-mode windows, the PIF options take effect only in 386 Enhanced mode.)

Figure 22.11 shows that the Advanced Options dialog box is divided into four segments: Multitasking Options, Memory Options, Display Options, and Other Options. Using these options, you can adjust your PIF for best performance and memory usage.

Multitasking Options

These options control how a DOS application shares processing time with other DOS applications. When you are running two (or more) DOS applications at the same time and one (or more) of them is running in the background, you need a way to control how much processor time each application gets in relation to the other applications. Windows enables you to control this ratio through the Multitasking Options group.

The ratio of processor time between all Windows applications and all DOS applications is set in a different way. Set this ratio by running the 386 Enhanced program in Control Panel. The settings in the Scheduling group control the ratio of processing time between Windows and all DOS applications.

Setting	Description
Background Priority	Type a value between 0 and 10,000 to specify the background priority for this DOS application. The default background priority is 50. This value is meaningful only when compared with the Background and Foreground Priority settings for the other running DOS applications.
	To figure the percentage of processor time allocated to a DOS application, total the Foreground Priority for the active DOS application and the Background Priority for all DOS applications running in background at that time. Divide the priority (Foreground or Background Priority) of an application by the total. For example, the total priority of three applications is 200 (one foreground application with a priority of 100 and two background applications with a priority of 50 each). The background activity gets 50 of a total 200, or 25 percent of the processor time allocated to DOS applications. (The ratio of DOS-to-Windows-application priority is set with the 386 Enhanced program in Control Panel.)
	If an application's Execution: Background check box is unchecked, the application cannot run in the background. Therefore, any number you enter in the Background Priority box has no effect. You can change an application's background or foreground setting while it is running by changing the Settings Priority options in the Control menu of the DOS application's window.
Foreground Priority	Type a value between 0 and 10,000 to specify the foreground priority for the application. The default foreground priority is 100. The value has no meaning unless another DOS application is running in the background.
Detect Idle Time	Choose this option so that Windows gives processor resources to other applications when this application is idle (waiting for input from you, for example). This option enhances the performance of your computer, and you should choose it in most cases. If an application is running slowly, deselecting this option may help in some circumstances.

V

Running and Customizing

Memory Options

Setting	Description
EMS Memory Locked	Choose this option to prevent the application's expanded memory from swapping to the hard disk. This setting improves the application's performance because the application remains in memory. Choosing this option, however, can force other applications to swap more frequently and therefore slow their performance.
XMS Memory Locked	Choose this option to prevent the application from swapping memory to the hard disk. Checking this check box improves the application's performance because the application remains in memory. Choosing this option, however, can force other applications to swap more frequently and therefore slow their performance.
Uses High Memory Area	Choose this option to enable the application to use the high-memory area (HMA). If HMA is available, each application can allocate its own HMA.
	HMA is used by some memory-resident utilities, such as networks. If a memory-resident utility is using HMA when you start Windows in 386 Enhanced mode, no other application can use HMA.
	Choose Uses High Memory Area for most applications. This option makes more memory available for the application, if necessary. If the application does not use the additional memory, HMA is not wasted. The default setting of 1024 gives the application as much extended memory as it requires, up to 1024K or until no more memory is available.
Lock Application Memory	Choose this option to prevent conventional memory from swapping to the hard disk. Choosing this option improves the performance of this application but decreases overall system performance. Use the settings described earlier in this table to lock EMS and XMS memory.

> **Note**
>
> DOS 5.0 can use HMA. If you are using DOS 5.0 and have the line DOS=HIGH in your CONFIG.SYS file (which enables DOS to use the HMA), the HMA is not available to DOS applications running in Windows. The check box for Uses High Memory Area, therefore, should be unchecked.

Display Options

Some applications directly access the computer's hardware input and output ports to control the display adapter. Windows must monitor the application's interface with the hardware ports to ensure that when you switch applications, the video display is restored correctly. Use the default settings for most applications.

These selections control the amount of memory Windows reserves for the application display when the application starts. Generally, you should not change these settings. If you change the application's display mode during operation, Windows releases unused memory to other applications if you go to a less memory-intensive mode; Windows attempts to use additional memory if you go to a more memory-intensive mode. If additional memory is not available, the screen image may be lost. Use the High Graphics and Retain Video Memory options to ensure that memory is available if you lose the display when you switch graphics modes.

The first three options in the following list are Monitor Ports selections:

Setting	Description
Text	Choose this option to have Windows monitor video operations when the application is running in text mode. Few applications require this option.
Low Graphics	Choose this option to have Windows monitor all video operations when the application is running in low-resolution graphics mode. Few applications require this option.
High Graphics	Choose this option when the application displays graphics in high-resolution graphics mode. EGA and VGA graphics adapters display applications in high-resolution graphics mode. The High Graphics option requires about 128K of memory. Choose this option and the Retain Video Memory option to make sure that you have enough memory to run any application. Be aware, however, that these options reduce the amount of memory available to all applications.
Emulate Text Mode	Choose this option to increase the rate at which the application displays text. Leave this option selected for most applications. If your application has garbled text, if the cursor appears in the wrong place, or if the application doesn't run, try clearing this check box.
Retain Video Memory	Choose this option so that Windows retains extra video memory and does not release it to other applications. Some applications, such as Microsoft Word, use more than one video mode. When Word switches from text to graphics mode, Windows usually releases the memory for the video mode that is not in use. If memory becomes scarce, Word may not be able to switch back to a previous video mode. Choosing this option and the correct video-memory option ensures that you always have enough memory available to switch back to an application and to view the screen.

Tip
IBM's VGA display adapter is not affected by the settings you make in the Monitor Ports options. The adapter ignores any settings you make.

Running and Customizing

V

(continues)

Setting	Description
	The application may lose its display if you select this option under low-memory conditions and then change to a more memory-intensive video display. The display is lost because Windows cannot dynamically free the memory needed for the new display mode.

Other Options

These options enable you to customize Windows even further in 386 Enhanced mode.

Setting	Description
Allow Fast Paste	Usually, this option is selected by default. Most applications can accept information pasted from the Clipboard, using the fastest method. If you paste into a DOS application and nothing happens, clear this check box in the application's PIF.
Allow Close When Active	Choose this option to enable Windows to close the application without requiring you to use the application's Exit command. Also choose this option to exit Windows without closing all active DOS applications first. Because you do not have to exit the application before closing the window, no reminder to save work in progress appears. Windows does display a message box, asking whether you are sure that you want to close the active application.
Reserve Shortcut Keys	Specify the key combinations that you want to be available for an application when it runs in the foreground. Usually, these key combinations are reserved for use by Windows. This option enables your application to use special keys that Windows may otherwise reserve for its use. Two more shortcut keys are available in 386 Enhanced mode than in Standard mode: Alt+Enter, which toggles a DOS application between full screen and windows; and Alt+space bar, which activates an application window's Control menu.
Application Shortcut Keys	Specify the key combination you want to use to activate the application so that the application moves from background to foreground. The shortcut combination must include Alt or Ctrl. You can include combinations of letters, numbers, and function keys. To specify a shortcut-key combination, choose this option and press the key combination you want to use. For example, choose this option and press Alt+W. (To remove the current shortcut key, choose this option and press Shift+Backspace.) Choose your shortcut-key combinations carefully. After the application is loaded, the specified shortcut keys activate that application and do not work as shortcut keys for other applications.

Be Careful When You Choose the Allow Close When Active Option

Checking the Allow Close When Active check box can result in loss of data and file damage. This option enables Windows to close an application before the application has the chance to close its open files. The files may be damaged, and you lose any changes made to these files.

This problem occurs most frequently with accounting and database software. These applications keep files open while operating. If you quit the application with Allow Close When Active selected, the open files may be left open, ruining the data files with which you were working.

Customizing DOS Applications with Multiple PIFs

Sometimes, you may need to start the same DOS application in different ways. You can create a different PIF for each of the ways in which you want the DOS application to run. Assign a different program-item icon to each PIF, or start each PIF directly from File Manager. For example, you may want to specify different start-up directories for different types of work, or you may want to specify a different application macro to run for each of the PIFs.

You also may want a different memory configuration for the different times you run the application. For example, you may need to invoke WordPerfect with a large amount of memory reserved.

Another good use for several PIFs is to invoke specific applications parameters. Suppose that you want to start WordPerfect 5.1 with the /m-macroname parameter so that WordPerfect runs the macro specified by macroname. You can type the following command at the DOS prompt:

WP /M-MACRONAME

You can enter this start-up command and the argument in the Optional Parameters text box of PIF Editor when you create the WordPerfect PIF. If you start WordPerfect this way, the macroname macro runs when WordPerfect starts. This macro may load documents or change default settings. You also may want to run WordPerfect with large memory limits when you are working on a book and want WordPerfect to run faster, or you may need to run WordPerfect with minimum memory limits to run WordPerfect alongside other applications in Windows Standard mode.

Controlling DOS Applications

Windows adds a great deal of power to your work, even if you don't run Windows applications. You can run, and switch among, multiple DOS and Windows applications. If you work with DOS applications, this feature enables you to copy a table of numbers from Lotus 1-2-3 and paste them into WordPerfect. You also can copy a number from an accounting or checkbook application, such as Quicken, and paste it into Lotus 1-2-3. You can copy and paste information, minimize and maximize the application, and move the window or icon. The time savings you gain makes using Windows with DOS applications worthwhile.

Switching among Applications

Windows uses the same key combinations to switch among all applications, whether they are Windows or DOS applications.

The following table highlights ways in which you can switch among DOS applications.

To Switch, Press...	When DOS Applications Are...
Alt+Tab	full-screen or windowed. Each application's title bar appears. Releasing the keys displays the application.
Alt+Enter	full-screen or windowed. Each windowed or full-screen application appears.
Ctrl+Esc	full-screen or windowed. This shortcut key displays a Task List of all applications that are running. Select the desired application.
Double-click window	windowed. Click the background window to make it active in the foreground.

To switch from an active DOS application to another application, perform the following steps:

1. Press and hold down the Alt key, and press Tab. Keep holding down Alt and pressing Tab until the window or title bar of the application you want to activate appears.

2. Release Alt.

If the DOS application is running in a window, a blank window or icon with a title appears each time you press Alt+Tab. When the title for the application you want appears, release Alt. By showing only the titles and empty windows as you press Alt+Tab, Windows can switch among applications quickly.

If the DOS application is running in a full screen, a title bar appears at the top of the screen. Each time you press Alt+Tab, the title bar of another application appears. Release Alt when you see the title bar of the desired application. The selected application becomes active.

You also can switch among applications by pressing Alt+Esc. This procedure takes longer if you have multiple applications running in Windows. Pressing Alt+Esc immediately activates the next application, which may not be the one you want. Activating this application takes time. After the application is active and the screen is drawn, you must press Alt+Esc again to activate the next application. A faster method is to press Alt+Tab until you see the title of the application you want.

You also can switch to Task Manager by pressing Ctrl+Esc. When Task List appears, you can select the application you want to activate.

Some DOS applications occasionally suspend the keyboard. During these times, pressing Alt+Tab, Alt+Esc, or Ctrl+Esc may not work. To switch back to Windows, return to the application's standard operating mode (this action may require pressing Esc) and then press Alt+Tab or Ctrl+Esc. If you are displaying a graph in 1-2-3 Release 2.01, for example, press Esc to return to the spreadsheet or menu and then press Alt+Tab.

If you are running Windows in 386 Enhanced mode and have DOS applications in windows, you can click the mouse to move from window to window. Position the windows on-screen so that each window is visible, and switch among them.

Printing and DOS Applications

Windows and DOS applications work differently when printing under Windows. When you print from Windows applications and have Print Manager enabled, scheduled multiple print jobs print without conflict. DOS applications, however, are a different story. Written for a single-tasking environment, DOS applications expect to have exclusive rights to the printer. Furthermore, these applications aren't written for Windows and therefore don't use Print Manager. This limitation is no problem if you are running in Standard mode, in which Windows applications are suspended while you are working in a DOS application. In 386 Enhanced mode, however, in which you can multitask a mix of Windows and DOS applications, the potential for conflict exists, with two or more applications attempting to print to the same printer at the same time.

> **Note**
>
> When you are printing directly to a network printer queue, most of these conflicts are averted, because Print Manager is disabled and the network handles the scheduling of print jobs from both DOS and Windows applications.

Windows handles these conflicts by letting you specify whether printing should continue in the Windows application or in the DOS application. If you are in 386 Enhanced mode and you try to print from a DOS application, and Windows already is printing, Windows displays a Device Conflict message box. The message box informs you that the applications have conflicted with Windows. You then must assign the printer to Windows or to the DOS application. If you assign the printer to Windows, printing continues in the Windows application, and the DOS application receives a printer-not-ready message, which prevents it from printing. If you assign the printer to the non-Windows application, Print Manager suspends printing from the Windows application until you exit the DOS application. Print Manager then continues from the point where the conflict began.

You can turn off the Device Conflict error message. To turn off the message, choose the 386 Enhanced icon in the Main Group of Control Panel. Choose the Never Warn option for the printer or communications port you are using. To control device contention, follow these steps:

1. From the Main program group in Program Manager, open Control Panel.

2. Choose the 386 Enhanced icon.

3. From the Device Contention list, select the port that may have a problem (almost always COM1).

4. Specify how you want Windows to handle a device contention by choosing one of the following options:

Option	Description
Always Warn	Displays a message when a problem arises. You can specify which application has priority access to the port. Generally, you should choose this option.
Never Warn	Enables any DOS application to use the port at any time. This option can cause contention problems.

Option	Description
Idle	Enables the port to remain idle for the number of seconds you specify (1 to 999) before the next application can use the port without the warning message appearing. Choose this option if an application pauses between printing, such as a 1-2-3 print macro that prints multiple but separate pages or a communication application that logs on to a database, downloads information, and then logs on a second time for more information.

5. Choose OK.

Using the DOS Application Control Menu

In 386 Enhanced mode, all DOS applications have an application Control menu similar to that in Windows applications. Use the application Control menu to copy and paste information, to minimize and maximize the application, and to control the application's use of system resources.

Whether the DOS application is in a window or full-screen, you can activate the Control menu by pressing Alt+space bar. If the DOS application is in a window, you also can activate the Control menu by clicking the Control-menu box to the left of the window title. Figure 22.13 shows the Control menu.

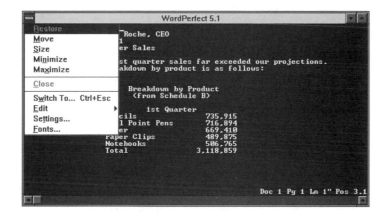

Fig. 22.13

The application Control menu for a DOS application.

If you activate the Control menu when the application is full-screen, Windows puts the application in a window and then brings up the Control menu. The applications don't appear in a standard-size window. WordPerfect

5.1, for example, appears in a half-screen window, and Lotus 1-2-3 Release 3.1 appears in a full-screen window.

In the Control menu, you see the commands that **R**estore, **M**ove, or **S**ize a DOS application window. (Because the application is in a window, you also can use the mouse to accomplish these tasks.) The Mi**n**imize and Ma**x**imize commands shrink the application to an icon or expand an icon to a window or full screen. Because the application's icon also has a Control menu, you can restore or move the icon just as you manipulate a windowed or full-screen application.

Changing Font Size in DOS Application Windows

You can make a DOS application easier to read by changing the size of the font used in a DOS application window. To be in a window, you must run the DOS application in 386 Enhanced mode. To change the font size, perform the following steps:

1. Open the DOS application's Control menu by clicking it or by pressing Alt+space bar.

2. Choose the **F**onts command. The Font Selection dialog box appears (see fig. 22.14).

Fig. 22.14
Use the Font Selection dialog box to set the character size in a DOS window.

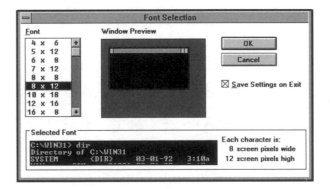

3. From the Font list, select a font size.

   The Window Preview and Selected Font boxes show you how the font looks on-screen.

4. To save this size for the next time you run this application, check the Save Settings on Exit check box.

5. Choose OK.

Changing the font size doesn't affect how a DOS application prints or operates; it only helps you make the DOS application more readable when you are working in a window.

Setting up DOS Applications for 386 Enhanced Mode

When you run Windows in 386 Enhanced mode, you can run a DOS application in a window. You can multitask DOS applications with both DOS applications and Windows applications. Some issues may arise, however, when you decide how DOS applications share computer power and communications ports with Windows applications.

Controlling Processor Sharing between DOS and Windows Applications

If you run multiple applications at the same time in 386 Enhanced mode and each application uses part of the processor's calculating power, the performance of all the applications diminishes. With the 386 Enhanced program in Control Panel, however, you can specify how much processor time all Windows applications share in relation to all DOS applications.

To schedule different amounts of processing power among Windows and DOS applications, follow these steps:

1. Open Control Panel from the Main group window in Program Manager.

2. Choose the 386 Enhanced icon. (This icon appears only when you are working in 386 Enhanced mode.) The 386 Enhanced dialog box appears (see fig. 22.15).

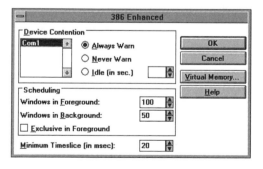

Fig. 22.15
The 386 Enhanced dialog box.

3. Choose one of the following Scheduling options:

Option	Use
Windows in Foreground:	Controls the proportion of processor resources allocated to Windows applications when a Windows application is in the active window. Type a larger number than the one in the Window in Background box to provide more processing power for the Windows application in the active window. Use a number from 1 to 10,000. Usually, you want this number to be much larger than the one in the Windows in Background box so that the active Windows application operates faster and doesn't keep you waiting.
Windows in Background:	Controls the proportion of processor resources allocated to Windows applications when no Windows application is active. Type a larger number than the one in the Windows in Foreground box to add more processing power to the Windows applications in the inactive windows. Use a number from 1 to 10,000. (This option slows the performance in the window in which you currently are working.)
Exclusive in Foreground:	Ensures that Windows applications always receive 100 percent of the processing time when a Windows application is in the active window. This option puts inactive DOS applications on hold.

4. Choose OK.

If you work mostly with Windows applications, and if the DOS applications rarely need to work rapidly when they are inactive, check the Exclusive in Foreground check box or enter a high number in the Windows in Foreground box.

In a PIF, you can control the multitasking settings for an individual DOS application. These settings control how the application multitasks with other DOS applications. You control these settings in the Multitasking Options section of a PIF's Advanced Options dialog box.

Using a Mouse in DOS Applications

If the DOS application supports a mouse and the Windows 3.1 mouse driver is loaded, you can use the mouse normally when the application is running in a full screen. You can do all the things that the application usually enables you to do with a mouse—bring up menus, select objects, and so on. If the DOS application is in a window (386 Enhanced mode), the mouse is under Windows control, and the application cannot use the mouse to bring up a menu or select objects. You can use the mouse, however, to select areas to copy or to choose commands from the Control menu.

A DOS application that doesn't support a mouse still can use a mouse for some Windows features when the application is running in a window. You can use the mouse to select areas to copy or to choose commands from the Control menu.

Scrolling in DOS Application Windows

While a DOS application is in a window, you can use the mouse as you do in any window to click the Minimize and Maximize buttons or to resize the window by dragging an edge. When an application is too small to appear in the normal application screen, vertical and horizontal scroll bars appear. You can use keystrokes or the mouse to scroll the window and display the DOS application screen. You cannot scroll to see more than usually appears on a single screen. With the mouse, you also can select areas of a DOS text or graphics screen to copy.

When you run a DOS application in a window, the Control menu includes a Scroll command. This command, which is in the Edit submenu, enables you to scroll with the keyboard. You use this command to see parts of the file that do not fit on-screen. This command scrolls the application's full screen of information in the window. You cannot scroll the window over more information than appears in the application's normal DOS screen.

To scroll with the keyboard, open the Control menu by pressing Alt+space bar, choose Edit, and then choose the Scroll command. The window title changes to show that you are in scrolling mode. If you are working in WordPerfect and the window title is WordPerfect, the window title changes to Scroll WordPerfect. Now press the arrow keys, PgUp, PgDn, Home, or End to scroll the window. When you finish scrolling, press Esc or Enter to exit scrolling mode.

Copying and Pasting Information between Applications

When you run DOS applications under Windows, you can copy and paste information among applications. Although you can copy and paste with DOS applications, such as Lotus 1-2-3 for DOS and WordPerfect 5.1 for DOS, you don't have access to the more powerful features of Windows, such as a common menu system, linked data, and embedded objects.

DOS applications running under Windows can use the Windows Clipboard. This feature enables you to copy data from a DOS application to a Windows application, from a Windows application to a DOS application, or between two DOS applications. Windows keeps the copied information in the same Clipboard used by all Windows applications. When the information is copied, you can paste it into a Windows or DOS application.

Copying and Pasting DOS Graphics May Produce Varying Results

Some DOS applications handle screen graphics in nonstandard ways. This limitation may make capturing the contents of a screen in graphics mode difficult or impossible. You may find that the color palette changes or that text characters disappear when they are copied from a DOS application and pasted into another application. However, you can capture full or partial screens from many applications and then paste them into Windows applications, such as Windows Write, Ami Pro, Word for Windows, Microsoft Excel, Aldus PageMaker, and Aldus Freehand. Most DOS and Windows applications can copy and paste text and numeric data indiscriminately, if the receiving application is in a mode that can receive the text or numbers you type.

Running DOS Batch Files

You can run DOS batch files from within Windows by creating a PIF for them. Creating a PIF for a batch file is the same as creating a PIF for any application. Although you can run some DOS batch files without creating a corresponding PIF, the following sections illustrate some of the advantages of running batch files from a PIF.

Running a Batch File from a PIF

You can run a batch file from a PIF in the same way you run any DOS application. By creating a PIF to prepare Windows for the batch file, you can set up the Windows environment correctly. For example, you may want to load a terminate-and-stay-resident (TSR) application along with one of your DOS applications.

To run a TSR and then a DOS application in the same DOS session, use the Notepad accessory to create a batch file like the following:

```
C:\tsrpathname\tsr.EXE
C:\application_pathname\application.EXE
```

Save this batch file with the extension BAT.

Create a PIF to run this batch file by using the path name and file name of the batch file entered in the Program Filename box. When the PIF runs, the file first opens a DOS session with the parameters set by the PIF. Then the PIF runs the batch file. The batch file loads the TSR and then loads and runs the application. When you quit the application, the session ends, Windows re-captures the memory, and the window closes (if a window was used).

When you create a batch file to run more than one application (for example, a TSR and a DOS application), enter in the PIF the settings for the most de-manding application in the batch file. The DOS session started by the PIF has the settings for the most difficult-to-operate DOS application.

The following batch files illustrate how you can run batch files to perform chores or procedures that are unavailable through File Manager. This one-line batch file prints a list of the files and directory names in the current directory to most non-PostScript printers connected to the LPT1 parallel port. After the batch file runs, you need to take the printer off-line and press the form-feed button to eject the page.

Type **DIR>LPT1** in Notepad, and save the file with the name DIRPRINT.BAT. Open PIF Editor; then open the **F**ile menu and choose the **N**ew command. Type **DIRPRINT.BAT** in the Program Filename box. Then open the **F**ile menu and choose Save **A**s, and enter a file name.

You now can print the current directory by selecting DIRPRINT.PIF from File Manager. If you use this command frequently, you may want to use the **N**ew command with the Program Item option in Program Manager to create a program-item icon that starts this PIF and prints the directory. When the batch file runs, the DOS session closes, and control returns to Windows.

Keeping a DOS Session Open After a Batch File Finishes Running

When you run a batch file under Windows, whether or not you run it from a PIF, the DOS screen closes, and control returns to Windows. Windows re-claims the memory that the batch file used.

You may want the DOS window or screen to remain open so that you can read results from a DOS application. When you are writing batch files to run from PIFs, you may want to see the batch-file operations on-screen to ensure that they run correctly. If the window or screen immediately closes when the batch file finishes running, you probably cannot see what happens.

Tip
When you run a PIF that keeps the DOS screen open, don't forget to type **EXIT** and press Enter to return to Windows.

To make Windows execute the batch commands and then keep the DOS screen open, you must add the line C:\pathname\COMMAND.COM as the last line of your batch file (where *pathname* is the directory containing COMMAND.COM). In a network, you can use the variable name %COMSPEC% instead. %COMSPEC% is a DOS environment variable that stores the location of DOS. Because %COMSPEC% always contains the current location of the COMMAND.COM file, no matter how the system is configured, you will want to use it as the last line of any batch file for which the DOS screen should remain open.

For example, if you want a batch file to display file names in wide format for the current directory and then keep the list on-screen, the batch file appears as follows:

```
DIR /W
%COMSPEC%
```

Creating a Program Item Icon for a Batch File

After you create a PIF that runs your batch file, you can assign a program-item icon to the PIF so that you can run the PIF by choosing an icon in Program Manager. To create a program-item icon for your batch file, complete the following steps:

1. In Program Manager, activate the group window in which you want the icon to appear.

2. Open the **F**ile menu and choose **N**ew.

3. Select the Program Item option, and choose OK.

4. In the Description box, type the label for the icon.

5. In the Command Line box, type the path and file name for the PIF. Use the Browse button to find and select the file if you cannot remember the name.

6. Choose the Change Icon button.

7. In the File Name box, type the name of the file containing icons. (If you do not have a library of icons, enter the name of a file that contains icons that came with Windows. These files usually are located in C:\WINDOWS\PROGMAN.EXE or C:\WINDOWS\MORICONS.DLL.) Then choose OK.

8. From the Current Icon list, select the icon you want to use in Program Manager.

9. Choose OK twice.

Ensuring that Batch File Variables Have Enough Memory

DOS reserves a small amount of memory in which to store names and numbers. This memory is the DOS environment. Usually, the DOS environment stores information such as COMSPEC (the location of COMMAND.COM), PATH (directories in the path), and PROMPT (the appearance of the DOS prompt). The DOS environment also can store variables used by batch files. Variables are changeable items in a batch. For example, if a batch file asks that you type a number, the number is stored in an environment variable.

The amount of memory available in the DOS environment is important if you want to run, from within Windows, batch files that use a large number of variables. Batch files that create DOS menuing systems, batch files that ask for many user prompts, or batch files that set up networks all need a larger DOS environment than Windows usually sets aside.

One way to expand the DOS environment is to use Notebook to add the following line to your CONFIG.SYS file:

```
SHELL=C:\pathname\COMMAND.COM /E:512 /P
```

This line loads COMMAND.COM with an environment of 512 bytes. If you are using DOS 3.0 or 3.1, use the blocks of memory instead of bytes. To calculate blocks, divide the memory (512) by 16 for an environment parameter of /E:32. The /P parameter indicates that COMMAND.COM is loaded; you must include this parameter.

Because the amount of memory required by or used for the DOS environment area may change, you may want to use the PIF to expand the environment memory and to run the batch file or application. The following modifications to a PIF expand the DOS environment so that it can store variables that can be used by the batch file:

Program file name:	COMMAND.COM
Title:	`file name.PIF`
Optional parameters:/E:	`384 /C C:\pathname\file name.BAT`

These changes create a DOS environment of 384 bytes and then run any application or batch file (COM, EXE, or BAT) that follows the /C. In this case, the batch file called file name.BAT runs.

Passing Variable Data from a PIF to a Batch File

You can pass variable data from a PIF to a DOS batch file. This procedure enables you to create a batch file that changes the way it operates depending upon which variables are passed to it. For example, the same batch file can add different directories to the DOS PATH, depending on which PIF ran the batch file. With this arrangement, you can set up a program-item icon tied to each PIF so that double-clicking an icon adds a new directory to the PIF. You also can create a PIF that prompts you to enter information. The batch file then uses that information to operate. This example is just one way in which you can control DOS from within Windows.

Use Notepad to create a batch file that adds a variable directory name to the current DOS PATH. (By adding a directory to the PATH, you can run any file in the PATH from anywhere on the disk without entering the file's full path name.) Save the following one-line batch file to the name PATHCHNG.BAT:

```
SET PATH=%PATH%;%1
```

This line tells DOS to attach a directory name stored in the variable %1 to the current path, stored in the variable %PATH%. The PATH then should be set equal to this new path that includes an additional directory. The variable %1 stores what is entered in the Optional Parameters line of the PIF that ran PATHCHNG.BAT.

If you occasionally need to add the Paradox 3.5 directory to your DOS path, for example, you can create a PIF with C:\PDOX35 in its Optional Parameters box. The Program Filename should be PATHCHNG.BAT. When the PIF runs, the optional parameter C:\PDOX35 is stored in %1 in the DOS environment. The PATHCHNG.BAT batch file runs. The SET PATH line then adds the directory in %1 to the existing PATH.

You can make this type of PIF more flexible by typing a question mark in the Optional Parameters box. When the PIF runs, Windows prompts you for the optional parameter. What you type in the prompt box is stored in the variable for use by the batch file.

You can enter multiple variables in the Optional Parameters box. Separate each variable with a space. Each variable then is passed to the batch file as %1, %2, %3, and so on, depending on the order in PIF Editor.

Passing Variable Data from a Batch File to a PIF

Just as a PIF can pass variable data to a batch file, a batch file can pass variable data to a PIF. In a batch file, the DOS command SET can store a value in an environment variable. The contents of the environment variable then can be retrieved by using the variable name enclosed in percent signs, %variable%. That variable then can be read by a PIF. The Program Filename, Window Title, Optional Parameters, and Start-up Directory boxes in PIF Editor can receive DOS environment variables.

Changing the Settings of a Running Application

Besides using PIF Editor to define PIF option settings, you can change some PIF options while the application is running in 386 Enhanced mode. You can change an application's display option between full-screen and windows. You also can change the percentage of processor time the application receives when it is active or in the background.

To change settings for an application running in 386 Enhanced mode, follow these steps:

1. Press Alt+space bar to open the Control menu.

2. Choose the Settings command. A Settings dialog box for the application appears (see fig. 22.16).

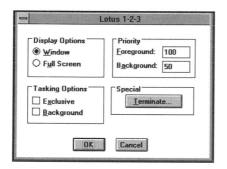

Fig. 22.16
Changing applications as they run with the Settings dialog box.

3. Choose the option you want to change.

The following sections list the options you can change as the application runs.

Switching Back to Full Screen

If you press Alt+space bar while running a full-screen DOS application in 386 Enhanced mode, the application is put in a window, and the Control menu appears. To return to full-screen mode from a window, press Alt+Enter. Alternatively, open the application's Control menu and choose Settings; select Full Screen; and choose OK.

Some applications, such as Microsoft Word for DOS, use Alt+space bar for their own purposes. Remember to reserve this shortcut key in the PIF for the application if you want to retain the shortcut key for the application's purposes and you do not want to return to Windows. If the application uses Alt+space bar, open the Control menu by pressing Alt+Enter.

Display Options

The Display Options change how the application appears. A faster method of switching display options is pressing Alt+Enter to alternate between full-screen and windowed modes.

Option	Description
Window	Displays the application in a window
Full Screen	Displays the application in a full screen

Tasking Options

The Tasking Options control how much of the computer's processing power is used. Choose either or both of these options.

Option	Description
Exclusive	Puts the processing of other applications on hold while the active application runs. If the DOS application is in a window, Windows applications continue to run, but DOS applications stop.
Background	Runs this application in the background when other applications are active. The application's use of processing time depends on the advanced 386 Enhanced mode PIF settings or the settings in the Priority Options section.

Priority Options

The Priority Options control the priority of processor time when the application is running in the foreground or background. The actual amount of time allocated to the application depends on the priority settings of the other applications. The numeric settings and allocation of processor time between applications are described in detail in the Background Priority section of "Advanced PIF Options for 386 Enhanced Mode" earlier in this chapter.

Option	Description
Foreground	A numeric setting that is the weighted amount of processor time as compared with all running applications
Background	A numeric setting that is the weighted amount of processor time as compared with all running applications

Special Setting

Use the Terminate option as a last resort. Choose this option when you cannot exit or quit the application in any other way. Terminate closes the application and gives you the chance to return to Windows to save open files in other applications. Save the files in all other applications, and then close the applications and exit Windows. If you are unable to exit Windows, press Ctrl+Alt+Del.

If you choose a PIF to start a DOS application but the application does not start or operate correctly, use PIF Editor to edit the PIF.

Following are some of the most common problems and their solutions:

Problem	Solution Using PIF Editor
Application file not found	Check the file-name extension in the Program Filename text box.
Application file not found	Check the application path name in the Program Filename text box.
Associated files not found	Type the application's path name in the Start-up Directory text box.
Insufficient memory to start	Increase the KB Required setting. You may need to increase the EMS and XMS KB Required settings if your application requires EMS or XMS memory.
Add-in applications don't run	Increase the KB Required setting.
Special keystrokes don't work	Reserve keystrokes for the application's use in the Reserve Shortcut Keys group (choose the Advanced button in a 386 Enhanced mode PIF to see these options).

Enhancing DOS Application Performance

You can use four steps to enhance the performance of DOS applications running in Windows:

1. If you operate in 386 Enhanced mode, use normal Windows techniques to make an application faster, such as running it full-screen or running in Exclusive mode.

2. Use the techniques described in Chapter 24, "Installing and Optimizing Windows 3.1," to enhance Windows' overall performance by increasing memory and disk performance.

3. Customize the application's PIF to clean out settings designed to handle worst-case situations, such as high-resolution graphics.

4. Go through a triage procedure that balances certain Windows features against the memory cost that they incur, such as the capability to copy a graphic screen.

Make Significant Performance Improvements in Two Areas

You probably will get the most significant performance improvements by making two improvements to your hardware. For a few hundred dollars, you can add memory to your computer so that it has at least 4M and then set up the SMARTdrive software to increase apparent disk performance.

For even less cost, use disk-defragmenting software to compact and defragment your hard disk so that it works more efficiently. After you defragment your hard disk, create a permanent swap file if you are running Windows in 386 Enhanced mode. These changes, along with increased memory, improved hard disk performance from defragmenting, and a permanent swap file, give you significant performance improvements.

Operating DOS Applications Efficiently

The following list presents a few simple tips on operating DOS applications. These tips should make your DOS applications run faster.

- In Standard or 386 Enhanced mode, shut down applications or documents that you are not using. These documents consume memory and may consume computer processing time.

■ Fine-tune your system according to the tips in Chapter 24, "Install-ing and Optimizing Windows 3.1," so that Windows runs faster. In most cases, the small cost of bringing your computer's memory up to at least 4M is well worth the significant increase in Windows' perfor-mance, and you do not have to perform the arcane manipulations with memory and configuration files.

■ Defragment your hard disk and set up a permanent swap file if you run in 386 Enhanced mode. Defragmentation means that all files are in order, and you can retrieve data faster than if your data is fragmented. A permanent swap file enables Windows to swap information between memory and hard disk much faster.

■ In 386 Enhanced mode, operate DOS applications full-screen whenever possible. Press Alt+Enter to toggle the application between full screen and windows.

■ In 386 Enhanced mode, don't operate DOS applications in the back-ground if the application does not need processing while it is in back-ground.

■ In 386 Enhanced mode, if you decide that you need more processing speed in the active DOS application, press Alt+space bar to open the Control menu. Choose the Settings command, select the Exclusive check box, and choose OK. This action gives the application maximum processor time while the application runs full-screen.

■ In 386 Enhanced mode, control the ratio of computer time that Win-dows applications and DOS applications receive. Use the 386 Enhanced application in Control Panel to change the Scheduling group so that Windows applications receive a lower weighting for computer time while operating in the background. (This change decreases the perfor-mance of all your Windows applications.)

Improving Performance with Swap Files

When you start a DOS application in Standard mode, Windows creates a space on the hard disk to store that application when you switch away from the application. This space is a temporary application swap file. (These files are different from the temporary or permanent swap files used in 386 En-hanced mode and described in Chapter 24, "Installing and Optimizing Windows 3.1.")

In Standard mode, Windows cannot run a DOS application and Windows applications at the same time, as it can in 386 Enhanced mode. In Standard mode, you also cannot run two DOS applications at the same time. When you have one or more DOS applications open, you switch to an application to use it or switch away from the DOS application when you want to use another application.

When you switch away from a DOS application, the program is copied from RAM to the temporary application swap file on the hard disk. Swapping the DOS program from memory makes memory available for Windows or another application. The number of swap files that can be created on your hard disk is governed by the amount of free space available on the hard disk. When you quit an application, Windows deletes the swap file.

Temporary swap files are hidden and use names starting with ~WOA. Never delete these swap files while Windows is running. Usually, these files are put in the TEMP directory specified in the AUTOEXEC.BAT file. If your AUTOEXEC.BAT file does not specify a TEMP file, the files are stored in the root directory of the first hard disk. You can define where you want application swap files to be located by entering a setting in the [NonWindowsApp] segment of your SYSTEM.INI file. For example, the following line places temporary swap files in the C drive in the directory TEMPSWAP:

```
swapdisk=C:\TEMPSWAP
```

You can use Notepad to edit the SYSTEM.INI file. Save the SYSTEM.INI file and restart Windows for the changes to take effect.

> **Note**
>
> Use the swap-disk setting in the SYSTEM.INI file to specify the fastest hard disk you have as the location for the application swap files. The disk should have at least 512K of available free space.
>
> Generally, using a RAM disk as a location for the temporary application swap files is not a good idea. Using the RAM as part of SMARTdrive usually is more efficient.

Frequently running a disk-defragmenting application increases the performance of your hard drives by making them more efficient. This increased performance enables you to switch among DOS applications more rapidly.

Improving Performance by Changing Standard PIF Options

Before changing an option in a DOS application PIF, be sure to read the description of that option in Chapter 24, "Installing and Optimizing Windows 3.1." Following are the PIF options for real or Standard modes that help you increase memory:

Option	Description
Video Mode	Affects the amount of memory reserved for the application's display. Set this option to Text to reduce the amount of memory set aside for the application and to make more memory available elsewhere. The application must run in text mode and cannot display high-resolution graphics. If you change modes, such as switching from text to graphics mode in 1-2-3, you may not be able to switch from the application to Windows. You must quit the application to return to Windows.
KB Required	Using a number higher than the minimum necessary to get the application started wastes memory. This number specifies the minimum amount of conventional memory required to start the application, not how much memory is allocated to the application. If you receive an out-of-memory warning before the application starts, you do not have sufficient available memory to start the application. Reduce the memory specified by this setting. If the application starts but later displays its own out-of-memory warning, use one of the other techniques to free more memory.
XMS Memory	Affects the amount of extended memory reserved for the application. (Most applications do not use extended memory; Lotus 1-2-3 Release 3 does.) If the application does not use extended memory, set the XMS Memory: KB Required and XMS Memory: KB Limit options to 0.
No Screen Exchange	Affects the memory set aside for screen images copied to the Clipboard when you press Print Screen (PrtScrn) or Alt+PrtScrn. You cannot copy and paste the application's display when this option is active, but more memory is available for the application. If you are not copying and pasting between DOS applications, you can turn this option off to save memory.
Prevent Program Switch	Affects how you return to Windows. This option makes more memory available for the application, but you have to quit the application to return to Windows. This option makes switching between applications difficult and basically does away with the advantages of using DOS applications with Windows.

Improving Performance by Changing PIF Options in 386 Enhanced Mode

Before changing an option in a PIF for operation in 386 Enhanced mode, be sure to read the description of the option in Chapter 24, "Installing and Optimizing Windows 3.1." Following are the PIF options for 386 Enhanced mode that help you free memory:

Option	Description
KB Required	Affects the amount of memory reserved for an application's program code. If the application starts but later runs out of memory, try reducing the KB Required setting to free more memory. If the application uses extended or expanded memory, you may have to increase the XMS Memory or EMS Memory settings.
Display Usage	Affects whether the application runs in a window or full-screen. Run the application in a full screen to use less memory and operate faster. You also can switch between full-screen and windowed mode at any time by pressing Alt+Enter.
Execution	Other DOS applications stop when Exclusive is selected and when the application with this setting is in the foreground (active) and full-screen. This option prevents simultaneous operation of applications and releases more memory and processor time to the application in the foreground. When Execution is Exclusive, set Display Usage to Full Screen for maximum benefit; otherwise, Windows uses part of the system resources.

Note

You do not have to use EMM386.EXE to emulate expanded memory when you are running Windows in 386 Enhanced mode. In 386 Enhanced mode, Windows simulates expanded memory. You can use EMM386.EXE, however, to create upper-memory blocks (UMBs) in which to load device drivers. Loading device drivers in upper memory, or *loading high*, increases the amount of conventional memory available.

Before changing an option in a PIF for operation in 386 Enhanced mode, be sure that you understand the option. The various options are described in various sections of this chapter. The PIF options for 386 Enhanced mode that help manage multitasking are listed in the next table.

Check the Detect Idle Time Option

If an application is extremely slow, Windows may be assuming that the application is idle frequently; Windows then may be relinquishing the application's share of processor time to other applications. To improve performance, try clearing the Detect Idle Time check box under Multitasking Options in the application's 386 Enhanced PIF dialog box. If this action does not improve performance, check the Detect Idle Time check box so that the performance of other applications is not reduced.

Quick Screen Refresh with Windowed Applications

When you run DOS applications in a window in 386 Enhanced mode, you may notice a delay in the application's screen refresh. This delay is due to Windows multitasking; Windows gives part of the processor time to all running applications. You can affect the rate at which Windows updates the display of DOS applications running in a window. A setting in the SYSTEM.INI file—WindowUpdateTime—controls the priority given to updating DOS applications running in a window. If your SYSTEM.INI file does not include a WindowUpdateTime line, you must insert it yourself. Full-screen DOS applications are not affected by the WindowUpdateTime setting. You should add the following setting to your SYSTEM.INI file:

```
[386Enh]

WindowUpdateTime=700
```

WindowUpdateTime is the priority given to updating the windowed DOS applications when Windows has other tasks running in the background. Increasing this setting gives more time to the windowed DOS application. The default is 50. The maximum value allowed is 1000.

Advanced PIF options available to applications running in 386 Enhanced mode also make a difference in memory and processor performance. The following list shows the advanced PIF options that you can change to make a difference in performance.

Advanced Option	Description
Multitasking	Affects the percentage of processor time the application receives when the application is in the foreground or background and Execution Exclusive is not selected. The Foreground and Background Priority settings determine the percentage of processor time given the application as a weighted portion of the time given all the running applications. Detect Idle Time should be selected so that other applications can run while Windows waits for input from the user.

V

Running and Customizing

Advanced Option	Description
EMS Memory	Affects how Windows emulates expanded memory in 386 Enhanced mode. Usually, if you leave KB Required at 0, Windows allocates as much memory as is needed, up to the amount specified in KB Limit. To limit memory use, set the maximum amount of expanded memory in the KB Limit text box. The Locked option prevents Windows from swapping this memory to disk. Locking memory increases application speed by enabling this application to keep memory. Locking memory, however, also limits the memory available to other applications and can slow their performance.
XMS Memory	Affects an application's use of extended memory. Few applications require this option, so set KB Required and KB Limit to 0. If an application uses extended memory, you can set the Locked option to increase performance by locking memory so that other applications cannot use it. Locking memory, however, slows the performance of other applications because they cannot use the memory.
Uses High Memory Area	Affects the high-memory area (HMA) of extended memory (the first 64K of extended memory). This option tells Windows that the application is allowed to use high memory. HMA, when available, increases application performance. Set this option unless a network driver or other utility is loaded into HMA before Windows is started. If HMA is in use when you start Windows, no applications running under Windows can use HMA. In 386 Enhanced mode, each DOS application can access its own HMA, because HMA is duplicated for every DOS session in this mode. Keep this option selected because if HMA is available and the application uses it, more memory is available to the application. If the application does not use HMA, no memory is wasted.

Note

One of the most significant improvements offered by DOS 5.0 is the capacity to load most of the operating system into extended memory. Like Windows, DOS 5.0 has a memory manager—HIMEM.SYS—that enables DOS to access extended memory. Before DOS 5.0 can use extended memory, the HIMEM.SYS memory manager must be loaded with a DEVICE=C:\WINDOWS\HIMEM.SYS line and a DOS=HIGH line in the CONFIG.SYS file. Notice, however, that you should use the Windows HIMEM.SYS, not the one in DOS Version 5. DOS loads most of the operating system in HMA. When DOS is loaded into the high-memory area, the HMA is not available to DOS applications running under Windows.

Advanced Option	Description
Lock Application Memory	Affects the application by locking it in memory and not allowing the application to swap to the hard disk as long as the application is running. This option increases the performance of the application but decreases the performance of Windows and other applications.
Display Options	Affects the amount of memory reserved for video modes. To save memory, choose the Text option and run your application only in text mode. To make additional memory available to the system, clear the Retain Video Memory option. This action may improve speed by increasing available memory, but with most applications, you cannot be in a high-resolution video mode, switch to another application, and then switch back. When you switch back, the screen does not refresh.

Note

The high-memory area is the first 64K of extended memory. You must have the Windows memory manager—HIMEM.SYS—or some other, compatible memory manager loaded to make this 64K available to Windows or any application that requests it. If you do not have a memory manager, no application can access the high-memory area. See Chapter 24, "Installing and Optimizing Windows 3.1," for a discussion of HMA.

Note

The speed of DOS applications in 386 Enhanced mode is greatly improved by turning off all the Monitor Ports options in the application's PIFs. By default, the High Graphics option is on; the High Graphics option takes up approximately double the memory of the Low Graphics option. All the Monitor Ports options should be turned off unless you are having trouble when you switch from Windows to your application.

V

Running and Customizing

Changing Performance While Running in 386 Enhanced Mode

When you change PIFs, you are making permanent changes in the way a DOS application performs. However, you can make some temporary changes even as an application is running in 386 Enhanced mode. You can use the Settings command in an application's Control menu to change the display option, the processor priority, and the tasking options, all of which affect performance.

To change performance while an application is running, follow these steps:

1. Open the Control menu and choose the Settings command.

2. To change performance, choose one of the options in the following chart:

Option	Description
Display Option	Choose Full for less memory use; select Window for more memory use. (Press Alt+Enter while the application is running.)
Priority	Type a number for the Foreground and Background weighting. The size of this number, relative to the corresponding numbers of other running applications, determines how much processor time the application receives.
Tasking Options	Choose Exclusive to suspend other applications while this application is in the active window. If this application is in a window, other Windows applications can run, but DOS applications are put on hold. Use the Exclusive and Full Screen display options together to dedicate the maximum amount of computer resources to the active application when it is full-screen. Background enables this application to run in the background.

Balancing Windows and DOS Applications

Getting your system to run Windows applications and DOS applications smoothly usually is a matter of fine-tuning the DOS application's PIFs. You also can use settings in the 386 Enhanced application in Control Panel to balance computer use between all DOS and all Windows applications.

Windows applications share CPU time equally; therefore, no foreground or background relationship exists among Windows applications. DOS applications, because they were written for a single-tasking system, expect exclusive use of the CPU. By necessity, if you run multiple applications at the same time in 386 Enhanced mode and each application uses part of the processor's calculating power, the performance of all the applications diminishes. With Control Panel, however, you can specify how much processor time all Windows applications share in relation to all DOS applications.

To schedule different amounts of processing power between Windows and DOS applications, follow these steps:

1. Open Control Panel from the Main group window in Program Manager.

2. Choose the 386 Enhanced icon. (This icon appears only when you are in 386 Enhanced mode.) The 386 Enhanced dialog box appears.

3. Choose one of the following Scheduling options:

Option	Use
Windows in Foreground:	Type a large number if you want more processing power for Windows applications than for DOS applications. Use a number from 1 to 10,000. Usually, this number needs to be much larger than the Windows in Background text box entry so that the active application operates faster and doesn't keep you waiting.
Windows in Background:	Type a larger number than the one in the Windows in Foreground box if you want more processing power for the Windows applications in the inactive windows. Use a number from 1 to 10,000. (This selection slows the performance in the window in which you are working.)
Exclusive in Foreground:	Check this box to ensure that the active application always gets the maximum amount of processing time. Applications in the background are left on hold.
Minimum Timeslice	The length of time given to each DOS application is controlled by the Minimum Timeslice setting. This setting determines the amount of time (in milliseconds) that a DOS session or DOS application controls the CPU before Windows can switch to another process. If no other process needs the CPU, the DOS session can have the CPU longer than the Minimum Timeslice. Windows always gives the DOS session CPU time at least equal to the Minimum Timeslice. The default is 20 milliseconds.

4. Choose OK.

Using WINSTART.BAT To Load TSRs

Windows has a file similar to the AUTOEXEC.BAT file. When Windows loads, it looks for a file called WINSTART.BAT, and if that file is found, it runs any commands in that file before loading. This batch file must be located in the Windows directory and executes only if you start Windows in 386 Enhanced mode.

V

Running and Customizing

If you start a TSR in WINSTART.BAT, the TSR is available only in Windows applications. Any DOS applications you start after loading Windows cannot use the TSR.

If a TSR is loaded before you start Windows, that TSR loads every time you start a DOS application or DOS session in Windows. Loading the TSR in each DOS application's memory area this way, whether or not the TSR is needed or wanted, is a waste of memory. Using WINSTART.BAT saves memory.

If you want the TSR to be available to a single DOS application, have the DOS application's PIF run a batch file that starts the TSR and then starts the application.

From Here...

In this chapter, you learned how to run and switch between DOS applications, as well as how to control the way Windows works with your DOS programs. From this point, you may want to review the following chapters of this book:

- Chapter 1, "Operating Windows," gives a basic understanding of how Windows functions—including how the keyboard, mouse, and icons behave—is essential to properly and effectively using DOS applications under Windows.

- Chapter 21, "Installing and Configuring Windows Applications," helps you to use your programs within Windows.

- Chapter 24, "Installing and Optimizing Windows 3.1," shows you how to set up many of your DOS applications up automatically to work within Windows, and how to optimize Windows to benefit the way your DOS applications perform.

Chapter 23

Introducing Visual Basic for Applications

For several years, Microsoft has hinted to the press and developers that its long-range strategy includes a common application programming language to be used in all of Microsoft's applications. This language would be founded on BASIC, the most widely known computer language, and would provide power users and developers with a common application language (also known as *macro language*) between applications. This feature would reduce learning time and support costs. In addition, this language would provide the means for developers to develop systems that integrate multiple applications so that they can work together to solve a business problem.

That long-awaited language is Visual Basic, Applications Edition (known commonly as Visual Basic for Applications, or VBA). The first two Microsoft products to include the language are Excel 5 and Microsoft Project. Visual Basic for Applications promises to be the most common Windows programming language, enabling power users and developers to apply it to each of Microsoft's applications. After all the major Microsoft applications, such as Access and Word, include Visual Basic for Applications, integrating applications will be significantly easier.

This chapter examines Visual Basic for Applications as it exists in Excel. The Visual Basic for Applications language is both a superset and subset of Visual Basic 3 for Windows. If you are familiar with Visual Basic 3 and familiar with Excel, you should be able to learn Visual Basic for Applications fairly quickly. Visual Basic for Applications is similar to but different from Access Basic and Word Basic. If you know either of these languages, you will find that Visual Basic for Applications applies similar concepts.

If you are an experienced Excel 4 macro programmer, you may face making the transition to Visual Basic for Applications with mixed feelings. Visual Basic for Applications in Excel is completely different from the Excel 4 macro language. You probably have Excel systems that use the existing Excel 4 language and have also logged hundreds of hours learning Excel 4 and developing programs in its language.

The process of switching to Excel 5's Visual Basic for Applications requires effort, but making the transition is easier than learning to develop Excel 4 macros. You don't have to switch immediately from the Excel 4 macro language to Visual Basic for Applications, because VBA lets you run your current Excel macro applications and programs with the Excel 4 macro language. Microsoft has promised that Excel 6 also will be able to run Excel 4 macros.

Nevertheless, you may want to begin making the transition to Visual Basic for Applications immediately, for the following reasons:

- If you learn and support one application's use of Visual Basic for Applications, you will find it much easier to learn and support Visual Basic for Applications in other applications.

- The language is based on Visual Basic, one of the most widely used Windows development languages.

- Microsoft has hinted that future Macintosh versions of the applications will contain Visual Basic for Applications. This means that the integrated applications that you develop in Windows will be portable to the Macintosh.

- You can copy applications that you write in Visual Basic for Applications into Visual Basic, compile them in Visual Basic, and run them as Visual Basic programs that control Excel and the other applications that will have the Visual Basic for Applications language.

- Visual Basic for Applications does not require you to select objects to change their properties. For example, when you use Visual Basic for Applications, you can make a range on a worksheet bold or clear without having to activate the worksheet and select the range.

This chapter gives you an overview of the structure and tools available in Visual Basic for Applications. In this chapter, you learn how to:

- Understanding the way Visual Basic's Object model has properties and methods

- Navigate to or describe an object's location within the application

- Understanding the way each object has methods that act as adverbs or built-in code that can affect an object

- Change objects with a minimal amount of code writing

- Store data or an object's location in a variable

- Draw a dialog box

- Get help and examples with the Visual Basic for Applications language

Major Differences between the Languages

The old Excel 4 macro language and the new Visual Basic for Applications language have some major differences between them. This chapter discusses these differences. However, if you are familiar with BASIC or Pascal, you should probably find Visual Basic for Applications fairly straightforward.

When you write or record a Visual Basic program, the individual program is known as a *procedure*. Each procedure is like an Excel 4 macro. Procedures are kept on a Visual Basic sheet known as a *module*. You can have as many modules and procedures in a workbook as you want.

Understanding the Visual Basic Object Model

The Visual Basic for Applications language is object-oriented. It is does not fit the full definition of an object-oriented language. The Visual Basic for Applications language is based on the Visual Basic programming language, and features extensions that enable it to control the different types of objects in Excel. In Visual Basic for Applications as implemented in Excel, the language's objects are Excel objects, such as workbooks, ranges in a worksheet, and charts. When Microsoft releases Visual Basic for Applications for implementation with Microsoft Word, the object model will be one that works with the objects found in a word processor, such as documents, paragraphs, lines, bookmarks, and tables.

The Visual Basic for Applications language consists of two general types of components: Visual Basic language statements and functions, and the Excel object models.

The Visual Basic language's statements are commands that produce some action, such as controlling the flow of the program. An example of Visual Basic's statements is If...Then...Else. This statement tests whether a condition is true and performs an action accordingly, as follows: *if* that condition is true, *then* perform some action; if the condition is not true (*else*), then perform a different action. Functions are Visual Basic commands that return a result. For example, the Date command returns the current date in the computer system.

The Excel object models include objects, properties, and methods that describe Excel and its contents. Excel objects are items in Excel that you can change. Such items include workbooks, worksheets, chart titles, and ranges on a worksheet. Each object has its own set of properties, which are attributes or characteristics that describe the object. If you want to set the value of cell A1 to 5, for example, you use a line such as the following:

```
Range("A1").Value=5
```

In this example, Value is a property of Range. Other properties of Range are Font, Formula, Height, Hidden, Style, and Left.

Each object also has related methods. Methods are actions inherent to an object. To remove the contents of the cell that just had its value changed, for example, you can use the following when Clear is a method of Range:

```
Range("A1").Clear
```

Other methods that you can use on Range are Activate, AutoFill, Borders, CheckSpelling, Copy, Delete, and Sort.

You can obtain additional information on the topics discussed in this section from Excel Help. Open the **H**elp menu and choose **C**ontents. Select the topic "Programming with Visual Basic," and then choose one of the following topics: "Functions," "Methods," "Objects," "Properties," or "Statements."

> **Note**
>
> If you are familiar with the Excel 4 macro language, you can find statement and function equivalents and tips on converting applications by opening the **H**elp menu, choosing **C**ontents, and then selecting Reference Information. From the next screen,

select "Microsoft Excel Macro Functions Contents." When the Excel 4 Macro Help appears, select "Visual Basic Equivalents for Macro Functions and Commands." A bar of alphabetical buttons appears. Click on the button that matches the first letter of the Excel 4 command for which you want a Visual Basic for Applications equivalent. For example, if you click on E, Help displays a list of Excel 4 macros that start with *E*. If you search this list for the Excel 4 command Echo, which turns off screen updating, you will see that the Visual Basic for Applications equivalent to this command is the following:

```
Application.ScreenUpdating = logical
```

Using Containers To Specify Objects

Objects can be confusing because Excel has so many of them, and some objects are implied. Implied objects are not typed in the code. To understand how to specify or navigate to the object that you want to affect, you need to be familiar with a few important concepts.

Think of each object as a container that can hold smaller objects, which in turn can contain smaller objects, and so on.

The largest object is the Application object. When run from within Excel, the Application object always refers back to Excel, the application from which the procedure ran. This helps your Visual Basic program understand which program is being controlled when the Visual Basic procedure is controlling other applications as well as Excel.

One of the objects within the Application object is Workbooks. Workbooks is a *collection*, which is a group of objects. The Workbooks object is a collection of all the open workbooks. You can use a Visual Basic For Each…Next statement, for example, to loop through each workbook in the Workbooks collection. If you want to refer to a specific workbook, you can use the following:

```
Application.Workbooks("Book3")
```

To refer to a specific worksheet in Book3, you can add the following:

```
Application.Workbooks("Book3").Worksheets("Sheet1")
```

To specify the first row, use the following:

```
Application.Workbooks("Book3").Worksheets("Sheet1").Rows(1)
```

To specify the first cell in the first row, use the following:

```
Application.Workbooks("Book3").Worksheets("Sheet1").Rows(1).Cells(1)
```

V

Running and Customizing

Finally, to set the `Formula` property to `Hi` in the first cell of the first row, use the following:

```
Application.Workbooks("Book3").Worksheets("Sheet1").Rows(1).Cells(1).
_Formula="Hi"
```

This quickly becomes cumbersome if you have to specify so many objects continually. But you don't. If you are referring to objects within Excel, you don't have to specify `Application` at the beginning of each line. And if the worksheet on which you are working is active, you don't have to specify the `Workbooks` and `Worksheets` objects. Finally, if the cell in which you want to put information is active, you don't have to specify the row or cell position. Instead, you can use a form such as the following:

```
ActiveCell.Formula="Hi"
```

The object model provides many such shortcuts. For example, you can refer to active objects with the statements such as `ActiveWorkbook`, `ActiveSheet`, `ActiveWindow`, and `ActiveCell`. These are actually properties of the application that return the name of the currently active object.

Another shortcut is to use `Selection` to refer to the currently selected object, as in the following example:

```
Selection.Font.Size=24
```

Using *With* To Reduce Code Size

One additional way in which you can reduce the amount of Visual Basic code that you write is to use the `With` clause. The `With` clause enables you to repeat several operations on the same object.

For example, if you turn on the Visual Basic recorder when you format selected cells with the Format menu's Cells command, you see the following code:

```
Sub Formatter()
    With Selection
        .HorizontalAlignment = xlLeft
        .VerticalAlignment = xlBottom
        .WrapText = False
        .Orientation = xlHorizontal
        .AddIndent = False
    End With
    With Selection.Font
        .Name = "Arial"
        .FontStyle = "Bold"
        .Size = 11
```

```
            .Strikethrough = False
            .Superscript = False
            .Subscript = False
            .OutlineFont = False
            .Shadow = False
            .Underline = xlNone
            .ColorIndex = xlAutomatic
        End With
    End Sub
```

In the first With clause, the object (the current selection) has the selection's properties changed by the options in the Alignment tab of the Format Cells dialog box. In the second With clause, the Font tab of the Format Cells dialog box changes properties. By using the With clause, you do not have to repeat Selection or Selection.Font on each line.

> **Note**
>
> As you probably inferred from the object model description, Visual Basic for Applications does not require that you select cells to change them or put something in a cell or range. As the example in the previous section demonstrates, however, specifying an object when it is not active can result in long lines of code.

V

Running and Customizing

Getting and Giving Information Using Parallel Syntax

Visual Basic for Applications makes it easy to get or set information about an object. The structure of Visual Basic for Applications statements is similar whether the statement reads the current property of an object or whether it changes the property of an object. This similar structure between statements that get and set information make Visual Basic for Applications easier to remember and program with.

For example, you use the same syntax to change a cell to bold and to find out whether the cell is bold. In this example, the object is the range A1, and the property to be changed is Font.Bold. Therefore, to change cell A1 to bold, use the following:

```
Sub BoldMaker()
    Range("A1").Font.Bold = True
Sub End
```

If you want to determine whether A1 is already bold, you use the same object and properties, but on a different side of the equal sign. In the following code, the variable b stores the True or False result that indicates whether A1 is bold:

```
Sub BoldChecker()
    b = Range("A1").Font.Bold
    MsgBox "Is the cell bold? " & b
Sub End
```

In this example, Font.Bold determines whether the object Range(A1) is bold and returns True or False. If the cell is bold, the MsgBox function displays the following message:

```
Is the cell bold? True
```

> **Note**
>
> The MsgBox function can display only results that are text. Therefore, MsgBox normally could not display the logical values of True or False from b. However, by joining the text message in quotation marks with the True or False result stored in b, the b is coerced into becoming text that MsgBox can display.

Referencing Objects in Visual Basic

In Visual Basic for Applications, you do not have to select an object before you determine its properties or before you change its properties. In Excel, you still must refer to a cell or range to change it.

> **Note**
>
> You cannot use Visual Basic for Applications objects such as Range and Cells as a line of code by themselves. Instead, you use them to specify the object on which to apply the property or method, as in the following:
>
> ```
> Cells(1,2).Formula="Hello World"
> ```
>
> You can also specify where information is coming from, as in the following:
>
> ```
> Content = Cells(1,2).Formula
> ```

You can refer to the active cell as the following:

```
ActiveCell
```

To refer to a cell or range using a text reference, use one of the following forms:

```
Range("B12")
Range("B12:C35")
Range("MonthReport")
```

The first range is the single cell B12 on the active sheet. The second is the range B12:C35 on the active sheet. Finally, the MonthReport is a named range on the active sheet. You cannot use any of these objects by themselves; you must follow them with a property or method.

If you want to refer to a cell or range by numeric position or a numeric offset in a row or column, use one of the following forms:

```
CELLS(1,3)
CELLS(x,y)
```

If you need a specific location on a specific sheet in the active workbook, use the containers that contain the object that you want to specify, as in the following example:

```
Worksheets("Sheet6").Rows(3).Cells(2)
```

Other objects that are useful are Rows and Columns. If you need to offset the top-left corner of a range, use the Offset method. To resize a range, use the Resize method.

> **Note**
>
> As a shortcut to writing cell or range objects on the active worksheet, use the brackets ([ ]) as an abbreviation, as in the following:
>
> ```
> [C14].Value=5
> ```
>
> This code puts 5 in cell C14 on the active worksheet. You can even use the following shortcut notation, which stores three times the content of the worksheet's cell B12 in the active worksheet's cell C14:
>
> ```
> [C14]=[B12]*3
> ```

Using Variables To Store Information

In Excel 5, names define ranges on a worksheet, but variables store value, formulas, or references in Visual Basic for Applications. You also can assign data types to variables so that they store only specific types of data—for example, text or integer numbers. Data typing can reduce troubleshooting problems later because it prevents you from putting the incorrect type of data in a variable.

Another advantage to Excel 5 variables is that you can *scope* them so they are available only within the Visual Basic procedure that contains them, to other procedures within the module, or to other modules globally.

Storing Objects in Variables

In Excel 5, you may need to store references in a variable if you have objects that you want to refer to repeatedly throughout your Visual Basic procedure. To store an object for later use, use a Set statement such as the following:

```
Set FutureObj=ActiveWorkbook.Sheets("Sheet6").Range("B36")
```

Then you can simply type this variable rather than the full object specification, as in the following example:

```
FutureObj.Font.Bold=True
```

Creating Dialog Boxes in Visual Basic for Applications

Dialog boxes are easy to draw and display in Excel 5. In Excel 5, you insert dialog sheets into a workbook and then draw the dialog box directly on the sheet. Excel 5 offers more items that you can place on a dialog box. In addition to all the dialog items that are available in Excel 4, you also can include spinners and scroll bars (sliders). Spinners (increment/decrement arrows) are double-headed arrows that enable you to scroll quickly through numbers. Scroll bars include a scroll box that the user can drag to a new position within the scroll bar to specify a number. Use scroll bars to enable users to select a number quickly from a wide range.

Figure 23.1 shows a simple scrolling list in a dialog box on the dialog sheet named Dialog1. You use the buttons located on the Forms toolbar to draw and test objects on a dialog box. When each object is drawn, it is given a name by Excel. In this figure, the list box is selected, so you can see the name of the list box, List Box 4, in the reference area at the top left of the figure. (You can change the name.) In your Visual Basic for Applications code, you can refer to this list box object by its name, for example, ListBoxes("List Box

4"). To fully specify the location of this list box, you should also specify the dialog sheet containing it, as in the following:

```
DialogSheets("Dialog1").ListBoxes("List Box 4")
```

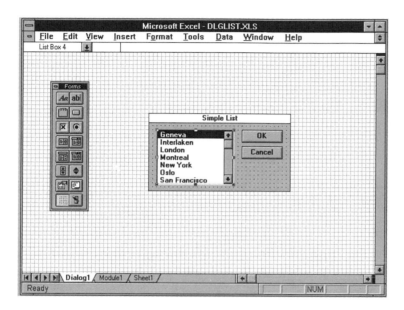

Fig. 23.1
Use the tools on the Forms toolbar to draw dialog box items on a dialog sheet.

When you write a Visual Basic for Applications program, you can get or set information in a dialog box just by referring to the object in the dialog box, and then specifying the property for that object that you want to get or set. For example, you may want to set the contents of an edit box to its default contents. After the user has entered something in the edit box you want to get the information out of the edit box.

The Visual Basic procedure shown in figure 23.2 begins by defining two variables, dlgCity and iCitySelection. The variable dlgCity is a variable that refers to the DialogSheets("Dialog1") object. It is used throughout the procedure instead of retyping DialogSheets("Dialog1") each time the dialog sheet is referenced. The ListFillRange property describes the range on Sheet1 that contains the contents of the list. The ListIndex property is then used to set the default of the list box to the first item, in this case Geneva.

V

Running and Customizing

Fig. 23.2

This code sets the contents of the list box, displays the dialog box, and puts your selected city into a range on the worksheet.

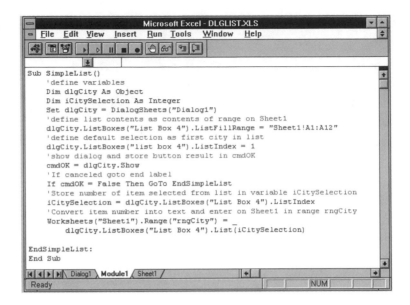

```
Microsoft Excel - DLGLIST.XLS
File  Edit  View  Insert  Run  Tools  Window  Help

Sub SimpleList()
    'define variables
    Dim dlgCity As Object
    Dim iCitySelection As Integer
    Set dlgCity = DialogSheets("Dialog1")
    'define list contents as contents of range on Sheet1
    dlgCity.ListBoxes("List Box 4").ListFillRange = "Sheet1!A1:A12"
    'define default selection as first city in list
    dlgCity.ListBoxes("list box 4").ListIndex = 1
    'show dialog and store button result in cmdOK
    cmdOK = dlgCity.Show
    'If canceled goto end label
    If cmdOK = False Then GoTo EndSimpleList
    'Store number of item selected from list in variable iCitySelection
    iCitySelection = dlgCity.ListBoxes("List Box 4").ListIndex
    'Convert item number into text and enter on Sheet1 in range rngCity
    Worksheets("Sheet1").Range("rngCity") = _
        dlgCity.ListBoxes("List Box 4").List(iCitySelection)

EndSimpleList:
End Sub

Dialog1  Module1  Sheet1
Ready                                    NUM
```

To show the dialog box, the code only needs to show the dialog sheet containing the dialog box. Because the variable dlgCity refers to `DialogSheets("Dialog1")` the dialog box can be displayed with the following:

```
dlgCity.Show
```

If the user clicks the OK button in the dialog box, True is stored in `cmdOK`. If the user clicks the Cancel button, False is stored in `cmdOK`. When `cmdOK` is False the procedure ends by going to the label `EndSimpleList` at the end of the procedure.

If the user click OK, the `ListIndex` property stores the number of the item selected from the list box in the variable `iCitySelection`. The variable `iCitySelection` is then used to pull from the `List` property the actual text that was selected from the list. For example, if the second item in the list was selected, `iCitySelection` stores the number 2 and *object*.`List(2)` returns the text of the second item in the object's list.

The text of the selected item is then entered in a named cell on the worksheet. The worksheet and named cell are specified by the following:

```
Worskheets("Sheet1").Range("rngCity")
```

Getting In-Depth Help On-Line

One of the best sources of technical information on Visual Basic for Applications is the on-line Help. To get to the Help index for programming, open the **H**elp menu and choose **C**ontents, and then choose "Programming with Visual Basic." The Visual Basic Reference screen displays.

A good way to begin learning details is to click the Objects link. This displays an alphabetized list of all objects. When you select an object from the list, Help displays the object description and examples. When viewing an object's Help screen (see fig. 23.3), you can choose the Methods or Properties link at the top of the Help screen to learn more about related methods or properties. Links that are labeled "Example" are links to a segment of sample code that you can copy from the Help file, paste into a module sheet, and run.

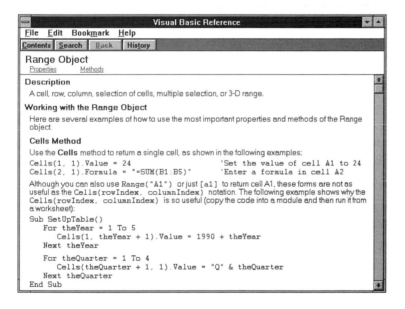

Fig. 23.3
The Help screens
in VBA are
extensive.

Debugging Tools

Visual Basic has far more debugging capability than Excel 4 macros.
It provides three tools to help you debug:

Tool	Description
Breakpoints	Breakpoints are conditions you specify that stop the procedure and send the program into break mode. The procedure stops before running the code that contains the breakpoint. Once in break mode, you can step through the procedure and examine variables.
Debugging buttons	The Visual Basic toolbar contains debugging buttons that display whenever a module (Visual Basic sheet) is active. Using these buttons, you can run one statement or procedure, set breakpoints, or examine values.
The Debug window	This window displays over your application as it runs. In the window, you can watch the resulting values and expressions as your procedure runs. Also, you can change values in this window to see how they affect your procedure.

From Here...

To learn more about Visual Basic for Applications, you should use Excel 5 or Visual Basic (refer to the following chapter).

- Chapter 21, "Installing and Configuring Windows Applications," describes the most effective way to install Excel 5 or Visual Basic in Windows.

Que publishes many good books that cover Excel 5 and Visual Basic, including the following:

- *Using Excel 5 for Windows* is the internationally best-selling book on Excel 5.

- *Using Visual Basic 3* and *Using Visual Basic for Applications* are comprehensive books that cover each version of Visual Basic.

- *Visual Basic for Applications by Example* and *Visual Basic 3 By Example* are both written for beginners and are filled with programming examples.

Part VI

Installing Windows

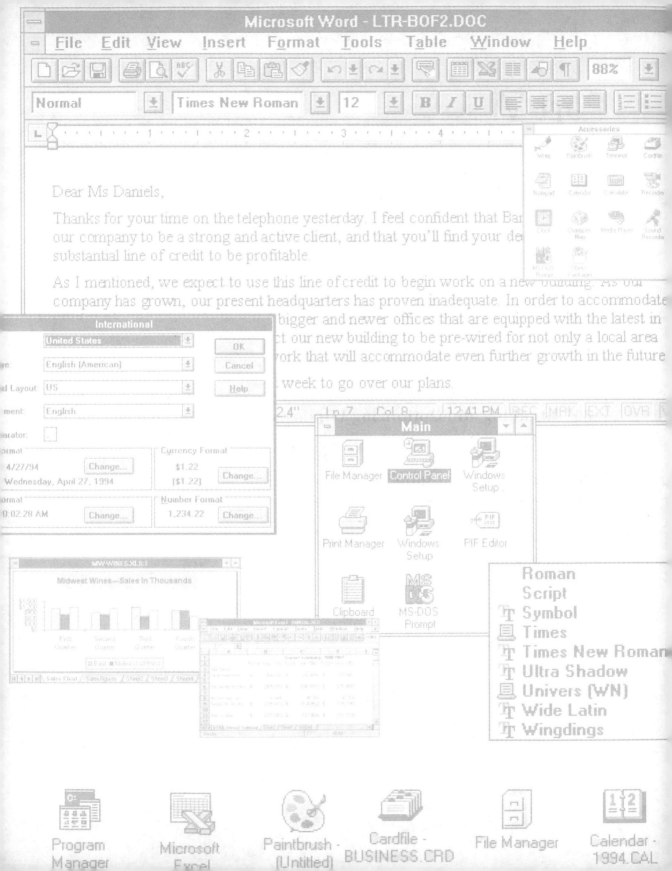

Microsoft Word - LTR-BOF2.DOC

File   Edit   View   Insert   Format   Tools   Table   Window   Help

88%

Normal   Times New Roman   12   **B** *I* U

Dear Ms Daniels,

Thanks for your time on the telephone yesterday. I feel confident that Bar
our company to be a strong and active client, and that you'll find your de
substantial line of credit to be profitable.

As I mentioned, we expect to use this line of credit to begin work on a new building. As our
company has grown, our present headquarters has proven inadequate. In order to accommodate
bigger and newer offices that are equipped with the latest in
ct our new building to be pre-wired for not only a local area
work that will accommodate even further growth in the future

week to go over our plans.

International

United States   OK

English (American)   Cancel

Layout: US   Help

ment: English

arator:

ormat   Currency Format
4/27/94   Change... $1.22   Change...
Wednesday, April 27, 1994   ($1.22)

ormat   Number Format
0:02:28 AM Change...   1,234.22   Change...

Main

File Manager   Control Panel   Windows Setup

Print Manager   Windows Setup   PIF Editor

Clipboard   MS-DOS Prompt

MW-WINES.XLS:1

Midwest Wines—Sales In Thousands

First Quarter   Second Quarter   Third Quarter   Fourth Quarter

Roman
Script
Symbol
Times
Times New Roman
Ultra Shadow
Univers (WN)
Wide Latin
Wingdings

Program Manager   Microsoft Excel   Paintbrush - (Untitled)   Cardfile - BUSINESS.CRD   File Manager   Calendar - 1994.CAL

Chapter 24

Installing and Optimizing Windows 3.1

The Windows installation process is very easy and graphical. However, there are decisions you need to make before you begin your installation process. There are also a number of maintenance tasks you should perform if you want Windows to install and perform at its best performance. If you inherit an existing installation of Windows or just want to fine-tune its performance, this chapter also includes information on how to optimize the hardware, DOS, and Windows so that Windows operates at its optimum.

Following the screens during the Windows installation process is fairly easy, although there are a few choices you have to make which this chapter can give you guidance with. The value in this chapter comes from its recommendations on how you can improve Windows performance by more than three-fold. In this chapter, you learn how to:

- Prepare your hard disk before installation

- Select printers and other options during installation

- Manually modify your AUTOEXEC.BAT and CONFIG.SYS files to improve performance if you are using a version of DOS prior to DOS 6

- Use MemMaker in DOS 6 or greater to optimize your computer's memory by modifying the AUTOEXEC.BAT and CONFIG.SYS files

- Use DoubleSpace in DOS 6 or greater to double your hard disk size without losing Windows performance or Windows virtual memory

- Manage your hard disk on a continuing basis to keep Windows and applications running at peak performance

Installing Windows 3.1

The Windows Setup program guides you through installing Windows. If you are unfamiliar with computers, you should use Express Setup. This application determines your hardware and software and makes appropriate selections for you. You are asked which type of printer your computer uses and where the printer is connected.

If you are familiar with computers and want to install only parts of Windows or make changes during installation, you should use Custom Setup. Custom Setup enables you to add printers and select hardware that may be different than what is detected by the Setup program. If your hard disk is low on available storage, you may want to use Custom Setup to install parts of Windows rather than the full Windows and all accessories. You can run Setup at any time to add Windows features or accessories that you did not install initially.

If you already have Windows 3.0 installed, you should install Windows 3.1 over the existing version of Windows. This type of installation preserves your current settings, application groups, and custom drivers. Drivers for existing printers are upgraded. Installation should take no more than 20 to 30 minutes.

Before You Install Windows

For Windows to operate correctly, Microsoft recommends that your hardware and software meet the following requirements:

- IBM Personal System/2, Personal Computer AT, COMPAQ Deskpro 286, or a compatible computer that uses an 80286, 80386, 80386SX, 80486, or Pentium processor

- 1M (megabyte) or more of memory on an 80286-based PC or 2M or more on an 80386 or 80468. (Memory above 640K should be configured as extended memory. Refer to your hardware installation manual for this information.)

- VGA graphics adapter cards supported by Windows

■ A hard disk with 5M to 10M of available storage

■ At least one 1.2M or 1.44M floppy disk drive

■ MS-DOS 3.1 or higher

These recommendations from Microsoft should be considered the minimum requirements to get Windows to run. More realistic recommendations for doing productive work, however, are as follows.

■ A 25MHz 80386 processor at a minimum. Newer applications such as Excel 5, Access 2, and Word 6 for Windows may require medium-performance 80486 computers for good performance. (It's just not cost-effective anymore to buy an 80386 computer.)

■ 8M or more of memory if you are going to run two or more applications (that's one reason you got Windows, right?)

■ 30M or more of hard disk space. Windows may take as much as ten, but you should also have an additional 10M for temporary Windows files and a permanent swap file of 1 to 10M. The more storage you can allocate to a permanent swap file the better your performance will be. At approximately 10M, the marginal performance improvement from a permanent swap file begins to decrease.

▶ "Running Windows 3.1 with DOS 6," p. 841

■ MS-DOS 6 or higher. MS-DOS 6 gives you additional tools you can use from within Windows such as Anti-Virus, Backup, and Undelete. MS-DOS 6 also includes MemMaker, a utility that automatically analyzes your hardware and software and creates the optimal AUTOEXEC.BAT and CONFIG.SYS files so that your computer uses memory most efficiently. Doing the same job manually is very technical and very error prone. MS-DOS 6 also includes disk compression software that can double your hard disk space at only a 5 to 10% speed degradation.

To run multimedia applications in Windows, you need a Multimedia Personal Computer (MPC) or an MPC upgrade kit to upgrade your existing computer.

Optional equipment supported by Windows includes the following:

■ One or more printers or plotters supported by Windows

■ A mouse (highly recommended)

■ Pen computer systems (add-in software available with pen system)

VI

Installing Windows

▶ "Using Windows for Workgroups 3.11," p. 857

■ A Hayes, MultiTech, or TrailBlazer (or compatible) modem for communications using Terminal

■ Major networks, such as Novell NetWare, 3Com, LANtastic, VINES and LAN Manager. If you plan to run Windows with a network you should use Windows for Workgroups 3.11 or higher. That version of Windows is designed to install and work better with networks.

Windows 3.1 can run in two different modes: standard mode and 386 Enhanced mode. Standard mode is used on all 80286 computers and 80386 computers with 2M of memory or less. 386 Enhanced mode is used on 80386 computers with more than 2M of memory. Standard mode enables you to switch among multiple applications, but DOS applications that are not *active* (full screen) do not run. These applications are suspended until they are activated again. 386 Enhanced mode enables you to run multiple applications, and DOS applications that are in *background* (in a window behind) can continue to run. Both modes enable Windows applications to run. The computer and minimum memory requirements for these modes are as follows:

	Standard Mode	**386 Enhanced Mode**
Processor	80286 or higher	80386 or higher
Memory	1M (640K conventional and 256K extended)	2M (640K conventional and 1024K extended)
Storage	5M to 9M hard disk	5M to 10.5M hard disk

When you install Windows, the Setup application checks to see what equipment you have installed and tries to determine the equipment's manufacturer and type. Windows is usually correct, but if you want to confirm the list, use Custom Setup so that you can review the hardware list. To speed the installation process, you may want to make a list of the following information before you install Windows:

■ The drive and directory name that you want to contain Windows.

■ Manufacturer and model number of your computer. If you cannot determine your exact computer model and your computer has an MCA bus, choose an equivalent IBM PS/2 model. If your computer has an EISA bus, choose an equivalent COMPAQ model. Most computers have an EISA bus.

■ Type of display adapter. Most computers have VGA or SuperVGA adapters.

■ Manufacturer and model of your printer.

■ Printer port(s) that your printer(s) is (are) connected to. Most printers connect to the parallel (LPT1 or LPT2) ports. Some older laser printers use a serial port (COM1 or COM2).

■ Communication information if you are using a serial printer connected to a COM port or if you connect your computer to a phone line with a modem. Include baud rate, number of bits, stop bits, and parity. Find this information in your printer or modem manual, from your dealer, or from the manufacturer.

■ Mouse manufacturer and type (if you have a mouse).

■ Type of keyboard.

■ Make and model of multimedia adapters (if you have multimedia capability).

■ Type and version of the network you are on (if you are connected to one). Your system administrator can help you with this information.

If you are uncertain of the manufacturer or type of equipment you use, check your manuals or sales receipts or call your dealer or corporate personal computer support line.

Before you install Windows, you need to make sure that you have 5M to 10M of storage available on the hard disk on which you are installing Windows. Use the DIR command to find the available storage. You can install Windows on any hard drive; Windows does not have to be installed on drive C.

Note

Windows runs and switches between applications faster if you prepare your hard disk properly before installing Windows. Because Windows frequently reads and writes information to disk as it operates, the information on your disk needs to be stored as compactly as possible without wasting space. A disk defragmenting or disk optimization application can rearrange files on disk to increase your hard disk performance.

Preparing Your System

After you have made a list of your equipment, you are ready to install Windows. If you are unfamiliar with computers, you should use the Express Setup. If you are familiar with computers or need to customize the installation, use the Custom Setup.

Complete the Paperwork

Before you install Windows, you may want to prepare for the installation by completing the following optional steps:

1. Protect your original disks from change. On 1.44M (3 1/2-inch) disks, slide open the write-protect tab (a square sliding button). On 1.2M (5 1/4-inch) disks, put a write-protect tab (an adhesive patch) over the square notch on the disk's edge. Copy the original disks onto a set of backup disks and store the originals at a separate site.

2. Complete the registration forms and mail them back to Microsoft while you are waiting for following portions of the installation to complete. Microsoft uses the registrations to send you special offers on related software, and newsletters containing tips and informing you when updates to Windows are available. You may not get discount pricing on upgrades unless you are registered.

Tuning Your Hard Disk Before Installation

As Windows runs it reads sections of its code from disk. This means that a fast hard disk can speed up how fast Windows and its applications run. It also means that taking the time to maintain a clean, well organized hard disk pays you back with higher performance. Before you install Windows or any Windows application you should do the following maintenance to your hard disk.

Your first cleanup job is to remove old applications and data files that you no longer need. The more space and larger contiguous space you have on your hard disk, the more it helps Windows. If you have previously run a version of Windows on the computer, look for a TEMP directory located off the root directory or underneath Windows. The \TEMP directory contains temporary files that can be deleted so long as Windows is not running when you delete them.

Your second cleanup job is to remove lost clusters from your hard disk. Lost clusters occur when programs are interrupted when they are working with files on disk. This may happen when power is lost while an application is running, an application may fail and the computer must be restarted, the disk has a hardware problem, or the application is poorly written and writes incorrect files to disk. Lost clusters are like links of a broken chain that have been left laying scattered across the hard disk. One section of the chain does not know where other sections are located. Without being able to relink the section the chain remains unusable. In the case of a file, the sections take up disk space, but their data is not accessible to the application. DOS comes with a utility to remove lost clusters from your hard disk. To use it, follow these steps:

1. Start your computer and exit any applications and version of Windows. Return to the DOS prompt which usually looks like the following:

   ```
   C:\>
   ```

2. Type the command **CHKDSK /F** and press Enter.

   This command runs the check disk command. With the /f switch it finds and reattaches fragmented files.

3. If you have fragmented files DOS displays a message similar to the following:

   ```
   6 lost allocation units found in 2 chains.
   Convert lost chains to files (Y/N)?
   ```

4. Press **Y** and press Enter.

DOS reconnects the clusters and stores them in the root directory. When it is done, the screen displays statistics about the disk such as how large it is, how many directories, how many files, and so forth.

Rejoined clusters are stored in the root directory (usually C:\) with a file-name pattern such as the following, in which #### is a number:

```
FILE####.CHK
```

Use the ERASE command to delete these unnecessary files from your hard disk. Use a wild card such as the following to erase all the files found by check disk:

```
ERASE FILE*.CHK
```

VI

Caution
Do not run chkdsk /f while Windows is running—it may damage Windows and may destroy the data of any open application.

The third task you must do is to defragment your hard disk. Defragmenting produces a hard disk that has larger blocks of available space. This is not normally the case. When DOS stores a file on disk it looks for an available space and stores what it can in that location. If the file can't all fit in a single location on disk, as much of the file as can fit is written in the space. A pointer,

Installing Windows

an address, is also written that gives a forward reference to the next blank space where more of the file is written. Some files may be divided into hundreds of small sections that are scattered all over the disk. Reading such a file takes considerably more time than reading a file that is in one contiguous chunk. When you defragment your hard disk a utility aligns all the chunks of a file so they are all adjacent. This makes all the files faster to read and leaves larger chunks of unused hard disk where new files can be stored.

If you are using DOS 6 on your computer a defragmenting utility comes with it. Some third party utilities such as Norton Desktop also include a *defrag* utility. If you have DOS 6 you can defragment your hard disk by following these steps.

1. Start your computer and exit any applications and version of Windows. Return to the DOS prompt.

2. Type the command **DEFRAG** and press Enter.

   This command runs the defrag disk command. If your hard disk has MS-DOS 6 DoubleSpace, the command automatically runs the DoubleSpace defragmenting utility.

3. The program displays a list of the hard drives on your computer. Use the arrow keys to select the drive where you want to install Windows. Press Enter or choose OK.

4. After analyzing your hard disk the defrag program makes a recommendation. Use the arrow keys to select (the default) or deselect the recommendation, and then press Enter.

   Defragmenting a large, badly fragmented hard disk may take considerable time, stretching into hours. Defragmenting a well maintained hard disk may take only a few minutes. If you are defragmenting a DoubleSpace disk the time may also be lengthy.

The percentage of defragmenting completed appears on-screen. When defragmenting is complete a message is posted on-screen.

Protecting Your Computer During Windows Installation

Windows installation is normally a very easy and straightforward process, but there are a few precautions that you should take. Windows may, for example, write an old SMARTDrive file over a newer SMARTDrive file. Or, if you have an unusual system with unique drivers, hardware that the installation program cannot recognize, unusual video, or an unrecognizable BIOS, the Windows installation may fail, leaving you with a computer that won't start.

If you are installing a Windows upgrade over an existing version of Windows, you should use File Manager in your current version of Windows to copy onto a floppy disk the files WIN.INI, SYSTEM.INI, files that end with .GRP, and any application files that end with .INI. If you are unable to get the upgrade version of Windows working, you can reinstall your original version, copy these INI files back, and retain your custom settings and Program Manager groups.

DOS and Windows both use a memory manager called SMARTDrive. If you install a newer version of DOS and then install an older version of Windows, your computer may be left using an old version of SMARTDrive. This is easy to prevent. At the DOS prompt, type the following and then press Enter:

C:\AUTOEXEC.BAT

Look for a line containing the file name SMARTDRV.EXE. Notice the directory indicated for the file.

Switch to that directory with a command such as the following:

```
CD \DOS
```

Type **DIR** to see the data of the SMARTDrive file. Write down this date. After you install Windows recheck the AUTOEXEC.BAT file to see if a SMARTDRV.EXE file in the C:\WINDOWS directory is being used. Check the date on this SMARTDRV.EXE file. If the SMARTDrive file in the DOS directory is more recent, edit the AUTOEXEC.BAT file so the directory for the more recent SMARTDRV.EXE is used. You can use the Windows Notepad application to edit and save the AUTOEXEC.BAT file.

To ensure that you are not left with a computer that doesn't start, make backup copies of your AUTOEXEC.BAT and CONFIG.SYS files to a *bootable* floppy disk. This disk can be used to start and repair your computer.

To create a bootable floppy disk with these backup files, follow these steps,

1. Format a disk using the following command:

   ```
   FORMAT A: /S
   ```

   This command creates a disk that can start the computer if the disk is in drive A when the power is turned on.

2. Copy the AUTOEXEC.BAT and CONFIG.SYS files onto the disk. These files are in the root directory. Use commands such as the following:

   ```
   COPY C:\AUTOEXEC.BAT A:
   COPY C:\CONFIG.SYS A:
   ```

VI

Installing Windows

If the computer doesn't restart after installing Windows, turn off the power, put this disk in drive A:, and then turn the power back on. The computer should restart. Rather than deleting all the files you have installed you may want to call the Microsoft telephone support line, listed in Chapter 26, for aid in determining the driver or file that is not working correctly. Chapter 27 includes numerous installation trouble-shooting tips.

Installing Windows on a DoubleSpace Disk

Tip

You can tell which version of DOS your computer uses by typing **VER** at the DOS prompt and pressing Enter.

Windows installs and runs well on a disk compressed with DOS 6 DoubleSpace. You must be aware, however, that the Windows swap file and temporary files should not be put on the compressed disk.

If you are going to install Windows on a disk with DoubleSpace you must determine which drive contains the DoubleSpace host drive. This is the drive on which you should put your TEMP directory and the swap files required for 386 Enhanced mode. Most computers that are not on a network use the H drive as the DoubleSpace host drive. (Even if your computer has only a single hard disk, a portion of it may be partioned off to act as a separate drive.)

▶ "Doubling Your Hard Disk with DoubleSpace," p. 842

If your hard disk uses DoubleSpace, you can learn which drive is the host by typing **DBLSPACE** at the DOS prompt and then pressing Enter. Select the drive you want to check and press Enter. Disk statistics appear on-screen. Use the arrow keys to select **S**ize and press Enter. Additional disk statistics appear and show you the uncompressed host drive. In this Change Size window, you can also change the *New free space* on the host drive. The permanent swap file used with 386 Enhanced mode is set during installation. You can reset it from Control Panel at any time.

Preparing Third-Party Memory Managers

If you plan to use a non-Microsoft memory manager such as QEMM386, 386Max, or Blue Max, you should be aware of specific setting require-ments. Many of these are outlined in two files that come with Windows: README.WRI (a Windows Write file) and SETUP.TXT (a text file). Both are included in the Windows 3.1 directory. You should read these files before using a memory manager.

To install Windows without interference from these memory managers, *remark out* the DEVICE= line referring to your memory manager before you install Windows. Remark out lines by opening the CONFIG.SYS file, located in the root directory, with a text editor. Type the word **REM** before the DEVICE= line that loads your memory manager. Save the file back to the same name. Now restart your computer and install Windows. After you read the files in Windows, you can make the adjustments necessary to use your memory manager.

> ### Note
>
> If you have trouble installing Windows due to a terminate-and-stay-resident program, remove the TSR load line from CONFIG.SYS and restart your computer so that the TSR does not load. Then restart the Windows installation.

Preparing Memory Management

If you are installing Windows on a computer that uses DOS 6, you can use the MemMaker utility that comes with DOS 6 to prepare your AUTOEXEC.BAT and CONFIG.SYS files so that they optimize the use of memory. You should run MemMaker before installing Windows so that Windows can make its modifications to a correctly configured AUTOEXEC.BAT and CONFIG.SYS.

Controlling the Setup Options

Express Setup and Custom Setup begin with a DOS segment that uses keyboard controls. The DOS part of the installation process appears in two colors, and characters appear as they do at the DOS prompt (c:\). After the initial software is installed, the Setup program changes to a Windows screen. At that point, you can use normal Windows keystrokes or mouse controls.

At almost any time during the installation, you can get Help by pressing F1, the Help key. This key is the same Help key used in Windows and Windows applications. To exit from a Help window, press the Esc key if you are in a DOS screen. If you are in a Windows screen and the Help window is on top, press Alt, F and then X (Alt, **F**ile, E**x**it).

During the DOS segment of the installation, use the following controls. A status line at the bottom of the screen lists available controls.

Action	Key
Move highlight to select next item	Up/down arrow key
Select an option or move to next screen	Enter
Help from a Setup screen	F1

(continues)

Action	Key
Back up in Help screens	Backspace
Exit the Setup program	F3
Return from Help to Setup	Esc

During the Windows segment of the installation, use the following controls:

Action	Key
Help while in a screen or dialog box	F1
Move between areas in a dialog box	Tab
Select the current item in the dialog box	Space bar
Choose a button (OK, Cancel, etc.)	Click the button
Select a check box or option button	Click the check box until an X appears or click the option button until its center is dark
Scroll through a list and select an item	Click the up or down arrow to the right of the list. Then click an item in the list.

The current item in a dialog box is surrounded by dashed lines. A current button, such as OK or Cancel, has a bold border.

To click something with the mouse, move the mouse until the tip of the mouse pointer, usually an arrow, is over the item. Then gently but quickly press and release the left mouse button.

Starting Windows Setup

To install Windows, complete the following steps:

1. Start your computer. If your computer starts automatically with Windows or an application running, return to a DOS prompt, such as C:\.

2. Put Disk 1 of the Windows disks in a disk drive, and close the door.

3. Type the drive letter, followed by a colon, (for example, **A:**), and press Enter to switch to that disk drive.

4. Type **SETUP,** and press Enter.

5. Read and follow the on-screen directions. Watch the status line at the bottom of the screen to see what keys to press in response to on-screen directions.

You are given two alternatives for installation, Express Setup or Custom Setup. If you are unfamiliar with Windows or with computers, choose Express Setup. The differences between these choices are described in the following two sections.

If a previous version of Windows is detected, you are given the option of upgrading the older version using the same directory or of installing Windows 3.1 in a new directory. Upgrading an older version of Windows preserves Windows settings, updates printer drivers when necessary, and preserves drivers that Windows does not recognize. Approximately 5M of additional free space on the hard disk are needed to upgrade from Windows 3.0 to Windows 3.11.

> **Caution**
>
> If you choose to have Windows 3.1 and Windows 3.0 installed at the same time, ensure that the PATH in the AUTOEXEC.BAT does not list both directories at the same time. Listing both directories causes improper operation and may corrupt system files.

At the beginning of the Windows segment of the installation, you are asked to enter your name and company name. You must enter a name. The name is used to notify anyone who reinstalls the software that Windows has been previously installed. Press Tab to move between the two text boxes. Use the arrow keys, Backspace, or Del to edit what you type. You are given a chance to make corrections.

You are asked to insert additional disks as you complete installation steps. Insert these disks as the Setup program requests, and then follow the on-screen instructions.

> **Note**
>
> If you are installing Windows on a network or installing Windows on your own system, which is connected to a network, you should probably use Windows for Workgroups. You should read Chapters 25 and 26 and check with your network administrator for the best method of installing. The file NETWORKS.WRI contains information in a Windows Write format about installing Windows on a network.

VI

Installing Windows

When you have finished installing Windows, three large buttons appear: **R**eboot, Restart **W**indows, and Return to MS-DOS. The selections you made during setup do not take effect until you restart your computer by rebooting. To choose Reboot, click that button or press R.

Rebooting restarts your computer without turning off the power. Memory is erased, and DOS is reloaded. The AUTOEXEC.BAT and CONFIG.SYS files are reread, which configures your computer with the selections you made during setup. If you chose not to let Windows Setup modify AUTOEXEC.BAT and CONFIG.SYS, Windows may not run correctly even after you reboot. Modify these files as needed.

Installing Windows Using Express Setup

When you begin the Windows setup, you are asked whether you want to do an Express Setup or Custom Setup. The Express Setup uses settings and hardware configuration that the installation application has determined run on your system. These settings and installation configurations can be changed later if necessary (see "Changing the Setup after Installation"). Some of the things that the Express Setup does for you are as follows:

- The AUTOEXEC.BAT and CONFIG.SYS files are automatically modified.

- Windows is installed in C:\WINDOWS unless drive C does not have enough room. In that case, the installation application searches for a drive with enough room. If not enough room is available for a full version of Windows, Express Setup installs a smaller set of Windows and accessory applications.

- If you previously had Windows 3.0 installed, Express Setup reinstalls the same printers. If you did not have Windows 3.0 installed, Express Setup prompts you for which printer and connecting port to use.

- Express Setup searches your hard disk for applications and creates icons and group windows for Windows applications and many DOS applications.

- Express Setup gives you a short tutorial on using a mouse and Windows.

Tip
In most cases, you should use Express Setup. If Express Setup does not work correctly, you can install or reinstall other items or features of Windows at a later time by rerunning Setup.

Setup asks you to select the printers you use and which ports they are connected to. You are given the option of going through a mouse and Windows operations tutorial.

Installing Windows Using Custom Setup

After Setup starts, you have the option of doing a Custom Setup. The Custom Setup enables you to select specifics of how Windows is installed. You can see or select changes as they are made. You should use Custom Setup if you are familiar with computers and want to cross-check the installation process or select different hardware configurations than those automatically selected. Some of the steps that Custom Setup executes are as follows:

■ Shows you a list of the hardware detected. You can accept or change the detected hardware, which is useful if the type of mouse or video adapter has been incorrectly detected.

■ Shows you the changes Custom Setup makes to AUTOEXEC.BAT and CONFIG.SYS and enables you to edit the changes. You have the option of accepting the modifications, rejecting the modifications, or making manual changes.

■ Enables you to select the drive and directory name where Windows will be installed

■ Enables you to select the Windows components (such as screen savers, wallpaper, and sounds) and accessory applications to be installed

■ Gives you full control over installing printers

■ Enables you to select which Windows and DOS applications are set up with icons and windows

■ Gives you the opportunity to take a short tutorial on the mouse and Windows

In Custom Setup, you need to make choices from dialog boxes in the Windows screens. If you are familiar with Windows operations, use normal Windows selection techniques with the keyboard or mouse. For example, to select any item in a dialog box, press and hold down Alt; then press the underlined letter in the item you want to select. Release both keys. If you are selecting a group of option (round) buttons, you can move among them by pressing the arrow keys after the group has been selected. The button with the dark center is selected.

To edit text in a name or text box, hold down the Alt key as you press the underlined letter to select that text box. A flashing cursor, the insertion point, appears in the box. Type the text. To edit existing text, move the insertion point with the left- or right-arrow keys and then use the Del key to delete characters to the right, use the Backspace key to delete characters to the left, or type new characters at the insertion point.

During installation, you are asked where you want to install Windows. The default choice is as follows:

```
C:\WINDOWS
```

You can edit this path name so that Windows is installed on a different hard drive or directory. To edit, press the arrow keys to move from character to character, the Del (Delete) key to delete to the right, the Backspace key to delete to the left, and the character keys on the main keyboard to type characters.

Windows also asks whether it can make changes to the AUTOEXEC.BAT and CONFIG.SYS files. You are given three choices for these files:

- You can accept all changes. Copies of the old files are saved to backup files.

- You can modify changes. A dialog box shows you the original and proposed files. Use the Tab key to move into the top list and edit the proposed changes. Press the arrow keys to move around in the text and press Backspace or Delete to remove text. Type new text at the insertion point.

- You can reject all changes.

◄ "Adding and Configuring Printers," p. 284

You are given a chance to install printer and plotter drivers, which tell Windows how to communicate with a printer or plotter. You do not have to install printer or plotter drivers at this point, although it is a convenient time. You can install drivers later, using Control Panel.

Troubleshooting

◄ "Adding and Configuring Printers," p. 284

My printer is not one of the printers displayed during installation.

A temporary solution is to check your printers manual and see if your printer has any emulation modes. An emulation mode makes a printer behave like a printer from a different manufacturer or of a different model. See if you can switch your printer into an emulation mode and then use the Windows printer driver for that emulated printer. Another alternative is to select a printer driver for the previous model of the printer from the same manufacturer. The final, and least acceptable solution, is to use

► "Finding Help, Support, and Resources," p. 1,008

the Generic/Text Only printer driver. This prints alphanumeric characters to any printer, but you cannot print with formatting, styles, or graphics.

The long-term solution is to find the correct printer driver for your printer. Call the printer manufacturer to see how to obtain a driver for Windows 3.1. Nearly all printers manufactured in the last few years have Windows drivers. You can also check the Microsoft Download service, MSDN, and download printer drivers over the telephone directly from Microsoft. You can use Windows Terminal and its default settings to download drivers. Once you receive the appropriate printer driver you can add it to Windows.

Select the names that match your equipment and choose **I**nstall. Choose **C**onnect to connect your printer to the port where it is physically attached. Choose **S**etup to change the paper orientation (vertical or horizontal printing), paper size, number of copies, font cartridges, and so on. Choose S**e**t as Default Printer if you want to make a printer the default. These settings can be changed later from an application's printer setup command or from Control Panel. Don't forget to use the Help information available by pressing F1 (Help).

Caution

Each printer has different setup options, and if your printer includes a memory option, be sure to specify how much memory your printer has. (The HP Laserjet III, for example, has a memory option.) If Windows does not know how much memory is available, it may display an erroneous message stating that it does not have enough memory to print.

◀ "Customizing Groups," p. 95

When you finish installing printers, Windows asks whether you want it to search your hard disk for Windows and DOS applications. If you choose this option, Windows makes a list of all applications on your hard disk. You are given an opportunity to put the names of these applications into a special group window. Each application is represented by a small picture. These pictures, called *icons*, make starting an application easy. You probably should select the applications you recognize and have them put into a group. You can add or remove applications in a group window at any time after Windows is installed.

VI

Installing Windows

Learning from the Setup Files

◄ "Using
Windows
Write," p. 335

At the end of the Windows installation, you are given an opportunity to read files that Setup copied into the WINDOWS directory. You can read the files from the installation application when it asks you to, or you can complete the installation of Windows and read the files with Write, a small word processor that comes with Windows. The names of the files are as follows:

Tip

Learn additional installation and troubleshooting tips by using Windows Write to read the WRI files or read-me files.

README.WRI	Current updates to the user manual
PRINTERS.WRI and fonts	Additional information about configuring printers
NETWORKS.WRI	Information about installing Windows on networks
SYSINI.WRI	Information about modifying the SYSTEM.INI file (described in Chapter 24, "Installing and Optimizing Windows")
WININI.WRI	Information about modifying the WIN.INI file (described in Chapter 24, "Installing and Optimizing Windows")

Installing Unlisted Printers

If you cannot locate a printer driver from your printer's manufacturer, Windows offers a temporary solution. One of the choices for a printer driver is Generic/Text Only. Using the Generic/Text Only printer driver enables you to print text and numbers on most printers. However, you cannot print with special capabilities, such as underline, bold, or graphics.

Check with the Microsoft telephone support line listed in Chapter 2 and your printer manufacturer for a printer driver for your printer or for a compatible driver. Windows has hundreds of printer drivers available. Microsoft maintains a Windows Driver Library (WDL) containing device drivers supported by Windows 3.1. You can obtain a copy of this library through Microsoft forums on CompuServe, GEnie, ON-Line, or other public bulletin boards. You also can receive a driver by calling Microsoft. Refer to Chapter 2 or 27 for their phone numbers.

When you receive a printer driver to match your equipment, you can install the driver without reinstalling Windows. Use Control Panel to add the new printer driver.

Running Windows After Installation

► "Troubleshooting
Windows,"
p. 979

After you install Windows and reboot, you can start Windows from the DOS prompt, such as c:>, by typing win and pressing Enter. Windows starts in the most efficient mode for your processor and memory configuration.

If the screen goes blank when you start Windows, you may have installed Windows with an incorrect graphics adapter. To fix this problem, find out what kind of graphics adapter you have (you may need to call the manufacturer) and repeat the installation. Turn off and restart your computer and repeat the installation process, specifying a different graphics adapter.

Changing the Setup after Installation

After Windows is operating correctly, you can make modifications to the way Windows is installed without reinstalling the entire Windows application. You may want to change the installation, for example, if you have a portable computer running Windows. When you are on the road, you need to use the plasma or LCD screen in the portable, but when you are at the office, you want to use a high-resolution color monitor. Instead of reinstalling Windows to get the new video driver, you can use the Windows Setup program to switch between the drivers you use. Windows Setup also is useful when you buy and attach a new keyboard or mouse or when you attach your computer to a network.

The Windows Setup program is located in the Main group window of Program Manager. To change the setup of the display, keyboard, mouse, or network after Windows is installed, follow these steps:

1. Activate Program Manager, and then activate the Main group window.

2. Choose the Windows Setup icon.

3. From the Windows Setup dialog box, choose the **O**ptions menu and select the **C**hange System Settings command.

   From the Change System Settings dialog box, you can change installation settings without reinstalling Windows.

4. Select the pull-down list of the setting you want to change by clicking the related down-arrow icon. You also can press Alt+*letter* to select the list and then press the down-arrow key to pull the list down.

5. Select from the pull-down list the type of device you want installed by clicking it or by pressing the up- or down-arrow keys.

6. Choose OK or press Enter.

7. If a special driver is required, you may be asked to insert one of the original Windows disks or a disk sent by the manufacturer of your display, keyboard, mouse, or network.

Tip
If you have any difficulty running Windows, try reading through the text file SETUP.TXT or the Windows Write file README.WRI, located in the Windows 3.1 directory.

VI

Installing Windows

8. After the new setup has been created, you must restart Windows for the changes to take effect. You are given the choice of restarting Windows or returning to DOS. If you need to change hardware—such as attaching a new keyboard or mouse or connecting a new display—return to DOS, make the new connection, and then restart Windows.

If Windows or a Windows application does not behave correctly after changing the installation, check the Windows Setup dialog box to see whether you have the correct settings. Return to the original settings if necessary or reinstall Windows if appropriate.

Enhancing Windows Performance

Tips and tricks are available for improving the performance of Windows throughout this book, but the factors that have the greatest effect can be summarized as follows:

- How you use Windows

- Hardware capability (speed of CPU, video adapter, and hard disk)

- Memory optimization

- Hard disk performance

In far too many cases, Windows users begin trying to increase performance by making adjustments in the WIN.INI and SYSTEM.INI files that yield only small improvements in performance. If you want large improvements, start with changes that make the biggest improvements and then work down to the small fine-tuning.

Before you begin optimizing a computer for Windows, check to make sure that you don't have operating habits that drain performance, such as keeping many applications loaded that you aren't using. Honestly evaluate the hardware and upgrade the critical areas, such as meeting a minimal memory limit of 4M for multiple applications and realizing that 8M yields far faster performance. Next, optimize the performance of the hardware by improving the efficiency of the memory and hard disk. This is described at the beginning of this chapter on how to prepare your computer before installing Windows. Finally, improve Windows efficiency by conserving resources and making fine adjustments to Windows internal operating methods.

Working Efficiently in Windows

You can follow some common guidelines that help you operate Windows and applications faster and more efficiently. These guidelines don't require any technical adjustments; they only require that you adjust the way you work.

- When you run Windows, consider the hardware's capabilities. If you operate a 486 machine with 16M of memory, you can probably run as many applications as you want without worrying about performance. But if you have an 80386 machine with two or three megabytes of RAM, expect performance to deteriorate if you try to run more than one large application at the same time.

- Limit the number of loaded or running applications. Even idle applications use computer resources, slowing the performance of the application you are currently using. Weigh the time an application takes to open against the performance degradation you experience.

- Operate DOS applications full-screen rather than in a window. Use windowed DOS applications only when you copy and paste between these applications.

- Turn off processing for DOS applications that reside in the background and that don't need to use processor time. Chapter 22 describes how to improve DOS application performance.

- Use printer fonts and Windows screen fonts for normal work that doesn't demand special sizes or styles. Font scalers, such as Adobe Type Manager and TrueType, give you extra capabilities but are slower than Windows screen fonts.

- Limit the display of graphic features in Windows applications. Many Windows applications come with useful graphical features, such as icon bars or special page display options. Although convenient, these features usually degrade the application's performance. If performance is sluggish and the Windows application has a draft mode, use draft mode. If you don't need the graphical features, try turning off these features—performance probably will improve.

- Limit the number of open windows on the desktop. These windows occupy the computer's memory and your memory. Too many document windows slow performance and can confuse you. In some applications, such as word processors, document length can affect performance, so having multiple short documents rather than one long document is a good idea.

VI

Installing Windows

Providing a Good Environment for Windows

The first step in optimizing the system is to verify that the hardware is config-ured properly and that the system environment is set up to work smoothly with Windows.

Before you install or optimize Windows, be sure that the hardware and operating system are working correctly. Checking these parts of the system may seem obvious, but you can easily spend hours investigating a *problem* in Windows, only to find that the problem is part of the basic computer configuration.

Protect What You Have When You Install Windows

One step you can take prior to changing the system configuration or install-ing a new application is to prepare a diskette that you can use to boot the system. If the hard disk's AUTOEXEC.BAT or CONFIG.SYS files are incorrectly changed, you can restart the computer from the disk. This disk also can be used to copy back the original AUTOEXEC.BAT and CONFIG.SYS files.

Another disk that contains files for the minimum system configuration is an essential tool for troubleshooting. In a minimum configuration, CONFIG.SYS and AUTOEXEC.BAT files are limited to the command lines needed to run the computer, and nothing else. When you experience a problem with Win-dows, or any other application, you can use this disk to start Windows in as clean a configuration as possible. Then, if you can't reproduce the error, you can assume the error may have occurred because of an incorrect line in one of these files. (If you recently installed new application software and Win-dows suddenly doesn't work, the culprit probably is the new application, which incorrectly modified the CONFIG.SYS or AUTOEXEC.BAT.)

Install the Correct Version of DOS

To ensure that Windows runs smoothly on your computer, verify that the operating system (DOS) is installed and configured properly. You find out which version of DOS is installed by typing VER after the DOS prompt and pressing Enter.

Get MS-DOS 6. Upgrading to MS-DOS 6 is worth the low cost, even if you run only a few DOS applications. DOS 6 enables you to configure the system to maximize the memory available for DOS sessions, whether or not you run applications in Windows. Written to work well with Windows, MS-DOS 6 offers you the best opportunity for compatibility and includes some useful new utilities.

Disable Shadow RAM

Some systems have the capability of loading ROM (Read-Only Memory) into RAM to improve performance. RAM is faster than ROM, so this practice results in increased performance on the system. Unfortunately, this practice also consumes conventional memory and may be incompatible on some hardware with Windows. If you run many DOS applications and are tight on conventional memory, run the computer's setup software and disable Shadow RAM before you install or run Windows. Your computer's setup software or procedures should be described in the manuals that come with your computer.

Storing TEMP Files in a Special Directory

Windows creates temporary files when running. These files act as a temporary working space for applications and windows. (These temporary files are different from the permanent swap files used by 386 Enhanced mode or the DOS swap files.)

From a housekeeping standpoint, specifying where Windows stores temporary files is a good idea. If the computer ever loses power or an application fails and the old temporary files aren't cleaned up by default, you will know where to look for the files so that you can erase them. These temporary files begin with ~ and have the file extension TMP.

Caution

Never erase temporary files while Windows is running. Always exit Windows before erasing temporary files.

A simple line in the AUTOEXEC.BAT file enables you to set a TEMP variable that specifies where on the hard disk to place temporary files. During setup, Windows inserts this statement for you. If Windows is on drive C, for example, the following line is inserted:

```
SET TEMP=C:\WINDOWS\TEMP
```

You can keep this setting, or you can change the setting by editing the AUTOEXEC.BAT with the Notepad. If you edit the SET TEMP line, you must create the directory named by SET TEMP. Use the MD command in DOS or File Manager to create this directory.

When choosing a directory for temporary files, keep the following guidelines in mind:

VI

■ Pick the fastest drive available.

■ Set TEMP to a directory (not the root directory). Temp files are easiest to manage if they are placed in a TEMP directory under the root, not under Windows.

■ Make sure that 2M to 4M of free disk space is available for the temporary files on the selected drive.

■ Do not put the TEMP file directory on a disk compressed by DoubleSpace (DOS 6) or a third-party disk compression program.

Putting temporary files on a compressed disk slows down Windows operation because each time a temporary file is read or written it must be compressed or decompressed. Put the TEMP directory on the host drive, usually the H drive. The host drive is the decompressed drive that is created to work with your compressed drive. If your computer already has a TEMP directory on its compressed drive you can easily fix it by creating a directory on the host drive and changing the AUTOEXEC.BAT file. Use File Manager to create a TEMP file on the host drive. Then open the AUTOEXEC.BAT file in Windows Notepad. Find the line that looks like the following:

```
SET TEMP=C:\TEMP
```

Change it to the following:

```
SET TEMP=H:\TEMP
```

Now save the AUTOEXEC.BAT to the root directory. The next time you restart your computer the new TEMP directory takes effect. Once you have exited Windows, you can switch to the old TEMP directory and delete all the temporary files it contains.

Use the Most Recent Versions of the Windows Drivers

Be sure that you update the AUTOEXEC.BAT and CONFIG.SYS files to include only the latest versions of Windows memory and device drivers. Improvements were made to most of the drivers since Windows 3.0 was introduced, and you cannot substitute an old driver for a new one just because both drivers use the same name. If you install Windows 3.1 over the top of a previous version of Windows, the drivers are automatically updated.

EMM386.SYS and SMARTDRV.SYS, used in previous versions of Windows, were replaced with EMM386.EXE and SMARTDRV.EXE. Usually, you should use the latest version of a Windows driver, regardless of whether the source is a DOS upgrade or a new release of Windows. If you have two copies of the same driver, use the driver that displays the most recent creation date and delete the older driver from the system.

Note

Many hardware manufacturers introduced upgrades to Windows device drivers. Check with the manufacturer of the equipment to be sure that you have the most recent driver.

You can download new drivers directly from the Microsoft Download by dialing (206) 936-6735. The modem settings to connect to this bulletin board are,

Variable	Setting
Baud rates	1200, 2400, 9600
Data Bits	8
Stop Bits	1
Parity	None

Separate Windows and Windows Applications on the Disk

In the past, installation guides for some Windows applications recommended that you install application files in the Windows directory. Microsoft Excel is a good example. The problem with this advice is that no easy way exists to tell which files belong to the application and which files belong to Windows. This kind of installation makes upgrading Windows, or the application, difficult. Most applications enable you to upgrade over an older version in the same directory, but this procedure requires that you trust the installation application to remove old files. Unfortunately, application upgrades can neglect to delete old application files from the system, which subsequently can cause compatibility problems.

You can save work by installing each Windows application in a separate directory on the hard disk. Be sure that you also store data and applications in separate directories, which prevents having to cull the data from the application directory before you delete an outdated application from the disk.

Protect Your Initialization Files

Windows uses two initialization files to store information needed to run Windows on a computer. WIN.INI contains settings that relate to applications and to your preferences for the Windows environment. SYSTEM.INI contains information related to system hardware. In the past, Windows applications made use of WIN.INI to store different types of information, from preferences for screen display to default settings for fonts. Increasingly, Windows applications are being written to make use of their own INI files instead of cluttering the WIN.INI file.

Before upgrading Windows or a Windows application, make copies of the WIN.INI and SYSTEM.INI files to disk or another directory. Sometimes an installation application adds lines to the WIN.INI file without deleting lines its earlier version left behind. Unless you plan to run both versions of an application, you probably don't want both sections in the WIN.INI file. Keeping a copy of the WIN.INI prior to the upgrade allows you to recognize which sections to remove. In addition, it is sometimes helpful to know just what sections of the INI file an application affects. If you later decide to remove the application, you can edit the INI file to remove unnecessary commands.

Using Memory Efficiently

The performance of Windows is strongly influenced by the way you configure the computer's memory. In many ways, Windows memory management is a balancing act—each time you make use of a disk enhancer, such as SMARTDrive or a RAM disk, you must weigh the enhanced performance against the cost of the memory used. The more memory you have available for applications to use, the more applications you can run in Windows. On the other hand, dedicating portions of the memory to performance enhancement, thereby excluding them from use by applications, makes Windows sessions faster. There is really no single solution.

Memory management techniques are worth exploring, whether the supply of system memory is minimal (4M) or plentiful (8M or more). The less memory available, the greater the need to manage memory wisely. On the other hand, those with the luxury of plentiful extended memory have more options available for optimizing Windows. In either case, it is important to understand a bit about the memory on the system and how Windows uses it in each of its two operating modes. This section covers the basic concepts of memory, its use by Windows, and some of the tools for managing memory.

Understanding Memory

Figure 24.1 illustrates the areas of Random-Access Memory (RAM) in a 286, 386, or 486 machine.

The first 640 Kilobytes (K) of memory is known as *conventional memory*. If you run DOS applications, this memory may be the computer's most precious resource. Conventional memory is the original location of the DOS operating system, hardware device drivers, and other system software. Before the advent of 286 computers, conventional memory also was the only memory available to applications. DOS developers had to write applications that fit in whatever conventional memory remained after DOS and other system software was loaded. Most DOS applications still maintain compatibility with older computers by running within the confines of conventional memory.

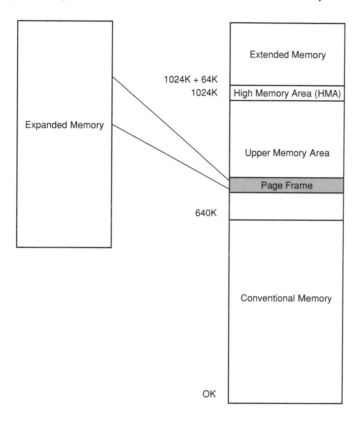

Fig. 24.1
Computer memory architecture.

The Upper Memory Area (UMA) is the memory between 640K and 1024K, which traditionally is reserved for use by accessory cards (such as a video adapter), Read-Only Memory (ROM), and the ROM BIOS. In a 286 computer, this area of memory still is largely unavailable to applications. Using the features of DOS 5 or other memory management software on an 80386 or 80486 processor, your computer can use this part of memory for device drivers and memory-resident applications. (See the section "Configuring Memory under DOS 5.0" later in this chapter.)

◀ "Creating and Using PIFs," p. 741

Expanded memory (or EMS memory) was designed to get around the 640K memory limit on DOS applications. EMS memory comes as an add-in board

VI

Installing Windows

you install in the computer, and an Expanded Memory Manager (EMM) enables applications to use the board. Only applications written to work with an EMM can take advantage of expanded memory. EMS memory overcame the problems of being unable to exceed the 1024K memory barrier by redirecting the addresses within the area shown in figure 25.1 as the Page Frame. The EMM works by mapping small chunks of memory in and out of a sliver of memory in the UMA. These portions of memory are known as *pages,* and the section of UMA is a *page frame.* The application looks at the memory area in the UMA shown as the Page Frame, but the application actually sees an area in the expanded memory. For years, expanded memory was the only additional memory available to application developers and, as a result, a variety of popular DOS applications require expanded memory to work. Because of the technical limits inherent in EMS, Windows doesn't use expanded memory, but you still can run DOS applications that require expanded memory. (See Chapter 22, "Running, Installing, and Configuring DOS Applications," to learn how to configure DOS applications to use expanded memory.)

Extended Memory (XMS memory) is the area of memory above 1024K on 286, 386, and 486 computers. Extended memory mounts on the system board of the computer or on special add-in boards you install. Unlike expanded memory, extended memory doesn't need to be mapped in and out of the UMA to work. This advantage makes applications faster and easier for the programmers to write. XMS memory does require the use of an extended memory manager to coordinate its use by multiple applications. Windows doesn't differentiate between conventional memory and extended memory—it combines conventional and extended memory into a single source of memory that it can access directly when this memory is needed.

The *High Memory Area* (HMA) is the first 64K of extended memory above 1024K. If you have DOS 5.0, you load most of DOS in HMA, freeing an additional 45K of conventional memory for DOS applications. (The remaining portion of HMA is used for system resources.)

By using a special area of the hard disk as an extension of RAM, *virtual memory* is a mechanism for increasing the amount of memory available to applications. Using virtual memory, you may be able to run more applications at the same time than is normally possible when using the physical memory on the system.

Virtual memory is available in Windows 386 Enhanced mode on 386 or 486 machines. When physical memory is tight, Windows begins to move 4K *pages* of code and data from memory to the hard disk to make more room in physical memory. Windows uses a *least-recently-used* technique to move pages of memory to the disk, selecting first the pages of code and data not recently accessed by an application. If an application requires a piece of data no longer in physical memory, Windows retrieves the information from disk, paging other information from memory to make room.

To applications running in Windows 386 Enhanced mode, no difference exists between physical memory on the system and virtual memory on the disk. Windows can use up to 64M of memory (16M of physical memory and 48M of virtual memory on the hard disk) with this technique.

The use of virtual memory slows Windows operation. Calculation-intensive applications, such as worksheets, may run significantly slower if virtual memory is used.

Understanding How Windows Uses Memory

A major benefit of Windows is multitasking capability. Although only one application can use the computer processor at a given instant, in Windows, multitasking means that you can run multiple applications at the same time. Windows uses different methods to achieve multitasking in standard and 386 Enhanced modes, primarily because standard mode must work within the confines of the 80286 processor.

Memory Management in Standard Mode

In standard mode, Windows applications are multitasking, but DOS applications are single tasking. This means that multiple Windows applications process information at the same time. A DOS application, however, operates in full-screen mode and monopolizes the processor, requiring all other applications to be suspended while the DOS application is active.

Windows applications can use either conventional or extended memory. DOS applications, however, run only in conventional memory. When you start a DOS application, Windows swaps the current application out of memory and writes an *application swap file* to the disk. If Windows and Windows applications are currently running, these applications are moved together to separate swap files on the disk, leaving behind only the portion of code needed to run the Task Switcher.

DOS applications aren't designed to multitask. Because Windows isn't in memory when a DOS application runs, Windows cannot provide multitasking capabilities. In standard mode, the only portion of Windows that remains in memory after a DOS application loads is the Task Switcher needed for Windows to restore itself. The Task Switcher responds to an Alt+Tab, Alt+Esc, or Ctrl+Esc key combination and swaps the active DOS application to disk to make room for Windows and any active Windows application.

When you press Alt+Esc to switch between DOS applications or to Windows, the active DOS application is moved to a separate application swap file on the disk. Each DOS application has an application swap file. Windows and all open Windows applications share one Windows swap file.

By default, application swap files are stored in the directory identified by the TEMP variable in AUTOEXEC.BAT. Swap files begin with a tilde (~) and have the extension, SWP. You can view the files from File Manager, using the **V**iew By File **T**ype command and then marking the Show Hidden/**S**ystem Files check box.

Caution

Do not delete swap files while Windows is running.

Memory Management in 386 Enhanced Mode

In 386 Enhanced mode, both Windows and DOS applications multitask. Windows uses the special capabilities of the 80386 and 80486 processors to create a virtual machine for each DOS application's exclusive use. The *virtual machine* is a simulation of an 8086 processor and inherits the conventional memory configuration present before you start Windows. In 386 Enhanced mode, Windows and Windows applications are contained in one virtual machine (the system VM), and each DOS application is contained in a separate virtual machine.

Imagine these virtual computers, stored end-to-end in the length of conventional through extended memory. Moreover, each virtual machine uses an image of the original conventional memory for DOS and TSRs loaded before Windows 3.1 starts.

This explains why having a well-configured and uncluttered conventional memory area is important. You duplicate this area for each virtual machine used by a DOS application. Clutter and waste becomes clutter and waste multiplied by the number of DOS applications running. If you optimize the use of this memory, loading drivers in upper memory and moving part of DOS to the HMA, you maximize conventional memory available *to every virtual machine.* If you neglect to clear TSRs and unnecessary applications from the AUTOEXEC.BAT, these applications are loaded in the original conventional memory area, and each virtual machine created includes a copy of the TSR.

Running Windows 3.1 with DOS 6

There are a number of advantages to upgrading your computer to DOS 6. Not only do you get file management utilities that run within Windows, Undelete, Backup, and Anti-Virus, you also get MemMaker and DoubleSpace. MemMaker is a program that analyzes your hardware, AUTOEXEC.BAT, and CONFIG.SYS files and then creates new AUTOEXEC.BAT and CONFIG.SYS files that optimize the use of memory. It does this by moving memory-resident programs and drivers into the upper memory area. The result is more room for Windows and applications in the limited conventional memory. No longer do you have to be a Windows whiz kid. You can just run MemMaker.

The DoubleSpace program compresses a hard disk so that you can get almost twice the amount of storage. Because compression and decompression take time it can degrade Windows performance by 5 to 10%, but this is usually worth it for the disk-space.

If you are installing DOS 6 on a computer that currently runs Windows you will want to remark out the SMARTDRV.EXE line in the AUTOEXEC.BAT file before installing. Use Windows Notepad to type REM at the beginning of the AUTOEXEC.BAT line containing SMARTDRV.EXE, save the file, and restart your computer. DOS 6 installs a new SMARTDrive with new settings. You can remove the old remarked out line if DOS 6 correctly installs.

Optimizing Memory with MemMaker

Before you run MemMaker, you can help it be more efficient by organizing your AUTOEXEC.BAT and CONFIG.SYS files so that the drivers with the largest memory requirements come first in the listings and therefore are loaded into memory first. Delete any drivers or memory-resident programs that are not needed.

After you install DOS 6, you should run MemMaker by typing **MEMMAKER** at the DOS prompt. Do not be in Windows when you run MemMaker. The screens are explanatory, and you can get help by pressing F1.

MemMaker gives you the options of either an Express or Custom setup. In nearly all cases, select the Express setup. You are asked if you use any programs that require expanded memory (EMS). You should select Yes for this option only if you run DOS applications that require EMS.

Tip
Before running MemMaker, quit any applications, but start any hardware or memory-resident programs such as network drivers.

VI

Installing Windows

If you are not sure whether you need EMS, select No to give Windows and its applications more memory. If you later run an application and a warning message states that expanded memory or EMS is not available, you should exit Windows, rerun MemMaker, and select Yes in response to the EMS question.

When you run MemMaker, it restarts your computer twice so that it can check the modified memory configurations. When MemMaker is complete, it displays a table showing you how much memory is available and how much was freed by running MemMaker. If you want to accept the changes, press Enter. If you want to disregard the changes, press Esc.

> **Note**
>
> MemMaker stores your original AUTOEXEC.BAT and CONFIG.SYS files as AUTOEXEC.UMB and CONFIG.UMB. You can restore your original AUTOEXEC.BAT and CONFIG.SYS files by typing the following command at the DOS prompt when Windows is not running:
>
> **MEMMAKER \UNDO**

Doubling Your Hard Disk with DoubleSpace

Tip
You can see if DoubleSpace is installed and which drive is the host by exiting Windows, then typing **DBLSPACE /L** at the DOS prompt, and pressing Enter.

DOS 6 comes with a hard-disk compression program known as DoubleSpace. This program stands between the hard disk and memory and uses mathematical formulas to compress data before it is written onto the disk from memory. Conversely it decompresses data as it reads it from the disk and puts it into memory. The time it takes to compress and decompress data reduces performance by 5 to 10 percent during disk-intensive procedures. In most cases, the doubled disk space is worth it.

> **Troubleshooting**
>
> *After installing DoubleSpace, my computer runs three or four times slower. The Microsoft manual says there should only be a 5 to 10 percent performance decrease due to DoubleSpace.*
>
> DoubleSpace may have removed your permanent swap file. Without a permanent swap file, Windows runs much slower. This happens when the uncompressed host drive created by DoubleSpace does not have enough room for a permanent swap file. To fix this you can exit Windows, rerun DoubleSpace and resize the host drive to allow more room for a permanent swap file. Once the host is resized you can re-create a permanent swap file on the host. This procedure is described in greater detail in this section.

Caution

DoubleSpace uses a RAM resident program, DBLSPACE.BIN, to access drives compressed with DoubleSpace. This takes approximately 40K of memory. If your system is already low on conventional memory, and nothing more can be loaded into high memory, you should not use DoubleSpace. If you do have high memory available you can move DBLSPACE.BIN out of conventional memory by running MemMaker after you install DoubleSpace. Never delete the file DBLSPACE.BIN.

Run the DoubleSpace program by typing **DBLSPACE** at the DOS prompt. Windows must not be running. The DoubleSpace program prompts you and provide guides on how to run the program. Press F1 for help with the current screen.

During DoubleSpace installation, you are prompted to specify the size of the *host drive*, which is a virtual drive that DOS uses during compression and decompression. The host drive is not compressed, so it is slightly faster.

Note

If you have already created a host drive that is too small for a permanent swap file, you can resize the host and compressed disk. To resize these disks, type DBLSPACE at the DOS prompt and press Enter. When the DoubleSpace screen appears, select the compressed disk and press Enter. Choose the **S**ize button to display a screen that enables you to resize the host drive.

DoubleSpace recommends a host size of 2.5M, but you nearly always want it larger. Calculate an approximate host size from the following table. In the table a larger permanent swap file is recommended for computers that have less memory. Making the permanent swap file larger adds marginal performance after approximately 10M, so a very large permanent swap file is usually not worth the trade for lost disk space.

Memory	Host Size
4M RAM	10M for permanent swap file 2M for TEMP files in the TEMP directory 2.5M for host operation 14.5M total host size
8M RAM	7–8M for permanent swap file 2M for TEMP files in the TEMP directory 2.5M for host operation 12.5M total host size

VI

Installing Windows

After DoubleSpace is complete, it shows you the new size of the original disk and the drive letter and size of the host drive.

Once DoubleSpace is complete you must move the permanent swap file to the host drive. To do this, follow the instructions in the section titled "Setting Up the Swap File in 386 Enhanced Mode" later in this chapter.

You may also want to move the TEMP directory to the host drive. This gives Windows a slight performance increase during disk intensive commands. The earlier section in this chapter titled "Storing TEMP Files in a Special Directory" tells you how to move the TEMP file by adding a directory to the host drive and modifying the AUTOEXEC.BAT file.

Running Windows 3.1 with DOS 5.0

One benefit of using DOS 5.0 is that you can load most of DOS into extended memory without using a third-party memory manager. If you load the operating system in extended memory, you save approximately 50K of conventional memory. You also can load device drivers and terminate-and-stay resident (TSR) applications in extended memory and, therefore, save even more conventional memory. This procedure frees more memory for DOS applications running under Windows.

DOS 5.0 is equipped with HIMEM.SYS, an extended memory manager that allows DOS 5.0 to load most of the operating system, device drivers, and TSRs above conventional memory. The significance is that by loading most of the operating system, the device drivers, and TSRs above conventional memory, more conventional memory is available for DOS applications. When used on a 286, 386, or 486 PC, HIMEM.SYS provides HMA and XMS memory to DOS applications that can use it.

HIMEM.SYS opens three areas of memory above the 640K barrier that you can make available to applications:

- *Upper Memory Area (UMA)*. Consists of the memory between 640K and 1024K. DOS 5.0 can load device drivers and memory-resident applications into the upper memory area. UMAs are created only on the 80386 and 80486 families of processors.

- *High Memory Area (HMA)*. The first 64K of memory above 1024K. DOS 5.0 can load a portion of the operating system into the HMA.

- *Extended Memory* (XMS). Includes all memory above 1024K.

You load HIMEM.SYS by entering a line, such as the following, in the CONFIG.SYS file:

DEVICE=C:\DOS\ HIMEM.SYS

Windows usually adds this line for you during installation. Windows uses the same memory manager, HIMEM.SYS, as DOS 5.0. Use the memory manager file that has the most recent date.

After the HIMEM.SYS memory manager loads, another line in the CONFIG.SYS loads most of DOS into the High Memory Area. The line DOS=HIGH must be in the CONFIG.SYS file *after* the HIMEM.SYS line.

To load device drivers in upper memory, the PC must have an 80386 or 80486 processor, and you must add device driver commands similar to the following listing to the CONFIG.SYS file, below the HIMEM.SYS statement:

```
DOS=HIGH, UMB
DEVICE=C:\DOS\EMM386.EXE RAM
DEVICEHIGH=C:\DOS\ANSI.SYS
```

The DEVICEHIGH command loads the ANSI.SYS driver in upper memory.

> **Note**
>
> EMM386.EXE is incompatible with Windows running in standard mode. You must remove or disable the DEVICE=C:\DOS\EMM386.SYS RAM command in the CONFIG.SYS file if you run Windows in standard mode.

To load TSRs into upper memory, the PC must have an 80386 or 80486 processor, and you must include the following line in the AUTOEXEC.BAT file:

```
LOADHIGH TSRname
```

You must have the DOS=UMB statement and the statements in the CONFIG.SYS file for loading HIMEM.SYS and EMM386.EXE.

> **Caution**
>
> Loading TSRs—whether or not in upper memory—before loading Windows is not recommended.

Tip

Many applications require that you load the ANSI.SYS driver before you can type certain characters. You can load this driver in upper memory by using the DEVICEHIGH command and save valuable conventional memory.

VI

Installing Windows

DOS 5.0 installs a file named WINA20.386, which must be present in the root directory. WINA20.386 is a driver that enables Windows to run DOS 5.0 even if DOS is loaded into HMA via the DOS=HIGH command. This is pertinent only to 386 Enhanced mode.

You can load device drivers in upper memory, which enables you to load selected drivers in high memory in the same way a TSR is loaded in high memory. To load a device driver in upper memory, after the HIMEM.SYS, EMM386.EXE, DOS=HIGH, and UMB lines, add a command in CONFIG.SYS similar to the following line:

```
DEVICEHIGH=C:\path\devicefilename.ext.
```

Optimizing Hard Disk Performance

Besides an adequate amount of memory, the hardware resource most responsible for Windows performance is the hard disk. Most people consider the hard disk primarily as a storage area for applications and data. The hard disk, however, performs an additional function, serving as swap space for information that Windows moves to and from memory as needed. Because Windows accesses the hard disk so often, the drive's capability to move information to and from the disk directly affects performance. The most important areas you can change that affect hard disk performance for Windows are shown in the following list:

- Amount of free space

- Regular use of CHKDSK

- Amount of disk fragmentation

- Efficient use of SMARTDrive

- Creation of temporary and application swap files

Increasing Available Space

As Windows works, the hard disk is used to store temporary files. Because Windows frequently reads and writes these files, the efficiency of the hard disk affects Windows performance. If a large amount of storage is available on the hard disk, however, Windows can more easily find available and efficiently located space. Some procedures described in following sections of this chapter, such as creating swap files, are easier to apply if the hard disk has adequate available space.

The easiest step you can take to maximize free space on a hard disk is to delete all unnecessary files. If possible, make a backup of the disk before deleting files. This way, if you make a mistake and delete important files by accident you can still recover the data.

Erase data files and old applications from File Manager. Any files that you are unsure of or that begin with a ~ (tilde) should be erased from DOS only when Windows is *not* running.

Begin by deleting old applications and data you no longer need. If you do not use the Windows accessories, such as Cardfile, Paintbrush, Calendar, and Calculator, you may want to delete their EXE files and the associated help files from the Windows directory.

Next, delete the *temp files* left behind by applications that terminated unexpectedly. These files usually end in the extension TMP or SWP and begin with a ~ (tilde). (Make sure that you erase these files from DOS when Windows is not running.) If you have one, clean out the TEMP directory. The TEMP directory is identified in the AUTOEXEC.BAT file with the statement SET TEMP=*path*. This directory is where temporary files should be stored. Finally, consider using a tape drive or other storage medium to archive historical data. If you haven't used the data in months, you probably should archive.

Using the CHKDSK Utility

After deleting unnecessary files, use the DOS command CHKDSK to find and recover lost file clusters (also known as *allocation units*). A *file cluster* is the smallest unit that can store a file on the hard disk. When applications terminate unexpectedly, a number of these clusters often are left on the disk, unaccounted for and inaccessible by the applications. As an analogy, these clusters are similar to scraps of paper, as though you started to write a sentence and then left the work unfinished.

CHKDSK finds and links the unfinished ends of lost clusters to other clusters beginnings—converting them to files that you can inspect or delete. Converted clusters appear in the root directory with a file name similar to FILExxxx.CHK. If these files contain text, you may be able to read the contents with the Notepad.

To use CHKDSK, first exit Windows. (Never use CHKDSK from within Windows; doing so may destroy applications and data.)

At the DOS prompt, type the following line:

```
CHKDSK /F
```

If CHKDSK encounters lost clusters, you are asked if you want these clusters converted to files. Press **Y** and press Enter to proceed with the conversion. You are then shown how many clusters were found and how much storage

VI

Installing Windows

space was recovered. Next, display the directory of the root for files that end with CHK by typing the following line at the DOS prompt:

```
DIR C:\*.CHK
```

Check these files with Notepad for lost data you may want to recover, and then delete them.

Defragmenting Your Disk

Information written to a hard disk is not necessarily stored in a *contiguous* (adjacent) block. Rather, fragments of information are more likely spread across the disk wherever the system can find room. The more you use the hard disk, the more fragmented the disk becomes. Obviously, the drive takes more time to hunt for information located in several places than it takes to fetch the same information from a single location. Because of this extra time, disk fragmentation can slow the computer's operation considerably.

Fortunately, a number of applications that compact the hard disk by restructuring files into contiguous blocks and moving free space to the end of the disk are available. DOS 6 includes the DEFRAG command, which you can use to defragment your disk. DEFRAG is described at the beginning of this chapter. A large block of contiguous free storage on the hard disk can be used by temporary and permanent swap files in 386 Enhanced mode and by temporary application swap files in standard mode. All of these applications can improve Windows performance.

After you *defragment* the disk, you may want to put the defragmenting utility in the AUTOEXEC.BAT so that it compacts the disk on start-up. This reduces the time for defragmenting to a few seconds. The improved performance of the hard disk is well worth the investment.

Using SMARTDrive To Increase Disk Performance

SMARTDrive is a disk cache, a hard disk enhancement software package that comes with Windows. A *disk cache* works by reducing the amount of work Windows must do to write and read information to and from the hard disk. SMARTDrive sets aside an area of extended memory, known as a *cache*, which acts as a high-speed reservoir of disk information for Windows. When Windows needs a piece of data from the hard disk, Windows first checks to see whether the information is in the cache. Because the cache is electronic memory, the retrieval can be hundreds or even thousands of times faster than a mechanical disk drive.

If Windows doesn't find the needed data in the cache and must read new data from disk, the cache receives a new store of data. SMARTDrive has a good hit rate for guessing which information will be needed next and for storing that information in the cache.

A disk cache also can speed the process of storing information on a disk. Rather than writing information to the disk, Windows writes to the cache, which enables an application to continue a task without taking the time to access the hard drive. When the system has a spare moment, SMARTDrive moves the information from the cache to the disk. Although the increased performance is noticeable, this caching operation may not be noticeable to the user.

As mentioned previously, Windows and MS DOS 5.0 and 6 both come with the SMARTDrive disk-caching application. The SMARTDrive application that comes with Windows 3.1 is an improved version of the application that came with Windows 3.0 and DOS, so be sure that you use the most current version.

Note

If you upgrade DOS after you install Windows, check the AUTOEXEC.BAT file to see the directory from which SMARTDRV.EXE is being loaded. Check both the DOS and WINDOWS directory to see which contains the more recent SMARTDRV.EXE file. If necessary, edit the AUTOEXEC.BAT file so that the most recent SMARTDRV.EXE file is the one that is loaded.

SMARTDRV.EXE is an application that you can run from the DOS prompt. During Setup, Windows installs SMARTDRV.EXE as the first line in the AUTOEXEC.BAT file. Because of this location in the AUTOEXEC.BAT file, SMARTDrive runs immediately on start-up and is then installed in the CONFIG.SYS file with a line similar to the following:

```
DEVICE=C:\WINDOWS\SMARTDRV.EXE
```

Caution

Do not use SMARTDrive with other disk-caching software. DOS disk-caching software cannot run with Windows. If you use a replacement for SMARTDrive, it must be designed for Windows.

To load SMARTDrive so that you can view the current settings, type **SMARTDRV** or **SMARTDRV /S** at the DOS prompt. When you run with /S switch, SMARTDrive statistics display on-screen. A table similar to the following appears on-screen:

VI

Installing Windows

```
Microsoft SMARTDrive Disk Cache version 5.0
Copyright 1991,1993 Microsoft Corp.
Cache size: 2,097,152 bytes
Cache size while running Windows: 2,097,152 bytes
Disk Caching Status
drive     read cache      write cache     buffering
----------------------------------------
  A:        yes           no              no
  B:        yes           no              no
  C:*       yes           noyes           no
  H:        yes           no              no
*DoubleSpace drive cached via host drive.
Write behind data will be committed before command prompt returns.
For help, type "Smartdrv /?".
```

`Cache size` is the size of the SMARTDrive disk cache when Windows is not running. The SMARTDrive application picks a value based on the amount of extended memory in the computer. The performance gains afforded by SMARTDrive tend to drop off after 2M.

`Cache size while running Windows` is the minimum size of the SMARTDrive disk cache when working in Windows. In 386 Enhanced mode, Windows reduces the SMARTDrive cache to the minimum value and retains use of the extra memory until you exit. In standard mode, SMARTDrive works with HIMEM.SYS to *dynamically allocate* memory to Windows when memory is tight and take back memory for use by the cache when more memory is available.

The `Disk Caching Status` reports the drives on which read and write caching is currently in effect. The read cache holds information read from the hard disk. Information needed by an application can be supplied from the cache instead of being read from the disk. The write cache holds information to be written to the disk. When the computer and Windows are less busy, the information in the write cache is written to disk. By default, write cache is disabled for diskettes.

Increasing Performance with Swap Files and Virtual Memory

Swapping is the process of freeing space in memory by moving information to the hard disk. Nearly all applications use some kind of swapping when working. Swapping, however, encompasses a broad category of operations that involve memory and hard disk space. An application swap file, for example, differs in operation from the swap file used by the Virtual Memory Manager in 386 Enhanced mode.

The following definitions may help you to sort out the major uses of swap files and temporary files.

File	Definition
Virtual Memory Swap File	Single file on the hard disk, either temporary or permanent, that is treated by the 386 processor as extended memory. Increases memory recognized by Windows 386 Enhanced mode by the amount of disk space allocated to swap file.
Application Swap File	File created for each DOS application running in Windows standard mode. Stored by default in the TEMP directory named by the variable in AUTOEXEC.BAT. Provides appearance of multi-tasking by providing a space to store inactive applications when other applications are loaded and running in memory.
Temporary Files	Files used by applications to hold information temporarily swapped out of memory. Stored by default in the directory named by the TEMP variable in AUTOEXEC.BAT.

Setting Up the Swap File in 386 Enhanced Mode

Windows uses disk swapping as a way of expanding the apparent memory of the computer when Windows runs in 386 Enhanced mode. Disk swapping occurs when Windows lacks enough RAM to load an application, and must move some or all of a Windows or DOS application out of memory and to a hard disk.

◀ "Enhancing DOS Application Performance," p. 784

> **Note**
>
> Don't confuse virtual memory swap files used in 386 Enhanced mode with *temporary application swap files* used by DOS applications when running in Windows standard mode. These files are different. Temporary application swap files, which aren't used by Windows in 386 Enhanced mode, are used by DOS applications.

VI

Installing Windows

When you run Setup, Windows examines the available space on the hard disk and looks for a large contiguous (single continuous piece) of storage. If Setup finds a large enough contiguous section of storage, a permanent swap file is created. The permanent swap file, 386SPART.PAR, is installed in the root directory of the drive selected by Windows. A small companion file, SPART.PAR, is located in the Windows directory.

If Windows finds no suitable space for a permanent swap file, a temporary swap file is placed on the drive that contains the SYSTEM.INI file. The temporary swap file is known as WIN386.SWP. If insufficient space is available for a temporary swap file, no swap file is created. In this case, Windows performance can become significantly slower.

Swap files are system files and, although you can see these files by displaying hidden files with the **V**iew menu in File Manager, do not delete them. If needed, use the 386 Enhanced application in Control Panel to remove virtual memory, which is described later.

You can change the type or size of the virtual memory you have. You can increase Windows performance by creating a larger permanent swap file. To make a larger permanent swap file, you need to delete unused files and clean up the hard disk. You also may need to defragment the disk so that the available storage is in a contiguous area.

A permanent swap file is composed of a contiguous (nonfragmented) portion of the hard disk where data is stored as a continuous section. Because parts of a permanent swap file are read in a continuous stream, this kind of file may be much faster than a temporary swap file. If you don't have much available storage on the hard disk or if the available storage is dispersed over the disk, use a temporary swap file. (The permanent swap file is not really permanent on the hard disk and can be removed with the 386 Enhanced program in Control Panel.)

Before you create a permanent swap file, run a disk defragmenting program. Defragmenting speeds the performance of both temporary and permanent swap files and increases the available space for a permanent swap file.

◀ "Doubling Your Hard Disk with DoubleSpace," p. 842

> **Note**
>
> If your computer uses DoubleSpace to double the size of the hard disk, make sure that the swap file is set to the host drive, the uncompressed drive. A swap file assigned to a compressed disk cannot be used by Windows.

> **Caution**
>
> If your computer shows a drastic performance decrease after installing DOS 6 and DoubleSpace, the permanent swap file may have been removed. Running DoubleSpace may set the permanent swap file to zero size. Read the section on DoubleSpace to learn about DoubleSpace and its uncompressed host drive. Read this section to learn how to create a new permanent swap file on the host.

Note

By default, Windows creates the temporary swap file in the directory that contains the SYSTEM.INI file, which usually is the WINDOWS directory. You can specify, however, a temporary swap file drive and size in the [386Ehn] section of the SYSTEM.INI file. A MinUserDiskSpace line controls the minimum amount of disk space to allocate for the temporary swap file, and a MaxPagingFileSize line controls the maximum size of the temporary swap file. PagingDrive specifies the drive on which to create the temporary swap file. The following example creates a 2M temporary swap file on drive D:

```
[386Enh]
PagingDrive=D
MaxPagingFileSize=2048
MinUserDiskSpace=1024
```

You can create or change the swap file by selecting the 386 Enhanced icon in Control Panel from the Main program group. Select the **V**irtual Memory option button. The **V**irtual Memory dialog box appears (see fig. 24.2). The Type and Size indicators show the kind and size of virtual memory currently specified.

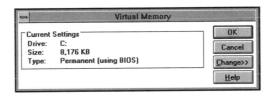

Fig. 24.2
The Virtual
Memory dialog
box.

To change the size, location, and kind of swap file Windows uses, follow these steps:

1. Open Control Panel from the Main group window in Program Manager.

2. Choose the 386 Enhanced program. The 386 Enhanced dialog box appears.

3. Choose the **V**irtual Memory button.

   Windows scans the disk for available storage; then the Virtual Memory dialog box appears. The current settings appear. If these settings are acceptable, choose Cancel twice and don't follow the remainder of these steps.

VI

4. Choose the **C**hange button.

   The dialog box expands and configuration options for a virtual memory swap file appear. Depending on whether you choose a permanent or temporary swap file, the dialog box changes options and displayed information.

5. Make the changes, then choose OK twice, and close Control Panel.

After you choose the **V**irtual Memory button, the **D**rive, **T**ype, and New **S**ize of swap file currently assigned to 386 Enhanced mode are shown in the New Settings portion of the dialog box. The options and the maximum and recommended size of swap file change, depending upon the type of swap file you select from the drop-down list. Figures 24.3 and 24.4 show the different views.

Fig. 24.3
These settings appear when you configure a temporary swap file.

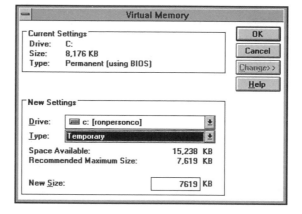

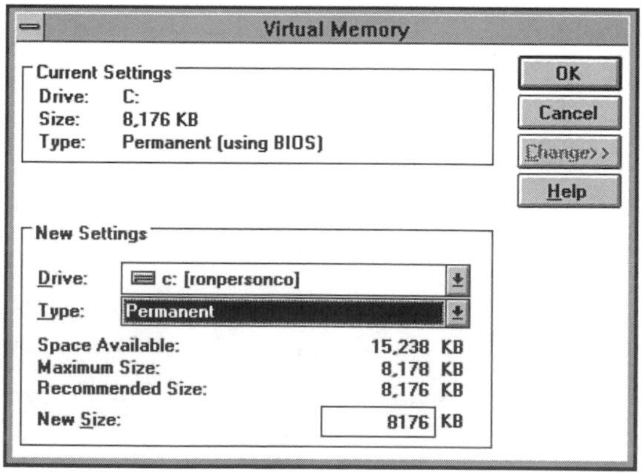

Fig. 24.4
These settings appear when you configure a permanent swap file.

> **Caution**
>
> Never put the permanent swap file on a compressed drive. If you use DoubleSpace, put the permanent swap file on the host drive.

If you are setting up a temporary swap file, the New **S**ize text box indicates the maximum amount of disk space Windows can allocate to the swap file during a Windows session. A temporary swap file shrinks and expands according to demand for memory, and the New **S**ize value indicates the maximum size to which the file can grow. The Recommended Maximum Size (entered by default in the New **S**ize text box) is based on the space available.

If you are configuring a permanent swap file, the New **S**ize text box indicates the amount of space to allocate to a permanent file on the hard disk. Maximum Size is roughly one half of the contiguous space available on the disk. (Windows displays a warning message if you try to set a larger New **S**ize value.) Usually, allocating the largest possible swap file is a good idea, but no more than three or four times the amount of the physical memory. If you have 4M of RAM, for example, allocate a swap file of 16M or less.

From Here...

This chapter should help you install Windows and optimize its performance. For more information about installing Windows, Windows applications, and troubleshooting problems during installation, refer to the following chapters:

- Chapter 21, "Installing and Configuring Windows Applications," gives you some tips on how to install and uninstall applications.

- Chapter 22, "Installing and Configuring DOS Applications," discusses the use of PIF files by DOS applications to set up Windows so that they can run properly.

- Chapter 25, "Installing Windows for Workgroups 3.11," tells you how to install and use Windows for Workgroups 3.11.

- Chapter 26, "Networking Windows 3.1x," teaches you how to make Windows run on a Novell network.

VI

Installing Windows

Using Windows for Workgroups 3.11

This chapter discusses the differences between Windows for Workgroups and Windows running as a stand-alone program, what you need to know before installing Windows for Workgroups, and finally, the specific instructions for installing Windows for Workgroups. This chapter teaches you how to implement Windows for Workgroups as an independent *peer-to-peer* network. The next chapter teaches you how to implement Windows for Workgroups integrated with a Novell network.

In this chapter, you learn how to:

■ Understand the difference between Windows and Windows for Workgroups

■ Install and configure Windows for Workgroups

Understanding Differences between Windows and Windows for Workgroups

Understanding the differences between regular Windows and Windows for Workgroups is critical to understanding how to set up a workgroup environment using Windows for Workgroups. You can use Windows in many different environments and even can install the program in computers without network adapters or any other means of communicating with other computers. This environment is called the stand-alone environment.

You can use Windows in conjunction with a LAN (Local-Area Network) and a network operating system, such as Novell NetWare 2.2 or 1, LAN Manager, or Banyan Vines. Windows is considered *network aware*—that is, if installed on an active network, Windows can detect the network's presence and load the necessary support drivers, if these drivers are available. (For information on installing and using basic Windows on a Novell network, see Chapter 26, "Networking Windows 3.1x," or refer to *Networking Windows 3.1*, published by Que Corporation.)

In actuality, Windows for Workgroups is Windows with enhancements. Visually, the sole differences between the two programs are in their initial sign-on screens (one reads "Windows" and the other "Windows for Workgroups") and the different icons present in Program Manager's Network group of Windows for Workgroups: the Mail, Schedule+, NetWatcher, WinMeter, Net, Remote Access, Network Setup, Log On/Off, and Chat icons. In addition, two new icons are added to the Control Panel: Networks and Fax (if installed). Coverage of these enhanced features has been presented throughout this book.

Because Windows for Workgroups is designed as a network operating system in its own right, a computer running Windows for Workgroups is by definition part of a "user community." Windows is designed only for a computer acting as a client; Windows for Workgroups is designed for a computer acting as a peer (a client and a server). Windows "takes" network resources; Windows for Workgroups "gives" and "takes" network resources.

One conceptual difference between Windows and Windows for Workgroups is in how the two programs handle files. Windows relies on outside utilities to regulate access to its files. Windows for Workgroups provides that capability through File Manager. Restricting another user's access rights to a file in Windows requires an outside utility such as Novell's FILER, which you can use to alter the access rights of users to certain files or directories.

Windows for Workgroups operating in stand-alone mode acts exactly like Windows. When operating on a LAN, however, Windows for Workgroups gives its users the capabilities of sharing directories and regulating access to those directories.

When setting up an office to use Windows for Workgroups, those users whose duties require them to have private printers can retain their own devices, even under a shared-printer system. Office workers who don't require separate printers, on the other hand, readily can access all the shared printers of the workgroup whenever necessary.

The Windows Calendar enables you to schedule appointments and to view your schedule by month or by day. Windows for Workgroups Schedule+, however, is a much more comprehensive package and is oriented to project management.

Schedule+ enables you to create a "project." You can create "tasks" that can be assigned to projects and prioritized. You can have tasks scheduled automatically by following the instructions in Chapter 6, "Using Schedule+." You can view at any time the projects you have created and their tasks in various ways.

Because Windows for Workgroups is on a LAN, Schedule+ enables one computer to share its schedule with other computers. This way, workgroup members can coordinate their schedules in a way that the Windows Calendar cannot.

Planning Your Workgroups Network

Before you set up your Windows for Workgroups network, you need to think about how you want to define a workgroup in your office. This section covers defining a workgroup, cabling, and placing users on the network. You also need to understand exactly what Windows for Workgroups has to offer for you and your office.

Defining a Workgroup

The concept of the *workgroup* lies at the very heart of Windows for Workgroups. A workgroup can consist of a group of users, a unit of organization in your office, or even the computers the workgroup members use. Working with Windows for Workgroups is much easier if you focus first on setting up your own workgroup instead of trying to deal with users and computers individually.

One of the first things you need to decide when setting up your Windows for Workgroups network is what workgroups you want to define for your network. This decision influences everything else you do from this point on. Initially, you need to ask yourself the following questions:

- How can you break the work in your office into groups?

- Whose work is similar to that of others in the office?

VI

Installing Windows

■ How many people do you want in each workgroup?

■ Can all networked computers be physically connected by appropriate cables?

Recognizing that users in one workgroup don't require a separate cable system from users in another workgroup is an important first step in organizing your workgroups. A LAN usually is organized so that *all* computers in the office are cabled together. A computer can belong to only one workgroup at a time, although many workgroups can operate on a single LAN.

The workgroup name you assign any particular computer when first starting Windows for Workgroups determines the workgroup to which that computer belongs. You can change this name at any time through the Windows Control Panel. Changing the workgroup name for a single computer in the network puts that computer into a new workgroup. (See "Selecting Network Names" later in this chapter.)

Every computer running Windows for Workgroups maintains a network database containing the following information:

■ The name for every computer on the network

■ The name of the workgroup each computer belongs to

■ The logon names and passwords of users on the network

■ The default workgroup, computer name, and logon name usually assigned to each computer

When you change the workgroup name usually assigned to a specific computer, the database is updated accordingly. If the workgroup name doesn't exist, a new entry for the new workgroup is created in the database. If you change the name of a computer, the database is updated. If you change the logon name to a name that doesn't exist, you must give the network a new password, and the database is updated.

You can change the name of a computer at any time. When it starts running Windows for Workgroups, other computers on the network are notified of any changes.

The database is "distributed" to all computers on the network running Windows for Workgroups. Computers carry a complete copy of all database elements specific to their workgroup. Computers carry a partial copy of database elements for other workgroups. If a computer needs to know more information about another workgroup, for example, when connecting a drive to a computer in another workgroup, it queries that computer at that time for the needed information.

Organizing Your Office into Workgroups

A LAN can accommodate hundreds of computers connected together. Because Windows for Workgroups operates on top of DOS rather than being a full-fledged network-operating system such as UNIX or LAN Manager, however, you may need to limit the number of users in a workgroup to fewer than 20 for the best results. A reasonable number of people assigned to a single workgroup ranges from eight to 16. In small offices or departments, assigning everyone to the same workgroup often is the easiest way to set up your LAN.

Workgroups are usually logical groupings of users. The decision to organize workers in your office into specific workgroups generally is based on several factors, such as the following:

- Who needs to share files with whom?

- Who needs to share printers with whom?

- Which users must interact with the work of other users?

Often the nature of the work in your office suggests a logical organization for your workgroups. In the case of a law firm, for example, work may fall clearly into certain categories determined by job description: attorneys, secretaries, paralegals, and administrative staff. In such a case, you may create workgroups for each work category, or you may decide to divide the office into two overall workgroups: LAW and ADMIN. Attorneys, paralegals, and secretaries then may be assigned to the workgroup LAW, and administrative staffers may be assigned to the ADMIN workgroup.

In this example, the attorneys, paralegals, and secretaries need to share files because of the way their work interconnects. Paralegals present technical summaries of case law to the attorneys; attorneys develop the information and produce rough drafts, notes, and dictation; and the secretaries review these drafts and organize the work into final form. The attorneys and paralegals then can review these final documents and suggest changes. The administrative staff has little or no interaction with the work of these professionals. Members of the workgroup ADMIN are concerned solely with such duties as accounting, office management, network administration, and PC support.

Sharing resources within a workgroup is far easier than doing so outside a workgroup. For your network to operate as efficiently as possible, therefore, you must determine which users in the network need to share files and printers most, making them candidates for being put in the same workgroup. After you determine these needs, you can decide best what workgroups to set up and which computers to assign to each workgroup.

You can assign all LAN users to a single, large workgroup, of course. Such an approach, however, has a distinct disadvantage: to maintain a secure system, you must assign a separate password to every user with access to the workgroup's shared directories. This process not only consumes time, but also increases the likelihood of lost passwords. Maintaining the network thus becomes more work.

Rather than create one single workgroup with many users, using Windows for Workgroups, you can create several different workgroups, each with fewer users, to keep your network more manageable. The advantage of keeping workgroups small is similar to the advantage of using smaller directories and subdirectories on your hard drive. Although you can store several hundred files in a single directory, you may find keeping track of all those files difficult. By creating several topical subdirectories for each directory and organizing files into the appropriate subdirectories, you easily can find the similarly grouped files.

Cabling Workgroups and Networks

Ideally, all network users are connected to the same network cabling system. In practice, however, connecting all users to the same network cabling system isn't always possible. Users on a WAN, or Wide Area Network, may be located in different buildings, across town, or even in a different city from one another. (In such cases, you may want a more powerful network operating system than Windows for Workgroups—NetWare 3 or 4, for example.)

Even within the same office or the same building, network cabling limitations may prevent you from placing all your computers on the same cable system. Thin, coaxial Ethernet cable, for example, limits the network to a length of 3,035 feet of cable (including repeaters), which may not be enough to reach all the computers you want to connect. You also must consider such physical barriers as office partitions, walls, drop ceilings, and so on when calculating how far your network's cable must reach.

When necessary, you can use a hardware device known as a *bridge* to extend your network beyond the physical limitations of the cable. A bridge joins two cable systems, enabling Windows for Workgroups to treat the two LANs as one. When using thin Ethernet cable, for example, a bridge can extend the maximum cable length of the network to 6,070 feet.

Bridges are sold in several different configurations, depending on the vendor. Some vendors sell a "plug and play" box. This bridge is about the size of a small computer with two built-in network adapters, or a network adapter and an adapter to be used with a remote phone connection. Phone connections can include a standard dial-up line, or a dedicated or leased line. With these types of bridges, all you need to do is plug them in.

Other vendors sell you the software and, sometimes, specialized hardware. This style of bridge must often be installed on a regular PC. Often you must supply your own network adapters. This type of bridge often costs less but has a more involved installation procedure.

You can use as many bridges as you want within the specifications of the type of network you are setting up. Thin Ethernet, for example, can have no more than 30 nodes on a single trunk segment (or branch of the network). This means you can have up to 30 bridges on a single trunk segment. If you also have computers on the same segment, subtract the total number of computers from 30. The remainder is the number of bridges you can have on that trunk segment.

You also can extend a network's cabling limitations by using a device called a *concentrator* or *hub*, available from such vendors as Synoptics. Synoptics has developed a concentrator that you can use to cable together twisted-pair (10BaseT) Ethernet adapters. You can connect each Synoptics concentrator to another concentrator separated by as much as 1.24 miles of fiber-optic cable.

Most hubs have a BNC connector (or, in the case of Synoptics, a fiber-optic connector) that enables them to be cabled together in a bus fashion, one after another. You attach a "T" connector to the BNC connector on each concentrator and cable the concentrators together, "T" to "T." Like bridges, the limit to the number of concentrators on a single thin Ethernet trunk segment is 30 nodes. Because a concentrator counts as an active node, you can have a maximum of 86 concentrators cabled together using thin Ethernet cabling. You also can connect concentrators using twisted-pair cabling. Due to timing problems, however, any two workstations should have no more than four concentrators between them.

VI

Installing Windows

Most Ethernet adapters have a special 15-pin port known as an *AUI* (Attachment Unit Interface) port. This port was originally intended for use in Thick Ethernet networks. A *transceiver* was attached to the AUI port, and a cable was run from the transceiver to the Thick Ethernet backbone. The purpose of the transceiver is to boost the signal to support the added length of cable between the computer and the network cabling. One use of this port today is to convert a network adapter from thin or thick Ethernet to twisted-pair. Transceivers are available that fit onto the 15-pin AUI port of a standard Ethernet adapter and offer a twisted-pair Ethernet jack. This jack is referred to as an *RJ-45* connector, and resembles a large modular telephone jack.

Placing Users on a LAN

Users are people in the workgroup who are logged onto the network. After users log on, Windows for Workgroups can track them. Windows for Workgroups uses the logon name mainly to set up users' schedules, send electronic mail, and allow access to shared resources. (You assign a logon name for a user during that user's first Windows for Workgroups session.)

The physical location of users on the LAN doesn't matter when you are using Windows for Workgroups in your network. Five users sitting in a row in the same room each can belong to a different workgroup, and two users in separate rooms across the building can belong to the same workgroup. A particular computer located anywhere on the LAN functions just as effectively as any other computer connected to the network.

Understanding Network Messaging

Each computer running Windows for Workgroups is part of a community of computers that send out messages to verify that every computer on the network is still active. Each computer needs to know that the other computers—especially those that share resources—are still available for access. Computers sharing files and printers with other computers also need to transmit data over the LAN. The term *network messaging* describes such computer-to-computer communication.

All communication between networked computers takes place in short bursts of information known as *packets*. If you copy a shared file from one computer to another, for example, Windows for Workgroups breaks down the overall file into smaller pieces, or packets, of information. These packets are transmitted in sequence from the sending computer to the receiving computer. The receiving computer reassembles the individual packets back into the original file.

Networked computers use such packets to prevent one computer from tying up the entire LAN while transmitting a large file (a process known as "hogging the bus"). Using packets makes communications over the LAN smoother.

Limiting the Number of Users on the LAN

In theory, a LAN can accommodate hundreds of users. In practice, however, the network starts to slow down when many users are accessing the LAN heavily. The more users need to read or write shared files, the greater the usage of the LAN. Finally, the LAN reaches a saturation point, where too many users are sharing files at the same time, and the LAN seems to slow down. In some cases, error messages may appear in programs running on users' computers. These error messages can include the following:

    Network Drive No Longer Accessible

or

    Network Printer Unavailable

The LAN doesn't have problems reading and writing to files on your own hard disk. The problem—and the subsequent slowness of the LAN—arises mainly when you share files with other computers on the network. A copy of the shared file has to travel over the LAN from the source computer into your computer's memory. Data traveling on the LAN is referred to as *traffic*.

> **Note**
>
> In network terms, "slow" doesn't mean that the transmitting speed of the network adapter changes. The term actually refers to a slowdown of response time on the LAN—that is, each user on the network must wait longer while the LAN handles the needs of so many users.

To understand network traffic better, think of the LAN as a one-lane highway. Each computer on the network is like an exit that doubles as an entrance. Each packet of information is like a car trying to access or leave the highway. Your "car" cannot get onto the highway until the next car has gone by—especially if that other car is now entering or exiting the highway through your entrance. The more cars using the highway, the longer you must wait to get on, just as with a very congested highway. Conversely, the

VI

Installing Windows

fewer cars passing your entrance, the faster you can get on. After you are on the highway, you must drive at a certain, set speed (the network's "speed limit"), because—unlike on real highways—everyone on the LAN highway travels at the same speed. (You cannot break the network's speed limit to reach your destination computer sooner.)

Certain types of programs cause greater network traffic congestion than do others. Database programs, for example, tend to place the heaviest amount of traffic on the LAN, because such programs make frequent reads and writes to files. (Database programs include Access, dBASE IV, Paradox, and FoxBASE.)

Windows for Workgroups puts no set limits on the number of users who can connect to a network. Certain warning signs do exist, however, that the network is becoming too congested. Watch for the following conditions:

- More than 60 users are logged onto and using the same LAN.

- More than 50 percent of the users sharing files on a LAN are using a database program.

- Users are starting to complain that the system seems slow when they share files or printers.

To resolve the problem of congestion, try these solutions:

- *Split the network into smaller, separate networks.* Doing so reduces traffic but doesn't enable *any* user on one LAN to exchange data with other users on another LAN. This option lightens network traffic, thus reducing congestion but also reducing flexibility.

- *Split the network into smaller networks connected through bridges.* A bridge filters out traffic not meant to go onto another network. You can split up the network by workgroups, for example, and place a bridge between the networks. This option enables any user to exchange information with any other user. Bridges can cost anywhere from $1,500 to $10,000.

- *Migrate to a faster type of network adapter.* For example, consider FDDI, which transmits at a speed of 100 million bits per second (mpbs), compared with 2.5 mbps for ARCnet and 10 mbps for Ethernet. This option is very expensive. FDDI cards and concentrators can cost up to 10 times the cost of Ethernet. Switching the cable to fiber is also expensive.

■ *Redistribute the programs and data to the computers that use them the most.* Although this option is the least expensive of the available options, it can be time-consuming and defeats the purpose of having a network in the first place.

■ *Migrate to a higher-powered operating system such as NetWare 3.1x or 4.x, or LAN Manager.* This option can be expensive, however.

Certain programs are available to monitor the use of a LAN, including WinMeter, which is included with Windows for Workgroups.

Programs that monitor other network operating systems (such as NetWare or LAN Manager) also exist. You can use these programs with Windows for Workgroups if the programs are DOS-based and compatible with the packet structure used by Windows for Workgroups. Unfortunately, many network monitoring programs written for other operating systems (such as UNIX) enable you to monitor the health of the LAN but don't give you information about Windows for Workgroups packets. Be sure that you are aware of the extent of such programs' compatibility with your system before you buy any for your network.

Note

The packet structure used by Windows for Workgroups is the same as that of LAN Manager. The name of the protocol driver file is PROTMAN.DOS. The drivers for the network adapter cards are NDIS drivers, which have been used by many computer systems in the past 10 years and are an industry standard. Some LANs—NetWare networks, for example—use another type of protocol known as IPX (Internetwork Packet eXchange). NetWare adapter card drivers follow Novell's ODI (Open Data-link Interface) specification.

Installing and Configuring Windows for Workgroups

This section addresses how to install and configure Windows for Workgroups. There are three possible types of installations:

■ New installation

■ Upgrading from Windows 3.1 to Windows for Workgroups version 3.11

■ Upgrading from Windows for Workgroups versions 3.1 to 3.11

VI

Installing Windows

You first learn how to install a new version of Windows for Workgroups on a new computer. After this, you learn about upgrade issues. Because most of the installation process is identical to the installation process for Windows, this section focuses on installation issues unique to Windows for Workgroups and networking.

Installing a New Copy of Windows for Workgroups on a New Computer

The installation procedure for a new copy of Windows for Workgroups is similar to a standard Windows installation. You need to locate Disk 1 of the set of Windows for Workgroups disks, move to drive A:, and type the following:

SETUP

As in Windows, there are two setup options:

- Express Setup

- Custom Setup

Custom Setup gives you greater control over settings for your computer and changes to various files (AUTOEXEC.BAT and CONFIG.SYS, for example). Both options scan your hard drive for a copy of Windows, and will upgrade it to Windows for Workgroups if you give SETUP the approval.

Basic Setup

SETUP detects the type of hardware you have in your system and displays the results, giving you the chance to override any values. After you specify which directory will contain Windows for Workgroups, a series of files are copied to the designated directory. The Windows kernel starts, and an initial registration screen appears. Enter your name, company, and product number to continue. The product number is located on a blue-bordered, glossy card included with the distribution disks and manuals, with the words, "Your Guide to Service..." at the top.

A selection screen appears next, asking you which Windows components you want to install. The choices include: ...*Components You Select*, *Printers*, and *Applications Already on Hard Disk(s)*. This screen allows you to install all or part of the product. Table 25.1 summarizes the components you can install, along with their size in bytes. If you select all components, the total disk space required is 5,169,738 bytes (5M).

Table 25.1	**Windows for Workgroups Components**	
Component	**Size**	**Description**
Readme Files	338,944	Files containing information about Windows and the latest updates
Accessories	4,143,890	Calculator, Notepad, Clock, and so on
Games	509,187	Minesweeper, Solitaire, Hearts
Screen Savers	55,920	Flying Windows, Stars, and so on
Wallpapers, Sounds	121,797	Argyle, Egypt, Ding Sound, and so on

At this point, SETUP begins to copy files from the distribution disks to your computer's hard drive. When the appropriate files on one disk have been copied, you are prompted to insert the next disk. There are a total of eight disks in the distribution set. Disks 6, 7, and 8 contain a series of printer and network adapter drivers.

Printer installation comes next. At this point, you should indicate either the printer you plan to connect directly to this computer, or a printer the user of this computer will use across the network. Continue to select any printers the user of this computer might use. (See Chapter 9, "Printing with Windows," for more information.)

Each printer should be assigned to the port to which it is physically connected. If the printer is a network printer, the assigned port does not have to physically exist. If there are more printers than physical ports, you can assign the network printer to a previously assigned port (LPT1, for example) and reconnect the printer later on.

Network Setup

Figure 25.1 illustrates the Network Setup dialog box. The first option button you need to select is the **N**etworks button. Click this button to begin configuring your network adapter.

VI

Installing Windows

Fig. 25.1
Windows for
Workgroups
installation—the
Network Setup
dialog box.

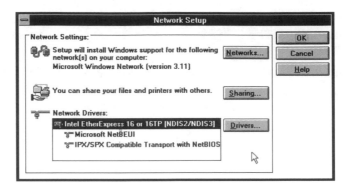

The next dialog box you see, Networks, is shown in figure 25.2. You can select any of three options:

- **N**o Windows support for networks

- **I**nstall Microsoft Windows Network

- In**s**tall Windows support for the following network only

Fig. 25.2
Windows for
Workgroups
installation—
Networks dialog
box.

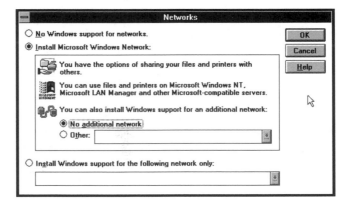

The first option installs Windows for Workgroups with no network support. Select this option if your computer has no network adapter installed. Selecting this option will not enable you to use certain features of Windows for Workgroups, such as electronic mail or file and printer sharing.

The second option allows you to install the basic networking facilities provided with Windows for Workgroups in addition to other network operating systems (such as Novell's NetWare or Banyan System's Vines).

The third option installs support for only one type of network, which is one of the following:

- Unlisted (you need to supply the drivers)

- 100% MS-Net (any network system compatible with Microsoft Networks)

- Artisoft LANtastic

- Banyan VINES

- BW-NFS (Network File System)

- DEC (Digital Equipment Corporation) PATHWORKS

- IBM (International Business Machines) OS/2 LAN Server

- Microsoft Windows Network

- Novell NetWare

- SunSelect PC-NFS

- TCS 10Net

MS-Net-compatible systems include:

- 3Com 3+Share

- Ungermann-Bass Net/One

Network Adapters

Network Adapters are boards installed in a PC that give you access to a LAN. Popular types of adapters include the following:

- Ethernet

- Token Ring

- ARCnet

- FDDI (Fiber Distributed Digital Interface)

A network adapter is installed into a PC, and is then cabled to other network adapters, forming a LAN. Some network adapters can be directly cabled together.

(continues)

VI

Installing Windows

(continued)

An example of this type is thin coaxial Ethernet adapters, also referred to as 10BASE2 Ethernet. A "T" connector is connected to the jack on the back of the adapter, which resembles a cable TV jack. A length of cable is run from "T" connector to "T" connector until all computers are joined together. The open ends of the cabling are capped by connectors known as *terminators*. The terminators prevent excess electrical signals from traveling across the LAN.

Other types of network adapters, including twisted-pair Ethernet (referred to as 10BASET Ethernet), Token Ring, and ARCnet, are connected together using a type of junction box. The name for this box differs depending on the type of network adapter. For Ethernet it is called a *hub* or *concentrator*. For Token Ring it is called a *MAU* or *MSAU* (Multi-station Attachment Unit). For an ARCnet adapter it is called a hub. In the case of an FDDI adapter, the cabling is specialized fiber-optic cabling. FDDI adapters can be cabled directly together in a daisy-chain fashion, or can be patched into an FDDI concentrator.

Network adapters differ in how they access the network and their raw speed of transmission. Ethernet adapters, for example, wait until the network is clear before transmitting information. If two happen to transmit at the same time, a *collision* occurs, and both adapters time out for a random period of time. In the case of Token Ring, the Token Ring adapter waits for a special signal known as a *token* before transmitting information.

Parts of this chapter cover native Windows for Workgroups networking. The next chapter covers connectivity to a Novell network.

Once you have chosen the type of network you want to support, select the OK button. You return to the Network Setup dialog box. The next option button to select is **S**haring. This button brings up Sharing dialog box, shown in figure 25.3, which gives you a choice of what types of resources you want to share from this computer. Choices include directory sharing and printer sharing.

Fig. 25.3
Windows for Workgroups installation— Sharing dialog box.

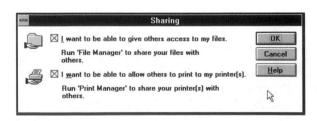

If you place a checkmark next to the Directory Sharing icon, you will be able, at any time after the installation is completed, to designate files or directories to be shared with other network users.

If you place a checkmark next to the printer sharing icon, you will be able, at any time after the installation is completed, to designate a printer to be shared with other network users.

The last option button you can select in the Network Setup dialog box shown in figure 25.1 is **D**rivers. Select this button when you are ready to select the driver for your network adapter. Figure 25.4 shows the Network Drivers dialog box.

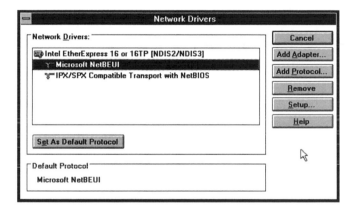

Fig. 25.4
Windows for Workgroups installation— Network Drivers dialog box.

Adding a Network Adapter. From the Network Drivers dialog box, you need to select the Add **A**dapter button. You then see the Add Network Adapter dialog box, which contains a list of network adapters (see fig. 25.5). Select the adapter that is installed in your computer. If your network adapter is not on the list, you must select the Unlisted or Updated Network Adapter option and have a disk with Windows for Workgroups drivers available.

VI

> **Note**
>
> Windows for Workgroups drivers may not be identified as such on the disk provided by the vendor of your network adapter. You must also bear in mind that the drivers which will work with your adapter may be located in a subdirectory on the vendor disk. Other labels that may work with Windows for Workgroups include NDIS and LAN Manager.

Installing Windows

Fig. 25.5
Windows for
Workgroups
installation—the
Add Network
Adapter dialog
box.

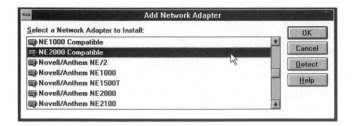

If you are not sure what type of network adapter is installed in your computer, you can select the **D**etect option button. This invokes a utility which senses network adapters and returns the signature programmed into the adapter. This option does not work in all cases, and may cause the installation to crash. If this happens, you can always restart the installation.

Configuring a Network Adapter. After you have selected a network adapter, you need to supply configuration information about the adapter. Not all adapters use the same types of settings. Table 25.2 summarizes the possible types of settings for network adapters.

It is best if you document the settings when you first install your adapter. If you are unsure of the settings, consult the documentation provided with the adapter, and enter the default values at this time. If these values do not correspond with the actual settings of the card, you can make changes at a later time. Write down each setting and save this information for future reference.

Table 25.2 Network Adapter Settings	
Setting	**Description**
Base I/O Port	This setting represents an address your computer uses to access information coming from the LAN or going out to the LAN. This address is actually the first address of a block of addresses. The range of addresses is typically 8, 16, or 32, depending on the type of network adapter.
I/O Channel Ready	Possible values for this include *late, early,* or *never.*

Setting	Description
Transceiver Type	This setting is used to select which connector you plan to use on the back of your network adapter to connect to the LAN. For Ethernet, choices include *Thin, Thick,* or *Twisted Pair*.
	Thin uses the BNC connector, which resembles a cable TV connector. Thick uses the 15-pin connector (also known as the *AUI* (Attachment Unit Interface) port. Twisted Pair uses the RJ-45 connector, which looks like a large modular telephone jack. Settings for Token Ring include the 9-pin connector (Type 1 cable), or the RJ-45 connector (also called the *UTP*—Unshielded Twisted-Pair connector).
DMA Channel	Some adapters use DMA (Direct Memory Access) to facilitate the transfer of information between the LAN and the memory of the computer. Select a number that is not used by any other board in this computer. Values range from 1 to 7.
Interrupt	The interrupt number is used by the computer to identify which board is signaling it for attention. Values range from 2 to 15.
Base Memory	This number represents a memory address used by the adapter to buffer information coming to and from the LAN. In some cases, this address could represent the address of a ROM chip on the network adapter containing programming code needed by the driver for the adapter.

Note

The Base I/O Port maps to a register on the network adapter itself. When the computer needs to transmit information on the LAN, it places the information into a buffer. The network adapter driver then divides the information into smaller units known as *packets*. The packets are then encoded for the type of network adapter and transmitted across the LAN, byte by byte. Each byte is stored in the register represented by the Base I/O Port. In a sense, the Base I/O Port is like a diving board: this is where a byte "jumps off" and dives into the LAN.

VI

Installing Windows

Adding a Protocol to a Network Adapter

Now that you have selected a network driver, you need to add a protocol. Protocols are standards regulating how information is to be sent and received. Protocols are associated with network operating systems. Novell networks, for example, use a proprietary protocol known as *IPX/SPX* (Internetwork Packet Exchange/Sequenced Packet Exchange). Microsoft networks (including LAN Manager and Windows NT) use a protocol known as *NetBEUI* (Network Basic Input/Output System—NetBIOS—Extended User Interface).

Network Adapters and Protocols

Network adapters control the physical transmission of information across the LAN. An FDDI adapter, for example, transmits information as pulses of light. An Ethernet adapter transmits information as a +2.5 or –2.5 volt electrical square wave. In addition, network adapters format the information to be transmitted into *frames* of data, adding an adapter-specific header. The header includes the source address of the adapter itself, and the destination address. A trailer, appended after the data itself, often contains a checksum for error detection.

Protocols, on the other hand, dictate *how* the information is to be transmitted. Protocols take information to be transmitted across the LAN, such as a file or a print job, and break it down into smaller units known as *packets*. A header is added to each packet identifying its sequence number and logical network information.

If you plan to use Windows for Workgroups only with other Windows for Workgroups computers, or if you plan to use only Microsoft products (such as Windows NT or LAN Manager), select the Microsoft NetBEUI protocol. If you plan to integrate Windows for Workgroups with another operating system, select the protocol associated with that system. In the case of a Novell network, for example, you would also need to select IPX/SPX Compatible Transport with NetBIOS.

After being selected, each protocol can be configured. To configure the protocol, select the **S**etup option button. Figure 25.6 shows the setup dialog box for the Microsoft NetBEUI protocol.

Fig. 25.6
Windows for Workgroups installation—setup for the Microsoft NetBEUI protocol.

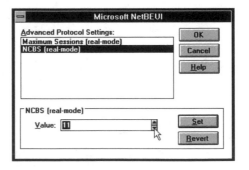

Settings for the NetBEUI protocol include Maximum Sessions and NCBS. Maximum Sessions refers to how many network users are allowed to access resources on this computer simultaneously. Values can range from 3 to 117. Values for NCBS can range from 7 to 25. Changes made to a protocol are saved in the PROTOCOL.INI file. If you make a change and then want to set this value back to its default, select the **R**evert button.

When you are done configuring the desired protocols, you can designate one of them as the default. To do so, select the desired protocol and then select the S**e**t As Default Protocol button. To remove a protocol, select the **R**emove button. When you are done with the Network Drivers dialog box, select the C**l**ose button. You are now ready to continue with the installation.

Selecting Network Names

The next task is to decide on names for your new network. The names you need to select include the following:

- User name
- Workgroup name
- Computer name

The *user name* is the name of a person who will use this computer. A computer can have more than one user name. You can add additional names after the installation. When the user first turns on the computer, he or she is prompted for a user name and a password. User names can be up to 20 characters long. When choosing the name, you should avoid duplicate user names in the same office. Some companies choose to use the first initial of the first name followed by the last name, for example.

The *workgroup name* is the name of the workgroup in which this computer is a participant. Workgroups are logical divisions of your network. Computers should be assigned to workgroups as indicated by the needs of your office or department. You can have more than one workgroup on a LAN. Users are not locked into one workgroup; however it is much easier for them to access resources inside their own workgroup. You can change the workgroup name assigned to a computer any time after the installation.

VI

Installing Windows

The *computer name* is a means of identifying the computer itself as a network resource. Computer names may be assigned based on location or based on the name of the person who uses the computer most frequently. In some companies, each employee has his or her own computer. In this case, it might make sense to name the computer after the employee. In other cases, computers are moved or are assigned to more than one person. If this is the case, you may need some other sort of designation.

Fill in the Network Names dialog box with the appropriate names and select OK. At this point, SETUP copies the driver files for your network adapter. If you have a disk supplied by the vendor of your network adapter, you can select the **B**rowse button to search the disk for the directory containing the Windows for Workgroups drivers (this is often in a subdirectory labeled *NDIS*).

After these files have been copied, SETUP continues the standard Windows installation by modifying your CONFIG.SYS and AUTOEXEC.BAT files (if you indicate Yes when the dialog box appears), setting up the Program Manager screen, setting up Program Groups, and installing applications as icons. When the installation is complete, you need to reboot your computer to load the network drivers and then restart Windows for Workgroups.

Several README files of interest are included with the product. These contain the latest information not included in the manual. The README files are installed only if you select this option at the beginning of your installation. The two files of interest to network users are README.WRI and NETWORKS.WRI. You can access these by opening the Windows Write utility from the Accessories group.

Confirming INI and Other File Modifications

After installation, you may want to view modifications made to the following files:

- CONFIG.SYS

- AUTOEXEC.BAT

- WIN.INI

- SYSTEM.INI

- PROTOCOL.INI

In the examples shown in this section, Windows for Workgroups has been installed in the C:\WFW directory. There are two primary changes to the CONFIG.SYS file:

```
DEVICE=C:\WFW\SMARTDRV.EXE /DOUBLE_BUFFER
DEVICE=C:\WFW\IFSHLP.SYS
```

SMARTDRV.EXE has been tremendously improved in Windows for Workgroups. This version of SmartDrive (version 5.0) is a 32-bit version that uses several techniques to improve the speed of disk access to files. The IFSHLP.SYS file is used to allow your computer to share files and printers.

> **Caution**
>
> The IFSHLP.SYS driver is incompatible with certain other networks, including LANtastic and LAN Manager. If you experience difficulties using Windows for Workgroups in conjunction with one of these other networks, remove the DEVICE=IFSHLP.SYS command from your CONFIG.SYS file. After you remove this driver, however, you lose the ability to share files or printers from this computer.

Changes to the AUTOEXEC.BAT file include the following:

```
C:\WFW\NET START
C:\WFW\SMARTDRV.EXE
```

The NET START command starts the Windows for Workgroups upper-level communications protocols. Windows for Workgroups uses the NetBEUI protocols, which function at the same level as other well-known protocols such as TCP/IP. The SMARTDRV.EXE command enables SmartDrive version 5.0. Both the NET and SMARTDRV commands have additional parameters, which are beyond the scope of this chapter. To obtain a list of parameters, issue the command followed by /?. To get help on SMARTDRV, for example, type the following:

```
SMARTDRV /?
```

Changes to the WIN.INI file include the addition of new sections based on your activities across the network. If you map a permanent drive letter to another computer, this action might be recorded as follows:

```
[MRU_Files]
Order=a
a=\\EVEREX\DBASE4
```

In the preceding example, the first available drive letter is assigned to the computer EVEREX and the directory C:\DBASE4 on that computer.

VI

Installing Windows

Changes to the SYSTEM.INI file are more extensive. Although not case-sensitive, auguments following a parameter are normally in lowercase. This example shows them in uppercase for emphasis and readability. The following is an example of changes made to this file:

```
[boot]
network.drv=WFWNET.DRV

[boot.description]
network.drv=Microsoft Windows Network (version 3.11)
secondnet.drv=No Additional Network Installed

[386Enh]
network=*VNETBIOS,*VWC,VNETSUP.386,VREDIR.386,VSERVER.386
netheapsize=20
device=ifsmgr.386
device=vcache.386
device=vshare.386
netmisc=ndis.386,ndis2sup.386
netcard=ee16.386
transport=nwlink.386,nwnblink.386,netbeui.386

[vcache]
minfilecache=512

[Network]
winnet=WFWNET/00025100
multinet=NONET
FileSharing=YES
PrintSharing=YES
LogonDisconnected=YES
EnableSharing=YES
UserName=DOUG
Workgroup=R&D
ComputerName=ADS486
Comment=Doug Bierer
logonvalidated=NO
reshare=YES
reconnect=YES

[network drivers]
netcard=exp16.dos
transport=NDISHLP.SYS,*NETBEUI
devdir=C:\WFW
LoadRMDrivers=NO

[NWNBLink]
LANABASE=1

[Password Lists]
*Shares=C:\WFW\SHARE000.PWL
DOUG=C:\WFW\DOUG.PWL
```

Table 25.3 summarizes the more important network-related parameters in the SYSTEM.INI file. A comprehensive listing of the SYSTEM.INI parameters is presented in the "read me" file SYSINI.WRI. Note that some parameters can be changed using Notepad, some through the Control Panel—Networks menu, and others through Network Setup (in the Network group).

Table 25.3	**SYSTEM.INI Networking Parameters**	
Section	**Parameter**	**Description**
[Network]		
	AuditEnabled=YES | NO	If this parameter is set to YES, Windows for Workgroups will record network events. This is explained later in the section on *NetWatcher*.
	ComputerName=*name*	This parameter indicates the name of your computer, which will be advertised on the network. The initial value is specified during setup.
	EnableSharing=YES | NO	The default for this setting is YES. When set to NO, files and printers on this computer cannot be shared.
	FileSharing=YES | NO	When set to NO, files on this computer cannot be shared. The default is YES.
	KeepConn=*nnn*	This parameter tells Windows for Workgroups to wait *nnn* seconds before killing an unused network connection from another computer. The default is 6 seconds. Increase this value if other computers need to access this computer at intervals throughout the day but there will be periods of inactivity.
	MultiNet=*name*	This specifies what other types of networks you have added support for. Examples for *name* include *NetWare3* for Novell NetWare version 3.x.

(continues)

VI

Installing Windows

Table 25.3 Continued		
Section	**Parameter**	**Description**
	NoProtocolErrMsg=YES | NO	Set this value to YES if you have a portable computer that is not always connected to the network. The default setting of NO causes an error message to appear when you run Windows for Workgroups and the network is not connected.
	PrintBufTime=*nnn*	This parameter specifies the time, *nnn* seconds, Windows for Workgroups should wait before releasing a print job. This is sometimes referred to as an *end-of-job timeout*. Decrease this value if you want documents released more quickly. Increase this value if you find you are getting partial print jobs.
	PrintSharing=YES | NO	When set to NO, printers on this computer cannot be shared. The default is YES.
	Username=*name*	The default username for this computer. *Name* defaults to the computer name until after you log in for the first time.
	WorkGroup=*name*	The default workgroup this computer belongs to. *Name* is established during setup.
[Network Drivers]		
	DevDir=*path*	This parameter specifies the *path* to the drive and directory that contains the PROTOCOL.INI file. The default is C:\WINDOWS.
	LoadRMDrivers=YES | NO	When you first set up the networking features on your computer, you will need to specify which network card you have installed, and its driver. At that time, this parameter changes to YES. The *RM* stands for Real Mode.
	NetCard=*filename(s)*	This parameter specifies a list of filenames representing the real mode drivers needed for the network adapter in your computer.

Section	Parameter	Description
	Transport=*filename(s)*	The list of filenames after this parameter represent the filenames of the drivers for the various protocols used by your computer.

[Password List]

	*Shares=*path*	*Path* represents the drive, directory, and filename of the file that contains passwords for shared directories or printers.
	Username=path	You may see a series of usernames and filenames. This represents the password files maintained for users of this computer.

[386Enh]

	EMMExclude=*range*	You may need to exclude a range of memory addresses to protect the operation of your network adapter. A Token Ring adapter, for example, often uses the range D000:0000 through D3FF:FFF. To prevent Windows for Workgroups from using this memory space, use this setting.

EMMExclude=D000-D3FF

	LocalReboot=ON I OFF	When set ON, this setting specifies whether you can use Ctrl+Alt+Del to quit an application that has crashed without restarting Windows for Workgroups. If set OFF, pressing Ctrl+Alt+Del reboots the computer. Leave this at the default (ON) if others are sharing resources from this computer.
	Netcard=*filename(s)*	This is a list of virtual device driver filenames used to initialize your network adapter if real mode drivers are not loaded on your computer.

(continues)

VI

Installing Windows

Table 25.3	Continued	
Section	**Parameter**	**Description**
	NetHeapSize=*size*	This parameter specifies the *size* in bytes of the buffer used for transfers to and from the network. This setting is not used by the default protocol, NETBEUI.386. Increase this setting if you have enough RAM in your computer, you are using real mode protocols (such as IPX/SPX), and you are experiencing slow network throughput.
	NetMisc=*filename(s)*	This setting lists virtual device driver filenames used to enable network communications protocols and the network adapter in your computer.
	Network=*filename(s)*	This parameter lists filenames that implement upper-level protocols which run the client and server portion of Windows for Workgroups.
	SecondNet=*filename*	*Filename* represents additional network drivers if you have specified support for additional networks other than Windows for Workgroups.
	Transport=*filename(s)*	Lists the filenames used to implement the middle-level communications protocols that govern the exchange of data on the network. The default is the Microsoft NetBEUI protocol implemented by the file *netbeui.386*.

Upgrading from Windows or Older Versions of Windows for Workgroups

When performing an upgrade, SETUP detects existing versions of Windows or Windows for Workgroups. You are prompted to install Windows for Workgroups in another directory or overwrite the existing version. Program groups and icons are not affected by the upgrade. When done, the final version resembles your previous version. The difference is that the older Windows kernel is replaced by the Windows for Workgroups kernel, and the utilities are replaced by the newer utilities.

If your previous version of Windows was an older version of Windows for Workgroups, the name and password file is maintained. You will have to log in as the same user name and use the same password as before. In addition, network adapter settings are retained.

A Windows for Workgroups feature added to standard Windows is referred to as a *Workgroup Add-On for Windows*. This term is used in the Microsoft Windows documentation when referring to a Windows workstation that you plan to upgrade to Windows for Workgroups.

From Here...

For more information on Windows for Workgroups, refer to the following chapters:

- Chapter 15, "Using Windows for Workgroups Mail and PC Fax," discusses the uses of Mail and PC Fax.

- Chapter 16, "Using Windows for Workgroups Schedule+," teaches you how to use Schedule+.

- Chapter 17, "Using Clipbook Viewer, Chat, and Pop-up," explains these very important options.

- Chapter 18, "Using Windows for Workgroups Management Tools," is a discussion of management tools available.

VI

Installing Windows

Chapter 26

Networking Windows 3.1x

Using Windows 3.1 on a LAN presents several new challenges that don't affect non-LAN Windows users. You will have to carefully consider how you can configure Windows to give you the right balance of usability, performance, ease of maintenance, and administration.

In this chapter, you learn how to:

- Use the Setup program to install Windows on a LAN server or workstation
- Install printers and queues
- View and edit Windows system files
- Optimize Windows performance on a LAN
- Perform common tasks such as logging on and printing
- Install applications in Windows

Installing Windows 3.1x on a LAN

Perhaps the most frequently asked question about networking Windows is, "Where should I install Windows?" The issue is whether to place Windows itself on the file server or on the user's local hard disk. There is no simple answer that satisfies everyone's needs. Networks are like snowflakes: each one is different. This should be obvious to anyone who has had to work with more than one network for any period. Different LANs use different hardware, PCs, LAN adapters, cabling, and printers. Different LANs have a wide array of software applications installed. In addition, users do not have the same degree of skill or proficiency in using their PC or the network.

Therefore, different environments dictate various solutions. The same solution is not always available for all of the users connected to the same network. In addition to these needs, the network administration team must strike a balance between four different requirements of any network:

- *End User Freedom.* How much flexibility is the user allowed over their own Windows configuration?

- *Ease of Administration.* How much control over the user does network administration need to allow for effective management and maintenance?

- *Performance.* How do the different ways of installing Windows affect performance for the user and for the network at large?

- *Reliability.* How do the different ways of installing Windows affect reliability for the user and for the network at large?

In addition to the question of where to install Windows, you also have to determine where you are going to put its virtual memory swap files and its temporary files. These files do not necessarily reside in the same location as Windows. Since virtual memory swap files and temporary files can affect performance, you want to carefully consider their location in deciding how you install Windows.

The next three sections discuss the possible answers to the question posed above. You may find that you have to employ all of the solutions due to the diversity of your network. In short form, there are three ways you can run Windows in a network environment:

1. Full workstation installation

2. Network installation to the user's local drive

3. Network installation to the user's private network directory

When To Use a Full Workstation Installation

A full workstation installation (also called a stand-alone installation) means that you install a working copy of Windows 3.1x on the user's local drive. The user can run Windows without being logged into the file server or attached to the network. You must have this type of installation if the users have a portable computer that they take away from the office and run Windows. Other users prefer this installation, as it performs its operations at a faster rate than a workstation which runs Windows from a server.

Full workstation installation is appropriate for portable PC users and those users who do not rely much on the network administrator for help in solving problems or configuring their machine. Since you install Windows completely on the user's PC, the network supervisor has little control over what happens on that PC.

This is the default installation method done by the Windows 3.1x Setup program. To install Windows 3.1x with full workstation installation, make your master Windows directory on the file server the default or put the Windows Disk #1 in drive A and make drive A the default. Then type **SETUP** at the system prompt.

Note

If this type of installation is performed using the Windows distribution disks, the workstation does not need to be logged on to the network.

Understanding the Advantages and Disadvantages

It is important to understand how this installation method affects the user's PC, how it affects the performance of the network, and how it affects the administrative aspects of managing the network. Too often, LAN administrators make installation choices without understanding the implications of the decision. In discussing the advantages and disadvantages, you look at the issue from the perspective of a LAN administrator. From the user's perspective, things might look differently.

Advantages

1. *No usage of file server disk space.* This method places all of the Windows files on the user's PC. This is only an advantage when this method is used for all of the Windows users on the file server, otherwise you have not gained anything. In a network installation, only one master copy of Windows has to reside on the file server. It can be used by any number of users, up to the limit of the software license.

2. *Reduced network traffic.* Loading Windows 3.1x from a local disk instead of from a file server keeps the traffic associated with loading Windows off the LAN cable. Since the LAN cabling can be a bottleneck in the network, this may be an important factor in the decision to install Windows locally. In addition to the loading of Windows, Windows uses many different dynamic link libraries (DLLs). Installing Windows locally can reduce the load associated with loading the Windows DLLs.

VI

Installing Windows

3. *Improved Windows load time.* Loading Windows from a local disk may reduce the amount of time it takes to load Windows if the local hardware performs faster that the combination of the file server's hardware and the LAN cabling system. However, only the time it takes to load Windows itself is improved unless all of the user's applications are installed on their local drive. Sometimes the load time from the file server is less than the load time from a local drive.

4. *Windows hardware configuration files match the machine.* SYSTEM.INI is a hardware-specific configuration file. With a local installation, SYSTEM.INI should reflect the settings needed for the machine.

5. *User can run Windows when the network or file server is down or unavailable.* If you install Windows locally, users may run Windows when the network is not running or when they are not connected to the network. This can be very useful for users who have notebook or portable computers. To gain this advantage you also have to install the users' applications on their local drive.

Disadvantages

1. *Large amount of disk space is required.* Windows 3.1x consumes approximately 9-14M of the user's disk space depending upon the installation options chosen. If you are installing on a portable PC, you need disk space for the applications, as well. Major Windows-based applications require a minimum of another 8-12M apiece.

2. *Performance improvement offset by applications on the file server.* If your motivation for installing Windows locally is to improve disk I/O performance, you may find that the gain is negligible due to applications that run from the file server. The only way you gain disk I/O performance is to install every application the user needs on the local drive. Depending upon your server's hardware and NetWare's file caching abilities, you may not see much gain loading Windows from the local drive at all.

3. *Administration of user's PC is decentralized.* Since all of the user's Windows files are local, you cannot manage the user's environment, in most cases, without having physical access to the user's machine. In addition, updates to the Windows 3.1x files require you to copy these files to each affected user's machine. While this is okay for a few of your users, I doubt that you want to support several hundred users this way.

4. *Shared PCs present configuration problems.* If different users use the machine, you have to figure out how you will maintain user-specific configuration files.

Files Copied to User's Disk

Full installation to the user's local drive creates a pair of directories. During installation you indicate the target directory where Windows will be installed. The default name for this directory is WINDOWS. Beneath the target directory, the Setup program creates the SYSTEM directory. The Setup program places approximately 125 files that use about 4.5M of disk space in the WINDOWS directory. Into the SYSTEM subdirectory, the Setup program copies approximately 115 files that use about 5.5M of disk space.

The target directory contains all of the Windows bundled programs like Calendar, Notepad, Cardfile and their related help, and DLL files. It also contains the bit-map wallpaper files, screen-saver files, sound files, the Windows INI files , PIF files, the group GRP files, and the program (WIN.COM). Windows INI files, in this directory, can be viewed and edited with the Notepad applet or with a similar editor that loads and saves ASCII files.

The SYSTEM directory contains the Windows core executable files and their DLL files, the TrueType font files, the fixed screen fonts, hardware drivers, the screen grabbers, and the NetWare drivers.

When To Perform a User Workstation Installation From a Network Drive

This method of installing Windows places only a small group of files on the user's local drive. These files are limited to the Windows INI files, GRP files, the initial PIF files, and WIN.COM. This method dictates that the major files needed to run Windows are installed in a shared directory on the file server. To run Windows, you need a search path to the Windows directory on the file server.

If centralized network administration is important, or you do not want to install Windows individually for each user, you ought to consider this method. If local disk space is limited, this approach minimizes the amount of disk space needed on the local drive.

Understanding the Advantages and Disadvantages

It is important to understand how this installation method affects the user's PC, how it affects the performance of the network, and how it affects the administrative aspects of managing the network. As in the previous section, you look at the issue from the perspective of a LAN administrator. From the user's perspective, things might look differently.

VI

Installing Windows

Advantages

1. *Limited usage of local disk space.* This method places most of the Windows files on the file server. The small group of files needed locally require 150K or less disk space.

2. *Centralized updating of Windows files and drivers.* Since all of the core Windows files reside on the file server, it is easier to install updated versions of these files.

3. *NetWare security controls usage.* Since the bulk of the files needed reside on the file server, NetWare's trustee rights and security privileges control what the user may run or access. The user cannot run, modify, or delete Windows unless they have proper rights.

4. *Improved Windows load time.* Loading Windows from the file server may reduce the amount of time it takes to load Windows if the file server and network hardware perform faster than the local drive.

5. *Windows configuration files match the machine.* SYSTEM.INI is a hardware-specific configuration file residing on the local drive. With a local installation, SYSTEM.INI should reflect the settings needed for the local machine.

Disadvantages

1. *Increased network traffic caused by Windows.* Loading any application over the network increases traffic. Windows is another large application that can generate significant traffic. You should carefully consider the impact of Windows on your network throughput.

2. *Administration of user's PC is mixed.* Since some of the user's Windows files are local, you cannot completely manage the user's environment, in most cases, without having physical access to the user's machine. While this is okay for a few of your users, it is unlikely that you want to support several hundred users this way.

3. *Shared PCs present configuration problems.* If different users use the machine, you have to figure out how you will maintain user-specific configuration files.

Files Copied to User's Disk

Windows 3.1x copies a small group of files to the user's local drive. Table 26.1 lists the files that Windows installs.

> **Note**
>
> WIN.COM is not Windows! It is a program that launches Windows. Setup creates WIN.COM and this program is specific to the hardware specified during the Setup program.

Table 26.1   Files that Windows' Network Installation Places on the User's Local Drive

File Name	Extension
WIN	INI
MOUSE	INI
CONTROL	INI
WINVER	EXE
_DEFAULT	PIF
DOSPRMPT	PIF
PROGMAN	INI
MAIN	GRP
ACCESSOR	GRP
GAMES	GRP
STARTUP	GRP
WIN	COM
SYSTEM	INI

When To Perform a User Installation to a Private Directory on a Network Drive

The final variation of the Windows 3.1x installation methods places all of the information on the file server. This method puts all of the shared Windows files into a shared directory on the file server, and all of the user-specific information into a private user directory on the file server. You must use this method for diskless workstations. Additionally, this is the recommended method if you have users who boot from a floppy disk. The only difference between this method and the previous method is the user's target directory.

VI

Installing Windows

Understanding the Advantages and Disadvantages

It is important to understand how this installation method affects the user's PC, how it affects the performance of the network, and how it affects the administrative aspects of managing the network.

Advantages

1. *No usage of local disk space*. This method places all of the Windows files on the file server.

2. *Centralized updating of Windows files*. It is easier to install updated versions of these files since all of the core Windows files reside on the file server.

3. *NetWare security controls usage*. Since all of the files needed reside on the file server, NetWare's trustee rights and security privileges control what the user may run or access. The user cannot run Windows unless that user has proper rights.

4. *Centralized administration is possible*. Since all of the files needed to run Windows reside on the file server, the network administrator has complete control over the user's environment. This makes administration of the network and troubleshooting much easier for the network administrator.

Disadvantages

1. *Large amount of file server disk space is required*. Windows 3.1x consumes approximately 15M of the file server's disk space, but you also need disk space for the applications. Major Windows-based applications require another 845M apiece.

2. *Network traffic for Windows is increased*. Because all files are on the file server, all DLLs, swap files, and temporary files must reside on the file server, too. This can greatly increase the traffic demands on the network.

3. *Shared PCs present configuration problems*. If users use different machines, you have to figure out how you will maintain user-specific configuration files and machine-specific files. Chapter 6, "Advanced Data Sharing," discusses how to manage these files.

Files Copied to User's Network Directory

The files copied to the user's private directory on the file server are the same as those installed in the previous method. The only difference between these two installation methods is the target directory is on the file server instead of on the user's local drive this time.

Virtual Memory Swap Files and Networks

Windows 3.1 uses the Intel 80386 and 80486 CPU's ability to use *virtual memory*. Virtual memory has its roots in mainframe technology going back to the early 1970's. In those days, memory was very expensive. Nobody could afford to purchase all of the memory they wanted. As mainframe operating systems became able to multitask programs, these systems needed more memory to run these programs.

The idea behind virtual memory is very straightforward. With virtual memory, you treat a portion of your disk space as if it is memory. The memory addresses available can exceed the physical memory of the computer, allowing large programs to run. The computer allocates memory in sections called pages. Data stored in memory pages that are in use but not needed are swapped out to disk based upon the least-recently-used (LRU) algorithm. This frees more real memory for programs that need to manipulate data or for more programs. Figure 26.1 illustrates how paging memory works.

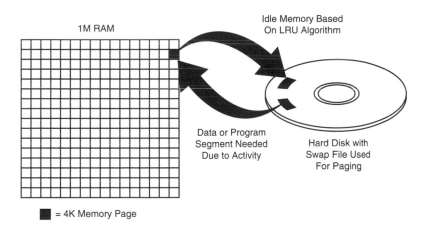

Fig. 26.1
Virtual memory.

VI

Windows 3.1 takes advantage of virtual memory, allowing you to load and run more programs than the memory of your PC normally permits. To accomplish this task, Windows uses a swap file.

Choosing Permanent Versus Temporary Virtual Memory Swap Files

Windows has two types of virtual memory swap files that you can use, *permanent* or *temporary*. Windows only uses one or the other, not both. You can create the swap file during Windows installation or from the Control Panel's 386 Enhanced mode option.

If possible, try to keep the virtual memory swap files on the user's local drive. This reduces the traffic on the network and the disk I/O load on the file server. If you cannot put the virtual memory swap file on the local drive, make sure that you define the size of the temporary virtual memory swap file on the file server, as described below. Otherwise, Windows creates excessively large swap files on the file server (see the following section, "Temporary Virtual Memory Swap File Rules"). In deciding between temporary and permanent swap files, there are several rules you should keep in mind. These rules are discussed in the following sections.

Permanent Virtual Memory Swap File Rules. There are several rules that Microsoft left out of the Windows documentation that pertain to your virtual memory swap files. The following guidelines help you better manage these files.

1. There are two files that comprise the permanent virtual memory swap files—386SPART.PAR and SPART.PAR.

2. The swap file itself (386SPART.PAR) is a hidden, system file in the root directory of the target drive.

3. The permanent virtual memory swap file (386SPART.PAR) must be on a local hard disk. You cannot put it on a file server drive or floppy disk.

4. The permanent swap file must be on an uncompressed volume or a compressed volume that offers support for permanent swap files. Most disk compression schemes are not compatible with permanent swap files.

5. Windows creates the permanent swap file from contiguous free disk space. If you need to optimize your disk, remove any existing permanent swap file first, then optimize, and then re-create the swap file. Make sure your defragmentation utility can skip hidden system files. If you want a large file you should run a disk defragmentation utility, such as Norton's Speed Disk, before creating the permanent swap file.

6. Once created, the permanent swap file must not be moved; otherwise, you get a corrupted swap file message. This happens because Windows creates the second file (SPART.PAR) in your Windows directory that points to the specific location of the swap file. SPART.PAR is a read-only file and is not hidden like 386SPART.PAR.

Temporary Virtual Memory Swap Files Rules. The following guidelines should be followed when you use temporary swap files instead of a permanent swap file set:

1. The temporary swap file is used if Windows cannot locate the permanent swap files.

2. A temporary swap file can reside on a local hard disk or on a network file server volume.

3. The file name of the temporary swap file is WIN386.SWP, and its location is the WINDOWS directory by default. However, the file name and location can be controlled with the PagingFile setting in the [386Enh] section of SYSTEM.INI file.

4. The default size of the temporary swap file is approximately 50% of free disk space, or 4 times the amount of physical RAM installed in the PC—unless you change the PageOverCommit statement in SYSTEM.INI. You can control the size of the temporary swap file by changing the MaxPagingFileSize setting in the [386Enh] section of the SYSTEM.INI file.

Note

The Windows 3.1 programs and documentation state that temporary swap files must reside in an uncompressed disk volume. You cannot place the swap file on a disk area that you are compressing with a program such as Stac Electronics' Stacker.

However, this is not true. You can edit SYSTEM.INI and set the [386Enh] section's PagingDirectory variable to a directory and a file name on a compressed volume.

Obviously, you pay a performance price whenever Windows writes or reads the swap file located on the compressed drive, because the data must be compressed before it is written and uncompressed when it is read.

Understanding Temporary Virtual Memory Swap Files and NetWare

Users who have diskless PCs or floppy disk-based PCs must have their swap file on the file server because they do not have a local hard disk. This presents three problems for you to solve:

First, you have to make sure that the temporary swap file resides in a directory where the user has create, write, file scan, read, and delete rights. This setting is in the [386Enh] section of the SYSTEM.INI file:

```
PagingFile=d:\path[\filename]
```

LAN administrators usually put this file in the user's home directory on the file server, because Windows creates a swap file for each user and the temporary swap file always uses the same name unless specified.

Second, you have to control how large of a temporary swap file Windows creates on the server with the [386Enh] section of the SYSTEM.INI file:

```
MaxPagingFileSize=n
```

VI

Installing Windows

The variable *n* is the number of kilobytes to allocate to the temporary swap file.

Otherwise, Windows attempts to use up to 50% of the volume's (or logical drive's) free disk space, or 4 times the amount of RAM installed on the user's PC. In addition, NetWare 2.x file servers allocate all of this disk space immediately. This uses up your disk space unnecessarily and makes Windows boot up very slowly. Each successive Windows user gets a swap file that is 50% smaller than the previous user. Worse yet is that NetWare 2.x usually crashes when you completely fill a volume! Fortunately, NetWare 3.x does not allocate the disk space until Windows actually writes the data to the server.

Third, you must consider the amount of disk space Windows allocates to the swap file in the user's disk space limitations in NetWare. Since Windows does not read the NetWare bindery information, Windows tries to allocate as large a swap file as allowed. However, when Windows tries to write to the swap file, the NetWare disk limitations control writing to the file server. If the user's limits prevent Windows from writing to the swap file, an application error occurs.

The problem is that there is no easy way to coordinate user disk space limitations and the temporary swap file size when the swap file resides on the file server. As the user stores more data on the server, his free disk space diminishes, but the MaxPagingFileSize setting remains constant. This causes the user to get an application error at some point. All you can do is periodically check the user's free disk space and compare it to the swap file size and adjust one or the other to compensate for the changes.

Understanding Windows Temporary Files

Not to be confused with virtual memory swap files, Windows and Windows-based applications rely heavily on temporary files. For example, if you use the Windows print spooler (as opposed to a network print spooler), the output is sent to a temporary file and then to the printer. Another example is all of the programs that have an undo option on their Edit menu. In order to "undo" something, you must have stored the data prior to the change. The data is stored in a temporary file.

The element that determines where the temporary file is stored is the DOS variable called TEMP, in most cases. Surprisingly enough, much of the disk I/O traffic that people think is virtual memory swap file traffic is actually temporary file traffic. Depending upon the application, some applications write the entire file to a temporary file while others write only the data that is being changed.

The recommendation is to keep this traffic local, first of all. The TEMP variable should always be directed to a local drive, not the network file server.

Tip
In a NetWare environment, you can assess your temporary file usage by applications by temporarily assigning the DOS TEMP variable to a directory on the file server. You can use NetWare's Monitor program to see what files are opened by an application.

Second, if possible, use a logical RAM drive for temporary files. There is no faster I/O than from a RAM drive.

The Bottom Line

So where do you install Windows? It depends on what you are trying to accomplish. Here are some general recommendations:

Best Performance at All Costs

If your mission is to have the fastest possible Windows installation, even if it means more work for a network administrator, install Windows using the following considerations:

1. Install enough RAM on the machine that is executing Windows. You won't have to worry about a virtual memory swap file, and you will have enough memory for a 4-8M RAM disk for temporary files.

   If you cannot afford enough RAM, make sure that you use a permanent swap file and make sure that your DOS TEMP variable is directed to your local disk drive.

2. Install Windows and applications on the local hard drive. This keeps this traffic off of the network and applications usually load faster from a local drive than from a network file server.

   The downside is that in a network environment, this is the worst administrative model because everything is on the user's local PC. Therefore, changes and updates are, at best, difficult.

Best Administration with Some Performance Loss

1. Install enough RAM on the machine that is executing Windows. You won't have to worry about a virtual memory swap file, and you will have enough memory for a 4-8M RAM disk for temporary files.

   If you cannot afford enough RAM, make sure that you use a permanent swap file and make sure your TEMP variable specifies a directory on your local disk drive.

2. Use a network installation, keeping all of Windows core files on the file server and the user-specific files in the user's network directory. This allows the network administrator to easily make changes as needed to both Windows files and user files.

   The downside here is slower program loading from a file server and the traffic on the network that is generated from running all applications from the server.

VI

Installing Windows

Using the Windows Setup Program

You install Windows 3.1x using the Setup program found on the first disk. Regardless of the type of installations you choose for your users, you want to put a copy of all of the Windows files into a master Windows directory on the file server. This allows you to run Setup from the file server without having the Windows disks. The files on the Windows disks are in a compressed form and cannot be used directly from the floppy. To uncompress the files and copy them to the file server use the following command from the system prompt:

SETUP /A

> **Note**
>
> Compressed files on the Windows disks have an underscore (_) as the last character of the file extension. Setup decompresses the file and changes the extension to the proper value. This way you do not have to worry about accidentally copying a compressed file over an uncompressed one in the master Windows directory. Windows operation may fail if it encounters a compressed file that should be uncompressed. This was a problem with Windows 3.0 since the compressed files had the same name and extension as the uncompressed ones.

You should have approximately 485 files and 16M of disk space used by the entire Windows file set. If you use network installations, you map the master Windows directory as a user search drive. This makes it easy to update drivers when Microsoft develops new ones. You merely have to replace the old driver with the new one in the master Windows directory. To install Windows as a network installation use the following command from the system prompt:

SETUP /N

The Setup program prompts for a target directory. You enter a directory on the user's local drive or a directory in the user's private area on the file server. Windows puts only the user-specific files into this directory, as discussed earlier, in the section "When To Perform a User Workstation Installation From a Network Drive" and in the section "When To Perform a User Installation to a Private Directory on a Network Drive."

If the user needs a full, working copy of Windows installed, you run Setup with no command-line options. This creates a working copy of Windows in the target directory as discussed earlier, in the section "When To Use a Full

Workstation Installation." Table 26.2 lists the Setup program options. Many sections later in this chapter discuss other options for the Setup program.

Table 26.2	Setup Program Options
Option	**Usage**
none	Installs a working copy of Windows into the target directory
/a	Installs all Windows 3.1x files into the target directory and marks them read-only
/b	Installs Windows 3.1x for a monochrome display adapter
/h:*filename*	Installs Windows 3.1x using a batch process governed by a parameter file
/i	Ignores the automatic hardware detection information
/n	Performs a network installation of user-specific files from a server
/o:*filename*	Uses the INF file specified rather than SETUP.INF
/s:*filename*	Uses the INF file indicated and a path for the Windows disks
/r	Rebuilds corrupted Windows group files
/t	Searches for incompatible software that should not be used while running Setup

Using Automated Setup Parameter Files

In addition to the standard methods of running Setup, you can run this program in a batch mode by using the following syntax:

Setup /h:*filename* [/n]

The file name refers to a parameter file that you create that contains the setup information needed for this installation. You can create several different parameter files for different circumstances. Disk #1 of your Windows 3.1x disks contains a sample parameter file, SETUP.SHH.

The parameter file used by Setup /h is an ASCII file that contains the following sections as outlined in table 26.3.

VI

Installing Windows

Table 26.3 The INI File	
Section Name	**Usage**
[sysinfo]	Determines whether the configuration screen appears during Setup
[configuration]	Specifies the specific hardware devices installed in the PC
[windir]	Indicates the target directory to install Windows into
[userinfo]	Registers the user and company information
[dontinstall]	Indicates specific Windows components that are not installed
[options]	Specifies various Setup options to be run
[printers]	Determines which printer drivers are installed
[endinstall]	Selects options for updating the user's CONFIG.SYS and AUTOEXEC.BAT and what happens at the end of Setup

When run with the /h option, the Setup program still uses SETUP.INF, CONTROL.INF, and SYSTEM.INI files that are in your Windows master directory. The parameter file usually has an extension of .SHH.

Editing the [sysinfo] Section

This section has only one statement. It determines whether Setup displays the System Information screen. The default is no.

```
showsysinfo=no¦yes
```

Editing the [configuration] Section

This section describes the various devices that are installed on the PC. This section has several parameters as shown in table 26.4. You need one entry for each item in the leftmost column.

Table 26.4 [configuration] Options		
Setting	**Allowed Values**	**Usage**
machine=	ibm_compatible	MS-DOS System
	ast_386_486	AST Premium 386/25 and 386/33
	at_and_t	AT&T PC
	everex_386_25	Everex 386/25 or Compatible

Setting	Allowed Values	Usage
	hewlett_packard	All Hewlett-Packard machines
	ibm_ps2_70p	IBM PS/2 Portable 70
	ibm_ps2_l40sx	IBM PS/2 Model 40 Laptop
	ncr_386sx	All NCR 80386 and 80486 PCs
	nec_pm_sx+	NEC Powermate SX Plus
	nec_prospeed	NEC ProSpeed 386
	toshiba_1200xe	Toshiba 1200XE
	toshiba_1600	Toshiba 1600
	toshiba_5200	Toshiba 5200
	zenith_386	All Zenith 80386 machines
	att_nsx_20	AT&T NSX 20 Safari Notebook
	apm	MS-DOS system with Automatic Power Management
	apm_sl	Intel 80386SL-Based system with Automatic Power Management
display=	8514	8514/a
	8514s	8514/a (Small fonts)
	plasma	Compaq Portable Plasma
	egahires	EGA
	egahibw	EGA black and white (286 only)
	egamono	EGA Monochrome (286 only)
	hercules	Hercules Monochrome
	mcga	IBM MCGA (286 only)
	olibw	Olivetti/AT&T Monochrome or PVC Display
	ct441	QuadVGA, ATI VIP VGA, 82c441 VGA
	tiga1	TIGA (Small Fonts)
	tiga2	TIGA (Large Fonts)

VI

Installing Windows

(continues)

Table 26.4 Continued		
Setting	**Allowed Values**	**Usage**
	vga	VGA
	vga30	VGA (version 3.0)
	vgamono	VGA with Monochrome display
	svga	Super VGA (800x600, 16 colors)
	v7vga	Video 7 512k, 640x480, 256 colors
	v7c	Video 7 512k, 720x512, 256 colors
	v7d	Video 7 1M, 800x600, 256 colors
	v7e	Video 7 1M, 1024x768, 256 colors, large font
	v7f	Video 7 1M, 1024x768, 256 color, small fonts
	xga16	XGA 640x480, 16 colors
	xgasm	XGA (Small Fonts)
	xgalg	XGA (Large Fonts)
	xgalo	XGA 640x480, 256 colors
mouse=	hpmouse	HP Mouse
	lmouse	Logitech Mouse
	ps2mouse	Microsoft or IBM PS/2 Mouse
	genius1	Genius Serial Mouse on COM1
	genius2	Genius Serial Mouse on COM2
	msmouse2	Mouse Systems serial or bus mouse
	msmouse1	Mouse Systems serial mouse on COM2
	kbdmouse	Olivetti/AT&T Keyboard mouse
network=	3open	3Com 3+ Open
	3share	3Com 3+ Share
	lantastic	Artisoft LANtastic
	banyan	Banyan Vines
	dlr	IBM OS/2 LAN Server

Setting	Allowed Values	Usage
	pclp	IBM PC LAN Program
	lanman	Microsoft LAN Manager
	msnet	Microsoft Network (or 100% compatible)
	novell	Novell NetWare
	pathworks	DEC Pathworks
	10net	TCS 10Net
keyboard=	t3s0alat	All AT type keyboards (84-86 keys)
	t1s2at&t	AT&T "301" keyboard
	t1s4at&t	AT&T "302" keyboard
	t4s0enha	Enhanced 101 or 102 key US and Non-US keyboards
	t3s0hp1	Hewlett-Packard Vectra keyboard (DIN)
	t4s40oliv	Olivetti 101/102 A keyboard
	t1s0oliv	Olivetti 83-key keyboard
	t3s10oliv	Olivetti 86-key keyboard
	t2s1oliv	Olivetti M24 102-key keyboard
	t1s42oliv	PC-XT 83-key keyboard
	t1s0pcxt	PC/XT 84-key keyboard
language=	dan	Danish
	nld	Dutch
	enu	English (American)
	eng	English (International)
	fin	Finnish
	fra	French
	frc	French Canadian
	deu	German
	isl	Icelandic

(continues)

VI

Installing Windows

Table 26.4 Continued		
Setting	**Allowed Values**	**Usage**
	ita	Italian
	nor	Norwegian
	ptg	Portuguese
	esp	Spanish
	esn	Spanish (Modern)
	sve	Swedish
kblayout=	beldll	Belgian
	bridll	British
	cafdll	Canadian Multilingual
	dandll	Danish
	dutdll	Dutch
	findll	Finnish
	fredll	French
	candll	French Canadian
	gerdll	German
	icedll	Icelandic
	itadll	Italian
	latdll	Latin American
	nordll	Norwegian
	pordll	Portuguese
	spadll	Spanish
	swedll	Swedish
	swfdll	Swiss French
	swgdll	Swiss German
	nodll	US

Setting	Allowed Values	Usage
	usadll	US
	usddll	US-Dvorak
	usxdll	US-International

Editing the [windir] Section

This section has only one statement that indicates the target directory where Windows will be installed:

```
defdir=drive:\path
```

Editing the [userinfo] Section

This section is used to enter the user and company information for the registration section of Windows 3.1x. It is ignored when setup is run with the /n option since this data is entered when Setup /A is run. This section has the following syntax:

```
"User Name"
```

```
"Company Name"
```

Editing the [dontinstall] Section

This section allows you to omit certain portions of the standard Windows files when Setup is run. To omit a section, include its name in this portion of the parameter file. The section names are as follows:

readmes	The Windows read-me files
accessories	The Windows Accessories
games	Games
screensavers	The Windows 3.1x screen saver files
bitmaps	The Windows 3.1x wallpaper bit-map files

Editing the [options] Section

This section controls optional processes that can occur at the end of Setup. If you do not want any of these processes, omit this section, otherwise just list the processes beneath the section. For example, the following runs the Windows tutorial upon completion of the Windows Setup program.

```
[options]
tutorial
```

VI

Installing Windows

The optional processes are shown in table 26.5.

Table 26.5	[options] Setup Configuration Entries
Process	**Description**
setupapps	Allow the users to scan their drives for existing DOS and Windows applications.
autosetupapps	Automatically scan the user's path and set up all Windows and DOS applications found.
tutorial	Run the Windows tutorial at the end of Setup.

Editing the [printers] Section

This section installs the printer drivers that the user needs and assigns the printer to a Windows port. The ports that are available are:

LPT1:	COM2:	FILE:
LPT2:	COM3:	LPT1.DOS
LPT3:	COM4:	LPT2.DOS
COM1:	EPT:	LPT3.DOS

The syntax for the printers section statements is as follows:

```
printer name, port
```

Table 26.6 lists the printer drivers Microsoft supplies with Windows 3.1x.

Table 26.6	Windows Printer Drivers and Printer Names
Driver	**Printer Name**
TTY.DRV	Generic/Text Only
pscript.DRV	Agfa 9000 Series PS
pscript.DRV	Agfa Compugraphic 400PS
HPPCL.DRV	Agfa Compugraphic Genics
pscript.DRV	Apple LaserWriter
pscript.DRV	Apple LaserWriter II NT
pscript.DRV	Apple LaserWriter II NTX

Driver	Printer Name
pscript.DRV	Apple LaserWriter Plus
HPPCL.DRV	Apricot Laser
pscript.DRV	AST TurboLaser/PS
HPPLOT.DRV	AT&T 435
CITOH.DRV	AT&T 470/475
oki9ibm.DRV	AT&T 473/478
CITOH.DRV	C-Itoh 8510
CANON10e.DRV	Canon Bubble-Jet BJ-10e
CANON130.DRV	Canon Bubble-Jet BJ-130e
CANON330.DRV	Canon Bubble-Jet BJ-300
CANON330.DRV	Canon Bubble-Jet BJ-330
lbpiii.DRV	Canon LBP-4
LBPII.DRV	Canon LBP-8 II
lbpiii.DRV	Canon LBP-8 III
CIT9US.DRV	Citizen 120D
CIT9US.DRV	Citizen 180D
CIT24US.DRV	Citizen PN48
pscript.DRV	Dataproducts LZR-2665
diconix.DRV	Diconix 150 Plus
pscript.DRV	Digital Colormate PS
pscript.DRV	Digital DEClaser 1150
pscript.DRV	Digital DEClaser 2150
pscript.DRV	Digital DEClaser 2250
pscript.DRV	Digital DEClaser 3250
pscript.DRV	Digital LN03R ScriptPrinter
pscript.DRV	Digital PrintServer 20/turbo

VI

Installing Windows

(continues)

Table 26.6 Continued	
Driver	**Printer Name**
pscript.DRV	Digital PrintServer 40
EPSON9.DRV	Epson DFX-5000
HPPCL.DRV	Epson EPL-6000
HPPCL.DRV	Epson EPL-7000
pscript.DRV	Epson EPL-7500
EPSON9.DRV	Epson EX-800
EPSON9.DRV	Epson EX-1000
EPSON9.DRV	Epson FX-80
EPSON9.DRV	Epson FX-80+
EPSON9.DRV	Epson FX-85
EPSON9.DRV	Epson FX-86e
EPSON9.DRV	Epson FX-100
EPSON9.DRV	Epson FX-100+
EPSON9.DRV	Epson FX-185
EPSON9.DRV	Epson FX-286
EPSON9.DRV	Epson FX-286e
EPSON9.DRV	Epson FX-850
EPSON9.DRV	Epson FX-1050
HPPCL.DRV	Epson GQ-3500
EPSON9.DRV	Epson JX-80
EPSON24.DRV	Epson L-750
EPSON24.DRV	Epson L-1000
EPSON24.DRV	Epson LQ-500
EPSON24.DRV	Epson LQ-510
ESCP2.DRV	Epson LQ-570 ESC/P 2
EPSON24.DRV	Epson LQ-800

Driver	Printer Name
EPSON24.DRV	Epson LQ-850
ESCP2.DRV	Epson LQ-870 ESC/P 2
EPSON24.DRV	Epson LQ-950
EPSON24.DRV	Epson LQ-1000
EPSON24.DRV	Epson LQ-1050
ESCP2.DRV	Epson LQ-1070 ESC/P 2
ESCP2.DRV	Epson LQ-1170 ESC/P 2
EPSON24.DRV	Epson LQ-1500
EPSON24.DRV	Epson LQ-2500
EPSON24.DRV	Epson LQ-2550
EPSON9.DRV	Epson LX-80
EPSON9.DRV	Epson LX-86
EPSON9.DRV	Epson LX-800
EPSON9.DRV	Epson LX-810
EPSON9.DRV	Epson MX-80
EPSON9.DRV	Epson MX-80 F/T
EPSON9.DRV	Epson MX-100
EPSON9.DRV	Epson RX-80
EPSON9.DRV	Epson RX-80 F/T
EPSON9.DRV	Epson RX-80 F/T+
EPSON9.DRV	Epson RX-100
EPSON9.DRV	Epson RX-100+
EPSON24.DRV	Epson SQ-2000
EPSON24.DRV	Epson SQ-2500
EPSON9.DRV	Epson T-750
EPSON9.DRV	Epson T-1000

VI

Installing Windows

(continues)

Table 26.6 Continued	
Driver	**Printer Name**
FUJI24.DRV	Fujitsu DL 2400
FUJI24.DRV	Fujitsu DL 2600
FUJI24.DRV	Fujitsu DL 3300
FUJI24.DRV	Fujitsu DL 3400
FUJI24.DRV	Fujitsu DL 5600
FUJI9.DRV	Fujitsu DX 2100
FUJI9.DRV	Fujitsu DX 2200
FUJI9.DRV	Fujitsu DX 2300
FUJI9.DRV	Fujitsu DX 2400
PG306.DRV	Hermes H 606
pscript.DRV	Hermes H 606 PS (13 Fonts)
pscript.DRV	Hermes H 606 PS (35 Fonts)
HPPLOT.DRV	HP 7470A [HP Plotter]
HPPLOT.DRV	HP 7475A [HP Plotter]
HPPLOT.DRV	HP 7550A [HP Plotter]
HPPLOT.DRV	HP 7580A [HP Plotter]
HPPLOT.DRV	HP 7580B [HP Plotter]
HPPLOT.DRV	HP 7585A [HP Plotter]
HPPLOT.DRV	HP 7585B [HP Plotter]
HPPLOT.DRV	HP 7586B [HP Plotter]
HPPLOT.DRV	HP ColorPro [HP Plotter]
HPPLOT.DRV	HP ColorPro with GEC [HP Plotter]
HPDSKJET.DRV	HP DeskJet
HPDSKJET.DRV	HP DeskJet Plus
HPDSKJET.DRV	HP DeskJet 500
DJ500C.DRV	HP DeskJet 500C

Driver	**Printer Name**
HPPLOT.DRV	HP DraftPro [HP Plotter]
HPPLOT.DRV	HP DraftPro DXL [HP Plotter]
HPPLOT.DRV	HP DraftPro EXL [HP Plotter]
HPPLOT.DRV	HP DraftMaster I [HP Plotter]
HPPLOT.DRV	HP DraftMaster II [HP Plotter]
HPPCL.DRV	HP LaserJet
HPPCL.DRV	HP LaserJet Plus
HPPCL.DRV	HP LaserJet 500+
HPPCL.DRV	HP LaserJet 2000
HPPCL.DRV	HP LaserJet Series II
HPPCL.DRV	HP LaserJet IID
pscript.DRV	HP LaserJet IID PostScript
HPPCL.DRV	HP LaserJet IIP
HPPCL.DRV	HP LaserJet IIP Plus
pscript.DRV	HP LaserJet IIP PostScript
hppcl5a.drv	HP LaserJet III
pscript.DRV	HP LaserJet III PostScript
hppcl5a.drv	HP LaserJet IIID
pscript.DRV	HP LaserJet IIID PostScript
hppcl5a.drv	HP LaserJet IIIP
pscript.drv	HP LaserJet IIIP PostScript
hppcl5a.drv	HP LaserJet IIISi
pscript.DRV	HP LaserJet IIISi PostScript
PAINTJET.DRV	HP PaintJet
PAINTJET.DRV	HP PaintJet XL
THINKJET.DRV	HP ThinkJet (2225 C-D)

VI

Installing Windows

(continues)

Table 26.6	Continued
Driver	**Printer Name**
IBMCOLOR.DRV	IBM Color Printer
EXECJET.DRV	IBM ExecJet
oki9ibm.DRV	IBM Graphics
ibm4019.drv	IBM Laser Printer 4019
pscript.DRV	IBM LaserPrinter 4019 PS17
pscript.DRV	IBM LaserPrinter 4019 PS39
pscript.drv	IBM LaserPrinter 4029 PS17
pscript.drv	IBM LaserPrinter 4029 PS39
pscript.DRV	IBM Personal Pageprinter
pscript.DRV	IBM Personal Page Printer II-30
pscript.DRV	IBM Personal Page Printer II-31
proprint.DRV	IBM Proprinter
proprint.DRV	IBM Proprinter II
proprint.DRV	IBM Proprinter III
proprn24.DRV	IBM Proprinter X24
proprn24.DRV	IBM Proprinter X24e
proprint.DRV	IBM Proprinter XL
proprint.DRV	IBM Proprinter XL II
proprint.DRV	IBM Proprinter XL III
proprn24.DRV	IBM Proprinter XL24
proprn24.DRV	IBM Proprinter XL24e
PS1.DRV	IBM PS/1
IBM5204.DRV	IBM QuickWriter 5204
QWIII.DRV	6:unidrv.dll
HPPCL.DRV	Kyocera F-Series (USA)
HPPCL.DRV	Kyocera F-5000 (USA)

Driver	Printer Name
pscript.DRV	Linotronic 200/230
pscript.DRV	Linotronic 330
pscript.DRV	Linotronic 530
pscript.DRV	Linotronic 630
pscript.DRV	Microtek TrueLaser
pscript.DRV	NEC Colormate PS/40
pscript.DRV	NEC Colormate PS/80
NEC24pin.DRV	NEC Pinwriter CP6
NEC24pin.DRV	NEC Pinwriter CP7
NEC24pin.DRV	NEC Pinwriter P5XL
NEC24pin.DRV	NEC Pinwriter P6
NEC24pin.DRV	NEC Pinwriter P7
NEC24pin.DRV	NEC Pinwriter P9XL
NEC24pin.DRV	NEC Pinwriter P2200
NEC24pin.DRV	NEC Pinwriter P5200
NEC24pin.DRV	NEC Pinwriter P5300
HPPCL.DRV	NEC Silentwriter LC 860 Plus
pscript.DRV	NEC Silentwriter LC890
pscript.DRV	NEC Silentwriter LC890XL
pscript.DRV	NEC Silentwriter2 90
pscript.DRV	NEC Silentwriter2 290
pscript.DRV	NEC Silentwriter2 990
pscript.DRV	OceColor G5241 PS
pscript.DRV	OceColor G5242 PS
oki9ibm.DRV	Okidata ML 92-IBM
oki9ibm.DRV	Okidata ML 93-IBM

VI

Installing Windows

(continues)

Table 26.6 Continued

Driver	Printer Name
HPPCL.DRV	Okidata LaserLine 6
OKI9.DRV	Okidata ML 192
OKI9.DRV	Okidata ML 192 Plus
OKI9IBM.DRV	Okidata ML 192-IBM
OKI9.DRV	Okidata ML 193
OKI9.DRV	Okidata ML 193 Plus
OKI9IBM.DRV	Okidata ML 193-IBM
OKI9.DRV	Okidata ML 320
OKI9IBM.DRV	Okidata ML 320-IBM
OKI9.DRV	Okidata ML 321
OKI9IBM.DRV	Okidata ML 321-IBM
OKI24.DRV	Okidata ML 380
OKI24.DRV	Okidata ML 390
OKI24.DRV	Okidata ML 390 Plus
OKI24.DRV	Okidata ML 391
OKI24.DRV	Okidata ML 391 Plus
OKI24.DRV	Okidata ML 393
OKI24.DRV	Okidata ML 393 Plus
OKI24.DRV	Okidata ML 393C
OKI24.DRV	Okidata ML 393C Plus
HPPCL.DRV	Okidata OL-400
HPPCL.DRV	Okidata OL-800
pscript.DRV	Oki OL840/PS
DM309.DRV	Olivetti DM 109
DM309.DRV	Olivetti DM 309
HPPCL.DRV	Olivetti ETV 5000

Driver	Printer Name
HPPCL.DRV	Olivetti PG 108
HPPCL.DRV	Olivetti PG 208 M2
PG306.DRV	Olivetti PG 306
pscript.DRV	Olivetti PG 306 PS (13 Fonts)
pscript.DRV	Olivetti PG 306 PS (35 Fonts)
HPPCL.DRV	Olivetti PG 308 HS
pscript.DRV	DEVICESPECIFIC
PANSON24.DRV	Panasonic KX-P1123
PANSON24.DRV	Panasonic KX-P1124
PANSON9.DRV	Panasonic KX-P1180
PANSON24.DRV	Panasonic KX-P1624
PANSON9.DRV	Panasonic KX-P1695
HPPCL.DRV	Panasonic KX-P4420
pscript.DRV	Panasonic KX-P4455 v51.4
pscript.DRV	PostScript Printer
pscript.DRV	QMS ColorScript 100
pscript.DRV	QMS-PS 800
pscript.DRV	QMS-PS 800 Plus
pscript.DRV	QMS-PS 810
pscript.DRV	QMS-PS 820
pscript.DRV	QMS-PS 2200
pscript.DRV	Seiko ColorPoint PS Model 04
pscript.DRV	Seiko ColorPoint PS Model 14
HPPCL.DRV	QuadLaser I
HPPCL.DRV	Tandy LP-1000
HPPCL.DRV	Tegra Genesis

(continues)

VI

Installing Windows

Table 26.6 Continued	
Driver	**Printer Name**
pscript.DRV	Tektronix Phaser II PX
pscript.DRV	Tektronix Phaser II PXi
pscript.DRV	Tektronix Phaser III PXi
TI850.DRV	TI 850/855
pscript.DRV	TI microLaser PS17
pscript.DRV	TI microLaser PS35
TOSHIBA.DRV	Toshiba P351
TOSHIBA.DRV	Toshiba P1351
HPPCL.DRV	Toshiba PageLaser12
PG306.DRV	Triumph Adler SDR 7706
pscript.DRV	Triumph Adler SDR 7706 PS13
pscript.DRV	Triumph Adler SDR 7706 PS35
HPPCL.DRV	Unisys AP9210
pscript.DRV	Unisys AP9415
pscript.DRV	Varityper VT-600
pscript.DRV	Wang LCS15
pscript.DRV	Wang LCS15 FontPlus
HPPCL.DRV	Wang LDP8

Editing the [endinstall] Section

The final section of the setup parameter file declares procedures you want performed when Setup is finished installing Windows. The options available are described in table 26.7.

Table 26.7 [endinstall] Section Options	
Statement	**Usage**
configfiles=modify	This option causes Setup to make modifications to the user's CONFIG.SYS and AUTOEXEC.BAT file. It makes a backup copy of the original files with an .OLD extension.
configfiles=save	This option causes Setup to create suggested AUTOEXEC.BAT and CONFIG.SYS files in the user's Windows directory. These files have .WIN as their extension.
endopt=exit	This setting causes Setup to exit back to DOS at the end of the installation.
endopt=restart	This option causes Setup to exit to DOS and then restart Windows upon completion of the installation.
endopt=reboot	This option reboots the user's PC at the end of the Setup process.

Restricting Users' Ability To Run Setup

As the network administrator and the one responsible for keeping everything running, you have to decide if you allow the user to run the Setup program. The usual reason that a user might need to run this program is to change their hardware configuration. This happens when the user has a video adapter that offers several different choices for resolutions or when the user needs to install different printer drivers.

If your users do not need to re-run Setup for these reasons, you do not have to leave the Setup program in the user's Main group. The user can still run the program from the **F**ile menu, using the **R**un command, or from File Manager if the program resides in a directory where the user has access. You could rename the Setup program if you cannot prevent users from accessing it. The only sure-fire way to prevent the user from running Setup is to remove the program itself.

Another option is to restrict the user's usage of the Setup program to a network installation only. You can do this by changing a statement in the SETUP.INF file. The [data] section has a statement as follows:

```
NetSetup = FALSE
```

If you change this setting to TRUE, the user can only run a network setup. This limits the Setup program to updating the user's INI files to reflect the driver changes needed. Setup re-creates the user's group files, but nothing should be gained or lost. It prevents the user from making a full workstation installation to their local disk.

VI

Installing Windows

Installing Printers and Queues

When installing Windows interactively or from batch mode, you can install the printer drivers for the user. In a network environment, you must install the printer drivers for each printer on the network the user uses. The user's WIN.INI file records these drivers. If you are performing a full workstation installation, Setup copies the printer drivers needed into the user's Windows SYSTEM directory.

When you install the printers, you can also assign the printer to NetWare queues. The user's WIN.INI file records the queue assignments made in Windows 3.1x. Windows re-establishes the assignments each time the user starts Windows, which is a major enhancement from earlier versions of Windows. Since NetWare supports up to three active "captured" ports, you can have up to three queues pre-assigned to printer drivers. You can install other printers that the user can use, but you cannot make the needed queue assignments until the user wants to use the printer. Users can change queue assignments through Control Panel or Print Manager.

Installing printers requires several steps during installation. In addition, you need to be aware of a few options that are not obvious. This section points out these options and shows you sample screens so that you recognize these options when you run Setup.

Figure 26.2 displays the dialog box used to select printer drivers you want to add. In this example, an Apple LaserWriter is selected to be added as a network printer. The figure also shows that a Hewlett-Packard LaserJet Series II printer is installed.

Fig. 26.2
The Printers
dialog box.

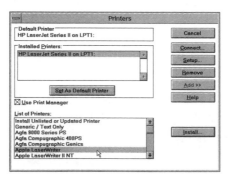

Once Windows has added the printer's driver to the Windows INI files, Setup displays it in the Installed Printers portion of the dialogue box (see fig. 26.3).

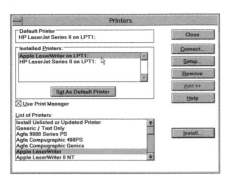

Fig. 26.3
The Printers dialog box showing the Apple LaserWriter as installed.

Once the dialog box lists a printer, you are ready to instruct Windows that the printer is a network printer. You select the **C**onnect button. The first task in the Connect dialog box is to select a port. This is the port that you are going to "capture." NetWare limits captures to LPT1, LPT2, and LPT3. Figure 26.4 shows the Connect dialog box with LPT1 selected.

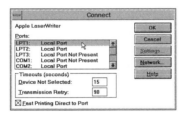

Fig. 26.4
The Connect dialog box.

After you choose the port, click the **N**etwork button to continue. Setup displays the Network - Printer Connections dialog box. This dialog box lists the available network print queues and the three ports that NetWare can capture. Choose the port and the queue you want to assign to the port, and then choose the Co**n**nect button to make the assignment. Note that if you mark the Per**m**anent check box, you are instructing Windows to re-assign this queue to this port each time you start Windows. Figure 26.5 shows the Network - Printer Connections dialog box with a queue assigned as a permanent assignment.

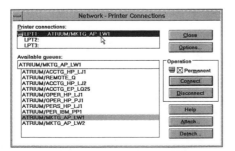

Fig. 26.5
The Network - Printer Connections dialog box.

After assigning the queue, you must configure the printer settings by choosing the **O**ptions button from the Network - Printer Connections dialog box. Windows requires this step because Windows does not use the NetWare print job information (PRINTCON.DAT). Figure 26.6 shows the default settings that the Printer Options dialog box uses. For Windows to interact properly with NetWare, you need to make sure that you use the following settings:

No Tabs

No Banner

No Timeout

Fig. 26.6

The default Printer Options for LPT1.

The **N**otify check box causes NetWare to send the user a message that indicates the job has been printed. **F**orm Feed causes NetWare to issue a form-feed command to the printer at the end of a print job. You use **C**opies to set the number of copies that NetWare prints. Fo**r**m Name establishes the name of the form that is loaded on this printer. You establish these names in NetWare using the PRINTDEF program. Figure 26.7 displays a properly configured Printer Options dialog box.

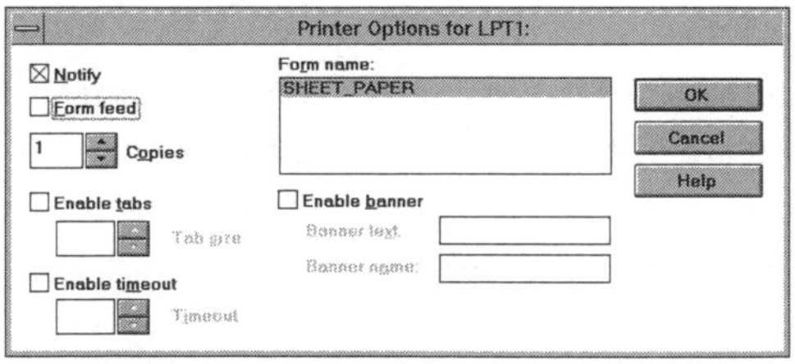

Fig. 26.7

The Printer Options for LPT1: dialog box.

Once the Printer Options dialog box is complete, choose OK to return to the Network - Printer Connections dialog box. Then, select the **C**lose button from the Network - Printer Connection dialog box to return to the Connect dialog box. Choose OK to return to the Printers dialog box.

The next procedure is to configure the printer driver for any printer options you may need. These options vary from printer to printer because different printers have different options. On laser printers, you have to check the amount of memory installed, the default paper tray, and any printer font cartridges you have installed. On Postscript laser printers, you have to decide if you want the Postscript header sent with each print job (generally you do), if you want the error handler installed (generally you do), and whether you are printing directly to the printer or to a file. For dot-matrix printers, you need to make sure that you set your graphics resolution properly and select your font cartridges.

Optimizing Windows 3.1x for Use on a LAN

The INI files control how Windows operates on your PC. Many of the settings in these INI files are important to consider when configuring Windows to run in a NetWare LAN environment. In this section, you learn about the settings that pertain to running Windows in this environment. For the purposes of this discussion, it does not matter, unless indicated, whether you install Windows locally on the user's PC or on the file server.

SYSTEM.INI

SYSTEM.INI is a critical Windows INI file. This file is the primary hardware configuration file for Windows. It also controls most of the multitasking options for using Windows. Each machine configuration requires a different SYSTEM.INI file.

Many of the settings in this file are not configurable. You modify others to change Windows' behavior when needed.

Important Settings for LAN Users

Some settings for this file need to be considered for potential change. Most of these settings affect the [386Enh] section since this section controls multi-tasking when running in 386 Enhanced mode.

> **Note**
>
> You can place commands in Windows INI files in any order within their appropriate sections. To add comments, precede them with a semicolon.

VI

Installing Windows

[386Enh] Section

The following settings control how Windows uses the upper memory area (UMA) when running DOS applications. Windows automatically scans the UMA for a place to put expanded memory page frames and translation buffers. Translation buffers allow Windows to translate MS-DOS and network application interface (API) calls from protected mode (Windows) to real mode (DOS). However, if your third-party memory manager already allocated the page frame, Windows uses the page frame from the memory manager.

If you only use the Windows memory manager and only have HIMEM.SYS in your CONFIG.SYS, you have to configure the UMA for the page frame location, otherwise your DOS applications won't find any expanded memory.

The problem is that Windows does not always accurately detect other device drivers and ROMs that use UMA address space. Therefore, you have to instruct Windows about which areas it can or cannot use.

EMMExclude

Syntax: `EMMExclude=`*Starting Hexparagraph-Hexparagraph range*

Default: The command is not included in SYSTEM.INI and there are no default settings.

Example: `EMMExclude=A000-EFFF`

This setting excludes a memory range from Windows. The paragraph and range must be an even multiple of 16K. Multiple lines can be used to exclude more than one range. Use this to avoid conflicts with ROM and RAM addresses used by other peripherals if you think Windows is not picking these addresses up properly. Many network administrators exclude A000-EFFF on all machines so that changes made in the UMA by the user do not affect Windows.

Several types of devices have known areas that you must exclude. Some of these are listed in table 26.8.

Table 26.8 Upper Memory Area Exclusions	
Device	**Exclusion**
AST Premium 386/25 and 386/33	E000-EFFF
Dell 386SX	C000-C7FF E000-FFFF
Dell Laptops	C000-C7FF E000-FFFF

Device	Exclusion
Epson	E000-EFFF
IBM PS/2 Laptop Model 40	E000-EFFF
NCR - All 80386 and 80486 Machines	C600-C7FF E000-EFFF
Toshiba 5200	C000-C7FF
Zenith - All 80386-based PCs	E000-EFFF
Almost all ARCnet Cards	D000-E000
Eagle/Novell Ethernet Remote Boot ROM	C000-DE00
Almost all VGA Adapters	C000-C7FF
Almost all SVGA Adapters	C400-C7FF
All systems using Plus Development Impulse drives	C000-DFFF

EMMInclude

Syntax: `EMMInclude=`*Starting Hexparagraph-Hexparagraph range*

Default: The command is not included in SYSTEM.INI and there are no default settings.

Example: `EMMInclude=B000=BFFF`

This setting specifies a range of memory that limits where Windows scans when looking for unused memory in the UMA area. More than one range can be specified with multiple lines. The paragraph and range must be an even multiple of 16K.

EMMPageFrame

Syntax: `EMMPageFrame=`*Hexparagraph*

Default: This command is not included in SYSTEM.INI. This allows Windows to scan the UMA for a suitable location on its own. Windows uses the page frame location established by a third-party, Windows-compatible memory manager.

Example: `EMMPageFrame=C400`

VI

Installing Windows

This setting specifies where Windows puts the 64K page frame used for EMS memory if no third-party memory manager has already established the location. You must use this setting if the only memory manager you have in your CONFIG.SYS is HIMEM.SYS. Otherwise, DOS applications do not receive any expanded memory.

EMMSize

Syntax: EMMSize=*kilobytes*

Default: This command is not included in SYSTEM.INI. Therefore, Windows uses the maximum amount of expanded memory possible.

Example: EMMSize=1024

This sets the total amount of memory that is available for expanded memory. Some applications, if running without a Windows program information file (PIF), grab all available RAM leaving none available for other applications. The symptom is that you cannot create another virtual machine. If set to zero, no expanded memory is available to these applications.

SysVMEMSLimit

Syntax: SysVMEMSLimit=*number of kilobytes*

Default: 2048

Example: SysVMEMSLimit=1024

This command establishes the maximum amount of expanded memory Windows is allowed to provide to all running DOS applications. A value of zero prohibits Windows from providing any expanded memory. A value of –1 allows Windows to create as much expanded memory as it needs until it runs out of memory. You need to use this setting if you have DOS applications that use extended memory; but, Windows does not have any extended memory to give because it has converted all extended memory to expanded memory for other DOS applications.

The next set of commands you should consider deals with serial ports. Windows supports up to four serial ports, COM1-COM4. Unfortunately, whenever you go beyond COM2, the Windows defaults don't work. The defaults listed in the following table illustrate the problem.

Port	I/O Port	IRQ
COM1	03F8	4
COM2	02F8	3
COM3	03E8	4
COM4	02E8	3

In industry standard architecture machines (ISA), interrupt channels must be unique or the machine crashes when both devices are active at the same time. Therefore, you usually have to take care to avoid conflicts with IRQ3 and IRQ4. If you reconfigure your COM ports on the PC, you must reconfigure SYSTEM.INI in Windows using the following commands.

COMxBase

Syntax: COMxBase=*address*

The *x* is replaced with any number from 1 to 4.

Default: See the preceding table.

Example: COM1Base=3F8h

This setting controls the I/O port used for serial ports. It can be changed via the Ports option of the Control Panel.

COMxIrq

Syntax: COMxIrq=*number*

The *x* is replaced with any number from 1 to 4.

Default: See the preceding table.

Example: COM1Irq=4

This setting controls the interrupt channel used for serial ports. It can be changed via the **P**orts selection of Control Panel.

network. The next section to consider is the devices needed to run Windows with NetWare. Novell wrote device drivers for interfacing NetWare with Windows. These devices are written into SYSTEM.INI when you run Setup if you have previously loaded the workstation's network shell software. The following is the normal line you should find in the [386Enh] section of SYSTEM.INI.

Syntax: network=*vnetbios,vnetware.386,vipx.386

VI

Installing Windows

The first driver listed, *vnetbios, is an internal driver to Windows. There is no external file for this driver. The other drivers, vnetware.386 and vipx.386, are external files. These files should be in the user's Windows SYSTEM directory or in the master Windows directory on the file server.

If your PC uses temporary swap files, the next two commands control the swap file. The Temporary swap file (WIN386.SWP) can be on the file server or on a local hard disk. For best performance, it is normally better to put the swap file on the local hard disk. This reduces traffic on the network and workload for the file server. In addition, file servers running NetWare 2.x allocate the disk space for the swap file right away, whether the space is ever needed or not. Fortunately, NetWare 3.x does not allocate the swap file space until it is actually written.

MaxPagingFileSize

Syntax: `MaxPagingFileSize=`*kilobytes*

Default: No default value. If Windows does not find a permanent swap file, it automatically uses a temporary swap file. If this command is missing from the user's SYSTEM.INI file, Windows uses 50% of the user's free disk space.

Example: `MaxPagingFileSize=1024`

Caution

If the temporary swap file is placed on the file server, you may have conflicts with NetWare's user volume and disk space limitations. Windows does not read the NetWare binderies to determine how much disk space the user has remaining. Windows only looks at free disk space. Therefore, it is possible for Windows to "allocate" more space to the swap file than NetWare allows Windows to write. NetWare controls all data written to the file server.

If you use the NetWare user disk space limitations and temporary swap files on the file server, you must plan for the user's temporary swap file in their disk space limitations. You also want to use MaxPagingFileSize to limit the swap file size.

You may still run into problems even having tried to allocate enough disk space to the user. This happens because the size of the user's temporary swap file is established by SYSTEM.INI and doesn't change dynamically as the user stores more real files on the file server. Eventually, you will still have a problem with the size of the swap file and the user's disk space limitations.

MinUserDiskSpace

Syntax: `MinUserDiskSpace=`*kilobytes*

Default: 500

Example: `MinUserDiskSpace=1024`

This command limits the size of the temporary swap file by forcing Windows to leave a certain amount of disk space free.

PagingDrive

Syntax: `PagingDrive=`*drive letter*

Default: The current drive when the user started Windows.

Example: `PagingDrive=c`

This command specifies where Windows creates a temporary swap file if it does not find a permanent swap file. If this is a NetWare file server drive, the drive must be mapped as a root directory.

PagingFile

Syntax: `PagingFile=`*path**filename*

Default: The current drive and directory when the user started Windows.

Example: `PagingFile=c:\temp`

This command specifies the name and path for the temporary swap file if no permanent swap file exists. This command overrides the PagingDrive command. You should use this setting whenever the temporary swap file resides on the file server.

The following commands affect how Windows handles multitasking. You use these commands to fine-tune how you want Windows to perform.

MinTimeSlice

Syntax: `MinTimeSlice=`*milliseconds*

Default: 20

Example: `MinTimeSlice=15`

VI

Installing Windows

MinTimeSlice determines how much time Windows must spend on an active task before it is permitted to switch to another task or virtual machine. Decreasing this value makes the foreground task run smoother at an overall cost of less performance. This happens because Windows spends relatively more time switching tasks and less time actually processing. On machines with clock speeds over 25MHz, you may find decreasing this value to be beneficial.

WinTimeSlice

Syntax: `WinTimeSlice=`*foreground priority,background priority*

Default: 100,50

Example: `WinTimeSlice=100,150`

This value sets the relative priority of all running Windows applications. These values are compared to the values of any running DOS program PIF settings to determine how much time is spent on Windows programs running in foreground or background.

Local

The next command is important for every SYSTEM.INI file. The Local command addresses how Windows handles devices in its multitasking machine environment. You can visualize the Windows environment as consisting of two components. One component is the virtual machines that contain DOS, drivers, and programs that are specific to that application and do not affect any other virtual machine. The other component is the part of Windows that is global and relevant to all virtual machines (see fig. 26.8). A simple question is, "Where do physical device drivers reside?" Because the hardware is shared by all virtual machines, you can easily understand that Windows device drivers must be a part of the global environment so that Windows can arbitrate between different programs that need access to a given device.

Syntax: `Local=`*device*

Default: CON

Example: `Local=MS$MOUSE`

The DOS device name must be in uppercase characters.

At this point in the file, add another line as follows: `Local=EGA$`

Some DOS programs reset the monitor upon exiting. Since the monitor is global to all virtual machines, this can cause the operation of other VMs to fail. Using Local=EGA$ localizes any monitor settings to that VM. The DOS device name, EGA$, must be typed in uppercase.

The CON device is the keyboard. The default setting makes the keyboard local to the foreground virtual machine.

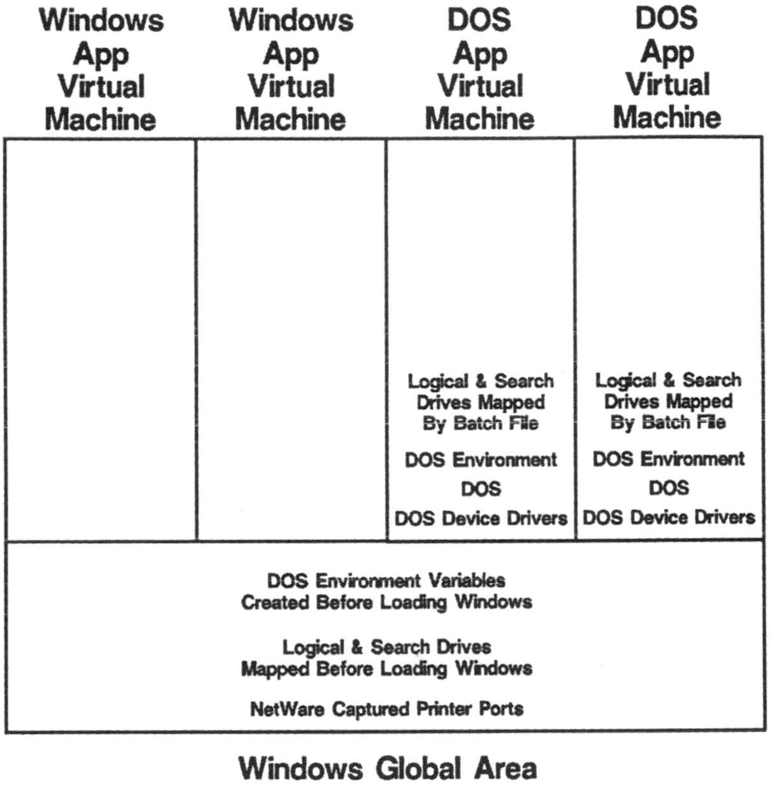

Fig. 26.8
Windows virtual machines and global areas.

Windows App Virtual Machine	Windows App Virtual Machine	DOS App Virtual Machine	DOS App Virtual Machine
		Logical & Search Drives Mapped By Batch File	Logical & Search Drives Mapped By Batch File
		DOS Environment	DOS Environment
		DOS	DOS
		DOS Device Drivers	DOS Device Drivers

DOS Environment Variables
Created Before Loading Windows

Logical & Search Drives
Mapped Before Loading Windows

NetWare Captured Printer Ports

Windows Global Area

[boot] Section

The [boot] section of SYSTEM.INI contains one line that must be present for Novell networks.

Syntax: `network.drv=netware.drv`

This command identifies the driver needed by Windows for NetWare. The NETWARE.DRV file must be in the user's Windows SYSTEM directory or in the master Windows directory on the file server.

[Boot.description]

The [Boot.description] section of SYSTEM.INI contains one line that must be present for NetWare LANs.

Syntax: `network.drv=Novell NetWare (version information)`

Setup uses this section to display the user's current configuration when Setup is run from Windows. There is no need to edit this section.

[NonWindowsApp] Section

The [NonWindowsApp] section contains just a couple of commands that you need to consider. Both commands concern DOS application parameters.

The first one is for users who run Windows in standard mode. Standard mode does not permit multitasking DOS applications. It does permit task-switching between DOS applications.

SwapDisk

Syntax: `SwapDisk=`*drive:path*

Default: The directory established by the DOS TEMP variable. If no TEMP variable exists, Windows uses the current directory when the user starts Windows.

Example: `SwapDisk=c:\swapcity`

When a user switches out of a DOS application in foreground, the DOS application is swapped out of memory onto disk. It remains there until the user switches back to the DOS application. Windows uses the swap area when it runs out of RAM for Windows applications, also.

CommandEnvSize

Syntax: `CommandEnvSize=`*bytes*

Default: The amount of environment space established by the SHELL statement in CONFIG.SYS.

Example: `CommandEnvSize=384`

This value establishes the amount of DOS environment space created in each virtual machine running a DOS application. The valid range is between 160 and 32,768 bytes. If the value entered is smaller than that already established for the DOS environment, this setting is ignored.

The preceding documented commands are the ones that are likely to need adjusting for your Windows environment. There are many other possible settings.

PROGMAN.INI

This is one of the critical INI files for Windows. It contains the information about the Program Manager groups. Listing 26.1 shows a sample of this file. The [settings] section displays the current settings for the user's window placements and the name of the user's display driver. The [Groups] section contains the name and path to the user's group files.

Note that one of the groups in the sample refers to drive T:. Shared groups can be on the file server as long as the user's PROGMAN.INI contains a valid path to the group. This allows the network administrator to update a group easily. The other example shows the use of a DOS Truename path to access a shared group on the file server. DOS Truename paths are one of the best kept secrets around. It is highly recommended that you use Truenames whenever you can to specify paths to network directories.

> **Caution**
>
> Never use a DOS Truename path in the Working Directory field of a Windows Program Properties! A severe bug in Windows 3.1x causes Windows to crash immediately upon entering a Truename path in this field.

Listing 26.1   Sample PROGMAN.INI File

```
[Settings]
Window=4 5 1019 673 1
display.drv=ULTRA.DRV
Order= 4 2 3 5 6 1
AutoArrange=1

[Groups]
Group1=C:\WIN31\MAIN0.GRP
Group2=C:\WIN31\ACCESSO0.GRP
Group3=C:\WIN31\GAMES.GRP
Group4=C:\WIN31\STARTUP.GRP
Group5=T:\WAPPS\GRP\TOOLS.GRP
Group6=\\ATRIUM\SYS\WAPPS\GRP\DTP.GRP

[restrictions]
NoRun=1
```

Please note that the `display.drv=` line in the [settings] section of listing 26.1 is updated each time you start Windows. The setting in PROGMAN.INI is replaced by the same value that is listed in your machine's SYSTEM.INI [boot] section.

VI

Installing Windows

The most important change to PROGMAN.INI for networks is the addition of the [restrictions] section. This section allows the network administrator to limit some aspects of Program Manager. Table 26.9 displays the settings for this section.

Table 26.9 PROGMAN.INI [restrictions] Settings	
Setting	**Values**
EditLevel=	Controls what the user can modify in Program Manager:
	0 - The user can make any changes they want.
	1 - The user cannot create, delete or rename groups. Disables **N**ew, **M**ove, **C**opy and **D**elete commands on the Program Manager **F**ile menu when a group is selected.
	2 - All restrictions from 1 plus the user cannot create or delete program items. New, Move, Copy, and Delete commands are completely disabled.
	3 - All restrictions from 2 plus the user cannot change command lines for program items. The text in the **C**ommand Line text box of the Program Properties dialog box cannot be changed.
	4 - All restrictions from 3 plus the user cannot change any program item information. None of the fields of the Program Properties dialog box can be changed.
NoClose=	0 - No restrictions.
	1 - The user cannot use the **F**ile E**x**it command. The user cannot use Alt-F4 to exit Windows. Use this option with extreme care! You have no way of making sure the user has closed all applications before turning the machine off. This can result in lost data and corrupted files!
NoFileMenu=	0 - No restrictions.
	1 - Removes the File menu from Program Manager. Users can only run programs by selecting their icon. However, users may still run programs from File Manager.
NoRun=	0 - No restrictions.
	1 - Disables the **R**un option in the **F**ile menu.
NoSaveSettings=	0 - No restrictions.
	1 - The user cannot use the **O**ptions **S**ave Settings command. Any changes made to the arrangement of windows and icons is not saved when the user exits Windows.

WIN.INI

This file is one of the most important files in Windows. It contains a wide array of information about the user's Windows environment. It can contain seventeen sections just for Windows. In addition, application software can add sections to this file.

[Windows] Section

This section contains settings usually affected by Control Panel. These choices are user-specific for the most part. There are a couple of network-oriented settings in this section:

Syntax: `NetWarn=x`

Default: `NetWarn=1`

x can be either 0 or 1. When NetWarn is 1, Windows warns the user if he starts Windows and the network is not running or if the user has not loaded the workstation shell software. When NetWarn is 0, no warning is displayed. All network options in Control Panel are disabled. You change this option through the Network option of Control Panel.

Syntax: `Spooler=x`

Default: `Spooler=YES`

x can be either YES or NO. If this option is set to YES, Windows prints all jobs to a temporary file before sending them to the printer or network queue. You should make sure that this value is NO when using a network queue. This option is changed with the **B**ackground Printing command from the Print Manager **O**ptions menu.

[extensions] Section

Windows uses this section to relate files with their source programs via the file's extension. Windows installs the default settings shown in listing 26.2. Third-party Windows applications may add other settings for their applications (see listing 26.3). Since applications are installed user-by-user, this section is user-specific, also. Note also that DOS Truenames can be used in the [extensions] section of WIN.INI to reference directories on a specific server and volume.

VI

Installing Windows

Listing 26.2   Default Extensions

```
[Extensions]
cal=calendar.exe ^.cal
crd=cardfile.exe ^.crd
trm=terminal.exe ^.trm
txt=notepad.exe ^.txt
ini=notepad.exe ^.ini
pcx=pbrush.exe ^.pcx
bmp=pbrush.exe ^.bmp
wri=write.exe ^.wri
rec=recorder.exe ^.rec
hlp=winhelp.exe ^.hlp
```

Listing 26.3   Sample Extensions from Microsoft Word, Lotus 1-2-3 for Windows, and Balance Monitor for Windows

```
wrk=z:\programs\123w\123w.exe ^.wrk
wks=z:\programs\123w\123w.exe ^.wks
wk1=z:\programs\123w\123w.exe ^.wk1
wk3=z:\programs\123w\123w.exe ^.wk3
wr1=z:\programs\123w\123w.exe ^.wr1
doc=C:\WAPPS\WINWORD\winword.exe ^.doc
dot=C:\WAPPS\WINWORD\winword.exe ^.dot
rtf=C:\WAPPS\WINWORD\winword.exe ^.rtf
bal=\\ATRIUM\SYS\PROGRAMS\BAL\BALMON.EXE ^.bal
```

[ports] Section

This section is one of the most misunderstood sections of this file. Listing 26.4 lists the default contents of this section. This section contains the configuration for serial ports as set in the Ports option of Control Panel. This section does not reflect the ports installed on the user's PC. These ports are the Windows driver names for the physical ports. With the exception of COM port settings, this section is the same for all users. Otherwise, you could not use a user's WIN.INI file on more than one machine without having to reconfigure Windows every time the user runs Windows.

Listing 26.4   WIN.INI [ports] Section

```
[ports]
LPT1:=
LPT2:=
LPT3:=
COM1:=9600,n,8,1,x
COM2:=2400,e,7,2
COM3:=4800,n,7,1,p
COM4:=9600,n,8,1,x
```

```
EPT:=
FILE:=
LPT1.DOS=
LPT2.DOS=
```

[fonts] Section

Here is a real problem section. So far, WIN.INI has contained user-specific information. If this trend held true throughout WIN.INI, the same WIN.INI could be used for each user, no matter which machine the user uses. Now, at the end of the [fonts] section, screen fonts are listed that are specific to the type of video adapter (see listing 26.5). This means that this WIN.INI won't work on a machine that doesn't have the same type of video adapter. These screen fonts are the fonts Windows uses for its own menus, icons, and dialog boxes. You need to solve this problem, or users won't be able to use any machine but their own.

Listing 26.5 Sample [fonts] Section of WIN.INI

```
[fonts]
Modern (Plotter)=MODERN.FON
Script (Plotter)=SCRIPT.FON
Roman (Plotter)=ROMAN.FON
Arial (TrueType)=ARIAL.FOT
Arial Bold (TrueType)=ARIALBD.FOT
Arial Bold Italic (TrueType)=ARIALBI.FOT
Arial Italic (TrueType)=ARIALI.FOT
Courier New (TrueType)=COUR.FOT
Courier New Bold (TrueType)=COURBD.FOT
Courier New Italic (TrueType)=COURI.FOT
Times New Roman (TrueType)=TIMES.FOT
Times New Roman Bold (TrueType)=TIMESBD.FOT
Times New Roman Bold Italic (TrueType)=TIMESBI.FOT
Times New Roman Italic (TrueType)=TIMESI.FOT
Courier New Bold Italic (TrueType)=COURBI.FOT
WingDings (TrueType)=WINGDING.FOT
Symbol (TrueType)=SYMBOL.FOT
MS Sans Serif 8,10,12,14,18,24 (8514/a res)=SSERIFF.FON
Courier 10,12,15 (8514/a res)=COURF.FON
MS Serif 8,10,12,14,18,24 (8514/a res)=SERIFF.FON
Symbol 8,10,12,14,18,24 (8514/a res)=SYMBOLF.FON
Small Fonts (8514/a res)=SMALLF.FON
```

The solution is rather simple, you have to add all of the screen fonts to the user's WIN.INI file. Listing 26.6 displays all of the screen fonts used by Windows. These have to be added to the user's [fonts] section of WIN.INI. The FON files for the particular video display still have to reside in the master Windows directory on the file server or in the Windows SYSTEM directory on the PC.

VI

Installing Windows

Listing 26.6   Windows Screen Fonts

```
[fonts]
Helv 8,10,12,14,18,24 (CGA res)=HELVA.FON
Helv 8,10,12,14,18,24 (EGA res)=HELVB.FON
Helv 8,10,12,14,18,24 (60 dpi)=HELVC.FON
Helv 8,10,12,14,18,24 (120 dpi)=HELVD.FON
Helv 8,10,12,14,18,24 (VGA res)=HELVE.FON
Helv 8,10,12,14,18,24 (8514/a res)=HELVF.FON
Courier 10,12,15 (CGA res)=COURA.FON
Courier 10,12,15 (EGA res)=COURB.FON
Courier 10,12,15 (60 dpi)=COURC.FON
Courier 10,12,15 (120 dpi)=COURD.FON
Courier 10,12,15 (VGA res)=COURE.FON
Courier 10,12,15 (8514/a res)=COURF.FON
Tms Rmn 8,10,12,14,18,24 (CGA res)=TMSRA.FON
Tms Rmn 8,10,12,14,18,24 (EGA res)=TMSRB.FON
Tms Rmn 8,10,12,14,18,24 (60 dpi)=TMSRC.FON
Tms Rmn 8,10,12,14,18,24 (120 dpi)=TMSRD.FON
Tms Rmn 8,10,12,14,18,24 (VGA res)=TMSRE.FON
Tms Rmn 8,10,12,14,18,24 (8514/a res)=TMSRF.FON
Symbol 8,10,12,14,18,24 (CGA res)=SYMBOLA.FON
Symbol 8,10,12,14,18,24 (EGA res)=SYMBOLB.FON
Symbol 8,10,12,14,18,24 (60 dpi)=SYMBOLC.FON
Symbol 8,10,12,14,18,24 (120 dpi)=SYMBOLD.FON
Symbol 8,10,12,14,18,24 (VGA res)=SYMBOLE.FON
Symbol 8,10,12,14,18,24 (8514/a res)=SYMBOLF.FON
Roman (All res)=ROMAN.FON
Script (All res)=SCRIPT.FON
Modern (All res)=MODERN.FON
```

Unfortunately, Microsoft does not yet use the TrueType fonts for its own system fonts. If Microsoft makes this change, these fonts will be obsolete.

[network] Section

This section records the permanent network connections established by the user in File Manager. It also records the permanent queue assignments and job settings for each. These options would be user-specific. Listing 26.7 displays a sample of these entries.

Listing 26.7   WIN.INI [network] Section Sample

```
[Network]
L:=[ATRIUM/SYS:USERS/HADER]
LPT2:=ATRIUM1/AP_LW1
LPT2-OPTIONS=128,1,8,0,0
LPT3:=ATRIUM1/HP_LJ1
LPT3-OPTIONS=128,1,8,0,0
```

[printerPorts] Section

This section lists the active and inactive printers installed for this user. You must install all of the printer drivers for each shared network printer as well as any private user printer in this section. You install printer drivers through the Windows SETUP program or through the Printers option of Control Panel. Listing 26.8 displays a sample of the entries in this section. Network printers a user can use are user-specific, but the user must have the correct drivers installed. The printer drivers needed come from this section. The drivers themselves must reside in the master Windows directory on the file server or on the local PC's Windows SYSTEM directory. This section can present a problem when users move around from machine to machine if Windows was installed on the individual PCs rather than a network installation.

Listing 26.8   WIN.INI. [printerports] Section

```
[PrinterPorts]
Apple LaserWriter=pscript,LPT2:,15,90
Canon Bubble-Jet BJ-10e=CANON10e,LPT1:,15,45
Epson LQ-2550=EPSON24,LPT1:,15,45
HP LaserJet Series II=HPPCL,LPT3:,15,45
```

[application] Sections

Every Windows application may make changes to WIN.INI for its own use. Most of the time, these applications add new sections to WIN.INI. These additions can be quite substantial. Listing 26.9 illustrates a change made to WIN.INI for Arts & Letters from Software Support Group, Inc. The application added its own information, the [a&l] section, for its own use.

Listing 26.9   WIN.INI Application Section

```
[a&l]
editor config=L:\WAPPS\A&L\STARTUP.DEF
editor=L:\WAPPS\A&L
backuppath=L:\WAPPS\A&L
symbols=L:\WAPPS\A&L\SYMBOLS
typefaces=L:\WAPPS\A&L\TYPEFACE
Editor Libraries=2
Editor Library1=L:\WAPPS\A&L\CUSTOM\Curves.yal
Editor Library2=L:\WAPPS\A&L\CUSTOM\*.yal
Editor Activities=2
Editor Activity1=L:\WAPPS\A&L\ACTIVITY\eless-b.yal
Editor Activity2=L:\WAPPS\A&L\ACTIVITY\*.yal
```

VI

Installing Windows

Windows application developers have the option to create their own INI files or add their data to WIN.INI. Separate INI files for each application are probably better because after a while it gets hard to tell which parts of WIN.INI belong to each application.

CONTROL.INI

CONTROL.INI contains the user's current color scheme selection as well as the available color schemes, custom color schemes, wallpaper patterns, screen saver options, and some installation options. A little known secret is that you can use CONTROL.INI to control the icons that appear in Control Panel.

Control Panel is not a Windows group, even though it has a similar appearance. You cannot rearrange the order of the icons and you cannot delete individual icons. The problem is that in a networked environment, you may not want your users to have access to all of the features that Control Panel permits. You can add a new [don't load] section anywhere in CONTROL.INI and type the name of the icon as it appears in Control Panel and set it equal to any non-blank ASCII value (see listing 26.10). The following example causes Control Panel's network, printers, and drivers icons to be omitted when the user loads Control Panel.

Listing 26.10   PROGMAN.INI Don't Load Section

```
[don't load]
network=yes
printers=no
drivers=some
```

You can also create a regular Windows group for the Control Panel Icons as another option. Control Panel is basically one program, CONTROL.EXE with related control panel files with a .CPL extension. Table 26.10 shows the CPL files and which Control Panel features they are used for.

Table 26.10   Control Panel Feature Files

Icon Name	CPL File	Windows Version
Colors	MAIN.CPL	3.1/3.11/WFW
Fonts	MAIN.CPL	3.1/3.11/WFW
Ports	MAIN.CPL	3.1/3.11/WFW
Mouse	MAIN.CPL	3.1/3.11/WFW

Icon Name	CPL File	Windows Version
Desktop	MAIN.CPL	3.1/3.11/WFW
Keyboard	MAIN.CPL	3.1/3.11/WFW
Printers	MAIN.CPL	3.1/3.11/WFW
International	MAIN.CPL	3.1/3.11/WFW
Date/Time	MAIN.CPL	3.1/3.11/WFW
Network	MAIN.CPL	3.1/3.11/WFW
386 Enhanced	CPWIN386.CPL	3.1
Enhanced	CPWIN386.CPL	3.11/WFW
Drivers	DRIVERS.CPL	3.1/3.11/WFW
Sound	SND.CPL	3.11/WFW
Big Cursor	BIGCUR.CPL	3.11/WFW
Display	CRTLCD.CPL	3.11/WFW
FAX	FAX.CPL	3.11/WFW
PCMCIA	WPCMINFO.CPL	3.11/WFW

To create an individual icon for a single Control Panel option, you create a Program Property for it and set the command line using the following syntax:

```
CONTROL.EXE CPL_file Icon_name
```

An example of the command line for a Program Property to run only the Color option of Control Panel is

```
CONTROL.EXE MAIN.CPL COLOR
```

Often in the network environment, you need to control the Control Panel options that users can access. The above two methods allow you to exercise that control.

How Windows Searches for INI Files

When you launch Windows, it starts up like most other software you have used in terms of how it locates its files—first looking for files in the current default directory. If it does not find a file in the current default directory, Windows uses your path to locate other files. Specifically, Windows searches the path for the directory where you installed Windows. The program that

VI

Installing Windows

performs these initial searches is WIN.COM. Windows expects to find all INI files in the same directory. Furthermore, Windows must find WIN.COM, PROGMAN.INI, and SYSTEM.INI in the same directory.

Having looked at all of the standard Windows INI files, you can sort them by their function as discussed at the beginning of the chapter.

1. Hardware Information

   SYSTEM.INI

   MOUSE.INI

2. User Preferences

   PROGMAN.INI

   WIN.INI

   CONTROL.INI

3. Application Information

   WIN.INI

Even though WIN.INI contains application-oriented information, it has to be treated as a user preferences file.

What Happens If Users Use Different Machines

If your users do not use the same machine all the time and if all of your PCs are not the same type and configuration, you have a problem with the way Windows finds its configuration files. Your users need the set of machine-specific files, SYSTEM.INI and MOUSE.INI, that match the machine they are using. These files are not user-specific, they are machine-specific. However, when a user moves to a different machine, the user still needs his user information files, WIN.INI, CONTROL.INI, and PROGMAN.INI.

If you have the same types of machines everywhere, you can use the same SYSTEM.INI, MOUSE.INI, and WIN.COM for everyone. Depending upon how you installed Windows, you put these files on the user's PC or in their personal directory on the file server. As long as your user's path contains this directory and a path to the Windows directory, they can run Windows without any INI file problems.

If your users always use the same machine, their SYSTEM.INI, MOUSE.INI, and WIN.COM are always the same files. Depending upon how you installed Windows, you put these files on the user's PC or in their personal directory on the file server. As long as your user's path contains this directory and a path to the Windows directory, they can run Windows without any INI file problems.

Presently, the only way to manage Windows in a LAN environment with different machines and users who move around is to develop a scheme to get the correct files to the user. Since you allow users to move around, you have to store user-specific files in their personal directories on the file server. Machine-specific files must be on the PC itself or in a directory on the file server than you select based upon the machine the user is using.

Figure 26.9 displays how this is done if the user launches Windows from their local drive. It does not matter if the user has a full copy of Windows on their local drive or just the files for a network installation. In a network installation, the user has a search drive to the Windows directory on the file server. The basic concept is that prior to starting Windows, you have to copy the user-specific files from the user's personal directory on the file server down to the machine the user is using. If the user is allowed to make changes to his environment, you have to copy the changed files back to the user's home directory on the file server. Otherwise, the changes made by the user will not be reflected when the user changes machines. This means you start Windows from a batch file. The batch file copies the user files to the machine and launches Windows. Then, the batch file copies the files back to the user's network directory when Windows is terminated.

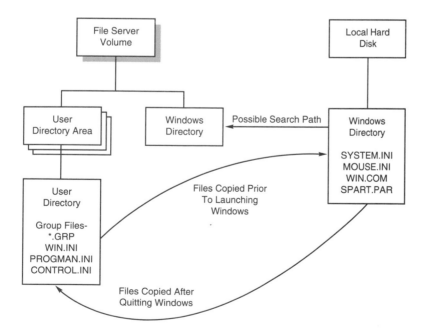

Fig. 26.9
Launching
Windows from a
local hard disk.

VI

Installing Windows

If you launch Windows from the user's home directory on the file server, then you must get the correct machine-specific files for the PC into the user's home directory. These files can come from the PC itself or from a network directory. You may want to establish a DOS environment variable to identify the machine type, such as PC_TYPE=VGAMSM3 for a 386-based PC with a VGA adapter and a Microsoft mouse. Then you could create a directory containing a WIN.COM, SYSTEM.INI, and MOUSE.INI for each machine type combination. Use the machine type variable as the file name. Also use a DOS variable to store the user's login name. For example, the VGAMSM3 would have the following files:

```
VGAMSM3.SYS - SYSTEM.INI File
VGAMSM3.MSE - MOUSE.INI File
VGAMSM3.COM - WIN.COM File
```

The batch file can have a very simple copy command substituting the variable name for the file name in the source:

```
NCOPY SYS:\CONFIG\%PC_TYPE%.SYS SYS:\USERS\%LOGIN_NAME\SYSTEM.INI
NCOPY SYS:\CONFIG\%PC_TYPE%.MSE SYS:\USERS\%LOGIN_NAME\MOUSE.INI
NCOPY SYS:\CONFIG\%PC_TYPE%.COM SYS:\USERS\%LOGIN_NAME\WIN.COM
```

Figure 26.10 illustrates the concept you can use for running Windows solely from the file server.

Fig. 26.10
Running Windows
from the file server.

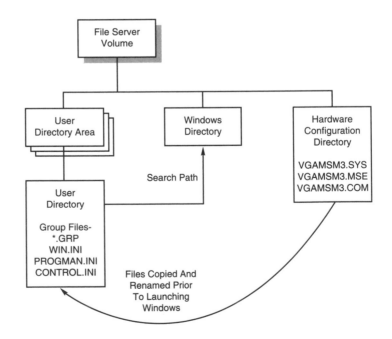

Figure 26.11 shows how to get the machine-specific files from the user's PC but launch Windows from the user's home directory on the file server. In both cases, the user needs a search drive to the master Windows directory on the file server. With these methods you usually do not have to worry about copying files back to their source since users typically do not change the hardware configuration.

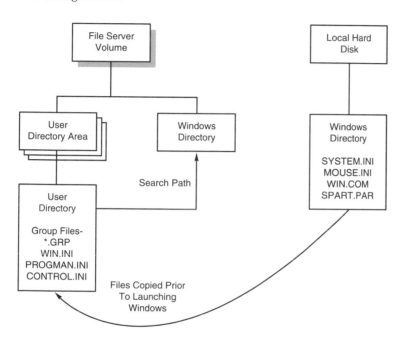

Fig. 26.11
Running Windows from the file server and local PC.

Logging On

If you use Windows 3.1x with Novell NetWare, you must log onto the file server prior to launching Windows. If you do not log on first, there is no way to have your default search drive mappings established as part of the global Windows environment. When you log into the file server first, the necessary drive and search mappings needed for the LAN carry into the Windows environment.

Since Windows 3.1x runs on the user's workstation, you need to make sure that the workstation is ready to run Windows by checking the workstation's configuration and software. Over the past two years nothing has been more challenging for network administrators than trying to stay up with the current releases of the NetWare shell files and how they should be configured for the Windows environment.

VI

Installing Windows

Beginning with NetWare 386 3.0, Novell segregated the DOS user's workstation software into two separate groups. The older and more commonly used workstation software is the *DOS Workstation Shell* and the newer software is the *DOS/ODI Workstation Shell*. These two different, yet overlapping, sets of files provide network services to the PC. Generally, either set can be used by a PC depending upon non-Windows networking issues.

Novell's DOS/ODI Workstation Shell software permits a PC to use both IPX/SPX and TCP/IP protocols simultaneously so that PCs connected to a network using TCP/IP can access the services of the TCP/IP hosts as well as the NetWare file servers that are available. As a part of NetWare, Novell only supplies workstation software for using IPX/SPX protocols. If you want to use TCP/IP protocols on the workstation, Novell offers another product called *LAN Workplace for DOS*. This software is used in conjunction with the DOS/ODI Workstation Shell software but cannot be used with the older DOS Workstation Shell software.

Most recently, Novell has developed a newer set of workstation shell modules called the DOS Requester. Since these modules replace one of the other modules with modules called VLMs (Virtual Loadable Modules), many people are calling these the VLM shells.

In deciding whether to use the DOS Workstation Shell software, the DOS/ODI Workstation Shell software or the VLM DOS Requester, the primary factor is the need to run both TCP/IP and IPX/SPX protocols or just IPX/SPX protocols and the version of NetWare and NetWare services you need.

Managing IPX.COM and IPX.OBJ

The program responsible for interacting with the PC's network adapter card and for building data packets according to the IPX/SPX protocols is IPX.COM. This program does not come in executable form on the NetWare disks. You have to create the executable module using a linker program provided by Novell in NetWare. The linker program for NetWare versions 2.1x is SHGEN and the linker for NetWare versions 2.2x and 3.1x is WSGEN. This program is on disks by the same name. The procedure for using the program is well documented in the NetWare installation manual.

You create IPX.COM from two independent pieces of software, the network adapter interface code and the NetWare interface code. The network adapter interface code is supplied by Novell for some network adapter cards or by the manufacturer of the network adapter card. The Novell-supplied modules are on a disk labeled LAN_DRV_001. The vendor-supplied modules are on a disk supplied by the vendor with the network adapter card. This disk must have a volume label of LAN_DRV_*xxx*, where *xxx* can be any three legal DOS characters. The NetWare interface code is a file named IPX.OBJ. This file is on the SHGEN or WSGEN disk.

The linker program links the network adapter interface code with the NetWare interface code to create IPX.COM. As Novell makes changes to their interface code, Novell releases new versions of IPX.OBJ on the CompuServe NOVLIB bulletin board. You must run version IPX.COM 3.10 with Windows. Version 3.10 is created from the IPX.OBJ file dated 3-10-92 (20,340 bytes). This file can be found in the NOVLIB file named DOSUP8.ZIP. This file is shipped on the Microsoft Windows 3.1x disk #2.

> ### Note
>
> Novell is likely to update IPX.OBJ again, after this book is published. To get the new files you have three choices: Call Novell and order an update if you know one is available; contact your local dealer; or get a CompuServe subscription and keep an eye on the NOVLIB forum and the New NetWare Uploads library.

IPX.COM is the first workstation shell module loaded into memory. It resides in base memory. Its size varies from about 15K to 30K depending upon the network adapter driver. Memory management software such as MS-DOS 5.0's LOADHIGH command, Quarterdeck Software's QEMM or Qualitas 386Max can load IPX.COM into the Upper Memory Area (UMA). For more information about the UMA, keep reading. The next section gets into this terminology in detail.

Selecting the Best NetWare Redirector

The NetWare redirector program routes commands and functions issued by the user or the application to either COMMAND.COM or to IPX.COM. COMMAND.COM processes the command locally, while IPX would put the request into a data packet and send it to the file server, hence the name Redirector.

In early versions of NetWare, there were different versions of the redirector for each major DOS version. This meant you had to update the redirector every time you upgraded someone's DOS version. Novell has since made the redirector universal for all versions of MS-DOS, PC-DOS, and Novell DOS saving you from a major maintenance nuisance. However, there are still three different versions of the redirector.

VI

Installing Windows

The three redirector programs are NETX.COM, EMSNETX.EXE, and XMSNETX.EXE. Running Windows 3.1x requires version 3.32 or later. If you do not have this version, contact your Novell dealer or download the latest DOSUP file from NOVLIB on CompuServe. From table 26.11, select the redirector you are going to use based upon where you want the program to reside in memory.

Table 26.11 NetWare Redirectors	
Redirector Program Name	**Memory Used**
NETX.COM	Base Memory
EMSNETX.COM	Expanded Memory
XMSNETX.EXE	High Memory Area

Sample Network Batch File

Listing 26.11 shows a sample batch file for loading the DOS Workstation Shell software and logging onto the NetWare file server.

Listing 26.11   Sample Network Login Batch File

```
NET.BAT
@ECHO OFF
CD \NET
IPX
NETX
CD\
F:LOGIN
```

This batch file illustrates the proper sequence for loading the DOS Workstation Shell files. It assumes the files reside in a directory called \NET on the current drive. The section later in this chapter called "Selecting Settings for SHELL.CFG or NET.CFG" explains why the batch file makes the NET directory current before loading the other modules. The batch file also assumes that the NetWare LOGIN directory is the logical drive F. This also assumes that CONFIG.SYS contains the setting LASTDRIVE=E. If LASTDRIVE is not E, then the LOGIN directory is not drive F but the next available drive letter.

Using the NetWare DOS/ODI Shell Files

The NetWare DOS/ODI Shell files were first shipped with NetWare 386 3.0 and have been shipped with every subsequent version of NetWare 2.x and 3.x. ODI is an abbreviation of Open Datalink Interface. The main issue behind ODI is the ability to support multiple network and transport protocols over a single LAN adapter card. If you do not plan to use multiple protocols and just use IPX/SPX protocols, you can use either the DOS Workstation Shell or the DOS/ODI Workstation Shell. Novell has mentioned that they may discontinue the DOS Workstation Shell software at some point which will force everyone to use the DOS/ODI Workstation software.

The major network and transport protocol suite that you need DOS/ODI for is TCP/IP. If you are using both TCP/IP networks and NetWare, you need to use this software. The modules that are part of the standard DOS/ODI Workstation Shell software are:

1. Link Support Layer program — LSL.COM

2. LAN Adapter Driver program — driver.COM

3. Protocol Management program — IPXODI.COM

4. Redirector Programs — NETX.COM, EMSNETX.EXE, XMSNETX.EXE

5. Netbios Emulation program — NETBIOS.EXE

6. Configuration file — NET.CFG

How To Use LSL.COM

The first module of the DOS/ODI Workstation Shell is the datalink support layer program LSL.COM. This program handles the interface between the network adapter and the physical cabling of the network. You should have version 1.21 or later to run Windows 3.1x. This program is the first module you load, and it resides in base memory. This program can be unloaded from memory (LSL U) when you are not logged into the network and if you are not currently using Windows.

Loading LAN Drivers

The program that controls the LAN adapter card is usually named after the model or name of the LAN adapter card itself. Novell supplies the modules listed in table 26.12. LAN adapter manufacturers such as Thomas Conrad,

Standard Microsystems Corp., and Intel Corp. provide drivers for NetWare with the LAN adapter card. Unlike the drivers used for the DOS Workstation Shell, these drivers are in executable form and no linking is required. These drivers are configured through the workstation shell configuration file—NET.CFG. The LAN driver loads into base memory.

Table 26.12 Novell-Supplied LAN Adapter Drivers		
Driver Name	**Size**	**Description**
3C1100.COM	12288	3Com 3C1100 3Station Ethernet MLID v1.00 (911112)
3C501.COM	11838	3Com 3C501 EtherLink MLID v1.20 (910319)
3C503.COM	14821	3Com 3C503 EtherLink II MLID v1.22 (910614)
3C505.COM	25117	3Com 3C505 EtherLink+ Ethernet MLID v1.20 (910729)
3C523.COM	12238	3Com 3C523 EtherLink/MC Ethernet MLID v1.20 (910729)
EXOS.COM	20194	Novell EXOS 205/215 Ethernet MLID v1.13 (911108)
LANSUP.COM	14094	IBM LAN Support MLID v1.20 (910430)
NE1000.COM	12717	Novell NE1000 Ethernet MLID v1.20 (910729)
NE1500T.COM	21840	Novell NE1500T Ethernet MLID v1.20 (911011)
NE2.COM	19210	Novell NE2 Ethernet MLID v1.21 (911104)
NE2-32.COM	12737	Novell NE2-32 Ethernet MLID v1.20 (910729)
NE2000.COM	13018	Novell NE2000 Ethernet MLID v1.34 (910603)
NE2100.COM	21836	Novell NE2100 Ethernet MLID v1.20 (911011)
NE3200.COM	19242	Novell NE3200 Ethernet MLID v1.00 (910903)
PCN2L.COM	14117	IBM PC Network II & II/A MLID v1.34 (910717)
TOKEN.COM	15663	IBM Token-Ring MLID v1.12 (910614)
TRXNET.COM	12128	Novell Turbo RxNet & RxNet/2 MLID v1.31 (910806)

Using the NetWare Protocol Managers

NetWare uses a set of network and transport protocols called IPX and SPX. These protocols are more than adequate for a self-contained NetWare LAN. However, other network and transport protocols exist. If you want to interconnect your NetWare LAN with other non-NetWare networks you have a problem because of the different protocols.

The most common network protocols used in non-NetWare LANs are TCP/IP. This set of protocols is widely used by universities, research centers, government agencies, the military, and many major corporations because the protocols allow networks of diverse systems comprising mainframes, minicomputers, workstations, and PCs. The wide-area network that most universities and agencies connect to is called the Internet. It is estimated that there are over 600,000 mainframes and minicomputers connected to the Internet worldwide. No one knows how many PCs and workstations are connected to the Internet.

The DOS/ODI Workstation Shell software allows multiple protocol set operation with a single LAN adapter card installed in the PC. You need a protocol manager program for each set of protocols. Novell supplies a protocol manager for its IPX/SPX protocols with NetWare. This program is IPXODI.EXE. You need version 1.20 of IPXODI for Windows 3.1x. Novell's optional software package, LAN Workplace for DOS, has a protocol manager program for using TCP/IP protocols with NetWare.

Selecting Settings for SHELL.CFG or NET.CFG

The DOS Workstation Shell software uses a configuration file called SHELL.CFG or NET.CFG. For the DOS/ODI Workstation Shell software this file must be NET.CFG. This file is an ASCII text file that all other NetWare workstation shell files read. This file is extremely important to the workstation because it configures the workstation shell software according to your network needs. All of the potential settings for this file are in your NetWare *Using the Network* manual. However, a few settings that are particularly important for NetWare and Windows 3.1x need to be discussed.

Show Dots = On

You need this setting for Windows 3.1x and NetWare directory compatibility. Windows and DOS use a directory notation of two periods (..) to denote the parent directory. NetWare does not use this convention in its directory structures. This causes a problem when working in a Windows File Open dialog box in some applications because you cannot move upline in the directory structure of a NetWare volume without this convention. The default setting for this parameter is Off. Without this setting you might not be able to move back up the directory structure by clicking the open folders above your current directory because they may not be displayed. Windows users are advised to use Show Dots = On for compatibility.

> **Note**
>
> Some NetWare-aware applications show the upline directories in the File Open dialog box without Show Dots = On because the application was designed to overcome this incompatibility.

File Handles = *x*

This shell setting controls how many files the workstation can have open on the file server simultaneously. The default setting permits 40 open files. This is probably enough for a DOS workstation but not enough for a workstation running Windows applications from the file server. The maximum value for this setting is 255. You have to estimate how many files might be needed for multitasking applications. The general range for this value is 60 to 100.

SPX Connections = *x*

More and more Windows applications are using NetWare's SPX protocol over NetWare's IPX protocol. SPX requires an acknowledgment from the recipient for each data packet sent. This assures the sender that the packet was received and that the recipient is ready for the next packet. During communication between an application running on a workstation and the file server, many separate SPX connections may be established to handle different aspects of the process. The default number of SPX connections permitted is only 15, not enough as more and more applications migrate to SPX protocols over IPX protocols. The recommended value for this parameter is at least 60. There is no easy way to find out how many SPX connections are needed without checking with the application software developer.

SPX Listen Timeout = *x*

SPX Listen Timeout governs how long the sender waits for the required acknowledgment from the recipient. If the acknowledgment is not received within this period, the sender assumes something has happened to the packet and retransmits the packet. Applications running under Windows may not receive the acknowledgments as quickly as they did when the application ran under DOS. Increasing this value may reduce traffic on the network caused by retransmission. Usually, this value is set between 2000 and 3000.

SPX Abort Timeout = x

SPX Abort Timeout determines how long the sender tries to maintain a connection when the recipient is not sending acknowledgment packets back to the sender. Once the timeout limit is reached the sender drops the connection. On large networks and in running Windows, this value should be between 3000 and 4000.

IPX Retries = x

IPX does not require the recipient of a data packet to send an acknowledgment back to the sender. Most IPX packets issued from a workstation request some data from the server. When the server starts sending data back to the sender, the sender knows that the server received the packet. If the sender does not receive any data back from the server it assumes that the packet got lost or destroyed. IPX Retries dictates how many times the sender retransmits the packet before giving up on the recipient.

Print Header = 255

NetWare creates a buffer for the initialization codes used to configure a printer at the start of a print job. The buffer is normally only 64 bytes. You need to increase the buffer size to its maximum value of 255 bytes. The initialization codes for PostScript printers and printers that use soft fonts are often longer than 64 bytes. Increasing this value for users who don't use soft fonts or PostScript printers has no negative impact.

Print Tail = 64

NetWare creates a buffer to hold the characters used to reinitialize the printer after a print job. These characters can exceed the default buffer size of 16 bytes. The maximum number of characters permitted is 255.

Printing to a Network Printer

When you print to a network printer in Windows, some of the way you set up printing must change. The following sections discuss how to install and use network printers using Windows.

Installing Printers and Queues

Windows represents a move toward a more integrated environment. One of the benefits of Windows is that you install printer drivers in Windows. By doing so, all Windows-applications can use the Windows printer drivers, eliminating the need for each application to have its own printer drivers. Unfortunately, this does not help your DOS programs that you run in Windows. You still need printer drivers for DOS applications.

VI

Installing Windows

Consequently, you still need to go through the process discussed so far in this chapter to set up the NetWare printing environment. Contrary to some people's opinion, Windows does not make the NetWare printing setup obsolete.

The first step is to install all of the printer drivers the user needs for any locally attached printers and any printers that the user can use that are shared printers on the network.

The Printers option in Control Panel gives you access to the printer setup information. Figure 26.12 displays the Printers dialog box, listing the printers that you installed during setup. The **C**onnect and **S**etup buttons permit you to change your queue assignments and printer configuration options. You can also add or remove printers using the appropriate buttons. When adding printers, you need to indicate the master Windows directory on your file server or you need the Windows installation disks.

Fig. 26.12

Control Panel's
Printers dialog box.

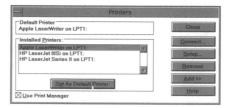

Windows records Printer drivers installed and their configurations in the user's WIN.INI file. Listing 26.12 reflects the sections of a typical WIN.INI affected by printer options.

Listing 26.12   WIN.INI Printer Settings

```
[Network]
LPT1:=ATRIUM/MKTG_AP_LW1
LPT1-OPTIONS=16,1,8,0,0,LST:,

[PostScript,LPT1]
ATM=placeholder

[HP LaserJet IIISi,LPT1]
paper=1
prtcaps=-4216
paperind=1
prtcaps2=31
prtindex=19
```

```
brighten=1
joboffset=1

[HPPCL5A,LPT1]
prtcaps2=31
cartindex=8

[PrinterPorts]
Apple LaserWriter=pscript,LPT1:,15,90
HP LaserJet IIISi=hppcl5a,LPT1:,15,45
HP LaserJet Series II=HPPCL,LPT1:,15,45

[devices]
Apple LaserWriter=pscript,LPT1:
HP LaserJet IIISi=hppcl5a,LPT1:
HP LaserJet Series II=HPPCL,LPT1:
```

Windows Port Names

When you install a printer driver in Windows, you select the port you want it assigned to. The ports available are:

```
LPT1
LPT2
LPT3
COM1
COM2
COM3
COM4
EPT:
FILE:
LPT1.DOS
LPT2.DOS
```

If the printer is attached to the PC, the physical port must be installed in the PC. If the port used is a serial port, COM1-COM4, you use Control Panel to set the port's parameters so that the Windows' configuration matches the physical settings.

The EPT port is an IBM enhanced printer port. You use this port on some IBM PS/2 models. The IBM Personal PagePrinter laser printer uses this port. This port is a proprietary interface from IBM and does not exist on the "clones." If you use this port, you need to make a change to your SYSTEM.INI file. You should add the following line to the [386Enh] section of SYSTEM.INI:

```
local=EPT
```

VI

Installing Windows

The local command makes the EPT device local to each virtual machine, rather than part of the global Windows environment. This means that Windows puts a copy of the driver in each virtual machine. This allows each virtual machine to have different register states for their program.

If you use the FILE option, Windows creates a print file for the job. You tell Windows a file name each time you print to this device, and Windows creates a disk file of the print job.

The LPT ports that have the DOS extension as part of their name are alternate LPT devices. These devices print through the PC's ROM BIOS rather than directly to the printer port, as Windows usually does. When you print using these device names, it appears that you are printing to a file. Since DOS does not write a file with the same name as one of its devices, it sends the data to the LPT port, dropping the extension. You can use this option to have two printers assigned to the same LPT port. You cannot assign these device names to NetWare queues.

Assigning Printers to NetWare Queues

All three LPT ports, LPT1-LPT3, can be assigned to NetWare queues. These ports do not have to be physically installed to be assigned to NetWare queues. You can select a queue through Control Panel, Print Manager, or the NetWare Tools program.

In Control Panel, you select the Printers option from Control Panel, and then select the printer you want to assign to a NetWare queue. Select the Connect button. Choose the LPT port you want to assign to the queue. Select the Network button while in the same dialog box. Select the LPT port again and the queue you want to use. If you want this assignment every time you use Windows, mark the Permanent check box. Now select the Options button to set the job parameters you want used with the NetWare queue. For Windows, you should use No Tabs, No Banners, and No Timeout. Finally, return to Control Panel using the OK or Close buttons.

In Print Manager, you can select a different queue by opening the Options menu (see fig. 26.13). From the Network - Printer Connections dialog box you select the LPT port you want to use, the queue you want to assign to it, and if you want to make the queue assignment permanent (see fig. 26.14). Then choose the Options button to set the job parameters for the queue (see fig. 26.15). Use the OK and Close buttons to return to Program Manager.

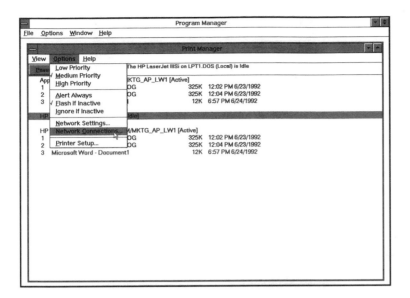

Fig. 26.13
Print Manager
Options menu.

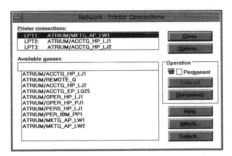

Fig. 26.14
The Network -
Printer Connec-
tions dialog box.

Caution

Be careful when choosing queues in Print Manager. Figure 26.11 shows how to get
the machine-specific files from the user's PC but launch Windows from the user's
home directory on the file server. In both cases, the user needs a search drive to the
master Windows directory on the file server. With these methods, you usually do not
have to worry about copying files back to their source since users typically do not
change the hardware configuration.You can assign any NetWare queue to any of the
LPT ports. Print Manager does not display which printer driver is assigned to the port.
Therefore, you can mistakenly assign the port to the wrong queue for the printer
driver you are using!

Fig. 26.15
The Printer Options
for LPT1: dialog box.

You can assign a queue to a port using the NetWare Tools program. You select the Printers icon from the Tools group (see fig. 26.16). From the Network
- Printer Connections dialog box you select the LPT port you want to use, the
queue you want to assign to it, and if you want to make the queue assignment permanent. Then select the **O**ptions button to set the job parameters
for the queue. Use the OK and Close buttons to return to Program Manager.

Fig. 26.16
The NetWare Tools
group.

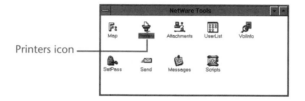

Printers icon

Caution

Be careful when choosing queues in NetWare Tools. You can assign any NetWare
queue to any of the LPT ports. Print Manager does not display which printer driver is
assigned to the port. Therefore, you can mistakenly assign the port to the wrong
queue for the printer driver you are using!

Using Windows Printers

In a networked environment, you almost always have multiple choices in the
printers that you can use. If you installed all of the printer drivers, you can
select any driver when you are ready to print. Most Windows applications
permit this ability. However, few Windows applications allow you to select a
different queue from within the application. You must first use Control
Panel, Print Manager, or NetWare Tools to choose a queue and the queue
options, as discussed previously.

In most Windows applications, you can select any of the printers you have installed in most Windows applications. For example, when you choose the **F**ile P**r**inter Setup command, Windows Write displays the Print Setup dialog box (see fig. 26.17).

Fig. 26.17
The Windows
Write Print Setup
dialog box.

If you select the Specific **P**rinter option button, your other printer choices appear (see fig. 26.18). The **O**ptions button displays a dialog box of other configuration choices available for the printer. This Options dialog box is different for various printer types.

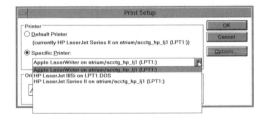

Fig. 26.18
The Specific **P**rinter
drop-down list.

One of the challenges that faces network users is the issue of fonts. Initially, fonts were built into the printer itself. You could only use the fonts that your printer had. Selecting a font was a simple matter of sending the appropriate control codes to the printer to select the font. Of course, you could not print the fonts from one printer on another printer. Everyone appreciates variety and control. We like to be able to select different type styles and sizes for different jobs. Since printers were very limited, the next step was font cartridges that could plug into the printer. These cartridges increased our choices and were usually good quality. Cartridges were limited in the variety of typefaces and sizes each could contain. Of course, you could only use those faces and sizes on the printer that had the cartridge.

Then Adobe's PostScript was built into laser printers. This meant that now you had 35 or more typefaces and these faces were scalable. Scalable fonts meant that you had a wide range of sizes available because the actual font was created on-the-fly by the printer. The problem was that PostScript printers are more expensive.

VI

Installing Windows

Next, soft fonts appeared. Soft fonts could be stored on the user's PC and downloaded to the printer when needed. Soft fonts initially were bit-maps, meaning that you have a separate file for each point-size and each style (bold, italic, etc.) for the typeface. This could result in many megabytes of disk space. Other soft fonts were scalable, outline fonts. These fonts had a file that stored the font's outline parameters. A font manager program used this information to create the font in the right size and style when you need it. This saves disk space but increases the demands on your processor. In addition, you had to download the entire font to the printer before you could use it. These fonts were almost exclusively limited to Hewlett-Packard laser printers (or compatible) and PostScript printers.

The problem for network users is how to guarantee that the font you need is available and can be downloaded to the printer. The danger in downloading entire fonts to the printer is that they are lost if someone shuts off the printer to clear a problem such as a paper jam. Downloading fonts on-the-fly means that each user must have the soft fonts and the soft font manager available on his machine. Another problem is how you do you send a file to another user who doesn't have the same fonts or software?

As the industry begins to move to graphic displays, users want to see what their document will look like before they print the document. This means that you need screen fonts that match your printer fonts. Since display adapters and printers use different technology, you couldn't necessarily use the same screen fonts and printer fonts.

You can see the complications of font technology on a stand-alone computer. It gets worse in networks where all of the users do not have the same type of display or printer. Apple Corporation developed an answer to these problems in a new font technology called TrueType. Microsoft includes TrueType with Windows 3.1.

The scalable nature of the fonts makes them economical in their disk space requirements. Each TrueType font style has a pair of files. One has an FON extension and the other has a TTF extension. I have installed 69 different typefaces on my system, resulting in 191 different fonts and 382 TrueType files. All of the FOT files are small, between 1300 and 1400 bytes, requiring only 253K. The TTF files vary between 9kb and 72kb. The total requirement for my 191 TTF files is 11.5M. Each style of a typeface (bold, italic, condensed, etc.) requires separate files. While this may seem like a lot of space for a single user, it is not much for a network. I recommend that you store your TrueType fonts in your master Windows directory on the file server.

Managing the Queue

The next topic of this chapter concerns managing the data once it is in a NetWare queue. Windows Print Manager is compatible with NetWare queues provided you used Setup /N when you installed Windows. Otherwise, you won't have the NetWare drivers needed.

Viewing and Managing Jobs with Print Manager

If you select Print Manager from Control Panel, a window appears that displays all of the print jobs in the queues that you are using (see fig 26.19). Unfortunately, Print Manager does not allow you to manage the queue. You can delete jobs in the NetWare queue using the Delete button. You cannot modify the job information.

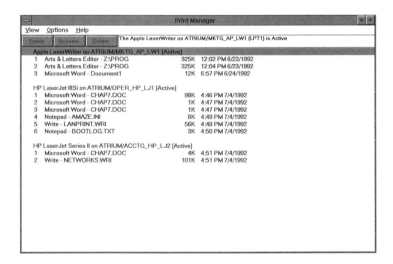

Fig. 26.19

The Print Manager window.

Print Manager does allow you to make some changes. The **O**ptions menu offers two network-related options (see fig. 26.20). The Network **C**onnections command allows you to change your queue assignments.

The **N**etwork Settings command displays a Network Options dialog box (see fig. 26.21). Mark the **U**pdate Network Display check box if you want the Print Manager's print job list updated as jobs are added or removed.

VI

Installing Windows

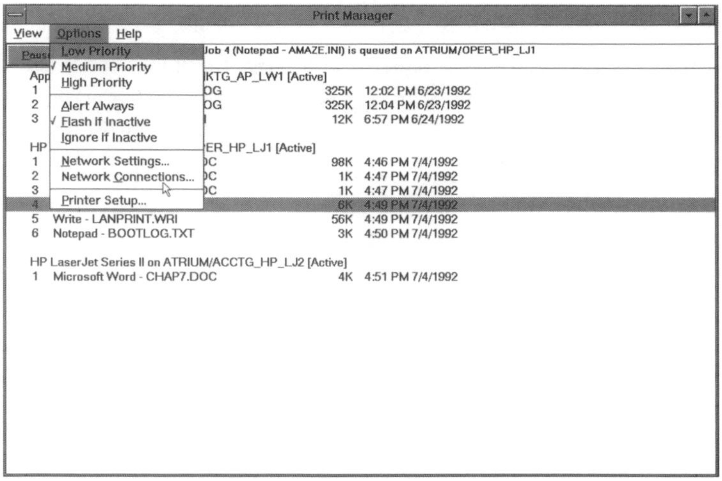

Fig. 26.20
The Print Manager
Options menu.

View	Options	Help	Print Manager

Job 4 (Notepad - AMAZE.INI) is queued on ATRIUM/OPER_HP_LJ1

Pause | Low Priority
✓ Medium Priority
App | High Priority | KTG_AP_LW1 [Active]
1 | | OG | 325K | 12:02 PM 6/23/1992
2 | Alert Always | OG | 325K | 12:04 PM 6/23/1992
3 | ✓ Flash If Inactive | | 12K | 6:57 PM 6/24/1992
| Ignore If Inactive |
HP | | ER_HP_LJ1 [Active]
1 | Network Settings... | DC | 98K | 4:46 PM 7/4/1992
2 | Network Connections... | DC | 1K | 4:47 PM 7/4/1992
3 | | DC | 1K | 4:47 PM 7/4/1992
4 | Printer Setup... | | 6K | 4:49 PM 7/4/1992
5 | Write - LANPRINT.WRI | | 56K | 4:49 PM 7/4/1992
6 | Notepad - BOOTLOG.TXT | | 3K | 4:50 PM 7/4/1992

HP LaserJet Series II on ATRIUM/ACCTG_HP_LJ2 [Active]
1 | Microsoft Word - CHAP7.DOC | | 4K | 4:51 PM 7/4/1992

Fig. 26.21
Print Manager
Network Options

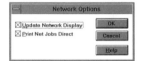

The **P**rint Net Jobs Direct check box should always be marked. If you do not mark this option, you invoke the Windows 3.1 print spooler. When the Windows print spooler is invoked, your print jobs are first printed to a temporary file in the location specified by the DOS TEMP variable. Once the job finishes printing to the temporary file, Windows then sends it to the NetWare queue. This has the effect of making it take longer to print your jobs when accessing a network printer.

If you want to edit print job information, the only solution provided by Microsoft or Novell is the tried-and-true DOS program Pconsole program from NetWare. You need to create a PIF for Pconsole and then add the PIF to one of your Program Manager groups. Then you can perform all of the normal Pconsole functions while using Windows.

If this isn't elegant enough for you, you can get a copy of QMGR.ZIP off CompuServe. It is a shareware package ($20.00) from Italy, no less! This is a fully-Windows Pconsole substitute for managing NetWare print queues and print jobs, allowing you to do all of the normal Pconsole activities plus a couple of extras, such as copying print jobs from one queue to another. You can filter the display to list only jobs from specific users. Also, the program adheres to all of the normal NetWare rights so it is user-safe. You can reach the author of QMGR.ZIP at the following address:

Giovanni De Giovanni
PR.ES srl
Corso Susa 242
10098 Rivoli-Torino
Italy
CompuServe ID: 73767,2111

Other Software for Managing Queues

A significant problem with Windows and NetWare together is that printer selection and queue assignment are not as integrated as they need to be. You can select a different queue easily enough with Control Panel, Print Manager, or NetWare Tools, but nothing checks to see if you have the correct printer driver assigned. Likewise, you can select a different printer driver in most Windows applications, but you usually cannot select a queue.

A few solutions exist to help solve these problems. They are regular commercial software applications. The first product focuses solely on the printer/queue selection issue. The software is WinQueue from North Shore Software. You license this product for your server. During installation you set up descriptions for the various network printers and the queues they are assigned to. The descriptions you create describe the network printer and appear in all Windows applications Printer Setup screens. You also set up the print job parameters for Windows to use. When a user wants to use a different queue/printer combination, they just open the normal Print Setup menu from their application. Figure 26.22 shows how this appears in a Microsoft Word 2.0 Print Setup window. WinQueue automatically matches up the Windows printer driver and NetWare print queue.

Fig. 26.22
The Word 2.0 Printer Setup dialog box, after WinQueue is installed.

Another product that is extremely useful is NetTools from Automated Design Systems. This product was designed initially as a replacement for Program Manager because of Program Manager's deficiencies in network environments. However, one of the nice features of Windows Workstation is that you create network printer assignments using their administrative option. Each printer/queue assignment is assigned an icon. The user's printer icons display on their desktop. When a user wants to select a different printer/queue combination, he merely double-clicks the printer icon on the desktop. Automated Design's product goes far beyond just printer selection capabilities. It addresses many other weaknesses of the NetWare/Windows combination. It deserves a good look from anyone installing Windows in a NetWare environment.

Saber Software's LAN Workstation is probably the most capable NetWare-aware Windows shell. It, too, replaces the Windows Program Manager with a look-alike that is designed for network administration. LAN Workstation offers the best INI file management system on the market and the printing module is very strong, as well. Novell licensed Saber's DOS menu product for NetWare 3.12 and 4.x. Another nice touch with this product is that you can use the same menu scripts for both your DOS users and your Windows users, which means less administrative headaches trying to maintain both environments.

Finally, Lanovation's LAN Escort rounds out the field for NetWare-aware Windows replacement shells. LAN Escort is the easiest of all of to set up and is ideally suited for smaller environments. This product continues to improve with each subsequent release. Like the others, it offers group administrative options for adding icons and groups to a user's Windows work area. It also offers better printer management for the network environment.

You can contact these vendors at the following addresses:

Product: WinQueue
North Shore Software
205 - 51551 Range Road 212A
Sherwood Park, Alberta
Canada T8G1B2
(403)922-5465

Product: NetTools
Automated Design Systems Inc.
375 Northridge Road
Suite 270
Atlanta, GA 30350
(404)394-2552

Product: Saber LAN Workstation
Saber Software Corp.
PO Box 9088
Dallas, TX 75209
(800)338-8754

Product: Lan Escort
Lanovation
1313 5th Street SE
Minneapolis, MN 55414
(800)747-4487

Installing Applications

When you install applications for the LAN environment you have additional concerns that you don't have when you install applications on a stand-alone PC. You must consider where configuration files are going to reside. You need to know how the application and its INI file interact. You also need to devise a plan for centralized administration of the software. The following sections discuss some of the details of installing applications for Windows running in a LAN environment.

Types of Windows Applications

Approaching this topic from an application point of view, you can group Windows applications into two groups: Mini-APPS and Major Applications. Installing and maintaining these two groups requires distinctly different approaches.

Mini-APPS

Mini-APPS can be distinguished from major applications by the following characteristics:

1. They do not have significant INI files of their own.

   Mini-APPS either do not use any INI file or they can re-create their INI file on-the-fly if they don't find it. The Windows Clock program is a good example of this type of Windows program. Clock does have an INI file it creates. However, if Clock can't find its INI file, it re-creates it. Of course, for the LAN administrator this means one less problem to worry about.

2. They do not make significant changes to any of the standard Windows INI files: SYSTEM.INI, WIN.INI, CONTROL.INI, MOUSE.INI, and PROGMAN.INI.

   The other place where applications keep configuration information is the standard Windows INI files. Mini-APPS do not make changes to these files.

VI

Installing Windows

3. They can be installed in a program group by dragging the file from File Manager and dropping it in the desired group.

   Simplicity is the key to Mini-APPS. They do not have a sophisticated installation program that you must run to install the application into a group.

The key to Mini-APPS is that the whole configuration file management issue is minimal. The only real work in managing Mini-APPS is organizing and distributing them to users.

Major Windows Applications

You can identify major Windows applications by any of the following characteristics:

1. They have significant INI files of their own that prevent them from running if they cannot locate their INI files.

   Major Windows applications may need their own INI files. If the application cannot locate its INI files, it won't run. Therefore, LAN administrators have to install the application's INI files for each user.

2. They make changes to the user's Windows INI files: SYSTEM.INI, PROGMAN.INI, WIN.INI, CONTROL.INI, or MOUSE.INI.

   If the application makes changes to standard Windows INI files, the network supervisor must plan on making these changes whenever the application is installed for a user. The network administrator must keep track of the changes made by various applications.

3. These applications normally have a "install" or "setup" program that you use to install the application.

   The installation program usually creates the application's INI files and writes changes to standard Windows INI files. Under normal circumstances, you cannot run the application without having run its installation routine.

The problem with major applications is that they are more sophisticated and the same techniques used for Mini-APPS won't work for installing and maintaining these applications.

Strategy for Managing Mini-APPS on a LAN

There is a straightforward and relatively simple method to installing and maintaining Mini-APPS on a LAN. Before the details, some assumptions are necessary:

1. You are going to install the Mini-APP's files on the file server so they can be shared by multiple users.

2. Different users have access to different Mini-APPS. Not every user is permitted to run every program. Furthermore, applications are generally shared by users within a group or department.

3. You want a centralized method for adding and removing these applications to a group's program set (i.e., the Program Manager group).

4. You have already organized the Mini-APPS into shared directories on the file server.

Setting up the Master Groups

The game plan is to create an environment that makes it easy to share these Mini-APPS with users on the LAN. I want to be able to give different applications to different groups with a minimal investment in time and energy.

1. Start by performing a network installation of Windows into a directory on the file server—Setup /N. This places a small set of files in the directory that uses less than 80K. You have to map a search drive to the master Windows directory on the file server to use this "user."

2. Now, create as many Program Manager groups as needed to put all of your Mini-APPS into a group. You are limited to 50 programs per program group. Make sure the Program Properties for each program contain a standard drive letter that is always available to your users. In figure 26.23, the standard Main and Accessories groups are left. Then, create two other groups, Accessories and Accessories 2, which contain all the Mini-APPS installed on the file server.

Fig. 26.23
Program Manager groups with Mini-APPS.

3. Next, create new Program Manager groups for the various departments by adding the group. Then drag the Mini-APP into the new group using the mouse and the Ctrl key. Dragging an icon while holding down the Ctrl key leaves the item in the original group and copies it into the new group. Figure 26.24 displays a sample group for the operations department.

Fig. 26.24

The Program Manager groups with the Operations group.

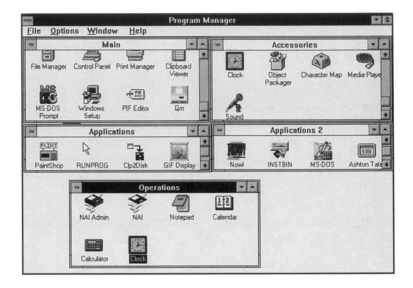

This process creates a new Program Manager group. The file created by my example is OPER.GRP. This group was added to the PROGMAN.INI file for this "user." Listing 26.13 displays a sample PROGMAN.INI for this "user."

Listing 26.13 PROGMAN.INI

```
[Settings]
Window=4 4 633 427 3
display.drv=vga.drv
Order= 1 2 3 4 5
AutoArrange=1

[Groups]
Group1=M:\WAPPS\MINIAPPS\MAIN.GRP
Group2=M:\WAPPS\MINIAPPS\ACCESSOR.GRP
Group3=M:\WAPPS\MINIAPPS\APPLICA1.GRP
Group4=M:\WAPPS\MINIAPPS\APPLICA2.GRP
Group5=M:\WAPPS\MINIAPPS\OPER.GRP
```

4. You can leave these new shared groups in the same directory they are in now. Flag the newly created, shared group file, OPER.GRP, shareable read-only so that users cannot make changes to this group. Give File Scan and Read rights to the NetWare Everyone group for this directory or give File Scan and Read rights to just the user group you are working on for this file, OPER.GRP.

5. Now, edit the PROGMAN.INI file for any user who is a member of the operations department and add this new group to the [Groups] section. Depending upon where you installed Windows for your users, the PROGMAN.INI file is on the file server in the user's private directory or it is in the Windows directory on their local drive. Obviously, it is easier for you if these files are all on the file server.

   When the user runs Windows, this new group appears in their Program Manager groups.

You can see from this example, managing the Mini-APPS on the network is not going to be a major task. You can create a very straight-forward process for adding new groups, adding new programs to groups and distributing these programs to end-users on the network.

Strategy for Maintaining Major Windows Applications

Because of the installation requirements of major applications, major applications can be a major nuisance on the network. Typically, these applications have a "setup" or "install" program that you must run to install these applications for each user. These installation programs usually are not designed for the network environment. This can lead to the network administrator having to visit each user's PC and install the application from the user's PC using the floppy disks that accompany the application. Therefore, to install several major applications for a user can take several hours of the network administrator's time.

Since many of these applications do not have network-oriented installation routines, most do not give you any game plan for avoiding the lengthy installation process. Therefore, if you want to avoid these long installations, you need to develop a process you can use. In the following sections, the process is outlined for you.

Keeping a "Clean" Copy of Windows

You start by installing Windows using SETUP /N to a target directory on the file server. This is your "clean user" copy of Windows. "Clean" here means that you have not installed anything other than the standard Windows groups and icons in this copy. You should have just the Main, Accessories, Games, and Startup groups. These groups contain only the default programs that Windows puts into the group. Next, you run SETUP /A to fully expand the Windows disk into a secondary "clean master" Windows directory (assuming you have already run SETUP /A and created a master Windows directory).

The reason behind creating the "clean" copies is to be able to track what the application's installation program does when you use it. Most application documentation does not tell you what changes the installation is going to make to your environment. Therefore, you want to always test-install applications to these "clean" Windows directories. If the goal is to eliminate the lengthy setup process with an alternate procedure, you must determine what the standard procedure does first. You use the "clean user" copy of Windows as your target user when you install the application. You use the "clean master" as your target network copy of Windows.

If you have several different hardware configurations and machine types, you may need to create a "clean user" copy of Windows for each. This is why you use the network installation method rather than making a full workstation copy of Windows.

You also want to back up these "clean" sets of files so that when you are finished, you can restore the files back to their "clean" condition.

The critical step is to use the "clean user" copy of Windows as the user target and the "clean master" as the Windows target of a test installation. You would map a search path to the "clean master" directory. Hopefully, the application asks for both a user directory, a program directory and a master Windows directory. Direct the user portion into the directory where your "clean user" copy of Windows resides. Direct the programs into a directory where you would normally keep the application's files. Direct the master Windows directory to where your "clean master" resides.

Ferreting out INI Files

After you install the application, you need to find out what the installation process accomplished besides copying the application files themselves into a program directory on your file server. You want to find out about the INI files and INI file changes made by the installation program.

The first place to look is in the program directory where the installation program put all the application's program files. You should look for any INI files placed in this directory. If any INI files exist, inspect them to see what type of information they contain. Remember, INI files contain three general types of information: User Preferences, Hardware Configuration, and Application Information.

Next, you look in the "user" directory where your clean copy of Windows resides for any new INI files. If any new INI files are there, you need to inspect them to determine the type of information they contain.

Finally, you need to see if any of your standard Windows INI files were updated by comparing a listing of the INI file prior to running the installation routine to a listing of the INI file after the installation. You need to document any new sections and any lines added to existing sections. Put copies of the new sections and changes into a separate text files. You need a way to merge these changes into the user's existing INI files.

You should also check to see if the installation made any changes to your AUTOEXEC.BAT and CONFIG.SYS files.

There are three reasons for collecting and analyzing all of this information:

1. If you plan to circumvent the application's installation process, you have to replace it with a process of your own that accomplishes the same tasks. Hopefully, your process is better designed for a network environment and takes less time.

2. You should always document any software that runs on your network. Collecting and categorizing this information is a normal part of the process you should be using for all applications.

3. Most Windows applications do not offer a de-installation routine. How can you tell which information you need to remove when you want to remove an application from the network? If you have documented what the installation process does, you can successfully rid yourself of the application and all of it's other data.

Installing Applications Without Disks

If the application does not offer a network installation process, and you don't want to have to use its regular installation process, you have to be able to reproduce what the installation program did. You can do this for users who will run the application from the file server. This means you have to figure

Tip

Neil J. Rubenking has written a utility that collects all the information that a Windows application-installation program creates or changes, and writes the data into a text file. The utility name is INCTRL (In Control).

VI

Installing Windows

out what new INI files your user needs and what changes are needed in any standard INI files. In plain terms, this means you have to copy the needed INI files to the user's directory and then you have to edit any standard Windows INI file for the changes needed.

The new INI files created by the application must be handled in the same manner as the configuration files discussed earlier in this book. Hardware files need to reside on the PC itself or in a directory you can locate based on the hardware. User-specific INI files need to be in the user's home directory on the file server or on the user's personal machine. Application INI files should be kept in the directory where the application was installed. You also need to decide how these files have to be copied when the user starts up Windows, if necessary. The utility INCTRL can be a big help in figuring out what the process is going to entail.

When you think about it, this sounds as if it could be as much trouble as running the installation program itself. When performing network installations of Windows applications, it takes almost the same amount of time to install the application by hand as it takes the install program. The benefit of manually installing the application is that you can exercise complete control over how it is done.

Aleph Systems, 7319 Willow Avenue, Takoma Park, MD 20912, CompuServe 71371,635, has a neat program called the Network Application Installer. In a nutshell, it allows you to automate the installation process by giving you a way to record the changes that need to be made to install a Windows application. It does not do your homework for you. You must still analyze what the installation program did when you installed the application. However, once you have found and analyzed the changes, this program records what you found and the gives you an easy way of adding the application to the user.

Setting up the Program Item Properties

The final step in setting up a Windows Application is creating its Program Item Properties from the **F**ile menu in Program Manager. Figure 26.25 displays a sample Program Item Properties dialog box for Word for Windows. After choosing the **F**ile **N**ew command in Program Manager, you select Program **I**tem in the New Program Object dialog box.

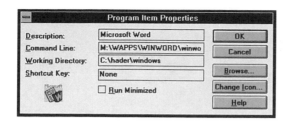

Fig. 26.25
The Program Item
Properties dialog
box.

Completing the Program Item Properties involves filling in the following fields:

1. **D**escription. This field contains the name that appears beneath the program's icon. When displaying this field, Windows 3.1x wraps up to three lines to avoid long descriptions overwriting adjacent icon descriptions.

2. **C**ommand Line. This field contains the name of the program you want to run, including the full path to the program. For applications to run from the file server, make sure that the drive letter you use is always mapped to the server and volume the application resides on.

3. **W**orking Directory. This field is one of the most important additions to Windows 3.1x for networks. This field establishes the user's default data directory when the application is run. Since Windows cannot map any data or search drives prior to launching a Windows application, many applications need an entry in this field to establish the user's data directory.

4. **S**hortcut Key. You use this option to establish a "hot key" combination for bringing this application from background into foreground.

5. **R**un Minimized. This option causes the program to minimize itself into an icon on the desktop when the program is launched. This is useful for programs such as third-party screen savers, the Windows Print Manager and other utilities that you may need most of the time.

6. Change **I**con. This option permits you to change the file name for the icon and the icon you use if the file contains more than one icon. Generally, Windows applications get their icon from the executable file of the application. Some programs such as PROGMAN.EXE contain multiple icons.

What's Missing To Make Windows Complete

Even though Windows and NetWare are likable, this combination is not yet a marriage made in heaven. There are several key areas that still need significant improvement. Windows is network able, but Windows is not designed for networks.

First, Windows and NetWare need better printer driver, queue selection, and NetWare print job integration. There is nothing in either product that keeps track of these three pieces to make sure that the user doesn't select a queue that is inappropriate for the type of printer driver the user has active. In addition, Windows does not use the NetWare print job definitions. Right now it takes too many steps for the user to select a different queue and printer, plus you have to leave Control Panel as a user program. Print Manager needs to be improved to allow the network administrator the ability to disable the Network Connections and Network Settings items.

Windows needs a script capability that allows network users the ability to map logical and search drives, issue Capture commands, and perform other housekeeping for any application, DOS or Windows-based. If the people from Automated Design Systems (Windows Workstation) and Saber Software (Saber Menu for Windows) can do it so can Microsoft.

The new restrictions of Program Manager are a nice addition, but similar restrictions are needed for File Manager. File Manager is still an open doorway to the user to run other programs than those that appear in their program groups. In addition, the ability to control whether the user is allowed to establish or change the Network Connections within File Manager is needed.

Microsoft must get the data types in the INI files straightened out. First of all, the hardware information (Fonts) that is in WIN.INI must be put into a separate file so that WIN.INI can be strictly a user-specific file. The same applies to PROGMAN.INI which now contains a device driver statement. The majority of the networks do not have all the same type of machines or users who use only one machine.

Better handling of shared machines and user options in a network environment would be a nice addition to Windows. Presently, network administrators have to be very aware of what is going on in Windows to be able to make it work on their network properly. There are too many quirky details the LAN supervisor must master.

Until these items are addressed, those attempting to network Windows with NetWare need to evaluate third-party software applications that help to eliminate or simplify these problems. The two premier products that you need to evaluate are Windows Workstation and Saber Menu for Windows. These two products offer excellent scripting abilities and offer solutions to dozens of other Windows/NetWare integration problems.

From Here...

No one ever said networking Windows was easy. This chapter discussed many of the important details that you need to consider when using Windows 3.1x in a NetWare LAN environment.

Refer to the following chapters for more information:

- Chapter 9, "Printing with Windows," discusses printing on a network.

- Chapter 15, "Using Windows for Workgroups Mail and PC Fax," shows you how to use these Mail and PC Fax in your workgroup.

VI

Installing Windows

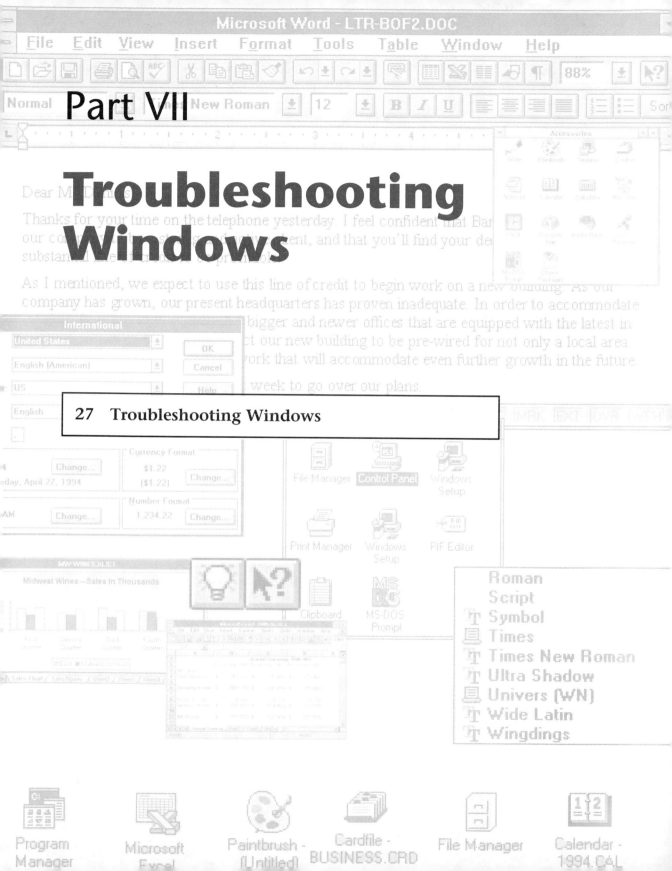

Part VII

Troubleshooting Windows

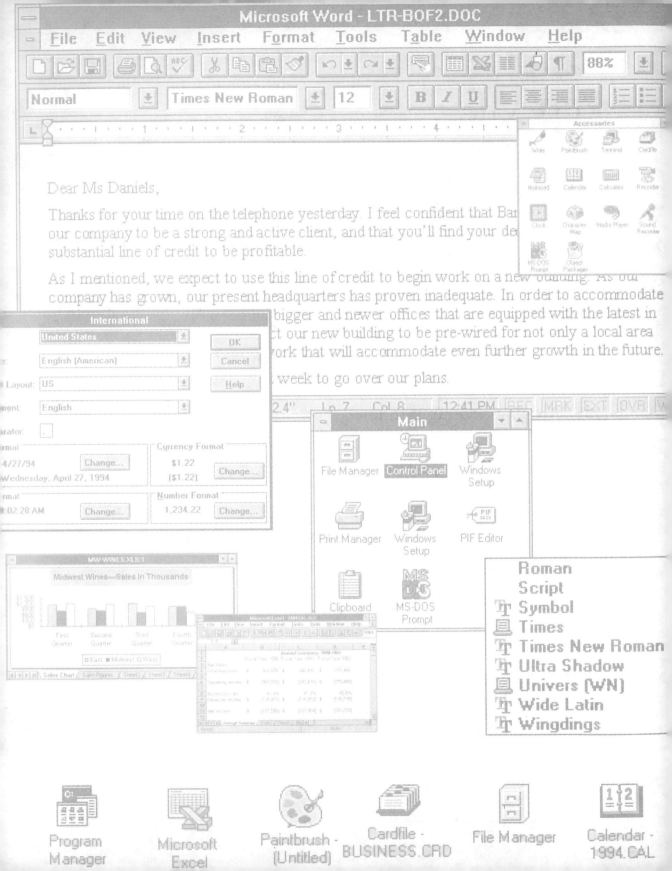

Chapter 27

Troubleshooting Windows

Windows 3.1 and 3.11 are stable operating environments that usually work well. But the very nature of complex software implies that problems can occur. Often, the solution is simple and quick to implement. At other times, a bit of research may be required to uncover the source of a problem and to devise a solution.

In this chapter you will learn how to:

- Solve installation problems

- Solve general Windows problems

- Troubleshoot application problems

- Respond to application failures

- Resolve memory conflicts

- Solve font and printing problems

- Solve network problems

- Resolve object linking and embedding difficulties

- Solve communication and port problems

- Find sources for help, support, and training

If you encounter a problem, this chapter is a good place to start. The simplest solutions are listed first in each section. Try these solutions first. If a simple solution doesn't solve the problem, go to the next step. Work through the steps until you find a solution that solves the problem. If none of the solutions solves the problem, call one of Microsoft's technical support lines. The support technicians use an on-line database of problems and solutions known as the Knowledge Base. The numbers for different technical-support telephone lines are listed at the end of this chapter.

Although encountering problems may be frustrating, working with any computer problem also can be educational, so consider these experiences to be a way to learn more about your computer. When the next problem arises, it may not seem so mysterious.

Solving Installation Problems

To install Windows, you typically insert the first of the Windows disks in drive A and type **A:SETUP**. Two setup options exist: Express and Custom. Usually, Windows performs the installation flawlessly, gleaning needed information about the computer without asking you any questions. If equipment is incompatible or the computer lacks the correct resources, however, an installation failure can occur. Several situations can cause an installation failure, so watch the progress of the installation; notice when a failure occurs and what message appears.

A Failure Occurs During the DOS Portion of the Installation

The first part of a Windows installation runs in DOS. During this time, the setup application checks the hardware and records information about the equipment for use later in the setup process. If Windows cannot recognize a piece of hardware, the installation may fail, and you must stop the installation.

To solve the problem, first find out exactly what kind of equipment you have in, and attached to, your PC (this investigation may take some research). Write down this information for use during the installation. Restart the installation, insert the disk and, at the DOS prompt, type the following command:

> **SETUP /I**

This command causes Windows to perform a custom installation without detecting the hardware. When prompted by the installation application, you must specify what kind of equipment you have.

If you are unsure what information about the equipment you need, try the installation even if you aren't sure that you can complete the process. When prompted for information about the equipment, write down the questions and then quit the installation. Try again after you get the needed information.

A Failure Occurs During the Windows Portion of the Installation

When the DOS portion of the installation is complete (during which the files needed by the installation routine are copied on the hard disk), Windows starts, and the rest of the installation runs from Windows. If a failure occurs during the switch from DOS to Windows, quit the installation and try one of the following solutions:

■ Close any memory-resident applications and restart the installation after restarting the computer. If memory-resident applications start each time you start the computer, you will have to edit the AUTOEXEC.BAT file (and possibly the CONFIG.SYS file) to remove memory-resident applications that start automatically. You can use the Windows accessory Notepad (if Windows is runnable) or a text editor to edit these system files, which are located in the root directory (exit all directories and subdirectories to get to the root directory).

■ Run the installation again, and choose Express rather than Custom Setup. Then make sure that the hardware descriptions and software settings are correct.

■ Make sure that you have the right version of DOS. You need to have DOS 3.1 or later to install Windows; to check which version you have, type **VER** at the DOS prompt and press Enter. If you have an earlier version of DOS, install a newer version and then install Windows. You will get better performance from DOS and Windows if you have DOS 6.2 or later. You can install DOS 6.2 on your computer even if you already have Windows installed. For more information, see Chapter 24, "Installing and Optimizing Windows 3.1."

The Installation Application Keeps Asking for the Same Disk

The Windows installation application prompts you for each disk by number, as needed. If you are repeatedly prompted for the same disk, even after you insert the disk, try one of the following solutions:

■ Make sure that you correctly specified the drive that contains the disk. Windows assumes that you are installing from drive A. If you are installing from drive B, be sure that you specify drive B in the dialog box that prompts you to insert disks.

■ Disk-cache applications on the hard disk can cache a disk. Remove from the CONFIG.SYS or AUTOEXEC.BAT file all lines that reference a disk-caching application (by typing **REM** at the beginning of the appropriate lines), and restart the computer. Then try the installation again.

■ If the installation application doesn't recognize that you changed the disk, you must add a line to the CONFIG.SYS file. This line sends a message to the computer, saying that you changed the disk. Add this line to the CONFIG.SYS file if you are installing Windows from drive A, a high-density (1.2M) drive:

DRIVEPARM=/D:0 /F:1

■ The /D:0 parameter specifies the drive. To use drive B rather than A, the command reads /D:1; for drive C, the command reads /D:2. The /F:1 parameter specifies the drive type; for a 160K, 180K, 320K, or 360K drive, the command reads /F:0 (zero); for a 3.5-inch 720K drive, the command reads /F:2; for a 3.5-inch 1.44M drive, the command reads /F:7; for a 3.5-inch 2.88M drive, the command reads /F:9.

The Installation Application Doesn't List Your Hardware

If you installed on your system hardware that Windows doesn't recognize during the installation, you may need a special driver for the hardware. (A *driver* is software that serves as a translator between hardware, DOS, and Windows.) First, however, find out whether the hardware is compatible with a similar piece of equipment that may be listed. If the equipment is compatible, choose the compatible equipment during the installation.

To acquire a driver, call Microsoft Product Support Services and ask whether Windows includes the driver you need. Ask for a copy of the driver you need. You can download drivers directly from Microsoft Download Services. If the driver you need is not available, contact the equipment manufacturer to see whether it offers a Windows-compatible driver.

You Don't Have Enough Hard Disk Space To Install Windows

Most people use the Express Setup to install Windows. If you lack the space on your hard disk to install Windows, choose the Custom Setup and install only the parts of Windows that you need. You can leave out certain accessories—for example, Windows Write, if you use Word for Windows as your word processor. You also may be able to do without Help files.

If you still lack space, scour the hard disk for files and applications that you can delete. (Look for big graphics files, which consume a great deal of disk space.)

Finally, to get rid of wasted disk space, run a disk-defragmentation utility on the computer.

If you are using DOS 6.2 or can upgrade to DOS 6.2 (which is worth it), you can run DoubleSpace. DoubleSpace is disk-compression software that comes with DOS 6.2 and later versions. It enables your computer to put almost twice as much data on your hard disk. The downside to DoubleSpace is that it slows performance by 5 to 10 percent. It also requires approximately 40K of memory, but the DBLSPACE.BIN program can be loaded into high memory so that it does not reside in conventional memory. Run MemMaker, a DOS 6.2 memory-optimization program, to move the DoubleSpace program into high memory. DoubleSpace and MemMaker are described in more detail in Chapter 24, "Installing and Optimizing Windows 3.1."

Windows Doesn't Start after Installation

If you cannot start Windows after installation, try one of the following solutions:

- Check to see whether you installed the wrong hardware. From the DOS prompt, change to the WINDOWS directory. Type **SETUP** and press Enter. Review the hardware settings to make sure that these settings are correct. If the settings are incorrect, change them.

- Close all memory-resident applications (TSRs). You may have to remove these applications from the AUTOEXEC.BAT file to prevent the TSRs from starting automatically (refer to "A Failure Occurs During the Windows Portion of the Installation" earlier in this chapter).

- Install Windows again, using the SETUP /I command (refer to "A Failure Occurs During the DOS Portion of the Installation").

■ If Windows won't start in 386 Enhanced mode even though you have a 386 or 486 computer, you may lack enough free conventional memory or disk space for Windows to run in 386 Enhanced mode. Use a text editor to edit the AUTOEXEC.BAT and CONFIG.SYS files; remove all memory-resident applications, network drivers, mouse drivers, and so on, and see whether Windows will start. If it does, run MemMaker in DOS 6.2 to configure your CONFIG.SYS file to optimize memory.

Getting the Mouse To Work

If the mouse doesn't work or behaves strangely, you may have a connection problem or a software problem, or something may be wrong with the mouse. Two kinds of mice are available: serial and port. A *serial mouse* attaches to a serial port of the computer; a *port mouse* attaches to a port on a board that you install inside the computer's system unit.

The Mouse Doesn't Work in Windows

A serial mouse must be connected to the COM1 or COM2 port. Although the port you choose doesn't matter, you must make sure that you connect the mouse before you start the computer (reboot if you plugged in the mouse after you started the computer).

The mouse may not work because of an interrupt conflict. Serial devices use *Interrupt Request Lines* to communicate with the computer, and only eight IRQ *interrupts* are available. If two devices are fighting for the same interrupt, a conflict develops. Suspect this problem if you have a lot of equipment attached to the computer. Check the IRQ interrupts for the other devices, and make sure that the mouse doesn't conflict with them. You can change an IRQ interrupt by choosing the Ports application from Control Panel, choosing **S**ettings, choosing **A**dvanced, and then selecting a different **I**nterrupt Request Line (IRQ) from the list.

The Mouse Doesn't Work in DOS Applications

To use a mouse in a DOS application, the mouse not only must be correctly installed in Windows, but also set up in DOS before you start Windows. The easiest way to get a mouse working in DOS is to make sure that the correct driver is included in the WINDOWS directory; then add a line to the CONFIG.SYS file or the AUTOEXEC.BAT file so that DOS sets up the mouse when you turn on the computer.

The Microsoft mouse uses the driver MOUSE.COM, which you set up in the AUTOEXEC.BAT file, or MOUSE.SYS, which you set up in the CONFIG.SYS file by adding the following line:

DEVICE = C:\WINDOWS\MOUSE.SYS

If the mouse still doesn't work, Windows may not support this mouse, and you need to purchase a different mouse that Windows does support. (First check with the mouse manufacturer to see whether the device emulates another mouse that Windows supports; if so, install the mouse with this driver and try again.)

If you use an IBM mouse with IBM mouse driver Version 1.0, you need a newer driver. Contact the dealer from whom you bought the mouse to get an updated driver, and install the driver in Windows, using the Windows Setup application in the Main group.

A final reason why the mouse may not work is that the monitor doesn't support a mouse in a DOS application that runs in a window. If you have a 16-color monitor with 800 x 600 resolution, make sure that you use the standard Super VGA driver that comes with Windows 3.1. The driver from earlier versions of Windows needs to be updated. If you have a monitor for which no driver is available in Windows 3.1, check with the manufacturer to see whether an updated driver is available for Windows 3.1.

The Mouse Pointer Doesn't Move or Jumps Around

If the mouse pointer appears on-screen but doesn't move, the wrong mouse driver is selected or an interrupt conflict exists. First suspect that the wrong driver is installed, because this problem is much easier to fix.

To check the driver, choose the Windows Setup application in the Main group in Program Manager. A dialog box appears, listing the equipment you installed during the Windows installation. If the mouse doesn't match the equipment settings, open the **O**ptions menu and choose the **C**hange System Settings command; from the **M**ouse list, select the correct mouse.

If this procedure doesn't work, check for an IRQ-interrupt conflict (refer to "The Mouse Doesn't Work in Windows" earlier in this chapter).

If the mouse pointer moves but jumps around on-screen, the mouse may be dirty, or an IRQ-interrupt conflict may exist. To clean the mouse, you usually can remove the ball easily by following instructions on the bottom of the mouse. Use a solvent to clean the ball; then replace it. (Don't lose the ball; this part is almost impossible to replace.) If cleaning doesn't work, an IRQ-interrupt conflict is the probable culprit.

Solving General Windows Problems

General Windows problems include difficulties with running Program Manager, File Manager, or Windows itself. This section of the chapter deals with applications, application failures, printing, memory, communication ports, and networks.

Problems in Program Manager

Program Manager is Windows' hometown. When you start Windows, you see Program Manager. When you run an application, you start from this part of Windows.

Program Manager consists of the Program Manager window, in which group windows exist that contain program-item icons. Group icons that represent closed group windows also appear inside Program Manager. Windows creates some of these group windows as part of the installation process; you create other group windows. The same is true of program-item icons; Windows creates some, and you create others.

Group windows and program-item icons are easy to create and to delete. To delete a group window or program-item icon, just select the icon and press the Del key. You can delete an icon accidentally in no time at all. Fortunately, deleting a group or icon doesn't delete applications or files; this action deletes only the group or icon.

If you believe that you are missing a group window or a program-item icon, create another window or icon. To create a new group window, open the **F**ile menu in Program Manager and choose the **N**ew command; then choose Program **G**roup.

To create a program-item icon select the group in which you want to place the icon, open the **F**ile menu and choose **N**ew, and select Program **I**tem. In the **D**escription text box, enter a name for the icon; in the **C**ommand Line text box, enter the application's path and name (choose **B**rowse if you're not sure where the application is located).

Slow or Odd Performance

If Windows begins running slowly after a time, three possible causes exist. One cause may be lack of memory; you may be running too many applications simultaneously for efficient operation. For a temporary fix, run fewer applications. For a better fix, add more memory to the computer (which doesn't cost much, and the speed improvement can be significant). If your computer uses DOS 6.2, run MemMaker to optimize memory. Windows also may be slow if the hard disk is full. Remove some unneeded files.

If you are running Windows on a 386 computer or better, make sure that you have created a permanent swap file. A *permanent swap file* is a contiguous section of hard disk used by Windows to store frequently used segments of the Windows program. If a permanent swap file is not created, Windows creates its own temporary swap file, but a permanent swap file is faster. A permanent swap file can be created only in a contiguous free space on the hard disk; it cannot be created on a disk that has been compressed with DoubleSpace or some other disk-compression software.

If your computer does not have a permanent swap file, use the 386 Enhanced program in Control Panel to create one on your fastest uncompressed disk. The permanent swap file should be larger than 1M. You will see performance increases as you add swap-file space up to 8M to 10M.

Adding DoubleSpace to a computer on which Windows is installed can remove the permanent swap file, making Windows perform significantly slower. Remedy the situation by recreating the permanent swap file, using the 386 Enhanced application in Control Panel. Put the permanent swap file on an uncompressed drive. If you have only a single hard disk, use the host drive for the DoubleSpace drive (usually, drive H). If the host drive is too small for an adequate permanent swap file, resize the host drive. You can resize the host drive by exiting Windows, typing **DBLSPACE** at the DOS prompt, and pressing Enter. Select the compressed drive and then choose **D**rive, Change **S**ize.

Another reason for Windows to be slow is that the hard disk has become fragmented. Computers save files in segments on the hard disk, and the segments may not be adjacent. Over time, you end up with a hard disk with pieces of files scattered across the surface in no particular order, which lengthens the time the computer takes to access these files. A disk-defragmentation application can speed the computer's operation (and usually free some disk space) by moving all fragmented files together.

If Windows suddenly begins behaving unpredictably and you cannot tell why, you may have accidentally erased files that Windows needs. If the problem seems to be with an application, you may need to reinstall the application. If the problem is in Windows, you may need to reinstall Windows. Don't delete files, however, unless you know for sure what the files are. Also, take care not to save the data files in application directories or the WINDOWS directory; this step lessens the chance that you will accidentally delete a file that the computer may need.

Erased or Lost Files

If you erased system or application files that the computer needs, you need to reinstall the application or Windows. If you accidentally erased data files that you need, restore these files from backup copies.

What? You didn't make a backup copy? In this case, stop what you're doing—don't do anything else on the computer—and use a file-recovery application, such as Norton Desktop for Windows, to recover lost files.

If you lose a file through no fault of your own, such as a power outage, many applications perform an automatic save, which often preserves at least part of your work. Check the application's documentation to see whether the application has the capability of backing up files when a power or application failure occurs. These backup files may have odd names and may be located in special directories; the documentation can tell you how to find these files.

Troubleshooting Windows Applications

Sometimes while you use an application, you press a key and the wrong thing happens. The first thing you should do is try again. If the incorrect response persists, check this section to see what may be happening.

If the system stops responding altogether, or *crashes*, see "Responding to an Application Failure" later in this chapter.

You Get the Wrong Result When You Press a Key

If you press a key in an application—usually, a shortcut key—and something that you didn't expect happens , a shortcut-key conflict probably exists. In many applications, you can assign custom shortcuts to the keyboard combinations. If you inadvertently assigned system-level shortcut keys to an application-level function, however, you get the wrong result when you press the keys. (The Ctrl+Alt+Del key combination, for example, reboots a computer. Don't assign this sequence to the function of making selected text bold.) The easiest solution to the problem is to change the shortcut in the application.

You also can change shortcut keys in a DOS PIF or in the Properties dialog box in Program Manager (select the program-item icon, and open the **F**ile menu and choose **P**roperties).

If you press a Windows shortcut key and the Windows function doesn't execute, a DOS application may be preempting the shortcut. Check the DOS application's PIF by using PIF Editor in the Main group in Program Manager, or check the DOS program-item icon's properties in Program Manager by opening the **F**ile menu and choosing **P**roperties.

An Application Runs Too Slowly

If the application begins running slowly, the computer lacks enough memory to run the application optimally. You need to free memory by closing other applications or by taking other measures (see "Solving Memory Conflicts," later in this chapter). Suspect low memory if the hard disk's light blinks frequently, which indicates that Windows is switching applications between memory and the hard disk because memory is low.

A full hard disk also can cause an application to slow. If you suspect that the hard disk is nearly full, save all work, and use File Manager to remove or back up unneeded files. (Don't put off this step: if the hard disk gets completely full, you cannot save to the hard disk, and the application may freeze.)

If applications run slowly when you run multiple applications or open very large files, you may need to set up a permanent swap file. Select the 386 Enhanced application in Control Panel; choose **V**irtual Memory and **C**hange; and change the **T**ype to Permanent.

When you change to a permanent swap file, Windows may suggest that you defragment the hard disk—a procedure that regroups scattered segments of files to make these files contiguous. Defragmenting a hard disk not only saves disk space but also speeds disk access because files no longer are scattered across the entire disk. You need a utility to defragment a hard disk.

Troubleshooting DOS Applications

DOS applications don't need Windows to run, but you gain many advantages when you run DOS applications in Windows. To run DOS applications, Windows uses files that are known as *PIFs*, or application information files. A PIF includes information about the DOS application's location on disk, as well as setup information that is standardized to work on all computers. Although the PIF settings may enable DOS applications to work on the computer, these files may not cause the DOS applications to work optimally on the computer. Chapter 22, "Running, Installing, and Configuring DOS Applications," tells you how to optimize DOS application performance by fine-tuning PIF settings.

Other reasons to edit a PIF include the following:

- The application is in a directory other than the directory listed in the **P**rogram Filename text box of the PIF.

- The **S**tart-up Directory, which specifies the data directory, is different from the directory that you want or the directory that the application expects.

- You want to start an application by using a special parameter.

- You want to ensure that an application swaps to disk when not in use, freeing more memory for other applications (the Prevent Program S**w**itch option).

- An application was upgraded and requires more memory.

- You want to increase the memory available to an application to increase its performance.

For more tips about improving DOS applications' performance, see "Solving Memory Conflicts," later in this chapter.

Installation and Setup Problems

Usually, when installing any software, you need to provide information about the equipment or software. Before you start an installation, find out exactly what equipment you have, how much memory your system has, and what software you previously installed and where on the computer the software is located. Check the application's documentation to see whether you can find a list of information needed during installation. As always, make sure that you have enough hard disk space before you begin the installation process, and (if possible) shut down all memory-resident applications. If you have difficulty when installing a DOS application, refer to the application's documentation.

Copy, Paste, and Print Screen Problems

If you cannot copy between a DOS application and other DOS and Windows applications, or if you cannot print the DOS screen in Windows, open the application's PIF and deselect the No Screen **E**xchange option. This option may be selected to save memory. (To edit a PIF, choose PIF Editor from the Main group; then open the **F**ile menu and choose the **O**pen command to open the PIF for the DOS application you want to change.)

DOS Font and Printing Problems

If you cannot change the font size in a DOS application, the application may be running in graphics mode rather than in text mode. Check the application's documentation to see whether you can switch to text mode.

Some display drivers don't support changing fonts in DOS applications running in a window. If you use a Super VGA monitor, make sure that you selected the Super VGA driver that comes with Windows 3.1. If this selection doesn't fix the problem, contact the video adapter manufacturer to see whether a new driver is available for Windows 3.1.

If you cannot get a driver that supports font switching in DOS applications, try adding the following line to the [NonWindowsApp] section of the SYSTEM.INI file:

```
FontChangeEnable = 1
```

Problems Switching Between Applications

If you cannot switch between applications, the DOS application's PIF may be set to prevent switching (which can save memory). If this is the case, the only way to get back to Windows is to close the DOS application. To change this, open the application's PIF and deselect the Prevent Program Switch option. (To edit a PIF, choose PIF Editor from the Main group; then open the File menu and choose the Open command to open the PIF for the DOS application you want to change.)

In PIF Editor, also check the Advanced dialog box and see whether any Reserve Shortcut Key options are selected. If they are, you cannot use these shortcut keys to switch between applications; try deselecting these options. In particular, deselect the Alt+Tab option.

If you switch between DOS applications in standard mode and a DOS application's screen does not redraw, edit the application's PIF and deselect the No Save Screen option. This option saves memory by not redrawing the screen but is suitable only for applications that can redraw a screen themselves.

If you are unable to switch from a DOS application, consider the following possibilities:

- Windows may not have reserved enough memory to save the video image of the application when you switch out of the application. Edit the PIF for that application to reserve a higher video mode. For example, if the current video mode is for text screens, select a graphics video mode.

- Check the PIF to ensure that the Prevent Program Switch option is cleared (standard mode only).

- Ensure that the application does not use the Directly Modifies options (standard mode only). Try clearing one or more of these options and rerunning the application.

- A very few applications take complete control of the keyboard, so Windows cannot receive any keyboard signals. You must quit such an application to return to Windows.

Be Cautious When Changing PIF Settings

When you change PIF settings, do not begin working on important data immediately. Run the DOS application as an experiment to see whether the new PIF setting runs the application and enables you to switch between applications. Some applications require specific PIF settings because of the way they work with the keyboard and video memory. If you cannot find a PIF setting that enables you to switch from that application to another, you must quit that application to return to Windows.

Performance Problems Running DOS Applications

DOS applications running in standard mode usually swap between memory and the hard disk, allowing more applications to fit in memory at the same time. If you assign a serial (COM) port to a DOS application, however, Windows assumes that you are doing so because you want to use the COM port to communicate via a modem. Swapping, however, interrupts modem communications, so Windows doesn't permit a DOS application assigned to a COM port to swap. Therefore, fewer DOS applications can run in standard mode, because saving memory by swapping between memory and the hard disk is impossible. To solve this problem, deselect the COM**1**, COM**2**, COM**3**, or COM**4** option in the PIF dialog box. (To edit a PIF, choose PIF Editor from the Main group; then open the **F**ile menu and choose the **O**pen command to open the PIF for the DOS application you want to change.)

If the system slows when you're running DOS applications, you may be running a DOS application in the background unnecessarily. In the PIF Editor dialog box, deselect the Execution **B**ackground option. (To edit a PIF, choose PIF Editor from the Main group; then open the **F**ile menu and choose the **O**pen command to open the PIF for the DOS application you want to change.)

In PIF Editor, type the maximum amount of extended memory needed by the application in the XMS Memory: KB Limit option. This setting prevents the application from using all the extended memory by setting an upper limit. Leave the setting at 0 to prevent the application from gaining access to any extended memory (except in the HMA), or set the option to –1 to give the application all the requested extended memory. Use the –1 setting only if the application requires large amounts of extended memory, because this setting may slow the system significantly.

Operation Problems Running DOS Applications

If you hear a beep when you try to switch from a full screen to a window, the application cannot run in a window. Press Alt+Enter to return to the full screen; if this step doesn't work, press Ctrl+Alt+Del to close the application without closing Windows.

If you're stuck in a DOS application after you marked (selected) text or after you scrolled, you still may be in the Windows editing mode, which prevents you from working with a DOS application. You can tell whether this problem exists by looking at the DOS application's title bar; if the bar still reads Select or Mark, a Windows operation still is incomplete. Complete the operation (by selecting text or by opening the Edit menu and choosing the Copy Enter command), or press the Esc key to return control to the application.

Capturing the Screen Doesn't Work

If you are unable to capture a DOS screen, check the following solutions:

■ Check the PIF to ensure that the No Screen Exchange option is deselected. Someone may have selected this option to make more memory available, but while No Screen Exchange is selected, this option prevents copying or cutting to the Clipboard.

■ Check the Reserve Shortcut Key option in the Advanced dialog box in PIF Editor to see whether the PrtScrn or Alt+PrScrn key combinations are reserved for the application's use. The application may use the key combinations, disabling them for Windows use.

■ Check the Video Mode if you are running in standard mode or the Video Memory if you are running in 386 Enhanced mode. Selecting a higher video mode to make more memory available for the video may enable you to capture screen data.

■ A final reason why you cannot capture a screen may be lack of memory. Close some applications to free memory.

Pasting Information Doesn't Work

If you are unable to paste information that you copied or cut to the Clipboard, check the following solutions:

■ Windows cannot paste graphics in a DOS application. Windows can paste graphics in Windows applications that can accept graphics.

■ Copied *text* from a DOS application actually may be graphics that appear as text on-screen. If so, Windows cannot copy the *graphical text* to another DOS application. You may be able to copy and paste the entire screen in the application instead.

■ Some DOS applications cannot handle the fast paste method used by 386 Enhanced mode. If you operate in 386 Enhanced mode and pasting does not work, modify the advanced portion of the PIF to clear the Allow Fast **P**aste check box.

Problems Closing DOS Applications

Quit a DOS application with the normal command used to quit the application. If the screen does not return to Windows immediately, press Alt+space bar to open the Control menu, and choose **C**lose. You can control how the window or screen for a DOS application reacts when the application closes via the **C**lose Window On Exit setting in the PIF. The application window will remain open if this check box is not checked.

Normally, you cannot quit Windows when a DOS application is running. If you try to quit Windows when a DOS application is active, Windows asks you to close the application first unless this PIF option has been selected.

If you are running Windows in 386 Enhanced mode and the Allow **C**lose When Active check box is selected in the application PIF, you can close Windows while that DOS application is running. This may result in loss of data and damaged program files, however, so this option should rarely be used.

If you are connected to a network while in a DOS application, disconnect from the network before you quit the application.

If a DOS application running under Windows terminates improperly, it prevents you from exiting the application. When a DOS application crashes, and you cannot exit the frozen application, you can use the **T**erminate option in the Control menu to terminate the application. Open the application's Control menu and choose the **S**ettings option; then choose **T**erminate to close the application. This option should be used only as a last resort.

Responding to an Application Failure

Errors in programming may cause Windows applications to try to use the memory that another application is using. This situation can cause a software failure, or *crash*. When this happens, you sometimes see a message advising you that the application encountered an unrecoverable error. The screen also may freeze and the application may become unusable.

Fortunately, if an application crashes, you may not have lost everything. You often can recover from a crash by shutting down only the crashed application. In many cases, you don't have to turn off the computer or restart Windows. You lose the data in the application that crashed (unless the application has a file-recovery utility, as Word for Windows does), but you may not lose data from other applications that were running at the same time.

If you encounter a message advising you that an application has terminated or if the screen freezes, press the following keys:

Ctrl+Alt+Del

A message appears, offering you three alternatives. The first choice is to press the Esc (Escape) key, which exits the message box. If you don't feel that the application really crashed, you can try pressing Esc to return to the application. If this step doesn't work (it probably won't), press Enter to exit the application and return to Windows. If this action doesn't work, you have to reboot the computer.

To recover from an application crash, follow these steps:

1. When you see a message advising you that the current application has terminated, press Ctrl+Alt+Del.

2. To close an application (and lose all changes you made during the current work session), press Enter. If this solution works, you return to Windows. Restart the application and continue working.

3. If you encounter another error message (rather than return to Windows), press Ctrl+Alt+Del again to restart the computer. You lose unsaved data in all applications that were running when the crash occurred.

A crash sometimes occurs for no apparent reason, and you must restart the application to continue. (If the application freezes, rather than simply shutting down, try the Ctrl+Alt+Del technique.) If the system crashes frequently, however, suspect a problem. One problem stems from using an older version of an application that is not compatible with Windows 3.1. If this is the case, call the manufacturer to see about getting an updated version of the application.

Another problem may be that your equipment is incompatible with Windows. Check to be sure that you're using the right driver. To learn more about hardware compatibility, use Windows Write to read the README.WRI or SYSTEM.WRI files provided in the WINDOWS directory.

Solving Memory Conflicts

Everything you do on the computer happens in memory, and the computer has only so much memory. Occasionally, memory becomes full. If this problem becomes a regular occurrence, consider adding memory; the cost per kilobyte is far less than in the past, and the improvement in speed can be amazing—especially if you jump from a 4M system to 84M. (Beyond 164M, the improvements are less noticeable.)

Out-of-Memory Errors

If you see an out-of-memory message when you try to start an application, you have too many applications running or too many documents open. When this happens, you are not out of extended memory—the type of memory you can buy in a store. Instead, Windows has run out of the memory that it uses to keep track of its own resources, such as the names and locations of open windows. If you cannot start a DOS application, try the following suggestions, or refer to the following sections on freeing memory in standard and 386 Enhanced modes. If you cannot start a Windows application, try the following suggestions:

- Close any applications you're not using. Close any memory-resident applications. In general, be sure that you really use any of the memory-resident applications that are set to start up automatically. If you don't, modify the CONFIG.SYS or AUTOEXEC.BAT file to remove memory-resident applications.

- Clear or save the Clipboard contents. From the Main menu, choose Clipboard Viewer. Then open the **F**ile menu and choose Save **A**s to save the contents, or open the **E**dit menu and choose **D**elete to delete the contents.

- Turn off desktop wallpaper, which uses a great deal of memory. From Control Panel, choose Desktop; in the Wallpaper group, choose None in the File list.

- Make sure that Windows has enough disk space available for swap files. If possible, set up a permanent swap file. In 386 Enhanced mode, choose the 386 Enhanced application in Control Panel and choose Virtual Memory; then choose Change and select Permanent as the swap file Type.

- Upgrade to DOS 6.2, and run MemMaker as described in Chapter 22, "Running, Installing, and Configuring DOS Applications." MemMaker optimizes the use of conventional memory. It takes drivers and software that would have consumed conventional memory and loads as many of them as possible into areas of high memory. This makes more room in conventional memory for Windows and Windows applications.

Memory Needs To Be Freed for DOS Applications in Standard Mode

A PIF is an application information file that Windows uses to run DOS applications. You can change some of the PIF settings to improve memory management. To edit a PIF, choose the PIF Editor application from the Main group in Program Manager. Then open the File menu and choose Open to open the PIF for the application that is causing the problem.

- For the Video Memory option, choose Text. This choice reduces the amount of memory Windows reserves for the application. Close the application before you make this change.

- In the Memory Requirements KB Required box, reduce the amount of memory required.

- If the application doesn't need extended memory, set XMS Memory: KB Required and KB Limit to zero.

- If you don't plan to use this application to take screen shots, select the No Screen Exchange option.

- If you won't need to switch between applications, select the Prevent Program Switch option. With Prevent Program Switch active, you must exit the application to return to Windows.

Memory Needs To Be Freed for DOS Applications in 386 Enhanced Mode

You can use PIFs to improve memory management in 386 Enhanced mode, just as you can in standard mode. Start PIF Editor as you did in the preceding section, and open the PIF for the application that is causing the problem. If none of the following suggestions helps, edit the PIFs for other DOS applications you may run at the same time you run the one that causes the memory overload.

- For the **V**ideo Memory option, choose Text. This choice reduces the amount of memory Windows reserves for the application. Close the application before you make this change. Deselect the Retain Video **M**emory option in the **A**dvanced dialog box.

- In the Memory Requirements: KB **R**equired box, reduce the amount of memory needed.

- Select the F**u**ll Screen option. Running a DOS application in a window takes more memory.

- Select the **E**xclusive option to run this application exclusively. With Exclusive selected, you cannot run other applications in the background.

- Run DOS applications full-screen rather than in a window to conserve memory. Switch between window and full-screen display by pressing Alt+Enter.

Solving Font and Printing Problems

In the days before Windows, printing was likely to cause problems for people. Windows greatly simplifies printing by using a common printer driver and by including Print Manager to manage printing. Occasionally, however, a problem crops up in the best of systems.

The Printer Doesn't Print

One of the most common problems you may encounter is when the printer simply won't print. Often, this problem is the easiest to fix, because the fault frequently is mechanical. Try one of the following solutions:

- Make sure that the printer is plugged in, turned on, and on-line (a light or message on the front of the printer usually gives you this information). Make sure that the printer has paper and that the paper is not jammed. Make sure that the printer lid or case is closed.

■ Make sure that the printer cartridge is firmly plugged in or that the ribbon or print wheel is correctly installed.

■ Make sure that you have the right cable and that the cable is functioning. You sometimes can borrow a cable from an identical printer that you know works to see whether a new cable is all you need.

■ Make sure that you selected the correct printer in the application. Make sure that the settings, such as paper orientation and source, are correct.

■ Make sure that the printer options and port are correct. You can use the Printers application in Control Panel to check printer settings and connections. With Print Manager enabled, you can use this feature to check settings and connections. (Refer to Chapter 9, "Printing with Windows.")

■ If you're trying to print on a network, make sure that you're connected to the network printer.

■ If you use a switch box to switch between printers, choose the Printers application in Control Panel and choose Connect. Turn off the Fast Printing Direct to Port option. You also can try connecting the printer directly to the computer without the switch box.

■ Test to see whether the computer and printer are communicating. One simple test is to exit Windows and use a DOS command to copy a small text file directly to the printer. (This procedure may work for dot-matrix printers and Hewlett Packard laser printers). For example, type the following command at the DOS prompt to print the AUTOEXEC.BAT file to a parallel printer on LPT1:

```
COPY C:\AUTOEXEC.BAT > LPT1:
```

■ For a PostScript printer, try copying the file TESTPS.TXT to the printer. (An Apple PostScript printer is likely to connect to a serial port, such as COM1, rather than to a parallel port.) Use the following command:

```
COPY C:\WINDOWS\SYSTEM\TESTPS.TXT COM1
```

If the file doesn't print when you use the DOS copy command, a problem may exist outside Windows—perhaps one of the mechanical problems listed previously. Check the printer's documentation.

Problems Printing from Windows

Make sure that the printer cable is connected and functioning properly. In Windows, all pin connectors must be working (which may not be the case with DOS applications). To test the cable, borrow another cable that you know works.

Windows stores information being processed for printing in a temporary file. If you cannot print from within Windows (but can from DOS), check to see whether a place (a directory) is available for the temporary files and whether enough space exists for the temporary files. To see whether a directory for temporary files exists, type **set** at the DOS prompt and press Enter. If you see a TEMP= line, a directory is set. If you don't see a TEMP= line, add the following line to the AUTOEXEC.BAT file:

```
SET TEMP=C:\TEMP
```

Check to make sure that you have a directory named TEMP, and make sure that at least 2M of free hard disk space is available on the computer. Then restart the computer and try printing again.

If you still cannot print, try the following possible solutions:

- If no specific driver for the printer exists in Windows and you selected a driver for a printer that the printer emulates, make sure that you chose the correct printer to emulate. Check the printer's documentation.

- If you're printing to LPT1 (a parallel port), choose the Printers application from Control Panel, and choose **C**onnect. From the **P**orts list, select LPT1.DOS (or LPT1.OS2) instead of LPT1.

- If a time-out message appears when you try to print, you can try one of two solutions. The easiest solution is to turn off Print Manager and print directly. (The computer takes longer to print because the file cannot be queued up for printing, as usually happens in Print Manager, but the printer doesn't take longer to print.) To turn off Print Manager, choose Printers from Control Panel and turn off the **U**se Print Manager Option. Another solution is to increase the printer's time-out settings. Choose Printers from Control Panel, choose **C**onnect, and increase the value for **D**evice Not Selected or **T**ransmission Retry. These values are the number of seconds before the computer gives up if the printer, or device, is not selected or if a transmission fails in some way.

- If you have a serial printer, look for an IRQ-interrupt conflict. If another serial device, such as a mouse, is using the same IRQ interrupt as the printer, one of the devices won't work. Refer to "The Mouse Doesn't Work in Windows" earlier in this chapter, or see Chapter 7, "Customizing with Control Panel."

Formatting Problems or Garbled Output

If the printed pages are formatted incorrectly, start by using Windows Write to read the PRINTERS.WRI file, and see whether you can find pertinent information specific to the printer.

If the PRINTERS.WRI file offers no help, make sure that the printer can print the fonts and sizes you specified in the application. Make sure that printer-configuration settings are correct. To check, choose Printers in Control Panel, and then choose **S**ettings (refer to Chapter 7, "Customizing with Control Panel"). Check all switches on the printer that control settings, such as page length and line feeds, to be sure that all settings are correct (check the printer's manual).

If printed text is garbled, make sure that you selected the correct printer as the default. In Control Panel, choose Printers; then select the correct printer and choose S**e**t as Default Printer. If the printer contains a cartridge, make sure that you select the correct cartridge. Try turning the printer off and then on again to clear the printer's memory of text that may be left over from a previous print. Test for a faulty cable by borrowing a cable that you know is functioning correctly.

If you use a serial printer, check the port settings. Choose the Ports application in Control Panel, and choose **S**ettings. Sometimes, choosing a lower baud rate can improve printing.

If the printer doesn't include a driver in Windows and you're emulating a printer that Windows does include, try emulating a different model.

If nothing else works, try selecting the Windows Generic/Text Only printer driver. Have the Windows disks on hand; then select Printers from Control Panel, and choose first **A**dd and then **I**nstall. Follow the screen instructions to install a printer. Choose **C**onnect to connect the driver to the same port as the printer.

Fonts Display or Print Incorrectly

Windows 3.1 comes equipped with TrueType technology, which shows you the same fonts on-screen that you see when you print, no matter what kind of printer you use. Windows comes with four TrueType fonts; you can add more easily. The four TrueType fonts are Times New Roman, Arial, Courier New, and Symbol.

Because you may have other fonts that you want to use, you also can turn off TrueType. If you don't see TrueType fonts listed in an application's font list, choose the Fonts application in Control Panel, choose **T**rueType, and select the **E**nable TrueType Fonts option. If you see only TrueType fonts in the application's font list but also want to see other fonts you have available, in the same TrueType dialog box, turn off the **S**how Only TrueType Fonts in Applications option.

If you cannot print TrueType fonts on a laser printer, you may be using an old print driver. Make sure you use a driver that came with Windows 3.1, or contact the printer's manufacturer for a Windows 3.1 driver.

If you use fonts other than TrueType fonts, what you see on-screen may not match what you see when you print. This can happen when you use printer fonts, for example, for which no corresponding screen fonts exist because Windows substitutes the closest TrueType font for the screen display. To solve this problem, use TrueType fonts for printing or use a printer font for which you have a screen font. In many applications, you can select an option to make only printer fonts available or to show fonts on-screen as they appear when printed. Check the application documentation.

If you installed a cartridge in the printer and cannot print the fonts, check to ensure that you selected the correct cartridge. Choose Printers from Control Panel; select the printer; choose **S**etup; and, from the Car**t**ridges list, select the correct cartridge. If the cartridge is correct, try turning off the printer and making sure that the cartridge is properly installed. (Often, firm pressure is needed to insert the cartridge.)

If you have trouble printing soft fonts, make sure that you haven't turned off the printer since you downloaded the fonts. If you turned off the printer, you have to download the fonts again. If this action doesn't work, check the font documentation to be sure that you installed the fonts correctly. You also need to download the fonts again if you changed the port connection.

If you use many soft fonts at once, try using fewer fonts. Many printers support only a limited number of fonts. The number of fonts you use also is limited by the size of the WIN.INI file, which can be only 64K. If WIN.INI is at the maximum size, use shorter paths for the soft fonts to conserve characters.

Text is Lost by the Printer

If the printer loses text, the cable or the port may be at fault. If you use a parallel printer (LPT) and suspect the cable, try another one that you know is working. If you use a serial printer (COM), change the port settings by choosing the Ports application from Control Panel and then choosing **S**ettings. Try selecting a lower baud rate from the list. If this step doesn't work, check to see that all settings are the same in DOS, Windows, and on the printer.

If only part of a page prints, the printer probably lacks sufficient memory. Graphics often present this kind of problem because these files are large. If possible, split the graphics so that fewer graphic images appear on one page. If you cannot do this, try a lower print resolution. If you run into this problem frequently, find out whether you can add more memory to your printer.

If you know that you have enough memory in the printer, choose the Printers application in Control Panel, select the printer and choose **S**etup, and make sure that the correct amount of memory is specified in the **M**emory list.

PostScript Printer Problems

If an out-of-memory message appears when you use a PostScript printer, you may be trying to use too many soft fonts. Try using printer fonts, or use fewer soft fonts.

If fonts are not the problem, try making changes in the printer's advanced options. Choose Printers from Control Panel; then select the printer and choose **S**etup, **O**ptions, and Ad**v**anced. In the **S**end To Printer As list, make sure that Adobe Type 1 is selected. Make sure that the C**l**ear Memory Per Page option is selected so that the printer's memory clears after each page prints. Select the Use Substitution **T**able option so that the printer substitutes built-in printer fonts for new fonts that you specify in the document. (To change the table, choose **E**dit Substitution Table and make selections for the table.)

If a PostScript printer doesn't respond, try increasing the transmission retry setting by choosing Printers from Control Panel, selecting the printer and choosing **C**onnect, and doubling the value in the **T**ransmission Retry text box.

Paintbrush Printing Problems

If a Paintbrush picture is printed smaller than normal, open the **V**iew menu and choose the **V**iew Picture command to see whether the picture looks OK. If necessary, open the **O**ptions menu and choose the **I**mage Attributes command to change the height and width of the image.

When you print, make sure that the **U**se Printer Resolution option in the Print dialog box is turned off. Check to make sure that the desired scaling is set (if set to less than 100 percent, the picture prints smaller than normal).

Solving Network Problems

If you have trouble connecting to a network or using Windows on a network, check this section for solutions. If none of these suggestions helps, use Windows Write to read the NETWORKS.WRI file in the WINDOWS directory. In general, you will find that Windows is much easier to use on a network if you use Windows for Workgroups 3.11. If the difficulty is with printing, refer to "Solving Font and Printing Problems," earlier in this chapter.

Cannot Connect to a Network Drive

If you cannot connect to a network drive, make sure that you use the correct network drivers. Choose the Windows Setup application in the Main group, and read the Network line. If the setting is wrong, open the **O**ptions menu and choose the **C**hange System Settings command; then choose a different driver from the **N**etwork list.

If the driver is correct, try exiting Windows and connecting from DOS. If you still cannot connect to the network drive, the problem is not with Windows but with the network.

Problems Running a Shared Copy of Windows

If you have trouble running a shared copy of Windows, make sure that both the personal Windows directory and the shared Windows directory are listed in the computer's path, with the personal Windows directory listed first.

Make sure that you always use the same letter to indicate the Windows drive when you connect to a network, because the first time you use this drive, Windows records the drive letter and always looks for needed files on this drive. (To change the drive letter, you must change the path to match.)

Problems Running Network Software

If you have problems running applications while the network software is loaded into high memory, try disabling the network software's high-memory-area options. For more information, check the network documentation.

If you have trouble running Windows while network software is loaded into upper memory, try loading the network software in conventional memory.

If network pop-up messages cause the system to crash, disable the messages. You also may be able to run an application such as WINPOPUP.EXE to display and dispose of the messages properly.

Solving Object Linking and Embedding Problems

Object linking and embedding (OLE) enables you to create compound documents made up of objects created by different applications. To create a compound document, the applications must be OLE-compatible.

Creating a compound document involves at least two applications: the *client* (primary) application, in which you embed objects; and the *server* (secondary) application, which you use to create objects to embed in the client application. Some applications can function as either a client or a server. An object embedded in a client application is linked to the server application you used to create the object.

Many Windows applications come with free OLE applications. Word for Windows, for example, includes Microsoft Draw, WordArt, and Equation Editor. When installed on the computer, these *applets* become available to all other applications that support OLE.

Server Unavailable During OLE

When you create, edit, or update an embedded object, the server application used to create the object must be available. If you see a message that the server application is unavailable, you must wait until the application becomes available, or you must switch to the server application and complete or end the current task. You may be able to choose Cancel to close the warning dialog box and try again later.

Cannot Open a Server Application

If you try to insert a new object from within a client application, and the server application isn't listed or doesn't start when chosen from the list, try one of the following solutions:

- Make sure that the application is registered in the registration database. The registration database tracks where server applications are located and what their capabilities are. Chapter 21, "Installing and Configuring Windows Applications," describes how to reregister an individual application or rebuild the entire registration database.

- If you moved an application to a new directory or drive, at which point it began to fail, delete the application and reinstall it in a new location.

- Make sure that the server application wasn't deleted from the computer.

- If you moved the server application, make sure that the directory where the server application is located is included in the AUTOEXEC.BAT file.

Pasting Problems

Applications that are sources or servers of data produce different results when their data is copied and pasted to another application. Some server applications are not capable of linking data, some can copy data to the Clipboard only in specific formats, and some applications cannot use OLE 2.0 embedding.

If you are trying to paste and link the contents of the Clipboard into a document, but the Paste Link command is unavailable (grayed out), first save the file you used to create the information. If the Paste **L**ink command still is unavailable, the application you used to create the information may not be a server application. If not, you can paste, but not link, the information into the document.

Solving Communication and Port Difficulties

Serial communications take place on the four COM ports available in Windows. Serial communications may include printing, faxing, scanning, operating a mouse, and modem transmissions.

Cannot Access a Serial (COM) Port

If you have trouble using your modem, check to see whether a port conflict exists, as follows:

■ First check to see whether another application is using the same port. If so, close this application.

■ Make sure that the port settings, including the IRQ interrupt, are correct. To learn more about changing the IRQ interrupt settings, refer to "The Mouse Doesn't Work in Windows" earlier in this chapter.

■ If the computer crashes when you try to use a serial port, an IRQ-interrupt conflict may exist. COM1 and COM3, for example, often use IRQ4, but COM2 and COM4 often use IRQ3. Some computers can share IRQ interrupts if you add the following line to the [386enh] section of the SYSTEM.INI file:

```
COMIrqSharing = true
```

If you suspect IRQ-interrupt conflicts, check the documentation that came with the serial devices to see what the IRQ-interrupt settings are. These default settings often can be changed so that all applications on the computer can exist harmoniously.

High-Speed Communications Problems

Windows enables communication at high speeds of 9600 bps, but at this speed, accidents sometimes happen. If you experience problems, try the following solutions:

■ If you have DOS applications running in the background, close them, or lower the background-execution priority of these applications in PIF Editor (by setting a lower value in the **B**ackground Priority option in the **A**dvanced dialog box).

■ Make sure that the computer is running as fast as possible; some computers slow to prolong battery life. Check the documentation.

■ Add a 16550A Universal Asynchronous Receiver Transmitter (UART) to the serial port. The UART buffers the serial-port data, which enables the port to run faster. (Windows' own buffering at times conflicts with some versions of UART; in this case, disable the UART's buffering by using the comxfifo setting in the SYSTEM.INI file. You can read about this setting in the SYSINI.WRI file in Windows Write.)

Lost Characters When Communicating through DOS

If you use a DOS communications application that uses the Xon/Xoff protocol, you may lose characters if other applications are running and slowing the system. If this is the case, include the following statement in the SYSTEM.INI file (X is the number of the COM port):

```
COMxProtocol = XOFF
```

Trouble Communicating through Windows Terminal

If the modem won't dial the phone number in a Terminal file, first make sure that the hardware is connected correctly. Then make sure that the correct COM port is specified; open the **S**ettings menu and choose the **C**ommunications command, and then check the **C**onnector option.

If the modem dials but doesn't establish a connection, the settings you chose for the remote computer may be wrong. The system and the remote system must use the same baud rate, data bits, parity setting, stop bits, and flow control. You have to contact someone at the remote site to discover the settings of the remote computer. On your system, change the settings to match the settings of the remote computer; open the **S**ettings menu and choose the **C**ommunications command, and then select the appropriate options.

If you can dial and connect but cannot send or receive a file, your computer and the remote computer may not be using the same *handshake protocol* (the flow-control method). Find out whether the remote system uses Xon/Xoff and whether the remote system uses hardware handshaking. Open the **S**ettings menu and choose the **C**ommunications command to change the **F**low Control settings to match the settings of the remote computer.

Finding Help, Support, and Resources

Information is often the hardest resource to obtain when dealing with Windows problems. The following sections list many resources to assist you in obtaining information, support, and training.

Telephone Support for Windows

Microsoft operates technical-support telephone lines from 6 a.m. to 6 p.m. (Pacific Daylight Time). Following are the most frequently used telephone support lines:

Topic	Telephone Number
Customer Service	(800) 426-9400
Upgrade Consulting Relations (Solution Providers) Authorized Training Centers Windows 3.1	(206) 637-7098
MS DOS 5 Setup	(206) 646-5104
MS DOS 5 Autoanswer	(206) 646-5103
MS DOS 6 (90-day)	(206) 646-5104
MS DOS 6 (pay)	(900) 555-2000
Visual Basic Startup	(206) 646-5105
Visual Basic Autoanswer	(206) 646-5107
LAN Manager	(206) 635-7020
SQL	(206) 637-7095
Languages/Hardware	(206) 637-7096

You can get telephone support for Microsoft applications at the following numbers:

Topic	Telephone Number
Access	(206) 635-7050
Excel for Windows	(206) 635-7070
Word for Windows	(206) 462-9673
Project	(206) 635-7155
PowerPoint	(206) 635-7145
Works for Windows	(206) 635-7130
MS Mail	(206) 637-9307
Word for DOS	(206) 625-7210
Excel for Macintosh	(206) 635-7080
Word for Macintosh	(206) 635-7200

VII

Troubleshooting Windows

Telephone Download of Windows Drivers

You can download new drivers directly from the Microsoft Download by dialing (206) 936-6735. You can use Terminal (the communication application that comes with Windows) to download drivers. Following are the modem settings you need to connect to this bulletin board:

Baud rates 1200, 2400, 9600

Data bits   8

Stop bits   1

Parity   None

Telephone Support for Non-Microsoft Applications

For technical or sales information regarding a major product, call one of the following support lines:

Manufacturer	Software	Support Line
Adobe Systems	Corporate	(415) 961-4400
	Technical (Adobe Type Manager, Adobe fonts)	(415) 961-4992
Aldus Corp.	Corporate	(206) 662-5500
	Technical (PageMaker, Persuasion, Freehand)	(206) 628-2040
Borland	Corporate	(408) 438-8400
	Technical (ObjectVision)	(408) 438-5300
Corel	Corporate	(613) 728-8200
	Technical (CorelDRAW!)	(613) 728-1990
Intuit	Corporate	(415) 322-0573
	Technical (Quicken)	(415) 322-2800
Lotus	Corporate	(617) 577-8500
	Technical (recordings) (1-2-3 for Windows, Ami Pro, Freelance)	(617) 253-9130

Manufacturer	Software	Support Line
Lotus	Technical (pay per call)	(900) 454-9009
Polaris	Corporate	(619) 674-6500
	Technical (PackRat)	(619) 743-7800
Symantec	Corporate	(310) 449-4900
	Technical (Norton Desktop for Windows)	(213) 319-2020
WordPerfect	Corporate	(801) 225-5000
	Technical (WordPerfect 5.1 for Windows)	(801) 228-9907

Computer Bulletin Board Forums

Computer bulletin boards are databases from which you can retrieve information over the telephone line by using Terminal, the communication application that comes with Windows. Some bulletin boards contain a wealth of information about Windows and Windows applications. One of the largest public bulletin boards is CompuServe.

CompuServe contains forums in which Windows and Windows applications can be discussed. You can submit questions to Microsoft operators, who will return an answer within a day. CompuServe also contains libraries of sample files, and new printer and device drivers. The Knowledge Base, available in Microsoft's region of CompuServe, has much of the same troubleshooting information used by Microsoft's telephone support representatives. You can search through the Knowledge Base by using keywords. The Microsoft region of CompuServe is divided into many different areas—for example, Windows users, advanced Windows users, Microsoft Excel, Microsoft languages, and sections for each of the major Microsoft and non-Microsoft applications that run under Windows.

After you become a CompuServe member, you can access the Microsoft user forums, library files, and Knowledge Base. To gain access to one of these areas, type one of the following GO commands at the CompuServe prompt symbol (!), and then press Enter:

Type	To Access
GO MSOFT	Overall Microsoft area
GO MSUSER	Overall applications and Windows areas
GO MSAPP	Microsoft applications areas

Chapter 12, "Using Windows Terminal," shows an example of how to log on to CompuServe and enter the Microsoft Windows and applications region. (You must join CompuServe and get a passcode before you can use the bulletin board.)

For more information, contact CompuServe at the following address:

CompuServe
5000 Arlington Centre Blvd.
P.O. Box 20212
Columbus, OH 43220
(800) 848-8990

Finding Consultants and Corporate Training

Microsoft Solution Providers train on, develop, and support applications written with Microsoft products for the Windows environment. Microsoft Solution Providers are independent consultants and training facilities that have met strict qualifying requirements imposed by Microsoft. To get the names and phone numbers of Solution Providers or Authorized Training Centers in your area, call Microsoft Customer Service at (800) 426-9400.

Appendixes

A Windows Files

B Windows INI Files

C Using the Keyboard To Control Windows

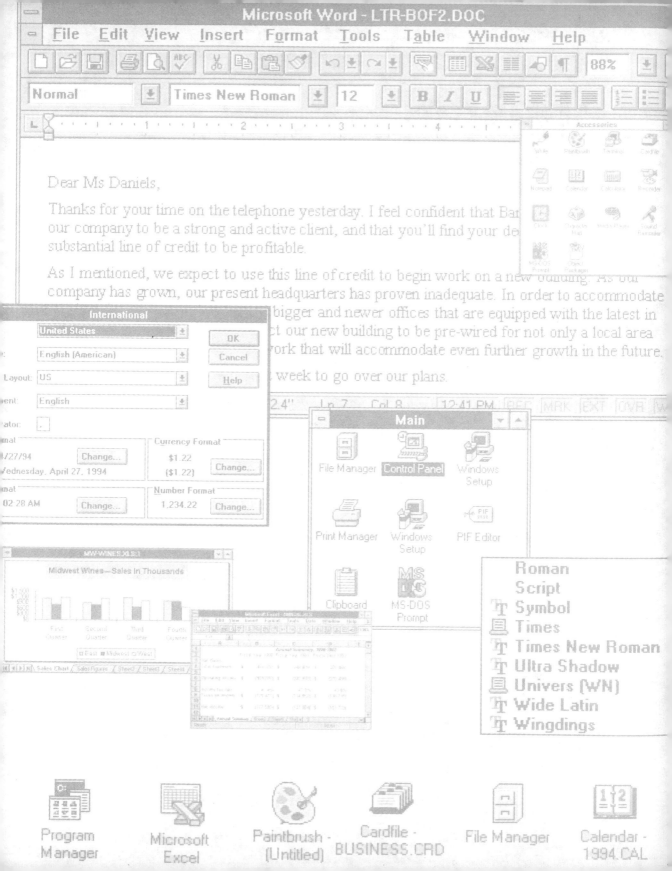

Windows Files

Windows creates a new operating environment for applications. Its functions are so complex and varied that it requires many files of different types. The lists in this appendix describe the different types of files required by Windows and which of these files you can safely delete to give your hard disk more space.

Main Windows Files

When you start Windows, multiple files are loaded through a chain of events. When you type **WIN** and press Enter, the file WIN.COM is run. This file, which is the Windows loader, checks the current hardware configuration and device drivers, and determines whether Windows should run in standard or 386 Enhanced mode. If WIN.COM is started on an 80286 processor or started with the command WIN /S, the DOSX.EXE file is run to start Windows in standard mode. If WIN.COM detects an 80386 or better processor and no /S switch is used on start-up, the WIN386.EXE file is run to start Windows in 386 Enhanced mode.

Table A.1 describes the main files that are used when Windows operates.

Table A.1 Main Windows Operating Files	
File	**Description**
KRNL286.EXE or KRNL386.EXE	These kernel files manage memory, schedule task executions, and load applications.
USER.EXE	This file controls interaction between user events, such as keyboard input and mouse actions, and the effect of those events on windows, icons, and other user interface items.

(continues)

Table A.1 **Continued**	
File	**Description**
GDI.EXE	The Graphics Device Interface controls the creation of images and other display devices.

Drivers, Fonts, and International Files

In the distant past, applications had to directly "speak to" and control devices such as printers. In Windows and Windows applications, the communication between Windows and its applications and hardware devices goes through *device drivers*. These drivers are separate entities that act as translators between Windows and different types of hardware. Each driver converts a standard set of Windows output into the signals understood by a specific model or a specific vendor's printer. A driver also tells Windows about the hardware's capability.

Having device drivers separate from Windows makes Windows *device-independent*. This independence is important. It means that Windows doesn't have to be upgraded each time a new set of printers, plotters, mice, or modems is released. Instead, each hardware vendor can write its own small-device driver to make sure that its hardware works with Windows.

Table A.2 describes some of the different types of device drivers used in Windows.

Table A.2 **Windows Device Drivers**		
Device Type	**Description**	**Example Files**
System drivers	Support access to system times, information about the disks, and OEM-defined system information.	SYSTEM.DRV for most systems; HPSYSTEM.DRV for HP Vectra in standard mode
Keyboard drivers	Support keyboard input and internationalization.	KEYBOARD.DRV for standard keyboards; KBDHP.DRV for HP keyboards
		KBDMOUSE.DRV for Olivetti/AT&T keyboard mouse

Device Type	Description	Example Files
Keyboard drivers	Support keyboard input and internationalization	KBD*??*.DLL for international keyboard libraries, where *??* is a two-letter identifier for the country
Mouse drivers	Support a mouse.	MOUSE.DRV for PS/2 or Microsoft mouse; MSCMOUSE.DRV for Mouse Systems serial/bus mouse
Display drivers	Support the display and cursors.	VGA.DRV for VGA display; VGAMONO.DRV for monochrome VGA
Communication drivers	Supports serial and parallel communications.	COMM.DRV for standard serial and parallel communication devices
Printer drivers	Support printers. Most printer drivers use a DRV or DLL file extension. The first portion of the file name usually is a readable abbreviation of the printer maker and model.	HPDSKJET.DRV for the HP DeskJet Series; HPPCL5A.DRV for the HP LaserJet III Series; EPSON9.DRV for the Epson 9-pin
PostScript description information	Give PostScript descriptions to specific printers.	HP_3D522.WPD for the HP LaserJet IIID PostScript; L200230&.WPD for the Linotronic 200/230
Network drivers	Provide the network connection to Windows utilities and accessories.	NETWARE.DRV for Novell NetWare 2.10 or later; NETWARE.HLP Help file for NetWare
Multimedia drivers	Provide multimedia support SoundBlaster for Windows	SNDBLST2.DRV for 2.0 DSP driver; MCICDA.DRV for MCI CD-audio driver
Font files	Provide fonts for system, raster fonts and vector fonts.	All these files end with FON; TrueType font files end with TTF

Appendixes

Files Supporting MS-DOS and MS-DOS Applications

To run MS-DOS applications, Windows uses a number of files for device drivers and memory management. Table A.3 describes some of the files that may be used for these purposes.

Table A.3 MS-DOS Support Files	
File	**Description**
EMM386.EXE	386 EMS manager.
HIMEM.SYS	XMS manager.
RAMDRIVE.SYS	RAMDrive utility.
SMARTDRV.EXE	SMARTdrive utility.
MOUSE.COM	MS-DOS mouse driver.
WINOLDAP.MOD and WINOA386.MOD	Supports data exchange between non-Windows applications and Windows. WINOLDAP.MOD is used in standard mode. WINOA386.MOD is used in 386 Enhanced mode.
*.2GR *.3GR	The "grabber" supports PrintScreen and copy-and-paste between non-Windows and Windows applications. The file name, indicated here by an asterisk (*), depends on the type of display you installed. 2GR grabbers are for 286 computers; 3GR grabbers are for 386 computers.

Files for Standard and 386 Enhanced Mode

In standard mode, WIN.COM detects an 80286 processor or the WIN /S switch and loads the DOSX.EXE file to act as the MS-DOS extender, allowing access to extended memory. Next, the kernel file, KRNL286.EXE, is loaded. Two more files also are loaded. WSWAP.EXE supports Windows applications in swap mode, and DSWAP.EXE supports non-Windows applications in swap mode.

In 386 Enhanced mode, WIN.COM detects a 386 computer and loads WIN386.EXE. WIN386 then looks in the [386enh] section of the SYSTEM.INI file for files that it should load. Special device drivers may be loaded separately. These device drivers have the file extension 386.

Windows Accessories and Utility Files

Windows loads many accessories and utilities if you use the Express setup. If you choose a Custom setup, you have the option of installing selected accessories or utilities. Table A.4 shows these ancillary files and the files associated with them. These files are located in the WINDOWS or WINDOWS\SYSTEM directory.

Table A.4   Windows Accessory Files

Application/Utility	Main File	Associated Files
Calculator	CALC.EXE	CALC.HLP
Calendar	CALENDAR.EXE	CALENDAR.HLP
Cardfile	CARDFILE.EXE	CARDFILE.HLP
Character Map	CHARMAP.EXE	CHARMAP.HLP
Clipboard	CLIPBRD.EXE	CLIPBRD.HLP
Clock	CLOCK.EXE	
Control Panel	CONTROL.EXE	CONTROL.HLP CONTROL.INI CPWIN386.CPL DRIVERS.CPL LZEXPAND.DLL MAIN.CPL MIDIMAP.CFG SND.CPL
Disk-cache utility	SMARTDRV.EXE	
Dr. Watson	DRWATSON.EXE	
File Manager	WINFILE.EXE	WINFILE.HLP
Help	WINHELP.EXE	WINHELP.HLP GLOSSARY.HLP
Media Player	MPLAYER.EXE	MPLAYER.HLP MMSYSTEM.DLL MMTASK.TSK

(continues)

Table A.4 Continued		
Application/Utility	**Main File**	**Associated Files**
Microsoft Diagnostics	MSD.EXE	MSD.INI
Minesweeper (game)	WINMINE.EXE	WINMINE.HLP
Notepad	NOTEPAD.EXE	NOTEPAD.HLP
Object Packager	PACKAGER.EXE	PACKAGER.HLP
Paintbrush	PBRUSH.EXE	PBRUSH.DLL PBRUSH.HLP
PIF Editor	PIFEDIT.EXE	PIFEDIT.HLP
Power Management Support	POWER.HLP	SL.DLL SL.HLP
Print Manager	PRINTMAN.EXE	PRINTMAN.HLP
Program Manager	PROGMAN.EXE	PROGMAN.INI PROGMAN.HLP
Recorder	RECORDER.EXE	RECORDER.DLL RECORDER.HLP
Registration Editor	REGEDIT.EXE	REGEDIT.HLP REGEDITV.HLP DDEML.DLL OLECLI.DLL OLESVR.DLL
Shell Library	SHELL.DLL	
Solitaire	SOL.EXE	SOL.HLP
Sound Recorder	SOUNDREC.EXE	SOUNDREC.HLP
System Editor	SYSEDIT.EXE	
Task Manager	TASKMAN.EXE	
Terminal (communications application)	TERMINAL.EXE	TERMINAL.HLP
Windows Tool Helper Library		TOOLHELP.DLL
Windows Tutorial	WINTUTOR.EXE	WINTUTOR.DAT
Write	WRITE.EXE	WRITE.HLP

Bitmaps, Screen Savers, Sounds, and Miscellaneous Files

Many additional files are located in the WINDOWS and WINDOWS\SYSTEM directories. Some of these files can be described by the categories in table A.5.

Table A.5	Miscellaneous Windows Files
File Type	**File Name**
Setup information file	*.INF
Registration information	*.REG
Read-me text files containing additional information	*.TXT
Read-me files opened with Write	*.WRI
Start-up logo code	*.LGO
Logo screen	*.RLE
INI templates	*.SRC
Bitmap wallpapers	*.BMP
Screen-saver files	*.SCR
Wave sound files	*.WAV
Temporary files	*.TMP

As you can see by the number of files used by Windows, it is a very complex program. Do not delete files with which you are unfamiliar. If you need to delete files to regain hard disk space, delete only those files listed in the following section.

Files You Can Delete To Regain Hard Disk Space

You can delete files from the WINDOWS or WINDOWS\SYSTEM directory to regain hard disk space, but you must be very careful. If you delete the wrong file, Windows may no longer run.

Appendixes

> **Caution**
>
> Do not delete files while Windows is running unless you are very sure of the file's function and know that the file will not be used while Windows is running. Under no circumstances should you delete a temporary file (*.TMP) while Windows is running. Doing so can cause you to lose part or all of a document and may cause Windows to be disabled. To delete files, exit Windows and then use the DOS command DELETE or ERASE.

Standard Mode Files

If you run Windows only in 386 Enhanced mode, you can regain more than 180K by deleting the following files:

    DOSX.EXE

    DSWAP.EXE

    KRNL286.EXE

    WINOLDAP.MOD

    WSWAP.EXE

    *.2GR

The asterisk (*) in *.2GR indicates that the file name may change, depending on the resolution of the screen. The file extension, 2GR, will be the same.

386 Enhanced Mode Files

If you never run Windows in 386 Enhanced mode, you can save more than 700K of hard disk space by deleting the following files:

    CGA40WOA.FON

    CGA80WOA.FON

    EGA40WOA.FON

    EGA80WOA.FON

    CPWIN386.FON

    DOSAPP.FON

    *.3GR

*.386

WIN386.EXE

WIN386.PS2

WINOA386.MOD

These files are not installed on 80286 computers, because an 80286 cannot run in 386 Enhanced mode.

Files Used by Non-Windows Applications

If you run only Windows applications, you can delete the files that Windows uses to deal with non-Window applications. Remove the following files to regain approximately 250K:

*.PIF

APPS.INF

CGA40WOA.FON

CGA80WOA.FON

EGA40WOA.FON

EGA80WOA.FON

*.2GR and *.3GR

DOSAPP.FON

DSWAP.EXE

WINOLDAP.MOD

WINOA386.MOD

> **Caution**
>
> If you remove the files that support MS-DOS under Windows, you will not be able to run the MS-DOS Prompt application from Program Manager.

Unused Accessories

You can remove from Windows features such as accessory applications and colorful gewgaws without degrading the program's performance.

Start Windows Setup by double-clicking the Setup icon in Control Panel; open the **O**ptions menu and choose **A**dd/Remove Windows Component. You can add or remove the following applications:

- Accessories such as Cardfile, Write, and Calendar. Look for the application with an EXE extension, the Help file with an HLP extension, and additional files with a DLL extension.

- Games

- Wallpapers and sound files

- Screen savers

Unused Drivers

If you remove a piece of hardware, such as a printer or sound card, you may never need that hardware's driver again. (Even if you did need it, you could reload it from the installation disks.) You can remove a device driver, such as a printer driver or multimedia driver, by using File Manager to search the WINDOWS and WINDOWS\SYSTEM directories for files with the DRV extension. If the name of the file obviously describes the device that you are removing, delete that file.

Deleting a driver's file doesn't delete the references to that driver in Control Panel or in applications. To remove a driver's references in Windows, follow these steps:

1. Start Control Panel (located in the Main group of Program Manager).

2. Start the Printer application or the Driver application.

3. Select the device that you no longer use; then choose the **R**emove button.

4. Choose OK.

Tip
Some graphics and presentation programs install megabytes of fonts you will never use. Delete what you don't use.

Fonts and Their Files

If you find that you don't use all the fonts installed on your computer, you can save disk space by removing the extra fonts. Fonts that you can delete safely are fonts used by unused devices, such as a plotter or printer. You also can delete TrueType fonts that may have been added when an application was installed but that you never use. Fonts on disk may range in size from as little as 17K to more than 80K.

To delete a font and its associated files, follow these steps:

1. Start Control Panel from the Main group of Program Manager.

2. Start the Fonts application.

3. Select the font you want to delete.

   Notice the font description, its size, and its use at the bottom of the dialog box. This information can help you decide whether to delete the font.

4. Choose the **R**emove button. A Remove Font dialog box appears.

5. Select the **D**elete Font from File check box; then choose Yes.

6. Return to step 3 to delete additional fonts and their files, or choose Close.

Caution

Don't delete MS San Serif, because it is used in dialog boxes. If you delete it, dialog boxes will be difficult to read.

Miscellaneous Files

You can regain more than 500K of disk space by deleting the files shown in table A.6. Delete only the files that you are positive are not being used.

Table A.6	Windows Files and Their Purposes
File	**Notes**
EMM386.EXE	Delete if you never use DOS applications that require expanded memory.
WOA or GRB	Make sure that you have exited Windows before deleting these files.
*.TMP	Make sure that you have exited Windows before deleting these files. If you created a TEMP directory and used a SET TEMP statement in your AUTOEXEC, all these files should be in the TEMP directory.
WIN386.SWP	Temporary swap file.

(continues)

Table A.6 Continued	
File	**Notes**
CLIPBRD.EXE	Delete the Clipboard if you will never copy or cut and paste to move data within or between applications.
MSD.EXE and MSD.INI	This is the Microsoft Diagnostics tool that Microsoft technical support may ask for to help resolve hardware incompatibilities.
PIFEDIT.EXE	PIF Editor is used to edit or create PIF files used to tune DOS applications. If you will not be using DOS applications, you can delete it.
PRINTMAN.EXE	Print Manager stores files sent to the printer so that you can print multiple files without waiting for the printer to finish. Delete this file if you want to print directly or if you use the network print spooler.
SYSEDIT.EXE	This simplified text editor automatically opens INI files, the AUTOEXEC.BAT file, and the CONFIG.SYS file. If you normally use Notepad to do this, you can delete SYSEDIT.EXE.
TASKMAN.EXE	Task Manager appears when you press Ctrl+Esc to switch to another application. If you switch between applications by pressing Alt+Tab or by clicking the application's window, you can delete TASKMAN.EXE.
RAMDRIVE.SYS	If your CONFIG.SYS doesn't load this file, you are not using a RAM drive, so you can delete this file.
MORICONS.DLL	Delete this file if your Program Manager doesn't contain custom icons that are stored in this file.

Help Files

You can delete the Help files from Windows and Windows applications under the following circumstances:

- You are super-adept at Windows and Windows applications.

- You have a good Que book beside your computer.

- You work in one of those companies that provides no computer training or manuals, so why should you need on-line help either?

To delete Help files, delete files ending with HLP. Delete them by specific application rather than with a wild card, *.HLP, so that you can select the help you remove. In some cases, deleting an application's HLP file disables its tutorial files as well.

Caution

You probably should never delete WINHELP.EXE, the Windows Help engine, which is the software most applications use to present the data in their HLP files. If you delete WINHELP.EXE, an application may not be able to give you help even if it still has its HLP file available.

Appendix B

Windows INI Files

The Windows program is composed of many files. The files that control the characteristics of Windows and its applications are called INI (often pronounced "in-eee") files. INI, which is the file extension for these files, is an abbreviation of *initialization*. These files are read when Windows or an application starts. The files control such things as the starting position and size of windows, printer configurations, and optional settings in applications.

INI files have gone through an evolution as Windows has evolved. In the first versions of Windows, all Windows and application environmental variables were saved in the file WIN.INI. As Windows became more robust and people began using more applications, the WIN.INI file became huge and unmanageable. The next evolutionary step was for applications to create their own application INI file, which was stored in either the application's directory or in the WINDOWS directory. With the release of OLE 2.0 in Windows 3.1, the advent of the *registration file* has relieved WIN.INI of even more burden. The REG.DAT file, edited with REGEDIT.EXE (as explained in Chapter 21, "Installing and Configuring Windows Applications"), stores information about an application's OLE 2.0 capability. As Windows evolves, the REG.DAT file will become a database of information about application capabilities and features.

Types of INI Files

The two INI files that you will hear discussed most frequently with respect to Windows itself are WIN.INI and SYSTEM.INI. Other INI files control the applications that come with Windows, such as CONTROL.INI, PROGMAN.INI, and WINFILE.INI. These INI files are stored in the WINDOWS directory. When you add an application to Windows, the application usually creates its own INI file in its directory or in the WINDOWS directory. These INI files usually use an abbreviation of the application's name as their file name. Table B.1 describes the different types of INI files.

Table B.1 Windows INI Files	
INI File	**Contents**
WIN.INI	Settings and characteristics of Windows
SYSTEM.INI it uses	Settings and characteristics of Windows and the hardware
CONTROL.INI	Colors, patterns, and printer configurations
PROGMAN.INI	Contents of groups in Program Manager
WINFILE.INI	Settings and characteristics of File Manager
application.INI	Settings and characteristics of the application

INI File Contents

INI files are nothing more than text files with a specific structure. The structure looks like this:

```
[section]
keyname=value
keyname=value
```

Windows and applications read the contents of INI files by searching for a specific section name and then reading the keyname and the corresponding value. In the PROGMAN.INI file, for example, you can disable the **R**un command in Program Manager's **F**ile menu by modifying the [restrictions] section like this:

```
[restrictions]
NoRun=1
```

As this example illustrates, most values used in INI files are Boolean. That means the values are TRUE (or 1) to turn that characteristic on and FALSE (or 0) to turn that characteristic off. You can add remarks or comments to INI files by typing a semicolon (;) at the end of a line, followed by the comment.

Modifying INI Files

Because INI files are text files, you can use most word processing programs or text editors to edit them, but this may not be the best way of making changes. Leave manual editing of INI files as a last-resort method; use it only if the section or keyname must be edited manually. To make changes to INI files, first try these methods:

- Use the commands in Program Manager to change the groups and items in PROGMAN.INI.

- Use the commands in File Manager to change the configuration, options, and views in WINFILE.INI.

- Use Control Panel applications to change fonts, colors, desktop patterns, hardware drivers, printers, and other elements in CONTROL.INI.

- Run the Windows Setup application (in Program Manager's Main group) if you want to change system settings, network settings, and keyboard or mouse configurations.

- Use the Printer Setup command or button (found in many applications) to change printer settings and to add or remove printers.

> **Caution**
>
> Because INI files are read only on start-up, changes you make to an INI file don't take effect until you restart Windows. Changes to AUTOEXEC.BAT or CONFIG.SYS don't take effect until you restart your computer.

If you need to change an INI file manually, you can use Notepad or Sysedit to edit the INI file. Notepad is a simple text editor located in the Accessories group (described in Chapter 14, "Using Desktop Accessories").

Sysedit (short for *system editor*) is a built-in editor that automatically opens INI files located in the WINDOWS directory as well as the AUTOEXEC.BAT and CONFIG.SYS files located in the root directory. Figure B.1 shows Sysedit with multiple INI files loaded. Notice that each INI file is in its own window; you edit and save each file separately.

Fig. B.1
Using Sysedit is
one way to edit
INI files manually.

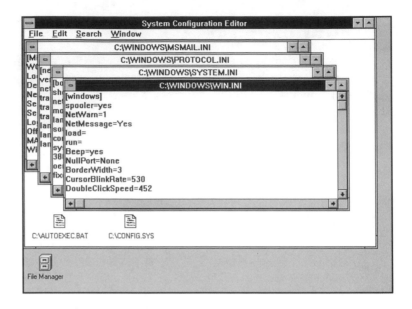

◄ "Using Desktop
Accessories,"
p. 463

To start Sysedit, open the **F**ile menu in Program Manager or File Manager, and choose the **R**un command. Type **sysedit** in the Command Line text box; then choose OK. When Sysedit is running, it uses commands that are very similar to Notepad's.

WIN.INI: Windows Initialization

The WIN.INI file contains many sections that control the Windows start-up characteristics. Depending on your selections during installation, from Control Panel or Network applications or within some Windows applications, your WIN.INI file may not contain all the possible sections or may contain sections that are not described here. Table B.2 lists the sections that appear in the WIN.INI file.

Table B.2 Sections in WIN.INI	
Section	**Description**
[windows]	Controls Windows' start-up size, applications that run or load on start-up, and so on
[Desktop]	Controls desktop appearance and the locations of windows and icons

Section	Description
[Extensions]	Associates data files with an application so that double-clicking a data file in File Manager or from an icon automatically loads the application and data
[intl]	Controls display characteristics for countries other than the United States
[ports]	Lists available ports
[fonts]	Lists screen font files
[FontSubstitutes]	Lists pairs of interchangeable fonts
[TrueType]	Describes characteristics for TrueType fonts
[mci extensions]	Associates files with Media Control Interface devices
[network]	Specifies network settings and connections
[embedding]	Lists the server applications for object linking and embedding (OLE); these lists also are kept in REG.DAT (described in Chapter 21, "Installing and Configuring Windows Applications")
[Windows Help]	Lists display and use characteristics for Help
[sounds]	Lists the sound files associated with events
[PrinterPorts]	Lists available printer devices
[devices]	Lists output devices to provide compatibility with previous versions of Windows
[programs]	Lists paths that Windows will use when searching for an application that has an associated file
[colors]	Specifies Windows colors

Appendixes

Note

Older Windows applications were designed to insert their application-specific information into the WIN.INI file. You may find some of this information under a heading such as [application]. Newer Windows applications use their own INI files and the REG.DAT file to record custom information.

SYSTEM.INI: System Initialization

The SYSTEM.INI file is located in the WINDOWS directory and contains global system information used by Windows during start-up. The SYSTEM.INI file contains the sections described in table B.3. Many of the sections shown here may not appear in your SYSTEM.INI file. You also may have sections that are not listed here. Additional sections may be necessary for video-display drivers, multimedia and sound-card drivers, and so on. The names of these sections may vary from manufacturer to manufacturer. If necessary keynames and values are missing, built-in settings are used.

Table B.3 Sections in SYSTEM.INI	
Section	**Description**
[boot]	Lists of drivers and Windows modules
[boot.description]	Lists devices changeable with Windows Setup
[drivers]	Lists of names used by driver files
[keyboard]	Lists of keyboard information
[mci]	Lists of MCI drivers
[Network]	Information on Windows for Workgroup network
[network drivers]	Information on network protocols and drivers
[NonWindowsApp]	Information for non-Windows applications
[standard]	Information for standard-mode Windows
[386Enh]	Information for 386 Enhanced-mode Windows

Caution

In general, avoid changing the SYSTEM.INI file manually. This file is best modified by making selections from the Windows Setup program. If you do manually edit this file, always make a backup copy of SYSTEM.INI to floppy disk or a different directory before editing. If Windows doesn't run correctly after restarting with your new settings, you can copy the backup version back into the WINDOWS directory.

PROGMAN.INI: Program Manager Initialization

The PROGMAN.INI file normally has two sections: [Groups] and [Settings]. If you are a system administrator who needs to modify Program Manager so that users cannot delete or create groups or icons, or if you need to control which applications can be started, you will want to add a [restrictions] section. Manually creating and editing the [restrictions] section and its keynames and values are described in detail in Chapter 3, "Controlling Applications with Program Manager."

CONTROL.INI: Control Panel Initialization

The sections in CONTROL.INI contain values for the latest settings of the applications in Control Panel. Control Panel is located in the Main group of Program Manager. CONTROL.INI is easiest to modify through the use of applications located in Control Panel. Table B.4 describes the sections.

Table B.4 Sections in CONTROL.INI	
Section	**Description**
[current]	Current color scheme
[color schemes]	Specifies colors used in each color scheme
[Custom Colors]	Specifies custom colors in the color palette
[Patterns]	Specifies colors used in the bitmaps that create patterns
[MMCPL]	Settings for the multimedia items
[Screen Saver.*]	Specifies settings for the screen saver
[Userinstallable.drivers]	Specifies drivers and settings for multimedia
[drivers.desc]	Specifies the multimedia control devices, MIDI Mapper, and Time
[installed]	Specifies the current version of Windows and installed printers

Appendixes

WINFILE.INI: File Manager Initialization

WINFILE.INI contains only one section: [Settings]. This section specifies the options you choose from menu commands in File Manager, as well as the last screen location and size of File Manager.

Appendix C

Using the Keyboard To Control Windows

For many users, it is much easier to use the mouse to operate Windows. In Chapter 1, "Operating Windows," you learn how to use the mouse to work in the Windows environment. If you are a touch-typist or have an aversion to using a mouse, you can use the keyboard to accomplish the same operations you learn about in Chapter 1. In this appendix, you learn how to use the keyboard to control Windows, using a hands-on approach.

Understanding Keyboard Terminology

Table C.1 lists keyboard actions and keystrokes you need to know to control Windows from the keyboard. After you complete the step-by-step exercises in this appendix, you can refer back to this table when you need a reminder of how to use the keyboard in the Windows environment.

Table C.1 Keyboard Terminology	
Keystroke	**Keyboard action**
A comma indicates that you release the first key before pressing the second key. A plus (+) indicates that you press and hold down the first key and then press the second key.	
Alt, letter	Press and release the Alt key and then press letter. This action opens a menu without choosing a command.
Alt+letter	Press and hold down the Alt key as you press the underlined letter. This action opens a menu or selects an option in a dialog box.

(continues)

Table C.1 Continued	
Keystroke	**Keyboard action**
Letter	Press the letter in the command that is <u>underlined</u> on-screen to choose a command in a menu (this book shows the letter you are to press in bold type). Press **M**, for example, to choose the **M**ove command. You can press the uppercase or lowercase letter.
Arrow key	Press the appropriate directional arrow key.

Keystrokes To Control Windows

Alt+Esc	Activates the next application window or icon on the desktop. Pressing Alt+Esc does not restore icons into windows.
Alt+Tab	Activates the next application window or icon. Restores icons into windows. Only the application's title bar or a box displaying the application's name shows until you release Alt+Tab, making it faster to cycle through application windows than to use Alt+Esc.
Alt+Shift+Tab	Activates the previous icon or application. Restores icons into a window. Only the application's title bar or a box displaying the application's name shows until you release Alt+Tab.
Ctrl+F6	Activates the next document window (if an application has multiple document windows open).
Ctrl+Tab	Activates the next group window within Program Manager.
Ctrl+Esc	Displays the Task List window, from which you can activate an application by selecting from a list of currently running applications.
Alt+space bar	Selects the Control menu for the active application icon or window so that you can control the location, size, and status of the window.
Alt+hyphen (-)	Selects the Control menu for the active document window within the application window so that you can control the location, size, and status of the document window.

Keystrokes To Control the Menus

Alt	Activates the menu bar.
Alt, letter	Selects the menu indicated by letter (letter is <u>underlined</u> on-screen; letter is displayed in bold in this book).
Letter	Chooses (executes) the command in the menu indicated by letter.
Arrow keys	Selects but does not choose the next menu (use the right or left arrows) or the next command (use the up or down arrows).

Enter	Chooses (executes) the selected command in the menu.
Esc	Closes the current menu without making a choice. Press Esc a second time to deactivate the menu bar and return to the document.

Keystrokes To Control Dialog Boxes

See table C.3 in the section "Selecting Options from Dialog Boxes," later in this appendix, for more information.

Arrow keys	Selects or scrolls file names in a list box. Selects round option buttons in a group.
Tab	Selects the next text box, list box, group of options, or button.
Shift+Tab	Selects the previous text box, list box, group of options, or button.
Alt+letter	Selects the option, text box, or list box specified by letter (letter is <u>underlined</u> on-screen; letter is displayed in bold in this book).
Space bar	Selects or deselects the active check box or button.
Enter	Chooses the bold or outlined button (usually the OK button). This action completes the command or opens another dialog box.
Esc	Closes an open dialog box without making any changes.

Controlling Windows and Icons

You can control windows with the keyboard using the Control menu. Every application and document window has a Control menu that can be accessed using the keyboard. In an application window, the Control menu icon looks like a space bar in a box and is located to the left of the title bar. To activate the Control menu with the keyboard, press Alt, space bar. In a document window within an application, the Control menu icon looks like a hyphen in a box. If the document is in its own window, the icon is located to the left of its title bar. If the document is maximized, the icon is to the left of the File command. To activate the Control menu with the keyboard, press Alt, hyphen (-). An application's Control menu is shown in figure C.1.

Many of the commands in a document Control menu are the same as those in an application Control menu. The application Control menu, however, controls the application window; the document Control menu controls the document window within the application. The commands in a Control menu are given in the following chart.

Fig. C.1

The Control menu and its commands can be accessed using the keyboard.

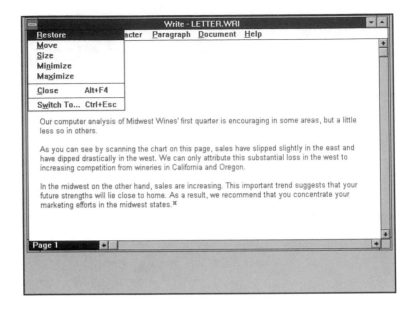

Command	Action
Restore	Restores an icon or maximized window to its previous window size. The shortcut-key combination is Ctrl+F5 (for a document window).
Move	Moves the currently selected icon or window to a new location when you press the arrow keys. The shortcut-key combination is Ctrl+F7 (for a document window).
Size	Resizes a window by moving its edge. The shortcut-key combination is Ctrl+F8 (for a document window).
Mi**n**imize	Minimizes a window into an icon. In most cases, this command applies only to application windows.
Ma**x**imize	Increases an application window or icon to its full size. The shortcut-key combination is Ctrl+F10 (for a document window).
Close	Exits an application or closes a document window. If changes were made to the current file since the last save, the application asks whether you want to save the file. The shortcut-key combinations are Alt+F4 (for an application window) and Ctrl+F4 (for a document window).
S**w**itch To	Displays the Task List so that you can switch to a different application. Available in applications Control menu only. The shortcut-key combination is Ctrl+Esc.

Command	Action
Next Window	Activates the next document window in applications that enable multiple documents to run simultaneously; works only when multiple document windows are open. The shortcut-key combination is Ctrl+F6.

Moving a Window or an Icon

You can use the **M**ove command in the Control menu to move a window using the keyboard. Try moving the Program Manager window using the keyboard by following these steps:

1. Activate the Program Manager window if it is not already the active window by pressing Alt+Tab until the box for Program Manager appears, and then release both keys.

2. Select the Control menu by pressing and releasing the Alt key and then pressing the space bar.

3. Choose the **M**ove command, either by pressing the letter M on the keyboard or by using the down-arrow key to select the command and pressing Enter.

   A four-headed arrow appears in the title bar, and the window borders turn gray.

4. Press the arrow keys to move the shadowed borders to where you want the window and press Enter.

You can also use the keyboard to move a group or program item icon.

To move a program or group icon with the keyboard, press Alt+Esc to select the icon. Press Alt, space bar to display the Control menu, and then select **M**ove from the Control menu. Press the arrow keys until the icon is where you want it.

Changing the Size of a Window

You can also use the keyboard to change the size of a window. Change the size of the Program Manager window, using the following steps:

1. Activate the Program Manager window if it is not already the active window by pressing Alt+Tab until the box for Program Manager appears, and then release both keys.

2. Select the Control menu by pressing and releasing the Alt key and then pressing the space bar.

3. Choose the **S**ize command, either by pressing the letter S on the keyboard or by using the down-arrow key to select the command and pressing Enter.

    A four-headed arrow appears in the window, as shown in fig. C.2.

Fig. C.2
Use the arrow keys to pick the side you want to move.

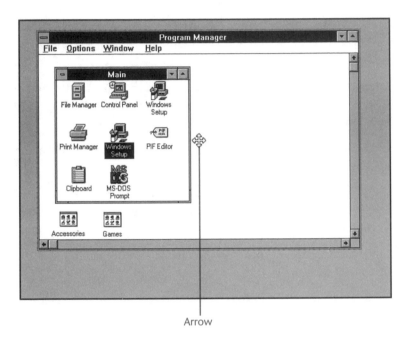

Arrow

4. Press the arrow key that points to the edge you want to resize.

    A double-headed arrow jumps to the edge you selected (see fig. C.3). To change two sides at the same time, press the arrow key that points to the first side you want to resize, and then press the arrow key for one of the two sides that join the first side. A double-headed arrow appears at the corner that is the intersection of the two sides.

5. Press the appropriate arrow key to move the selected edge.

6. When the window is the size you want, press Enter. Press Esc to leave the window unchanged.

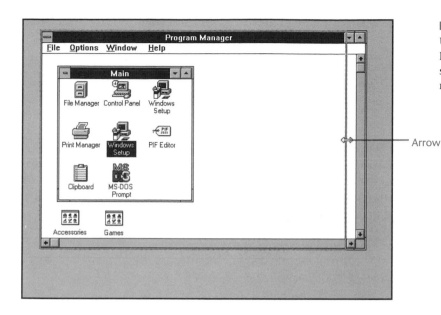

Fig. C.3
Use the arrow
keys to move the
selected size to a
new position.

Arrow

Appendixes

Maximizing and Restoring Windows

Often you will want to maximize application and document windows to full
size to give you as much working space as possible. Use the Control menu to
maximize the Main program group—a document window within the Program Manager window—by following these steps:

1. Activate the Main group window by pressing Ctrl+Tab until the Main
   group is selected.

   If the Main group is reduced to an icon, press the Enter key after the
   icon has been selected to restore the icon to a window.

2. Select the Control menu by pressing and releasing the Alt key and then
   pressing the hyphen key.

3. Choose the Ma**x**imize command, either by pressing the letter X on the
   keyboard or by using the down-arrow key to select the command and
   pressing Enter.

4. Restore the Main group to a window by opening the Control menu as
   in step 2 and choosing the **R**estore command.

When a window is maximized, the Maximize command is unavailable (appears in gray). The same is true for the **R**estore command when the window is already restored. You can use the same procedure to maximize and restore application windows. The only difference is that you press and release the Alt key and then the space bar to open the application Control menu instead of the document Control menu.

Minimizing Windows

Often, you will want to minimize applications to an icon on the desktop to make room for other applications and reduce the clutter on the desktop. You can minimize an application from the keyboard using the Control menu. Try minimizing the Program Manager window by following these steps:

1. Activate the Program Manager window, if it is not already the active window, by pressing Alt+Tab until the box for Program Manager appears, and then release both keys.

2. Select the Control menu by pressing and releasing the Alt key and then pressing the space bar.

3. Choose the Minimize command, either by pressing the letter N on the keyboard or by using the down-arrow key to select the command and pressing Enter.

4. Restore Program Manager by pressing Alt+Tab until the box for Program Manager appears and then releasing both keys.

   Alternatively, press Ctrl+Esc to display the Task List, select Program Manager from the list, and press Enter. A third method is to press Alt+Esc until the icon is selected, then press Alt, space bar to display the Control menu. Use the down-arrow key to select **R**estore, and then press Enter.

Starting Applications

You can start an application from Program Manager using the keyboard by selecting the program item icon and pressing Enter. Start the Write application using the keyboard by following these steps:

1. Activate the Program Manager window, if it is not already the active window, by pressing Alt+Tab until the box for Program Manager appears, and then release both keys.

2. Activate the Accessories group window by pressing Ctrl+Tab until the Accessories group window is selected. If the window is reduced to an icon, press Ctrl+Tab until the icon is selected and then press Enter.

3. Use the arrow keys to select the program item icon for the Write application.

4. Press Enter.

The Write window appears on the screen, as shown in figure C.4.

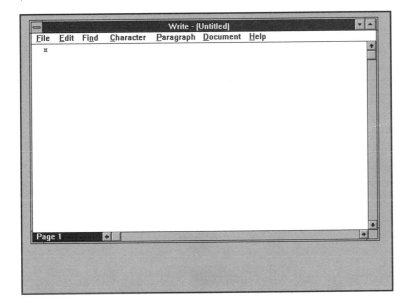

Fig. C.4
You can open applications from Program Manager using the keyboard.

Working with Applications

In this section you learn how to work with menus and dialog boxes by using the keyboard. You also learn how to use the keyboard to move around in a document and to select and edit text. You will use the Write application that you opened in the preceding section to learn how to work with applications, using the keyboard.

Scrolling in a Document

You can scroll through a document using the keyboard with the arrow keys and several other keys on the keyboard. Table C.2 summarizes the keyboard actions that work in most applications for moving around a document. Many applications have other shortcut keys for moving and scrolling in a document. When you use the keyboard to move around a document, the insertion point moves with you. When you use the mouse to scroll in a document, which you learned in Chapter 1, the insertion point does not move as you scroll. You must click in the document to reposition the insertion point.

Table C.2 Keyboard Methods for Moving in a Document	
Keyboard Action	**To**
Left- or right-arrow key	Move left or right one character
Up- or down-arrow key	Move up or down one line
Ctrl+left- or right-arrow key	Move left or right one word
Ctrl+up- or down-arrow key	Move up or down one paragraph (in some applications)
Home	Move to left margin
End	Move to end of line
Ctrl+Home	Move to top of document
Ctrl+End	Move to end of document
PgUp and PgDn	Move up or down one screenful

Editing with the Keyboard

When you start typing in an application, what you type appears in the document at the insertion point—the blinking vertical bar you see on-screen. Most applications push existing text to the right to make room for the new text. Some applications allow you to select an *overtype* mode by pressing the Insert key. Be careful when you work in this mode, as it is easy to type over existing text inadvertently. To delete text to the left of the insertion point, press the Backspace key. To delete text to the right of the insertion point, press the Del key.

Typing and editing text is the same in nearly every Windows application. After you practice the techniques described in this section, you can type and edit text in other applications.

In the following steps, you type a list in Write, which you opened in the previous section, and make a simple editing correction to the list. Follow the steps and remember to include the misspelled word Raketball.

1. Type the following lines and press Enter at the end of each line:

   Things to do today

   Complete cash flow analysis

   Plan next quarter's goals

   Raketball at 7:00

2. Change Raketball to Racquetball by using the keyboard.

   Use the arrow keys to move the insertion point between the k and the e in Raketball. Press the Backspace key to delete the letter k and type **cqu**. The result of your typing is shown in figure C.5.

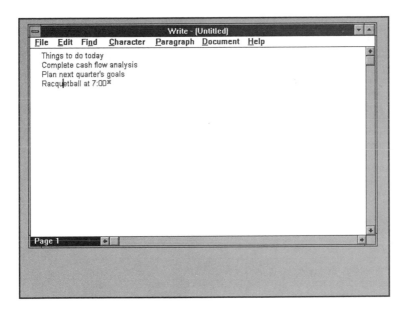

Fig. C.5
The Write word processor with the corrected list.

3. Practice using the keyboard to move around the file in Write, using the keyboard actions described in the preceding section.

Selecting Text and Objects

Knowing how to select text and objects in Windows applications is essential, because all Windows applications operate on the *select then do* principle. This means that you must select the text or object before you issue any commands to do something to it. Selecting the text or object tells the application what to apply the command to.

To select text with the keyboard, position the insertion point at the beginning of the text you want to select, press and hold down the Shift key, use arrow keys to move to the end of the text to select, and then release the Shift key. To select a word using the keyboard, hold down Ctrl+Shift while you press the left- or right-arrow key. To select a length of text with the keyboard, position the insertion point where you want the selection to start, hold down the Shift key, and scroll to the end of the selection by using any keyboard scrolling technique.

To select an object with the keyboard, position the insertion point beside it, hold down Shift, and press an arrow key to move over the object. Selected objects, such as graphics, usually appear with *selection handles* on each side and corner.

The following table summarizes the shortcut keys that work in many Windows applications for selecting text:

Key	Action
Shift+left arrow or Shift+right arrow	Adds the next adjacent character to the selection
Shift+down arrow	Selects to next line
Shift+up arrow	Selects to preceding line
Shift+PgUp or Shift+PgDn	Selects to top or bottom of page or screen
Shift+Home	Selects to beginning of line
Shift+End	Selects to end of line
Ctrl+Shift+left arrow or Ctrl+Shift+right arrow	Selects a word each time you press the left or right arrow
Ctrl+Shift+Home	Selects to start of document
Ctrl+Shift+End	Selects to end of document

Shortcut Keys for Editing

Some Windows applications include shortcut keys for editing text. These keys may work in some parts of the application, such as a formula bar, but may not work in others. Experiment to find the shortcuts that can help you.

Practice selecting text in the Write document you created in the previous section:

1. Use the arrow keys to position the insertion point to the left of the T in Things.

2. Press and hold down the Shift key as you press the right-arrow key.

   Holding down the Shift key selects text as the insertion point moves.

3. Move the insertion point to the beginning of a word and hold down the Ctrl and Shift keys and press the right-arrow key to select the word.

   You can select multiple words by repeatedly pressing the right-arrow key as you hold down the Ctrl and Shift keys.

4. Try out the other shortcut keys for selecting text listed in the preceding table.

Choosing Menus and Commands

If you are a touch-typist, you may prefer to access the menus and dialog boxes in your Windows applications by using the keyboard instead of the mouse. After you learn the methods for working with menus and dialog boxes using the keyboard, it is easy to use these methods in any application.

To choose a menu command with the keyboard, follow these steps:

1. Press and release the Alt key to activate the menu bar.

2. Type the underlined letter in the name of the menu you want.

3. Type the underlined letter in the name of the command you want.

   or

   Press the down arrow to select the command you want and then press Enter.

Another way to choose commands with the keyboard is to press and release Alt and then press Enter to open the first menu, press the left and right arrows to open adjacent menus, and then press the up and down arrows to select the command you want from the open menu. Press Enter to choose the selected command.

If you are using the keyboard, press Esc to back out of a menu without making a choice and press Esc a second time to return to the document.

Use the keyboard to boldface some text in the Write document by following these steps:

1. Select Things in the document, using the techniques you just learned.

2. Press Alt,C,B.

   Next to many menu commands you will see a shortcut key listed. You can issue commands using these shortcut keys to save time. To boldface the selected text, for example, you can press Ctrl+B.

In addition to the shortcut keys listed in the menus, most applications have many keyboard shortcuts for issuing commands. Refer to the documentation or on-line help to learn these keyboard shortcuts.

Selecting Options from Dialog Boxes

Many commands require more information from the user before the command can be carried out. When you select the **C**haracter **F**onts command in Write, for example, Write needs to know what font you want to use. Whenever you see three periods after a menu command, called an *ellipsis*, that means a *dialog box* will appear when you select the command. Figure C.6 shows the Font dialog box for Write.

Fig. C.6
Many commands use a dialog box to get more information from the user.

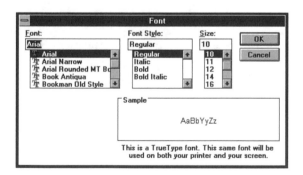

Table C.3 summarizes the different parts of a dialog box.

Table C.3	Areas of a Dialog Box
Area	**Use**
Text box	Type text entries manually. Press the Backspace key to erase characters if you make a mistake.
List box	Select a listed item by scrolling through the list and selecting one item. The selected item appears in highlighted text (and also may appear in the text box above the list).
Drop-down or Combo list box	Display the list by selecting the list and then pressing the down-arrow key. Press the down-arrow key to select the item you want from the list.
Option button	Select one option from a group of option buttons. (You can select only one option button in each group.) Option buttons are round and have darkened centers when selected. To remove a selection, select a different option in the same group.
Check box	Select multiple options from a group of check boxes. Check boxes are square and contain an X when selected. To deselect a check box, select it a second time.
Command button	Complete the command, cancel the command, or open an additional dialog box for more alternatives. Pressing Enter chooses the command button that appears in bold.

Appendixes

You can select from dialog boxes in one of two ways with the keyboard. With the faster method, you use Alt+*letter*. You press and hold down Alt while you press the underlined letter in the name of the item you want. With the second method, you move among items in a dialog box by pressing Tab.

To select from a group of round option buttons, access the group of option buttons by pressing Alt+*letter*, where *letter* is the underlined letter in the name of the group of option buttons. A dashed line encloses the active option button. Move the selection to another button in the same group by pressing the arrow keys. Use the Communications dialog box in the Terminal application to learn how to select an option button:

1. Open the Terminal application, which is located in the Accessories group.

2. Press Alt, S, C to open the Communications dialog box shown in figure C.7.

Fig. C.7

The Communications dialog box in Terminal has option buttons, check boxes, and a scrolling list.

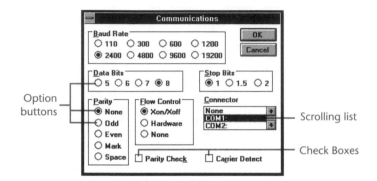

3. Press Alt+B to select the **B**aud Rate group and then use the arrow keys to select a new baud rate.

To select a check box, press Alt+*letter*, where *letter* is the underlined letter in the name of the check box. Each time you press Alt+*letter*, you toggle the check box between selected and deselected. An x appears in the check box when the box is selected. You also can toggle the active check box between selected and deselected by pressing the space bar. A dashed line encloses the active check box. Try selecting a check box in the Communications dialog box:

1. Press Alt+k to select the Parity Chec**k** option.

2. Press Alt+k again, or press the space bar, to deselect the option.

To select from a list of alternatives in a scrolling-list box, select the list box by pressing Alt+*letter*, where *letter* is the underlined letter in the name of the list box. When the list box is active, use the up- or down-arrow key or PgUp or PgDn to move through the list. The text in reversed type is selected. (To display a drop-down scrolling list by using the keyboard, press Alt+*letter* to activate the list and then press Alt+down-arrow to drop the list. Select items by pressing the up- or down-arrow keys.) Select a new communications port in the Communications dialog box:

1. Press Alt+C to select the **C**onnector scrolling-list.

2. Use the up- and down-arrow keys to make a selection from the list.

To edit text in a text box with the keyboard, select the text box by pressing Alt+*letter* or by pressing Tab until the text box is selected. (All text inside the box usually is selected.) To replace selected text, begin typing; the new characters you type replace the selected text. You can also edit the existing text using the arrow keys to move the insertion point, and the Backspace and Del keys to delete characters.

Try selecting a text box in the Save As dialog box in Terminal, using the following steps:

1. Press Esc to close the Communications dialog box.

2. Press F, A to open the File Save As dialog box, shown in figure C.8.

3. Press the Tab key twice to move the focus away from the File **N**ame text box.

4. Press Alt+N to reselect the File **N**ame text box.

5. Use the arrow keys to edit or retype the text.

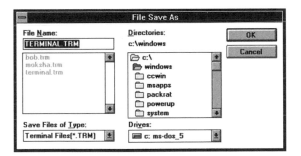

Fig. C.8
You can select and edit a text box using the keyboard.

Appendixes

To select a command button, press Tab or Shift+Tab until a dashed line encloses the name of the button you want. Press Enter to select the active button shown by the dashed enclosure. You can select the button in bold, usually the OK button, at any time by pressing Enter. Press Esc to choose the Cancel button and escape from a dialog box without making any changes.

Changing Directories in a List Box

When you save and open files in a Windows application, you often will need to switch directories. Try selecting different directories in the Save As dialog box in Terminal, using the following steps:

1. Press Alt, D to select the Directories list. You can also press Tab to advance to the Directories list.

2. Select the root directory by pressing the up-arrow key and pressing Enter.

   The open current directory is listed above the list box and is represented by an open folder in the list box. Notice that when you select a new directory, any subdirectories for that directory are listed below the directory.

3. Move back to the \WINDOWS directory by using the down-arrow key to select *windows* in the list and pressing Enter.

Switching between Applications

In Chapter 1, you learn how to switch among applications by using both the mouse and the keyboard. Unless you can see the window for the application you want to switch to, it is much more convenient to use one of the keyboard methods for switching among applications. For the sake of review, the two most useful keyboard methods for switching among applications are presented here. To switch from one application to another using the first method, follow these steps:

1. Hold down the Alt key and press the Tab key until a box appears on-screen listing the application you want to switch to (see fig. C.9).

2. Release both keys.

   If the application was reduced to an icon, it is restored when you switch to it using this method.

To switch to another application using the second method, follow these steps:

Tip

Even when you don't want to switch to another application, you can open the Task List if you lose track of what applications you have opened. When in doubt, press Ctrl+Esc to display a listing of all open applications.

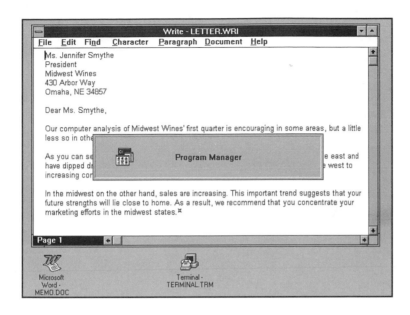

Fig. C.9
Press Alt+Tab to
switch to another
application.

1. Press Ctrl+Esc to display the Task List, shown in figure C.10.

2. Use the arrow keys to select the application you want to switch to from the list.

3. Press Enter.

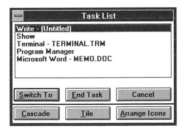

Fig. C.10
The Task List can
be used to switch
to another
application.

From Here...

This appendix showed you how to operate your windows applications using the keyboard. To learn more about operating Windows and Windows applications, refer to the following chapters:

Appendixes

■ Chapter 1, "Operating Windows," describes how to use the mouse and some of the most important keys to control and operate Windows.

■ Chapter 2, "Getting Help," teaches you how to access hundreds of pages of on-line help to make applications easier to use and make you more productive.

Index of
Common Problems

(continues)

If you have this problem...	You'll find help here...
DOS: Running DOS batch files from Windows	p. 776
DOS: Windows doesn't find the PIF when running the application	p. 750
DoubleSpace causes computer to run more slowly	p. 842
Electronic support	p. 84
Embedding: Cannot open a server application	p. 1006
Embedding: Editing embedded objects	p. 215
Embedding: Resolution changes when editing an embedded graphic	p. 215
Embedding: Server is unavailable during OLE	p. 1005
Embedding: Updating embedded objects	p. 216
Erased or lost files	p. 988
File Manager: Backing up important files	p. 165
File Manager: Changing the display's sort order	p. 145
File Manager: Confirmation messages are annoying	p. 148
File Manager: Deleted the wrong file or directory	p. 159
File Manager: Displaying files with certain extensions	p. 141
File Manager: Finding lost files or directories	p. 136
File Manager: Hidden or system files aren't listed	p. 148
File Manager: Renaming files or directories	p. 158
File Manager: Virus scanning	p. 168
Font files take up too much disk space or memory	p. 281
Fonts display or print incorrectly	p. 1002
Fonts don't appear in the font list	p. 292
Fonts you have are not TrueType fonts	pp. 275, 277
Fonts: Can't change font size in a DOS application	p. 991
Formatting changes from one session to the next	p. 281

(continues)

If you have this problem...	You'll find help here...
Help: Copying Help information for editing	p. 80
Help: Customizing Help to meet your needs	p. 76
Help: Defining unknown Windows terms	p. 75
Help: Marking Help topics you use often	p. 78
Icon names are hard to read	p. 239
Icon titles overlap and aren't readable	p. 102
Icons change by themselves	p. 101
Icons for running applications disappear	p. 93
Icons move by themselves	p. 112
Icons: Changing the icon for a program or packaged object	pp. 100, 226
Icons: Program you want doesn't have an icon	p. 50
Installation: Failure in DOS portion of installation	p. 980
Installation: Failure in Windows portion of installation	p. 981
Installation: Insufficient hard disk space	p. 983
Installation: Setup keeps asking for the same disk	p. 981
Installation: Windows doesn't start after installation	p. 983
Installation: Your hardware isn't listed	p. 982
Keyboard: Producing international characters	p. 248
Keys: Wrong result when you press a key	p. 988
Keystrokes don't repeat quickly enough	p. 246
Linking: Editing linked data	p. 208
Linking: Link button or command is dimmed	p. 203
Linking: Linked data changes to errors when updating	p. 206
Linking: Preventing accidental link updates	p. 228
Linking: Updating linked data	p. 210
Memory: Out of memory/insufficient memory	pp. 735, 836, 996
Menu command is grayed	p. 32

If you have this problem...	You'll find help here...
Menu doesn't match the one in this book	p. 33
Menu: Wrong menu is open	p. 60
Mouse buttons are backward for left-handed user	p. 247
Mouse doesn't work in DOS	p. 984
Mouse doesn't work in Windows	p. 984
Mouse pointer doesn't move or jumps around	p. 985
Mouse: Double-click speed is too slow or too fast	p. 248
Multimedia: Adjusting MIDI equipment settings	p. 684
Multimedia: Driver for your equipment isn't listed	p. 666
Multimedia: Embedding sound and video in applications	p. 680
Multimedia: Playing animation, MIDI, and AVI files	p. 676
Multimedia: Upgrading your equipment	p. 662
Multimedia: Using Video for Windows 1.1	p. 714
Network: Can't connect to a network drive	p. 1004
Network: Problems running a shared copy of Windows	p. 1004
Network: Problems running network software	p. 1005
Networks: IFSHLP.SYS driver is incompatible with your network	p. 879
Networks: Unknown adapter type	p. 874
Notepad: Finding specific entries	p. 469
Notepad: Horizontal scroll bar is missing	p. 466
Notepad: Text doesn't wrap automatically	p. 465
Paintbrush: Can't see the whole image	p. 395
Paintbrush: Changing current line width or shape	pp. 369, 390
Paintbrush: Changing the current color	p. 368
Paintbrush: Circles aren't perfectly round	p. 383

(continues)

If you have this problem...	You'll find help here...
Printing: Serial devices don't work	p. 253
Printing: Setting up a new printer in Windows	pp. 284, 293
Printing: Stopping the printer temporarily	pp. 298, 305
Printing: TrueType fonts print slowly	p. 273
Printouts are garbled or formatting is wrong	p. 1001
Program Manager disappears	pp. 104, 113
Program Manager doesn't start	p. 49
Program Manager returns to old settings	p. 90
Recorder: Interrupting the recording process	p. 448
Recorder: Macro shortcut key conflicts with application shortcut key	p. 452
Recorder: Nesting macros/using subroutines	p. 449
Recorder: Recording a lengthy macro	p. 443
Recorder: Recording mouse actions	pp. 447, 448
Recorder: Stopping a macro in progress	p. 455
Recorder: Tracking the prerequisites for a macro	p. 447
Recorder: Using macros with selected text or graphics	p. 447
Recorder: Using macros with Terminal	p. 444
Registration database is corrupt	p. 726
Screen capture doesn't work	p. 993
Serial (COM) port can't be accessed	p. 1007
Sharing data with users who don't have the server application	p. 206
Sharing DOS and Windows files	p. 197
Sharing printers across a network	pp. 314, 320
Sound: Assigning sounds to system events	p. 675
Sound: Choosing equipment	p. 663

(continues)

If you have this problem...	You'll find help here...
Terminal: Saving settings	p. 416
Terminal: Transferred file is unusable	p. 436
Terminal: Trouble communicating	p. 1008
Terminate-and-stay-resident applications cause problems	pp. 721, 737, 820
Time: Displaying the Windows clock	p. 501
Training	p. 85
Window doesn't show all the icons	p. 46
Window is too big or too small	p. 42
Window: Creating personalized group windows	p. 95
Window: Wrong application window is active	p. 63
Window: Wrong document window is active	p. 57
Windows slows down or acts strange	p. 986
Workgroups drivers aren't identified	p. 873
Workgroups: Attaching files to a Mail message	p. 531
Workgroups: Changing an appointment in Schedule+	p. 585
Workgroups: Changing your Mail password	p. 549
Workgroups: Chat background color isn't what you selected	p. 639
Workgroups: Chatting on-line with your workgroup	p. 636
Workgroups: Confirming receipt of a Mail message	p. 536
Workgroups: Creating templates for Mail messages	p. 521
Workgroups: Disconnecting a user connected to your computer	p. 648
Workgroups: Displaying the ClipBook	pp. 626, 635
Workgroups: Faxing from your computer	p. 560
Workgroups: Finding a time when users are available for a meeting	p. 606

(continues)

If you have this problem...	You'll find help here...
Workgroups: Finding Mail addresses	p. 522
Workgroups: Finding specific Mail messages	p. 529
Workgroups: Keeping a "To Do" list	p. 595
Workgroups: Logging on and off your system	p. 652
Workgroups: Monitoring network activity on your computer	p. 645
Workgroups: No Postoffice exists	p. 554
Workgroups: Preventing pop-up messages from popping up	p. 643
Workgroups: Printing Mail messages with embedded objects or attached files	p. 529
Workgroups: Saving Clipboard entries	p. 629
Workgroups: Scheduling a meeting	p. 603
Workgroups: Scheduling recurring appointments	p. 588
Workgroups: Scheduling resources	p. 609
Workgroups: Sending a pop-up note to your workgroup	p. 640
Workgroups: Setting up reminders for Schedule+ appointments	p. 588
Workgroups: Sharing ClipBook pages	p. 630
Workgroups: Sharing resources by remote access	p. 653
Workgroups: Storing Mail messages	p. 538
Workgroups: Time sharing on network needs adjustment	p. 651
Workgroups: Turning off the Chat sound	p. 640
Workgroups: Viewing ClipBook contents	p. 626
Workgroups: Viewing the event log for your computer	p. 649
Workgroups: Working off-line on a networked computer	p. 577
Write: Enhancements don't appear on-screen or in print	p. 347

Index

Symbols

A

X–Y–Z

GO AHEAD. PLUG YOURSELF INTO MACMILLAN COMPUTER PUBLISHING.

Introducing the Macmillan Computer Publishing Forum on CompuServe®

Yes, it's true. Now, you can have CompuServe access to the same professional, friendly folks who have made computers easier for years. On the Macmillan Computer Publishing Forum, you'll find additional information on the topics covered by every Macmillan Computer Publishing imprint—including Que, Sams Publishing, New Riders Publishing, Alpha Books, Brady Books, Hayden Books, and Adobe Press. In addition, you'll be able to receive technical support and disk updates for the software produced by Que Software and Paramount Interactive, a division of the Paramount Technology Group. It's a great way to supplement the best information in the business.

WHAT CAN YOU DO ON THE MACMILLAN COMPUTER PUBLISHING FORUM?

Play an important role in the publishing process—and make our books better while you make your work easier:

- Leave messages and ask questions about Macmillan Computer Publishing books and software—you're guaranteed a response within 24 hours
- Download helpful tips and software to help you get the most out of your computer
- Contact authors of your favorite Macmillan Computer Publishing books through electronic mail
- Present your own book ideas
- Keep up to date on all the latest books available from each of Macmillan Computer Publishing's exciting imprints

JOIN NOW AND GET A FREE COMPUSERVE STARTER KIT!

To receive your free CompuServe Introductory Membership, call toll-free, **1-800-848-8199** and ask for representative **#597**. The Starter Kit Includes:

- Personal ID number and password
- $15 credit on the system
- Subscription to CompuServe Magazine

HERE'S HOW TO PLUG INTO MACMILLAN COMPUTER PUBLISHING:

Once on the CompuServe System, type any of these phrases to access the Macmillan Computer Publishing Forum:

GO MACMILLAN   **GO BRADY**
GO QUEBOOKS   **GO HAYDEN**
GO SAMS   **GO QUESOFT**
GO NEWRIDERS   **GO ALPHA**

Once you're on the CompuServe Information Service, be sure to take advantage of all of CompuServe's resources. CompuServe is home to more than 1,700 products and services—plus it has over 1.5 million members worldwide. You'll find valuable online reference materials, travel and investor services, electronic mail, weather updates, leisure-time games and hassle-free shopping (no jam-packed parking lots or crowded stores).

Seek out the hundreds of other forums that populate CompuServe. Covering diverse topics such as pet care, rock music, cooking, and political issues, you're sure to find others with the same concerns as you—and expand your knowledge at the same time.